TEXAS AGGIES GO TO WAR

NUMBER 104

Centennial Series of

the Association of

Former Students,

Texas A&M University

TEXAS AGGIES GO TO WAR

In Service of Their Country,

Expanded Edition

Henry C. Dethloff

with JOHN A. ADAMS, JR.

Foreword by GEORGE H. W. BUSH

Texas A&M

University Press

College Station

This paper meets the requirements of
ANSI/NISO Z39.48–1992 (Permanence of Paper).

Binding materials have been chosen for durability.
∞

Unless noted, all illustrations, excluding maps, are courtesy of the
Cushing Library, Texas A&M University, College Station.

Library of Congress Cataloging-in-Publication Data

Dethloff, Henry C.
Texas Aggies go to war : in service of their country / Henry C. Dethloff
with John A. Adams, Jr. ; foreword by George H. W. Bush.—Expanded ed.
      p. cm.—(Centennial series of the Association of Former
      Students, Texas A&M University ; no. 104)
   Includes bibliographical references and index.
   ISBN-13: 978-1-60344-077-6 (pbk. : alk. paper)
   ISBN-10: 1-60344-077-1 (pbk. : alk. paper)
   1. Texas A & M University—Alumni and alumnae. 2. Military education—Texas.
   3. United States—Armed Forces—Recruiting, enlistment, etc. 4. Texas A & M
   University—Students. 5. Soldiers—United States. I. Adams, John A., 1951–
   II. Title. III. Series.
U430.T37d48 2008
355.0092′2764—dc22
                                                          2008015457

CONTENTS

MAPS

TABLES

FOREWORD

To Aggies Who Have Served and Supported Our Military Forces, Past and Present:

I have often said that a successful life, by definition, includes service to others. The George Bush Presidential Library shares not only a campus with Texas A&M University but also a commitment of service to country that is so well reflected and documented by this history of Texas Aggies in war.

Since the university's founding in 1876, Texas Aggies have provided exemplary leadership and service to their state and their country in peace and in war. They have served in the U.S. Army, Navy, Air Force, Marines, and Coast Guard; they have served in combat and as engineers, in food services, supply, and as training officers capably meeting the diverse needs and tasks of modern warfare.

Students and graduates of Texas A&M have fought for their country in all of this nation's wars, great and small, since 1898. Fully one-half of all those who had attended the A&M College since its founding served in the armed forces of the United States during World War I. Many were pioneers in tank and air warfare.

More than twenty thousand Texas Aggies fought in World War II, twenty-nine of them as flag officers, on every battlefield from Pearl Harbor and Corregidor through North Africa, Italy, France, and Germany and across the vast Pacific Ocean. They flew with Doolittle over Tokyo, were on the raid at Dieppe, led the charge up the cliffs at Normandy, and fought in the Battle of the Bulge. Many of them died in those devoted efforts. In all, seven Aggies received the Medal of Honor, the nation's highest award for service.

In more recent times, Texas Aggies fought in Korea, Vietnam, Grenada, Panama, and the Persian Gulf. Even now, many are in Iraq and Afghanistan.

Texas Aggies Go to War: In Service of Their Country is a remarkable story, one that makes me value and admire my adopted university all the more.

George H. W. Bush
Forty-first President of the United States

PREFACE

This is a history of Texas Aggies in war and the way in which they, as citizen soldiers, have answered the call to arms. It is admittedly a story that can never be fully put into words or pictures because the soldiers, sailors, marines, and aviators, who all have unique personalities, are a book and a story unto themselves. In this narrative we present an introduction, an outline, an image, and a perception of the manner in which Texas Aggies have served, fought, and died for their country since the first Aggie soldiers entered combat in the Spanish-American War. In its broader context, this is the story of Texas A&M's Corps of Cadets; the militia tradition; the National Guard; the reserves; the ROTC; the U.S. Army, Navy, Marines, Air Force, and Coast Guard; and national defense. It is a tale of global involvement and a record of the constant vigilance, effort, and sacrifice needed to maintain national security, world peace, and the survival of democratic society. This story illustrates the value that training at Texas A&M and in the Texas A&M Corps of Cadets has provided to the nation at critical times in our history. We hope these examples will encourage future generations to continue the legacy.

In May, 2004, Texas A&M University president Robert Gates explained in an address that he came to Texas A&M to conclude a lifetime of public service "because of the still powerful traditions and spirit of Texas A&M, because of its proud patriotism, and because of its extraordinary history of service to the nation." Texas A&M is a unique American institution, he said, "not because we are a world-class research and teaching university—which, of course, we are. . . . A&M is unique because of its history, its spirit, and its traditions. . . . The Corps of Cadets is the living, daily representation at Texas A&M of the spirit, the traditions, the values, and the history which set us apart from every other great school in America."

The inspiration for this book comes from the former students of Texas A&M University whose remarkable record of military service for more than a hundred years is a story that has never been told. On behalf of those fifty thousand or more Texas Aggie service members, several sponsoring former students have initiated this writing, research, and information-gathering project and have positioned themselves as editors, advisors, and counselors to see it through to completion and publication. They have, in the course of the project, received considerable assistance and encouragement from the extended family of former students. Those sponsors, who constitute an advisory committee for the history project, include C. C. Taylor ('51), Maj. Gen. William A. Becker ('41),

James K. B. Nelson ('49), and William C. Lonquist ('48). The project has been funded by contributions made through the Texas A&M Foundation under the management of the Texas A&M University Press. Royalties received from the sale of the book have been designated for the Eternal Aggies Corps of Cadets Endowment at the Texas A&M Foundation.

This narrative history is one of several intended products of this effort. A permanent electronic directory, http://lib-oldweb.tamu.edu/aggiesinwar, sponsored by the Texas A&M University Libraries, has been building since the inception of the project and is available to the public for research. In conjunction with the electronic directory, David A. Chapman, university archivist, is editing a volume titled *Those Who Served: A Directory and Record of Texas Aggies in Military Service since 1898*, which is planned as the next phase of the project. The University Archives has also become a repository for Aggies in war files, letters, records, and photographs collected from veterans, their families, and the public.

Primary resources for the project include the historical files and records of the Association of Former Students. These have prominently included letters, memoranda, and photographs, some of which date back to the Spanish-American War, and the accumulated killed in action files, most of which relate to World War II. In addition, the lists and memos accumulated in the commemorative efforts of the university, such as the World War I Trees Memorial files, the Memorial Student Union files, the Vietnam Memorial file, and the Muster celebration files have been exceptional sources of comments, documentation, and illustrations. Texas Aggies have often celebrated their Musters virtually in the midst of battle. Since the inception of this work, these materials have been transferred to the University Archives for preservation and access.

Particularly valuable primary sources include the interviews and oral histories with veterans. Terry A. Anderson and the authors conducted a considerable number of interviews during the course of the work, but many of the real historical treasures have been the oral histories completed by Anderson and Robert A. Calvert under a special oral history program conducted by the university in the 1980s. Thousands of pages of firsthand accounts of war and military service were accumulated during the course of this effort and are now on deposit in the Texas A&M University Archives. The *Texas Aggie, Battalion, Bryan–College Station Eagle, Houston Chronicle, Dallas Morning News, Austin Statesman, San Antonio Express,* and other state and local newspapers have been an important resource, as have the occasional published memoirs and reminiscences of former students.

The electronic files and directory materials, including the AggieNetwork, have been an important research resource as have the letters, memoranda, and diaries sent to the Texas A&M University Archives by veterans of the various classes in response to solicitations from the sponsors and through the good efforts of the class agents. Suggested readings at the close of each chapter provide the opportunity for readers to gather further information on the wars, battles, or periods covered in the narrative history and include many of the materials the authors consulted in the course of the work.

The authors are very appreciative of the considerable support they have received from the Texas A&M University Press and its director, Charles Backus; the Texas A&M University Libraries, Dean Colleen Cook, and former Dean Fred C. Heath; the Association of Former Students, including its executive director, Porter S. Garner III, and staff; former *Texas Aggie* editor Jerry C. Cooper ('63); director of communications and *Texas Aggie* editor Joan Tatge; David A. Chapman ('67), university archivist; and Bill Page, director of the Government Documents Department, TAMU Libraries. The authors would like to thank them all for their contributions to the project.

By soliciting information from former students and reviewing and commenting on each of the preliminary drafts of this book, the sponsors have been vital facilitators of the work. They have contributed significantly in many ways to the final product. In addition, we wish to specifically recognize and thank Roger A. Beaumont, Jerry C. Cooper, and sponsors C. C. Taylor and Major General Becker for their crucial role as monitors, editors, and critics throughout the several drafts of the book, and Col. James Woodall ('50), Lt. Col. Donald R. "Buck" Henderson ('62), and Lt. Col. Gerald R. "Jake" Betty ('73) for their help and encouragement. The authors acknowledge all responsibility for errors and regret the inevitable error of omission, which they perceive to be one of the greatest problems in producing such a narrative. We hope that those oversights will result in new books and articles that will more completely document how Texas Aggies have served their country.

TEXAS AGGIES GO TO WAR

THE A&M COLLEGE OF TEXAS AND THE MILITARY TRADITION

The battleship *Maine*, sent to Havana harbor to protect American citizens from
the ravages of rioting and rebellion, mysteriously exploded on February 15,
1898, with 260 of her crew perishing. Americans, already ignited by a common
cause—"Cuba Libre!"—to free Cuba from the Spanish empire and end alleged
atrocities, were now invited by the sensationalist American yellow press to
"Remember the *Maine*!" This appeal struck a particular chord among students
of the Agricultural and Mechanical College of Texas, who were often called
upon to "Remember the Alamo." Thus, in March, a month after the *Maine* exploded and before an American declaration of war, students of the college—all
members of the Corps of Cadets and trained in the military arts, petitioned their
college president, Lafayette Lumpkin Foster, for permission to organize a regiment for "war against Spain."[1]

Less than a decade later, in March, 1917, anticipating another war, the students, faculty, and board of directors of the A&M College joined together to
offer themselves and the college's facilities and equipment to the U.S. government "for military purposes." Fully one-half of all those who had attended the
A&M College since its founding in 1876 served in the armed forces of the United
States during World War I, including 1,233 officers ranging in rank, according
to the Texas A&M *Biennial Report*, from 2 brigadier generals to 530 second lieutenants. Some served in the Marine Corps, others in the U.S. Air Corps, Navy,
and Merchant Marine. Of those who served, 25 are known to have received
France's Croix de Guerre posthumously, and 12 earned the U.S. Distinguished
Service Cross.[2]

Hundreds of Texas Aggies had been mobilized for war in 1940 even before
the Japanese bombs dropped on Pearl Harbor. Some were already in combat,

fighting under the flags of Canada, Great Britain, and France. Some were at Pearl Harbor on December 7, 1941; many more were in an American fortress on Corregidor Island in the Philippines, "the American Alamo of World War II." On San Jacinto Day, April 21, 1942, some four months after Pearl Harbor, Maj. Gen. George F. Moore, a 1908 graduate, and twenty-five other former students of the A&M College were in an American fortress on Corregidor Island. Their muster was interrupted by Japanese shells, and within two weeks all were dead or imprisoned.[3]

During World War II more than twenty thousand students of the A&M College served in America's armed forces, more than from any other single American college or university. They served both in combat and in capacities, functions, and places that reflected the enormity and complexity of modern warfare. Aggies representing all branches of the armed services were at Pearl Harbor, on Corregidor, with Doolittle at Tokyo, on the raid at Dieppe, in North Africa and Italy, on the Rapido River, at Normandy, in the Battle of the Bulge, in Germany, and in the Pacific Islands. Some commanded POW camps, some governed captured territories or cities, many were instructors and training officers, and others helped perfect tank, radar, and rocketry warfare. Texas A&M's fourteen thousand officers in service exceeded the number from the U.S. Military Academy. More than one thousand former students gave their lives in the service of their country during that conflict. Twenty-nine Texas Aggies served at flag rank during World War II.[4]

After World War II numerous Aggies remained on active duty, and hundreds of newly commissioned lieutenants from Texas A&M entered service. Many of these Aggies found themselves in Korea in 1950 and the years following. One Aggie recalled that he was peeing in the Yalu one moment and fleeing southward past Seoul through South Korea to the sea the next.[5] By 1968, more than half a million American soldiers were deployed in combat in South Vietnam, many of them Texas Aggies. While it was a tragic distinction, "more second lieutenants from Texas A&M University were casualties in Vietnam than were the graduates of any other university in the nation," notes historian Tom Pilkington. In that difficult war, each soldier had to decide "within your own mind and soul . . . what you think is right, and then do the best job you can," as Louis Newman III ('66), another Aggie soldier and recipient of the Silver Star and Bronze Star, commented.[6]

"Actions," "engagements," "conflicts," and antiterror "initiatives" have been occurring on an increasingly global scale, whether in Korea, Lebanon, Quemoy and Matsu Islands, Vietnam, the Congo, Panama, Libya, Somalia, Haiti, the Persian Gulf, Afghanistan, Kosovo, or Iraq. In every instance Texas Aggies have been there in the service of their country. Aggies on the ground in the Euphrates Valley fought the enemy in the Gulf War with infrared detection devices and radar scopes while warding off mosquitoes with their "arthropod repellent lotion." As robotic spy planes reconnoitered the deserts of Afghanistan or "smart" bombs fell on al-Qaeda mountain positions, Aggies such as 2nd Lt. Michael A. Kelley ('89) sought out the enemy in their underground labyrinths, donned biological decontamination kits, and dug and covered their "cat-holes" in the desert with their e-tools (entrenching tools) while confronting terrorism face-to-face.[7]

Different worlds, different wars, different times—but, through it all, Texas Aggies were serving their country in the armed forces. Military service has forged a major bond between the former students from the nineteenth to the twenty-first century—more than 125 years. War, combat, and military training, as an intrinsic part of Texas A&M's historic experience, has helped mold the unique psyche and character of Texas Aggies who were the archetypal "citizen soldiers."[8]

It is notable that this once relatively obscure and remote institution of higher education—an agricultural and mechanical college—Texas' first public institution of higher learning, should become a major school for military training. It is an unusual institution, too, in that its students should, over the course of a century, be so publicly and consistently committed to the concept of service to and defense of the nation.

Indeed, it was for peace, not war, that the college was established, or so its founders thought. The college began enrolling its first students on Monday, October 2, 1876, to prepare young Texans for what one member of its board of directors described as another kind of warfare, "industrial warfare," which, he believed, would become the greatest warfare of the present and future centuries.[9] In 1876, industrial warfare was something new and largely unknown in the United States, especially in rural, pioneering, frontier, war-ravaged Texas.

What Texans knew and had experienced and what those first fifteen- and sixteen-year-old A&M students knew and had lived with was war of the more traditional variety. Although born during a civil war in a culture strongly molded by frontier violence and reared during the upheaval of civil disobedience and Reconstruction, the students of the A&M College became strong partisans of discipline and order. Indeed, the Texas Revolution, the Mexican War, the Civil War, military occupation, and, throughout it all, Indian warfare, banditry, and depredations on the still unsettled Texas frontier dominated the lives and lore of Texans during the four decades from the inception of the Republic of Texas to the inauguration of the state's first public institution of higher learning. No wonder then that, when they founded their college, Texans embraced the wording of the Morrill Land-Grant College Act, approved by Congress in July, 1862, during the maelstrom of the Civil War. It stated that the purposes of the colleges thus endowed should be "to teach such branches of learning as are related to agriculture and the mechanic arts . . . without excluding other scientific and classical studies and including military tactics."

Numerous other land-grant colleges accepted the charge to include military tactics within the curriculum, but Texas A&M became more military and service oriented than most, largely because many Texans in the nineteenth century believed that the state's role in education should focus on preparing citizens to be jurors, voters, and soldiers. Many were firmly convinced that military training ensured the "good order and conduct" of the students.[10] Although maintaining student discipline may have been a factor in the embrace of military training by the college's administrators and faculty, it was by no means critical. There were, after all, relatively few students enrolled in the A&M College of Texas during its early years. And they were physically isolated—four miles from the nearest town—and even at their worst behavior threatened only wolves and the wilderness prairies.

Engineering provided one foundation for the school's military education and training. The discipline of engineering originally emerged from military necessity. The first modern engineers were military engineers who built fortifications, walls, moats, fortresses, and towers or, conversely, destroyed, tunneled under, bridged, scaled, or otherwise circumvented those fortifications.[11] In 1802, recognizing the synergy of engineering and military training, Congress and Pres. Thomas Jefferson created the Corps of Engineers, to be stationed at West Point, which was to "constitute a military academy." They also settled the burden of military education and training "on the shoulders of the civilian colleges of the individual states."[12] This responsibility of military training and education, coupled with incentives for training in the agricultural and mechanical arts, marked the beginning of the land-grant college system.

Jefferson believed that national defense rested primarily upon the shoulders of the armed citizenry, the militia, and the states and that the maintenance and training of citizen-soldier armies was primarily the business of the states. That concept was formalized in 1862 by the Morrill Act, which, "in effect, passed responsibility for the pre-commissioning education of reserve officers to the states and their basically civilian institutions." Its provisions for education in agriculture, engineering, and military training embraced the "American System of Education," which would prepare American youths "to discharge, in the best possible manner, the duties they owe to themselves, to their fellow-men, and to their country."[13]

Alden Partridge, a member of the first graduating class of the U.S. Military Academy at West Point in 1806 and considered to be the spiritual father of the Reserve Officer Training Corps, was singularly responsible for formulating the American system of education, which proposed to "combine civilian and military studies in order to produce enlightened and effective citizen-soldiers." His work set the tone and style of the educational reform ideas under which Texas A&M was founded.[14]

The Civil War and the South also influenced Texas A&M's military heritage by reinforcing the equation of military service and martial valor to honor, patriotism, civic duty, and virtue. Considered to be as valuable for the citizen as it was for the soldier, military training helped instill "morally correct behavior in the character of future engineers, farmers, teachers, and attorneys." The ideal citizen was "self-reliant, outwardly moral, mindful of his rights and civic responsibilities, and most importantly, eager and capable of bearing arms in self-defense or for the public good."[15]

While Texas A&M shared both the Jeffersonian and the Southern heritage, it was nevertheless distinctive among such institutions because of having been uniquely molded by the Texas frontier experience and by Texas independence. As a *Texas* school, its combination of civilian and military studies held a stronger meaning than elsewhere. Throughout Texas' brief forty-year history, first as a republic and then as a state of the Union, peace had been the exception and war the rule. In the autumn of 1835, armed conflict between Texans and Mexican military forces began at Gonzales, Goliad, and San Antonio. Texas declared its independence from Mexico on March 2, 1836, while the defenders of the Alamo were besieged by the armies of Santa Anna. The Alamo fell on March 6. Texas troops under Col. James W. Fannin surrendered at Goliad and on March 27 were massacred by their captors. Finally, with a volunteer citizen army, Gen. Sam Houston defeated the Mexican armies in the Battle of San Jacinto on April 21, 1836. For the next ten years the Republic of Texas survived continuing conflicts with Mexico, including two brief occupations of San Antonio by Mexican troops in 1842 and Indian wars along its ill-defined western frontier. The defense of the Republic of Texas depended, for the most part, on poorly organized local militia of all able-bodied males between the ages of 17 and 50, who were subject to call in an emergency.

The admission of Texas as a state of the Union in 1845 and the outbreak of the Mexican War reaffirmed the citizen soldier, volunteer tradition. Volunteer Texas Rangers, some six thousand strong, assisted the armies of Gen. Zachary Taylor and Gen. Winfield Scott as did other Texas volunteer units. Taylor accepted several companies of Texas Rangers with reluctance, but he soon discovered that their fighting instincts and their knowledge of the terrain were indispensable. When combat began, General Taylor asked the governor of Texas for four Ranger regiments—two mounted and two on foot.[16] At the close of the war, Ranger companies continued to patrol the western frontiers but were gradually supplanted by regular U.S. army garrisons.

In 1861, when Texas seceded from the Union, federal troops were withdrawn, and the Rangers and militia again assumed responsibility for frontier defense. Indeed, the necessities of regional security as well as Texas' recent history and strong sense of independence mitigated against a total commitment of Texas troops to Confederate commands in the eastern theater of war. But what the Texans lacked in numbers outside of Texas was compensated for by their ferocity in battle. Thus, in the Army of Northern Virginia, Hood's Texas Brigade was in the forefront of combat, while the 8th Texas Cavalry (Terry's Texas Rangers), Lawrence Sullivan Ross's Brigade, and Granbury's Texas Brigade fought on battlefields from Arkansas through Mississippi, Georgia, Tennessee, and the Carolinas.[17]

Following the Confederate surrender at Appomattox, Federal troops (backed by returning former Confederate soldiers) assembled on the banks of the Rio Grande in 1865 and 1866 and prepared for yet another war, this time against Mexico's emperor Maximilian, who was aided by French and European power. After France withdrew its support, Maximilian was executed by Mexican nationalists, and the threat of war passed. The danger to Mexican sovereignty and American borders had been stymied in good measure by the massing of American armies on the Rio Grande. Texans now faced military occupation on the one hand and the resurging Indian wars in the west on the other. The Texas legislature mustered two Ranger forces—a home-guard frontier battalion designed for Indian warfare and a special force to guard the southern border from attack across the Rio Grande. Major battles with Indians—most prominently the Red River War along the course of the river running west of present-day Fort Worth and the Palo Duro engagements in the Texas Panhandle in 1874, and intermittent sorties across the Rio Grande throughout the decade by ranger units and regular army units—meant that, in 1876, the year when the A&M College of Texas began instruction, a state of war existed in the state. The U.S. Army seems to have agreed that this was the case because, in 1876, the army began constructing one of Texas' last frontier fortifications, Fort Sam Houston, adjoining San Antonio. Troops previously stationed at the Alamo were transferred to the fort in 1879, and the military post has remained in continuous service ever since.[18] The seeming permanence of war and the tradition of the volunteer militia and Ranger units made military training at A&M a more serious and more accepted component of the land-grant college mission than elsewhere.

One student who entered in 1876, when asked why he had enrolled in the college, replied that he wanted to learn how to fight Indians and hunt buffalo. Qualified students had the option of pursuing a field of study in agriculture, mechanics and engineering, or language and literature. With six faculty on hand and few courses offered, in reality all of the students received much the same course work whatever their chosen field of study. In addition, all of the students were required to participate in military training, be members of the Corps of Cadets, and wear uniforms. Throughout the nineteenth century, the A&M campus was a military encampment. Detractors called it a "military peacockery."[19]

In the 1870s, there were no real guidelines for configuring military training in land-grant colleges. Programs varied depending on the experiences and whims of the school administrators and their governing bodies. Texas A&M's more rigorous version of military training was heavily based on the college's first commandant of cadets and instructor of military tactics (and mathematics), Robert P. W. Morris, who at age twenty-two was the youngest member of the faculty and a graduate of the Virginia Military Institute. Morris wrote the policies, organized the Corps of Cadets, and established the regimen for military training.[20] Military instruction, the Corps of Cadets, and the *Rules and Regulations*, modified over time, were the dominant features of student life on the A&M campus for most of the next one hundred years.

Military training at Texas A&M received a stimulus and a bit of standardization under an 1866 congressional authorization to assign active or retired military officers to land-grant colleges as professors of military science and tactics on the army's payroll. Capt. George T. Olmstead, the first assigned military officer and commandant of the Corps of Cadets, joined the faculty in 1878. In the eyes of the cadets, Olmstead stood "seven feet tall." He imposed a new regimen of order and discipline sustained by a rigorous program of military training and instruction.[21]

Even so, regional defense continued to occupy the concerns of the Texas legislature, which, in 1879, reorganized the state militia as the Volunteer Guards and provided a small salary for those called to active duty. Although Indian warfare diminished considerably with the capitulation of Comanche and Kiowa warriors in 1875 and the resettlement of those tribes into the Indian Territories, sporadic incursions across the Rio Grande and Apache raids in more remote western areas of Texas continued.[22] The classic western frontier was vanishing but not completely gone, and one of its legacies was the continuous reinvigoration of the Texas militia citizen-soldier tradition.

After 1890, this culture was further enhanced with the appointment of retiring Texas governor Lawrence Sullivan ("Sul") Ross as president of the A&M College. Ross was born in 1838 in the Iowa Territory, where his father was Indian agent. The family moved to Texas and, in 1849, settled at Waco Village, where "Sul" Ross, still a youth, had his first taste of Indian warfare. Ross's service with the U.S. Army, interspersed with his college education, eventually led to his killing of the Comanche chief, Nocona, and his rescue of Nocona's wife, Cynthia Ann Parker, who had been taken captive by the Comanches in a raid on Fort Parker twenty-five years earlier.[23]

When the South seceded from the Union, Sul Ross joined the 6th Texas Cavalry and for the next four years fought at Pea Ridge, Corinth, Vicksburg, Atlanta, Nashville, and elsewhere, including some daring raids behind Union lines. In Arkansas, he led a three-week incursion aimed at destroying supply routes, disrupting communications, and undermining morale. Ross sometimes literally tied his men in the saddle to keep them moving. In 135 separate battles during the war, he had seven horses shot out from under him and survived without a scratch. After Confederate brigadier general Ross's Texas Cavalry Brigade surrendered to Union armies at Jackson, Mississippi, in May, 1865, Ross returned to Waco. In 1886, he became governor of Texas and served until 1890, when he accepted the presidency of the A&M College.[24]

Upon his arrival at Texas A&M, Sul Ross was considered a living legend and the personification of the volunteer Texas Ranger and the citizen soldier. He reaffirmed the school's commitment to the Corps of Cadets, military training, and combat readiness. Moreover, he felt an overriding and deep personal obligation to prepare American youths "to discharge, in the best possible manner, the duties they owe to themselves, to their fellow-men, and to their country." Ross, along with his commandant of cadets and faculty, began preparing the students of Texas A&M for the "great hive of industry" as engineers, architects, agriculturists, physicians, lawyers—and soldiers. Student life at Texas A&M became, if it had not been so before, the lifestyle of a military encampment, including twenty-four-hour guard duty, drills, musters, inspections, and cannon and small-arms firing practice. The call to arms—to a war against Spain—came very soon.

Suggested Readings

Adams, John A., Jr. *Keepers of the Spirit: The Corps of Cadets at Texas A&M University, 1876–2001* (College Station: Texas A&M University Press, 2001).

Andrew, Rod, Jr. *Long Gray Lines: The Southern Military School Tradition, 1839–1915* (Chapel Hill: University of North Carolina Press, 2001).

Cutrer, Thomas. *Ben McCulloch and the Frontier Military Tradition* (Chapel Hill: University of North Carolina Press, 1993).

Dawson, Joseph G., III, ed. *The Texas Military Experience, from the Texas Revolution through World War II* (College Station: Texas A&M University Press, 1995).

Dethloff, Henry C. *The Centennial History of Texas A&M University, 1876–1976* (College Station: Texas A&M University Press, 1975), 2 vols.

Rose, Victor M. *Ross' Texas Brigade: Being a Narrative of Events Connected with Its Service in the Late War between the States* (1881; repr., Kennesaw, Ga.: Continental Book, 1960).

Simons, William E. *Professional Military Education in the United States: A Historical Dictionary* (Westport, Conn.: Greenwood Press, 2000).

Spurlen, Charles D. *Texas Volunteers in the Mexican War* (Austin, Tex.: Eakin Press, 1998).

Webb, Walter Prescott. *The Texas Rangers: A Century of Frontier Defense* (Austin: University of Texas Press, 1965; repr., 1993).

In contrast to students at most colleges and universities, Texas Aggies marched to a different drummer. The college reported as of December, 1898, that eighty-nine men were in the army, sixty-three of whom were officers or noncommissioned officers. The Spanish-American war marked a transition for the United States. And it was a maturing, sobering experience for Texas Aggies and but a premonition of greater, more dangerous things to come.

CUBA LIBRE TEXAS AGGIES AND THE SPANISH-AMERICAN WAR

On Tuesday, April 19, 1898, near the close of the nineteenth century, the U.S. Congress recognized the independence of Cuba and authorized the use of the armed forces to drive the Spanish out. When Spain then declared war on the United States, Congress issued a call for volunteers. Among the Aggies who signed up were a lieutenant colonel (George W. Hardy), a major, a regimental sergeant major, fifteen captains, ten first lieutenants, eight second lieutenants, six first sergeants, thirteen sergeants, five corporals, and twenty-two privates. Others not included in that 1898 count, such as Bonney Youngblood ('02), James Fred Stalcup ('04), and George N. Hope ('04), came to the A&M College after active service. Most of the students and former students served in the 1st, 2nd, 3rd, 4th, and 5th Regiments of the Texas Volunteer Guard. Aggie volunteers fought and served in Cuba, Puerto Rico, Hawaii, and the Philippines, while others were stationed at various posts in staging areas scattered across the United States.[1] How did the United States and these Texas Aggies become embroiled in this not-so-splendid little war that held such momentous consequences for America and helped build the reputation and tradition of the A&M College of Texas as a war school?

The prospect of America's entry into war of any kind seemed unlikely in 1890, particularly to the three hundred student cadets of the A&M College of Texas, who were living a rather isolated existence about four miles from the nearest town, Bryan. There seemed to be little reason to support Pres. Lawrence Sullivan Ross's determination to emphasize the military features of the college. Threats from hostile Indians, Mexico, or other antagonistic nations were not apparent. For the most part, by 1890, war and preparation for war had rapidly receded into the background of the American vision. Congress pegged Regular

Army enlisted strength at a mere twenty-five thousand men, most of whom were stationed in frontier outposts in the West and Southwest. The navy, considered among the largest and most modern in the world during the Civil War, had "dwindled into insignificance."[2]

Americans built railroads and factories, mechanized their farming, enlarged their cities, and rested comfortably for a time in their own splendid isolation. The level of comfort diminished rapidly because of falling farm prices, unemployment, and labor strife, accompanied in 1893 by the particularly violent Pullman railroad strike and the onset of America's first modern depression. The army shifted its troops from the frontier posts in the West to the industrializing urban centers to discourage labor strikes and help contain violence. Civil unrest rather than war was on the public's mind. State militias or home guards, once the heart of civil defense, declined from disuse or lack of funding. In many states, volunteers lacked training, weapons, and discipline but retained some viability as social and fraternal organizations. Thus, Texas A&M's preoccupation with military training and discipline at the dawn of the modern era was something of an anomaly among American institutions of higher learning.

In 1893, a visiting legislative committee concluded (without enthusiasm) that no student could graduate from the college without attaining a certain proficiency in the military department. The regimen of the school still required all students to be members of the Corps of Cadets, wear uniforms, attend lectures on military tactics, and participate in drills and reviews. As the 1895 student yearbook, the *Olio*, explained, "we dress alike, eat alike and sleep alike."[3]

Although the A&M College campus had all of the character of a frontier military post, including the posting of round-the-clock perimeter sentries, the nature of the nation's frontier had begun to change significantly. A new kind of frontier loomed on the horizon. American international trade and commerce had begun to expand, increasing contact with foreign naval and military forces, some friendly, some hostile. Those contacts revealed a gap between American weaponry and the modernization under way in Europe and the Pacific. In 1882, alerted to the growing numbers of foreign naval vessels off America's coasts, Congress authorized the loan of cannon and mortars to state militia units to help them train for coastal defense. The Texas Militia and the A&M College were armed under those provisions. Then, in 1883, conscious of America's growing overseas investments and global competition, Congress appropriated additional funds to begin four decades of naval expansion and modernization.

Moreover, in the late 1880s and early 1890s, labor strikes and violence in the cities, coupled with an outbreak of Indian raids in the West, forced the army to alter its traditional view that state militias and local guard units competed with the Regular Army for men and money. Army commanders began to view the state militia as a useful pool of reserves. State militias began the conversion from local defense forces to national guards, a manpower pool that was trained to federal standards to provide skilled reserves for the Regular Army. In this context the state militia, state volunteers, and college military training programs began receiving more attention and support from the federal government.[4] That changing attitude soon impacted military training at Texas A&M and other land-grant colleges.

These events also brought into focus the inherent conflict between state troops and federal authority. Could state national guard units be ordered to foreign service? Should state militias or national guards be used primarily to provide a trained personnel reserve for the Regular Army? Should they retain autonomy from federal forces? The Spanish-American War settled those issues for the most part. Those who fought in that war were from the United States, not from Texas, Ohio, Michigan, or some other state, despite the name the volunteer units may have retained.

Thus, the Spanish-American War was a pivotal conflict in many respects because it decided the relationship between the state militias and the national armies. The war loosened the foundations of American isolationism. It redefined America's perception of war, peace, frontiers, and home defense. Home defense became protection of the nation rather than of the community or state. The frontier was that uncertain area of contact between the United States and other nations. Preparing for war, however, was hardly a vital concern for most Americans in the late 1800s.

The United States went "stumbling unprepared into war" even though the fighting bore the label "made in the United States." The war has been attributed largely to the emotional rhetoric of the new mass-circulation yellow press (so named because of the pulp content of the paper) and to Cuban immigrants living in the United States who had been defeated in a ten-year revolution between 1868 and 1878. They were described as agitators and professional enthusiasts of liberty who had no real stake in the island and had become disassociated with life there.[5]

Earlier revolts in Cuba had been encouraged and abetted by American filibusterers and adventurers. In 1873, Spain seized the *Virginius*, an American commercial ship running arms to revolutionists, and peremptorily executed the captain and fifty-two members of the crew and passengers. With its armed forces dismantled and dispersed, the United States protested loudly but took no action. In 1886, after the collapse of the revolt, Spain abolished slavery in Cuba. As sugar and tobacco cultivation soared, imports competed with the products of American manufacturers. Since Americans attributed declining farm prices in part to foreign competitors, Congress enacted very high protective tariffs targeted at Cuban sugar imports. Cubans, in turn, blamed their resulting depression and hard times on Spain, and, in 1895, Cuba began another revolt for independence. The insurgents, employing the strategy of hit-and-run raids, burned cane fields, employed various acts of sabotage, and used tactics similar to those exploited so effectively by a latter-day Cuban revolutionary, Fidel Castro. The American public, thrilled by the distorted media portrayals of a democratic revolution in nearby Cuba, as well as American investors with stakes in Cuban lands, sugar mills, and factories, were strongly influenced by the sensational stories circulating in the yellow-press newspapers.

Under a new leader, Gen. Valeriano Weyler, Spanish forces in Cuba acted vigorously to quash the 1895 rebellion, forcing potentially hostile civilian populations into reconcentration areas, destroying rebel villages and farms, executing captives on the spot, and generally intimidating civilian populations. William Randolph Hearst's *Journal* captured the public's imagination with lurid prose characterizing Weyler as a "butcher" and a "brute, the devastator of haciendas, the destroyer of families, and the outrager of women, whose animal brain runs riot with itself in inventing tortures and infamies of bloody debauchery." Joseph Pulitzer's *World* asked whether there were "no nation wise enough, brave enough and strong enough to restore peace to this blood smitten land?"[6] All the while, Pres. William McKinley remained aloof, pursuing a policy of non-involvement, peace, and quiet diplomacy.

For the most part, the citizens of Bryan and the students at Texas A&M paid little attention to the rising rhetoric about Cuba until January, 1898, when the local newspaper, the *Bryan Eagle*, began reporting Cuban affairs in more detail. That same month a riot swept through Havana that resulted in the destruction of several newspaper offices and "caused apprehension among manufacturers, financiers and others that business affairs might be unsettled." Cuban police restored order, arrested the riot's leaders, and planned to try them by court martial. Spanish authorities also prohibited the publication of daily newspapers and foreign dispatches without previous censorship by authorities. Meanwhile, American naval units located along the East coast, including the armored cruisers *Maine* and *Marblehead*, were ordered to take on coal and be ready to "proceed to sea should occasion require."[7]

President McKinley decided that the presence of the *Maine* in Cuban waters might alone preserve America's interests in Cuba and encourage an early and peaceable resolution of the conflict. Thus, the *Maine*, 319 feet long with a crew of 354 officers and men and one of the most modern warships in the American fleet, steamed into Havana harbor on January 25, 1898. On February 15, about 9:40 in the evening, an explosion ripped the *Maine* apart, sinking it almost instantly and killing most of the crew. Initial reports from Capt. Charles D. Sigsbee speculated that the *Maine* had been sunk by an internal explosion—or by a submarine mine.[8]

John C. Hemment, a photographer and journalist who wrote and published one of the earliest accounts of the Spanish-American War, had recently photographed the *Maine* and described her as "beautiful, graceful, and majestic in all her strength, floating lazily on the waters of Chesapeake Bay." Upon arriving in

Havana harbor, he was shocked by the sight of the sunken ship: "When I saw her now, an unrecognizable mass of twisted, mangled, charred scrap iron, formerly the home, now the sepulcher, of so many brave men, it would be difficult to portray accurately my emotions. The vessel was lacerated and mutilated beyond recognition. A single mast alone remained. Her massive steel beams and girders were bent and twisted. Her funnels and ventilators were rent and distorted. I was overcome."[9]

The American press, including the *Bryan Eagle* and the general public, soon determined that Spanish treachery had destroyed the *Maine*. A military court of inquiry concluded that the ship had indeed been sunk by a submarine mine (although a later analysis indicates the explosion may have been due to faulty ventilation).

A wave of "belligerent enthusiasm" swept the United States. Thousands of citizens and National Guard units deluged state and federal authorities, offering to volunteer for service. Cadets at the A&M College petitioned their president, L. L. Foster, for permission to organize a regiment in case of war against Spain. The commandant of the Corps of Cadets, Lt. George L. Bartlett, was ordered to active duty, promoted to major, and sent to Tampa, Florida, in anticipation of the likely upcoming campaign. Meanwhile, Cuban revolutionaries were encouraged by the prospect of American assistance, and Maximo Gomez pledged to lead the peoples' armies against Havana as soon as the American fleet opened fire and to "keep on fighting until Havana surrenders or nothing is left of it but a heap of ruins." Cuban sympathizers in the United States, such as Emile Nuñez, landed arms and ammunition and some independent adventurers to assist in the overthrow of Spanish rule. On March 3, the *Bryan Eagle* quoted Nuñez, who had just arrived in Tampa from Cuba, that "Cuba is now almost free."[10] Counseling calm, President McKinley sought a diplomatic solution—not war with Spain.

For a while, Congress seemed of much the same opinion. Then, in a rare show of accord, it unanimously approved a defense appropriations bill intended to arm and equip the navy and make the army combat ready. The latter meant, for the most part, restoring Civil War–era cannon to working condition and placing orders for modern Mauser and Krag-Jorgensen-type rifles as opposed to the black-powder Remington (trapdoor-type) rifles that were still being issued to some troops.[11]

While the president continued to press for a peaceful solution to the Cuban problem, the situation began to spiral out of control. Several states appropriated funds to equip and muster their troops for service against Cuba. The Texas governor sent the Texas Rangers to the Rio Grande to guard the boundary against possible attack from pro-Spanish and anti-American elements in Mexico. When the Texas Militia went on alert, its units, scattered throughout the state, began to fill their ranks and conduct more serious drills and musters. The

Department of the Navy began to stow munitions and coal aboard vessels and ready them for combat. That readiness extended to the Asiatic Squadron in Yokohama, Japan, under the command of Adm. George Dewey.[12] Rhetoric and journalistic reports about freeing Cuba began to be interspersed with references to Spanish control of the Philippines, Puerto Rico, and Hawaii.

Meanwhile, McKinley, stirred to action by the *Maine* incident and the publication of a letter from the Spanish minister in Washington, D.C., criticizing the president as a "bidder for the admiration of the crowd," demanded through the Department of State that Spain grant the Cuban rebels an armistice and end the reconcentration system. By April 9, 1898, Spain formally agreed to both of these demands but declined to accept the unspoken requirement that Spain grant Cuba independence. On April 15, President McKinley presented Congress with a message that declared the Cuban situation a nuisance and a menace to national peace and security. He urged that American life and property in Cuba be protected. Finally, on April 19, by a joint resolution, Congress approved a declaration of war against Spain with the stipulation that Cuba be free and independent and the statement that the United States had no intention of annexing the island. Congress failed to mention Puerto Rico, Guam, Hawaii, or the Philippines.

On April 22, Congress authorized the president to call 60,000 volunteers to arms for a one-year term of service. Two days later, Congress approved an increase in the levy to 125,000 volunteers to accommodate the wholesale enlistment of state guard and militia units whose individual members refused to volunteer unless their entire unit was accepted. Then, on April 30, Admiral Dewey met and destroyed the Spanish Fleet in Manilla Bay.[13]

The bill enabled state troops to become, en masse, a part of the Regular Army. By June of 1898, the Texas Militia was essentially reconstituted as the Texas Volunteers, comprising five infantry and two cavalry regiments, plus two batteries of artillery. Most of the 284 officers and 2,739 men from Texas in the Spanish-American War served in the Texas Volunteers, as did most of those who volunteered from the A&M College of Texas.[14]

George W. Hardy was among those who served. He completed his studies at the A&M College in 1879 and moved to Corsicana. In 1889, Hardy joined the Texas Militia and was elected captain of the Garrity Rifles, a company of the 4th Texas Volunteer Guard, a state militia unit. During the next ten years he was promoted to lieutenant colonel. In June, 1898, Gov. Charles A. Culberson sent Hardy's unit to Camp Tom Ball, near Houston, where they were sworn in for a one-year tour of service with the U.S. Army as members of the 4th Texas Volunteer Infantry. Hardy remained on active duty in Texas until he was honorably discharged with his regiment at San Antonio in March, 1899.[15]

Similarly, Joseph F. Nichols ('89), a member of the Scott (later Ross) Volunteers while at the A&M College, was captain of Company E, 5th Regiment of the

Texas Militia at Greenville when the Spanish-American War began. In April, 1898, Nichols enlisted as captain of Company C, 3rd Texas Volunteers, under the command of Regular Army officers, and served until February, 1899, at a number of Texas posts, including Fort Bliss, Camp Mabry, and Fort Clark. P. C. Gebhart ('02) volunteered for the 2nd Texas Volunteers and remained on active duty in Texas until his discharge at Dallas on November 9, 1898. Gebhart then enrolled at Texas A&M, where he played on the football team until 1901, when his "Father objected to my playing foot-ball and declined to permit me to return evidently feeling that I was not doing much more than playing foot-ball."[16]

Among others who spent the war in Texas were the Hutson brothers, Will ('95) and Henry ('96), sons of Charles W. Hutson, a professor at A&M (and brothers of twins Sophie and Mary, as well as Ethyl, who were among the first women to take classes at A&M College in the 1890s). Writing to his mother on June 3, 1898, Henry said he was serving as officer of the day for his unit in Galveston and that volunteers were being turned away because the unit was full. Will Hutson, who joined Troop G, 1st Texas Volunteer Cavalry, as first sergeant, explained in a letter home in late October that the boys who had been in Cuba were already back and few wanted to remain in service any longer. Among Texas Aggies serving at home and abroad, several were in the hospital corps, one was a trumpeter, one a Rough Rider with Colonel Woods and Theodore Roosevelt, and one a Missouri Regular.[17]

Despite the rhetoric and enthusiasm, the rapid and large-scale recruitment efforts produced soldiers with little or no training and antiquated equipment. The navy, on the other hand, thanks to modernization and a substantial ship-building program over the past decade, was much better equipped despite inadequate funding and reduced opportunities for training, maneuvering, and firing practice. Naval vessels during this period had tended to remain inactive, in port, and on exhibit—at considerably less operating cost than required for steaming and naval maneuvers. Both the army and navy had little experience in the complexities of modern warfare, which first emerged on a large scale during the American Civil War and which now became critical.[18]

Remarkably, the War Department in 1898 overcame tremendous difficulties in mobilizing an army from virtually nothing and fielded what proved to be a sufficient fighting force. Initial plans called for the assembly of the army at Tampa, Mobile, and New Orleans, while the state volunteers went mainly to the old Chickamauga, Georgia, battlefield. Later, with an eye on the Pacific, the War Department added San Antonio and San Francisco as muster points. Meanwhile, the navy imposed a blockade on Cuban ports including Havana, Matanzas, Mariel, and Cardenas, effectively sealing off Havana and other seaports connected to Havana by rail. As war plans matured, smaller gun-running expeditions brought food, supplies, and ammunition to isolated rebel groups in Cuba. Meanwhile, state volunteer units were directed to assemble within their states to receive weapons, uniforms, and field equipment and then to move as units to designated, and widely scattered, war encampments.[19]

Adm. Pascual Cervera y Topete sailed from Spain on April 24 with a formidable Spanish fleet, including the cruisers *Viscaya* and *Infanta Maria Teresa*. Throughout May, the eastern seaboard of the United States waited anxiously for a possible Spanish attack on its coastal cities. Rumors were rife, and millions of Americans evacuated their homes there. An additional thirty thousand volunteers were sent to Chickamauga to prepare for homeland defense, delaying the planned expedition to Cuba. The news that the Spanish fleet was in the Gulf of Mexico led the War Department to order additional regiments of the Texas Volunteer Infantry to New Orleans and Mobile for coastal defense.[20]

Claude Stanley, a Texas A&M student who joined the Texas Volunteers, sent the *Bryan Eagle* a personal account of his move to Mobile. Stanley volunteered with other Texas Aggies for service at the onset of war and trained for almost a month at various posts scattered throughout Texas. Along with his fellow troopers he boarded the train at Camp Mabry in the early morning of May 20 and headed northward through Rockdale, Palestine, and Longview, where they transferred to another train, which took them to Marshall, Shreveport, and then south to New Orleans:

> Every town, no matter how small gave us a grand reception. The fair sex seemed to be more enthusiastic than the men. At Rockdale we were received with a brass band and the shooting of anvils. At Palestine we stopped for dinner, which consisted of black coffee, two hard tacks, and canned beef. At Longview we were transferred . . . and while there we had a jolly time with the girls. Longview has lots of pretty girls, but none that will compare with Bryan's. At Marshall we had supper . . . (hardtack and sardines). We arrived at Shreveport after dark but there was a crowd of boys and girls there to give us a send off. When we reached New Orleans we stopped overnight . . . (and had old chuck, hardtack and sardines). We arrived here (Mobile, Alabama) . . . worn out from our trip and half starved to death besides!
>
> We sleep in tents of five men to a tent. Each man has a pair of blankets. He sleeps on one and covers with the other one, and his coat for a pillow . . . and that is the life of a soldier.
>
> Yours to the front, Claude Stanley[21]

Stanley fared much better in his transition to military life than did Bonney Youngblood, who enlisted in the Texas Volunteer Infantry at the age of sixteen and received orders to a camp in Miami, Florida. Shortly after he arrived he "took measles, malaria and typhoid, all at the same time" and came near "passing on." His military career ended prematurely with an honorable discharge in October, 1898. After taking a year to get well, Youngblood enrolled at Texas A&M, where he received a degree in agriculture in 1902.[22]

Company A, 1st Texas Volunteers, at Camp Cuba Libre, Jacksonville, Florida. Capt. George McCormick ('91) (first row, center left), commander, holds one of the company mascots. At top right is Lt. Milby Porter ('97).

Youngblood's experiences in the Spanish-American War were typical of those of many veterans. Disease caused more casualties than combat during that conflict. Although relatively few of the 225,000 or so volunteers called to arms actually fought in Cuba, thousands became ill. Most of the volunteers had no medical screening of any sort, and for those who were unwell, the only cures were in the traditional folk medicines. Pharmacology and hygiene were then in their infancy, and the germ theory of disease had been in acceptance for less than two decades.

In Tampa alone, for example, where additional units of the army's V Corps prepared for transfer to Cuba and Puerto Rico, 4,122 soldiers were reported sick on a single day, July 27, 1898—most of them down with yellow fever and dysentery. Almost 21,000 soldiers, mostly volunteers, composing roughly ten percent of the total volunteer force, contracted typhoid fever. While the mortality rate from typhoid peaked at 5.89 per 1,000 in September, 1898, sanitation measures implemented by the U.S. Surgeon General's office and devised by a special task force headed by Maj. Walter Reed began to reduce the drastic toll of disease at army encampments.

The Spanish-American War was an important learning experience for modern medicine, but not until 1901, long after operations ended in Cuba, did Walter Reed discover that the mosquito carries yellow fever, while his studies of typhoid, completed in 1904, significantly enhanced the medical world's understanding of the causes and spread of that illness.[23] Disease, of course, was a fact of life in those times and thus no deterrent to the rush to arms. The sighting of a powerful Spanish fleet in the Atlantic, however, caused considerable alarm.

About May 12, the Spanish fleet was sighted steaming westward from Martinique toward an "unknown destination," and, on May 14, an American consul reported Spanish ships off Curaçao, a Dutch island colony near Venezuela. Expecting the Spanish fleet to make for Havana, Santiago, or Puerto Rico, the U.S. Navy Department dispatched the fast modern cruisers and battleships under Adm. Winfield S. Schley, popularly referred to as the Flying Squadron, from its position off Hampton Rhodes, Virginia (where it was stationed to defend the Atlantic coast against Spanish attack), to the Caribbean. There it was to aid Adm. William T. Sampson in the search for Cervera's fleet. But again the Spanish disappeared from view. Finally, word came that the Spanish fleet had moved into Santiago harbor, and on June 1, Sampson's fleet joined Schley in an attempt to form a blockade. A coal carrier, the *Merrimac*, was sunk in the harbor entrance, but the heroic effort failed to provide an effective barrier.[24]

Having located the Spanish fleet and in theory isolating it, the War Department firmed its plans for landing an expeditionary force in Cuba. The strategy was to capture Santiago by land, blockade the harbor by sea, and force the surrender of the Spanish fleet. The army's V Corps, with 815 officers and 16,072 enlisted men, plus a cavalry division (accompanied by eighty-nine newspaper reporters), constituted the attacking force that was to join with the Cuban insurrectionists. The War Department correctly estimated the Spanish forces defending Santiago to have in the neighborhood of 12,000 officers and men.[25]

The Rough Riders, an elite cavalry unit expected to lead the attack, waited anxiously for the invasion of Cuba. Headed by Col. Leonard Wood and Lt. Col. Theodore Roosevelt, the Rough Riders recruited most of their men in the Southwest, including Texas, the Oklahoma Territory, New Mexico, and Arizona. The cavalry regiment assembled in San Antonio, Texas, in May and early June, 1898, for several weeks of intensive training, some parading, and no little partying. During one celebration Teddy Roosevelt rode his horse into the bar of the Menger Hotel. Finally, on May 29, about five hundred strong, with fifteen hundred horses and mules, the regiment boarded a train for Tampa, Florida. En route, food, illness, poor sanitation, and dwindling supplies quickly created problems. The planned forty-eight-hour trip turned into a four-day ordeal, exhausting travel rations. Once in Tampa, with no coherent organization for transportation to Cuba, the Rough Riders seized the troop carrier *Yucatan* for the voyage but were forced to leave behind most of their horses and mules. Indeed, during the six weeks or so that the V Corps assembled at Tampa, the scene ranged from something resembling a reunion to a county fair to a major disaster. Finally, on June 13, the army set sail for Cuba.[26]

On June 22, the army, with assistance from naval officers on the scene, began landing operations at the village of Daquiri, located east of Santiago along the southeastern coast of Cuba. The landing or "invasion" meant ferrying troops and equipment back and forth in the few boats available and literally throwing horses and mules over the side of the boats in the hope that they might survive and swim to shore. Many did, but some of them swam out to sea instead. Fortunately, Spanish forces did not oppose the landing.

Once ashore, troops and "dismounted" cavalry began the march along trails and roads through the town of Siboney. Following an initial skirmish at Las Guasimas, the army began climbing toward the heights surrounding Santiago, where resistance stiffened. During the approach, American forces lofted a hot-air observation balloon that created more problems than it solved. The balloon attracted Spanish infantry and cannon fire. Unfortunately, it floated over the leading units of the 71st New York Volunteers, who were showered with the bombardment and forced to halt. Soldiers in the rear, including the Rough Riders, pressed forward at the same time, creating a horrendous congestion at the beginning of what became the famous Battle of San Juan Hill. The Rough Riders and 10th Cavalry finally pressed through the snarl and led the attack up the slopes on July 1, pausing in the midst of battle when their own artillery began raining down on their positions. Finally, after almost fourteen hours of uninterrupted charging and fighting, the Spanish troops withdrew, leaving the Americans in control of the hills around Santiago harbor.[27]

The costs had been high. Some 1,475 Americans were killed or wounded, and the city had not surrendered. At first it was unclear whether this battle had been a victory or a defeat, but the uncertainty ended on July 3, when Admiral Cervera's fleet sailed out of Santiago into the open jaws of the American navy, comprising five modern battleships, two cruisers, and an assortment of associated ships—and was destroyed. Gen. José Toral subsequently surrendered the city of Santiago on July 16. In neighboring Puerto Rico, beginning on July 25, civilian populations welcomed the arrival of American troops. U.S. forces, mostly volunteers, began leaving Cuba on August 6, and hostilities against Spain officially ended on August 12.[28] Insofar as combat in Cuba and the outcome were concerned, this had been a "splendid little war," but in terms of planning, preparation, management, supply, and logistics, it had been a near disaster. The war, however, reverberated in strange and distant places.

As U.S. combat forces withdrew from Cuba, an occupation army of approximately thirty thousand soldiers began arriving from the United States into the new island republic. Among them were Texas Aggies such as Lt. Milby Porter (who prepared a photographic record of his military service) and Capt. George McCormick, both officers of Company A, 1st Texas Volunteer Infantry. They had

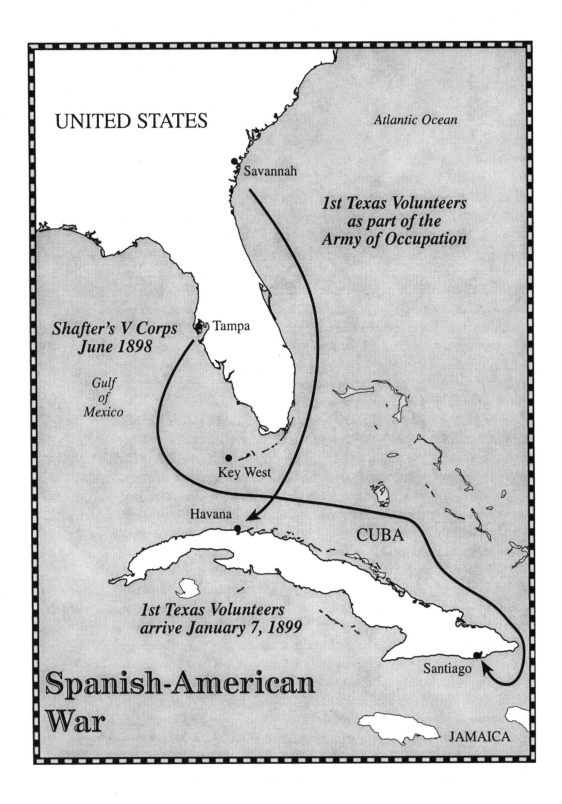

UNITED STATES

Atlantic Ocean

Savannah

*1st Texas Volunteers
as part of the
Army of Occupation*

*Shafter's V Corps
June 1898*

Tampa

Gulf
of
Mexico

Key West

Havana

CUBA

*1st Texas Volunteers
arrive January 7, 1899*

Santiago

Spanish-American
War

JAMAICA

The army of occupation arrived in Cuba on January 1, 1899. The entire thirty-thousand-man army can be seen snaking from the port toward the encampment.

arrived at Camp Cuba Libre near Jacksonville, Florida, at the beginning of the war to serve as local defense forces, should Spain attempt to invade, and to provide reserves for the expedition to Cuba if needed. At the end of the war, the 1st Texas Volunteers were transferred to Camp Onward near Savannah, Georgia, awaiting shipment to Cuba. They embarked on December 27, 1898, aboard the transport ships *Mobile* and *Kilpatrick*. When they arrived at Havana on January 1, Lieutenant Porter explained, one of the soldiers' first actions was to remove the Spanish flag that was flying over El Morro castle at the harbor entrance.[29]

Lieutenant Porter, Captain McCormick, and many of the Texas A&M volunteers completed their one-year tour of duty and returned to the States before the end of 1899. Others, including H. E. Rawlins ('83), remained in Cuba until 1906, working on what he described as "the rehabilitation of the island country." Maj. George T. Bartlett, A&M's former commandant of cadets, who had been assigned to the 3rd Artillery at the beginning of hostilities, remained in Havana for several years, first as chief clerk of the army's commissary department and then with the U.S. Army Engineers as "inspector of masonry," supervising the paving of Havana's streets.[30]

As it turned out, the war had much more to do with developments in the Pacific than with Cuba, and combat continued far beyond August 12, when

Cuban revolutionaries such as these on the streets of Havana in 1898 assisted in the overthrow of the Spanish colonial regime and the establishment of an independent government.

Spain and the United States formally agreed to end the hostilities. The agreement provided for the surrender of Manila in the Philippines to American forces the next day.

The destruction of the Spanish fleet at Manila by Admiral Dewey had increased America's interest in establishing a Pacific presence, especially in Hawaii and the Philippines. Following a revolt in 1893, the U.S. Senate had rejected a treaty annexing Hawaii to the United States, clinging to the idea that the United States should remain protected and isolated behind the two oceans and benign British naval power. However, when American isolationism crumbled during the next half-dozen years as friction developed with Britain and Germany, naval technology began to advance rapidly. Some Americans became intrigued by the prospect of the United States becoming a global commercial power. Thus, when President McKinley ordered the invasion of Cuba, he had also ordered American forces to land in the Philippines with the intention of assisting Filipino insurrectionists under Emilio Aguinaldo to attain independence for that country. The army sent around sixty thousand soldiers to San Francisco in preparation for an expedition to the Philippines, but by the time the

American troops began arriving there, their mission had changed. Americans now sought "law, order, and civilization" for the Filipinos, not independence from Spain. However, tension between insurrectionist troops and U.S. occupation forces in Manila led to hostilities in February, 1899. During the campaigns in the Philippines, American casualties were twice those in Cuba. Filipinos continued to resist American rule with intermittent fighting until almost 1935.

Texas Aggies among the Philippine expedition's VIII Army Corps were Lt. Charles C. Todd ('97), Collin C. Brown, and Eugene Appleby. Todd fought against Spanish forces and was wounded in action near Manila. Brown and Appleby, on the other hand, fought against Aguinaldo's Filipino forces. Todd was the first Aggie to receive a direct commission in the Regular Army and was among the first troops to land in the Philippines. He had served as first captain of the Corps of Cadets and gave the valedictory address at his graduation. In his speech he lauded the benefits of a solid education and stressed duty to one's country. He cited the great contributions of the college's president, Lawrence Sullivan Ross, to the well-being of the school and Ross's service to the college and the state: "It is not the nature of a Texas boy to forget an action of this kind. . . . Your image is so engraved upon the hearts of the students of this college as to live forever."[31] Todd's call to service had come sooner than expected.

Shortly after the war broke out, he was ordered to active duty and reported to San Francisco to join the first contingent of American troops headed for the Philippines. He fought with the insurrectionists against the Spanish and was wounded in one of his first combat encounters. By September, 1899, Todd was back in College Station, Texas, where he addressed the Young Men's Christian Association, urging cadets to make the best use of their time and opportunity— because their knowledge and morals would soon be put to the test. And in that, he was also correct. Todd later studied law and returned for a time to the A&M College for a two-year stint as commandant of the Corps of Cadets before entering the practice of law.[32]

As Todd was returning to College Station, two of his former fellow students, Brown and Appleby, were boarding ship in San Francisco to join the fight against Filipino insurrectionists. These two composed a travelogue about their war experiences, and it was published in the campus *Battalion* in March, 1900: "At exactly 4 o'clock on the evening of September 30, 1899, the transport Sheridan, having on board the 33rd Infantry, swung out into the bay, 'mid a mighty shout from the thousands on shore and slowly steamed out towards the setting sun on her long and tedious voyage to the Orient. As we steamed past the battleship *Iowa* she dipped her flag for us, and her band played The 'Stars and Stripes Forever,' and our band responded with 'I don't care if you never come back.'"[33]

After a short stop in Honolulu, the ships left for the Philippines and arrived in Manila Bay on October 27. Following a number of night encounters with hostile Filipino forces along the eastern coast, the troop ships embarked for the north-central coast of Luzon, where the navy bombarded the shore for several hours and then landed troops under heavy fire at the village of San Fabian. "We were not long," wrote Appleby and Brown, "in getting into the thickest of the fighting after this date, and we drove them over rivers, across mountains and through the mud, killing them and capturing them until we broke up the army and put the American flag in all their seaport cities."[34]

The Spanish-American War brought substantial changes in America's status among the nations of the world and in the perceptions Americans had of themselves. Among other things, this conflict reinforced the A&M College's commitment to military training and the beginning of a long history of service to the country in time of war. In view of the institution's contributions to the war effort, the inspector general recommended that in the future the army should issue regular commissions to the college's best students, such as Charles C. Todd.[35] The war changed Texas A&M and, indeed, America's role among the world's nations to an extent not fully realized for many years: "The Spanish-American War: Those Who Served the Good Effects of the Military Instruction Given to the Students of This Institution Are Shown Very Plainly by the Number of Ex-students and Alumni of This College That We Find Taking Part in the Late War with Spain, and the Comparative Good Ranks Held by All."[36]

As of December, 1898, the college reported that eighty-nine men were in the army, sixty-three of whom were officers or noncommissioned officers. There were others who came to Texas A&M after their term of service or who were unaccounted for in the 1898 report, some of whom are included in table 1. Unfortunately, the college failed to include the names of all those who served, and the record is thus incomplete.

The most immediate consequence of the war was that Cuba became free and independent. Qualifications in the peace settlement included a proviso for a permanent U.S. military base at Guantanamo Bay, a promise by Cuba to repay debts owed American citizens, a requirement that Cuba not enter into any treaties that might be detrimental to U.S. interests, and a condition that Cuba acknowledge the right of the United States to intervene at any time to protect its interests on the island. In the settlement following the surrender, in exchange for $20 million, Spain ceded the Philippines, Puerto Rico, and Guam to the United States. The Philippines remained a U.S. possession until it became a republic in 1946.

As the *Bryan Eagle* observed, America astonished the whole world in that war by recruiting, mustering, equipping, and readying a volunteer army of 261,400 men. And despite mismanagement and confusion, the United States surprised itself by becoming, almost overnight, a global power, a role inconsistent with the nation's history and traditions and with the values of many Americans.

TABLE 1. Texas Aggies in the Spanish-American War

Name	Rank/Enlisted Grade or Rate	Class
Franklin, R. Hadley	1st Lieutenant	1880
Hardy, G. W.	Lt. Colonel	1880
Rogers, Robert Allan	Major	1881
Swain, Mark Sims	Captain	1888
Nichols, Joseph F.	Captain	1889
Anderson, William D.	Captain	1890
McCormick, George, Jr.	Captain	1891
Middlebrook, Robert Moore	Sergeant	1891
Cook, Edgar A.	1st Lieutenant	1892
Cottingham, Wesley P.	Sergeant	1892
Perlitz, Willie E.	1st Lieutenant	1893
Abbott, Elisha G.	1st Lieutenant	1894
Ferguson, Alex M.	Sergeant (Regular Army)	1894
Fowler, E. G. Rees	Captain	1894
Rose, Wilton F.	Captain	1894
Bloor, Alfred Wainnerwright	Sergeant	1895
Holman, James Richard	Captain	1895
Hutson, William Ferguson	1st Sergeant/1st Lieutenant	1895
McDonald, Hugh F.	1st Lieutenant	1895
Watts, Arthur P.	(?)	1895
Blount, John F.	(?)	1896
Cushing, Dan	Corporal	1896
Hutson, Henry L.	Corporal/1st Lieutenant	1896
Moursund, E. M.	Corporal	1897
Perkins, Frank Dudley	(?)	1897
Porter, Milbey	Lieutenant	1897
Rollins, Henry M.	Corporal	1897
Stalcup, James Fred	(?)	1897
Stewart, Charles R.	(?)	1897
Todd, Charles C.	2nd Lieutenant (RA)	1897
Appleby, Eugene	(?)	1898
Brown, Collins C.	(?)	1898
Rawlins, H. E.	(?)	1898
Robson, C. Guy	Regimental Sergeant-Major	1898
Youngblood, Bonney	(?)	1902
Gebhart, P. C.	(?)	1902
Hope, George N.	(?)	1904
Moore, Minor	(?)	

Suggested Readings

Brands. H. W. *Bound to Empire: The United States and the Philippines* (New York: Oxford University Press, 1992).

Cosmas, Graham A. *An Army for Empire: The United States Army in the Spanish-American War* (1971; repr., Shippending, Penn.: White Mare, 1994).

Linn, Brian McAllister. *The Philippine War, 1899–1902* (Lawrence: University of Kansas Press, 2000).

Millis, Walter. *The Martial Spirit: A Study of Our War with Spain* (Boston: Houghton Mifflin, 1931), pp. 109–39.

Rickover, H. G. *How the Battleship Maine Was Destroyed* (Annapolis, Md.: Naval Institute Press, 1995).

Roosevelt, Theodore. *The Rough Riders* (1902; repr., New York: De Capo Press, 1990).

Trask, David. *The War with Spain in 1898* (New York: Macmillan, 1981).

French army tank company commander George P. F. Jouine ('07), the most decorated former A&M student of World War I, understood the mechanics of tanks and knew how best to use them on the battlefield. Jesse Easterwood ('09), on loan to the United Kingdom's Royal Flying Corps, piloted one of the first Handley Page heavy bombers in a night attack against a German-held railroad junction and flew sixteen missions behind German lines. He intermittently served with the Italian and French air forces.

3

BORDERING ON WAR

The kind of soldiers he got for the occupation of the Philippines, said Col. Luther R. Hare, the hard-charging, hard-cursing veteran of Little Big Horn, who commanded the 33rd Infantry (nicknamed the "Texas Regiment"), were "1,200 sharpshooters and 1,300 crapshooters." In 1899, although the U.S. Army had begun to demobilize even before the ink had dried on the Treaty of Paris ending the war with Spain, the War Department hastily recalled volunteers to deal with the Filipino insurrection. Most of the volunteers were short-timers. The sharpshooters, if not crapshooters, included Texas Aggies Collin Brown and Eugene Appleby, among others. But the nine-month service obligation of most of the volunteers meant that personnel strength eroded rapidly. Indeed, just the transit to and from the Philippines could consume much of the term of enlistment.[1]

By 1904, the Regular Army numbered fewer than 100,000 men, while reserve or National Guard units declined to about 70,000. Most state governments chose not to fund a traditional militia, and the federal government provided little financial assistance for such efforts. Moreover, for more than a decade after 1900, the meager congressional appropriations for the army went primarily to the Corps of Engineers for the construction of dams, bridges, harbors, and dikes—and not for military defense or training.[2]

In 1915, Theodore Roosevelt's comment that the United States had been entirely unprepared for war in 1898 applied equally to the state of readiness in 1917. Running with William McKinley, Roosevelt won the vice presidency in 1900, and upon the assassination of McKinley by the anarchist Leon Czolgosz in September, 1901, he became president. "T. R." handily won reelection in 1904 as a progressive, moderate-reform candidate, but, other than modernizing the navy, Roosevelt and his successors did little to strengthen the military forces of the country at the level that was the norm in Europe. This lack of preparation can be attributed in part to the tradition of the citizen soldier, which held that any adult male with a gun in hand to defend the country was thereby a soldier. In reality, at the dawn of the twentieth century, untrained citizens could no longer be considered soldiers. Even so, professional military training languished after the Spanish-American War as it had before the conflict. Thus, on the eve of World War I, the United States was unprepared for war.

Although Secretary of War Elihu Root sought to improve the processes for mobilizing citizen soldiers and professed to be extremely proud of the volunteers' efforts in the war against Spain, he noted that "The great lesson of our wars is that they must be carried to a conclusion by citizen soldiers and these soldiers must be trained. To throw untrained citizens into the field is nothing short of death by government order."[3] Thus, in 1903, Congress passed legislation that integrated federal and state guard units into a more uniform and better-trained pool of citizen soldiers between the ages of eighteen and forty-five. State militias now had to conform to federal standards of discipline, armament, organization, and pay. Moreover, the president of the United States was given the authority to call the National Guard units to active duty.[4] While the new legislation helped create a uniform, state-based National Guard, both federal and state financial support for military training declined, as did the public's enthusiasm for and participation in the National Guard, militia, and the Regular Army.

Texas A&M, where enthusiasm and support for military training remained strong, was again an exception. Students there felt even more obligated to serve in their country's military forces. Indeed, military training on campus became more pronounced, purposeful, and focused. After 1900, the corps training included sham battles, a spring march to the Brazos River, and more intense instruction in military tactics. The cadet uniform also reflected more closely the Regular Army uniform. In deference to Spanish-American War veterans and warm Texas weather, cadets wore the floppy, western-style campaign hat with a center crease, a dark blue woolen shirt, loose trousers, and an optional pair of canvas leggings.[5]

The military caste of the college was further enhanced when the army assigned a series of very able and determined professors of military science and tactics to the Texas A&M campus. During this period, annual inspections and program reviews conducted by the War Department consistently ranked the A&M College as one of the top ten "distinguished" military programs in the United States. Its growing recognition as a reputable military institution contributed to a doubling of the student body enrollment between 1903 and 1909—from 354 students to 711. Pres. Robert Teague Milner (1908–1913) routinely boasted that "A&M had the world's largest student body under military discipline."[6] Because of the continuing decline in the Regular Army's authorized strength, only a few A&M graduates went directly into military service, but a significant number joined the Texas National Guard, thus becoming members of the "ready" or active reserve.

Legislation was enacted in 1912 that allowed Regular Army volunteers, after serving for four years, to transfer to an active reserve status and permitted those already discharged from active duty to volunteer for a reserve army unit. This action in effect created the basic army reserve structure as it exists today. However, by 1914, because the reserves were unfunded, very few men leaving the army had volunteered for active reserve service.[7] As a result, the United States was ill prepared for the two very different wars that now threatened its security. One was in Europe, Africa, and Asia Minor; the other was on the nation's southernmost boundary, adjacent to Texas on the Rio Grande.

The war across the sea was such as the world had never before seen. At a time when British and French casualties in single battles often exceeded 100,000 men, the total strength of the U.S. Army was 127,588 men, and its ready reserve National Guard numbered only 66,594. Thus, as U.S. Army chief of staff Peyton C. March noted later, the army in 1915 "was of no practical military value as far as fighting in France was concerned."[8]

In contrast, members of the Texas National Guard faced a more imminent threat. In the four decades before 1910, Mexico's turbulent politics and the presidency were dominated by Porfirio Diaz, whose victory over invading French armies on May 5, 1862 (Cinco de Mayo) made him a folk hero. Near the end of his days, despite tremendous economic progress, Mexico erupted again into revolution, a conflict fed by strong ethnic loyalties and anti-American sentiments that lasted a decade. Foreign investments, especially American-owned ones in railroads, mining, oil, agricultural development, and utilities, were now threatened with destruction and confiscation.[9] Political chaos reigned as lawlessness and violence arose precipitously along the Texas–Mexico Rio Grande boundary.

In early 1914, Pres. Woodrow Wilson secretly directed the army and navy to prepare, if necessary, for the invasion of Mexico to protect America's strategic interests, notably oil, copper, rubber, zinc, and silver. Subsequently, in mid-January, the secretary of war sent more than twenty-four thousand troops, many of them Texans and some of them Aggies, to Texas City, Texas, south of Houston, to guard the borders.[10]

On April 21, 1914, President Wilson ordered the navy to land marines and occupy the port of Vera Cruz, Mexico. This action was sparked by an incident on April 9 at Tampico, when Mexican authorities arrested a number of Americans without just cause and held them without specifying charges or permitting bail. In time, the prisoners were released, and Mexican authorities expressed their regret. The United States indignantly demanded an apology and a twenty-one-gun salute. When Mexico refused to comply, marines landed at Vera Cruz.

Argentina, Brazil, and Chile stepped in to help mediate the crisis, but the American fleet remained on patrol along the Mexican coast until November.[11] Tensions between the United States and Latin America had risen rapidly after 1900 as the former expanded its economic interests throughout the region. A capstone of that economic expansion was America's new Panama Canal, which opened for business in 1914.

Moreover, in August, 1914, war began in Europe. That continent had seen no major conflict since 1871, and it seemed incredible to most Americans and many Europeans that war should come now. In truth, since 1871, Europe had been arming and building alliances in preparation for combat. When, on June 28, 1914, a Serbian nationalist assassinated Archduke Franz Ferdinand of Austria on the streets of Sarajevo, Bosnia, a chain of coalitions and treaties came into play. Austria-Hungary demanded that the conspirators be brought to justice and that Serbia halt her anti-Austrian activities. Serbia and Austria-Hungary mobilized for war, triggering the mobilization of Russia, an ally of Serbia. Soon afterward, when Germany called its armies to the field to assist Austria, France reciprocated, and Great Britain then prepared to aid France and Belgium. Japan, allied with Great Britain, joined in, while Turkey sided with Germany. Italy remained neutral until April, 1915, and then joined the Allies.

On August 3, 1914, Germany declared war on France, and by September 5, German armies, slashing through neutral Belgium, were within thirty miles of Paris. The war assumed a scale and dimension never before imagined. On the 350-mile-long western front, massive armies fought with poison gas, tanks, aircraft, bombs, trenches, and bayonets. In one offensive at Arras, France, in the spring of 1917, British forces lost nearly 175,000 officers and men, a number exceeding the entire standing army of the United States at the time. In Russia, in the battle of Tannenberg in 1914, German armies under General von Hindenburg marched between two larger Russian armies and defeated both, taking 90,000 prisoners and most of Russia's war equipment. Between May and September, 1915, as Russian armies were driven out of Poland, they suffered a million casualties, and an equal number were taken prisoner. The Czarist government collapsed in 1917, and, following the Communist revolution in October, Russia withdrew from the war.

As battleships and submarines became the chosen weapons of naval warfare, the War Department and Congress grew increasingly concerned about the readiness of America's armed forces. However, it was not the war in Europe but the threat of conflict on the home front that triggered public alarm. Preparedness assumed a new urgency on March 9, 1916, when the Mexican rebel leader, Francisco ("Pancho") Villa, crossed the Rio Grande and raided Columbus, New Mexico, killing nineteen Americans. In response, President Wilson ordered Brig. Gen. John J. Pershing with 9,000 regulars and some 30,000 National Guard members (most of whom belonged to the Texas National Guard), joined

Europe 1914

- Allied Powers
- Central Powers
- Neutral Countries

NORWAY
SWEDEN
GREAT BRITAIN
DEN.
RUSSIA
NETH.
GERMANY
BELG.
FRANCE
AUSTRIA-HUNGARY
SWITZ.
ITALY
RUMANIA
PORT.
SERBIA
BULGARIA
SPAIN
MONT.
ALB.
GREECE
TURKEY

by almost 1,000 Texas Rangers dispatched by the governor, to the border of Mexico in pursuit of Villa's troops. The U.S. Army gathered near El Paso and crossed into Chihuahua, where it fought several skirmishes and scattered the Villistas but failed to capture Villa himself.[12]

In June, 1916, the immediate threat of war with Mexico, rather than the more distant concerns about the European conflict, caused Congress to pass the first comprehensive legislation on military policy, which allowed the Regular Army strength to expand beyond 175,000 men, while the National Guard could increase its numbers to 400,000. Meanwhile, as commander in chief, President

Wilson ordered the National Guard to the Rio Grande to guard the border against attack. By the late summer of 1916, more than 100,000 National Guard troops were positioned on the U.S.-Mexico border from Brownsville, Texas, to Yuma, Arizona—a distance of more than sixteen hundred miles.[13]

Among those troops were many Texas Aggies, including Oscar B. Abbott ('13) and John F. Ehlert and Claudius M. Easley, both of the class of 1916. Easley and Ehlert remained on active duty near Brownsville, Texas, for most of 1917. Following that crisis, both stayed on active duty through the two world wars. Much later, in another war, Easley, by then a brigadier general, died in combat on Okinawa. His Aggie classmate John Ehlert served overseas in World War I and rose to the rank of colonel during World War II, when he was wounded in combat.[14] Both attributed their training in the Texas A&M Corps of Cadets and their initial service with Gen. John J. Pershing's expedition in Mexico with greatly influencing their career choices and advancement. Indeed, Pershing in Mexico and the border defenses in Texas, rather than Germany and Europe, reinforced the military training regimen at Texas A&M and reinvigorated America's efforts to improve military training everywhere.

The new legislation also helped create a pool of trained reserves from which the army could rapidly recruit soldiers and find officers trained for combat leadership. It established the Officers' Reserve Corps (ORC) and provided federal funding for "civil education institutions" to train officers to be commissioned via the Reserve Officers' Training Corps (ROTC). The legislation applied immediately to all land-grant institutions, including Texas A&M. Pres. William B. Bizzell quickly asked the War Department for permission to establish an ROTC program. The army approved A&M's application in October, 1916, and instruction was scheduled to begin in September, 1917.[15] The ROTC afforded Texas Aggies more opportunities for direct commissioning in the armed forces following graduation. Prior to the institution of the ROTC, commissions were usually granted only after service in a noncommissioned status or upon the completion of special military training programs.

Victor A. Barraco, for example (a 1915 graduate who rose to the rank of general in World War II), recalled that he and twenty-two other Aggies were able to be commissioned in World War I only because they enlisted in the U.S. Marines and took training at Quantico, Virginia.[16] The ROTC, therefore, actually had no impact on preparing men for combat in World War I. The United States became embroiled in the war before the ROTC program could be implemented.

The conflict on the Texas border suddenly became curiously commingled with the slaughter and turmoil in Europe. Despite signs of reconciliation and pacification on the Texas border with Mexico, U.S.-Mexican relations suddenly deteriorated almost to the point of war. The American press revealed that Germany had proposed to Mexico that, if the United States entered the war against Germany and Mexico declared war on the United States, Mexico would receive great benefits if the Central powers won the war—that is, the territories the

United States had acquired from Mexico as a result of the Mexican War—including Texas, Arizona, and New Mexico—would be returned to Mexico. German foreign minister Arthur Zimmerman sent a secret telegram on January 16, 1917, to the interim government of President Carranza, which read in part as follows: "We intend to begin unrestricted submarine warfare on the first of February. We shall endeavor in spite of this to keep the United States neutral. In the event of not succeeding, we make Mexico a proposal of alliance on the following basis: Make war together, make peace together, generous financial support, and an understanding on our part that Mexico is to reconquer the lost territory in Texas, New Mexico, Arizona. The settlement in detail is left to you."[17]

Despite a tremendous outcry in the United States and demands for war, Wilson chose peace and formal diplomatic relations with Mexico by sending Ambassador Henry P. Fletcher to Mexico City. The United States indeed moved closer to a war in 1917—but not one with Mexico.

Despite America's efforts to remain neutral, the war in Europe inexorably pressed in upon American shores and interests. In 1915, a German U-boat had sunk an unarmed British passenger liner, the Lusitania, costing the lives of more than 1,100 civilians, including 128 American citizens. Commerce with Europe declined precipitously after 1914, and American merchant vessels were occasionally sunk by German submarines and raiders. After February, 1917, Germany began unrestricted submarine warfare. The Zimmerman telegram and reports of American ships being sunk by Germany pushed the nation to the edge of battle. On the A&M campus, the faculty and staff fully expected a declaration of war. Many of the students were already on active duty along the Rio Grande when, on March 17, 1917, A&M President Bizzell volunteered the entire college to the federal government as a military training site. By this action, Texas A&M became the first college in the nation to offer its facilities for wartime service.[18] Two weeks later, on April 2, President Wilson, with great personal reluctance, asked Congress to declare war on Imperial Germany and the Austro-Hungarian Empire. Upon the approval of the House and Senate, Wilson signed a declaration of war on April 6.

The coming of war had an immediate effect on life at Texas A&M. While most of the students welcomed the call to arms and mobilization, confusion nevertheless reigned. All Regular Army officers, including most of those assigned to military training duties at the colleges and universities, were immediately called to active duty. The ROTC training program, scheduled to begin in September, 1917, was suspended and not reactivated until 1920—after the war. In early 1917, to fill the immediate wartime need for officers, the War Department created more than forty "officer training schools" (better known in World War I as OTS) in diverse locations around the country. One of the first of those began operating at Camp Funston, near Leon Springs, Texas, northwest of San Antonio.[19]

By May, 1917, around 117 Aggie cadets, primarily seniors who were only a few weeks short of graduation, had signed in at Camp Funston for training.

The commander of the camp was Col. William S. Scott, former Texas A&M commandant (Sept., 1889–Aug., 1890). Other A&M cadets enrolled in officer training programs to become "ninety-day wonders" in camps scattered across the United States.[20] Unlike most other OTS candidates, many of the Texas Aggies had four years of military training and discipline to back up their ninety days of intensive training. The OTS program, however, was only a beginning in the massive officer-procurement effort needed to deal with an expansion of the army from about 250,000 to 4.2 million men. On May 19, Congress authorized the draft and provided new opportunities for enlistment.

Aggies who had not been admitted to OTS camps now enlisted, and the A&M campus became virtually deserted: Texas Aggies had gone off to war. Graduation ceremonies that had been scheduled for mid-June of 1917 were canceled because almost no seniors were still on campus. Indeed, no formal graduation ceremonies would be held at Texas A&M for the duration of the war inasmuch as there were very few students enrolled and eligible for a degree. In the case of the class of 1917, however, the college's administrators made special arrangements to hold commencement exercises "under a big oak tree" at Camp Funston, Leon Springs, where seniors in good standing, though now in the armed forces, received their diplomas. Within weeks, most of those Aggies also received their commissions as army second lieutenants. Before the end of 1918, ten members of the original 1917 class of Aggie officers trained at Camp Funston were killed in action in Europe. More than one thousand Texans, including many Aggies, were trained and commissioned over the course of a year in the OTS sessions at Camp Funston.[21] Many Texas Aggies had already followed other routes to war.

Some Aggies were in combat even before the United States became a belligerent. A particularly interesting group of soldiers, no more than a dozen, served with the Allied armies. By mid-1917, the annual *Alumni Directory* listed five Aggies who were known to be "somewhere in France," while unnamed others were thought to be overseas. Information about them was scant. Among the Aggies who were unquestionably at war was Bertus Clyde Ball ('13) of Alvarado, Texas, a surgeon in the French army. John Ashton ('06) was a veterinarian attached to the First Veterinary Hospital, Army Veterinary Corps, British Expeditionary Force. Nat S. Perrine ('17) enlisted and fought with the Fourth French Army and received the Croix de Guerre for gallantry in action.[22]

Perhaps the most remarkable "early" war experience was that of George P. F. Jouine, a 1907 civil engineering graduate from Houston, Texas, who, in 1914, decided to make his own way to the fighting. He sailed to France at his own expense, enlisted as a private in the French army, received a battlefield commission, and, despite six combat wounds, served thirty-four months on the front lines. With more than a dozen combat decorations from three nations, Jouine became the most decorated former A&M student of World War I.[23]

Jouine's most significant role was as commander of a tank company in early 1916. This revolutionary new war machine had been introduced by the British only months earlier and proved critical to the final outcome of the war. As a civil engineer, Jouine understood the mechanics of tanks, and, as a trained military officer, he learned how best to use the weapon on the battlefield. Jouine later pursued a successful career in engineering in Houston, Texas. Upon his death in May, 1957, his military decorations and his engineering library were donated to Texas A&M. He was also influential in creating a graduate fellowship in engineering. In recognition of his achievements, the Corps of Cadets has, since 1958, annually named the most outstanding scholastic cadet unit the "Jouine unit" in his honor.[24]

Texas Aggies also made significant contributions to early aerial as well as tank warfare. Only eight years after the historic flight of Orville and Wilbur Wright at Kitty Hawk, North Carolina, in December, 1903, aviation pioneer Lt. Robert G. Fowler flew his fragile single-stroke-engine Wright Flyer to a safe landing on Kyle Field on December 1, 1911. Cadets rushed to surround the little aircraft in delight and amazement, and Texas Aggies thus became infected with the excitement and wonder of flight.

Many of them, such as Jesse Easterwood of Wells Point, Texas, pioneered in military aviation. On April 7, 1917, the day after Woodrow Wilson signed the declaration of war, Easterwood left the A&M campus to enlist in the navy. He was sent to flight training school at the newly established U.S. Naval Air Service station at Pensacola, Florida, where he was among the first class of navy officers to qualify as aviators. Although he was commissioned as an ensign "with wings," there were no aircraft for him to fly. Consequently, the navy loaned him to the United Kingdom to serve with the Royal Flying Corps. After piloting one of the first Handley Page heavy bombers in a night attack against a German-held railroad junction, Easterwood flew sixteen missions behind German lines and intermittently served with the Italian and French air forces before being transferred back to an American unit. After the war, in early 1919, the War Department sent this highly decorated officer to the Panama Canal Zone. His assignment was to bolster the American forces that were defending the area and to provide more leverage in America's ongoing dispute with Columbia over reparations for the loss of Panama. Easterwood also provided support for America's interests in Nicaragua, where U.S. Marines had intervened several times since 1912. Thus, Easterwood left the big war in Europe for a cluster of small wars in Central America. Soon after arriving in Panama, he died in an airplane accident at Coco Solo and was posthumously awarded the Navy Cross. In May, 1941, the A&M board of directors named the new college-owned airport on the west side of the campus in Easterwood's honor. In doing so, they stated that "his life and activities best typify the spirit of the A&M College."[25]

Thus, even before U.S. forces arrived in Europe, Texas Aggies had found their

The tank and aircraft were introduced as the major new weapons of warfare during World War I. The Renault tank pictured here was used by Lt. Otto G. Tumlinson ('18) and others in France. George P. F. Jouine ('07) sailed to France at his own expense in 1914, enlisted as a private in the French army, received a battlefield commission, and became the most decorated former A&M student of World War I as a tank company commander. Gen. A. D. Bruce ('16) fought with the 2nd Infantry Division's machine gun battalion in the war and rose from the rank of lieutenant to lieutenant colonel. He became the army's leading expert in tank destroyer tactics.

way to the battlefront. In his annual message to the alumni in 1917, President Bizzell praised the response of his former students who were serving their country: "Thousands of graduates and seniors promptly responded to the request of the War Department for enlistment in the Officer Training Corps. The military training offered at the College gave the graduates and advanced students an unusual advantage in meeting the exacting requirements at Camp Funston and at the other camps throughout the country. The unusual proficiency of Agricultural and Mechanical College men immediately attracted the favorable attention of the officers of the Army and won for them confidence and esteem of

The Curtiss JN-4 ("Jenny") two-seat biplane (of which there were many variations) pictured next to the Academic Building on the Texas A&M campus was the primary training aircraft used by the army. Military aviation came of age during World War I, and a substantial number of Texas Aggies were pioneers in air combat.

the highest military experts in the country. . . . After forty years the military instruction of the college has received ample vindication and justified those who succeeded in including military science as a required subject in the land-grant colleges."[26]

By 1917, Texas A&M had produced a significant proportion of the nation's agricultural, mechanical, civil, and electrical engineers, and its officer production exceeded that of most military institutions. This, however, was only the beginning.

In the summer of 1917, as the nation began sending its citizen soldiers to the great war in Europe, Gen. John J. ("Blackjack") Pershing, the newly selected commander of the American Expeditionary Force (AEF), faced the daunting challenge of raising, training, equipping, and shipping an army "over there" for a new style of warfare on a massive scale that U.S. forces had never before experienced. The first units of the AEF arrived in France in July, 1917, and began moving into positions along the battlefront near Verdun in October. American soldiers, however, were not committed to combat until the spring of 1918, when they were thrown into the breach to help stop the German offensive that brought the enemy to within fifty miles of Paris. In the initial action only about

TABLE 2. Degrees Granted, 1876–1917

Year	Literary	Agri-culture	Mech. Eng.	Civil Eng.	Elec. Eng.	Textile Eng.	Arch. Eng.	Chem. Eng.	Archi-tecture	Deceased	Yearly Total
1878	2										2
1879	16	2		2						7	20
1880	5			2						2	7
1881	2									1	2
1882			12							3	12
1883			8							4	8
1884		3	9	2						3	14
1885		2	8							1	10
1886		3	8							2	11
1887		1	10							4	11
1888		7	5	5						4	17
1889		6	3	10						5	19
1890		7	3	4						1	14
1891		4	6	6						1	16
1892		7	7	11						1	25
1893		6	1	6						3	13
1894		8	7	17						3	32
1895		8	8	11						2	27
1896		7	5	9						3	21
1897		6	7	13						7	26
1898		11	7	6						3	24
1899		8	10	3						3	21
1900		8	8	9						1	25
1901		6	8	6						2	20
1902		8	9	13						2	30
1903		1	16	20						2	37
1904		6	9	21						2	36
1905		19	7	11	1						38
1906		8	7	16	9	3	3			1	46
1907		10	3	20	11	1				1	45
1908		17	7	14	9	3				1	50
1909		9	1	15	14	1	3			1	43
1910		12	2	25	24		3	1		1	67
1911		20	18	29	20	2	5	2	1	5	97
1912		28	9	29	26	1	5	1	1		100
1913		46	8	31	19	3	4	2	1		114
1914		34	8	9	14		2		1		68
1915		52	5	10	12	2		5	2	1	88
1916		64	12	14	15	1	4	5	4		119
1917		75	8	15	25	2		1	9		135
Total	25	519	269	414	199	19	29	17	19	83	1,510

TABLE 3. World War I Officer Production

School	Officers	Enlisted	Total	General Officers	Killed or Died
Texas A&M	1,233	984	2,217	0	54
VMI	1,176	231	1,407	5	57
VPI	638	1,657	2,297	2	24
Clemson	U	U	1,549	0	25
Norwich	345	147	495	2	16
N. Georgia	U	U	371	0	10
Penn. Military	208	142	350	4	12
Citadel	276	40	316	0	16

U = Unknown or unavailable

Source: Texas A&M *Alumni Quarterly*; John D. Kraus Jr., "Civilian Military Colleges in the Twentieth Century," PhD diss., University of Iowa, 1978, p. 487; William Couper, *One Hundred Years at V.M.I.* (Richmond, Va.: Garrett and Massie, 1939), pp. 226–27; VMI Museum.

27,500 American soldiers were in combat, but by late summer American armies with several hundred thousand men played an increasing role in the counterattacks that ended the war in early November. Despite having been unprepared for war, the United States, within approximately eighteen months, produced more than 80,000 officers in their special ninety-day training camps and expanded the size of the standing army from about 250,000 at the war's start to more than 4 million by its conclusion.

In World War I, for the first time, American civilians who were called into service received intensive training before going into battle. The army organized, manned, and trained 55 divisions and sent 42 of those to France before the war's end. Although many of these units arrived without artillery, tanks, gas masks, or modern rifles, by the time they entered combat most of them were reasonably well equipped, trained, and ready to fight. By any standards, mobilization was a remarkable achievement. For the Texas Aggies who went "over there" in 1917 and 1918, following in the footsteps of A&M Cadets Ball, Ashton, Perrine, Easterwood, Jouine, and others who preceded them to Europe for service in the Allied armies, the battle had just begun.

Suggested Readings

Dunn, Timothy J. *The Militarization of the U.S.–Mexico Border, 1978–1992: Low-intensity Conflict Doctrine Comes Home* (Austin: CMAS Books, University of Texas Press, 1996).

Eisenhower, John S. D. *Intervention! The United States and the Mexican Revolution, 1913–1917* (New York: W. W. Norton, 1993).

———. *Yanks: The Epic Story of the American Army in World War I* (New York: Free Press, 2001).

Hart, John M. *Empire and Revolution: The Americans in Mexico since the Civil War* (Berkeley: University of California Press, 2002).

Roosevelt, Theodore. *America and the World War* (New York: C. Scribner's Sons, 1915).

Tuchman, Barbara. *The Guns of August* (New York: Macmillan, 1962).

Chapter 3

Capt. Charles T. Trickey ('17) flew unarmed reconnaissance missions behind enemy lines to detect troop movements and warn the Allies of forthcoming German attacks. During one of these forays, an incendiary bullet passed through and instantly ignited Trickey's gas tank, which was situated between the pilot's seat in front and Trickey in the back. As fuel spilled into Trickey's compartment, he immediately "climbed out on the wing of the machine, thus enabling the pilot to make a safe landing behind their own lines." In less than an hour, the crew were in the air again in another aircraft.

4

OVER THERE

"The state of war between the United States and the Imperial German Government which has been thrust upon the United States is hereby formally declared" (U.S. Congress, April 6, 1917). When the United States entered World War I, the standing army was composed of only 170,000 men and was limited by law to no more than 286,000. But a month later, following the declaration of war, Congress approved the Selective Service Act, which required all males between the ages of 18 and 45 to register for the draft and provided for the conscription of those who might be needed. A few weeks later Pres. Woodrow Wilson selected General Pershing to command the American forces in Europe. Congress and the War Department anticipated raising an army of only about 500,000; few envisioned that almost 3 million American troops would be in France by late 1918.[1]

General Pershing's command experience with around thirty thousand troops on the Mexican border provided little precedent for the size and complexity of the armies that would become the American Expeditionary Force (AEF) and ultimately nearly one-third of all Allied troops deployed on the western front. Two months after the declaration of war, American citizens began registering for the draft, and, by September, 1918, more than 24 million men had signed up— nearly half of all adult male Americans. Ultimately, some 4,100,000 men were inducted into service.[2]

Many Texas Aggies, as we have seen, were already in the air and on the battlefields of Europe in the summer of 1917, as students began leaving the A&M campus and mobilization began in earnest. Students, faculty, and administrators who remained on campus were no less committed to the war effort. The administration defined the college's war mission as providing men for military service, making facilities and faculty available for war training courses, helping to increase food and feed production, and developing conservation programs that would more effectively channel food to the army and national defense needs while sustaining the general public welfare. In promoting and encouraging agricultural production and conservation critical to the war, the college became a public relations and educational interface with the Texas public. In Texas, this was particularly critical and timely because the state was experiencing one of the longest droughts in its history. President Bizzell, who had no military experience, nevertheless had a solid grasp of the urgency of the situation. Immediately after the declaration of war, he went to Washington, D.C., to seek funding for the development of campus military training programs, equipment, and additional training staff for the college. He constantly reminded students, faculty, and the public that, in this war effort, everyone—students, faculty, farmers, engineers, priests, and ministers—was a soldier.[3]

In late April, 1917, after the commandant of the Corps of Cadets, Col. C. H Muller, and his assistant, Lt. W. H. Morris, left the campus for active service, the college hired Col. Charles J. Crane (1881–1894), former A&M commandant and a retired Regular, to oversee the corps for the duration of the war. To assist Colonel Crane, Bizzell secured the services of Capt. William Martin, a returning veteran of service with Canadian troops in France. Martin gave the cadets a first-hand knowledge of and insight into trench warfare. A&M College's *Alumni Quarterly*, published in January, 1917, three months before America's entry into the war in Europe, announced that "a large number of vacancies now exist in the grade of second lieutenant in the line Army." Created to help alleviate that shortage, the Officers Reserve Corps (ORC) became the primary mechanism for the entry of young officers, who received readiness training at Camp Funston and other places.[4] Probably the greatest initial impact of the Selective Service Act was to trigger large-scale enlistments.

In addition to the commissioning of the class of 1917 at Leon Springs in June, former students, undergraduates, and some faculty now entered service in large numbers. Among those who left the campus to go to war in 1917 were Isaac S. ("Ike") Ashburn, secretary to the board of directors, who left his duties at the college to serve as a major with the AEF. Dana X. Bible, who had come to A&M as head football coach in 1917, resigned after the close of one of A&M's most successful seasons to become a fighter pilot. By Christmas of 1917, virtually all of the members of that championship team were in the army. Coach Bible completed aviation ground school in Austin, earned his wings at Love Field in Dallas, and became a U.S. Air Service pursuit pilot in the 22nd Aero Squadron of the First French Army. Team members who entered service included Jack Mahan, Roswell ("Little Hig") Higginbotham, Tim Grisenbeck, Scotty Alexander, and Kyle ("Slippery") Elam. Higginbotham, who returned after the war along with Mahan to play on the 1919 and 1920 A&M teams, coached baseball at Texas A&M

and Southern Methodist University until recalled to active military duty in 1942. Rising to the rank of lieutenant commander in the navy, "Little Hig" was killed in a plane crash at Quonset Point Naval Base in 1943, a casualty of yet another war.[5]

Considering the belated effort and the size of the undertaking, the United States did a remarkable job of mobilizing for war. To a great extent, events at the A&M College of Texas reflected what was happening at other American colleges and universities. Students from the class of 1918 were placed on active duty before completing their semester courses. The college's board of directors announced that those cadets who were "called to colors" would receive full credit for academic courses, and the fees they had paid would be refunded for courses they had not been able to complete.[6]

As the civilian student population on the A&M campus dwindled, military personnel arrived to attend specialized training programs taught by the faculty and staff with the assistance of army and navy personnel. The Electrical Engineering Department conducted a radio communication and repair program for the U.S. Air Service; the Signal Corps taught a course in "buzzer practice," or telegraphy; and the Mechanical Engineering Department directed a course in motor-truck mechanics and aviation repair. Science and physics faculty taught meteorology under a special program developed by the U.S. Weather Bureau, while other engineering and agriculture faculty and staff taught basic courses in horseshoeing, machining, blacksmithing, carpentry, general mechanics, and other such skills. By September, 1918, 3,648 soldiers had trained on the campus in war-oriented subjects. Academics in the traditional sense had been displaced since most civilians and soldiers "had their hearts and minds in the war."[7]

In the autumn of 1918, the War Department organized the Student Army Training Corps (SATC), which allowed all males over eighteen years of age to register for the draft, immediately be inducted into the army as a private, and return to class (with pay) to prepare for attending an officer training school. The SATC curriculum was aimed at one overriding objective: to produce army officers in short order. In intensive twelve-week programs, students attended classes designed to enable them to complete college in less than two years.[8]

Aggies from the Dallas A&M Club undertook a unique mobilization initiative to form a cavalry regiment composed primarily of present and former A&M students. Initiated in February, 1918, the plan called for volunteers to sign up and train with the Texas State National Guard. Once the regiment attained full strength and training was completed, the unit was to be nationalized into the army and sent to France, much as the Texas State Militia had been nationalized during the Spanish-American War. The leaders of this effort included former cadets Joe Utay ('08), Thomas H. Barton ('01), Marion S. Church ('08), and Richard H. Standifer ('08). Even before receiving authorization from the War Department in Washington, they began recruiting and equipping the unit with

While Aggies served at the front, Texas A&M's campus became a war-training camp for students and for the military with specialized training programs offered for the army in aviation maintenance, auto repair, radio communications, meteorology, horseshoeing, and blacksmithing.

private funds. In July, 1918, they were designated the 3rd Regiment of the 1st Brigade of Texas Infantry and were popularly known simply as the "A. and M. College Regiment."[9]

Recruiting advertisements in Dallas and east Texas newspapers called for "red-blooded Texans." By October, the A. and M. College Regiment, under the command of Col. Aba Gross ('96) of Waco, was at full strength, had passed all federal inspections, and awaited mobilization.[10] Before Washington granted approval, however, the armistice dashed the hopes of these Aggie citizen soldiers serving in France. Most Aggies found their way to the battlefields through more conventional channels.

From June, 1917, through June, 1918, the effort of mobilizing, training, and transporting an army to France consumed the nation. Following a brief stop in

England, Pershing arrived in Boulogne, France, on June 13, 1917, with his staff of thirty-one and a small contingent of troops. A graduate of the West Point class of 1886, Pershing had fought at the battle of Wounded Knee as a young cavalry trooper in 1890, and, during the Russo-Japanese War, he was a foreign observer attached to the Japanese army during its Manchuria operations in the early 1900s. However, it was his outstanding performance in combat with the 9th Cavalry Regiment during the Spanish-American War that brought him to the attention of then Col. Theodore Roosevelt. After "T. R." became president in September, 1906, he promoted the forty-six-year-old soldier from the rank of captain to brigadier general, passing over 909 competing regular officers. In May, 1917, after commanding intervention forces in Mexico, Pershing became head of the AEF with orders to form a general staff and prepare to sail for France. When he arrived on the front, Allied personnel and resources were nearly exhausted. France had lost almost a quarter of her adult male population in the war with Germany over the past three years. Pershing formally announced the arrival of the American armies in France on July 4, 1917, with the memorable words "Lafayette, we are here."[11]

By late summer of 1917, virtually the entire Regular Army of the United States—composed of the 1st Division (the "Big Red One"), the 2nd Division, and the 26th Division—was en route to France. In late October, the 42nd ("Rainbow") Division, so named because it was composed of National Guard units from twenty-six states, joined to form four vanguard units. These divisions, averaging a thousand officers and twenty-seven thousand troops each, were the only divisions to train solely in France. While many of the National Guardsmen in the 42nd Division had limited combat experience in Mexico or on the border, in Europe they quickly learned how much the scope of land warfare had changed. Their experience of pursuing Pancho Villa across the Rio Grande in south Texas was very different from the trench war, gas, stalemate, and attrition they faced on the western front.[12] In fact, there was little in the annals of warfare that could compare with those new horrors.

As Pershing awaited the balance of the army to arrive from the States in the latter half of 1917, he had three main priorities: to staff, train, and equip the army and establish his field command headquarters; to prevent the Allies from gaining control over his troops and committing them piecemeal in combat; and to develop the logistical support and communications needed to support his army in the field. These objectives required levels of planning and coordination previously unheard of. Pershing assigned a young, freshly minted major, George C. Marshall, the task of developing and coordinating troop training and gave him near carte blanc authority. Thus, planning and coordination became George Marshall's great forte in both World War I and II. To fashion a command and staff structure adequate to the task of managing the increasingly complex AEF, Pershing adapted the French model. He restructured the three traditional army staff elements of administration, intelligence, and operations into the five staff functions much like those the U.S. Army uses today: G-1, administrative policy; G-2, intelligence; G-3, operations; G-4, training; and G-5, coordination.[13]

Eager to escape the confines of Paris, Pershing selected the small town of Chaumont as the site for the headquarters of the AEF. He became painfully aware of the fact that an army of 170,000 or 500,000 or even a million men would be inadequate to the task at hand. He concluded that the situation required an American response of not less than 1 million men, with 3 million being a realistic commitment, and he cabled the War Department to this effect. As British prime minister Lloyd George noted in his memoirs, "The reservoir of French manpower had almost run dry and ours was approaching exhaustion."[14]

Pershing strongly resisted British and French demands that American troops be used as replacements for their combat losses. With the support of the president and Congress, Pershing refused to commit U.S. troops to battle other than as American units, under both American officers and the American flag. Despite a few exceptions to that policy, Pershing prevailed. As a result, most U.S. troops arriving in France did not enter combat in 1917 but focused on becoming trained and properly armed and equipped. By December, 1917, Pershing still had fewer than 175,000 men in France, and most of the American effort during the last six months of 1917 focused on his third priority: logistics.[15]

The logistics of transferring, outfitting, and supplying a 1-, 2-, or 3-million-man army thousands of miles from home was an unprecedented challenge. The near-debacle associated with landing around 20,000 troops in Cuba in 1898 offered no real guidelines, but the experience made it clear that extreme caution and concern were paramount. The scale of World War I logistics was completely different from what it had been in the Spanish-American War. As Pershing's staff focused on the buildup and supply of the AEF, they drew upon the experiences and counsel of the British and the French. The armies of the United Kingdom had encountered numerous pitfalls in supplying their troops across the Channel. They found that the seaports and rail lines worked best when managed by civilian experts. Since sea, rail, and land routes as well as supply and storage areas in France would be the lifelines of the AEF, Pershing decided to avoid the prime French ports in the north of the country, which the British were using, since they were highly susceptible to German attack by sea and air. Instead, he selected three ports farther to the south and west, in the Bay of Biscay: Bassens (Bordeaux), La Pallice (La Rochelle), and St. Nazaire (Nantes).[16]

As it turned out, locating the American forces' ports and supply depots in the south of France provided an immediate strategic benefit. Those locations put merchant ships laden with troops and war matériel beyond the range of the more than one hundred German U-boats in operation in the North Atlantic and the English Channel.[17] This strategy ultimately proved invaluable. After the British convoy troopship *Tuscania* was sunk on February 5, 1918, taking with her more than one hundred soldiers and sailors (including the first A&M man to lose his life in World War I, Norman G. Crocker ('17) of Center, Texas), not one troopship calling on the southern French ports was lost to German naval warships or U-boats.[18]

Texas Aggies proved particularly proficient in warfare logistics. By 1917, Texas A&M had graduated more than nine hundred students in engineering. Almost two-thirds of the college's living graduates from 1878 through 1917 were engineers, most of them mechanical, civil, electrical, and chemical (see table 2). Most Aggie engineers had experience in private-sector railroad construction and operation, building construction, municipal services, manufacturing, and so on, while graduates in the classes from 1916 to 1920 usually enlisted or went directly on active duty via the OTS training camps and served mainly as combat officers. The older A&M graduates tended to serve in logistical and engineering roles—building, maintaining, and operating the critical supply depots and transit centers. Many of these Aggies had business and engineering expertise particularly relevant to the needs of the military forces moving to Europe. According to Frank E. Vandiver, historian and former president of Texas A&M and a Pershing biographer, logistics, including the ability to transfer, equip, and supply the army, not only shaped America's combat strategy and tactics but also decided the outcome of the war.[19]

Edward B. Cushing ('80), who served as assistant manager for the Southern Pacific Railroad for three decades, played a major role in AEF logistics. By 1915, an avid A&M alumnus and former chair of the board of directors, Cushing had become a campus hero as an A&M advocate in Texas' political arena. When war was declared, Cushing, now in his midfifties and initially rejected for induction in the army under the ORC program, pressed his case for service with higher-ups in Washington. As a result of his efforts, in April, 1917, he received a direct commission as a major in the 17th Engineer Regiment that was being activated in Atlanta, Georgia. By August, 1917, Cushing was in France serving as director of debarkation at the ports of Antwerp and Brussels. In early 1918, the army moved him to the Railroad Transportation Corps, and in May, he became one of the chief AEF transportation officers charged with overseeing the Mediterranean supply ports and depots.[20]

Officers such as Cushing and Maj. William F. Hutson ('95), who understood and were experienced in moving people and supplies, contributed enormously to the success of the American armies in combat. A veteran of the Spanish-American War, Hutson had also been a managing engineer with the Southern Pacific Railroad. Commanding the 1st Battalion of the 17th Engineers, he built docks, warehouses, and railroads at the Port of St. Nazaire. The major challenges confronting the AEF engineers were improving the ports for troop debarkation and massive, expedited cargo handling, building adequate storage facilities, and then expanding the French double-track rail system for the fast transit of troops and supplies to the field. During this work, Hutson and his fellow officers published the "OoLaLa Times," a regimental newspaper "from somewhere in France" that provided updates and stories on unit personalities and events. The newspaper became "must" reading back in College Station, Texas. Other Aggie engineers active in France during the early stages of the war were Lt. Homer A. Jopling ('17), Detached Wagon Co. no. 1, 23rd Engineers; Lt. William T. Jones ('14), 111th Engineers; Lt. Horace Boyett ('11), 307th Engineers; and Lt. Preston M. Geren ('12) and Lt. Oscar A. Seward ('07), both of the 315th Engineers. Lt. Palmer H. Olsen ('16) and Lt. Eddie L. Jarrett ('06), both of the 316th Engineers, and Lt. Howard F. Ellis ('15) arrived in France in August, 1917, and served as aides-de-camp to former A&M commandant Gen. William Scott.[21]

Of the hundreds of Aggie engineers who served in France, most were drawn from their civilian work to perform similar tasks for the American Expeditionary Force. Tyree L. Bell ('12), for example, a captain of the A&M football team, enlisted, rose to the rank of major, and was sent by the army to the Royal Technical Institute at Glasgow, Scotland, to study dock and harbor engineering before taking charge of construction at the embarkation camp at Bordeaux, France. The expertise Bell acquired in World War I was again put into play in the construction of military facilities in World War II and throughout four decades of engineering work across the state of Texas.[22]

Other Aggie engineers provided frontline support as the AEF began its major offensive in the autumn of 1918. G. P. F. Jouine ('07), who had worked for the Corps of Engineers on the Mississippi River, was experienced in the construction of railroads, bridges, dams, ports, and levees as well as in irrigation projects. He and other Aggie engineers provided support in bridge and rail repair, removal of barbed wire, road improvements, and the construction of forward supply depots and airfields, which were often conducted under hostile fire. Captain R. B. Pearce ('11), 310th Engineers, summed up his firsthand observations following the Meuse-Argonne offensive: "We did not go over the top but were under shell fire all the time, and sometimes it got pretty hot. It was a great experience and I would not take anything for it. However, several times last October [1918] I would have sold it [the experience] awfully cheap."[23]

Forty-two of the eighty American divisions scheduled to be sent to France for the planned Allied summer offensive of 1918 actually saw service there. By April, 1918, one year after the United States declared war, with Pershing commanding nearly 430,000 American troops in Europe, it had become increasingly evident that the year of decision might be 1918. Russia's withdrawal from the war following the Bolshevik Revolution allowed the chief of the German general staff, Field Marshall Erich Ludendorff, to transfer vast numbers of troops and supplies to the western front. Beginning on March 21, 1918, German

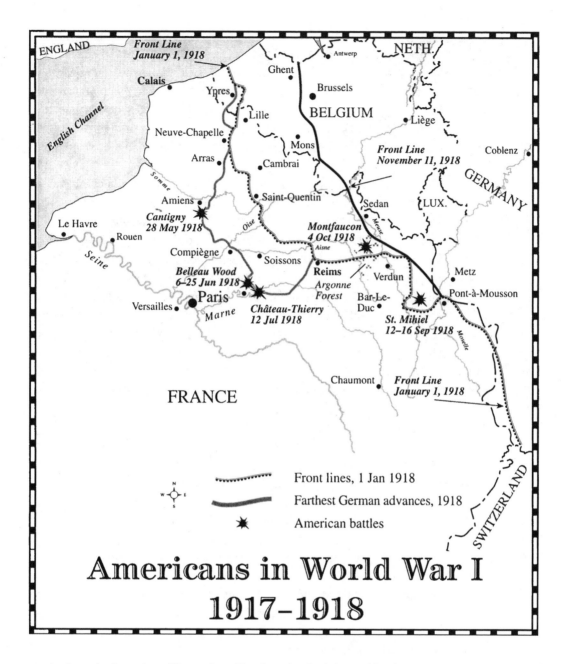

ENGLAND

Front Line
January 1, 1918

Ghent

Antwerp

NETH.

Calais

Ypres

Brussels

BELGIUM

English Channel

Lille

Liège

Coblenz

Neuve-Chapelle

Mons

Front Line
November 11, 1918

GERMANY

Arras

Cambrai

Somme

Amiens

Saint-Quentin

Sedan

LUX.

Le Havre

Cantigny
28 May 1918

Rouen

Oise

Montfaucon
4 Oct 1918

Meuse

Metz

Compiègne

Soissons

Aisne

Seine

Belleau Wood
6–25 Jun 1918

Reims

Verdun

Pont-à-Mousson

Paris

Argonne
Forest

Bar-Le-
Duc

St. Mihiel
12–16 Sep 1918

Moselle

Versailles

Marne

Château-Thierry
12 Jul 1918

FRANCE

Chaumont

Front Line
January 1, 1918

SWITZERLAND

N
W ✧ E
S

Front lines, 1 Jan 1918

Farthest German advances, 1918

★ American battles

Americans in World War I
1917–1918

armies launched a series of five major offensives that had three objectives: (1) to
strike and split the British and French before the American forces grew any
larger; (2) to capitalize on the low morale and exhaustion of the French along
the front lines and, through bold action, capture Paris; and (3) given the possibility that German arms might not achieve total victory, to put Germany in a
better position to demand favorable peace terms from the Allies.[24]

The Germans' spring offensive forced Pershing to commit U.S. forces to
battle—ready or not. The first German attack fell against the British sector in

Flanders near Ypres and the French sector between Cambrai and St. Quentin. The British fell back fifty miles but held, suffering heavy losses. After further blows in the north, the German armies struck the French, whose lines began to crumble at Cantigny-Montdidier. In a tense confrontation, the top Allied generals agreed to accept French marshal Ferdinand Foch as generalissimo, and Pershing was persuaded to deploy U.S. forces in support of the hard-pressed French. Thus, on the night of April 24, 1918, the 1st Division moved into position to assist the French.

While training had been intense, Pershing was rightly concerned about the impact of this new style of modern warfare on his men and the lack of the "weapons of choice" on the western front. When American units arrived on the battlefield, they had no tanks, large field guns, or airplanes other than equipment borrowed from the Allies, and they were sometimes armed with outdated rifles. However, they had no choice but to fight since the French position at Cantigny was critical. However, before the American forces could counterattack, Ludendorff launched his third attack from Chemin des Dames toward the Marne River. Despite the mounting threat, the Big Red One pushed forward in late May to surround and capture Cantigny. Aggie engineer Hamlet P. Jones ('13) of Kaufman, a Leon Springs OTS graduate, was killed in the assault while leading his men "over the top." Fighting was fierce, but the Americans overran German advance front lines at Cantigny.[25]

Meanwhile, the German offensive had made significant advances at Chateau-Thierry. In a bold move, German infantry captured a bridge across the Marne, only 55 miles by road northeast of Paris. From a distance of 75 miles, a German long-range naval gun began lobbing shells into downtown Paris. In an urgent call to Pershing, French general Henri Pétain requested that all available American divisions be directed to Chateau-Thierry to defend the capital. The only two AEF divisions not fully committed at the time were the 2nd Division, which was in the process of relieving the 1st at Cantigny, and the 3rd Division near Verdun, which was in its final stages of field training. Pershing ordered both to move with haste toward the Marne. In early June, elements of the 2nd Division moved into position for an attack on the region between the small villages of Belleau and Bouresches. The battles for Hill 142 and Belleau Woods were two especially fierce encounters between the Americans and the Germans.[26]

When the 5th U.S. Marine Regiment attempted to take Hill 142, it quickly became engaged in fierce close-quarter combat with Germans in the surrounding woods. By mid-June, 1918, the 2nd Division had taken its objective but at great cost—more than 9,000 casualties out of a total infantry strength of 17,000. Lt. Hugh McFarland ('17), 82nd Infantry Regiment, was wounded in action at Belleau Woods, as was Lt. Durant S. Buchanan ('17), who was wounded twice and awarded the Croix de Guerre for "bravery and valiant service." Among those killed in action were Aggie marine 1st Lt. Thomas R. Brailsford ('17) of

October, 1918, 1st Lt. Eben Herbert Mills ('13)
(standing near the propeller), somewhere in France.

Latexo, Texas, and 1st Lt. Edmund L. Riesner ('16) of Houston. Marine corporal Eric A. Goldbeck ('19), who left college as a sophomore to enlist on the day war was declared, Lt. Frank W. Slaton ('12), and Sgt. John P. Thompson ('19) of Navasota, Texas, were reported lost in action around Chateau-Thierry.[27]

By midsummer, the first three offensives had cost the Germans nearly 500,000 casualties, including 95,000 KIAs (soldiers killed in action) and 35,000 POWs (prisoners of war). Despite the very heavy losses and difficulties in replenishing their supplies, the German high command decided to launch yet another massive attack on Chateau-Thierry in early July. At this time, the American armies had introduced the use of the U.S. Air Service to scout the enemy lines for troop movements and artillery emplacements. Unarmed reconnaissance missions like those flown by Capt. Charles T. Trickey ('17) detected troop movements and forewarned the Allies of the coming German attack. (The danger and daring of these flights is described at the beginning of this chapter.)[28]

During the battles of July and August, 1st Lt. Eben Herbert Mills ('13) flew reconnaissance at the front. Upon America's entry into the war, Mills, a San Antonio native, enlisted in the aviation section of the Reserve Corps in June, 1917. By October, he was in France. After completing flight training in Issoudon in April, 1918, he received his commission and was at the front when the German offensive began.

The development of U.S. air power during World War I was dramatic. Military aviation came of age then, and a substantial number of Texas Aggies were pioneers in air combat. In April, 1917, the United States had only two military airfields and 55 training aircraft, of which 51 were deemed obsolete. By October, 1918, just prior to the Chateau-Thierry-Soissons engagements, the U.S. Air Service had reached levels sufficient to neutralize the previously pronounced German air superiority with 2,500 aircraft and more than five thousand pilots. At the close of the war, American pilots had brought down 755 confirmed enemy aircraft, while losing only 357.[29]

In mid-July, German troops began attacking across the Marne River in force, bringing them on the march to Paris through the Sumelin Creek Valley, where the U.S. 3rd Division met them. Fighting was at times hand to hand, with heavy casualties on both sides. Capt. George F. Wellage ('16) of Eagle Pass, Texas, and commander of Company D, 23rd U.S. Infantry, was among those commended for bravery and awarded the Distinguished Service Cross (DSC), an honor second only to the Medal of Honor. The *Alumni Quarterly* reported, "The particular exploit in which Captain Wellage figured was the smoking out of a German machine gun nest; a duel with two German officers in which one was killed and the other brought back a prisoner."[30]

Lt. Max D. Gilfillan ('17) and Durant S. Buchanan ('17) were both wounded in action. Though injured, Gilfillan led his men to their objective. He was cited for bravery by General Pershing and decorated with the Croix de Guerre. Texas A&M's losses in this pivotal engagement included Lt. Benjamin H. Gardner Jr. ('14), Pvt. Edwin M. Gorman ('18), and Capt. James G. Ellis Jr. ('18) of the 27th Ambulance Company, who was killed in action while assisting the wounded. The Americans blunted the attack and forced at least a temporary German withdrawal, but the Allies received no real respite.[31]

On the heels of the action at Chateau-Thierry, a counteroffensive began near the city of Soissons. On July 18, the U.S. 1st and 2nd Divisions, along with the 1st Moroccan Colonial Division and the French 58th and 69th Divisions, continued the battle with an attack along the Aisne River to Soissons. The first two American divisions led the assault, while the 3rd Division continued its drive past Chateau-Thierry toward Fismes. One soldier with the 1st Division recalled that "as this was a rail head the wounded began coming in, ambulance after ambulance and the trains couldn't take them away fast enough so they were put on the ground around the depot. . . . They came in most all nite and the Germans were over head but luckily no bombs were dropped. . . . Some of the boys went west [were killed] and some to the hospitals as they do all the time while at the front."[32]

Despite heavy American casualties, the attack succeeded. The offensive resulted in the capture of 3,800 prisoners and sixty-eight field guns. Moreover, the drive at Soissons finally began to turn the tide of the battle in favor of the Allies. The five summer offenses by the Germans had been stopped in their tracks, but the costs were again high. The 300,000 American troops who participated in the combat of July, 1918, suffered nearly 50,000 casualties.[33]

At Soissons, Maj. Andrew D. Bruce ('16), commanding the 4th Machine Gun Battalion; Marine company commander Capt. Hugh McFarland ('17); and platoon commander Lt. Herbert W. Whisenant ('16 and a graduate of the first officers training camp at Leon Springs) all received the Distinguished Service Cross. Wounded in the battle were Lt. Paul B. Dunkle ('17), Capt. Merlin Mitchell ('17), Pvt. Leland Douthit ('17), and Lt. Col. Earl Graham ('16). Infantry captain Haydn P. Mayers ('14) was killed in action and posthumously awarded the DSC for extraordinary valor in trying to bring one of his wounded men back to the American lines.[34]

Also awarded the DSC and killed in combat at the battle of Soissons was Lt. John H. Moore ('15) from DeKalb, Texas, who was assigned to the 3rd Machine Gun Battalion. He attended OTS at Leon Springs and fought in six major engagements. Lieutenant Moore's bravery, reflecting that of the other combatants who received the DSC, was described by his commanding officer in a letter to his family in Texas:

> I am enclosing herewith a citation for conspicuous gallantry in action for your son. He displayed coolness and courage in handling his section under violent bombardment, advancing to the second objective, assisted infantry in reducing enemy machine gun nests, advancing towards the third objective he encountered a most severe artillery bombardment, was knocked down and stunned by the concussion; as soon as revived by his men, struggled to his feet, rallied and reorganized his section, started to lead them out of the shelled area; he himself reconnoitering in advance to locate a less dangerous place and while so doing was killed, his sacrifice enabling most of his men to go on.
>
> In the death of your son the battalion and Expeditionary Forces have sustained a great loss. We honor his memory as he made the supreme sacrifice gallantly doing his duty as a leader of men. Surely there is reward for one who gives up his life so unselfishly and so nobly.[35]

At the time of the battle of Soissons, in mid-1918, the *New York Times* estimated that more than one-third (535) of all living Texas A&M "graduates" (1,425) were on active duty—a greater percentage than any other college or university in the United States could claim.[36]

During the summer and early fall of 1918, Pershing's army increased by 250,000 men per month. While some Allied leaders felt the momentum had shifted in their favor, the war was far from over. The sheer size of the AEF, two million strong by early September, created logistical bottlenecks and delays. Never before in the history of warfare had so much manpower and so many supplies been moved so far and so fast to be concentrated in one location. The United States sent not only men but also an enormous quantity of war matériel and food to the front. In France, the Quartermaster Corps of the AEF's Services of Supply handled 7.2 million tons of equipment and supplies, including 27,000 standard-gauge freight cars and more than 1,700 hundred-ton locomotives. In addition, the army shipped and fed more than seventy thousand mules and horses. These supplies and the timely delivery of men and munitions to the front lines proved crucial in the final campaigns of the war, from September through late October, 1918.[37]

As the last major battle involving U.S. troops in World War I began—the Meuse-Argonne offensive—Pershing reorganized the AEF to better manage line and staff functions. Before the attack, he had created the First U.S. Army, which was composed of the I, IV, and V Corps. With the support of the French 15th Colonial Division, he launched a massive strike in early September across the Meuse River at St. Mihiel to "straighten out the line."[38] By September 16, the German army had withdrawn, and the Allies had attained their objectives. Maj. William H. Morris, assistant Texas A&M commandant in 1916 and 1917, penned the following account from the battlefield:

> The Ninetieth Division was in the St. Mihiel drive and my regiment, the 360th Infantry, was on the right flank of the whole thing. My battalion led the regiment "over the top" twice and took [Bois le Prêtre] and Hill 327, which the French have not been able to take in four years. Lieutenant Harry Burkett '17 and William Francis '15, old A. and M. men, were with my battalion in the drive. The work of Burkett can not be too highly praised and Francis was the bravest little fellow of them all and showed absolutely no fear of death whatsoever. I wish you would tell Dr. Francis that I said no officer could show more bravery and sand [grit] than he did.
>
> My battalion took both objectives assigned to it, the first in an hour and forty-seven minutes, and the second in an hour and fifty minutes. We went through the hardest kind of high explosive barrage, gas and machine gun fire. We stayed in the front lines during the offensive for seven days before we were relieved. It rained most of the time and the shelling was heavy. Before that time we had been in the lines twelve days: so we practically faced the enemy nineteen days before relieved.
>
> It takes battle to show what an officer is made of. Several have been relieved from command. . . . Strength of character and leadership are two requirements of an officer. It takes a long time to determine these two things and a battle is the supreme test.
>
> Two more days and we are off to the front again. Give my best to all, especially the boys [of the Corps of Cadets].[39]

This first all-American offensive at St. Mihiel resulted in more than seven thousand casualties. Among those wounded in action was Maj. Ike Ashburn, commander of the 358th Infantry Regiment. Although he sustained a severe neck wound and was temporarily paralyzed, he remained in command, and his unit seized its objective. Ashburn's Distinguished Service Cross citation noted that, while wounded, he "led his unit with exceptional daring and effect until he was incapacitated by a second wound."[40] After recovery, Ashburn joined the 90th Division command staff for a short period and, after discharge from the army, returned to Texas A&M to become commandant of the Corps of Cadets from September, 1919, to December, 1923.

Lost in action at St. Mihiel were former cadets Lt. Vories P. Brown Jr. ('08) of San Antonio, Pvt. Romeo Willis Cox ('13) of Childress, infantry company commander Capt. Samuel R. Craig ('17) of El Campo, Lt. Charles Houser ('16) of Eagle Pass, Capt. Herbert N. Peters of Sabinal (who was posthumously awarded the Distinguished Service Cross), Lt. Ferdinand Regenbrecht ('17) of Sealy, and infantry Capt. George F. Wellage ('16), who was killed instantly by shrapnel on September 12, 1918.[41]

In early October, the Allies launched their last and greatest offensive in the Meuse-Argonne Valley north of the battered fortress complex at Verdun. It was this action that brought the war to a close. As Pershing committed nine divisions against heavy resistance, the initial effort was brought to a standstill, but by October 10, the German army had been pushed out of the Argonne region. With overall American troop strength in France exceeding 2.8 million in mid-October, the Yanks had turned the tide. Writing his sister, 1st Lt. Eben Mills stated that his present job was to "observe the German retreat." Nine Aggies died in action during this final offensive, including Lt. Robert W. Nolte ('13) of New Orleans (awarded the DSC for valor in the battle of Blanc Mont on October 9, 1918) and infantry Lt. John C. McKimmey ('18) from Gustine, Texas, who was also the recipient of the DSC and the Croix de Guerre at St. Etienne.[42]

Following the Argonne campaign, Germany sued for peace. And so it was that on November 10, 1918, the day before the armistice ending the first Great War, a group of young men signed a letter addressed to their "Brother Alumnus" of the Agricultural and Mechanical College of Texas, noting that at that moment and at that place the atmosphere of old A. and M. pervaded a high-ceilinged dining room "somewhere" in France: "[I]ts walls have echoed to a 'Chigarro garem' and 'rough tough, real tuff' in good old A. and M. style. . . . Now we pledge [toast] A. and M. and you and all our brothers overthere and overhere in the wine of France." So wrote Texas Aggie Lt. C. H. Harrison ('12), Lt. J. M. Kendrick ('15), Lt. W. T. Donoho ('13), Capt. C. A. Biggers ('14), Lt. Dillon T. Stevens ('13), Capt. R. B. Pearce ('11), Lt. Martin M. Daugherty ('16), Lt. T. K. Morris ('16), Lt. John Fires ('12), Lt. Quinlan Adams ('12), and Lt. Mark P. Thomas ('17).[43] The next day, November 11, one of the world's bloodiest conflicts concluded, with more than 5 million casualties among the Allied powers and another 3.5 million among the Central powers.

As the guns fell silent, all of the combatants were exhausted and welcomed

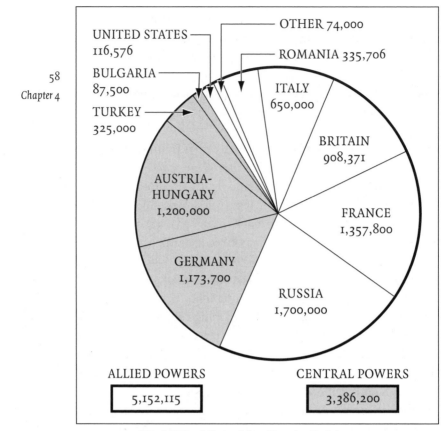

TABLE 4. World War I Casualties (Deaths Only)

the November 11 armistice. The Great War marked a major change in the character of warfare and in the processes and mechanisms by which the United States would prepare, recruit, and train future armies. Texas A&M's participation in the war had been exemplary. More than two thousand Aggie graduates and former students served in the armed forces, a number greater than any college or university could claim. By October, 1918, more than half of all living Aggies were in uniform, including some from almost every A&M class from 1880 to 1921. Seven hundred of those were graduates, of which 95 percent were commissioned officers. Fifty-four A&M service men died during the war; two-thirds of those were killed in action, and the others in training accidents (primarily aviation related) and from disease.

During the war, the Association of Former Students authorized a fifteen-by-twenty-six-foot banner of the "best-quality bunting" to be our "service flag." Some two thousand stars were placed on the periphery representing each man in service, and a center square of gold stars stood for those who made the supreme sacrifice. It was first hung in the assembly building named "Guion Hall" and later displayed in the Academic Building, where it remained through World War II.

TABLE 5. Texas Aggies: World War I Deaths

Name	Branch of Service	Class	Death	Date	Where
Capt. Joseph D. Carter	USA	1900	T	Mar. 19, 1919	Verdun, France
1st Lt. Corey V. Woodman	USAAS	1907	I	Dec. 5, 1918	Mardi, California
1st Lt. Vories P. Brown Jr.	USA	1908	KIA	July 14, 1918	Alsace, France
Capt. George L. Harrison	USA	1908	KIA	Sep 14, 1918	Tuiacount, France
Capt. James G. Elhs Jr., Medical Corps	USA	1910	KIA	July 3, 1918	Maine, France
Lt. Jesse L. Easterwood	USN	1911	T	May 19, 1919	Panama
Pvt. John L. Matthews	USA	1911	T	Feb., 1918	France
Maj. Benjamin F. Wright	USA	1911	KIA	Oct. 8, 1918	Champagne, France
1st Lt. Graham D. Luhn	USA	1912	KIA	Oct. 8, 1918	St. Etienne, France
1st Lt. Robert W. Nolte	USA	1913	KIA	Oct. 9, 1918	Argonne, France
Pvt. James R. Findlater	USA	1913	I	Oct. 8, 1918	Merritt, NJ
Capt. William F. Bourland	USA	1913	KIA	Oct. 9, 1918	Bois de Nancy, France
1st Lt. Richard P. Woolley	USA	1913	I	Jan. 16, 1918	Nice, France
Cpl. John B. Murphy	USA	1913	KIA	July 20, 1918	Missy-Aux-Borx, France
Capt. Herbert N. Peters	USA	1913	KIA	Sept. 26, 1918	St. Mihiel, France
1st Lt. Frank W. Slaton	USA	1913	KIA	July 20, 1918	Soissons, France
Pvt. Romero W. Cox	USA	1913	KIA	June 19, 1918	St. Mihiel, France
1st Lt. Hamlet P. Jones	USA	1913	KIA	May 18, 1918	Cantigny, France
2nd Lt. Benjamin H. Gardner Jr.	USA	1914	KIA	July 18, 1918	Maine, France
Capt. Hadyn P. Mayers	USA	1914	KIA	July 21, 1918	France
1st Lt. Charles E. Rust	USAAS	1915	KIA	Oct. 11, 1918	France
2nd Lt. John H. Moore	USA	1915	KIA	July 18, 1918	Soissons, France
Capt. Geo F. Wallace	USA	1916	KIA	Sept. 12, 1918	St. Mihiel, France
1st Lt. Edmund L. Riesner	USMC	1916	KIA	June 10, 1918	Belleau Woods, France
1st Lt. Charles Hausser	USA	1916	KIA	Sept. 12, 1918	St. Mihiel, France
1st Lt. Cyrus E. Graham	USAAS	1916	T	Nov. 9, 1918	France
Cpl. Walter G. Bevill	USA	1917	I	Mar. 31, 1918	Camp Pike, Arkansas
1st Lt. Thomas R. Brailsford	USMC	1917	KIA	June, 1918	Belleau Woods, France
Capt. Samuel R. Craig	USA	1917	KIA	Sept. 14, 1918	St. Mihiel, France
1st Lt. James F. Greer	USAAS	1917	T	Oct. 21, 1918	France
2nd Lt. Elmer C. Allison	USAAS	1918	T	Feb. 19, 1919	March AFB, California
1st Lt. Farris S. Anderson	USA	1918	KIA	Oct. 13, 1918	Attigny, France
Pvt. Norman G. Crocker	USA	1918	KIA	Feb. 5, 1918	HMS Tuscania
Pvt. Edwin M. Gorman	USMC	1918	KIA	July 18, 1918	Maine, France
2nd Lt. Luke W. Loftus	USA	1918	KIA	Aug. 27, 1918	Nogales, Arizona
2nd Lt. Willford McFadden	USAAS	1918	KIA	Oct. 7, 1918	France
2nd Lt. John C. McKinney	USA	1918	KIA	Oct. 9, 1918	St. Etienne, France
1st Lt. Harry L. Peyton	USAAS	1918	Training	Mar. 28, 1918	San Antonio, Texas
1st Lt. Wendell F. Prime	USA	1918	KIA	Nov. 6, 1918	Sassey, France
1st Lt. Ferdinand Regenbrecht	USA	1918	KIA	Sept. 19, 1918	St. Mihiel, France
Cpl. Charles L. Teague	USA	1918	KIA	July 19, 1918	Argonne, France
Sgt. John P. Thompson	USMC	1918	KIA	June 3, 1918	Chateau Thierry, France
Jim Woodson *		1918			
Pvt. Horace C. Yates	USA	1918	I	Oct. 18, 1918	Travis, Texas

(continued)

Name	Branch of Service	Class	Death	Date	Where
C. Barfield *		1919			
Pvt. Richard P. Bull Jr.	USA	1919	I	Oct. 17, 1918	Austin, Texas
Pvt. Marson F. Curtis	USA	1919	KIA	Oct. 23, 1918	Argonne, France
Capt. Eric A. Goldbeck	USMC	1919	KIA	June 7, 1918	Chateau Thierry, France
2nd Lt. William G. Thomas	USAAS	1919	T	Sept. 22, 1918	France
Edwin B. Crook *		1921			
2nd Lt. Walter S. Keeling	USAAS	1923	T	Sept. 10, 1918	Ft. Worth, Texas
L. S. Suber *					
John H. Burford *					
A. G. Hays *					

Sources: *Directory of Former Students, 1876–1949* (College Station: Texas A&M, 1973), p. xxvi; "Gold Book," *Alumni Quarterly* (Aug., 1919): 1–26; "Our Roll of Honor," *Alumni Quarterly* (Aug., 1918): 21–46; *Longhorn* (1919): 5, 155–56.

Key

USA	U.S. Army	T	Training
USAAS	U.S. Army Air Service	I	Illness
USMC	U.S. Marine Corps	KIA	Killed in Action
USN	U.S. Navy	*	Data not available

Other memorial traditions still visible on the campus are the fifty-four oak trees that were planted around the main drill field in March, 1920, and the American flags that still fly on the perimeter of Kyle Field during football games, representing each man lost in service. In addition, a nine-ton granite monument was dedicated by Gov. Pat Neff in 1924 to honor World War I sacrifices. The "West Gate Memorial" now stands on the corner of Simpson Drill Field.

In addition, out of World War I came the "Aggie War Hymn," the first verse of which was composed by an Aggie marine, Pvt. James Vernon ("Pinky") Wilson ('20) while he was standing guard duty on the Rhine River in occupied Germany. The hymn has become one of the most memorable Aggie legacies of World War I, which is appropriate since the war was a watershed for Texas A&M. The college emerged from the conflict even more deeply committed to military training. The obligation of service to country has thus become an even stronger part of the Aggie tradition.

Academically, Texas A&M sought ways to channel its wartime experiences to enhance and expand its academic and research programs. The shortage of engineers both during and after the war spurred efforts to build programs that soon become pioneering departments, especially in aeronautical and chemical engineering. Concurrently, A&M's civil and mechanical engineering programs achieved a new level of recognition. Overall, the war contributed to a further

Texas Aggies declared a "strike" and marched to Bryan in celebration of Armistice Day, November 11, 1919. By October, 1918, more than half of all living Aggies were in uniform, most of them as commissioned officers.

strengthening of Texas A&M's engineering, agriculture, and military training programs.

Officer training was significantly transformed in the war's aftermath. By late December, 1918, the SATC officer training program was replaced by a reinvigorated Reserve Officer's Training Corps. At Texas A&M, the emphasis placed on military training and tactics before World War I had greatly benefited the nation. During the decade following World War I, A&M continued to refine its military program and received recognition by the War Department as one of the country's top ten distinguished military programs. During the postwar years, more than a dozen Aggie World War I veterans were promoted to general officer rank. Those included George F. Moore ('08), Victor A. Barraco ('15), George Beverley ('19), Ralph R. Thomas ('21), Nat S. Perrine, Oscar B. Abbott ('13),

C. M. Easley ('16), Harry H. Johnson ('17), John A. Warden ('08), Howard C. Davidson ('11), Douglas B. Netherwood ('08), A. D. Bruce ('16), William E. Farthing ('14), and Jerome J. Waters Jr. ('13). In time, these men would constitute a critical element of the World War II officer corps. As Texas A&M achieved recognition for the measure of service its former students gave to the country, the college was widely seen as the epitome of those educational institutions that produced citizen soldiers.

Suggested Readings

The Americans in the Great War: Michelin Illustrated Guides to the Battlefields (1914–1918) (France: Michelin, 1920), 3 vols.

Ayers, Leonard P. The War with Germany: A Statistical Summary (Washington, D.C.: GPO, 1919).

Ferguson, Niall. The Pity of War (New York: Basic Books, 1998).

"Gold Book: A Tribute to Her Loyal Sons Who Paid the Supreme Sacrifice in the World War," Alumni Quarterly (Texas A&M Alumni Association, Aug., 1919).

March, Peyton C. The Nation at War (New York: Doubleday, Doran, 1932).

Pershing, John J. My Experiences in the World War (New York: Frederick A. Stokes, 1931).

Stallings, Laurence. The Doughboys: The Story of the AEF, 1917–1918 (New York: Harper and Row, 1963).

Taylor, A. J. P. The First World War: An Illustrated History (New York: Perigee, 1963).

Vandiver, Frank E. Blackjack: The Life and Times of John J. Pershing (College Station: Texas A&M University Press, 1977).

Hitlerism in Germany is the greatest menace
that has ever threatened civilization.
—*Battalion* (November 8, 1933)

BETWEEN THE WARS, 1919–1941

The November, 1918, armistice that ended the World War I brought a sense of relief to the Aggies, the nation, and much of the world. At the close of hostilities, letters and telegrams to the *Alumni Quarterly* reflected excitement, thankfulness, and sheer relief. Infantry Lt. C. M. Copeland ('18), for example, felt lucky to be alive: "If the war had not ended when it did I fear I would not have been left to tell the story. I pulled through with a whole skin though there were a few times during the last month when I wasn't absolutely sure my lucky star was still shining." Corps of Engineers Lt. Horace Boyett ('11) commented, "I was fortunate enough to go through without a scratch," and infantry Capt. Harry J. Burkett ('17) concluded, "This method of fighting is not a winter sport by any means. Many of us got through safe, some were hit and nicked up a bit, and others have gone west."[1]

The Great War, the war to end all wars, had taken a tremendous toll and both scared and scarred an entire generation. Americans quickly came to believe that "there ain't going to be no war no more." The nation set about demobilization and the pursuit of peace with a passion and an intensity greater than that which had galvanized support for the war effort. Disarmament and isolationism displaced war and international cooperation. The Senate refused to ratify the Treaty of Versailles ending the war and committing the United States to membership in the League of Nations. Two years later, the Washington Naval Conference focused on peace and the territorial rights of other nations, disavowed aggression, and invoked disarmament. The Five-Power Naval Treaty of 1922, which reduced naval armaments, effectively sank more battleships than had been sunk during the war—most of them American. Even then, Pres. Calvin Coolidge vetoed the meager funding provided by Congress that would have helped maintain the country's assigned level of tonnage. Preparedness and military training received largely token support. Army strength declined to pre–World War I levels, approaching 118,000 by 1937, when war and destruction were already being visited upon Asia and eminent in Europe. In effect, from 1919 through 1939, war had not been abolished but rather ignored. Small wars, often obscure to the American consciousness, displaced great wars.

The seeds of World War II were sown at least in part in the settlements reached at the end of World War I. Germany lost its borderlands, its colonies, and its sense of security. The costs and depredations of war, followed by $33 billion in war reparations exacted on Germany at the Paris Peace Conference, brought on an economic collapse in 1923 that contributed to the rise of Adolf Hitler and the radical National German Socialist Workers (Nazi) Party. In Italy, Benito Mussolini seized power in 1922 and established a Fascist dictatorship, then turned his armies to the conquest of Ethiopia in 1935. Japan, allied with the West late in the war, received the Chinese province of Shantung on the north coast in compensation and began an era of militarization and expansion throughout the Pacific, threatening both American territories acquired as a result of the Spanish-American war and Western trade interests in the Far East. Meanwhile, the United States diligently pursued peace, prosperity, and isolation from the affairs of the world. Pres. Warren G. Harding sought to restore "normalcy." But things would never again be the same.

While Americans focused on healing and renewal, the age of the automobile fueled a social and economic revolution. The boom of the "Roaring Twenties" was followed by the economic convulsions of the Great Depression. Through boom and bust, American citizens diligently pursued a policy of disarmament, military downsizing, and isolation. During these same years, 1919 to 1939, the A&M College of Texas and the Texas Aggies generally proceeded along a path different from that of the broader society. Contrary to most schools and colleges, Texas A&M came to embody military training and preparedness. Its citizen soldiers grew in numbers and in their knowledge of war.

Veterans who returned to the campus were changed by the war. And when they arrived back at A&M, they found an altered campus environment. One of the most noticeable differences had to do with the Aggie uniform. The old-style cadet "grays" were gone forever, replaced by the olive-drab khaki clothing and campaign hats of World War I and the U.S. Regular Army.[2]

The adoption of the regular military uniform was both symbolic and significant. It meant that, rather than rejecting war and its experiences as American society at large was doing, Texas A&M sought to incorporate those experiences, as well as the uniform, into its postwar military and academic environment. Faculty and administrators perceived military training and technical training as complementary processes. Pres. William Bizzell and Frank C. Bolton, professor of engineering and director of war educational activities for the college, headed the postwar restructuring.[3]

More than most colleges and universities with military training programs, Texas A&M saw the massive demobilization as an opportunity and a challenge. Meanwhile, the War Department explored means of maintaining a viable trained army, sustaining a high level of military preparedness, and capitalizing on the war's lessons. It was on this common ground that A&M sought to strengthen the Corps of Cadets and military training in the 1920s and 1930s. The college's administrators and former students believed that the education of engineers, agriculturalists, and business graduates—coupled with ROTC—produced a better-trained, better-educated, and better-disciplined workforce. In addition, that same civilian workforce constituted a pool of technically trained officers that might be needed for modern warfare. Beyond that, military training complemented Texas' pioneering past, its Southern military background, its agrarian-based militia tradition, and the lifestyle of the Corps of Cadets, which had been a part of the school since its founding in 1876. Thus, unlike many institutions in the post–World War I era, at Texas A&M, military training and education were believed to be eminently compatible and complimentary.[4] Faculty, administrators, directors, and A&M's former students for the most part appreciated and endorsed the college's "military features."

The primary vehicle for integrating military training and academics at the A&M College was the traditional Corps of Cadets, now strengthened and focused by the ROTC. Immediately following the cessation of hostilities in December, 1918, the War Department suspended training under the SATC program and advised institutions such as Texas A&M, which had wartime training programs, to apply for ROTC training or to activate their program if one had already been approved. Texas A&M moved quickly to begin its ROTC curriculum, which had been approved before the war, with an expanded military staff. President Bizzell prevailed upon the War Department to reassign Col. Charles H. Muller (formerly at A&M in 1916 and 1917) as professor of military science and tactics (PMS&T). He came in January, 1919, and was supported by a staff of thirty-one. Muller had distinguished himself in France and acquired an appreciation of the role of the ROTC in the postwar period. In addition, as part of the military training program, the college's engineering and science schools began to place more emphasis on "technical" training, which could benefit the more complex nature and needs of the specialized branches of the armed forces.[5]

Thus, implementing the new ROTC program melded well with the spirit and traditions of the Corps of Cadets as well as with the academic programs of the college. The ROTC compartmentalized its program and training curriculum along the lines of the army's branch structures, including the infantry, field artillery, signal corps, ordnance, coast artillery, and chemical warfare. The signal corps, or communications, option at Texas A&M was actually a continuation of the war training program managed by the Department of Electrical Engineering, and the field artillery program had been active on the campus since the beginning. One benefit of the military-academic alliance represented by the inauguration of the ROTC program was that it gave A&M students and faculty access to some of the latest technology and equipment, especially in radio and communications, aviation, and chemical engineering.[6]

In January, 1919, the War Department authorized the detailing of a field artillery unit to the college with additional officers and "at least 100 horses . . . for use in drill and for instruction in equitation," as well as the transfer of a large number of guns and equipment for training. In April, "Battery 'A,' Field Artillery, Texas A&M College ROTC" was formally organized. Whereas infantry training and smooth-bore cannon had been the main focus of the Corps of Cadets since 1876, cadets now worked with modern artillery pieces, caissons, and limbers (still drawn by six-horse teams). The *Battalion*, which returned to print in March, 1919, hailed the advent of the new artillery unit on campus with this front-page headline: "The Men behind the Big Guns Always Win."[7]

Aggies celebrated Armistice Day on the first anniversary of the end of the Great War, November 11, 1919. Former Texas A&M commandant of cadets Gen. William S. Scott (1889–1890) awarded commissions to sixty officers from the classes of 1917 and 1918 who had completed their degrees upon their return to campus. These new lieutenants were the first of more than 5,200 commissioned at Texas A&M between 1918 to 1941 as student enrollments and the Corps of Cadets' strength surged.[8]

This growth of military training at the college came as both the Regular Army and the reserves were rapidly being reduced in size, despite Congress's approval in 1920 of a new National Defense Act expanding the size of the peacetime Regular Army to 280,000 enlisted men and 17,700 officers. As part of an attempt to create a much larger National Guard and reserve, provisions were made for expanding the ROTC cadet training programs by including a requirement of summer camp attendance, similar to the World War I Leon Springs encampment prior to commissioning. While Texas A&M produced larger numbers of officers and trained personnel in the 1920s and 1930s, there were fewer opportunities for active military service. As Congress reduced its annual appropriations for the military, the authorized strength of the active and reserve forces continually declined. Personnel strength was first reduced to 150,000 in 1921 and then to 137,000 in 1926; in the years just before World War II, only 118,750 troops were funded. Throughout this period the size and the morale of the armed forces plummeted as millions of men were discharged from active duty and many more reduced in rank "to meet the needs of the service."[9]

One irony of the postwar cutbacks was that campus ROTC programs in general and Texas A&M's in particular flourished in spite of the difficult period for the active-duty military. By 1920, army ROTC units were established at 191 colleges and universities. By law, each program and the staff of the on-campus units had to be regular army officers. Thus, assignment to campus duty, while deemed out of the mainstream of day-to-day army activities, became an important mechanism for preserving an active-duty officer corps at a relatively low cost. In addition, national defense legislation in 1916 had created the U.S. Army Veterinary Corps and provided support for studies in veterinary medicine at Texas A&M.[10] Other special academic subjects such as aeronautical engineering received direct congressional support.

In December, 1920, the War Department approved air service training at Texas A&M and allocated a single-engine bi-wing Douglas DH-4 aircraft equipped with a machine gun, bomb sights, and "dummy drop bombs" to the program. Many Aggies became enamored of flight—if they were not already. Wartime flight training and mechanics programs had strengthened A&M's attachment to aviation. Indeed, Aggies had already had an early exposure to flight, which may explain the remarkable number of students who served as pilots in the Canadian, British, French, and American air services during World War I.[11]

Under ROTC's auspices, Texas A&M instituted a rigorous flight training program for cadets. The curriculum included pilot instruction, engine mechanics, instruments, aerial gunnery, and photography as well as procedures for liaison with infantry and cavalry ground units (known as "close air support"). Students who excelled in campus flight training were then channeled to six weeks of summer camp at a U.S. Army training field. ROTC-based air service training, coupled with the early 1911 exposure to aviation, bolstered Aggies' enthusiasm for flight and led many into air combat during the ensuing wars—and some eventually into space.[12]

Oddly enough, in the same year that the War Department approved an ROTC flight training program, it also authorized A&M's first cavalry unit, enabling cadets to be mounted on fifty "especially selected cavalry horses" with the expectation that the number would grow yearly. While the cavalry may not have fit the profile of a technical school, it certainly reflected the Texas heritage of riding the range, ranching, and the Rough Riders. By the close of 1920, the Corps of Cadets consisted of nine infantry companies, three signal corps companies, two artillery batteries, and the cavalry troop.[13]

In their enthusiasm for flight, artillery, the cavalry, and military training in general, Texas A&M's students and faculty were unique. Texas A&M did not mirror what was occurring on the national scene, where the overriding themes of returning to "normalcy" meant diminishing all things military.[14]

The idea of abolishing war captured America's imagination in the 1920s. Not only did Americans look inward and become more isolationist, but the media and the public also began to view military issues with some disdain. Security, it was believed, could best be achieved through disarmament. In turn, to disarm meant there would be little need of an army, navy, or air service and that indeed the country could return to its roots, that is, to dependence on a constabulary homeland force or state militia. Pacifism, isolationism, disarmament, and the remarkable economic boom of the 1920s, abetted by a series of multinational armaments treaties, all reduced the United States to a third-class military power. By the late 1920s, despite the lessons that one might draw from the Great War, "disarmament became a strange American obsession."[15]

In the wake of the bitterness of the postwar Paris Peace Conference and the failure of the United States to participate in President Wilson's vaunted League of Nations, the country entered into a series of accords, beginning with the Washington Conference of 1921–1922, designed to limit any potential arms race and to reduce misunderstandings between the principal powers—the United States, Britain, France, and Japan.[16]

The first of several agreements was the Four-Power Treaty, in which the signers with possessions in the Far East agreed to respect each other's claims and possessions. In case of a dispute, all of the parties were to be consulted. A Nine-Power Treaty followed, aimed at preserving the territorial integrity of China and as well as supporting the Open Door Policy, which provided foreign powers with equal access to China's trade. Finally, the Washington Naval Treaty of 1922 provided a parity in the tonnage of battleships and aircraft carriers among the United States, Great Britain, Japan, France, and Italy, thus establishing a global balance of sea power that was intended to deter war. The five nations would be bound by a ratio of 5 for the United States and Great Britain, 3 for Japan, and 1.75 for France and Italy. In retrospect, however, rather than implementing peace and security, this treaty seriously undermined American and British security in the Pacific.

Japan had emerged from its traditional insular and isolationist past at the beginning of the twentieth century to join the United States, Great Britain, and other nations in an international expedition to break the siege of Peking during the Boxer Rebellion. Subsequently, Japan became a major contender for territories and trade in Asia and the Pacific. By virtue of the Russo-Japanese War (February, 1904, to September, 1905) and the destruction of the Russian fleet in the battle of Tsushima Straits in May, 1905, Japan acquired Russia's interests in Manchuria, half of Russia's Sakhalin Island, and an open door to Korea. Admiral Togo's victory has been compared to Lord Nelson's defeat of the French at Trafalgar (exactly one century earlier) in terms of its impact on the balance of power among nations. Over the years and in part by virtue of the Anglo-Japanese Alliance and Japan's association with the Western powers during World War I, Japan's influence in the Pacific and in the global community grew steadily.[17]

However, Japan now felt both slighted and threatened by the Washington Naval Treaty and consented to accept the reduced naval tonnage only if the United States agreed not to fortify its Pacific holdings and islands—excepting Hawaii. The British assented to similar limitations. Notably, air power and air bases were neither addressed nor considered by military and naval planners in

1922, a strategic omission that would much later be partly alleviated by the innovation of the aircraft carrier. Even as the U.S. Navy scrapped more than thirty-five of its capital ships under the terms of the treaty, congressional appropriations for naval activities were cut back by half, and army and navy personnel were also reduced. Despite material decreases in American armaments in the Pacific, the Japanese military continued to regard the 1922 Washington agreement as a catastrophic event.[18]

Over the next dozen years or so the participants in the Naval Treaty conducted further negotiations and signed additional agreements and "pacts" that presumed to abolish war with a broad stroke of the pen. The result was that Japan slowly narrowed the perceived armament gap between itself and the United States. Moreover, it was nearly impossible to monitor the construction of secondary vessels as light cruisers, destroyers, or submarines and other auxiliary ships as agreed to under the treaties. By late 1933, Japan and Germany flatly rejected any limits and ratios as they rearmed and expanded their armed forces, while the United States persisted in reducing its armaments. War was one step closer—but still seemed far away.[19]

In the context of those times, the Corps of Cadets and the emphasis on military training at the A&M College of Texas were anomalies. The corps continued its steady growth and production of officers throughout the 1920s. When Col. Ike Ashburn left the commandant's office in late 1923 to become executive secretary of the Association of Former Students, he was replaced by Col. Charles C. Todd ('97), the first career officer alumnus of Texas A&M to be selected as commandant. In 1898, Todd, along with two former cadets, Frederick E. Giesecke ('86) and Edwin J. Kyle ('99), had earlier filled the commandant's position on an interim basis.[20]

Despite the fact that Texas A&M at the time mustered the largest uniformed corps in the nation, active-duty assignments after graduation were limited by persistent army manpower reductions. Following graduation, most Aggies joined active reserve programs, and some of these moved to and from active duty when opportunities for service arose. Aggies brought to industry the special training and technical experiences provided by the military that were unavailable to the graduates of "nonmilitary" colleges and universities. Cadets had practical military and technical experiences during their mandatory attendance at army summer camp and, during the regular school year, technical instruction under the auspices of the School of Military Science and Tactics. This instruction included aviation, supply (agriculture, animal husbandry, veterinary medicine), signal corps (communications and electrical engineering), troop movements (port or road construction and maintenance by civil and mechanical engineers), and extensive hands-on gunnery training. Thus, skills taught by army veterans, along with the leadership opportunities provided by the corps, coupled with traditional academic studies, proved valuable assets in civilian employment. Most significantly, the ROTC became the primary mechanism for creating a reserve pool of trained officers.[21]

In this environment, the Corps of Cadets and ROTC at Texas A&M continued to prosper, and by 1927, corps enrollment totaled nearly 2,600 cadets. Each year, the college won recognition by the War Department as a distinguished military program, one that was ranked in the top five among nearly 125 ROTC colleges and universities nationwide. At the close of the decade, the army added an engineering program to A&M's ROTC organization, which already included infantry, field artillery, signal corps, cavalry, and air service.[22] Throughout the 1920s, the military cast of the A&M College became more pronounced.

By the mid-1930s, concern about the clearly deteriorating state of national security began to grow. A decade of talks on disarmament and respect for territorial rights was shattered by the Japanese invasion of Manchuria in 1931. Beginning that year, cadets at the Japanese naval academy at Etajima completed an annual exercise as a core portion of their curriculum to study and answer the following question: "How would you carry out a surprise attack on Pearl Harbor?"[23] All the while, America's war-planning exercises were based on the premise that a Japanese-American military confrontation in the Pacific would necessarily focus on the Philippines.

While clearly not representative of mainstream America and perhaps because of their unique focus on military matters, Texas Aggies in the early 1930s seemed to have an intuitive sense of an impending military crisis. Thus, in February, 1932, a *Battalion* editorial suggested that the worldwide depression and the rise of military conflict in the Far East might ultimately lead to young Americans being sent to war.[24]

Disarmament, military training, and prohibition became big issues on the A&M campus in the spring of 1932. A survey indicated that the student body was overwhelmingly opposed to both disarmament and prohibition and strongly favored ROTC and military training. Not only was that contrary to national public opinion, but the nationwide rhetoric against war and rearmament actually intensified following the Japanese invasion of Manchuria. Many Americans recoiled at the thought of possible U.S. intervention in a "foreign" war. Indeed, military training and ROTC came under specific attack. The rising tide of anti-militarism seemed to turn in December, 1933, following the U.S. Supreme Court's decision to uphold the right of the University of Maryland to require students to enroll for military training courses.[25]

A different ruling might well have ended Texas A&M's requirement that the all-male student body be enrolled in the Corps of Cadets and participate in military training. In Texas, unlike in Maryland, however, neither the students nor the public challenged A&M's military status. In 1932, the Corps of Cadets prospered even as depression-era conditions worsened and 2,294 banks failed. When Franklin D. Roosevelt took office as president in March, 1933, a little more than a month following the accession in January of Adolph Hitler as chancellor of Germany, more than fifteen million Americans were out of work, and newspapers and radio commentators warned of the imminence of war in Europe. The *Battalion*'s reporters also expressed alarm: "Hitlerism in Germany is the greatest menace that has ever threatened civilization."[26]

In 1933, Chief of Staff Gen. Douglas MacArthur estimated that the U.S. Army, with approximately 14,000 officers and 122,000 enlisted men, ranked only seventeenth among the armies of the world.[27] There was much cause for concern about the state of the nation's defenses. Nevertheless, unnoticed by most Americans between 1920 and 1940 and despite the dwindling support and size of American military forces, U.S. service personnel were present in nearly every corner of the world.

During those years many Texas Aggies participated in U.S. military operations in China, Nicaragua, Haiti, the Dominican Republic, and Honduras. In addition, they served in American posts overseas such as Hawaii, the Philippines, and Panama or as military attachés in foreign consulates and embassies. George Fleming Moore ('08), for example, began the first of four different tours of duty at Corregidor in 1925. Ion M. Bethel ('25), following his enlistment in the Marine Corps in November, 1918, returned to A&M to graduate and then went back to active military service. His thirty-three-year career included two tours in China (1927–1928 and 1935–1937). Bethel's experience proved critical to America's operations in the Pacific during World War II, when he coordinated logistical operations for the Peleliu invasion in the fall of 1944. He retired a major general in 1958.[28]

William L. Lee, a 1927 graduate of Texas A&M, served under Gen. Douglas MacArthur and Gen. Dwight D. Eisenhower in the Philippines between 1935 and 1938. During that period Colonel Lee was placed in charge of training and building a regional air defense and became known as the "father of the Philippine Air Force." His duties included teaching Dwight Eisenhower how to fly. A "Flying Tiger" of the American Volunteer Group at the onset of World War II, Lee won promotion to brigadier general and during the war commanded the Thirteenth Air Force in the Philippines and the Forty-ninth (Heavy) Bomb Wing and the Fifteenth Air Force in Italy. Lt. Gen. Andrew Davis Bruce ('16) was one of many Aggies who served in the Panama Canal Zone (33rd Infantry Division) in the 1920s and 1930s.

Others included Brig. Gen. Kyle L. Riddle ('37) and Brig. Gen. Robert M. Williams ('38). Williams began his overseas military career as a company commander of the 5th Infantry Regiment stationed in the Canal Zone. His units trained and operated in the Republic of Panama and in other locations in Central America. Brig. Gen. Aubry Lee Moore ('23) of the U.S. Air Force included a stint at Schofield Barracks, Hawaii, where he was engineering officer for the 19th Pursuit Squadron in 1934 and 1935. John F. Davis ('11) served as a brigade commander for the government of Guatemala between 1935 and 1937.[29] These examples suggest that while U.S. military forces remained relatively small during the two decades following World War I, many of the officers acquired significant overseas experience and some combat awareness.

Moreover, the size of America's military forces in the 1930s was deceptive. While army troop strength declined to only about 140,000 officers and enlisted men, a trained cadre of military personnel was warehoused in the depression-relief agency, the Civilian Conservation Corps (CCC), with an average participation of about 350,000 men between 1933 and 1941. The CCC played a major role in mobilizing for war.

For example, Gen. Ion Bethel also served in the 1930s as a CCC commander. The limited size of the military led the War Department to assign its Regular and reserve officers to duty assignments with the CCC, thus retaining them in a pay status and in a form of active duty. During the summer of 1933, A&M's PMS&T, Lt. Col. Ambrose R. Emery, and his staff of nine Regular Army officers were assigned to CCC camp duty throughout the Southwest. They supervised civilians in reforestation, road construction, and erosion-prevention projects and taught basic military skills such as close-order drilling and taking orders. Haynes W. Dugan ('34), author of the history of the class of 1934, concluded, "This experience obviously stood them in good stead in the years ahead when an army had to be made of civilians."[30] A sizable number of the army's officers and NCOs in World War II were CCC veterans.

Gen. Bernard A. Schriever ('31), who served as a CCC camp officer in New Mexico, explained that the "CCC was a great program to develop many future leaders" for the armed forces. Schriever, A&M's second four-star general, served as a combat pilot in World War II and went on to become the primary architect of the 1950s' intercontinental ballistic missile (ICBM) program as well as a major player in the manned space program in the 1960s.[31] New Deal recovery programs such as the CCC afforded transitional training and enabled the War Department to protect the active-duty officer pool of the armed forces and to build a reservoir from which to recruit soldiers.

One Aggie's unique experience involved a classic conflict over the effectiveness of naval air power in war. The "old Navy" (gun-club) tradition held that the battleship reigned supreme at sea. Brig. Gen. Billy Mitchell, among others, argued that, in modern warfare, air power and aircraft carriers should replace or at least supplement the traditional navy. Mitchell demonstrated his theory in a series of dramatic tests that sunk the heavily armored, former German battleship *Ostfriesland* and three decommissioned U.S. battleships—*Alabama*, *Virginia*, and *New Jersey*. George H. Beverley, who attended Texas A&M between 1915 and 1917 before entering military service in World War I, was one of those pilots who bombed the *West Virginia* and the *New Jersey* in 1923. Despite the complete destruction and sinking of the four ships, U.S. naval officials dismissed the demonstration as "artificial," and Mitchell was soon court-martialed for insubordination and other charges.[32]

Mitchell, of course, was eventually vindicated. Air power and the carrier often determined the course of war, especially in the Pacific, during World War II. And Beverley rose to the rank of brigadier general, serving first as USAF technical supervisor for the central United States from 1938 through 1942 and then commanding general of the Fifty-first Carrier Wing and the Fifteenth Air Force Service Command during World War II. The battleship-air controversy continued to rage until well into World War II. The dispute is perhaps best and most vividly demonstrated by a photograph of the USS *Arizona* featured in the November 29, 1941, army-navy football program in Philadelphia, which is captioned as follows: "A bow-on view of the USS *Arizona* as she plows into a huge swell. It is significant that despite the claims of air enthusiasts no battleship has yet been sunk by bombs."[33] Nine days later, the *Arizona* was bombed and torpedoed by Japanese aircraft and sunk at Pearl Harbor, costing the lives of more than eleven hundred American sailors.

By the mid-1930s, as the Japanese expanded their sphere of influence in Asia and Hitler mobilized Germany and occupied the Rhineland, it became increasingly evident to many military planners that the United States should address its military preparedness. However, Congress, responsive to the public's antiwar sentiments, passed three neutrality acts authorizing the president to halt the sale or shipment of munitions to belligerent nations. Even so, a poll of college students conducted in 1933 indicated that more than one-third would refuse to fight in any war and another one-third said they would fight only if the United States were attacked. In 1936, almost half a million students boycotted classes for a day in an antiwar strike.[34] Those sentiments were obviously not shared by the students at Texas A&M.

While, in 1936, with the overt threat of war rising sharply, the U.S. Army was for the most part poorly equipped and ill trained. It was in this context, in May, 1937, upon returning from a fishing trip to Galveston, that Pres. Franklin D. Roosevelt visited the A&M college campus and used that rostrum to question the past path of pacifism and disarmament. In what were billed as informal remarks to some twenty thousand visitors assembled in Kyle Field, Roosevelt said that it was time "to think in terms of preservation of the nation. Coming here today is a great inspiration to me."[35] FDR's annual message to Congress in January, 1938, stressed the same theme he had covered at Texas A&M: America's military forces were utterly inadequate and it was time to rearm. The pressures became greater when Hitler and Mussolini signed the Rome-Berlin Axis pact in 1938. Rearmament did indeed come—but only later and under more desperate circumstances.

Nevertheless, for the Texas Aggies, there were some positive spin-offs from Roosevelt's 1937 visit to the A&M campus. He authorized the Reconstruction

Finance Corporation to "loan" Texas A&M $2 million to build dorms and new facilities to assist in expanding the Corps of Cadets and the training of more officers. As a result, the college added 1,315 cadet rooms, including the new Duncan Dining Hall, the single largest project since the opening of the college. Federal and state funds also became available for enlarging the college-owned Easterwood Airport to facilitate the expansion of its air training ROTC programs, for the construction of a military science building (better known as the Trigon), and for the renovation of Guion (Assembly) Hall. During the same week that the new corps dorms in the Quad became ready for occupants, France and Britain declared war on Germany—on September 3, 1939.[36]

Other changes at the A&M College during the 1930s better prepared the Corps of Cadets for war. Corps enrollments grew rapidly during the decade, with some 4,933 students enrolled and in uniform in 1937. In addition, more active-duty assignments became available. Congress enacted legislation enabling one thousand reserve officers to return to active duty for a one-year tenure. Fifty of those could become eligible for a permanent appointment in the Regular Army. Another program allowed the army to recruit one hundred new lieutenants from colleges and universities nationwide. Under that program, the A&M commandant submitted four names from the class of 1935 for consideration: Raymond L. Murray, Bruno A. Hochmuth, Odell M. ("Dog Eye") Conoley, and Corps Cdr. Joe C. McHaney, all of whom received regular commissions (and in time, excepting McHaney, became Marine Corps general officers).[37]

Col. George F. Moore ('08), one of the best-known A&M graduates in the army at the time, returned to the college as commandant and professor of military science and tactics in late 1937. A career military officer, he reorganized the Corps of Cadets and expanded its training programs to encompass state-of-the art methods in military tactics and leadership, including the continued use of mounted cavalry units as well as horse-drawn artillery. The first full-scale peacetime maneuvers involving both the National Guard and reserve components were held in Louisiana in the summer of 1940. These exercises highlighted the generally unprepared state of the army. As Haynes Dugan, a decorated World War II veteran, commented, "It was one of the last times that horse cavalry in divisional strength was used. The horses, imported from the high country of New Mexico and Arizona, died in droves. It gave one much to ponder."[38] Except for limited development of tank warfare, artillery, and the air corps instruction, the army and ROTC training of that era differed little from that of 1920.

In early 1939, before World War II began in Europe, the board of directors of the A&M College, as their predecessors had done long before the United States declared war on Germany in World War I, offered the services of the college to the national government. They offered to help in any conceivable way to aid in the defense of the country. Some Aggies acted independently. Charles Monroe Johnson ('39), for example, felt so strongly about the war in Europe that, in May,

Smoke rises from the battleship USS *Arizona,* which was sunk during the surprise Japanese attack on Pearl Harbor on December 7, 1941. One of the few points of resistance was from an antiaircraft battery on Hickham Field, commanded by Lt. Roy W. Gillette ('40).

1940, he hitchhiked to Canada, joined the Canadian Seaforths, and fought the Axis powers for the next five and a half years. In September, 1940, Congress passed a selective service act that created a mechanism for building a new army of citizen soldiers. The process began that same month by calling National Guard units to active duty. Texas A&M's commandant, Col. George F. Moore, received orders to return to the Philippines, where he had served two previous tours of duty. He selected thirty-five young graduating Aggies to precede him to his new post: the Rock—Corregidor.[39]

Other 1940 graduates, including Lt. Roy W. Gillette, went to Hickam Field adjoining the American naval base at Pearl Harbor, Hawaii, where he was assigned to Battery K, 64th Coast Artillery, which was the only antiaircraft battery there. Robert Bruce Gregory Jr., from Nederland, Texas, attended the A&M College from 1937 to 1939. He then enlisted in the navy in October, 1939, and was assigned to a destroyer stationed at Pearl Harbor in 1940. In August, 1941,

Section of horse artillery of the 1st Cavalry Division, Fort Bliss, Texas, 1941.

Franklin Roosevelt and British prime minister Winston Churchill met at sea "somewhere in the Atlantic" and issued a communiqué that would become the text of the Atlantic Charter and a statement of Allied war aims. By December, 1941, Texas Aggies were in military service at diverse locations in the United States and throughout the Pacific, southeast Asia, and Central and South America. Many more would soon follow. Some of these were at the campus theater on Sunday, December 7, 1941, watching "A Yank in the R.A.F." when war struck.[40] "Yesterday, December 7, 1941, a date which will live in infamy, the United States of America was suddenly and deliberately attacked by naval and air forces of the Empire of Japan."[41]

Suggested Readings

Adams, John A., Jr. *Softly Call the Muster* (College Station: Texas A&M University Press, 1994).

Beard, Charles A. *American Foreign Policy in the Making* (New Haven: Yale University Press, 1949).

Chapman, David L. *Wings over Aggieland: The Fledgling Years, 1911–1941* (College Station, Tex.: Friends of the Sterling C. Evans Library, 1994).

Kaufman, Robert G. *Arms Control during the Pre-Nuclear Era: The United States and Naval Limitations between the Two World Wars* (New York: Columbia University Press, 1990).

Macaulay, Neill. *The Sandino Affair* (Chicago: Quadrangle Books, 1967).

Miller, Edward S. *War Plan Orange* (Annapolis, Md.: Naval Institute Press, 1991).

Mitchell, William. *Winged Defense* (New York: G. P. Putnam and Sons, 1935).

Spector, Ronald H. *At War, at Sea: Sailors and Naval Combat in the Twentieth Century* (New York: Viking, 2001).

Tansill, Charles C. *Back Door to War* (Chicago: Henry Regnery, 1952).

Watson, Mark S. *The War Department: Chief of Staff, Prewar Plans and Preparations* (Washington, D.C.: GPO, 1950).

The legend of the '42 Corregidor Aggies "drinking a toast in water to the heroes of 1836" came to symbolize the nation's resolve to wrest victory from the jaws of defeats suffered during the first six months of American combat in World War II. That legend came alive with a movie, *We've Never Been Licked*, which was filmed on the Texas A&M campus in 1943.

WE'VE NEVER BEEN LICKED

On Sunday morning, December 7, 1941, 366 Japanese fighters and bombers, supported by a fleet of midget submarines, struck the Pacific fleet anchored in Pearl Harbor and other bases on Oahu. In less than two hours, most of the American naval force in the Pacific lay in ruins, including four battleships: the *West Virginia, California, Oklahoma,* and *Arizona,* the latter carrying 1,177 American seamen with it to the bottom. The surprise attack eliminated a total of nineteen American warships and 188 aircraft while almost 2,200 men were killed and another thousand wounded. Floyd Buchel ('36) was at Pearl Harbor that day "and has not been heard from since other than he was missing in action. His mother died . . . still thinking that her boy would come home one day."[1] He never did.

Seaman 1st Class Buck E. Jordan ('51), whose ship, the USS *Argonne*, a repair vessel, was itself at dock for repairs, had temporary duty at the ammunition depot on Magazine Island, a few hundred yards southeast of "Battleship Row," when the attack began. He and others on duty ran to the tip of the island in time to watch the "first Jap plane drop his torpedo into the water toward the battleship *Oklahoma*. . . . The Japanese planes that flew by us were so low, we could see the eyes and teeth of the pilots as they dropped their torpedoes. . . . Soon we were pulling injured sailors from the water all around the island."[2] Jordan survived Pearl Harbor, the first day of war, and five years of battle in the Pacific. In 1945, he was present on the last day of the war at the signing of the peace treaty aboard the battleship *Missouri*.

When the attack came at 7:55 A.M. on Sunday morning, the men of Battery K, 64th Coast Artillery, who manned the only operational antiaircraft battery on Hickam Field, rushed to the ammunition shed only to discover that it was locked. Because it was Sunday, the officers who had the keys had not yet arrived for the day's duties, but the delay was short lived. Within minutes, Lt. Roy W. Gillette ('40) turned up with the key and took command, and the battery commenced firing at the enemy, providing one of the few points of resistance at Pearl Harbor. Gillette acted like a "true officer" during that infamous attack, one of his gunners declared years later.[3]

Almost simultaneously, Japanese forces struck the American islands of Midway, Wake, and Guam and were followed within days by invading troops. Japanese aircraft attacked Hong Kong, bombed Singapore, and invaded Malaya and the Philippines. Japanese troops occupied Bangkok, Thailand, on December 9, and that same day attacked Tarawa and Makin in the Gilbert Islands. On December 20, Japanese forces seized Mindanao in the Philippines. Among those captured were Capt. Sydney R. Greer ('35), a former Texas Highway Department engineer who was in charge of construction at the Del Monte airfield on Mindanao. Hong Kong surrendered on Christmas day. On December 30, Japanese forces began an attack on the Bataan Peninsula and the island fortress of Corregidor in Manila Bay.[4] Texas Aggies were there in considerable numbers.

Known as "the Rock" to its defenders, Corregidor was long considered the linchpin of American defense in the Pacific. The battle for Corregidor had deep roots. Indeed, the Japanese-American confrontation in the Pacific, a vast area of more than 68 million square miles, began in 1898, with the treaty that ended the Spanish-American War. At that time, the annexation of Hawaii and the United States' occupation of the Philippines aroused strong hostilities in Japan and spurred the island empire to expand its own spheres of influence in the Far East. Japan's remarkable victories in the Russo-Japanese War and Admiral Togo's destruction of the Russian fleet caused considerable alarm in America's military and diplomatic circles and forced a radical change in U.S. military planning.[5]

In May, 1905, following Japan's victory over Russia at Tsushima Straits, located south of Korea, the War Department began developing a series of broad strategic war plans. These documents were given color-coded designations to describe potential enemies and allies. For example, Germany was code-named "Black," Britain "Red," and Mexico "Green," while "Orange" was assigned to Japan. The United States was code-named "Blue." Thus, the Orange Plan or War Plan Orange (WPO-3), which was based upon the possibility of hostilities with Japan, established an anticipated U.S. response to an attack. In the early years, these strategic plans, some of which were later grouped into the "Rainbow War Plans," were little more than abstract exercises. Some of them, especially those anticipating a clash with Japan in the Pacific, were constantly updated to reflect changes in the region.[6]

As WPO-3 defined it, the center of the American military presence in the Pacific was the island of Corregidor in Manila Bay in the Philippines. Due largely to Manila's well-protected harbor and strategic importance, Corregidor became the centerpiece of American security in the eastern Pacific. In most war-gaming scenarios, military planners assumed that a first strike by the Japanese would come against U.S. naval and army installations in the Philippines. In response, American war planners envisioned a deployment of ships and troops across the Pacific from Hawaii to relieve the Philippines, nearly five thousand miles (and many weeks) distant.[7] Therefore, American fortifications would have to withstand an attack for months, if not a year, until relief arrived.

Military preparations for defending the Philippines began in earnest when the army decided to begin building fortifications there after World War I. The Philippines, however, posed a strategic dilemma. Consisting of more than 7,100 islands, the archipelago would be hard to defend. Military planners thus decided to focus on defending Luzon and the strategic area encompassing the capital of Manila, including the Bataan peninsula, Subic Bay, and Corregidor. In 1923, a joint army-navy board chaired by John J. Pershing, U.S. Army Chief of Staff, General of the Armies, concluded in its report to the army and navy secretaries that, within the guidelines of the Orange Plan, the primary mission in the Pacific was to hold Manila Bay at all cost:

> The islands were of great strategic value to the United States for they provided the best available bases for military and naval operations in the Far East.
>
> That their capture by Japan would seriously affect American prestige and make offensive operations in the western Pacific difficult.
>
> That the recapture of the islands would be a long and costly undertaking, requiring a far greater effort than timely measures for defense.
>
> That the national interest and military necessity require that the Philippines be made as strong as possible in peacetime.[8]

Despite treaty restrictions imposed in 1922, the United States began to fortify key locations in and around Manila. Since Corregidor received top priority, thousands of soldiers and laborers were quietly dispatched to Manila, Bataan, and Corregidor in the 1920s, including Col. George Moore ('08), who was then a coast artillery expert. The actual construction of the fortifications, however, failed to fulfill the military engineers' designs because of insufficient funding. Antiaircraft batteries, for example, were requested but not delivered. Many in the armed forces expressed concern that, unless large sums were spent on fortifying Corregidor and neighboring installations, the Philippine Islands could not be safeguarded. The War Department rejected these views from field commanders as too pessimistic and replied that "national policy dictated that the Philippines must be defended, no matter how hopeless the assignment seemed to those responsible for the defense."[9]

After duty assignments at a variety of locations, including additional service at Corregidor, Colonel Moore returned to Texas A&M to serve as PMS&T from mid-1937 until the fall of 1940. Handpicked for the commandant's position by then A&M board member and classmate Joe Utay ('08), the tall, lanky Moore was a near legend in his college days as a cadet. In addition to lettering in football in 1906 and 1907, he held a number of command positions in the Corps of Cadets and was a member of the Ross Volunteers and the "T" Association. His ability to kick a football "like an old stubborn mule" over a three-story building with spires (Ross Hall) earned him the nickname "Old Maud." Moore, the soldier, perceived his alma mater as a critical source of trained officers and military personnel. During his tenure as commandant, he was determined to strengthen the college's military curriculum and to facilitate the production of officers.[10]

When Moore arrived, the Corps of Cadet numbered 4,933 students, and the regular military staff assigned under the ROTC program had grown to seventeen officers and forty enlisted men. With housing and other facilities inadequate, Moore urged A&M's administrators and its board of directors to give priority to building dormitories for the military training program. Elliott Roosevelt, son of Franklin Roosevelt and a member of the board of directors from 1936 to 1938, was then living in Fort Worth and provided considerable assistance in obtaining loans from the Reconstruction Finance Corporation for new dorms and a mess hall that housed and served the Corps of Cadets. He and Moore argued that Texas A&M and the cadet corps constituted a critical source of officers for the armed services. And indeed, the construction of the dormitories had an immediate impact on corps enrollment. By September, 1940, its strength exceeded six thousand cadets.[11]

Later that year Moore was reassigned to his third tour of duty in the Philippines and promoted to the rank of brigadier general on January 29, 1941. The first graduate of Texas A&M to reach flag officer rank in the Regular Army, Moore received orders to report as commander of the garrison and harbor defenses at Corregidor. The highly fortified, tadpole-shaped island, which was only 3½ miles long and 1½ miles wide (1,735 acres), was considered the key to the defense of Manila Bay. The Rock's twenty-three batteries of 12- and 14-inch guns had a 360-degree traverse and could fire a 1,560-pound shell more than 16 miles, a powerful deterrent to enemy naval attack. Fort Mills and its three smaller fortresses (Forts Hughes, Drum, and Frank) on adjacent islands—Caballo, El Fraile, and Caraboa, respectively—boasted 40-foot thick steel-and-concrete-reinforced fixed-gun firing platforms. Deemed impregnable, this line of fortifications was dubbed "the Gibraltar of the East." There were, however, serious deficiencies in these defenses. Moore and the War Department knew that to relieve a siege at Corregidor in a timely fashion, as anticipated by War Plan Orange, would be nearly impossible. Furthermore, WPO-3 failed to foresee the enormous impact of airpower on a Pacific war, underestimated the magnitude and skill of the attacking enemy, and completely neglected to recognize the inability of the United States to rapidly respond to an attack in the Philippines if one occurred first on Hawaii.[12]

If the Rock and Manila were attacked, WPO-3 anticipated that the defenders

Brig. Gen. George F. Moore ('08), former commandant of cadets at Texas A&M, commanded U.S. forces on Corregidor. "The Rock," a key to the defense of Manila Bay, fell to Japanese attackers on May 6, 1942. During the final assault, 800 Americans and 1,200 Japanese were killed. Eighty-seven Texas Aggies were among the defenders of Corregidor and Bataan.

could withstand a siege for up to two years. In addition, a combined force of U.S. Army and Filipino Scouts would be expected to hold strategic positions in the Mariveles Mountains on the neighboring Bataan Peninsula, which juts out two miles across the water near Corregidor. The basic premise of WPO-3 collapsed with the surprise attack at Pearl Harbor, the subsequent landing of Japanese troops on Luzon, and the capture of Manila. About eight hours after the attack at Pearl (on December 8 in the Philippines because of the International Dateline), airmen watched almost helplessly as most of the aircraft at Clark Air Field and other key facilities were bombed and strafed at will by Japanese pilots. On December 10, Japanese troops landed on the northern coast of Luzon at Vigan, Aparri, and Gonzaga. On Corregidor, Moore was promoted to major general on December 18 and given more authority to prepare for the defense of the Rock.[13]

With Moore on Corregidor were a dozen young Aggie coastal artillery officers whom he had handpicked to join him. The coast artillery batteries were augmented by a regiment of infantry and antiaircraft batteries under the command of Lt. David Snell ('37) of Dallas. Aggies in this group from the classes of 1938, 1939, and 1940 included Capt. Wilbert A. Calvert ('38; Archer City), Capt. Henry J. Schutte Jr. ('39; Houston), Lt. William Boyd ('38; Amarillo); Lt. Lewis B. Chevaillier ('39; Marshall); Lt. Carl Perkins ('39; Beaumont); Lt. Clifton Chamberlain ('40; Wichita Falls); Lt. William A. Hamilton ('40; Dallas); Lt. Charlton Wimer ('39; San Antonio); Lt. Andy M. James Jr. ('40; Dalhart); Lt. Urban C. Hopmann ('39; Beaumont); Lt. Stanley Friedline ('40; Grand Saline); and Sgt. Hugh Hunt ('38; Carthage).

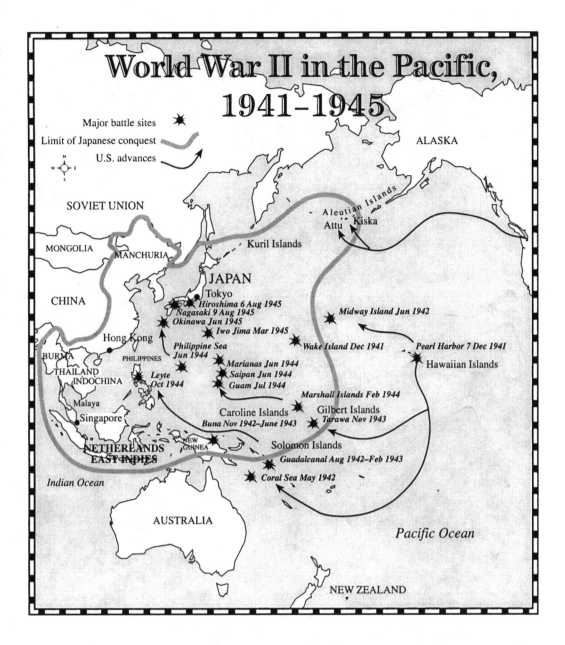

World War II in the Pacific, 1941–1945

Major battle sites
Limit of Japanese conquest
U.S. advances

ALASKA

SOVIET UNION

Aleutian Islands
Attu   Kiska

MONGOLIA

MANCHURIA

Kuril Islands

CHINA

JAPAN
Tokyo
Hiroshima 6 Aug 1945
Nagasaki 9 Aug 1945
Okinawa Jun 1945
Iwo Jima Mar 1945

Midway Island Jun 1942

Hong Kong

Philippine Sea
Jun 1944

Wake Island Dec 1941

Pearl Harbor 7 Dec 1941

BURMA

PHILIPPINES

Hawaiian Islands

THAILAND
INDOCHINA

Leyte
Oct 1944

Marianas Jun 1944
Saipan Jun 1944
Guam Jul 1944

Malaya

Marshall Islands Feb 1944

Singapore

Caroline Islands

Gilbert Islands
Tarawa Nov 1943

Buna Nov 1942–June 1943

NETHERLANDS
EAST INDIES

NEW
GUINEA

Solomon Islands
Guadalcanal Aug 1942–Feb 1943

Indian Ocean

Coral Sea May 1942

AUSTRALIA

Pacific Ocean

NEW ZEALAND

Additional Aggies on the Rock in command and staff positions were Maj. Paul A. Brown ('29) and Captains Cary M. Abney Jr., Chester A. Payton ('33), Stockton D. Bruns ('35), Roy M. Vick Jr. ('35), Willis A. Scrivener ('37), Graham M. Hatch ('31), William M. Curtis ('32), and Jerome A. McDavitt ('33). All were trapped on Corregidor. On December 24, with Manila surrounded, Gen. Douglas MacArthur, commander of American forces in the Philippines, relocated his command to Corregidor and declared Manila an "open city" in the hope that the Japanese would spare the capital from total destruction.[14]

MacArthur, his wife and son, and his staff took refuge with the defenders of Corregidor in the extensive Malinta tunnel complex. This underground catacomb cut out of solid rock over a period of thirty years was 1,450 feet long and 35 feet wide with a domed ceiling 20 feet high, augmented by numerous laterals and pockets. Of the twenty-five laterals, each about 200 feet long, only two had exits. In addition to housing headquarters units, the damp and smoky labyrinth included a three-hundred-bed hospital, an ammunition and supply depot, a makeshift dorm, and a motor pool. Although the fortress was bombproof, it lacked the resources to feed and house the 11,000 American and Filipino defenders now taking refuge on Corregidor. On the Bataan Peninsula, MacArthur had almost 65,000 troops and 26,000 civilians. His forces faced a Japanese army of comparable size, but they were backed by overwhelming sea and airpower. In January and February, 1942, Japan, now effectively in command of the South China Sea and the Pacific Ocean, intensified its bombing of both Bataan and Corregidor. Casualties mounted, and the bombing succeeded in disrupting the fortress's electrical power and supply of fresh water.

On February 20, Pres. Manuel Quezon of the Philippines was evacuated from Manila, and the next day President Roosevelt, as commander in chief, ordered MacArthur to leave Corregidor and transfer his command to Australia. Following the midnight departure of General MacArthur aboard PT-41 on March 11, 1942, Maj. Gen. Jonathan M. ("Skinny") Wainwright assumed command of the American forces. MacArthur's last words of encouragement to General Moore on the north dock at bottomside before boarding were to "hold Corregidor until he returned" and "George, keep the flag flying. I'm coming back."[15]

Upon MacArthur's departure, Wainwright, promoted to lieutenant general, moved his headquarters from Bataan to Corregidor, with Maj. Tom Dooley ('35) of McKinney, Texas, a former Aggie yell leader, as his aide-de-camp. Initial Japanese attacks on the northernmost defensive positions of American soldiers along the Mauban-Mabatang line on Bataan were blunted, but by mid-January, Japanese troops had forced Americans to give ground on the right sector of the lines. Afraid that his units might be flanked, General Wainwright ordered a withdrawal to a second line of defense along the Pilar-Bagac road north of Mount Bataan. Food, munitions, and medical supplies were exhausted, as were the troops. Sickness was rampant. The "battling bastards of Bataan" did much with very little:

> We are the battling bastards of Bataan,
> No mama, no papa, no Uncle Sam;
> No aunts, no uncles, no cousins, no nieces;
> No pills, no planes, no artillery pieces;
> And nobody gives a damn.
> —Frank Hewlett, Associated Press International

Throughout February and March, Japanese attacks increased as their armies were resupplied and reinforced. On April 9, the American field commander on

Bataan, Maj. Gen. Edward P. King Jr., decided that continued resistance was futile and thus agreed to an unconditional surrender. Thousands of the American survivors were able to take temporary refuge on Corregidor, which was also under continual air and naval attack.[16]

During those battles on the peninsula, both Wainwright and Moore spent considerable time outside the Malinta tunnel, even during heavy shelling, to inspire their troops and assess the garrison's operations. For his leadership under tremendous pressure and fire, General Moore was awarded the Distinguished Service Cross and cited for "extraordinary heroism in commanding the harbor defenses of Manila . . . during the siege of the Philippines; for gallantry in continually visiting the most exposed elements of his command. He repeatedly passed from one echelon to another during sustained hostile attacks, giving encouragement, directing operations, and by his courage and example, inspiring the heroic efforts of his command."[17]

Although, upon his departure, MacArthur had held out some hope that relief might soon arrive, none was available. As supplies on Corregidor ran short, it became apparent that the island, rendered increasingly barren by intense bombing, provided no cover for resupply or reinforcements. Furthermore, it provided no way to escape. Crowding on the Rock became acute as the survivors of Bataan, following the surrender of the peninsula, nearly doubled the population of the tiny island to more than eleven thousand. The enemy victory over the "battling bastards of Bataan" had cost the Japanese more than eight thousand killed and wounded, with American units and associated Filipino Scouts suffering at least half that number. On the Rock, rations were cut in half, unit formations were canceled, ammunition was scarce, water was critically short, and the Malinta tunnel was full of the sick and wounded.[18]

By April 21, Aggie Muster day, conditions on Corregidor had become desperate. In these darkest hours, Tom Dooley and the Texas Aggies on the Rock succeeded in making contact with the outside world. They showed their defiance of the Japanese and, more importantly, assured America that the "spirit of San Jacinto" was alive and well.

At about the same time that the defenders received word of a daring bombing attack on Tokyo led by Lt. Col. James H. Doolittle, Tom Dooley was compiling a roster of Texas Aggies on the Rock to embed in a United Press news story in order to confirm their whereabouts to their families back in Texas. Colonel Dooley explained the legendary Corregidor Aggie Muster at a very moving Muster presentation at Texas A&M on April 21, 1978: "General Moore wanted to discuss the thought of the upcoming April 21st. He knew I was an Aggie and said that he wanted to get a list of the Aggies still fighting there. Although the account nowadays says that they gathered on April 21st, it was impossible to congregate because they could not be spared from their [defensive] positions. So, we had a roll call, and a muster is a roll call. We got all the Aggies listed, and

I contacted one of the two correspondents still on the island. I don't remember whether he was UP or AP, but he was willing to use his carefully apportioned time—wire time—to get the story back to the States. We termed it the 'Aggie Story.'"[19]

The wording on the wire release made it appear that Texas Aggies on Corregidor drank toasts of water to the Texas heroes of 1836, sang A&M songs, told stories of their college days, and had their Muster interrupted by Japanese shells. There had actually been a roll call, as Dooley recounted, but no gathering. The roll call released in the news merely enabled families to know that their sons or husbands were alive and fighting. Still the old yell leader, Dooley recalled, "It gave a good plug for the state of Texas, and a good plug for Texas A&M." And, he added, if the worst occurred, releasing names at least helped establish relatives' claims to GI insurance policies.[20]

By capturing the imagination of a nation desperate for a ray of good news about the war effort, the wire story about the Texas Aggies had repercussions far beyond what Dooley or anyone may have anticipated. News of the Aggies on Corregidor spread through the leading papers and periodicals to the halls of Congress. The *Dallas Morning News* featured an article on General Moore that concluded, "The Japs will play hell rooting old Maud out of Corregidor." U.S. Rep. Luther A. Johnson of the Sixth Congressional District, the home of Texas A&M, and Texas Sen. Tom Connally entered the story of the Aggies and the Corregidor defenders into the *Congressional Record*. Following up on an earlier story, *Time* magazine ran an article on "Lone Star on the Rock," stating that "State proud Texans in the garrison of Corregidor celebrated San Jacinto. . . . [T]he Texas drawl and Texas Swagger is [sic] in uniform from Belfast to Calcutta to Pearl Harbor."[21]

There really was, however, no good news about the state of affairs on Corregidor. With the fall of Bataan, the enemy turned its full attention to the Rock. The War Department and MacArthur in Australia expressed grave concern. President Roosevelt wired General Wainwright and gave him full authority to "fight as long as there remains any possibility of resistance." Meanwhile, the Japanese assembled more than three hundred howitzers and artillery pieces on the tip of the Bataan Peninsula, ranging from 75 to 240 mm, to shell Corregidor from Bataan; they also launched a captive balloon for better fire direction and observation. After the defenders of the Rock trained their guns on the Japanese gun emplacements, they withheld fire because each gun was surrounded with American POWs. In addition to the land-based artillery barrages, between April 9 and April 30, 108 air raids pounded the defenders.[22]

After his departure, General MacArthur maintained a steady flow of information and comment from his headquarters in Australia about the doomed defenders of the Rock, now the last point of Allied resistance north of Australia and east of India. "Corregidor needs no comment from me," he said. "It sounds its own story at the mouth of its guns. It has scrolled its own epitaph on enemy tablets. But through the bloody haze of its last reverberating shot I shall always see the vision of its grim, gaunt and ghostly men still unafraid."[23] By mid-April, 1942, contact between Corregidor and the outside world had become infrequent, and by the end of the month it virtually ceased. In the final days, Wainwright and Moore dispersed their troops to defensive positions on the beach, first to escape the constant aerial bombardment that concentrated on "topside" (the tunnel area) and then to prepare for an amphibious enemy invasion at any time.[24]

As casualties mounted and water became scarce, on May 5, General Moore commanded all units to "prepare for probable landing attack." Preceded by massive artillery fire and heavy bombing, Japanese troops swarmed ashore at midnight. General Wainwright carefully described the magnitude of this combined land and air attack on Corregidor: "General Moore and I, making a careful check of that overwhelming artillery assault, discovered that the Jap batteries hit Corregidor with a five-hundred-pound 240 mm. shell every five seconds during an entire five hour period. The big shells whined in and struck us amid a shower of men, guns, dirt, rock, and debris with clock-like precision. They fell at the steady rate of twelve every minute, which meant thirty-six hundred of the shells for the five hours, enough shells to fill six hundred trucks.

"Moore and I, delving further into the mathematics of the fury, estimated at the end of the five incredible hours that the Japs had hit the Rock with 1,800,000 pounds of shells. These were statistics which ignored the other beating we took that day, for we also had thirteen air raids."[25]

Moore, in direct command of all infantry and U.S. Marine forces on the Rock, massed his troops to meet the invaders on the island's northern tip. The defenders met the Japanese on the coast and delayed the landing until 0230 but were gradually overwhelmed. With fighting reduced to hand-to-hand combat, Moore committed the first wave of his reserve force of 500 men at 0430 and launched a second U.S. counterattack at 0615. At daylight, with casualties mounting, the enemy was heavily reinforced with light artillery and tanks. By 0800, nearly 2,000 wounded and dead lay between the attackers and the mouth of the tunnel into the fortress. Since there were no litter bearers or medics, the walking wounded were either reinjured or even killed trying to withdraw to the tunnel. After conferring with Moore and Gen. Lewis Beebe, Wainwright, realizing that no relief was in sight, decided to stand down. He ordered that all weapons larger than a .45 caliber be destroyed along with classified documents. He then ordered the American flag lowered and burned.[26]

By noon on May 6, the Battle of Corregidor, one of the longest and fiercest defensive campaigns by the U.S. Army, was over. Nearly every inch of the island had been shelled. All foliage had been obliterated, and the pocked terrain looked like a moonscape. During the final one-day assault, 800 Americans and 1,200 Japanese had been killed.[27] The surviving defenders of Corregidor joined the American and Allied prisoners taken on Bataan and in earlier battles,

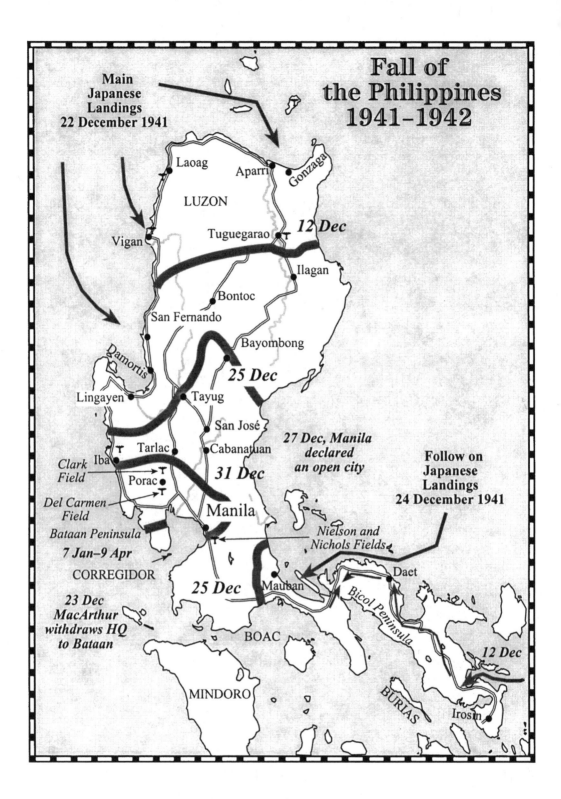

Fall of
the Philippines
1941–1942

Main
Japanese
Landings
22 December 1941

Laoag

Aparri

Gonzaga

LUZON

12 Dec

Vigan

Tuguegarao

Ilagan

Bontoc

San Fernando

Bayombong

Damortis

25 Dec

Lingayen

Tayug

San José

27 Dec, Manila
declared
an open city

Follow on
Japanese
Landings
24 December 1941

Cabanatuan

Clark
Field

Iba

Tarlac

31 Dec

Porac

Del Carmen
Field

Manila

Bataan Peninsula

Nielson and
Nichols Fields

Daet

7 Jan–9 Apr

CORREGIDOR

25 Dec

Mauban

Bicol Peninsula

12 Dec

23 Dec
MacArthur
withdraws HQ
to Bataan

BOAC

MINDORO

BURIAS

Irosin

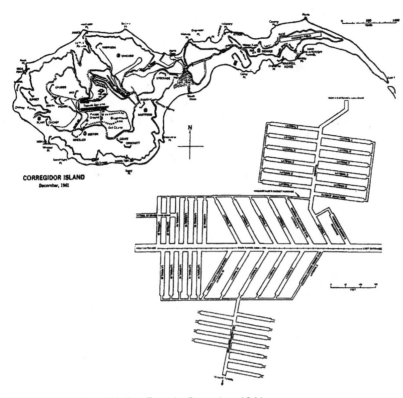

CORREGIDOR ISLAND
December, 1941

Corregidor Island and Malinta Tunnels, December, 1941

though they were not on the infamous death march. Largely through the efforts of Lt. Col. Jerome A. McDavitt ('33), the American Defenders of Bataan and Corregidor, Inc., have compiled a list of eighty-seven Texas Aggies who fought at Corregidor and Bataan. In 1969, their names were inscribed on a plaque that includes the following tribute: "With great humility and unbounded pride, we gratefully acknowledge and dedicate this plaque to all Texas Aggies who led and supported us during the gallant defense of Bataan and Corregidor from 8 December 1941 to 6 May 1942. The traditions of Texas A&M were never more manifest and may their service ever serve as inspiration to those who follow."

Even as the surrender was being completed, most of the more than 75,000 prisoners captured on Bataan and related campaigns were being marched by their Japanese captors nearly sixty-five miles up the Bataan Peninsula from Mariveles to the railhead at San Fernando. Making their way through humid jungles in 100-degree temperatures, those men would now be battling for survival in one of the most infamous episodes of the war: the Bataan Death March.

Given no food during the first three days of the march, the prisoners were allowed to drink only from filthy carabao (water buffalo) wallows. Starved and suffering from malaria, dysentery, and tropical diseases, the prisoners endured barbaric treatment from their captors. During the march, those who fell ill by the wayside were clubbed, beaten, bayoneted, and left to die. More than 9,000

TABLE 6. Texas Aggies Who Fought at Corregidor and Bataan

Maj. Gen. George F. Moore ('08)
Col. Edwin A. Aldridge ('16)
*Maj. Maynard G. Snell ('21)
Maj. John V. King ('22)
*Capt. Adolph H. Giesecke ('26)
*Lt. Col. Rufus H. Rogers ('26)
M/Sgt. William G. Boyd ('27)
Capt. John S. Coleman ('27)
*Maj. Clarence R. Davis ('27)
Lt. Col. E. T. Lewis ('27)
*Capt. Paul Brown ('28)
*Capt. John A. Bergstrom ('29)
Maj. Harry O. Fisher ('29)
*Capt. Jack W. Kelly ('29)
Capt. George H. Peets ('30)
Capt. Joseph R. Revak ('30)
Lt. James N. Roland ('30)
*Capt. Graham M. Hatch ('31)
*Capt. William M. Curtis ('32)
Maj. Oliver W. Orson ('32)
*Capt. George C. Brundrett ('33)
Capt. Aaron A. Gensberg ('33)
Capt. Jerome A. McDavitt ('33)
*Capt. Chester A. Peyton ('33)
*Capt. Cary M. Abney Jr. ('34)
Capt. Hervey H. Whitfield ('34)
Capt. Stockton D. Bruns ('35)
*Capt. Charles M. Dempwolf ('35)
Capt. Thomas Dooley ('35)
*Capt. Gus H. Frobel ('35)
*Capt. Sidney R. Greer ('35)
*Lt. James R. Oppenheim ('35)
*Capt. Roy M. Vick ('35)
Capt. Jack K. Walker ('35)
Capt. Floyd Buchel ('36)
*Lt. John B. McClusky Jr. ('36)
Capt. Travis E. Perrenot ('36)
Lt. Harry J. Schreiber ('36)
*Lt. Maxey Chenault ('37)
Lt. Jackson L. Grayson ('37)
*Lt. Clifford G. Hardwicke ('37)
*Capt. Willis A. Schrivener ('37)
Lt. David M. Snell ('37)
Lt. James Y. Alexander ('38)

Lt. William Boyd ('38)
*Lt. Edgar B. Burgess ('38)
Capt. Wilbert A. Calvert ('38)
Lt. W. P. Culp III ('38)
Capt. Frank Gensberg ('38)
Sgt. Hugh Hunt ('38)
Lt. William E. Lewis ('38)
*Lt. James B. Whitley ('38)
Lt. Lewis B. Chevaillier ('39)
*Lt. Hugh A. Derrick ('39)
Lt. Henry Dittman ('39)
*Capt. James R. Griffin ('39)
*Lt. Howard P. Hardegree ('39)
Lt. James M. Henry ('39)
Lt. Urban C. Hopmann ('39)
*Capt. Ross I. Miller ('39)
T/Sgt. John J. Moseley ('39)
Lt. John R. Noles ('39)
Lt. James M. Roland ('39)
*Capt. Henry J. Schutte Jr. ('39)
Lt. Charlton J. Wimer ('39)
Lt. Clifton H. Chamberlain ('40)
Lt. Roy H. Davidson Jr. ('40)
Lt. Robley D. Evans ('40)
*Lt. Stanley Friedline ('40)
*Lt. Orman L. Fitzhugh ('40)
*Capt. Paul R. Gregory ('40)
Lt. William Hamilton ('40)
*Lt. Marshall H. Kennady Jr. ('40)
*Lt. Melvin Ray Millard ('40)
*Lt. John W. Muse ('40)
Lt. Donald W. Petersen ('40)
*Capt. Carl H. Pipkin ('40)
*Lt. John Darrell Stukenburg ('40)
*Lt. Charles E. Gaskell ('41)
*Lt. Burt O. Griffin ('41)
*Lt. Andy M. James Jr. ('41)
WO Walter M. Lee ('41)
Lt. Tull Ray Louder ('41)
Lt. Robert C. Robbins ('41)
Lt. Travis J. Smith ('41)
Lt. James R. Davis ('42)
Lt. Roy D. Russell ('42)

*Killed in action or died while a POW

prisoners died on the march, including nearly 2,300 Americans. An additional 1,600 Americans died of maltreatment and starvation in June and July at POW Camp O'Donnell following the march. Air Force Capt. John S. ("Dusty") Coleman Jr. ('27) chronicled his experiences and the brutality of Bataan in his memoir, *Bataan and Beyond: Memories of an American POW*:

> We passed an artesian well, with lots of cold water squirting out, about one hundred feet from the road. A few of the men from the front of the column started running out to get water for their canteens. The front guard shot three of them before they stopped running for the water. There were already seven or eight bodies lying around the well. My fever was so high and I was so weak, I hardly remember that day. Just before sundown the head of the column started turning into a barbed-wire stockade. During the day's march, I had drifted back close to the rear. . . . It was hot and dry; no wind was stirring. I fainted or blacked out. Someone filled my canteen with water and bathed my face. I came to, but my head hurt so bad I could hardly stand to open my eyes. I lay there all night. An officer came to me the next morning and said, "If you can't make the march past one o'clock, you had better not start because they are not leaving anyone alive on the road."
>
> I noticed a buck sergeant in front of me staggering along. . . . He staggered out of the column to the right. The front guard turned around and shot him like someone shooting birds, just half aiming. The bullet hit him in the chest and the sergeant rolled against the curb on the street. The guard saw that he had not killed him, so he pushed out his rifle in one hand, like firing a six-shooter from the hip, and shot him again. This time the bullet hit the sergeant in the pit of the stomach. Then the guard rushed up to him and ran his bayonet through the chest. . . . After seeing this, I was determined not to fall out of the column.[28]

On April 8, 2nd Lt. William E. Lewis Jr. ('38) was captured on Bataan and survived the Death March. Soon after the war, he completed a detailed and descriptive sworn deposition of his experiences in captivity. After the surrender, Lewis said, the captives were held in a concentration area for two days and three nights with neither food nor water other than what was in their canteens when captured. On April 12, they were herded out of the containment area and began the eighty-seven-mile march to the town of San Fernando. There were no facilities, and no arrangements were made for food. The walk began at 7:30 or 8:00 in the morning and continued until a great number of the prisoners either fell out or lagged behind due to exhaustion. Then their captors would either bayonet the prisoners to prod them on or kill them outright: "I witnessed many Americans and Philippine Scouts and natives bayoneted or shot to death."[29]

When the mass of prisoners could no longer make progress, the guards halted the procession and gave them the "sun" treatment—forcing them to stand in the hot sun for two or three hours, during which many of the prisoners passed out. Most of them were suffering from dizzy spells, dysentery, and high fever: "The March consumed about nine days, only one night of which I can remember having any relaxation. We were forced to sleep and defecate in the same immediate area. In many cases our contingent would be forced into a compound which had been recently occupied by captured native troops and that had been contaminated beyond comprehension." The prisoners had their first meal—a small quantity of rice—after reaching San Fernando, near the Pampanga River. They were moved by narrow-gauge railroad from Pampanga to POW Camp O'Donnell: "The cars that were provided were very small box cars into which one hundred to one hundred and twenty men were forced. In the car in which I was riding, there were three or four prisoners who suffocated. They locked the doors on each side and we had no toilet facilities and no water."[30]

Two months later, those prisoners chosen by lot to be transported to Japan were transferred by cattle boat to Manila. There they were placed in the hold of a ship marked with a big white cross on the stacks, even though the vessels were also carrying seven to eight hundred fully equipped Japanese troops. Upon arrival in Japan after a ghastly voyage, they moved from the ship's hold, where the temperatures had hovered around 120 degrees, into sleet and freezing weather. As a result, many prisoners contracted pneumonia and died.

The survivors, including Lewis, were then shipped to Osaka and assigned to work in the Yodagawa steel mills (where Dusty Coleman was also interned). Lewis was assigned to a sandblasting room and given no respirator or other protection to prevent his inhaling the dust. The captives' diet consisted of about 350 grams of cooked rice per day with a bowl of hot liquid. Of the 400 men assigned to the mill with Lewis, about 240 survived. The ordeal did not end there, for in August, 1945, the prisoners were transferred to a POW camp, where their rations were cut to 268 grams per day. Soon Lewis, no longer able to work, was badly beaten by a guard with a bamboo kendo stick.[31] Despite all of that, he survived and was liberated at the close of the war.

Capt. Adolph H. Giesecke ('26) survived the march but died in Japan. Lt. Burt O. Griffin ('41), who was near death after being unloaded from the prisoner transport in Moji, Japan, "was a stretcher case and had to be left behind . . . when the other prisoners were moved on." Capt. Rudyard Kipling Grimes ('38), who commanded the 57th Infantry, Philippine Scouts, in combat against the Japanese, survived the march but died in the encampment on Luzon before the troop ships made the transfer to Japan.[32]

The American prisoners taken at Corregidor fared somewhat better than those on Bataan, if such horrors can be measured with any reasonable precision. For example, the Japanese chief of war prisoners at Thanbhyuzhat, Burma, where a few Aggies were eventually interned, "welcomed" the prisoners with these words: "It is a great pleasure to see you at this place. . . . You are only a few remaining skeletons after the invasion of East Asia [by the West] . . . and are pitiful victims." He lamented the past intrusion of the British and the Americans and explained that there was "no other reason [than that intrusion] for Japan to drive out the anti-Asiatic powers of the arrogant and insolent British and Americans." He promised that the "Great East Asia Co-Prosperity Sphere" would benefit everyone and establish lasting world peace. He regretted the "insufficiency of various items," promised to manage all of the prisoners, "who are merely rubble," according to military regulations, cautioned them against attempting to escape since the punishment "shall naturally be severe." He also explained that everyone must work and that "nobody is permitted to do nothing and eat."[33]

After the fall of Corregidor, those who had been taken prisoner were eventually parceled out to POW camps across Asia—to Java, Singapore, Burma, Thailand, French Indochina, Korea, Manchuria, and Japan. Of the original twenty-five Aggies on duty on Corregidor, twelve returned home alive. General Moore was moved more than four times to different camps and released in late August, 1945. After the war, he returned to serve a fourth tour in the Philippines as commanding general of the Philippines-Ryukyus Command. After four decades of service, Moore retired on July 31, 1949.[34]

Tom Dooley survived and was invited to be in the official party on the deck of the USS *Missouri* in Tokyo Bay along with Generals MacArthur and Wainwright on September 2, 1945, to witness the surrender of Japan. Returning Aggie defenders of the Rock, including Urban Hopmann, David Snell, Bill Boyd, Bill Hamilton, and Cliff Chamberlain, were decorated for their courage and bravery. Chamberlain, who spent 999 days as a POW, returned in time to be the keynote speaker for the 1945 Campus Muster in Guion Hall.[35]

The legend of the '42 Corregidor Aggies is portrayed in a movie produced by Universal Pictures and filmed on the Texas A&M campus in 1943. Written by Norman Reilly Raine, author of the World War II–era "Tugboat Annie" stories appearing in the *Saturday Evening Post*, the film tells the story of Brad Craig, who grows up in Japan, where his father is on overseas assignment before the war. On the eve of the Japanese attack on Pearl Harbor, Japanese students and a gardener are spies who attempt to steal a vital chemical formula from the A&M College laboratories. Craig foils the plot, but, because of his past friendship with the Japanese, he is accused of being a double agent and is drummed out of the cadet corps. At the end of the film, he turns up as an observer aboard a Japanese enemy aircraft. During an encounter with American fighters, Craig recognizes the voice of one of his Aggie friends ("Cyanide" Jenkins, played by Noah Berry Jr.), seizes control of the plane, and dives it into a Japanese carrier, earning redemption and honor for himself.[36]

In some respects, the movie *We've Never Been Licked* symbolizes the status of the war as of May, 1942. Corregidor had fallen, Manila was occupied, and the Philippines were lost. Indo-China, Thailand, Java, Malaya, New Guinea, Man-

We've Never Been Licked, filmed on the A&M campus in November, 1942, starred Noah Berry Jr., Robert Mitchum, Richard Quine, and the Corps of Cadets. The movie proved to be a great morale booster for the nation during the difficult years of World War II.

churia, and Hong Kong were firmly under Japanese control. American naval strength in the Pacific had been greatly diminished at Pearl Harbor. Burma, India, Australia, Alaska, and the western coast of the United States thus seemed vulnerable to Japanese attack. Those were dark and desperate days. The Nazis were renewing their offensives in Russia and threatened the Suez Canal in North Africa. U-boat attacks were increasing in the Atlantic, and American forces were not yet in combat in either North Africa or Europe. The movie reflects the underlying mood of the country in the first six months of war: America had been outscored for the moment but had never been defeated. Throughout 1942 and 1943, the United States underwent a remarkable mobilization, converting peacetime production to wartime manufacture and millions of its citizens to soldiers, sailors, aviators, and marines, while building tanks, airplanes, arms, munitions, and the greatest military force ever assembled. Uncle Sam needed soldiers. Of the millions mustered, some twenty thousand Texas Aggies served in many diverse ways around the globe. Finally, the United States and its allies began to counterattack and slowly—and at great cost—turned the tide of the war.

Suggested Readings

Adams, John A., Jr. *Softly Call The Muster: The Evolution of a Texas Aggie Tradition* (College Station: Texas A&M University Press, 1994).

Coleman, John S. *Bataan and Beyond: Memories of an American POW* (College Station: Texas A&M University Press, 1978).

Gailey, Harry A. *The War in the Pacific: From Pearl Harbor to Tokyo Bay* (Novato, Calif.: Presidio Press, 1995).

Lawson, Ted W. *Thirty Seconds over Tokyo* (New York: Random House, 1943).

Miller, Edward S. *War Plan Orange: The U.S. Strategy to Defeat Japan, 1897–1945* (Annapolis, Md.: Naval Institute Press, 1991).

Morris, Eric. *The American Alamo of World War II: Corregidor* (New York: Cooper Square Press, 2000).

Spector, Ronald H. *Eagle against the Sun: The American War with Japan* (New York: Free Press, 1985).

Wainwright, Jonathan M. *General Wainwright's Story* (New York: Doubleday, 1946).

More than 20,000 Texas Aggies served in World War II, including more than 14,000 as commissioned officers in all branches of military service. They served in combat on land, on the seas, and in the air. They also played many crucial combat-support roles. Some spent most of the war in technical research assignments, including radar and rocketry, and a remarkable number served in the military forces of Allied nations.

UNCLE SAM NEEDS YOU!

It was no accident that Texas Aggies were at Pearl Harbor, on Bataan, and at Corregidor when the Japanese forces struck. By December, 1941, the armed forces of the United States stood at 1.6 million military personnel, up from 222,000 who were in service at the beginning of 1940. Mobilization actually began in September, 1940, as units such as the Texas National Guard, reserves, recruits (including many who had served in the Civilian Conservation Corps), and almost half a million draftees entered the services. Following Pearl Harbor, inductions, training, and equipping rose precipitously, topping out with 14.9 million Americans in the armed forces at the close of the war. A total of 16.2 million served during World War II. Most of the Texas Aggie classes of 1940 and thereafter went into military service for the duration of the war as commissioned and noncommissioned officers. Texas A&M produced approximately one-third of the ROTC officers who took part in World War II, and they served in capacities and in places that reflected the enormity and complexity of modern warfare.[1]

They fought in combat and worked in support roles as engineers, supply officers, Signal Corps specialists, aviators, training officers, food service workers, transportation and logistics personnel, veterinarians, information and intelligence gatherers, mapmakers, and even morale officers. Some governed and headed security forces at strategic and critical outposts in the Philippines, Haiti, Panama, Brazil, Nicaragua, Samoa, Burma, and Alaska. Some had oversight of captured enemy cities, and others commanded prisoner of war camps.

After the fall of Corregidor, where Texas Aggies fought, as had their San Antonio predecessors, to the bitter, unsuccessful end, Japanese forces controlled the Pacific from the borders of India to the islands of Alaska. Germany had overrun Europe, and Paris had fallen. The French fleet, including two battle-ships, eight cruisers, and thirty destroyers, was scuttled at Toulon. Russia was near collapse as German armies besieged Leningrad and Stalingrad. With the capture of Tobruk and the loss of thirty thousand British soldiers, North Africa seemed open to German conquest.[2]

As America wrestled with the problems of preparing for war, the Texas Aggies of the class of 1941 graduated on Friday, June 6, the last commencement held on campus for the duration of the conflict. After participating in their formal commissioning ceremonies, those with reserve commissions reported for active duty while others went to their local draft boards. Billy J. ("Bill") Adams ('41), for example, was commissioned as an army second lieutenant on June 7. On Sunday, June 8, he reported for active duty at Fort Sam Houston in San Antonio. When Adams arrived, he headed the alphabetical list of new arrivals and won assignment as the post's officer of the day (OoD) for Monday, June 9. That same day, upon being assigned to the 15th Field Artillery, the alphabet again gave him duty for the following day as the unit's OoD. In July, Adams reported to Fort Sill, Oklahoma, for field artillery training school, where he was given command of a newly formed antitank platoon—with no antitank guns.[3] These were common experiences in the early days of the war.

The guns would come later, while the training came sooner, thanks to another Texas Aggie, Maj. Gen. Andrew Davis Bruce, a 1916 A&M graduate who had left the battlefields of France in 1918 a lieutenant colonel (at the age of twenty-three) and an experienced combat officer in tank warfare. When World War II began, Bruce was sent to Texas to organize a tank destroyer command, which he located near Killeen, and named the post for Confederate Gen. John Bell Hood (1831–1879), "whose enemies never saw his back." His program established the basic model for armored (and antitank) warfare. While he served in North Africa and Europe, Bruce subsequently commanded the 77th Infantry Division in combat at Guam, Leyte, Kerama Rotto, Ie Shima, and Okinawa and served as occupation governor of Hokkaido, Japan. Later he served as deputy commander of the Fourth Army and commandant of the Armed Forces Staff College, retiring as a lieutenant general in 1954. At that time, Bruce returned to Texas to serve as president and then chancellor of the University of Houston.[4] Two Aggies who trained under General Bruce were Bill Adams and Kay Halsell II, both second lieutenants.

Halsell, from the class of 1936, had remained in the active reserves and in April, 1941, decided to opt for a one-year active-duty assignment, which turned into six years. His first post was at Fort Ord, California, with the 7th Division Artillery. There he was assigned to the 26th Field Artillery Brigade, which proudly boasted a new 105-mm-howitzer battalion. It also had three historic horse-drawn light battalions with matched teams of black-and-white horses: the 74th, 75th, and 76th Field Artillery, which had achieved fame in the battles of the Argonne forest. Within six weeks, the horses were retired from active duty, and the battalion became fully mechanized.[5]

In November, Halsell was transferred to become the executive officer of a new antitank battery. Then "all hell broke loose" on December 7. Halsell's antitank unit was rushed off to San José, California, to help guard Moffett Field against a possible Japanese parachute attack. Someone, probably a Japanese submarine, actually did shell the beach, Halsell recalled. After the immediate threat had passed, his unit formed the core of the new 826th Tank Destroyer Battalion, which was assigned to secure March Air Force Base against attack. Soon thereafter, the battalion was transferred to Fort Hood, Texas, for antitank training, which at the time, Halsell recalled, "was foundations and no buildings . . . the boondocks." When a visiting general told the men it would take a lot of "guns and guts" to win the war, Halsell heard someone in the crowd muttering, "it would take a whole lot of guts because we don't have any guns." In time, his antitank battalion was reformed as an amphibious tractor battalion to prepare, with the 1st Cavalry (which included more than thirty Texas Aggie officers), for assaults on the Admiralty Islands, Leyte, and Luzon. Kay Halsell ended the Pacific campaign with the occupation forces in Osaka, Japan, and closed his military career as a brigadier general.[6]

After completing the antitank training program at Fort Sill, Bill Adams joined the 9th Infantry Division for maneuvers at Fort Bragg, North Carolina. He recalled distinctly that, in December, the division finally began to receive their new 105-mm howitzers, and none too soon. Adams was at the 26th Field Artillery Battalion's motor pool when news came of the attack on Pearl Harbor and soon received orders to return to Fort Sill as an instructor in the Officer Candidate Field Artillery School, where he spent most of the war. He then served with the 20th Infantry Division in Kentucky, where his group helped organize and train the cadre who became the core elements of units designated for deployment to the Pacific and Europe.[7] ROTC-trained Texas Aggies such as Adams were a major source of officers who were able to conduct specialized military training and OCS programs.

Frederick H. Weston ('30), who, in 1967, completed thirty-five years of military service at the rank of major general, made unique contributions to military training during World War II. While serving with the 7th Cavalry Regiment before the outbreak of the war, Weston was assigned to the War Department's morale branch. There he incorporated physical conditioning and mental examinations into the training process. An advocate of army-operated off-duty activities for military personnel, Weston helped create the military's Special Services programs. His book, *Personal Affairs for Military Personnel and Aid for Their Dependents*, triggered the organization of the army's information program. Weston later became a recognized expert on mobile warfare, light armor, and air-cavalry operations, which he helped pioneer.[8]

Brig. Gen. Aubry Lee Moore ('23) enlisted as a flying cadet in November, 1927. He became deputy chief of air staff in 1942, assistant chief of air staff for the China-Burma-India operations in 1943, and chief of staff for the Tenth Air Force in 1944.

Texas Aggies played a large role in the inception and development of the U.S. Army Air Corps and provided pilots, training officers, engineers, and numerous air force generals. Pilot training was particularly urgent during the mobilization of 1940 and 1941, and military aviators and flight instructors remained scarce at the outbreak of World War II. Among those entering the officer corps were many Texas Aggies who possessed an unusual expertise in aviation, both technical and practical. In the interwar years, Aggies showed an affinity for flying, and Aubry Lee Moore from Frost, Texas, was one of many who found a home in the army's fledgling air corps in the 1920s and 1930s. After graduating in 1923 with a reserve commission in the field artillery, Moore found a job supervising weaving at a Brenham cotton mill but soon decided his future should be in war rather than weaving. After enlisting as a Flying Cadet in 1927 and completing his flight training at Kelly Field, Moore became a second lieutenant in the Regular Army.[9]

Moore was a section chief at the U.S. Army Air Corps' headquarters in Washington, D.C., when the bombs rained down on Pearl Harbor. In June, 1942, he became deputy chief of air staff and was instrumental in establishing air bases and organizing the newly created air corps units. For his outstanding service he received the Legion of Merit. In October, 1943, as the United States launched its counteroffensives in the Pacific, Moore was assigned to the China-Burma-India Theater of Operations and in early January, 1944, became chief of staff for the Tenth Air Force in support of Allied troops fighting in Burma.[10]

During his four years as a student, William L. Lee served in the Texas National Guard and, upon graduation in 1927, joined the air corps, completed flight training, and was sent to the Philippines in 1935. There he was responsible for organizing and training the fledgling Philippine air force. During his years there, Lee worked with Gen. Douglas MacArthur and was instrumental in planning and developing American air defenses. When war began, Lee commanded the Thirteenth Air Force, which was based in the Philippines. Following the invasion of Sicily in July, 1943, Brigadier General Lee was transferred to the Fifteenth Air Force's 49th (Heavy) Bomber Wing in Italy.11

Similarly, Robert Francis Worden ('33) from El Paso enlisted in the U.S. Army Air Corps after graduation and received his pilot's wings at Kelly Field. Later he was appointed as a second lieutenant in the Regular Army and spent most of the war as a flight instructor. In March, 1945, he was sent to Italy and ended the war as commander of the 49th Bomber Wing. Major General Worden retired from the air force in 1964 after serving with the Allied Commission in Rome and with air force headquarters in Washington, D.C.12

Officers who were involved in training programs during the early years of the war usually finished their tour in command combat positions. For example, Kyle L. Riddle ('37) from Decatur, Texas, received his pilot's wings and commission in the U.S. Army Air Corps Reserve at Kelly Field in February, 1939. After an assignment with the 8th Pursuit Group at Langley Field, he was transferred to Albrook Field in the Panama Canal Zone, where he spent three years organizing and training pursuit and fighter organizations for assignment to the new U.S. Air Corps, Panama and Caribbean Commands. His primary responsibility was to create combat training units to provide replacements for P-38 squadrons. Riddle assumed command of the 479th Fighter Group, which flew its first combat mission out of England in May, 1944, in support of the Allied invasion of Europe. His combat decorations included the Silver Star, Distinguished Flying Cross, and numerous other awards.13

Durant S. Buchanan ('17) began World War II as a Marine Corps training officer stationed in New Zealand and ended his tour as a major general commanding special troops in landings at Bougainville and Guam. His military career began in World War I with combat at Chateau Thierry and St. Mihiel. Maj. Gen. Bennett Puryear Jr. ('06), a brother of A&M's Dean Charles Puryear, commanded marine training units at Quantico, Virginia, and remained there throughout the war. Marine Brig. Gen. John T. Walker commanded the 22nd Marine Regiment during the assault and capture of Eniwetok Atoll in the Marshall Islands. For his extraordinary heroism, Walker received the Navy Cross.14

A navy flag officer, Rear Adm. Albert MacQueen Bledsoe attended Texas A&M for one semester in 1913 before receiving an appointment to Annapolis. During World War II he was director of service members in the Bureau of Navy Personnel. In 1944, Bledsoe commanded the USS *Denver* during the recapture of Corregidor and earned the Navy Cross in the battle of Leyte Gulf.15

Similarly, Aggie fighter pilot John H. Buckner transferred from John Tarleton College to Texas A&M in 1938 and later received an appointment to the U.S. Military Academy. After graduation he joined one of the many fighter squadrons that were mobilized throughout the country. In April, 1944, Buckner went to Europe as flight commander first of the 366th and later the 365th Fighter Squadron. Major General Buckner went on from that war to command the 18th Fighter-Bomber Group in Korea.[16]

Another aviator, Guy M. Townsend ('43), began his military service in October, 1941, when he left the A&M campus for air cadet training in California. Upon completion of that instruction, he was assigned to combat crew training for B-17 bombers. In August, 1942, Townsend was sent to the South Pacific for duty with the Thirteenth and then the Second Air Force. At the war's end he was a major with 450 combat hours in B-17s and B-29s in the Pacific theater and recipient of the Legion of Merit and Distinguished Flying Cross, among other service awards. After the war Townsend was at Edwards Air Force Base as a test pilot. As a brigadier general and flight test chief, he helped bring the B-52 into operational status. Townsend was the first military pilot to fly the B-47 Stratojet, B-50 Superfortress, and the B-52 Stratofortress. He logged more than 8,000 hours of flying time, 5,000 of which were in experimental test flights.[17]

Guy Townsend did a lot of flying, but Hiram Broiles is usually acknowledged as having spent more time in the air in World War II than any other American pilot. His flights and war experiences were extraordinary. A 1928 graduate, Broiles captained the Aggie baseball team, played two years of professional baseball, and then decided to join the army air corps. He earned his wings in 1932, but since the army air corps had no open slots, he flew as a commercial pilot with China National Air from 1933 to 1937 and returned to the United States as a pilot with United Airlines. When war came, Broiles was called to active duty in the air corps and assigned several unique missions. The first was to fly an advance party of Secret Service agents to Casablanca in December, 1942, in preparation for Franklin D. Roosevelt's historic meeting with British prime minister Winston Churchill, which was scheduled for January. The second assignment effectively took him around the world ten times. A member of the air transport command, Broiles piloted a specially outfitted B-24 called "Peeping Tom" with a crew assigned to film and map approaches to most of the airports that air force combat units around the globe might use. His crew surveyed almost every airfield and landing site in the world used by the air force in World War II, logging nearly 250,000 miles in the process. His crew also pioneered new air routes that bomber and transport planes could use to reach strategic areas. Broiles flew exploratory flights across the South Pacific and North Africa, as well as Arctic routes such as Nome, Alaska, to Siberia and to Europe via Greenland. After the war, Lieutenant Colonel Broiles went to work for the Federal Aviation Administration and returned to active duty during the Korean War.[18]

Two of A&M's most distinguished former students and later air force generals, Bernard A. Schriever and Alvin Roubal Luedecke, graduated respectively in 1931 and 1932. They achieved distinction in World War II and afterward pioneered in American missile and space-flight efforts. Luedecke began World War II with assignments as an air attaché in Panama and other South American embassies. He was chief of the air section, military intelligence, from 1942 to 1943 and, as major general, was deputy chief of air staff to the commanding general of the army air forces in the China-Burma-India Theater of Operations from 1943 to 1946.[19]

Luedecke's and Schriever's careers paralleled in many ways. Interestingly, one of Schriever's first duty stations after he earned his wings at Randolph Field was the Canal Zone, an area where Luedecke spent considerable time. After a brief stint as a commercial pilot, Schriever returned to active duty in 1938 as a test pilot at Wright Field in Ohio, received specialized training in aeronautical engineering, and soon afterward earned a master's degree in mechanical engineering at Stanford University. He spent most of the war in the South Pacific, as did Luedecke, flying sixty-three combat missions in B-17s and B-25s. At the close of the war Schriever was with the Far East Air Service, providing support for operations in New Guinea, Leyte, Manila, and Okinawa. Later Schriever became the organizing genius of the army's postwar missile program, winning promotions that ultimately led to four-star general.[20]

Alvin Luedecke made significant contributions with the Atomic Energy Commission and the National Aeronautics and Space Administration (NASA). For six years he directed nuclear tests on Eniwetok and Johnston Islands. After helping to organize NASA, he served as deputy director of its Jet Propulsion Laboratory at the California Institute of Technology. Returning to Texas A&M in 1968 as associate dean of engineering and coordinator of engineering research, Luedecke headed the engineering experiment station the following year. After the death of A&M's president Earl Rudder, Luedecke served as acting president (March–November, 1970).[21]

Manning Eugene Tillery ('26) joined the army air corps after graduation and spent most of his thirty years of service in supply and logistical support operations. He retired in June, 1956, at the rank of major general with the Legion of Merit and Commendation Ribbon. A contemporary, Robert B. Williams ('23) joined the air corps after graduation, earned his wings, and spent much of the war commanding the 49th Bomb Squadron and the 1st Air Division of the Eighth Air Force in Europe. He fought and retired as a major general in 1946, having earned the Distinguished Service Cross, Great Britain's Order of the Bath, and France's Legion of Honor and Croix de Guerre.[22]

George H. Beverley, an A&M student between 1915 and 1917, began World War II as the air force chief of technical inspection for the central United States. He assumed command of the 51st Troop Carrier Wing in Sicily in 1943, then

Gen. Alvin Roubal Luedecke ('32) was chief of the air section, military intelligence, 1942–1943, and deputy chief of air staff for the U.S. Army Air Force in the China-Burma-India theater in 1943. After retiring from the air force, Luedecke served as general manager of the Atomic Energy Commission, deputy director of California Institute of Technology's NASA Jet Propulsion Laboratory, director of the Texas Engineering Experiment Station, and acting president of Texas A&M University, March–November, 1970.

served as commanding general of the 15th Air Force Service Command. Howard C. Davidson, foster son of the college's dean of engineering, James C. Nagle, completed his junior year at A&M before transferring to West Point, where he graduated in 1915. During World War II, he commanded the Tenth Air Force in the Burma campaign in 1944 and 1945. Maj. Gen. Ralph Wooten ('16) headed the U.S. Army Air Force Technical Training School at Boca Raton, Florida, and Brig. Gen. William E. Farthing ('14) commanded the Seventh Air Force's base in Hawaii in 1942. Guy H. Goddard, a 1941 graduate of West Point who received a Master's degree in civil engineering from Texas A&M in 1947, trained engineer combat troops in Texas and elsewhere in the United States, then transferred to the Pacific theater to serve in various engineer combat battalions and finally as commander of the 836th Aviation Engineer Battalion. Goddard spent most of his thirty years on active duty in military engineering and construction work for the air force and retired a major general.[23]

Gen. George S. Patton Jr. called Otto P. Weyland ('23) "the best damn general in the air corps." Weyland was also the first Texas Aggie to attain the rank of four-star general. Born in Riverside, California, in 1903, Weyland moved with his family to Texas before World War I. At A&M he was a captain in the Aggie band, graduated in mechanical engineering, and was commissioned in the air reserve. After completing flight training in Texas, he received a Regular Army commission in the air corps. When war came, Weyland served as a flight instructor at Kelly Field, then commanded a fighter wing in Europe, where he

TABLE 7. Texas A&M's World War II General Officers Army and Air Force

Major Generals	Brigadier Generals
Bennett Puryear Jr. ('06)	Douglas B. Netherwood ('08)
George F. Moore ('08)	John A. Warden ('08)
Howard C. Davidson ('11)	William C. Crane Jr. ('10)
Roderick R. Allen ('15)	John F. Davis ('12)
Percy W. Clarkson ('15)	Jerome J. Waters ('13)
Edmond H. Leavey ('15)	Oscar B. Abbott ('14) .
Andrew D. Bruce ('16)	William E. Farthing ('14)
Ralph H. Wooten ('16)	Robert R. Neyland Jr. ('14)
Harry H. Johnson ('17)	Claudius M. Easley ('16)
Otto P. Weyland ('23)	Nat S. Perrine ('17)
Robert B. Williams ('23)	John T. Walker ('17)
	George H. Beverly ('19)
	John L. Pierce ('19)
	Arthur B. Knickerbocker ('21)
	Aubry L. Moore ('23)
	William D. Old ('24)
	William L. Lee ('27)
	Alvin R. Luedecke ('32)

fought in six major campaigns. As the war ended, he was commanding the Nineteenth Tactical Air Command, which provided air support for Patton's historic dash across France in the summer of 1944. After the war, he commanded the Tactical Air Command before leading the U.S. and UN Far East Air Forces (FEAF) during the war in Korea.[24]

George J. Eppright joined the army air corps after graduation in 1926, rose to the rank of colonel during World War II, and afterward worked in the experimental engineering and flight test divisions at Wright-Patterson Air Force Base in Dayton, Ohio. He retired from service in 1955. Robert R. ("Bob") Herring ('41) from Childress, Texas, flew sixty combat missions and served as chief staff intelligence officer for the Fifth Air Force in the Philippines near the close of the war. He was awarded the Legion of Merit, Silver Star, and Air Medal. After the war he was active in community affairs and the World Health Foundation.[25]

Jimmie Aston from Farmersville, Texas, enrolled in civil engineering in 1929. His senior year, he was captain of the football team, a member of the Ross Volunteers, and cadet colonel of the Corps of Cadets. He served as city manager for Bryan, Texas, and, in 1939, at the age of twenty-eight, became city manager of Dallas, Texas. His tenure there was relatively short. Aston retained his reserve commission and was called to active duty in the army air corps in 1941. After combat duty in both the Atlantic and Pacific theaters and receiving the Distinguished Service Medal, he ended the war as chief of staff for the air transport command.[26]

The extraordinary involvement of Texas Aggies in military aviation is documented not only by the unusual number of air force generals, pilots, combat missions, and decorations but also by the sobering statistics of A&M aviators who died in training and combat missions, especially in the early years. Hundreds of Texas Aggies died while pilots, instructors, or crew members in fighter, bomber, transport, and surveillance aircraft, as indicated in the sampling of letters and documents collected by the Association of Former Students in its effort to recognize Texas Aggies who have been killed in the service of their country:

Ted Chapman ('43) was killed in a plane crash on July 10, 1943, while serving as a second lieutenant in the army air corps.

Lt. Ray J. Canton Jr. attended from 1940 to 1942; he was killed in a plane crash near Highland City, Florida.

Lt. Joe Chamberlain ('42) was killed on May 30, 1943, flying out of Pyote, Texas. He was a navigator on a B-17.

First Lt. Austin Wilkins Clark was killed in a crash of two bombers on the west shore of the Great Salt Lake near Wendover, Utah. He attended A&M from 1937 to 1940, studied petroleum engineering, and became a pilot with the Royal Canadian Air Force in 1941.

Capt. Herbert Winfield Cumming ('41) was killed in action on November 7, 1943. Flight commander of a P-38 squadron, he was participating in a mission over northern France when his plane was shot down. Cumming parachuted into the English Channel but was never seen again.

Lt. Alfo Leroy Baker ('40) was killed in the crash of an army training plane near Victorville, California, on September 19, 1942. Baker entered the service in December, 1941, at Kelly Field.

Lt. James Hugh Brantley ('40) was killed in action over England on August 6, 1944. Brantley entered the air corps immediately after Pearl Harbor and received his silver wings at the Lubbock, Texas, airfield in September, 1942.

Capt. August J. Bischoff attended from 1939 to 1941. Upon graduation from A&M, Bischoff entered the chemical warfare service. In April, 1943, he transferred to the air corps and received his wings in December. He was killed in action in Romania on June 10, 1944.

Cadet James C. Black ('45) was killed in a plane crash near Merced, California, on February 1, 1944. He would have received his wings and commission in May, 1944. Black was a junior at A&M when he enlisted.

Lt. William Henry Baker ('42) was lost in a bombing mission over Germany. Baker participated in a commando raid over Dieppe on August 19, 1942.

Lt. Edmund F. Boyle ('41) went to Canada in August, 1941, and enlisted in the Royal Canadian Air Force. He was transferred to the USAAF and attached to the Eighth Air Force as a bomber pilot. Boyle was killed in action on April 22, 1944, when he was shot down over Dusseldorf, Germany.

Second Lt. James C. Barham ('36) was attached to the western division of the U.S. Air Corps Ferry Command. Barham was killed on January 16, 1942, near Las Vegas, Nevada. (On the same plane was Carole Lombard, famous motion-picture star.)

First Lt. Meinrad J. Endres attended from 1937 to 1939. Endres was one of four airmen killed on August 8, 1942, when a twin-motored bomber crashed in San Pablo Bay, California, ten miles north of the army air base at Hamilton Field.

Lt. Robert S. English attended from 1938 to 1941. Pilot of a B-17, he was killed when his plane was shot down near Paris while on a bombing mission.

Lt. Alfred A. Esposite attended from 1939 to 1942; he was killed over England on February 2, 1943, in a training accident.

Capt. Jerral W. Derryberry attended from 1937 to 1939; he was killed in a plane crash in California. Derryberry enlisted in the air corps on September 13, 1940, and received his wings in 1941. Captain Derryberry ferried B-17 bombers to England, North Africa, and Brazil.

Maj. Jeth Wesley Dodson ('32) was killed in a plane crash near Mobile, Alabama, on May 12, 1943. He was a signal officer at the headquarters of the Second Air Support Command, Barksdale Field, Louisiana.

Capt. Jessie C. Draper ('40) was commander of a flying training squadron at Williams Field, Arizona; he was killed on July 26, 1944, when his single-engine plane crashed thirteen miles west of Casa Grande, Arizona.

Capt. William Edwin ("Sheik") Davis ('29), U.S. Army Ferry Command, Romulus, Michigan, was killed on October 6, 1942, when his plane crashed and burned near Rock Springs, Wyoming.

Sgt. Ben Luker Dean attended from 1942 to 1943; he was a radio operator on a C-47 troop carrier plane and was lost in a storm off Cape Fear, North Carolina, on July 21, 1944.

Lt. Leslie Talbert Gordy ('44) was killed in a B-25 crash at Mather Field, California, on April 13, 1944.

Chief aviation machinist James H. Gulley ('42) was killed in a plane crash on February 17, 1944, in San Diego, California.

Sgt. Connie Claude Hagemeier attended from 1942 to 1943; he went missing on an overwater training flight from Pocatello, Idaho, to Hamilton Field, California, on October 6, 1943. The plane was never found, and the crew has officially been declared dead. Hagemeier was a gunner on a four-engine bomber.

First Lt. Charles D. Heller attended from 1935 to 1937; he was killed on July 11, 1943, while flying "the Hump" to Chengtu, China.

A/C Joe Berl Huddleston attended from 1940 to 1942; he was on a PBY aircraft that failed to return to Bronson Field, Pensacola, Florida.

Cpl. Earl E. Jackson attended from 1923 to 1925; he died on December 19, 1943, while stationed with the AAF in England.

Lt. Luther Gordon Kent Jr. attended from 1940 to 1942; he joined the air corps and received his wings and commission on December 5, 1943, at Foster Field, Victoria, Texas, where he served as an advanced pilot instructor. Kent was killed in a plane crash on October 13, 1944.

Second Lt. Boyd Knetsar ('39) was an instructor in the air corps at Albuquerque, New Mexico; he was killed in a plane crash on October 14, 1942.

Lt. Kenneth E. Krug Jr. attended from 1935 to 1936; he was killed on February 29, 1944, in an airplane crash in British Guiana, South America.

Lt. Rufus J. Lackland III attended from 1941 to 1942; he was killed when he and a cadet crashed in their plane on a routine training flight.

Capt. Henry Arthur Lewis attended from 1935 to 1939; he was killed when two flying fortresses collided over the Gulf of Mexico.

Lt. Beverly Earl Miller ('44) was a fighter pilot based in Naples, Italy; he was killed in January, 1944.

Lt. Henry R. Smith ('42) was killed at Enid, Oklahoma, on December 22, 1942, in a plane crash.

Capt. Eugene C. Tips ('13) was killed on January 2, 1941, in a plane crash.

Raymond Wilson attended for a few months in 1942 and joined the air corps; he was killed in a raid over Germany on January 11, 1944.[27]

Gen. George H. Beverley, while serving as chief of technical inspection for the air force, was particularly distraught over the large number of training accidents and combat fatalities. He supported the idea of adding one week of training to the cadet pilots' curriculum, but the demands of war were too great and the need for pilots too urgent.[28]

One Texas Aggie airman from Groesbeck, Texas, lived to tell the story of how he was shot down, bailed out, and was taken prisoner at Groesbeck, Holland, in March, 1944. S.Sgt. Lawrence E. Oliver, a tail gunner on a B-17 flying out of Suffolk, England, on a bombing mission to Munster, Germany, many years later recalled the following:

The Luftwaffe rose and hit us with everything they could put in the sky. From the coast going in all the way to the target and back into Holland we fought them. . . . Alexander, our ball turret gunner, reported gasoline pouring off the trailing edge of the wing. We were attacked again by FW-190s with one of them hanging behind our left wingman, rocking from side to side, blasting away. Finally, the B-17 pulled up, stalled, and went down. The Jerry was a cocky S.O.B. . . . but he misjudged his distance, and I blew his ass away. . . . Someone yelled "Fighters!" It was a frontal attack with 20mm cannon. The plane shuddered and the last shell exploded in the radio room and must have ignited the gasoline fumes because there was instant fire from the radio room forward. . . . I opened the door and pushed myself out. My landing sometime later was on the other side of the woods. I enjoyed 5 minutes of freedom, eventually ending up in Stalag Luft I . . . at a beautiful Barth on the Baltic, where seven sewers meet the sea.[29]

Texas A&M also sent pilots to the Marine Corps and navy. Homer S. Hill ('40) applied for navy flight school when the war began and received his wings in 1942. He spent most of the next two years as a marine combat pilot in the South Pacific and then, in 1944, became executive officer of a transport squadron. He also fought in Korea and Vietnam and retired a major general while earning the Distinguished Service Medal, Distinguished Flying Cross, and other awards.[30]

As with the army air force, navy and marine pilots also suffered very high losses, both in combat and in training. Cadet J. Neal Jones, who attended A&M briefly in 1942 before joining the naval air corps, died in a crash near the Naval Air Training Center at Kingsville, Texas, two weeks before he was to receive his wings. Lt. (jg) David E. Delong ('39) was killed when his plane went down in an "unrevealed" area in 1943. Ens. James M. Drummond ('41) was serving with the 21st Fighter Squadron stationed in San Diego when he was killed in a collision with another aircraft during a routine flight. Ens. Jeff G. Blair ('45) from Zwolle, Louisiana, crashed on the night of August 4, 1943, while piloting a navy plane. Lt. Granville William ("Bill") Cowan ('44) was lost during a naval combat mission, and 1st Lt. James Wilson Coke ('45), a Marine Corps pilot, died in a crash at El Centro, California, in February, 1943. Lt. (jg) George Lawrence Leger ('41) was killed during dive-bomber training at Corpus Christi, Texas, after having returned from combat in the South Pacific.[31] Flight at home or abroad was a hazardous business during World War II.

As Aggies entered military service in World War II, many of them continued to function much as they had in civilian life as petroleum, chemical, civil, and electrical engineers. In doing so they often made distinctive contributions to the war effort. John F. Younger ('37), for example, after completing his undergraduate degree in chemical engineering, worked for four years as a drilling mud engineer. He was called to active duty in 1941 to serve as a chemical warfare officer and spent most of the war in the Persian Gulf Command at Khorramshar, Iran, supervising shipments of chemicals, fuels, and explosives. In 1945, he was discharged at the rank of lieutenant colonel. Similarly, John W. Newton, a 1912 chemical engineering graduate, although not in uniform, served on the National Petroleum War Council and chaired a five-state refining council under the War Production Board's supervision. Another Aggie chemical engineer, George Demetrie Comnas ('35), designed a portable petroleum laboratory that was used in the North Africa campaign. After the war Comnas helped design and establish petrochemical plants in Spain, Greece, and Africa, which initiated revolutionary changes in those postwar economies.[32]

Chemical and electrical engineers were often given special assignments to develop new technologies of modern warfare. William C. Tinus, after earning his degree in electrical engineering in 1928, went to work for Bell Telephone Laboratories. In 1938, he began work on "radio object location," which laid the technical groundwork for American radar systems. When war came, Tinus's laboratory group helped design and refine the navy's first fire-control radar equipment, then participated in developing different radar systems for aircraft, naval vessels, submarines, and ground forces. He retired in 1968, after forty years with Bell Labs as vice president for military development and design engineering, having made exceptional contributions to the improvement of military electronic technology. Two other Aggies, Carter Coleman Speed ('36) and Travis M. Hetherington ('32), who also attended West Point, spent a substantial part of their World War II service heading the Army Air Corps Radar Training School, thus implementing the knowledge developed by Tinus and others at Bell Labs. Having been assistant director of the radio technical school in Sioux Falls, South Dakota, from 1939 to 1942, and director of the radar school in Boca Raton, Florida, from 1943 to 1945, Hetherington retired as a brigadier general after World War II. Speed, also a brigadier general, retired in 1946, following a term as commander of a squadron of the Fifty Air Force in Japan.[33]

Appropriately, many A&M electrical engineering graduates spent their military service in the Signal Corps. Tom J. McMullin ('36), who made his way to Texas from Ohio, studied electrical engineering and was active in the amateur radio club. After graduation, he applied for active duty in the army but was rejected because of color blindness. When war came, the army decided he was visually and otherwise qualified for a commission in the U.S. Army Air Signal Corps, and he then began five years of active duty in the States and in Europe.[34]

David K. Sain from Hughes Springs, Texas, received his degree in electrical engineering before his commission in the army in 1941. After attending signal school at Fort Monmouth, New Jersey, he spent most of the war in the Pacific theater in communications assignments and earned the Silver Star and the Army Commendation Medal. Colonel Sain closed his military career at Fort Huachuca, Arizona, in 1970, after heading the U.S. Army Strategic Communications Command.[35]

One Aggie who made exceptional contributions to electronic warfare earned an accounting and statistics degree in 1936. After Henry C. Wendler worked with IBM for six years, he was called to active duty fourteen months *before* the attack on Pearl Harbor to assist the War Department in the design and improvement of computer technology, which, in 1940, was still in its infancy. Wendler helped develop mobile machine records for army headquarters before transferring to the army air force, where he created a system of statistical control procedures adapted to computers. He helped provide statistical analyses for the D-day invasion and was involved in designing the transfer of major army air force efforts and resources from the European to the Pacific theater of operations. Wendler ended the war with Gen. Douglas MacArthur's headquarters in Manila and then with American occupying forces in Japan. He returned to IBM and in later years helped improve computing and data processing at Texas A&M University.[36]

As in World War I, many Aggie engineers, including Joe G. Hanover, a 1940 graduate in civil engineering, spent their war years in engineering support roles. Hanover went on active duty in February, 1941, and for the next four years served as a motor transportation officer and in related duties at camps in Texas, North Carolina, and California before being transferred to the Corps of Engineers. In early 1945, he was sent to Europe as a construction and labor supervisor and ended the war as commanding officer of the 1268th Labor Supervision Company in France. Active in the army reserves and Texas National Guard, Hanover was promoted to brigadier general in December, 1966.[37]

Frank H. Newnam Jr. ('31), a civil engineering graduate, worked for ten years with the Texas Department of Highways before serving with the U.S. Army Corps of Engineers. Sent to China, he supervised the engineering design and construction of highways, railroads, pipelines, buildings, and utilities related to the war effort. Another Texas Highways engineer, George P. Munson Jr. ('28), was called to active duty in October, 1941. In 1944, he commanded the 843rd Engineer Battalion, which helped remove obstructions and provide routes from the Normandy beachhead. The 843rd also assisted in the liberation of Paris and participated in the invasion of Germany. Munson returned to the Texas Department of Highways at the end of the war and was reactivated to command the 20th Engineer Brigade in Korea. He returned to Texas to build highways and remained active in the army reserves, retiring from service in 1965 at the rank of major general.[38]

While Andrew P. Rollins's one-year stint with the Texas Department of Highways was relatively short, his army engineering career spanned more than three decades. A 1939 civil engineering graduate, Rollins began active duty as a reserve officer in 1940 and received a Regular Army commission with the Corps of Engineers a year later. He served with the 27th Engineering Construction Battalion in the southwest Pacific. After the war, he served in Germany, Vietnam, and the United States as director for military construction and supervised the design and construction of the Saturn V launch facilities at Kennedy Space Center. In 1971, Rollins became deputy chief of the Army Corps of Engineers.[39] For many engineers like Rollins, Hanover, Newnam, and Munson, the work they performed in peacetime was much the same as what they accomplished during the war.

In addition, many Texas Aggies were neither pilots, engineers, combat officers, nor soldiers, but they nevertheless served their country during wartime as public relations officers, veterinarians, supply officers in charge of feeding the armies, and in numerous other roles. Lt. Col. Crawford H. Booth ('15) fought in Europe during World War I and then worked in the petroleum-refining business in Texas until called back to active duty for World War II as public relations officer at Camp Hood, Texas.[40]

One Texas Aggie who served the war effort in a very different way was Leldon Beard ('41), who entered service before graduation. He signed up as a flight engineer with Pan American World Airways and spent most of the war ferrying troops into and evacuating wounded soldiers out of the front lines. Although Beard was not in uniform, the air force awarded him an "honorable discharge," along with the American Defense Service Medal and other honors in recognition of his meritorious wartime service.[41]

Despite the rapid technical evolution of warfare, modern armies, just as they did in the days of Genghis Kahn and Napoleon Bonaparte, still traveled on their stomach. Veterinarians provided the interface between human and animal health and were critical in the acquisition, processing, and transport of food to the front. Aggie veterinarians performed a variety of essential duties during the war, from their primary responsibilities for food supplies and human health to helping fight a traditional horse-and-mule kind of warfare that still existed on the fringes of World War II. Robert H. Haight ('42), a veterinarian from Hollywood, California, received his commission in the veterinary corps soon after graduation from Texas A&M. His first assignment was as food inspector at Oakland Army Terminal, California, a major depot for food and supplies going to the Pacific theater. Haight recalls the huge storehouses filled with meat, fruits, vegetables, flour, sugar, and particularly butter (which was rationed to civilians) and Spam piled to the ceiling.[42]

In September, 1943, Haight arrived in Australia, where he was assigned to an Australian "horse outfit" to buy and train horses for service with General Stilwell's troops in the China-Burma-India theater. Because Japanese forces had the area closely guarded, the only way in was on horseback over the mountains. After the close of the war, Haight was part of a medical team that was sent to survey the damage from the atomic bomb at Nagasaki.[43]

One of Haight's classmates, Charles Van Loan Elia, also received his DVM in 1943 and was commissioned in the army veterinary corps. His first duty assignment, like Haight's, was at the Los Angeles port of embarkation, where he was responsible for the inspection and medical processing of horses, mules, dogs, and pigeons scheduled for shipment to American forces in China, Burma, and India. After the war, his duties took him from coast to coast and to Korea, the Ryuku Islands of Japan, and Alaska. In 1972, he became a brigadier general and chief of the U.S. Army Veterinary Corps.[44]

Ogbourne D. Butler ('39) graduated from Texas A&M in animal husbandry and in August, 1941, began active-duty service as assistant commandant of a school at Fort Sam Houston in San Antonio, Texas, that trained bakers and cooks for army mess halls and officers to supervise food service. After Pearl Harbor, Butler was assigned as a reconnaissance officer with an artillery battalion of the 2nd Division, which had distinguished itself in World War I. By 1943, he and the 2nd Division were in Great Britain and the following year at the front in Normandy. After the war Butler served as professor, department head, and vice-chancellor of Texas A&M while remaining active in the U.S. Army Reserve. He retired from service as a brigadier general commanding the 420th Engineer Brigade.[45]

One of Butler's contemporaries, Fred W. Dollar, hitchhiked from his home in Henderson, Texas, to the A&M campus in August, 1940, to begin work on a degree in agricultural economics. He paid his way through school waiting tables and doing odd jobs at Sbisa Dining Hall. Although it was not what he had planned, food services became Dollar's lifelong vocation in both war and peace. In May, 1943, he and most of the seniors were inducted into service. After basic training Dollar was sent to Officer's Candidate School in Fort Lee, Virginia. He received his commission in September, 1943, and immediately reported for duty with the LIV Quartermaster Corps, which was sent to England to help prepare for the invasion of Europe. On August 1, 1944, Dollar was on Utah Beach helping transfer food and supplies from ships into amphibious "ducks," which were protected from the crashing waves by a screen of sunken, obsolete ships. He spent the rest of the war in Europe supervising the distribution and preparation of food for combat troops. Dollar continued that work in Korea and retired in 1965 as lieutenant colonel. He returned to Texas A&M to work for several more decades as director of food services.[46] There are clearly many facets of modern warfare in addition to combat, ranging from food services to missile development, and Texas Aggies have served in almost every capacity.

They have also served in every theater of war. By mid- to late 1942, Allied and American forces began to slow the Axis's offensives in Russia, the Pacific, and North Africa. After the Battle of the Coral Sea in May and the Battle of Midway in June had stalled the Japanese advances in the Pacific, marines launched an Allied counterattack at Guadalcanal, and U.S. forces were deployed to the Aleutians. At Stalingrad, Russia, the Red army escaped the clutches of the Wehrmacht's pincers, while in North Africa, General Montgomery countered the German victory at Tobruk in June by defeating Rommel's armies at El Alamein.

In November, 1942, a quarter of a million U.S. and British troops landed in Morocco and Algeria in Operation Torch. Lt. Col. James Doolittle led a daring air raid over Japan in April. In mid-June, Allied forces, including 5,000 Canadian soldiers, 1,000 British, 50 American Rangers, two dozen Free French fighters, and at least one Texas Aggie staged a daring commando raid at Dieppe in German-occupied France. More than half of the Allied force was killed or taken prisoner, but the raid suggested that, even though the difficulties of opening a second front were formidable, the Axis's "Fortress Europe" was vulnerable. The Allied and American counteroffensive had begun, but the war would be a long, bloody, costly, and very complex struggle.

Suggested Readings

Boykin, Calvin C., Jr. *General A. D. Bruce: Father of Fort Hood* (College Station, Tex.: C&R Publications, 2002).

Boyne, Walter J. *Clash of Wings: World War II in the Air* (New York: Touchstone Books, 1997).

Moy, Timothy. *War Machines: Transforming Technologies in the U.S. Military, 1920–1940* (College Station: Texas A&M University Press, 2001).

Odom, William O. *After the Trenches: The Transformation of U.S. Army Doctrine, 1918–1939* (College Station: Texas A&M University Press, 1999).

Peña, William M. *As Far as Schleiden: A Memoir of World War II* (Houston: William M. Peña, 1991).

Underwood, Jeffery S. *The Wings of Democracy: The Influence of Air Power on the Roosevelt Administration, 1933–1941* (College Station: Texas A&M University Press, 1991).

Two Texas Aggies served with the Flying Tigers in China, and five were on the daring raid on Tokyo, including Doolittle's second-in-command, Maj. Jack Hilger ('32). Another five were part of the Lost Battalion, whose story was immortalized in the movie *Bridge on the River Kwai*. Ens. George Gay ('40) witnessed the Battle of Midway from a ringside seat in salt water. These Aggies fought in Alaska and the Aleutians, on Guadalcanal and New Georgia and were in the ill-fated raid on Dieppe and countless bombing runs over Germany.

COUNTERATTACK

In the spring of 1942, the Japanese onslaught in the Pacific seemed unstoppable. Manila, Hong Kong, Singapore, Bataan, and Corregidor had fallen. Japanese forces controlled Manchuria, Korea, and eastern China as well as the Philippines, Java, New Guinea, and the Solomon, Gilbert, Marianas, and Marshall Islands. In southeast Asia, they pressed into Burma and threatened India. The sea lanes to Australia and the American Samoan Islands lay unguarded. In the northern Pacific, Japanese troops seized Attu and Kiska Islands in the Aleutian chain, threatening Alaska and the west coast of the United States. Much of North Africa and most of Europe and Russia were occupied by Axis armies. In retrospect, however, the spring of 1942 marked the high point of Axis power and the beginning of the bitter, bloody battle to make the world once again safe for democracy.

In some respects the American and Allied counteroffensive had already begun. Indeed, it began before Pearl Harbor, before the United States officially entered the war, with the mobilization of National Guard units and the expansion of Regular Army and air corps active-duty billets. It began with congressional appropriations for hemispheric defense. It began as early as 1939, as young Americans flocked to the military service of other nations. Charles Monroe Johnson ('39), for example, who hitchhiked to Canada, joined the Canadian Seaforths, and served for the next five and a half years, exemplifies the spirit and commitment of those Americans who served. By December 7, 1941, many Americans and a substantial number of Texas Aggies were in combat in Europe, fighting under the flags of Canada, Great Britain, and France. In southeast Asia, others, including two Texas Aggies, fought for China as members of an independent, nonallied, American volunteer group (AVG) better known as the "Flying Tigers."

Almost eight months before Pearl Harbor, Pres. Franklin D. Roosevelt authorized members of the navy, Marine Corps, and army air corps to resign from their branch of service and volunteer to serve under Claire Lee Chennault, a former army air corps captain and air advisor to China to "help train Chinese aviators and protect China's skies." Chennault, with 300 volunteers, including 100 pilots and about 200 crew members, left for Burma aboard ship in July and August, 1941, as private citizens under contract with Central Aircraft Manufacturing Company. The group took up their posts and duties at a remote, abandoned RAF air base in the Burmese jungles 170 miles north of Rangoon and began training in a squadron of combat-ready P-40 Tomahawk airplanes. The P-40, Chennault told his pilots over and over, "has better armor, more firepower and can dive at an extraordinary speed. The Japanese are superbly trained pilots . . . their fighter planes [are] more maneuverable [and] have a better rate of climb but are more vulnerable than the P-40. . . . Use the P-40's good points and you'll stay alive and beat the enemy."[1] And they did.

It was already December 8 at the AVG base in Toungoo, Burma, when the Japanese struck Pearl Harbor. As Chennault put his aviators on high alert, among them was Charles R. Bond Jr., vice squadron leader of the 3rd Squadron, a Texan who began his military career by enlisting in the Texas National Guard (144th Infantry) in 1932. In March, 1938, Bond entered the army aviation cadet program, got his wings and a commission, and was on active duty as assistant operations officer, 49th Bomber Squadron, at Langley Field, Virginia, when he elected "inactive" duty in order to join the AVG. On December 12, Chennault sent Bond's "Hell's Angels" (3rd Squadron) to Rangoon to help the RAF, while the 1st and 2nd Squadrons remained at Toungoo to help defend Kunming, China, which came under Japanese bomber attack on December 18. The Flying Tigers were the first to counterattack the Japanese offensive, and by July 4, 1942, when the AVG was officially disbanded, its pilots had destroyed 217 enemy aircraft, with another fifty probable kills, in thirty-one air battles over Burma and China.[2]

Bond destroyed nine Japanese aircraft and was himself shot down twice. He received two medals from the Chinese government for his heroic actions, including the Fifth Order of the Cloud Banner and the Seven Star Wing Medal. He returned to active duty with the army air force in October, 1942, as commander of the 81st Fighter Squadron in Orlando, Florida, and in 1943 became chief of the air division, U.S. Military Mission, to Moscow, where he served as an aide to Ambassador Averill Harriman. Bond ended the war as a colonel, completed a degree in management engineering at Texas A&M in 1949, and returned to active duty. After various assignments in the United States, Italy, and Thailand, he retired in August, 1968, as major general and commander, headquarters, Twelfth Air Force, in Waco, Texas.[3]

When the AVG disbanded, several pilots, including David Lee ("Tex") Hill

('38), elected to stay in China as members of the China Air Task Force (CATF). The son of a missionary, Hill had been born in Korea in 1915, and his father later accepted a position at a church in San Antonio, Texas. In 1938, Hill completed flight training with the navy, was assigned to the *Saratoga*, and in 1941 volunteered for the AVG. During his seven months as a squadron leader with the Flying Tigers, he was credited with twelve kills. He returned to the States and to regular duty in early 1943 and was sent back to China in October to command the 23rd Fighter Group assigned to the newly formed Fourteenth Air Force, which included elements of the old CATF. Hill came back to the States in 1944 to take command of the 412th Fighter Group, which became America's first jet-equipped combat group.[4] Although small and unofficial, the battles of the Flying Tigers helped stem Japanese expansion and inspire America's counteroffensives in the Pacific theater.

Another early and wholly American counterattack against Japan involved a daring bombing raid over Tokyo led by Lt. Col. James Doolittle. The raid took place on April 18, 1942, on the heels of the surrender of Bataan and during Corregidor's last days, following the destruction of an Australian, British, Dutch, and American fleet off Timor and Java in February and early March, 1942, an action in which the American cruiser USS *Houston* was sunk. In those desperate times, Gen. Henry H. ("Hap") Arnold assigned Doolittle, a pioneering aviator who had broken speed records, performed remarkable aerobatics, and made significant contributions to aircraft flight and design, the job of leading a bombing raid over Japanese cities by launching sixteen modified B-25 bombers from an aircraft carrier. The carrier was to stealthily approach within 350 miles of Japan and launch thirteen bombers that were to hit Tokyo, while three additional aircraft were to target Nagoya, Osaka, and Kobe. The planes were to end their no-return mission by landing in Russia or China. The USSR, however, declined to allow the aircraft to land within its boundaries, and Chiang Kaishek, too, was unenthusiastic about a North China terminus because of the certainty of Japanese reprisals. The raiders thus decided to fly into China without "official" permission.[5]

In February, preparations for the attack began a world away on a remote airfield at Eglin Air Base in the Florida panhandle. Even those who were undergoing training were unaware of their target and who was to command the mission. The action was the first joint army-navy tactical operation since the Civil War. And in the middle of these preparations were a half-dozen Texas Aggies.[6]

The plan was simple yet in fact one of the most dangerous missions of the early war. To ensure deception, surprise, and maximum impact, a new approach was required. All of the air crew members were volunteers. Many of them became suspicious and probably concerned when a young navy ensign was sent to Florida to teach these hotshot air corps pilots how to take off in their B-25 bombers, named for famed aviator Billy Mitchell, in a very unorthodox manner and with twice the normal payload of bombs and fuel on one-third the customary length of runway. The mystery of the mission was further compounded when the crews learned that the commanding officer (CO) of the secret unit was none other than Lt. Col. Jimmy Doolittle, the famous aviator. Second in command was a Texas Aggie, thirty-three-year-old Maj. John A. ("Jack") Hilger of Sherman, Texas. Other Aggies on the mission were pilots Lt. Robert M. Gray ('41) of Killeen, Lt. William M. Fitzhugh ('36) of Temple, Lt. Glen C. Roloson ('40), and Lt. James M. Parker ('41) of Houston. In addition to instruction in short-field operations, precision bombing, and long-range fuel conservation, the pilots were taught to fly at low levels—very, very low— under what some claimed was beneath the height of telegraph lines.[7]

After their training in Florida was completed in late March, each crew was allowed to plot its own course to the West Coast to a marshaling area at Fort McClellan near Sacramento, California. They were instructed to do as much low-level flying on the way as possible. Any delay or aircraft problems would automatically scrub a plane and its crew from the mission. En route, Bob Gray, who was commander of aircraft number three, the "Whirling Dervish," detoured to land on a county road in central Texas to have lunch with and say farewell to his mom and dad. In Hilger's aircraft, plane fourteen, navigator Herb Macia looked out the window as the plane crossed into Arizona and commented to the crew:

> "That's where I was raised."
> "What in the hell's the name of that place?" Hilger asked.
> "Tombstone!" Herb said as the crew, unsure of their future, laughed like all get-out.[8]

Under tight security, the B-25s gathered at Alameda Air Station outside of San Francisco on April 1 and were loaded on America's newest carrier, the USS *Hornet*. Not until the carrier cleared the Golden Gate Bridge under the cover of a heavy fog and began sailing due west for Hawaii did Colonel Doolittle inform his pilots of their mission and target data. As he recalled, "America had never seen darker days. Americans badly needed a morale boost."[9] Shortly thereafter the captain of the *Hornet* broke silence to announce over the ship's loudspeakers, "The target of the task force is Tokyo. The army is going to bomb Japan, and we're going to get them as close to the enemy as we can. This is the chance for all of us to give the Japs a dose of their own medicine."[10] The *Hornet's* action report log notes that cheers from every section of the ship greeted the announcement: The mission was on.

The mission's planners had been very concerned about the possibility of detection by the enemy short of the launch point. The plan called for the *Hornet* to sail to within 450–500 miles of the Japanese Islands in order to enable the planes to hit their targets and proceed, they hoped, to safe areas in mainland

China. Steaming westward at 16 knots and fighting bad weather, the ships passed a number of fishing boats that could easily betray their presence, and the fears of the task force leader were confirmed. The raiders had likely lost the element of surprise.[11]

Undaunted, Doolittle, after conferring with Vice Adm. William F. ("Bull") Halsey, ordered his crews to man their planes. Thus, some 670 miles and a five-hour flight from their targets, on April 18, at 0800 Halsey gave the final orders to *Hornet* to turn into the wind at 22 knots and prepare to launch. In a driving rainstorm and as waves crashed over the carrier's ramp, Colonel Doolittle, at 0818, was first off the deck with a takeoff roll of only 467 feet of runway deck available. He was followed by Major Hilger's aircraft. In all, sixteen land-based bombers fully loaded with a ton of bombs each were launched from a carrier at sea, beginning America's first offensive strike against Imperial Japan.[12]

Although the physical damage was minimal, both the psychological injury to Japanese military leaders and the morale boost for the American public were tremendous. All of the bombers completed their assigned mission, and fifteen afterward made China, while the sixteenth landed in Vladivostok, Russia. The former commander of the Japanese imperial navy stated, "When it was learned who had commanded the enemy air group, Headquarters spokesman sarcastically pooh-poohed the attack as not even a 'do-little' but rather a 'do-nothing' raid. But the same could not be said of its impact on the minds of Japan's naval leaders and its influence on the course of the war at sea. Japan was vulnerable. From this standpoint the raid must be regarded as a 'do-much' raid."[13]

On battered Corregidor, radios picked up scattered reports of the raid. A Corregidor defender, Lt. William Boyd ('38), recalled, "When we heard the news, I think it was on April 21st, that bombers had bombed Tokyo we couldn't imagine at the time how they got close enough. . . . It was hard to believe . . . great news."[14] With reference to a popular novel and movie, *Lost Horizon* (1937), President Roosevelt commented that the "Doolittle Raiders" had come from "Shangri-La."[15] For the raiders, however, the actual bombing run over Japan was the easy part; the difficulty lay in reaching sanctuary in China.

Doolittle's crews discovered that the plane that was carrying the homing devices, crews, and supplies and flying ahead into China to rendezvous with and guide them to a safe haven had crashed with all aboard killed. Encountering dense fog over the China coast, Doolittle's B-25s scattered over a considerable area of the country, and the crews either crash-landed or bailed out. All of the aircraft were lost, three crewmen died in landing, and eight crewmen were taken prisoner. Of the eight prisoners, three were summarily executed, and one died in prison. Lieutenant Colonel Doolittle, along with Lt. James M. Parker Jr. ('41), who left campus to join the air force in October, 1940, Capt. Robert M. Gray, and Jack Hilger were among the survivors. Parker, who earned his wings at Moffett Field, recalled that "We hit Japan about thirty miles north of Tokyo.

Maj. John A. Hilger ('32) (center right), second in command to Gen.
James H. Doolittle, is escorted through a Chinese village to safety.

Right on a Japanese airfield. . . . We went down the island over the water to the tip of Japan. . . . At the tip of Japan there were four war ships there. They started firing at us. We changed speed and altitude and left them sitting there."

Halfway across the China Sea they hit fog and flew until "we ran out of gas and bailed out." Friendly Chinese troops found Parker and took him first to the capital of Hunan province. Several days later he, Doolittle, and the other survivors were feted and decorated by Madame Chiang Kai-shek in Chunking. Eventually Parker made his way to Calcutta, India, and back to the States in time to report for combat duty with the Twelfth Air Force in North Africa, where he copiloted with Jimmy Doolittle, now a general.[16]

Captain Gray also returned to combat but died in an airplane crash on October 18, 1942, six months to the day following the raid on Tokyo. Twelve other survivors of the raid were killed in subsequent actions before the end of the war. Also reported missing in action over North China on that day, April 18, was Texas Aggie pilot Bobby M. Godwin from Fort Worth, whose studies were interrupted by war and who, although it is unconfirmed, was likely a member of the ill-fated support plane that was to have guided the raiders to their rendezvous in China.[17]

Madam Chiang Kai-shek awards Brig. Gen. James H. Doolittle, Maj. John A. Hilger ('32), and Lt. Jack A. Sims the Order of Jung-Hui in Chunking, China, on April 29, 1942.

The bombs that fell on Japan caused minimal damage, but the raid gave the people at home "a little fillip," Doolittle said. "The news had all been bad until then." It also caused the Japanese to worry that they might be vulnerable, and it forced their air force to divert at least some of its aircraft and equipment to the defense of the home islands.[18] Nevertheless, Americans considered the raid to have been not just a "little fillip" but rather a devastating blow to the enemy.

Doolittle's attack greatly encouraged America's spirits during some very dark days of the winter and spring of 1942, when the enemy had been wreaking unparalleled destruction on the Australian, British, Dutch, and American allies in the Pacific. Japan accompanied the capture of Singapore and its 130,000 defenders on February 15 with an attack that same day on an Allied convoy that included four troop transports accompanied by the American cruiser *Houston*, a destroyer, and two Australian sloops, all of which were attempting to reinforce the garrison on Timor Island and subsequent naval engagements culminating in the Battle of the Java Sea. On February 18, Japanese troops began an amphibious landing on Java. The Allied command attempted to rush 32 P-40 crated aircraft aboard the USS *Langley* and another 27 aboard a freighter, the *Sea Witch*, to the beleaguered defenders. The *Langley* was sunk, and the *Sea Witch* was forced to withdraw.

Then, on February 27, virtually the entire Allied naval force available in the South Pacific, including the *Houston*, four Dutch light cruisers, six British destroyers, and five American destroyers, met the Japanese fleet with two heavy cruisers, a light cruiser, and seven destroyers supported by aircraft and submarines. The Battle of the Java Sea continued for two days and ended with the destruction of most of the Allied fleet that was engaged, including the sinking of the *Houston* in the final moments of the battle. Navy Lt. Ted Adair Hilger, brother of Doolittle's second-in-command, Jack Hilger, who left Texas A&M in 1931 to attend the U.S. Naval Academy, was one of the 361 survivors of the *Houston*'s 1,000-man crew. Hilger made it aboard the USS *Philsbury*, a destroyer that was soon wrecked during another Japanese attack within a few days of the sinking of the *Houston*. Hilger was reported "lost in sea action off the Java Coast."[19] Following the Battle of the Java Sea, the defending Dutch and Allied forces on Java surrendered unconditionally on March 8.

Among those captured were members of the 550-man 131st Texas National Guard Field Artillery Battalion, the "Lost Battalion," who began their grim odyssey in November, 1941, aboard a troop train bound from Texas for the West Coast. For many, it was their first trip out of Texas and their first ride on a train, and it also gave most of them their first glimpse of the Pacific. Sailing from San Francisco Bay aboard the army transport ship *Republic* on November 21, 1941, they arrived at Pearl Harbor on November 28. The ship refueled and sailed on December 1 as part of a large convoy bound for the South Pacific. Among those aboard were five Texas Aggies: 1st Lt. Isaac A. Morgan Jr. ('40) from Marshall; Maj. Winthrop H. Rogers ('28) from Wichita Falls; 1st Lt. J. B. Heinen Jr. ('34) from Dallas; Cpl. B. D. Fillmore ('43) from Jacksboro; Capt. Charles A. Cates ('30) from Decatur, and Pvt. James W. Smith ('42) from Willis Point. These men were captured by the Japanese on the island of Java and, with the other survivors of the 131st and the remnants of the USS *Houston*, spent the remainder of the war in captivity in Burma and Thailand working on the infamous 300-mile "Railroad of Death," which is portrayed in Pierre Boulle's novel, *Bridge over the River Kwai*, and the film based on it. Survivors point out that the story greatly understates the horrific conditions of the forced labor camps.[20]

At the dedication of the monument erected in the National Memorial Cemetery of the Pacific in Honolulu in 1994, Gavin Daws, an author whose books vividly describe the ordeals of American POWs in the Pacific, recalled the plight of the few hundred survivors of the *Houston* as they struggled ashore in Java. There they "were rounded up by the Japanese and herded into captivity, terrible-looking scarecrows in shorts made of sacking, green straw hats, sarongs, bits of Javanese blanket, anything and nothing, bodies starved and unwashed, salt-encrusted, soaked in fuel oil. . . . And several weeks later, into prison camp came marching more than 500 men in the uniform of the United States Army, and for a crazy second it was possible to believe that they were liberators. But no, it was the 131st Field Artillery, captives too."[21]

The loss of the Allied fleet and Java were devastating blows to the Allies and to American security. Japanese forces controlled Malaya, Burma, the Dutch East Indies, and Rabaul on New Britain and began an almost leisurely occupation of the Solomon Islands. The battles had only begun.

Japan next decided to strike southward against the east coast of Australia but was forced to turn back following the Battle of the Coral Sea in early May. Then its forces headed east to Midway, which is much closer to Hawaii and American shores, where they hoped to lure American carriers and naval vessels into a final battle, reasoning that the final destruction of the U.S. fleet would grant them uncontested control of the Pacific. In preparation, Japan began concentrating its navy near Rabaul and the Solomon Islands. Subsequently, one of the first great carrier battles of the war took place when the Yorktown and Lexington, with supporting warships, engaged the Japanese fleet, which had the Shokaku and Zuikaku and a light carrier, the Shoho. The Battle of the Coral Sea began on May 7. Japan lost the Shoho, and the Americans the Lexington, but the conflict deterred an imminent Japanese attack against Port Moresby and New Guinea. The Battle of the Coral Sea marked the first time that a Japanese advance had been halted.[22] (See map on p. 83.)

But Japan was unrelenting. As a prelude to a planned attack on Midway, Japanese amphibious forces planned to seize Attu, Kiska, and Adak in the Aleutian Islands. Dutch Harbor was bombed as part of a feint intended to lure the U.S. Navy to sea, force it to divide, and overwhelm it at Midway or in the Aleutians as opportunity allowed. The plan may well have succeeded, but naval cryptanalysts broke the Japanese navy's secret code, which indicated a probable concentrated attack against Midway rather than the Aleutians. The commander in chief in the Pacific theater, Adm. Chester Nimitz, withdrew his carriers and battleships to Pearl Harbor, ordered emergency repairs on the ships damaged at the Battle of the Coral Sea, and by the end of May had his battle group stationed some 350 miles northwest of Midway. Meanwhile, Japanese forces approached the Aleutians and on June 3 launched bomber attacks on Dutch Harbor; much farther south, they began a major attack at Midway the next day, June 4. The Battle of Midway raged for three days and concluded with four Japanese carriers and the American carrier Yorktown sunk, plus losses on both sides of dozens of accompanying vessels, hundreds of aircraft, and hundreds of seamen and aviators.[23]

Among the Aggies who fought in the Battle of Midway were Ens. George H. Gay Jr. ('40), Lt. Thomas H. Akarman ('40), and Maj. Earl O. Hall ('34), all of whom were pilots. Ensign Gay, from Waco, enrolled at Texas A&M in the fall of 1936 and decided to apply for flight school in 1939. After flunking his flight physical, he spent several months getting himself in condition to pass the navy physical, which he did in 1940, graduating from flight school in September, 1941. His unit, Torpedo Squadron 8, was aboard the USS *Hornet* with James Doolittle and Charles Bond from the AVG during the April, 1942, raid on Tokyo. Gay was disappointed that his squadron could not join in the raid, but his time came soon. The *Hornet* returned to Pearl Harbor and joined the *Enterprise* and other ships to form Task Force 16, under Rear Adm. Raymond Spruance, which Admiral Nimitz stationed near Midway in early June. When battle began on June 4, Ensign Gay's squadron, flying obsolete Douglas TDB-1 Devastator torpedo bombers, were among the first to attack the Japanese fleet.[24]

As the fifteen planes of Torpedo Squadron 8 pressed home their attack, one by one they were shot down. Injured by machine-gun fire and with his radioman/gunner mortally wounded, Gay made a final run on the carrier *Kaga* and, after launching his torpedo, pulled up and over the enemy ship only to be jumped by Japanese A6M Zero fighters, who forced him down into the ocean. Gay escaped from his cockpit and hid beneath a flotation device while the Japanese fleet passed over him. From there he watched U.S. dive bombers sink three Japanese carriers. Miraculously, he survived and was rescued by a Navy PBY aircraft. Back ashore, the navy doctors wondered how Gay had managed to keep his wounds clean and sterile: "Well, I soaked 'em in salt water for thirty hours," he explained. He lived to fight again another day, this time at Guadalcanal with Torpedo Squadron 11, and emerged from both encounters an American hero "during the dark days of 1942, when America desperately needed heroes." Nevertheless, Gay consistently argued that the real heroes were his twenty-nine fellow airmen of Squadron 8, who died during the Battle of Midway. In 1979, he wrote and published his own account of the Battle of Midway, titled *Sole Survivor: The Battle of Midway and Its Effect on His Life*.[25]

Earl O. Hall, from McGregor, Texas, joined the air corps in September, 1940, entered flight school, and earned his wings in April, 1941. He was at Hickam Field, Hawaii, when the Japanese attacked on December 7. In June, 1942, Hall, now a major and already the recipient of numerous decorations, including the Distinguished Flying Cross, was assigned to Task Force 16. He was lost during the Battle of Midway. A fellow Aggie airman, Lt. Thomas H. Akarman, who entered service as an aviation cadet a month after graduation, finished his pilot training and was commissioned in February, 1942. He survived the Battle of Midway in June but failed to return to his base after a bomb run over Rangoon, Burma, in November of that year.[26]

Midway was one of the most important naval battles of World War II, but it did not determine who would control the Pacific. Japan, despite its losses at Midway, still possessed more carriers and a stronger fleet in the Pacific than did the United States The view that Midway was the "Gettysburg of the Pacific War" became clear only after further naval combat in the Far East. The naval battles in the spring of 1942 had been costly to the Americans, but the battles of the Coral Sea and Midway finally blunted the enemy's advances. That, too, however, was not immediately clear to either the United States or Japan.

As part of the attack at Midway, Japanese forces launched a diversionary attack on Dutch Harbor, Alaska, on June 3. The attacking force consisted of two aircraft carriers, two cruisers, three destroyers, submarines, and four transport ships carrying twenty-five thousand troops who were to seize Dutch Harbor and spearhead the further invasion and occupation of Alaska. The Americans, however, responded quickly. In a matter of weeks a completely new airstrip was built at Umiak. The command of the 11th Air Force Bomber Group moved there from Anchorage only days before the invasion. Another existing airfield at Cold Bay had been improved and reinforced, and those installations provided a protective air umbrella over Dutch Harbor. Land-based fighters shot down numerous attacking aircraft and bombed and strafed the Japanese carriers, forcing them to withdraw. This left about forty additional Japanese fighters without a place to land, but the battle for the Aleutians was not ended.[27]

On June 7, the Japanese force, while turning back from Dutch Harbor, seized an opportunity to land small invading parties on the Aleutian islands of Attu and Kiska while foregoing a planned invasion of Adak. American land-based planes and a few smaller naval vessels offered resistance, but there were no defending ground troops. The invaders seized Attu with its thirty-nine Aleut natives and two missionaries and captured a ten-man weather crew stationed on Kiska. Even while these actions were under way, American and British reinforcements from Canada and the United States were en route to the Alaskan Command. The 54th Fighter Squadron, with P-38s and an Aggie flight surgeon, Mavis P. Kelsey ('32), left Seattle on May 25, bound for Alaska. They arrived in Anchorage on June 7, as Dutch Harbor was under attack.[28]

"There was so much war going on all over the world that people paid little attention to the Aleutian Campaign," Kelsey explains in his autobiography. However, he believed, only the quick concentration of American troops and aircraft in and around Fort Richardson and Anchorage prevented the Japanese from landing on the Alaskan mainland, an event, Kelsey said, "which would have quickly shifted our attention from the South Pacific." Soon after their arrival, on June 15, the 54th Fighter Squadron was "jerked up from camp and loaded on a small ship in Anchorage, destination not announced." Three days later they arrived at Cold Bay Harbor, a fishing village on the Alaska Peninsula, which was then being converted into an air base and frontier post. Kelsey recalled occasional earthquakes as well as "constant winds with frequent williwaws up to ninety miles an hour, accompanied by rain and fog. . . . The fierce winds blew snow and dust at the same time into one's clothing and tent. . . . We lost half the original pilots in our squadron to weather during the year we were there, [and] as many were shot down by the Japanese."[29]

One of Kelsey's most dangerous personal encounters was with brown bears rather than the enemy. During a recovery mission to a downed aircraft, the soldiers came fact to face with the bruins, some of whom had cubs, weighed up to 1,500 pounds, and took exception to the incursion into their territory. "We had army rifles, but they say that they won't stop these huge bears and once you shoot them they go wild and kill everything in sight." Kelsey's team carefully yielded to the bears' territorial rights. Fortunately, the bears, too, preferred evasion to confrontation.[30]

Conditions on the Alaskan frontier stabilized over the summer, and by fall the American fighters and bombers were launching repeated attacks on Japanese positions in Attu and Kiska. Americans soon occupied Amchitka, eighty miles from Kiska, and strengthened the garrison on nearby Adak. Major Kelsey served for a short time on Adak and Amchitka before he completed his Alaska tour as group surgeon of the 343rd Fighter Group and returned to the States in July, 1943. By that time Kiska and Attu had been reclaimed by the 7th Infantry Division. The retaking of Kiska was preceded by the withdrawal of Japanese occupiers; the action on Attu was marked by a considerable cost in lives lost in combat and limbs lost to trench foot.[31]

Roy Kasson Bliler ('50) was there and remembered it well. The purpose of the campaign, he recalled, "was to drive the Japanese out of the Aleutian Islands." When the Japanese had seized Kiska and Attu, the U.S. military really believed the enemy intended to advance southeastward down the West Coast of the United States. The Aleutian operations turned out to be "diversionary, but we didn't know it at that time." Bliler, who ended his World War II service in 1946 as a first lieutenant, then enrolled in Texas A&M. He had begun the war as a "Buck Sergeant, Grade 4, a three-striper" after being called to duty from the Texas National Guard on January 1, 1941. Bliler served as a navigator, and his B-25 bomber squadron was among those sent to Alaska in the spring of 1942. Like Kelsey, he ended up on Amchitka. During one of his bombing runs, his finger was torn by shrapnel and "bled like a stuck hog." The flight surgeon, Bliler recounted, poured alcohol on it and said, "Hell, it don't hurt, boy," as the wound continued to bleed profusely. But it certainly hurt.

Amchitka was a barren outpost, often shrouded in fog or lashed by powerful winds. When they weren't flying, the soldiers played poker and bridge and drank a lot of "torpedo juice" (grain alcohol). It was a place where nobody lasted much longer than six months.[32]

Bliler flew twenty-three combat missions during his first six months in the Aleutians, and his final sorties were flown against Attu and Kiska: "We bombed the Japs out of Kiska Island. They left, got on their boats and left. . . . We blamed the navy for letting them get away. Of course, you couldn't see your hand in front of your face, but we blamed the navy. The navy blamed the air force 'cause they didn't bomb them enough."[33]

Attu was a different story: "Attu was a blood bath. Attu was a terrible blood bath, and I didn't participate in it except for bombing. . . . Attu had Fish Hook Ridge on it. And those poor guys, they caught hell. . . . Our troops went in. . . . [They were] dumped in that cold water with no rubber boots, so their feet got wet immediately. And then the Japs let them come in. They came in, set up their tents, got all nice and situated, [and] then the Japs hit them in the valley. . . . [C]alled Massacre Valley. . . . [i]t was named for a battle with the Russians and the Aleut Indians. . . . They massacred the Aleut Indians. And [the Japanese] had a massacre that day. They caught our boys, pinned them down, they got frostbite and lost their toes. They ended up cutting a lot of 'em's toes off. We finally bombed them [the Japanese] off from that island."[34]

In the first amphibious landing of the war, the 7th Motorized Division, which had been training in the California desert for the invasion of North Africa, landed unopposed in dense fog and bitter cold at two points on Attu, which was defended by a well-entrenched force of about 2,600 Japanese soldiers. When the fog lifted, the American forces were subjected to a withering fire and could only cling to existence for the next five days, awaiting reinforcements. By May 20, Alaska's 4th Infantry Regiment had joined the 7th Division; the U.S. forces now totaled some 16,000 troops. But the unyielding Japanese launched a desperate and almost successful final attack on May 29, nineteen days after the start of the battle. When the fighting ended, most of the Japanese attackers were dead, either of battle wounds or suicide. In the fight, 549 Americans had died, and another 3,200 were wounded or suffered from exposure, while only 28 Japanese were taken prisoner.[35] By May 30, the battle for Attu was over. Kiska, with a far smaller defending force, was successfully evacuated under cover of heavy fog before the Americans invaded.

Even though the battle for Attu proved difficult and costly, it was an important beginning and characterized what would follow in the other island invasions. The recapture of Attu and Kiska began to relieve the immediate threat to Anchorage and major military posts in Alaska as well as to the west coasts of Canada and the United States, which were accessible to bombing raids from Aleutian and Alaskan bases.

On August 7, 1942, at the urging of the chief of naval operations and bolstered by the successes at the Battle of Midway, American forces launched the first major counteroffensive of the Pacific campaign in the Solomon Islands, where new construction of an airfield and fortifications on Guadalcanal and adjacent islands by the Japanese posed an increasing threat to Australia and the Far East. The 1st Marine Division, including the elite commando-type 1st Raider Battalion and the 1st Parachute Regiment, landed nearly 11,300 troops on Guadalcanal and another 3,000 in separate attacks on neighboring Tulagi, Gavutu, and Tanambogo Islands. During the first night of the campaign, the American forces lost three heavy cruisers: the *Quincy*, *Astoria*, and *Vincennes*, and the Australians lost the *Canberra.* The early-morning landing on the beaches had been unopposed, but, around noon, Japanese defenders struck with unmitigated fury, utilizing the then unprecedented banzai attacks. The American soldiers had never seen that kind of combat. Even wounded Japanese soldiers, when approached, would blow themselves up with hand grenades in a final act of defiance.[36] The war in the Pacific proved to be a terrible new kind of war.

The marines stood their ground in savage, hand-to-hand combat, then advanced toward their major objective, Henderson Field. After two weeks of unrelenting combat, the marines seized the airstrip, but the combat intensified when the Japanese brought in reinforcements. In early September, anticipating a major attack there, American marines took up positions along a rising ridge about one mile southeast of the field, an elevation soon known as "Bloody Ridge." On September 12, when about 2,000 Japanese troops struck the 840 entrenched marine raiders and parachute units on Bloody Ridge, the Americans held their ground under the directive "Nobody moves! Just die in your holes!" By sundown on September 14, following numerous banzai assaults, Bloody Ridge and Henderson Field remained in American hands. The costs had been horrific.[37]

Not until late spring, after being reinforced by the 2nd Marine Division, the 25th Infantry, and the Americal Division, was Guadalcanal "secure." Together, the U.S. and Japanese navies lost forty-eight heavy warships and thousands of seamen in what was one of the bloodiest, most protracted naval campaigns in history. On land, there were few prisoners, while some 1,600 Americans and almost 9,000 Japanese died in combat between August, 1942, and June, 1943. Despite this heavy toll, the battle for the South Pacific had only begun.

Among the Aggies who died in combat on Guadalcanal were Lt. (jg) Warren Kay Garrett ('45) from Ft. Worth, whose academic career at Texas A&M, like so many others, was cut short by war. He joined the navy air corps in 1941 and, during the Guadalcanal campaign, flew a dive bomber from the USS *Wasp.* On October 2, 1942, flying from Henderson Field, Garrett was directed to help protect a naval vessel that had just been hit by a torpedo. He died in the following action. Twelve days later, one of Garrett's classmates, Lt. Wiley H. Craft of Corpus Christi, who joined the Marine Corps air wing in 1941, died in action after taking off on a mission from Henderson Field. Soon after, in early November, an Aggie from Dallas, marine Lt. Samuel Thomas Gillespie, who also left the campus for active duty in 1941, died in air combat on Guadalcanal.[38]

The counterattacks in the Pacific and Southeast Asia moved slowly and painfully and at great human cost over the next three years from Guadalcanal toward the "land of the rising sun." New Georgia, Bougainville, Rabaul, New Britain (garrisoned by a one-hundred-thousand-man army), New Guinea, and ultimately the Philippines were the major objectives. After early frustrations, MacArthur and his air chief, Gen. George Kenney, devised leap-frog tactics that accelerated the pace of the advance. Americans selectively sought to "hit 'em where they ain't." But "they" were everywhere—and unyielding. The battles in Southeast Asia, Burma, Thailand, and China and throughout the south, central, and northern Pacific Islands were savage and relentless. And in almost every battle, Texas Aggies were there.

Throughout this period, Texas Aggies—many as soon as they came of age—left the campus or their homes in droves and joined the armed services. Cecil E. Lohn ('45) from Gainsville signed up with the air force, failed the physical, and then enlisted in the U.S. Army Coast Artillery. On his second day of active duty he was transferred to the air force, where he became a navigator on B-17s. His war service almost ended permanently during a bombing mission over Munich in January, 1945.

Wallace Jacob Albright joined the navy in September, 1942, served as torpedo man second class, and remained in service until January, 1946. Robert Leonard Skrabanek ('42) enlisted in the navy in November, 1942, received his commission the following March, and served most of his time in the Pacific theater aboard a variety of ships, including the carrier *Yorktown*. Later Skrabanek returned to Texas A&M to spend his civilian career in another kind of service—as a professor of sociology. In December, 1942, 1st Lt. Preston M. Geren Jr. ('45) began service and was mustered out after the war in April, 1946. Lindsey I. Lipscomb ('49) began service as an air force enlisted man in October, 1942, received his commission, and within the year was in combat as a B-24 bombardier and navigator.[39] These men are only a handful of the more than twenty thousand Aggies who served, many of them in combat in the South Pacific.

The attack on New Georgia began with landings on neighboring Vangunu Island in June and on the northeastern coast on July 5, 1943, headed by the marines' 1st Raider Battalion, with the army's 43rd and 37th Infantry Divisions and elements of the 25th Infantry Division. The Americans suffered heavy casualties, particularly in an advance on Bairoko beginning on July 20. South of Bairoko, where the 43rd led the attack on Munda Airfield, Japanese defenders virtually decimated the 43rd, forcing the commitment of the 37th, which was being held in reserve. The 37th went on line near the end of July. Capt. Felix B. Lester ('32) led Company B, 148th Infantry, 37th Division, in the final attacks on the Japanese positions. He died in that struggle on July 30, the day of his eleventh wedding anniversary. Munda fell to American arms on August 4, following a "masterful withdrawal" (similar to the Japanese evacuation of Kiska in the Aleutians) by the defenders to nearby Kolombangara Island.[40]

U.S. forces occupied New Georgia and bypassed heavily defended New Britain Island en route to New Guinea. Landings on New Guinea began in early September, 1943, and on the Admiralties in February, 1944. The campaign continued with amphibious landings along the northern coasts and marshes through snake-infested, insect-ridden jungles for almost a full year before Allied troops finally occupied Sansapor, on the northernmost tip of the island. In November, 1943, 1st Lt. John William Crow ('35) died in that action.[41] Crow had played guard on the Aggie football team during his student days and then coached at Allen Academy in Bryan, Texas, before going on active duty. The entire South Pacific and Southeast Asia were a maelstrom of combat from the time of the landings on Guadalcanal in October, 1942, through the end of hostilities in August, 1945.

In Burma, Japanese armies overwhelmed the defenders. Almost one hundred thousand Dutch, British, Australians, and the few American soldiers there surrendered in March, 1942. Survivors engaged the enemy in sporadic combat for the next several years. Finally, in July, 1945, under growing Allied reinforcements and pressure, the gaunt, starving Japanese survivors of their shattered Fifteenth Army withdrew into the surrounding jungles. Aggies were on the scene throughout that combat, and a number of them arrived in Burma as members of the Royal Canadian Air Force (RCAF). Flying officer William Byron ("Billy") Gibbs from Sweetwater, Texas, left A&M in June, 1940, to enlist in the RCAF. A fighter pilot, Gibbs was credited with shooting down at least seven Japanese airplanes before he was killed in early 1943. In related action in Ceylon, Lt. James A. Harris, who was enrolled at Texas A&M in September, 1934, joined the RAF in 1940. He was killed in action over Ceylon in the spring of 1943.[42]

Texas Aggie Brig. Gen. Victor A. Barraco ('15) was on duty on the perimeter at the gateway to these bloody battles in the South Pacific from July, 1942, to November, 1943. He was assigned as attorney general and provost marshal of the military government of American Samoa. One of twenty-two members of the Corps of Cadets who joined the Marine Corps in 1917, Barraco took basic training at Quantico, Virginia, was commissioned, and spent most of World War I on duty in the Virgin Islands and the West Indies. In December of 1940, he returned to active duty with orders to organize a marine battalion in Houston, Texas.[43]

Barraco's assignment to Samoa in the summer of 1942 came amid a buildup of forces for a counteroffensive in the South Pacific. His job was to help secure the perimeter, that is, American Samoa, and facilitate its use as a possible staging area for an assault on the Solomon Islands. In his own words, on Samoa he was "the law west of the Pecos." Barraco was the navy's bank for Samoa, the head of the labor and the customs boards, warden of prisoners, head tax assessor and collector, head of the department of agriculture, and fire marshal, among other roles. The U.S. War Department instructed him that his job in Samoa was "to get on with the war" in whatever way he could. In mid-1944, Barraco was assigned to the headquarters for the landing and invasion of Guam, which was scheduled for July, 1944. That assignment took him from the perimeter into the heart of the war in the Pacific.[44] Barraco's experiences on Samoa and Guam offer perspective on the many different, but no less critical, dimensions of war.

As American and Allied forces in the Pacific island-hopped, crawled, marched, flew, and sometimes literally swam their way through the war in 1942 and 1943, the Allies concentrated on building airbases, transferring supplies and war materials, and transporting troops to England in preparation for a counteroffensive in Europe. As Allied bombing intensified, British—and soon American—troops began to deter the Germans' advances and finally close in on the enemy in North Africa. In May, 1943, as the Attu and Guadalcanal campaigns ended, the Allied forces began a series of major offensives against what Churchill called the "soft underbelly" of Europe—Italy, via Sicily. In a sense, preparations for this attack had begun even before the United States entered the war.

The U.S. military began stationing observers in Great Britain even before Pearl Harbor and in 1942 began constructing supply depots and an elaborate network of army and air bases in England in preparation for the bombing and invasion of northern Europe. Deeply involved in the preparations was Capt. (later Brig. Gen.) James P. Newberry from Yoakum, Texas. Born in 1905, Newberry studied engineering intermittently at Texas A&M between 1923 and 1928, when he decided to learn to fly. Entering service as an air cadet, he won his wings and a commission in 1929, but, while assigned in 1931 to an observation squadron, he suffered a terrible accident. His plane, a Thomas-Morris 0-19, stalled and crashed. Newberry broke both ankles and his jaw, but three months later he was up flying again. In 1934, he became a supply officer and in 1941 was sent to the Burtonwood Air Depot in England as chief of supply. Newberry was on duty in Great Britain when Pearl Harbor was attacked and returned to the States in 1942 to a variety of duty stations before returning to Burtonwood in 1944, where he ended his tour.[45]

During the Battle of Britain and before America entered the war, Capt. Elbert B. ("Tex") Anding ('26) helped ferry aircraft from the United States to Britain. An electrical engineer, Anding held a variety of jobs before learning to fly and in 1929 worked as a pilot in Central America before enlisting in 1940 with the British Air Transport Auxiliary ferrying airplanes to England. In August, 1941, Anding was killed in a takeoff from a British air base.[46]

Another Aggie, William Pendleton Ballard Jr., died while transporting aviation fuel to England to be used by the bombers and fighters that had been ferried overseas. Enrolled at Texas A&M in 1941, Ballard enlisted for active duty in the navy in February, 1942. He asked for overseas duty and was promptly assigned as a seaman first class to a navy oil tanker. His ship sailed on September 3 and returned to New York after his first mission; Ballard then departed on another tanker on October 16. Eleven days later his ship was torpedoed and sunk. Ballard was saved by an escort vessel, but his rescue ship was torpedoed and sunk the very next day, October 28, taking Ballard with it.[47]

On August 19, 1942, one of the most dramatic and tragic missions combined air, sea, and infantry assault groups for a daring commando raid of occupied France fully two years before the Allied invasion at Normandy. Texas Aggies participated. American and British aircraft flew from their bases in England to provide cover for the raid on the German-occupied seaport of Dieppe, France. There on the coast, 5,000 Canadians, 1,000 British soldiers, 50 American Rangers, and two dozen Free French soldiers landed by sea and air drop. Unfortunately, the German defenders were ready. One thousand attackers were killed, and 2,000 soldiers, mainly Canadians, were taken prisoner. Their equipment and weapons were also captured. The remainder escaped in small boats but left most of their gear behind. Among those lost at Dieppe was Lt. William Henry Baker ('42) from Temple, Texas. Hitler is supposed to have said mockingly that the British had crossed the sea "to offer the enemy a complete sample of their weapons."[48] While more costly than Doolittle's raid over Tokyo, the raid on Dieppe nonetheless gave the Allies the impression that the Axis was in fact vulnerable.

At the same time, bases in England were being filled with American bomber and fighter squadrons that, by mid-July, 1942, began to bomb German targets throughout Europe. At the Casablanca conference, President Roosevelt and Prime Minister Churchill approved the combined bomber offensive named Operation Pointblank, and American bombing missions over Germany then began in earnest, targeting factories, munitions depots, railroads, and refineries and included some area, or "saturation," bombing. Attacks intensified from 1943 to 1944 and accelerated in late 1944 and early 1945 "to reach a degree of frightfulness that the world had never dared to contemplate." By the close of the war, the Royal Air Force and army air corps had dropped an estimated 2,790,000 tons of bombs on Germany and occupied territories. Most of those were unloaded after June 1, 1944, by which time the Allies had gained air superiority over Germany. The buildup, however, began slowly.

Six bomber crews of the American Eighth Air Force, commanded by Maj. Gen. Carl Spaatz, flew the first American mission from bases in England in company with RAF crews flying American-built Douglas A-20s (known as Bostons) on July 4, 1942. On August 16, the first heavy bomber mission using B-17s escorted by RAF Spitfires attacked rail yards at Rouen, France.[49] For the next three years, the United States organized and equipped the Ninth, Twelfth, and Fifteenth Air Forces and thus built a continually stronger presence in the skies over the Mediterranean and Europe. But throughout 1942 and 1943, the Luftwaffe and strong, concentrated antiaircraft fire inflicted heavy losses on Allied bombers and fighter escorts.

John H. Buckner ('40) had thought he wanted to be in the infantry until he saw the Corps of Cadets marching in the Battle of Flowers parade in San Antonio. Later he visited Kelly Field, crawled into some of the airplanes, and watched them fly. He then decided aviation was his calling. In 1939, Buckner received an appointment to West Point and in December, 1941, took an air corps option, receiving his wings in December, 1942. In October, 1943, Buckner went to England as a P-47 pilot with the Eighth Air Force, where he flew fighter escort for the bombers.[50]

Trains, bridges, and anything that looked like supplies were key targets for strafing and bombing attacks on German installations in France. On one bombing mission over France across the Channel from Dover, Buckner's plane was hit by flak. Although he lost an engine, he almost made it back to the coast of England before he was forced to bail out. When he left the plane, he stepped up on the side of the cockpit and jumped as far out as he could to avoid hitting the tail. When he pulled his parachute cord, the strap crossing his chest came up and bloodied his nose, but he made it into the water about fifty yards short of shore in the midst of a British minefield, where he was retrieved. Buckner saved the bloodied parachute, which was later transformed into his wife's wedding dress.[51]

Other Aggies who were engaged in bombing raids over Europe from British bases were less fortunate. Dallas native Lt. John Harold Allen ('42) arrived in England in November, 1943, and was killed in action a month later, when his B-24 was shot down while returning from a raid on German installations at Onsabruck, Holland. Lt. T. P. Aycock ('40), who also arrived in England in 1943, flew twenty-three missions to Germany as a bombardier on a B-24 before being killed over Germany on March 12, 1944. Another Aggie bombardier, Tech. Sgt. Thomas H. Gilliland ('42), died when his B-24 was shot down in 1942.[52]

Lt. Warren George Jr. ('41), a pilot, died in a raid over Bremen, Germany, on April 17, 1943. His Flying Fortress, nicknamed "Unmentionable," was one of sixteen bombers shot down during the raid. During George's relatively brief tour of duty in England, he flew twenty-one combat missions and received the Distinguished Flying Cross and other citations. S.Sgt. Robert C. Elliott, who left the campus before graduation to join the air corps in 1941, was a crewman on a B-17 that was shot down in a raid over Schweinfurt, Germany, in 1943. Elliott bailed out, but, before being taken prisoner by German military personnel, he fell into the hands of an irate mob of citizens who beat him mercilessly. Later, interned in a prisoner of war camp in Krem, Austria, Elliott collapsed. A casualty of war, he died in a veterans' hospital in the United States in 1947.[53]

The Allied air war over France and Germany in 1942 and 1943 forced the Germans to disperse their aircraft, armaments, and personnel over a broad geographic territory, somewhat diminishing their ability to bring massive troop concentrations to the key fronts in North Africa and Russia. Nevertheless, the air raids failed to seriously undermine the ability of the Axis to wage war. By late 1942 and into early 1943, Germany still controlled all of Europe, most of Russia, and much of North Africa. At the same time, the U.S. coasts were still considered vulnerable, and it wasn't until "after the invasion of North Africa [that] things changed," recalled Lt. Col. Glenn H. Reynolds ('41), who spent much of the war in command of an antiaircraft battery in Bermuda, the hub of antisubmarine patrols along the East Coast.[54]

The capture of Tobruk and thirty thousand Allied prisoners by Rommel's Afrika Corps in June, 1942, marked the high point of German control in North Africa. In the late summer of 1942, Gen. Bernard Law Montgomery was sent to assume command of Britain's much-battered Eighth Army in the western desert. He succeeded in repelling a German-Italian attack on Alexandria in late August and early September. During the battle, British bombers based in Egypt and Malta penetrated intensive German fighter and antiaircraft cover to deliver their payloads on German tanks and ground artillery. Very likely among the first Texas Aggies to engage in combat in North Africa, Lt. Roger Bentley Clements ('41) from Goldthwaite, Texas, took part in that action. He and a number of other students left the A&M campus in 1940 and made their way to Canada, where they volunteered for service with the RCAF. Clements was soon sent to Gibraltar and then to Malta, where Great Britain waged a desperate yet unremitting fight to hold fast to their last Mediterranean outposts against unrelenting German and Italian assaults by sea and air. On September 7, Clements and his two Canadian crewmen, flying their Wellington bomber in support of Montgomery's armies on the ground near Alexandria, were lost in action. The German offensive in North Africa had been blunted at least temporarily. Suffering from attrition and fuel and ammunition shortages, Rommel's armies had come under increasing pressure from British submarine and air attacks from Malta. While Rommel's armies withdrew toward Tunis seeking replenishment, massive Allied and American reinforcements (including a considerable number of Texas Aggies) began arriving in North Africa.

On November 8, 1942, a combined British and American army, under the command of Gen. Dwight D. Eisenhower, launched a three-pronged invasion of Vichy-controlled French North Africa at nine different landing sites. British units landed near Algiers and moved inland without resistance from the French. However, in separate landings by American forces at Oran, Safi, and Casablanca, the Vichy French soldiers offered stiff resistance. Meanwhile, German reinforcements arrived in North Africa, and Rommel's army dug in on the Mareth line as the Americans and Brits rushed in reinforcements and supplies. The Battle for North Africa—the springboard for a possible Allied invasion of Sicily and Italy—had begun.

Suggested Readings

Anderson, Terry H. *A Flying Tiger's Diary* (College Station: Texas A&M University Press, 1984).

Boyne, Walter J. *Clash of Wings: World War II in the Air* (New York: Simon and Schuster/Touchstone Books, 1994).

Fuchida, Mitsuo, and Masatake Okumiya. *Midway: The Battle That Doomed Japan* (Annapolis, Md.: Naval Institute Press, 1955).

Gailey, Harry A. *The War in the Pacific: From Pearl Harbor to Tokyo Bay* (Novato, Calif.: Presidio Press, 1995).

Lawson, Ted W. *Thirty Seconds over Tokyo* (New York: Penguin, 1944).

Morris, Eric. *Corregidor: The American Alamo of World War II* (New York: Cooper Square Press, 2000).

Nelson, Craig. *The First Heroes: The Extraordinary Story of the Doolittle Raid—America's First World War II Victory* (New York: Viking, 2002).

O'Donnell, Patrick K. *Into the Rising Sun* (New York: Free Press, 2002).

Lt. Gen. James F. Hollingsworth ('40), who would become the most decorated Texas Aggie general, got his baptism of fire as a captain in North Africa. Earning the Medal of Honor were Lt. Lloyd Hughes ('43) on a bombing run over Rumania; Lt. Thomas Fowler ('43) in tank battles leading to the capture of Rome; and S.Sgt. George Keathley ('36), who spearheaded the thrust through western Italy. Countless other Aggies flew missions in support of the advance on Germany.

NORTH AFRICA TO ITALY

North Africa was a trial by fire. "A callow, clumsy army" arrived there with little or no experience at war, sent by a nation that had little notion of how to act as a world power. It is where Americans began to learn both how to fight and how to act as a world power. It is where, observes Rick Atkinson, in his epochal *An Army at Dawn,* "Allied soldiers figured out, tactically," how to destroy Germans and where American soldiers became "killing mad." "We fought the hell out of them," recalled then Capt. James F. Hollingsworth, who arrived shortly after the initial landing and remained in the thick of the battle for North Africa.[1]

North Africa was a difficult war. It was political, tough, and strange, but then that is what war is about. American soldiers became blooded. American officers learned the art of war. Through North Africa lay the Allied road to Sicily and Italy, and from North Africa, Allied aircraft could strike at Rome, the Rhur, and the oil fields of Rumania. The Battle for North Africa marked the beginning of the liberation of Europe.

Allied planning for the invasion of Africa, designated Operation Torch, began in England in the spring of 1942 under the guidance of Gen. Dwight D. Eisenhower and British admiral Sir John Cunningham. That summer, in late August at El Alamein, the British Eighth Army, under Gen. Bernard Montgomery, succeeded in blocking Gen. Erwin Rommel's advance into Alexandria, Egypt, eighty miles short of his destination. Operation Torch proposed to insert a large Allied force into Morocco and Algiers, while British forces contained the Axis in Tunisia from the east. The invading forces, constituting the war's first joint army-navy amphibious landings, consisted of three major elements, including an eastern contingency with combined British and American units landing near Algiers. A central landing force under George Patton was to land at Oran, while western units, also under the command of General Patton, were to go ashore from the Atlantic Ocean into French Morocco. The invasion plan included the premise that Vichy French forces would be less likely to resist the Americans than the British, thus giving American armies the major role in the attack on French Morocco and central Algeria.[2] Among American and Allied officers who participated in the planning and the battles to come were Generals Mark Clark, Bernard Montgomery, George Patton, Terry Allen, and George H. Beverley ('19).

Arriving in London as inspector general of the Eighth Air Force, Brigadier General Beverley performed what he called "pick-and-shovel" work on the supply and maintenance portion of the invasion plan. Other than the problem of mastering the British telephone system, he said, the most crucial aspect of planning the invasion was to requisition enough transportation and to ensure that the ships, landing craft, trucks, tanks, and aircraft had enough fuel to do the job. Under his supervision preceding, during, and following the invasion, Allied forces established gasoline dumps of 55-gallon drums in scattered and often concealed locations along the coast of North Africa, thus solving, for the most part, the problem of fueling.[3]

The first invaders ashore in North Africa on October 22, 1942, were a single American general, Mark W. Clark, and a dozen commandos. Clark stepped from the submarine that had surfaced in the night off the coast of Algiers into a rubber folbot (folding boat), only to get flipped into the sea by an untimely wave. He and an accompanying commando were wrestled into another boat, and the party made its way to a point some two hundred yards off the coast of a fishing village, where they awaited a prearranged signal from the occupying Vichy French authorities. The signal came, and Clark waded ashore to meet with Gen. Charles Emmanuel Mast to discuss the possible surrender or nonresistance of the French armies to the American invaders. They hoped to deliver the French-controlled section of North Africa to the Allies without firing a shot. After almost twelve hours of discussion, Clark, still wet and bedraggled, returned to the submarine and reported to Eisenhower that the Americans might expect little or no resistance from the French.[4] That assessment turned out to be less than accurate.

Meanwhile, with the arrival of reinforcements and supplies, Montgomery's Eighth (British) Army launched an attack on German positions at El Alamein on the night of October 23 as American and British Torch invaders steamed toward the Mediterranean. The German defenders held firm for more than a week while losses on both sides mounted. Finally, a British thrust ten miles south of the coastal road and a decisive tank battle forced Rommel to begin retreating to the west out of Egypt into Tunisia.[5] Even as the Germans were entrenching themselves in Tunisia, the Allies began landing across the broad sweep of North Africa.

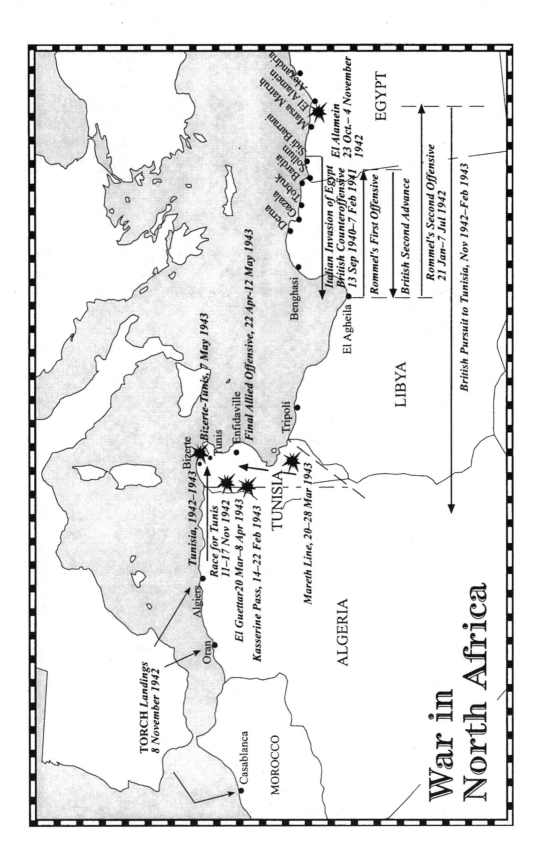

War in North Africa

MOROCCO

Casablanca

TORCH Landings
8 November 1942

Oran

Algiers

ALGERIA

Race for Tunis
11–17 Nov 1942

El Guettar 20 Mar–8 Apr 1943

Kasserine Pass, 14–22 Feb 1943

Tunisia, 1942–1943

Bizerte–Tunis, 7 May 1943

Bizerte

Tunis

Enfidaville

Final Allied Offensive, 22 Apr–12 May 1943

TUNISIA

Mareth Line, 20–28 Mar 1943

Tripoli

LIBYA

Benghasi

El Agheila

Italian Invasion of Egypt
13 Sep 1940–7 Feb 1941

British Counteroffensive
7 Feb 1941

Rommel's First Offensive

British Second Advance

Rommel's Second Offensive
21 Jan–7 Jul 1942

British Pursuit to Tunisia, Nov 1942–Feb 1943

Derna

Gazala

Tobruk

Bardia

Sollum

Sidi Barrani

Marsa Matruh

El Alamein

Alexandria

El Alamein
23 Oct.– 4 November
1942

EGYPT

On November 8, the Allies began pouring ashore at nine major landing sites along the coast of North Africa—from Safi, Fedala (near Casablanca), and Mehdia on the Atlantic coast of French Morocco to Oran and Algiers along the Mediterranean coast of Algeria. Patton commanded the U.S. Corps of three divisions, including the 3rd and the 9th Infantry and the 2nd Armored Division, most of whom landed at Safi and Fedala. The landing at Safi, 140 miles south of Casablanca, met little resistance but suffered 24 killed and another 25 wounded. The initial landing of Patton's 20,000 soldiers at Fedala went reasonably well, but the situation soon disintegrated. The Vichy French, contrary to expectations, put up a heavy resistance; meanwhile, French naval units from North African ports sailed out to give battle. Adm. Kent Hewitt's fleet eliminated these ships while the resistance on shore stiffened. Then, during the early phases of the battle for Fedala and Casablanca, an offshore storm halted the vital resupply of the invading armies, adding to the casualties and consternation of the American troops. At Mehdia, north of Casablanca, the landing was chaotic while the Vichy troops in the fortress, or "Kasbah," guarding the city again offered strong, unanticipated resistance.[6]

A direct attack by Allied naval units and marines on the port of Oran collapsed under misinformation, misdirection, and heavy French cannon fire aimed at the attacking naval vessels. Outside of the city, landing craft came ashore often miles from their designated rendezvous only to meet determined opposition. Throughout November 8 and 9, Allied reinforcements continued to flow into the battle from landing points to the east and west. Lt. (jg) Charles W. Gerhardt ('42) had left Texas A&M in 1941, before Pearl Harbor, to join the navy. He was now piloting a navy fighter assigned to the Atlantic fleet, providing air cover for the navy's amphibious landing at Oran. During the operations, his plane was shot down. After an hour at sea in the midst of the melee, he was rescued by a passing destroyer, which in turn was bombed by a Vichy bomber. Gerhardt took shrapnel in the leg but recovered and continued fighting in the North African campaign in the spring. Finally, after six months of almost uninterrupted combat, his plane was shot down, and he died in the closing months of the African campaign.[7]

One of Gerhardt's classmates, 1st Lt. Gambrell W. Haltom ('42) from Ft. Worth, was with the Signal Corps in the landings at Oran and continued in the thick of combat throughout the North African campaign until April of 1943, when he died in battle. During the landings at St. Cloud, west of Oran, assault units of the U.S. 1st Infantry Division (the "Big Red One") encountered heavy fire from a strong force of foreign legionaries, Tunisian infantry, and French paramilitary troops. Repeated attacks failed to dislodge the defenders, and Gen. Terry Allen, the division commander, decided to encircle the city and continue to press the enemy in a holding action while part of his troops bypassed Oran, moving westward along the coast toward Morocco. Finally, on the evening of November 10, American troops entered Oran and, after five hours of house-to-house combat, forced a surrender.[8]

Meanwhile, landings at Algiers encountered considerably less opposition than elsewhere. Hitting the beaches north and south of the city before dawn on November 8, the 34th Infantry Division arrived at the key Maison Blanche airfield, while British troops quickly secured a nearby airfield at Blida, south of Algiers. American aircraft began landing in Algiers in midmorning, long before firing ceased. By late evening, the French commander of Algiers surrendered the city to the U.S. forces, and negotiations began with Adm. Jean Louis Darlan for the surrender of the Vichy French throughout North Africa. Finally, on November 10, Darlan agreed, but the French government (under intense pressure from German occupation forces) refused to accept the surrender and removed Darlan from command, ordering the continued defense of North Africa against the Allies. Nevertheless, by November 11, the reality was that the Vichy French forces in North Africa, from Algiers westward through Casablanca, had capitulated.[9] The Battle for North Africa, however, was far from over.

Gen. George Patton, with the assistance of his Arabic interpreter, Col. Jack Nahas ('32) from Beaumont, a Signal Corps officer and graduate in electrical engineering, set up temporary headquarters in Casablanca, where critical supplies and reinforcements were soon funneled in to the North African armies. Nahas, born in Tripoli, Lebanon, had moved with his family to America in 1912. Because of Nahas's Arabic language skills and engineering background, Patton appointed him to take charge of the strategic port of Casablanca while he and Allied forces moved eastward toward Tunis.[10]

About ten days after the initial landings in North Africa, General Beverley and his staff followed the army ashore to supervise the distribution of fuel and supplies and the provisioning of the air force squadrons that were scattered along the coasts. One of Beverley's friends, Col. Demas T. ("Nick") Craw, who could speak French, was among the first ashore at Casablanca but was shot and killed by a "trigger-happy Frenchman." Beverley remained in Casablanca for only a short time before heading for Algiers, which was situated nearer the Tunisian front. Throughout North Africa and particularly over Algiers, the still powerful Luftwaffe continued to bomb and strafe American positions and engage American aircraft in combat long after the so-called cease fire by the Vichy. During one particularly heavy German air attack in Algiers, Beverley took refuge in the nearest bomb shelter, where entertainers from the USO (United Service Organizations) were helping bolster morale in the midst of the air raid. As Americans began to secure greater control of the skies over and the sea lanes to North Africa, the flow of food, supplies, armaments, and reinforcements to the Allies increased, while the German and Italian forces were less and less able to replenish their supplies and manpower.[11]

Even as the Americans began building up their supplies and troop strength immediately following the landings, the ever-robust German infantry and panzer units in Tunis were receiving reinforcements of men and matériel. In addition, the Luftwaffe increased its strikes on American positions throughout North Africa, and U-boats preyed upon American naval transport vessels and warships. Field Marshall Albert Kesselring, with Field Marshall Erwin Rommel and Col. Gen. Hans-Jürgen von Arnim, began preparing for not only the defense of Tunisia but also a counteroffensive against American and Allied invaders that might retrieve Algeria and Morocco. At the least, their orders were to hold North Africa at all costs.

Practically from the moment of the Allied landings, the Luftwaffe's bomber, fighter, and transport aircraft began arriving almost daily, carrying fresh troops and small arms. Axis armies consisted of almost half a million men, excluding the quarter-million Vichy French. Although outnumbered two to one, Rommel's panzer divisions boasted more than four hundred 60-ton Mark VI Tiger tanks armed with 88-mm cannon. The Americans' Sherman and General Lee tanks were no match for these weapons. Moreover, the German Wehrmacht could rely on its battle-seasoned troops, while the half-million-plus American troops were encountering combat for the first time. After handily defeating the Vichy French, the American and British forces now faced a formidable foe as they sought to dislodge the Germans from Tunisia.

Tank warfare and aerial combat intensified. The Allies launched their first attack against the German positions in Tunisia on November 25 and 26, anticipating an early end to the African campaign. There, for the first time in World War II, American tank and German panzer units met on the African desert, and the Americans were repulsed. In that action, 1st Lt. Frank Petty Haynes ('39) from Granger, who commanded a unit of Sherman tanks, was killed. The attackers were "too few, too weak, too dispersed, [and] too tardy."[12]

Unrelated to the attack on Tunis but relevant to the overall Allied successes, on the following day, November 27, French admiral Jean de Laborde made several important decisions. First, he rejected Admiral Darlan's proposal that he sail the French fleet out of its port in Toulon to join the Allied cause in Africa. Second, he refused to surrender the fleet to German occupying armies. Instead, he decided to scuttle the entire French fleet of 77 ships, including 3 battleships, 7 cruisers, and 32 destroyers.[13] Those ships would have provided a significant advantage to either the Germans or the Allies, had either one acquired them.

Subsequently, in early December, German counterattacks began testing the Allies' strengths and weaknesses on the perimeter of Tunisia, especially near Tebourba, where British and American units suffered heavy losses of tanks and men. For the most part, throughout December and January, the Allies clung desperately to their positions around Tunisia. During the subsequent offensives, Capt. James Hollingsworth took command of a company of the 67th

Armored Regiment of the 2nd Armored Division. His unit included three platoons of five tanks each. In the drive to Tunis, his first battle was an encounter with ten German tanks pulling antitank guns. The enemy left behind their antitank guns and crews while rapidly withdrawing, hoping to lure Hollingsworth's tanks into giving chase and coming within range of the antitank guns before their panzers counterattacked, a standard entrapment tactic of the Afrika Korps. Hollingsworth anticipated the maneuver, massed all of his firepower, and "killed every damn one" of the guns. He then gave chase to the tanks, but most of them escaped into the desert. Hollingsworth fought in the North African campaign for a month before participating in the battle for Sicily. S.Sgt. Gus Calhoun Caldwell ('41) from Lockhart, Texas, was another Aggie tank warrior who fought in North Africa before he was transferred to Italy, where he was killed in action in June, 1944.[14]

Among those who provided air cover for the American forces in North Africa was Jack Milton Ilfrey ('42) from Houston, one of the many who left the A&M campus before graduation. He completed his flight training at Luke Field, Arizona, only days after the attack on Pearl Harbor and was sent to England with a fighter squadron in early 1942. In November, he arrived in North Africa, flying a P-38 Lightning, which he named "Happy Jack's Go Buggy." On November 29, at the start of the Tunisian campaign, he assisted in shooting down an ME-110, shot down two ME-109s on December 1, and on December 26 downed two FW-190s over Bizerte-Tunis. Later he shot down an ME-109, damaged another, and in January destroyed yet another ME-109. He was the first Texas Aggie aviator to earn his "ace credentials" with five confirmed kills.[15]

Lt. Col. Hiram Broiles ('28) arrived in Casablanca in December with a planeload of army officers and agents who were to prepare for a war conference between Pres. Franklin D. Roosevelt and Prime Minister Winston Churchill. On January 14, 1943, when Roosevelt and Churchill announced that the United States and Great Britain would cease fighting only when the Axis powers accepted "unconditional surrender," peace seemed (and was) very far away.

But there were hints of better times. German advances had been stalled at Stalingrad, and Russian armies had launched a counteroffensive, effectively encircling the Germans. At the end of January, German armies, numbering 284,000 with arms and equipment, surrendered to the Russians. North Africa had been liberated from Vichy French control. Japanese advances were halted at Guadalcanal and in New Guinea, but Japan controlled the western Pacific and Asia from the borders of India to Alaska. Germany and Italy controlled Europe from the Mediterranean to the Baltic, and now German forces resumed the offensive in Tunisia.

On February 14, panzer units and infantry struck from the east and south through the Americans' forward positions at Kasserine Pass, while eliminating Iowa's 168th Infantry Regiment and destroying whatever Sherman tanks stood in the way. By February 19, the strategic Kasserine Pass into eastern Tunisia had been lost to Rommel's troops, and Germans were pouring northward toward Allied positions at Sbiba and eastward to the Algerian border. At that point, however, the attack stalled. Overextended and short on fuel, supplies, and munitions, Rommel began withdrawing on February 26. Operating under the U.S. II Corps, the U.S. 1st Armored Division and the British 6th Armored Division pursued the retreating enemy. Among them were three fellow Aggies, now cohorts in the 1st Armored Division. Lts. Robert L. Adams ('40) of Mabank, Gabe D. Anderson ('41) of Farwell, and Roy J. Chappell Jr. ('41) of Kaufman were commissioned together in 1941, assigned to the 27th Armored Field Artillery Battalion of the 1st Armored Division, and trained and deployed with it. Adams and Anderson went through the entire war as battery commanders with the 27th. Early in the North African fight Chappell's battery was overrun by German armored units; about six weeks later he was captured behind German lines and remained a prisoner for the duration of the war. Anderson received the Silver Star for heroic action in the Sicilian campaign.[16]

Gen. Terry Allen's 1st Infantry Division also fought Rommel's forces in the battle of Kasserine Pass. Among those with the 1st Division was 1st Lt. Jack E. Golden ('42), who completed tank destroyer training at Fort Hood before getting orders to head an antitank "cannon company" with the 16th Infantry Regiment of the Big Red One. Also participating was 1st Lt. John Pershing Gilreath ('42) from Memphis, Tennessee, who fought through North Africa and then in the invasion of Sicily. Later on Gilreath was killed in action in Italy. Through March, the Allies poured men, munitions, and aircraft into Tunisia and began moving toward the coastal cities of Tunis in the north and Gabes in the southeast, where American and British units fought fiercely. In one engagement, Capt. Walter P. Crump ('40) with the 1st Division died during an initial American thrust in early February, while Montgomery's British troops finally entered the city at the end of March. The enemy was being overwhelmed by the constant replenishment of American men, matériel, and aircraft, but the costs were high.[17]

Gen. James Doolittle's Western Air Command included the Twelfth Air Force and a number of Texas Aggies. Doolittle's copilot, Lt. James M. Parker ('41), had flown with him on the Tokyo raid and survived to fight with him again. Capt. Robert Edward Greenwell ('39) was a bombardier instructor in Midland for a year before joining Doolittle in April, 1943. Greenwell dropped bombs on Tunis, Sicily, Italy, and France until his death in November, when his B-17 was shot down over France. Capt. Kenneth McFarland Irby ('43) from Texarkana ferried replacements to North Africa during the final days of the Tunisian campaign and was killed when his troop transport plane crashed. That same month, May of 1943, S.Sgt. Lindsey C. Hoskins Jr. ('44) from Richmond, Texas, who had joined the air corps following the attack on Pearl Harbor, arrived in North Africa at the pinnacle of the battle for Tunisia and flew bombing missions over

Tunisia, Sicily, and Italy. He died on a mission over Sicily and Naples on May 11, just days before the final Allied victory in Tunisia.[18] The mission over Sicily and southern Italy was, in fact, a prelude to the Allies' invasion of Sicily and southern Europe.

Finally, on May 12, the German armies in Tunisia surrendered, and the Allies took nearly 238,000 veteran German and Italian soldiers prisoner. The Americans suffered more than 19,200 casualties in North Africa between mid-November and mid-May, 1943, including the 1,000 who were killed during the Operation Torch landings. More than 2,700 were reported killed in action, another 6,500 missing in action, and 9,000 wounded. British casualties were greater still, and the losses did not end with the surrender of North Africa. In June, Lt. Howard H. Brians ('42) from El Paso, a fighter pilot who entered combat in November, 1942, died when a grass fire ignited explosives aboard an abandoned German aircraft at a just-captured airfield. Another Aggie, 1st Lt. Harold B. Chamberlain ('34) from Beaumont survived combat but died of pneumonia in the spring of 1943. Lt. Walter Mark Cabaniss Jr. from Garland and Capt. Jack E. Golden survived North Africa but died in combat in France and Germany respectively.[19] Most of those who fought and survived in North Africa continued the fight through Sicily and Italy and into France and Germany.

Planning for Operation Husky, the invasion of Sicily, began soon after the Casablanca conference. Many people believed that the salvation of Russia and an Allied victory in Europe could be secured only by opening a second front in what some termed "the soft underbelly of Europe." General Eisenhower headed the overall planning and operations. British general Harold Alexander commanded the Fifteenth Army Group, which consisted of Patton's Seventh Army and Montgomery's (British) Eighth Army. As in Operation Torch, logistics, supply, and maintenance for the invasion became the responsibility of Gen. George H. Beverley, who later assumed command of the 51st Troop Carrier Wing. At dawn on July 10, 1943, the Allies began landing one hundred sixty thousand troops and six hundred tanks on the southern coast of Sicily under the cover of heavy naval bombardment and foul weather, while an army parachute unit dropped behind German positions.

At sea, transport ships unloaded armaments and men in the second great amphibious campaign of the war, while warships, such as the destroyer USS *Samuel Parker*, provided protective cover against the hoard of angry Luftwaffe fighters and bombers swarming from nearby airfields in Sicily and Italy. Lt. (jg) Robert J. ("Bob") Finlay ('38) from Brenham was gunnery officer aboard the USS *Samuel Parker* as she defended the landing craft and transports. During the engagement, Finlay's gun crews shot down eleven enemy planes. For heroism in that action he received the Silver Star.[20] The landing went better than expected, but enemy reinforcements had begun arriving as soon as the Allied invaders approached the coasts.

On July 11, the Axis forces, consisting of the Italian Sixth Army, two German

Line reached by
Allied forces in
Western Europe,
7 May 1945

AUSTRIA

Line reached by Soviet
forces, 7 May 1945

Bolzano

HUNGARY

Trento

7 May

Line reached by
Yugoslav partisans,
7 May 1945

Milan

Verona

Venice

Turin

30 April

Genoa

Bologna

15 Jan.– 8 April 1945

YUGOSLAVIA

GOTHIC LINE

4 Aug.

Pisa Florence

Evacuated by
German forces,
18 Sept.–Oct. 1943

GUSTAV LINE

Pescara

5 June

Jan. 15–May 11 1944

Adriatic Sea

CORSICA
(FRANCE)

Allies enter Rome
4 June 1944

Rome

Cassino

8 Oct.

25 Sept.

14 Sept.

Anzio

Capua

Benevento

Bari

Gaeta

Shingle
22 Jan. 1944

Naples

Taranto

Salerno

SARDINIA

Tyrrhenian Sea

Avalanche
9 Sept. 1943

Slapstick
9 Sept. 1943

Cagliari

3 Sept. 1943,
Italy surrenders

Catanzaro

9 Sept

Evacuated by
German forces,
18 Sept. 1943

Messina

Baytown
3 Sept. 1943

Palermo

Reggio di Calabria

Strait of Sicily

Catania

Ragusa

Siracusa

Operations
in Italy

Husky
10 July 1943

MALTA

0   Miles   100

Mediterranean Sea

panzer divisions, and one parachute division, launched a counterattack that for a time threatened to dislodge the invaders. The Allies, with heavy air superiority, finally forced the withdrawal of the defenders, and on August 17, Allied troops captured the northernmost city, Messina. Almost one hundred thousand of the Axis forces, however, escaped across the straits of Messina into Italy. Earlier American units had closed their attack toward Palermo, to the west of Messina. Following a costly battle, U.S. troops then seized the Biscari airfield and pressed northward into Palermo on July 22. In Rome, that action triggered a revolt against Benito Mussolini. The Fascist Grand Council asked King Victor Emmanuel to assume command of Italy's armies and appointed Marshall Pietro Badoglio to head the Italian government. The Nazis moved quickly to halt Italian defections, seizing Rome and Athens in early September and occupying positions that Italian troops had previously held.[21] By mid-1943, the battle for Italy and the rest of Europe had just begun.

U.S. fighter and bomber crews flew seemingly endless sorties over Sicily and Italy while suffering heavy losses from the Luftwaffe's fighter planes and ground-based antiaircraft emplacements. One of those who supported the Allied invasion of Sicily was 2nd Lt. Lloyd H. Hughes from Alexandria, Louisiana, whose 564th Bomber Squadron had recently arrived in North Africa. The Sicilian airfields now gave the Allies marginal access to Axis fuel refineries and storage facilities in Rumania. Thus, on August 1, 1943, even as the battle for Sicily raged, Lt. Hughes, piloting a B-24 Liberator bomber, began a dangerous two-thousand-mile mission (almost beyond the aircraft's range) to strike the refineries of Ploesti at nearly treetop level.

Hughes had volunteered for duty in 1942 prior to graduation, and, after flight training, he was speedily shipped to North Africa, where he remained virtually airborne until his death. On this particular mission, coming in at a very low level, his plane was among the last formation to attack and attracted extremely heavy ground fire. On the approach, his aircraft received several direct hits, causing sheets of gasoline to escape from the bomb bay and the left wing. Rather than make a forced landing and jeopardize his formation and the success of the attack, Hughes elected to continue the mission. He dropped his bomb load precisely on target and then, with his airplane blazing, attempted a forced landing. His plane crashed and was consumed. Hughes was the first Texas Aggie to receive the Congressional Medal of Honor in World War II "for conspicuous gallantry in action and intrepidity at the risk of his life above and beyond the call of duty."[22]

The strikes over Rumania continued until the end of the war at great cost to American aviators. Ray O. Hargis ('49; DVM), for example, from Natchitoches, Louisiana, was shot down on his first mission after being sheltered for almost nine months by the Belgian resistance. He was then taken captive and spent the rest of the war in a German prison camp.[23] By striking at the Germans'

Second Lt. Lloyd H. Hughes ('43).

vital fuel sources, those Allied missions began to have a serious impact on the German armies' ability to wage war. Even so, Allied forces on the ground at Messina and those who followed the withdrawal into Italy noticed little change in the tempo of battle.

On September 3, thirty days after the retreat of the Axis from Sicily, the British Eighth Army under Montgomery crossed the straits from Messina into Italy, where they planned to meet the U.S. Fifth Army under Gen. Mark Clark, which landed at Salerno on September 9. The Eighth Army was fortunate to make the crossing without opposition. However, during landings, the British X Corps in the Gulf of Salerno (south of Naples and Mount Vesuvius) and especially the U.S. VI Corp's 36th Infantry Division near the old Roman city of Paestum met strong resistance and suffered heavy casualties.

Theodore H. Andrews ('38) from Caldwell, Texas, and the 36th Division went back a long way. Andrews had enlisted and served with the 143rd Infantry Division of the Texas National Guard from 1934 through 1936. In 1940, he signed up for what he thought would be a one-year tour of active duty as executive officer of the 143rd Infantry. That year that stretched into a whole war and a military career from which Andrews retired a brigadier general in 1971. He was a first lieutenant and company commander with the 143rd Infantry at Salerno when, on September 12, five German panzer units initiated a fierce counterattack against the American lines.[24]

Among the Aggies with Andrews in the 36th at Salerno were Capt. John Letcher Chapin ('36), who commanded Company E of the 141st Infantry Regiment, and Lt. J. O. Beasley ('32) from Wells, Texas, who worked in chemical warfare. Beasley had been a scientist with the Texas Agricultural Experiment Station when he volunteered. Among others at Salerno were Capt. Gaines Maness Boyle ('39), artillery officer; Col. Richard J. Werner ('25), commander of the 141st; and Col. Percy W. Clarkson ('15), with the command staff of the 36th Division. Andrews, Werner, and Clarkson, all of whom served with the 36th at Salerno, ended their military careers as general officers. Boyle received the Silver Star, Purple Heart, and Bronze Star for distinguished service in Italy, which ended with his death on June 12, 1944. Chapin's company for the most part consisted of young Hispanic men who had dropped out of high schools in Bowie, Austin, and El Paso to volunteer for active duty. Lieutenant Beasley died in action at Salerno.[25]

The 36th held after being reinforced by the 45th Infantry Division, and the attacking panzer units finally began to withdraw northward to take up reinforced positions along the "Winter Line" (Gustav line) south of Rome along the Sangro River. There, in November and December, American soldiers, including the 36th, continued to press the attack. During this action on December 15, Capt. Charles H. Hamner ('40) led his company in the initial Allied assault on the enemy's fortified positions. "Leading his men in a fierce assault, he continued to discover and point out covered approaches while dangerously exposing himself to heavy enemy fire." Hamner was fatally wounded, but his "aggressive leadership, unfaltering loyalty, and calm determination inspired the successful accomplishment of the company's objective with a minimum of casualties to his men," so reads his citation for the Silver Star.[26]

The Allies failed to break through, however, and launched a second offensive on December 31 but again did not succeed in penetrating the lines. The Allies, headed by General Alexander's Fifteenth Army Group, next decided to attempt an assault on German positions at Cassino while Gen. Mark Clark's Fifth Army simultaneously flanked the line with a landing at Anzio. In order to establish a favorable base for the offensive at Cassino and to deflect the German forces from the landing at Anzio, the 36th Division made an attack across the Rapido River toward Cassino on January 14, 1944, capturing Mount Trocchio. The next day, a third assault on the line took place, led by British and Free French forces. When it was repulsed, the 36th Division across the Rapido was left in an extremely vulnerable position. "All day long on 22 January, troops that were across the Rapido were subjected to continuous enemy fire. Elements of the 143rd [Regiment] withdrew to the east bank of the river, and strong German counterattacks were thrown against elements of the 141st Regiment that remained." Among those who were still on the west bank of the Rapido was Capt. John Chapin. Although wounded on January 15 at the water line, Chapin left his hospital bed to rejoin his company for the Rapido attack. He explained that "I brought my boys overseas and I will take them home or die trying." He died trying. On January 22, the enemy rained artillery, mortar, and machine gun fire on the 141st, who soon exhausted their ammunition. Chapin was later found in his foxhole with his phone in one hand and his carbine in the other. He was posthumously awarded the Silver Star. After the war, in recognition of his "exceptional service and dedication to his men," the city of El Paso dedicated Chapin High School in his memory.[27]

The landing at Anzio began the same morning as the attack on the 141st and caught the Germans by surprise. Within twenty-four hours, thirty-six thousand troops were ashore, and the American units had suffered only thirteen killed in action. The next day, however, German aircraft dumped planeloads of bombs on the Anzio beachhead and on supporting ships offshore. An American destroyer was sunk, and casualties on shore rose precipitously. Even as reinforcements and supplies poured onto the beach and the Allies established a bridgehead several thousand yards inland, German resistance stiffened and soon counterattacked.

Fresh from the battles at Salerno, 1st Lt. Theodore H. Andrews was with the 36th Division at Anzio. He and Capt. Gerald P. Elder ('39) from Greenville, Texas, who was with the 45th Division, were among the one hundred fifty thousand soldiers who in mid-February were driven back to the beaches by a massive German attack. Lt. Elbert Sheridan Clark ('44) from Dallas flew his B-26 Marauder bomber in repeated low-level attacks on enemy positions at Anzio during the German assault. On February 12, his plane received a direct hit from enemy antiaircraft, and Clark was killed.

During the February battles at Anzio, the Allies dropped leaflets along the German positions, warning that bombs would soon be dropped on the monastery at Monte Cassino, which overlooked the German lines. Subsequently, on February 15, the monastery was destroyed, but the ruins remained a critical battle zone during the continuing Cassino conflict.[28] The Winter Line, despite the assaults and flanking action at Anzio, failed to collapse or even bend.

On May 11, the Allies opened with massive artillery barrages followed by an all-out assault, led by General Montgomery, against the German positions. The battle for Cassino ended with its capture on May 18, but the enemy continued to contest every advance along the Winter Line, while still containing the Anzio bridgehead. During the combat, Lt. Col. O. Wayne Crisman ('38) from Mansfield, Louisiana, an engineer with the 36th, led a critical charge through the German lines at Monte Artemisio, which helped open the way to Rome and earned him the Bronze Star. On May 23, 2nd Lt. Thomas W. Fowler, assigned to the 191st Tank Battalion, walked ahead of his unit with the 1st Armored Division to reconnoiter for mines. He came upon a completely disorganized infantry pla-

Second Lt. Thomas W. Fowler ('43).

toon wandering in the middle of a German minefield and took command of the men. Fowler then moved ahead alone. With his own hands he lifted antipersonnel mines out of the ground, clearing a path through the field. Returning for the infantry, Fowler led them through the minefield, made a reconnaissance into enemy territory, and then returned, still on foot, to lead the tanks through the now passable minefield. Scouting ahead, he encountered several dug-in German infantry, captured and dragged them out of their holes, and sent them to the rear. Then he destroyed their positions with grenades.[29]

Having led his tanks and troops a considerable distance ahead of the Allied lines, Fowler had his infantry dig in. Just as he was bringing up the tanks to provide support, the Germans counterattacked with infantry and Mark VI tanks. During the battle, an American tank was set afire. "With utter disregard for his own life, with shells bursting near him, he [Fowler] ran directly into the enemy tank fire to reach the burning vehicle. For a half-hour, under intense strafing from the advancing tanks, although all other elements had withdrawn, he remained in his forward position, attempting to save the lives of the wounded tank crew. Only when the enemy tanks had almost overrun him, did he withdraw a short distance where he personally rendered first aid to 9 wounded infantry men in the midst of the relentless incoming fire. 2nd Lt. Fowler's courage, his ability to estimate the situation and to recognize his full responsibility as an officer in the Army of the United States, exemplify the high traditions of the military service for which he later gave his life."[30] Thus reads Fowler's posthumous citation for the Medal of Honor.

The enemy withdrew but with great reluctance, all the while offering continuing resistance. The heavy assault at Cassino and along the Winter Line finally enabled the Anzio forces to break out of their containment on May 23 and join Montgomery's units in the advance to Rome. The German forces resisted every step of the way. During the drive to Rome, Capt. Otto Heye ('37) from Galveston, who was assigned to the engineer unit of the 36th Division, was killed in action. Finally, on June 4, the American troops reached the center of the Eternal City.

The next day, those same troops left Rome, moving northward in close pursuit of the withdrawing German armies. On June 6, along the coasts of Normandy, the Allied forces began the invasion of Europe. Despite the opening of a new front in France, the battle for Italy intensified rather than diminished. While the Allies diverted some of their troops and resources from the Italian peninsula to participate in the invasion at Normandy, the German armies in France were being reinforced with eight divisions shifted to that front from *outside* Italy, leaving their Italian forces essentially intact. This meant that the Fifth Army, although now joined by French and French Moroccan troops, had to do more with less.

Meanwhile, the withdrawal of the Axis from the vicinity of Rome into northern Italy was carefully staged. Temporary defensive positions just north of Rome had been established by the German Tenth Army even before the evacuation of the city, and from those positions they conducted strong rearguard protective actions and intermittent offensives covering the withdrawal northward.

The combat never ceased. Although now outnumbered but bolstered by increasing air support, the Allied armies "achieved the remarkable feat, in the circumstances, of keeping the Germans in motion for 64 days over a distance of 270 miles. They did not halt until they reached the outworks of the unfinished Gothic Line south of Florence on August 4, 1944."[31] As the Allies neared the line running roughly east to west from Pesaro on the Adriatic Sea through Florence to Leghorn on the Mediterranean, the fighting intensified, particularly in September and October, 1944, when the Allies still had aspirations of breaking through into that so-called soft underbelly and bringing the war home to Germany and to a close.

On August 25, the British Eighth Army surprised the Germans with a strike along the Adriatic coast, which brought them into Rimini by late September. To contain the offensive, General Kesselring diverted troops from the western segments of the line on the Mediterranean to the east, thus giving the Americans an opportunity to launch an attack on the west between Leghorn and La Spezia in mid-September. The U.S. 85th Division led the assault at Mount Altuzzo and were met with deadly automatic, small-arm, and mortar fire. All of the officers

S.Sgt. George D. Keathley ('37).

and noncommissioned officers with the 2nd and 3rd platoons of Company B, 338th Infantry Regiment, 85th Division, were killed.

At this critical moment, S.Sgt. George D. Keathley stepped forward, re-organized the survivors, and assumed command. Under constant fire, Keathley crawled from one casualty to another, collecting ammunition and administer-ing first aid. He visited all of the men in the command, giving them encourage-ment and ammunition and, when needed, medical attention. Two German in-fantry companies then counterattacked. "Keathley shouted his orders precisely and with determination and the men responded with all that was in them. Time after time the enemy tried to drive a wedge into S/Sgt. Keathley's position, and each time they were driven back, suffering huge casualties. Suddenly an enemy hand grenade hit and exploded near S/Sgt. Keathley, inflicting a mortal wound in his left side. However, hurling defiance at the enemy, he rose to his feet. Tak-ing his left hand away from his wound and using it to steady his rifle, he fired and killed an attacking enemy soldier and continued shouting orders to his men. His heroic and intrepid action so inspired his men that they fought with incomparable determination and viciousness."[32]

The Germans withdrew, leaving their dead and wounded. On September 17, 1944, Mount Altruzzo fell to the 85th Division. Keathley, who died on the battle-field, received the Congressional Medal of Honor for actions in keeping with the highest traditions of military service.

In October, the Fifth Army broke through the Gothic Line, crossed the Arno River, and moved within eight miles of Bologna. Lt. John F. Barnett Jr. ('35) from Palacios, Texas, with the 34th Division, 135th Infantry, Company K, who had been wounded in action near Cassino the previous February, had recovered to fight again. He died on the Gothic Line on October 13. On that same front, Pfc. John Daniel Connell ('44) from Bryan, Texas, a Browning-automatic-rifle (BAR) man with the 349th Infantry in the 88th Division, was killed on October 22, after having served for a full year of combat in Italy. Connell had already been wounded several times in previous engagements.[33] The German troops, however, essentially held the integrity of the Gothic Line until the end of the war, despite periodic ground attacks and frequent air raids.

During one of those air attacks in mid-December, Lt. Robert G. Johnson Jr. ('42) from Amarillo piloted a P-47 fighter plane in a strafing attack on La Spezia, on the west end of the Gothic Line. During the mission, his aircraft caught heavy flak from the antiaircraft batters. Johnson "disappeared into a heavy cloud formation and he has not been seen since." Johnson had completed seventy-five missions and twice received the Air Medal. Although the battle abated in December, it seemed to never end. At Leghorn, south of Florence on the western terminus of the line, Capt. John Poitevent Lackey Jr. ('40) from Rice, Texas, was killed in action near the end of January, 1945. In February, Pfc. Marvin Earl Hiner ('36) from Granbury, with the 87th Mountain Infantry, was killed by enemy artillery fire while on patrol at Mount Belvedere. Capt. Daniel L. Cajka ('39) from Wheelock was wounded in the final days of combat along the Gothic Line and died on April 25, 1945.[34]

In addition to the ground and air action along the Gothic Line, Italy continued to be the staging area for the Fifteenth Air Force's (and later the Twelfth Air Force's) strikes against Germany, Austria, and Hungary. At this time many Texas Aggies were attached to the Fifteenth Air Force and numbered heavily among the casualties in this theater of operations.

Lt. Joseph Pane Lindsly Jr. ('41) from Houston, twice a recipient of the Air Medal, died in combat over Sicily on January 21, 1944. Capt. Foster L. Cash ('40) from Pioneer, Texas, who was the squadron operations officer of a bombardment group of the Fifteenth Air Force, died over northern Italy while piloting a Flying Fortress in a raid on March 19, 1944. Lt. Norbert J. Gorski ('45) from Houston, Lt. Clarence Leroy Korth ('41) from Dallas, and Lt. Jack C. Herron ('46), all pilots, died in combat in April. Gorski, who flew a P-47 Thunderbolt, was serving with the Twelfth Air Force from a base near Pisa, Italy, when he was killed near Cassino. He had flown seventy-five missions and been awarded the Air Medal four times with three oak-leaf clusters. Herron was shot down on April 22 while strafing enemy positions near Cassino, while Korth was killed in a bombing raid over Belgrade, Yugoslavia.[35]

Sgt. John Lindsey Eddins ('41) from Kingsville, who began the war on the ground with the 85th Infantry, transferred to the air corps and served as a gunnery instructor before being assigned to a Liberator bomber. He and a crew of ten were killed in action over Italy in May, 1944, during the final battles over Monte Cassino. Lt. Lloyd W. Kelly ('39) from Wellington, Texas, a navigator on a B-24 stationed in Italy with the Fifteenth Air Force, had flown forty-five missions before he was killed over Munich, Germany, in July, 1944. Ploesti, Rumania, was a graveyard for many American fliers throughout the war, including Lt. Jim L. Kuykendall ('41), a P-38 Lightning pilot with the I Fighter Group of the 29th Fighter Squadron, and Lt. Brice C. Diedrick ('42) from Honey Grove. At the time of his death over Ploesti, Kuykendall had four German planes to his credit, with only one month of combat; he wore the Air Medal with three oak-leaf clusters, as well as four unit awards. Diedrick, who had served as a flight instructor in the States for a year before arriving in Italy, died over Ploesti when his plane exploded in midair.[36]

A nose gunner on a B-26 stationed in Italy with the Fifteenth Air Force, Sgt. Samuel David Lasser ('46) from Houston died in action on his thirteenth mission over Budapest, Hungary, in July, while Lt. Bland Massie Barnes Jr. ('47) from Galveston, Texas, with the 319th Fighter Squadron, 325th Fighter Group, crashed in August. He had flown thirty-one combat missions since his arrival in Europe in October, 1944, and had been awarded the Air Medal five times. Lt. Robert Martin Hyde ('45) from Higgins enlisted in the air corps in 1942, arrived in Europe in June, 1944, and was shot down in July in his P-51 while providing protection for a bombing raid over Austria. He parachuted out, was taken prisoner, and died in a German prison on August 11, 1944.[37] The toll continued to rise, both on the ground and in the air.

Lt. Maurice Block Jr. ('46) from Beaumont enlisted in the infantry in March, 1943, and qualified for flight training in the air corps. He was commissioned in March, 1944. In August, Block arrived at Naples, Italy, where he was assigned to the 319th Fighter Squadron, 325th Fighter Group. He nicknamed his plane, a P-51 Mustang, the "Third Dallas Blond." He was shot down over Yugoslavia on November 21 after flying thirty-three combat missions and earning numerous citations. Block made, his commanding officer wrote his parents, "the supreme sacrifice for a safer and better world of tomorrow."[38]

The battle for North Africa, Sicily, and Italy and the air combat over Europe were very costly for both the Allies and the Axis. Many American and Texas Aggie homes received communications from the War Department that informed their inhabitants of family members who had been "declared dead after being reported missing in action" or "killed in action. No other details received." That was true, for example, for 2nd Lt. Ben Prentice Gafford ('43) from Sherman and 2nd Lt. Joseph Brooks Dalton ('43) from Clint. In many homes, a gold star thus replaced the blue one.

As the war continued, American and Allied commitment intensified both in Europe and in the Pacific. The Allies did not break through the Gothic Line across Italy into northern Europe. However, that lengthy campaign forced the diversion of substantial Axis resources that could have been used to oppose the cross-channel invasion of France or to aid in a counteroffensive against advancing Russian armies in the east. North Africa, Sicily, and Italy were the precursors to the Allied invasion of Normandy and ultimately to the unconditional surrender of Germany.

Suggested Readings

Atkinson, Rick. *An Army at Dawn: The War in North Africa, 1942–1943* (New York: Henry Holt, 2002).

Blumenson, Martin. *Bloody River: The Real Tragedy of the Rapido* (College Station: Texas A&M University Press, 1998).

Botjer, George F. *Sideshow War: The Italian Campaign, 1943–1945* (College Station: Texas A&M University Press, 1996).

Higgins, Trumbull. *Soft Underbelly* (New York: Macmillan, 1968).

Jones, Vincent. *Operation Torch* (New York: Ballantine, 1972).

Kesselring, Albert. *The Memoirs of Field Marshall Kesselring* (London: Greenhill, 1997).

Lewin, Ronald. *Rommel as Military Commander* (New York: Barnes and Noble, 1998).

Strawson, John. *The Battle for North Africa* (New York: Charles Scribner's Sons, 1969).

While the Rangers led by Lt. Col. James Earl Rudder ('32) neutralized guns above the Normandy beaches, the XIX Tactical Air Command, led by Brig. Gen. Otto P. Weyland, pounded German strongholds. Lt. Felix Staffel ('45) parachuted behind enemy lines to fight house to house, and Lt. Jack Ilfrey ('42) became the first Aggie flight ace with five confirmed kills. Earning the Medal of Honor were Lt. Eli L. Whiteley ('41), who led fierce house-to-house fighting in Germany, and Lt. Turney W. Leonard ('42), who halted a German tank assault just before the Battle of the Bulge.

FROM NORMANDY TO THE GATES OF BERLIN

The final campaign to drive to the heart of the Third Reich began with an Allied landing on the beaches of Normandy, France, on June 6, 1944, accompanied by a renewed Red Army offensive against German forces in Poland, continued pressure on German defenses in Italy, and intensified bombing of greater Germany. Among the first ashore at Normandy was Lt. Col. James Earl Rudder, commander of the 2nd Ranger Battalion, whose job was to eliminate the German 155-mm battery overlooking Omaha and Utah Beaches. Other Aggies, including Lt. Felix Staffel ('45), parachuted behind German lines on D-day with the 101st and 82nd Airborne Divisions, while Aggie pilots, gunners, and navigators attached to the XIX Tactical Air Command under Brigadier General Weyland pounded the enemy from the air. Artillery officer Capt. Ogbourne D. Butler Jr. ('39) was bobbing in the choppy sea off the coast of Normandy in a Liberty ship while awaiting his turn to go ashore. Butler later recalled the D-day landing as the "greatest spectacle in the world. There were ships as far as you could see in any direction. Most of them were flying barrage balloons. There was still the firing from our warships, our destroyers, against shore batteries of Omaha Beach. There were landing parties going in. There was the overhead cover during the daylight hours from the American and British aircraft."[1]

Similarly, 2nd Lt. Lindsey I. Lipscomb ('49), who flew two combat missions from his base in England in support of the D-day invasion, said, "No one who flew that day and the next can ever forget the awesome, inspiring and frightening sight of the vast resources of the Allied Navies and Troops filling the English Channel and storming the enemy beaches." Lipscomb's war ended on Thanksgiving Day, 1944, when his plane was shot down over eastern Germany. All of the crew parachuted safely to the ground, "but four (the pilot, co-pilot, and two gunners) were found by civilians and killed—two of them with pitchforks." Lipscomb was taken captive by the military and interned for the duration as a POW.[2]

The planning for the invasion of Europe, Operation Overlord-Neptune, actually began in 1940, following the British exodus at Dunkirk. Subsequently, the North African campaign and the invasion of Sicily and Italy opened the gateway to Europe. In mid-January, 1943, President Roosevelt and Prime Minister Churchill agreed at Casablanca that the western Allies' priorities should be to rid Africa of German armies, invade Italy through Sicily, provide every assistance possible to Russia in the east, wage an unremitting air campaign over Germany, and prepare at the earliest possible time for a cross-channel incursion into France. The Allies' objective in the war was the full and unconditional surrender of Germany, Italy, and Japan. D-day, the Normandy invasion, popularly known as simply "D-day," was a pivotal moment in that effort.[3]

The Allies approached Normandy with a formidable assault force of some 1.6 million men who had been assembled, trained, and equipped in staging areas in England. The joint operation, comprising troops from the United States, the United Kingdom, and other nations, was headed by Gen. Dwight D. Eisenhower, supreme commander of the Allied Expeditionary Force. The action came at a time of peak mobilization in the United States. By mid-1944, the United States had more than 5.4 million men and women stationed abroad and another 7.5 million in service. A total of almost 15 million Americans would serve in the armed forces during World War II. The invading forces approaching Normandy now included a strong sprinkling of combat-experienced veterans from the North African campaigns, including Captains James F. Hollingsworth, and O. D. Butler. Butler went ashore with his artillery unit on D-day plus one and fought across Europe, remaining in the field for 289 days until wounded. Evacuated first to England for treatment, Butler was transferred to a recovery ward at Hammond General Hospital in Modesto, California, where he discovered wounded fellow officers and Aggies Frank C. Litterst Jr. ('43), who was returning from New Guinea; former Aggie fullback Jackson D. ("Jack") Webster ('43), who had been wounded while fighting with Patton's Third Army; Claude Lovett ('43); and James ("Monk") Vance ('41).[4]

Preparations for the invasion required increasing Allied control over the air and the destruction by bombing and strafing of German transportation, supply systems, and fortifications. This job became the primary work of then Brig. Gen. Otto P. Weyland, who assumed command of the XIX Tactical Air Command in February, 1944, and proceeded to direct air operations against the Axis powers. Among the numerous Texas Aggies under Weyland's command were Lt. Aubra ("Curtis") Fuqua Jr. ('45) and Lt. Warren N. Tomlinson ('41), each of whom flew thirty-five missions on B-17s, as did navigator Alfred H. ("Fred") Walker ('36), who was shot down over Inglestad, Bavaria, and held as a POW for nine months. Aggie B-24 pilots Maj. John Douglas Smith ('37), Lt. Col. Dexter Hodge ('39), Capt. Green R. Davis ('40), and Maj. Julian R. Thornton Jr. ('40) all earned the Distinguished Flying Cross (DFC) after flying twenty-five or more combat missions over Germany. Lt. Jack Ilfrey, the first Aggie to earn ace credentials, was flying P-38s in North Africa and was transferred to the 20th Fighter Group in England, where he participated in aerial combat over the English Channel and Western Europe.[5]

A primary air objective was to "liquidate" enemy radar installations along the coast, thereby contributing to the element of surprise and confusion during the early stages of the battle. The low-level bombing and fighter attacks against such installations were particularly costly. In early 1944, Aggie Lts. George L. Davis ('45) and Henry G. Goodwin Jr. ('43) were killed in action over Germany, while in April five more Aggies were lost over Germany and France, including B-29 bombardier Lt. John A. DeBell ('46) and turret gunner T/Sgt. Tommy Glass ('41) (on his sixth combat mission), as well as bomber pilots Lt. Raymond L. Gregg ('39), Lt. Edmund F. Boyle ('41), and Lt. John E. Harris ('42).[6]

During those operations, S.Sgt. Lawrence E Oliver ('50) from Groesbeck, Texas, with the 385th Bombardment Group, was a tail gunner on a B-17 flying almost daily missions out of England. On one mission his aircraft made it back to base "at dark-thirty with 78 holes in our plane, and already listed as MIA." On his last mission, on March 23, 1944, the Luftwaffe "rose and hit us with everything they could put in the sky." Two Folke-Wolfe F-109s targeted his aircraft, and the B-17 finally "pulled up, stalled, and went down." Oliver managed to steer clear of the tumbling aircraft and parachuted to earth. He was taken prisoner and brought to the nearest town, which happened to be Groesbeck, Holland.[7]

Weather was also a critical element in the success or failure of the planned invasion at Normandy. It was crucial to try to determine when inclement weather might, on the one hand, deter German air attacks on a slow-moving convoy or, on the other hand, impede the almost defenseless landing craft. Among those who helped pinpoint a window of opportunity was Edwin H. Ivey ('41) from San Antonio, whose vision problems sidetracked him from army air corps flight training into meteorology and weather forecasting. Ivey was commissioned a second lieutenant to serve with the 26th Weather Squadron stationed in Orlando, Florida. Their work was to provide weather services for the thirteen airfields under their jurisdiction, operate the Staff Weather Officers School, and forecast the weather for overseas theaters, particularly for Europe—and D-day.[8]

On the night of June 5, despite rough seas, heavy rain, poor visibility, and high winds, more than five thousand Allied ships, some towing artificial harbors, or "mulberries," to facilitate landings and cargo handling, moved into position off the coast of France. At 0200 hours on Tuesday morning, June 6, the waiting and preparations were over. The invasion had begun. Naval bombardments and aerial attacks against key targets were preceded by a parachute drop of the 82nd and 101st Airborne Divisions and the British 6th Airborne behind defensive positions on the German flanks in an attempt to secure key roads and bridges, seize the high ground, and confuse the enemy. Lt. Col. Bennie Zinn ('26) was with the 82nd Airborne in the glider landings at Normandy on D-day minus one. Fifteen minutes after the landing, "all hell broke loose." The Germans opened up with mortars and machine guns. Zinn set up a command post near St. Mère Eglise on the coast and that night finally made contact with the main assault units on Omaha Beach. Later, Zinn and the 82nd helped stall the German offensive in the Battle of the Bulge. After the war, Zinn became a veterans' service officer, whose job was to help in the restoration and return of veterans to civilian life.[9]

Spearheading the beach landings were special operation and Army Ranger units, including Rudder's Rangers, whose job was to neutralize key German gun emplacements and communications lines. One of the Allies' objectives was to confuse the enemy, whose high command believed the landings at Omaha and Utah Beaches were only a feint, or diversionary action, while the main landing was expected farther north at Pas de Calais. Field Marshal Erwin Rommel, popularly known as the "Desert Fox" for his exploits in North Africa, was also the overall commander of the German coastal defenses in France. On June 4, he returned to Germany to celebrate his wife's birthday and to urge Hitler to provide more reinforcements, including panzer divisions, to defend the French coast. Rommel had advised his staff that, when and wherever the Allies landed, "The first twenty-four hours will be decisive!" And to an aide, he had said as an aside, "for the Allies, as well as Germany, it will be the longest day."[10]

The airborne night assault operations were complicated and particularly hazardous. The units that dropped from the C-47s and C-46s were widely scattered. Although lost in the haze and fog, most of them recovered rapidly and reorganized. With the 101st was Felix Staffel, who earned his jump wings at Fort Benning, Georgia, trained in England, and jumped with the 501st Parachute Regiment at 0100 hours on D-day. As Staffel recalled, "The first few days in France were total chaos due to the paratroopers being dropped over a 100-square mile area containing both hedgerows and flooded areas. Both the 101st and the 82nd were all mixed up, and both divisions took heavy casualties the first several days, and it was basically every man for himself the first day. But we were operating as coordinated units by the end of day two." Fighting house to house in the city of Carentan, Staffel was wounded by shrapnel on D-day plus seven (June 13) and evacuated by LST (landing ship tank) to a hospital in England. On December 1, 1944, he returned to limited duty in France and was assigned primarily to guard bridges and key communications sites and to check for German infiltrators in U.S. uniforms.[11]

While thousands of soldiers landed in gliders, Louis Hudson ('44), a T-4 (technical sergeant trained in fire-control operations), parachuted behind enemy lines with the 82nd Division. Hudson left the A&M campus in March,

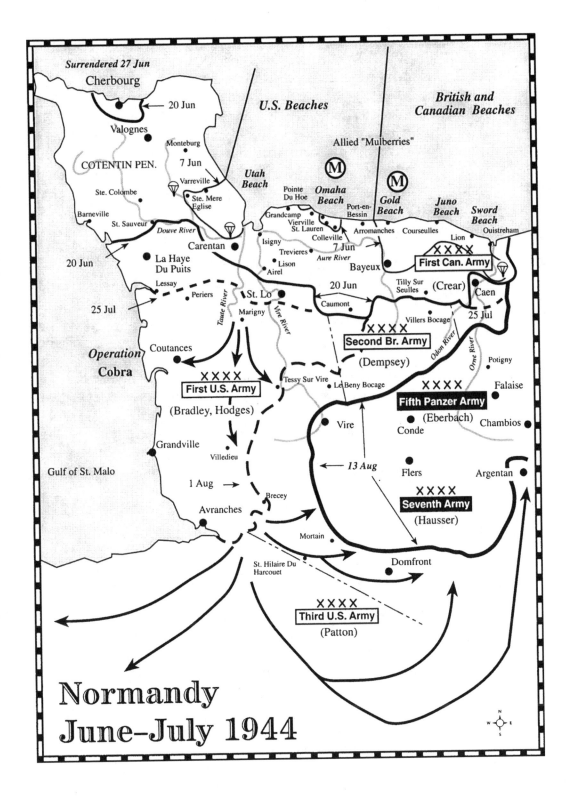

Surrendered 27 Jun

Cherbourg

20 Jun

Valognes

Monteburg

COTENTIN PEN.

7 Jun

Ste. Colombe

Varreville

Ste. Mere
Eglise

Barneville

St. Sauveur

Douve River

Carentan

20 Jun

La Haye
Du Puits

Lessay

25 Jul

Periers

St. Lo

Marigny

Operation
Cobra

Coutances

Taute River

Vire River

XXXX
First U.S. Army

(Bradley, Hodges)

Tessy Sur Vire

Grandville

Villedieu

Gulf of St. Malo

1 Aug

Brecey

Avranches

Mortain

St. Hilaire Du
Harcouet

U.S. Beaches

*British and
Canadian Beaches*

Allied "Mulberries"

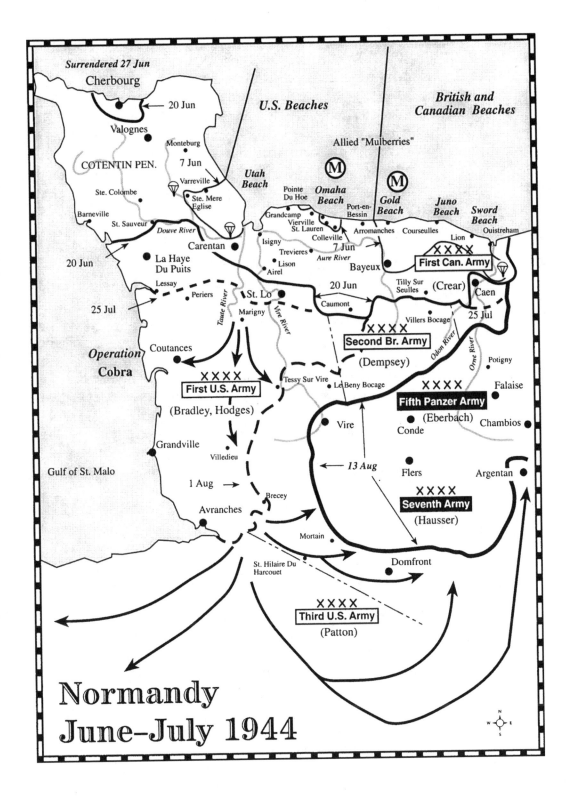

*Utah
Beach*

Pointe
Du Hoe

Grandcamp

*Omaha
Beach*

Port-en-
Bessin

*Gold
Beach*

*Juno
Beach*

*Sword
Beach*

Vierville
St. Lauren

Colleville

Arromanches

Courseulles

Lion

Ouistreham

Isigny

Trevieres

7 Jun

Aure River

Bayeux

XXXX
First Can. Army

Lison

Airel

20 Jun

Tilly Sur
Seulles

(Crear)

Caen

Caumont

Villers Bocage

Odon River

25 Jul

XXXX
Second Br. Army

(Dempsey)

Le Beny Bocage

Ome River

Potigny

Falaise

XXXX
Fifth Panzer Army

(Eberbach)

Chambios

Vire

Conde

13 Aug

Flers

Argentan

XXXX
Seventh Army

(Hausser)

Domfront

XXXX
Third U.S. Army

(Patton)

Normandy
June–July 1944

N
W   E
S

1943, with most of his classmates. They trained first in the States and then in England for a drop on enemy targets that were presumed to be in Belgium. The maneuver never materialized. Later, on June 6, the 82nd hit France. Not until after the war, Hudson recalled, did he discover that German panzer divisions had been held in reserve and not used during the initial landings. Had they been brought into action, he speculated, the entire invasion would have been quite different. American bazooka shells bounced off the panzer tanks. In fact, the infantry and airborne divisions began using the captured German bazookas (*panzerfaust*) against their own tanks. Hudson remained in action through the Battle of the Bulge and returned to Bryan, Texas, after the war to begin a long and giving career as a teacher and principal.[12]

Among the most visible special operations units at Normandy were the U.S. Army Rangers, whose job was to take the bluffs at Omaha Beach, including a network of pillboxes and heavy artillery. If the high ground were not taken and held, both the landing craft and soldiers coming ashore would be easy targets for the Germans. At the head of the 2nd Ranger Battalion was a former Aggie football player from Brady, Texas, Lt. Col. James Earl Rudder. His unit's dangerous and difficult assignment was to neutralize six 155-mm guns located on the cliffs of a small peninsula at Point du Hoc, overlooking the Omaha and Utah landing sites, emplacements that had been identified earlier by Allied intelligence analysts as "the most dangerous battery in France."[13] Rudder divided his five companies into two forces. The 225 men constituting Companies D, E, and F were to land, climb the one-hundred-foot-high position, and attack the enemy. Companies A and B, with a smaller force, were to land farther down the beach and approach Point du Hoc from the rear. The combined mission was to quickly destroy the guns. Rudder told the commanders of A and B Companies, "Now, if they [D, E, and F] don't make it up the bluffs, and we expect 80 percent casualties getting there—if they don't get up there within 30 minutes, you'll get the word—Tilt." From that point on, it would be every man for himself.[14]

Gen. Omar Bradley, commander of the American invasion forces, commented later, "Never has any commander been given a more desperate mission" than that assigned James Earl Rudder.[15] On the morning of D-day, after some delay and confusion during the landing, Rudder led his men in Companies D, E, and F up the precipice under heavy enemy fire. There they linked up with Companies A and B and continued to advance in close-quarter combat against the fortified positions. Despite being wounded twice, Rudder continued to lead the attack.

During the first thirty-six hours of fighting, more than half of Rudder's Rangers were killed or wounded as they resisted continual counterattacks by the Germans. The initial assault on Point du Hoc helped define the course of the invasion. It was, as Erwin Rommel predicted and as Cornelius Ryan described in *The Longest Day*:

Lt. Col. James Earl Rudder ('32) and his 2nd Ranger Battalion were assigned the task of neutralizing the six 155-mm guns located on the cliffs of a small peninsula at Point du Hoc. These emplacements were identified by prelanding intelligence as "the most dangerous battery in France."

. . . a wild, frenzied scene. Again and again the rockets roared, shooting the ropes and rope ladders with grapnels attached. Shells and 40-millimeter machine guns raked the cliff top, shaking down great chunks of earth on the Rangers. Men spurted across the narrow, cratered beach trailing scaling ladders, ropes and hand rockets. Here and there at the cliff top Germans bobbed up, throwing down "potato masher" hand grenades and firing Schmeissers [machine pistols] . . . as the attackers with tall, extended ladders, borrowed for the occasion from the London Fire Brigade, tried to maneuver closer in.

The assault was furious. Some men didn't wait for the ropes to catch. Weapons slung over their shoulders, they cut hand-holds with their knives and started up the nine-story-high cliff like flies. Some of the grapnels now began to catch and men swarmed up the ropes. Then there were wild yells as the Germans cut the ropes and the Rangers hurtled back down the cliff. . . . The Germans were leaning over the edge of the cliff, machine-gunning the

Rangers as they climbed. . . . By the end of the day there would only be ninety of the original 225 still able to bear arms.[16]

Rudder was awarded the Distinguished Service Cross (DSC) for extraordinary heroism for this action. The only message the Rangers transmitted from Point du Hoc was that they had taken their objective, destroyed the guns, and were holding their position.[17]

Down on the open beaches, thousands of soldiers waded ashore in the face of intense fire. The initial waves of the landing included one hundred fifty thousand men and fifteen hundred tanks divided into five assault divisions. One Canadian and two British divisions landed at Gold, Juno, and Sword Beaches to the east. To the west, two American divisions landed on Omaha, while another hit Utah Beach. Lt. Jack E. Golden ('42) from Seymour, Texas, assigned to the 16th Infantry Regiment, 1st Infantry Division, was at Omaha. He was awarded the Silver Star for valor on June 6 for his repeated efforts to rescue groups of his men who had been hit while in the water after the destruction of their amphibious craft; at the same time Golden continued to direct a fierce assault on the enemy.[18]

"My first thought at landing was, 'Am I going to come up out on the water?'" recalled infantry Capt. John F. Smith ('34). "Then some cursed soul grabbed me by the suspender and said, 'You're coming with us, Captain,' and I didn't know if I was grateful or not to him for saving my neck."[19] Later in the campaign, Smith, with the 359th Infantry Regiment, 90th Infantry Division, composed largely of men from Dallas and known as "Dallas's Own Regiment," survived wounds he sustained at the Battle of the Bulge. He earned the DSC and Silver Star in Luxemburg in January, 1945. Smith served his country again in Korea. Among those Aggies hitting the beach on D-day were future university president and historian Lt. Jim Dan Hill, 1st Infantry Division; future congressman Capt. Olin E. ("Tiger") Teague ('32) with the 314th Infantry Regiment, 79th Division; future oilman Capt. Johnny Mitchell ('34), Capt. Marion C. Pugh ('41), Lt. Jackson Webster ('43), and two future Medal of Honor winners, Lts. Turney W. Leonard ('42) and Eli Whiteley ('41).[20]

During the first two weeks of combat, from the D-day landing on June 6 until the beachhead was officially secured on June 20, Americans suffered 3,082 casualties (most of them on the morning of June 6 on Omaha Beach); the British lost 1,842 men, and the Canadians, 363. The battle continued both on land and in the air. Col. Tom C. Morris ('33), a reservist who had been called to active duty in 1941 before Pearl Harbor and whose orders (like those of so many others) after Pearl Harbor were changed to read "for the duration," came ashore on Omaha Beach on D-day plus one. Morris's 38th Infantry, 2nd Battalion, remained in the battle for Normandy for seventy-one consecutive days. They were first to enter and secure Trevières, France, making the first real break in enemy lines.

During those initial two weeks at Normandy, U.S. Army Air Corps pilots Lt. David R. Hughes ('46), Capt. Jack W. Cooper ('39), Lt. Clifford P. Garney ('40), Lt. Henry T. Gillespie ('38), Lt. Edwin R. Lewis ('42), and Lt. W. C. Jenn ('42) died in air-support operations. Maj. John Douglas Smith ('37), squadron commander of the 743rd Squadron, 455th Bomb Group, Fifteenth Air Force, flew thirty-five missions from bases in Italy in support of Allied landings between May, 1944, and April, 1945. Smith earned the DFC for exceptional valor over France on June 25, 1944. Many died in combat on the ground, including Lt. Ioland E. Dutton ('40), Lt. Ed A. Felder ('41), Capt. James H. Hinds ('15), Lt. William L. Hastings ('40), Capt. Ralph B. Hartgraves ('41), Lt. William L. Jameson ('34), Lt. John Ellzey ('41), and Lt. Henry D. Jackson ('42).[21]

Both Texas Aggies in service and their families kept the A&M campus posted, insofar as wartime censorship allowed, on the soldiers' whereabouts and welfare. The director of the Association of Former Students (AFS) and the editor of the *Texas Aggie* magazine received hundreds of letters, notices, and newspaper clippings from battlefronts worldwide—many of these reporting Aggies killed in action. Generally the first notice of the death of an A&M graduate came from the family, followed by a confirmation from the War Department. Letters such as the following began to fill the files at the AFS:

June 26, 1944
Dear Sir:

The War Department has notified me that my husband, First Lieutenant H. Douglas Jackson '42, was killed in action June 8 in France. Will you please include his name in "Silver Taps"? The following record of Douglas' military service and marriage is furnished for use in the column if it is customary.

H. Douglas Jackson was born in San Angelo on December 15, 1919; his parents are Mrs. Elizabeth Jackson of San Antonio and Dr. H. D. Jackson of San Angelo. He graduated from Texas A&M on May 15, 1942, and received his 2nd lieutenancy on May 16, 1942. He was married the same date to Miss Charlotte Dunaway of San Antonio and Shamrock. In addition to his wife and parents he is survived by his son, Robert Everett, who resides in Shamrock with his mother; one sister, Mrs. Lee M. Samson of San Antonio; and one brother, Gilbert Jackson of San Angelo.

Lt. Jackson reported for active duty at Camp Wolters, Texas, on May 18, 1942, and was later assigned to the 22nd Infantry, 4th Division, Camp Gordon, Georgia. The division trained at Fort Dix, N.J., Camp Gordon Johnston, Florida, and Fort Jackson, South Carolina. While on special duty at Fort George G. Meade, Md., Lt. Jackson received a written commendation from Maj. Gen. E. T. Reinhardt and for outstanding service in his regiment. He was commended by his regimental commander, Col. Harvey A. Tribolt. In July and August of 1943, Lt. Jackson was assigned to Wellfleet, Camp Edwards, Massachusetts, as an instructor in anti-aircraft firing. He was chosen to be in the first group on his division to take U.S. Army Ranger training. He received his 1st Lieutenancy on August 16, 1943.

Lt. Jackson embarked for overseas duty with the Fourth Division in transit for training in England until the invasion of France by the Allies. The Fourth Division took part in the fighting around Montebaury. Lt. Jackson was in Company D of the 22nd Infantry and was the 1st Platoon leader. Thank you very much.

Mrs. Charlotte Jackson[22]

These letters, collected in the Texas A&M Archives, preserve the personalities, the pain, and the agony of World War II.

The first two weeks of battle following D-day were critical. By mid-June, 1944, more than 315,000 U.S. troops with arms and supplies had come ashore, along with another 314,000 British and Canadian troops. The next phase involved a three-pronged inland advance. U.S. forces landing at Utah moved up the Cotentin Peninsula to capture the vital seaport of Cherbourg, while troops that landed at Omaha advanced southward toward Saint Lo. The third prong, the British and Canadian forces, attempted to move southeast and capture the town of Caen.[23] Resistance stiffened, but the Allies accomplished all three objectives by mid-July and then moved west and south toward Brest and Le Mans while regrouping for the drive toward Paris.

The Army Corps of Engineers began the work of repairing and reopening port facilities, rail links, and communications systems while building supply depots. A sixteen-inch ship-to-shore gasoline pipeline was installed at Cherbourg, and three pipelines were laid across France to the front lines. These would be extended each time the army pushed forward. In the Normandy countryside, combat involved advancing from hedgerow to hedgerow and field to field, much as it had in World War I. Similarly, cities and towns could be wrested from the defenders only by door-to-door and hand-to-hand combat.

Reinforcements and replacements continued to move across the English Channel to France. Lt. Searcy Bracewell ('38), who was admitted to the Texas bar in 1940, helped with the invasion planning and training in England and was assigned as assistant G-4 with Patton's Third Army staff. Sgt. Calvin C. Boykin Jr. ('46), with the 814th Tank Destroyer Battalion, 7th Armored Division, landed on Utah Beach on August 8 and fought through four campaigns in Europe. Boykin discovered years later that his high school friend from Big Spring, Texas, and fellow Aggie, Pvt. David V. Lamun ('46), 90th Infantry Division, had landed at Normandy on June 8 and was killed on July 6.[24]

General Eisenhower had originally intended to bypass Paris and establish a defensive line along the Seine River in order to prevent the German army from withdrawing into Germany. However, the pace of the Allied advance was so rapid that the supreme headquarters of the Allied Expeditionary Forces

(SHAEF) altered its plans and drove into Paris, which was captured on August 25, 1944. Although resistance in southern France diminished, the strategic ports of Le Havre and Antwerp in the north were not taken by Allied forces until early in 1945, as the Allied forces began the drive toward the Rhine. Casualties mounted as German armies battled to defend their homeland. Among the Texas Aggies killed in combat in July alone were Sgt. Rolland J. Bowman ('40), Lt. Earl V. Green ('42), Pvt. David V. Lamun, S.Sgt. James H. Japhet ('53), Lt. Michael J. Arisco ('42), Lt. John D. Ragland ('41), Capt. J. D. Holzheauser ('42), Capt. Woodrow R. Allen ('38), and B-24 navigator Lt. Jack H. Glenn ('45).[25]

Capt. W. R. Allen ('45), who headed the Comanche, Texas, Farm Security Administration before the war, was posthumously decorated for bravery as his unit fought to defend their position on the slope of Monte Castre, France, on July 11. With his unit "cut-to-pieces and isolated he had withstood repeated counter attacks by troops of the 'Das Reich' Division" and, in an effort to halt the enemy, called in friendly artillery on his own position. When informed that an enemy force double his was no more than 100 yards away, in his last transmission over the walkie-talkie he said while crawling through the underbrush, "I've no ammunition to waste; I'll wait until they get to 50 yards."[26]

A second major landing in France, Operation Anvil-Dragoon, took place on the French Riviera on August 15, 1944, with the assistance of the French Resistance. In the face of the rapid Allied advance, German forces withdrew up the Rhone Valley to avoid entrapment. After the key ports of Toulon, Marseille, and Lyons fell on September 11, the invading forces linked with the Normandy forces west of Dijon, thereby bringing all of southwestern France under Allied control. As the Allies advanced into northeastern France, casualties rose. In August alone, Texas Aggies killed in action there included Maj. Bailey G. Carnahan ('37), Lt. John G. Ellzey ('41), Lt. Frank P. Daugherty Jr. ('42), S.Sgt. Roy Hughes ('44), Maj. John L. Hanby ('40), Lt. William C. Richards ('40), Lt. Robert L. Ravey ('42), Lt. Theophilus Williams ('42), Col. Welborn B. Griffith Jr. ('23), and P-51 pilot Lt. Ferris S. Harris ('43).

By September, the Allied front stretched nearly four hundred miles from Switzerland across France and through the low countries of Belgium and Luxemburg to the English Channel and the North Sea. With forty-eight Allied divisions now in Italy and the European Theater of Operations (ETO), the advance slowed from mid-September until mid-December as winter set in with rain, mud, and snow. At the same time, the Allied troops encountered a more rugged terrain of wooded areas, rivers, and streams.

Progress was delayed even more by the increasing enemy resistance as the Allied armies approached the German border. In addition, invading forces had moved so rapidly that they outran their supply lines. Despite the establishment of a massive one-way truck route (it was crucial for trucks to reach the front lines with supplies, not for them to return) called the Red Ball Express, gas and ammunition ran short. So did infantrymen, as replacements slowed down. While the advance bogged down, Allied casualties continued to rise in ground combat and in the air. In September and October, 1944, Aggies killed in combat included pilots Capt. Phillip S. Isis ('39), a recipient of the DFC, and Maj. Raymond S. Carter ('42), who died in a bomber escort mission. Others lost in ground combat included Lt. William J. Collier Jr. ('34), Capt. Ballard P. Durham ('41), Capt. Allen W. Erck ('40) of the 3rd Armored Division, Capt. Abraham S. Kahn ('41) (who earned the Silver Star fighting in Belgium), and Lt. Harry P. Curl ('44).[27]

The Rhineland campaign, fought from October until mid-December, encompassed the west wall of the "Siegfried Line," Metz, Strasbourg, Saar, the Hürtgen Forest, and Arnhem in Holland and the Scheldt estuary in Belgium. In Holland, in Operation Market Garden in mid-September, 5,500 airplanes and 2,500 gliders transported more than 34,000 troops and 5,000 tons of supplies to the battlefield in an effort to secure the northern Rhine tributaries at Eindhoven, Nijmegen, and Arnhem. This airborne attack cost the Allies in excess of 13,000 casualties.

On October 20, units of the First U.S. Army captured the first German city, Aachen, despite fierce, bitter resistance. At the close of that battle, on November 4, American troops attacked the nearby small city of Kommerscheidt. There Lt. Turney W. Leonard's 100-man, twelve-gun, tank-destroyer company and 1,100 infantrymen became trapped between two German divisions. Leonard, who had been in the thick of the fighting since landing on Omaha Beach, had been cadet commander of I Company Infantry, a Distinguished Student, and honor military graduate (class of 1942) before entering the army. The overwhelming superiority of the enemy prevented Leonard's schoolmate and company commander, Capt. Marion C. Pugh, from making contact with his superiors. Pugh returned to division headquarters for reinforcements and ammunition, leaving Leonard in command. Lieutenant Leonard held out through the night under relentless attack.

Later Pugh returned with the news that no assistance would be provided and that his orders were to hold Kommerscheidt at all costs. With American casualties running very high, the Germans launched their final attack from three sides. Taking charge of the infantry, Leonard knocked out the attacking tanks. By this point, most of the American infantry officers were dead. Despite multiple wounds, Lieutenant Leonard regrouped those who were still able to fight and led a charge to high ground. Using only a submachine gun and grenades, he knocked out the snipers, a German half-track, and a .50-cal. machine gun. While directing fire that destroyed six German tanks, Leonard was hit by a high-explosive shell that tore off the lower part of his arm. Tying a tourniquet around the stump, he was last seen heading for a first-aid station (which was subsequently captured by the enemy). Leonard was never seen again. In the com-

Lt. Turney W. Leonard ('42).

mendation, Captain Pugh wrote that Leonard was "the bravest man he ever saw." For his superb courage, inspiring leadership, and indomitable fighting spirit during the fierce three-day engagement, Aggie Lieutenant Leonard of Dallas, Texas, was posthumously awarded the Congressional Medal of Honor. Fifty-six years later, as a salute between soldiers, German army Lt. Obit Volker Lossner, whose own grandfather had died near Kommerscheidt, helped a German family return Turney's Aggie ring to members of his family in ceremonies at Texas A&M on Veterans' Day, November 11, 2000. The ring is now on permanent display in the Sam Houston Sanders Corps of Cadets Center on the A&M campus.[28]

In addition to the heroism of Turney Leonard, the following Aggies received the Silver Star for valor in the battle of Metz and during the drive to cross the Siegfried Line: Maj. Albert L. ("Dutch") Sebesta ('32), Capt. Clint W. Braden ('40), Col. Sam L. Metcalfe ('17), Capt. Robert H. Ivey ('39), Capt. William B. Pace ('36), Capt. James F. House ('38), and Capt. Robert E. Adair ('37).[29]

By late November, heavy rain and severe cold further delayed the Allied advance. During the delays caused by the weather and the resupply of the Allies, the Germans regrouped and began planning a counterattack. Meanwhile, American battle casualties grew. From December 16 until January 2, 1945, more than 41,000 Allied officers and men died along the Siegfried Line. Among the A&M men killed in action were Lt. Arthur A. Cater ('46; Silver Star), Pvt.

Lynwood Beyer ('46), Lt. Ray E. Dickson Jr. ('37), Capt. Henry V. Baushausen ('35; Silver Star), PFC Max H. Barrett ('45), Lt. Garland E. Dennis ('43), Lt. Richard E. Alston ('44; Silver Star), Lt. Stephen C. Kaffer ('43), S.Sgt. Charles E. Kingery ('43), PFC Donald E. Hudson ('46; Silver Star), Sgt. Earl T. Brown Jr. ('46; Silver Star), and PFC Kenneth H. Doke ('46).[30]

By the winter of 1944, the Aggies at the front were students whose time on campus had been relatively brief and who, for the most part, were several years younger than those who had preceded them into service, as the United States desperately sought to replace the casualties and build army strength for the greater campaigns yet to come in Germany as well as in the Pacific theater.

As the war's dynamics began to change, the Rhineland campaign during the winter of 1944 marked the beginning of the end of the Third Reich. However, fighting an enemy defending its own lair, coupled with the bitter cold, fatigue, wounds, and death, placed enormous stress on the Allied soldiers. By December, 1944, Capt. Jack Golden had been in combat for nearly twenty-three months (except for a brief training period in England) and in action across North Africa, Sicily, and Italy. He was also in the first wave ashore on D-day. In a letter to his parents, dated December 12, 1944, shortly after becoming company commander, Golden applauded his dad's efforts to sell U.S. war bonds, hoping that it would help bring the war to an end more quickly. However, Golden was growing uneasy about news reports that civilians back home were more concerned about their own immediate interests than about making sacrifices for the war effort. His is a poignant firsthand view of war:

I hear my "pop" is really a bond seller. If the rest of the U.S.A. was like you then the boys at the front wouldn't have so much to be blue about. Sometimes after a hard day or a hard week we get to read a paper or magazine. We read about strikes, ammunition shortage[s], tire shortages etc. In the same paper we read about conversion into civilian production and things like that. Maybe the people at home expect us to understand these things. Maybe the boys in Paris, London, and the U.S.A. will, but not us. We can't understand why, if we walked across the island of Sicily fighting as we went, . . . defense workers [in the United States] can't get up thirty minutes earlier and walk two miles to work. Try and tell my boys tonight that the people of New England are cold. The snow is about two feet deep [here] and they don't dare build a fire. The wind has calmed down a little now and the snow has stopped falling, but their feet are still wet and their blankets damp, and there is always the chance that this may be your last night. Take one of my boys and take his neighbor who was lucky and got a defense job. One is dancing to keep warm in the snow, the other one dancing for relaxation from a hard eight hours at the plant. Sure we know that we have to have workers at home, but if we can do our job for 24 hours a day for five and six days at a time for the money Uncle Sam wants to pay us why can't those people work a little harder and a little longer for the money they are receiving. We can't go on strike, if we did we would have to take back the territory that so many of our buddies were killed in taking. We think in life and death, they think in money and shorter hours. Will boys who come home get jobs or will they be forgotten as quickly as they were in the last war. If we go home no one will understand us because they have never lived in the mud, snow and rain for day after day. They have never been bombed, straffed [sic] or been in an artillery and mortar barrage for hours.

We don't mind fighting. That is our job. I will try to explain. First, you get tired and more tired and after a while you can't run across open places and hit the ground as fast. . . . Also after a while you get so tired you stop doing the small things that are important to your safety and if you get tired enough you don't care whether you live or die. Do you understand?

I won't say I am not afraid because I am always scared to death. It was a game then. Now it is a job that has to be done and I try to do my job the best I can. What I mean by being scared now is that at one time I could walk through an artillery barrage without my heart jumping, but now I have a little faster heart beat when I am under fire and I move a little faster when I can. I guess I am not a young kid anymore, I am an experienced officer. I will never break down because I have my mother and daddy to back me up.[31]

By early December, the defeat of Germany seemed plausible. Indeed, after 120 days in action through France and Germany, Captain Golden's unit was moved to the rear for a much-needed 30-day R&R (rest and recuperation), but on December 16, after only 3 days of rest, the soldiers were called back into action as the war suddenly took a new, dangerous, and desperate turn.

With the snow waist deep in much of the Ardennes-Eifel region—an area of dense forest, rugged ravines, and narrow roads—the Allied forces assumed the terrain and weather would buffer them from counterattacks. Moreover, their intelligence reports indicated that the Germans were withdrawing across a broad front due to heavy casualties, short supplies, and pressures increasing in the east. Unknown to the Allies, Adolf Hitler, who had rejected a plan for an attack farther south, ordered a massive counterattack for November 25, Thanksgiving Day, under the code name "Watch on the Rhine." Growing more desperate, the Führer ordered an attack, asserting that "From the transport-driver and the drummer up to the General, boldness is the noblest of virtues, the true steel which gives the weapon its edge and brilliancy."[32] Citing the famed Prussian military strategist Karl von Clausewitz, he exhorted his troops to utilize surprise and speed. But because the Wehrmacht was unable to fully deploy its assault forces by Thanksgiving, the attack was delayed until December.

Hitler's battle plan called for twenty-five German divisions to hit the thin U.S. lines in the Ardennes region of Belgium and Luxembourg, cross the Meuse River, push northwest to recapture the port of Antwerp, and, by splitting the

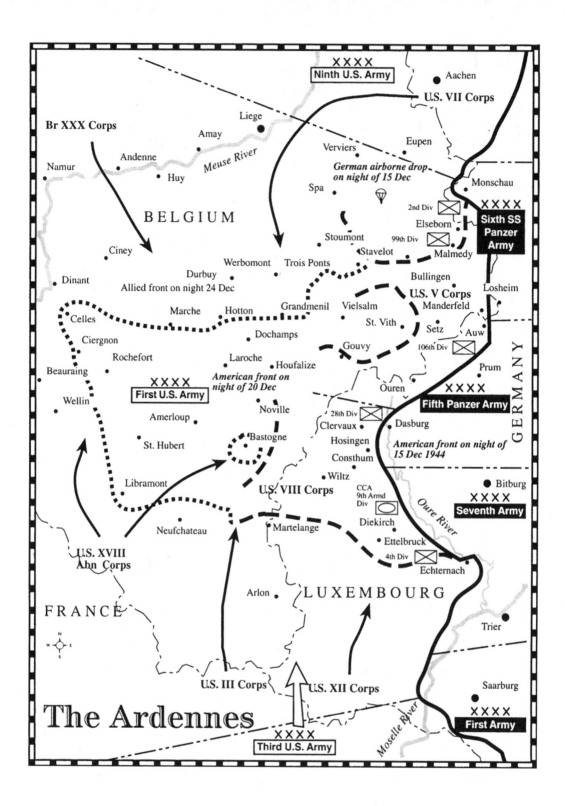

The Ardennes

British and American armies, turn the tide of battle in favor of the Reich.[33] A special German unit dressed in captured British and American uniforms and driving captured Allied trucks and tanks infiltrated Allied lines, causing general chaos and confusion in the rear. With this ruse they seized key bridges on the Meuse River. Under the code name "Herbstnebel" (Autumn Mist), the offensive began before dawn on the drizzling, cold morning of December 16. Allied reconnaissance planes were grounded because of the overcast. The Wehrmacht initiated a very heavy artillery barrage across a sixty-mile front followed by swift tank and infantry attacks that surprised the undermanned American forces. Lt. Ulrich W. Crow ('39) from Normangee, Texas, a platoon leader who landed at Omaha Beach with the 2nd Infantry Division, hastily withdrew his men into Rocherath, Belgium. Shrapnel hit him on the 18th, as German tanks moved through, but after recovery he returned to duty with the 720th Replacement Depot.[34]

Second Lt. James L. Huffines Jr. ('44) was there. Huffines left the campus in May, 1943, completed training, received his commission, and fought in the Ardennes, Rhineland, and Central European campaigns. After the war he returned and completed his degree in economics and accounting. A few years later, in 1950, Huffines was back at the front, this time in Korea, where he fought with the 66th Medium Tank Battalion. Sgt. A. P. Wiley Jr. ('46) was also in the Ardennes and Rhineland campaigns. He had arrived in France from England, where his 2nd Platoon, K Company, 120th Infantry Regiment, 30th Infantry Division, had been sent for "additional training" before heading for the front. The training lasted all of seven days. His outfit was near Malmedy, Belgium, ready to move forward, when suddenly the front lines moved to him on December 16. As his company headed into Malmedy, the roads were packed with troops streaming south, and on December 18 Wiley learned of the German breakthrough. On December 21, when K Company encountered the enemy, his platoon leader was killed and the platoon sergeant wounded. Wiley, then eighteen years old, stepped in to fill the void. On December 24 and 25, Allied planes bombed Malmedy and inflicted heavy casualties on Company K. Wiley and the remnants were assigned to L Company and then to I. Their number-one "minute by minute, hour by hour, and day by day concern was to survive what we were doing at that moment in time." They battled marauding German tanks and endured artillery and mortar fire, twelve inches of snow, and freezing weather, which brought on trench foot, frost bite, and gangrene. Wiley survived those ordeals and, by March, arrived with his company near Magdeburg, Germany, just west of the Elbe River. They were more than ready for the war to end.[35]

What had he and the 120th Regiment accomplished? "You took the high ground and town that was the key to the enemy's defense north of the L'Ambleve River. . . . You knocked the enemy out of Thirimont and off Hill 551. . . . You beat up four battalions from 2 regiments of [the enemy's] crack Parachute Troops. You knocked out 10 tanks and assault guns. . . . You captured more than

170 prisoners. You killed or wounded about 500 krauts. Above all you fought as the 120th always does, moving forward always despite casualties to take objectives assigned."[36] Wiley returned to Texas A&M, graduated with a business degree in 1949, and later founded the Wiley Lecture Series on the campus.

On December 16, when the German offensive began, Lt. William Peña ('42), with 3rd Battalion, 109th Infantry Regiment, 28th Infantry Division, had taken up a position in a farmhouse near Reisdorf across the Oure River from the German lines. "[J]ust before daybreak we began receiving the heaviest artillery and mortar barrage I had ever experienced. . . . I could not believe that the Germans had stored up so much fire power." German infantry soon arrived, and the battle began. The next day, December 17, Peña and his men saw a German fighter flying overhead—without a propeller. This was their first sighting of a jet. After close artillery fire was called in, the first German attack was turned back, but the fighting continued. For Peña, the war finally ended when his unit reached Schleiden, Germany.[37]

Lt. Col. Charles F. Girand ('31) from San Antonio had been in a "quiet sector" of the Belgian front in December, 1944, when his unit, the ill-fated 106th Infantry Division, took the brunt of the German offensive that struck with "pulverizing force." Girand and the 3rd Battalion were trapped behind German lines and fought their way back to the front, where they were immediately thrown into a counterattack. The 106th, which suffered 8,663 casualties during the Battle of the Bulge, was a part of the force that finally halted the German advance near Stavelot and Manhay, Belgium. After the battle, Girand wrote a letter home on January 8, 1945, describing some of the action. During the early years of the war, his wife and son had followed him from army camp to army camp:

> The third Bn. fought off thrust after thrust, until we were surrounded by the enemy. When we finally had orders to withdraw, I had doubts that we could get out. I called together some of the key officers and non-coms and explained the desperate situation to them, and told them it would take guts and ammunition to get us out; that I could furnish the ammunition if the men could furnish the guts. One of the men said that we needed only someone to give the word and we could get out if guts and ammunition was all that was required.
>
> . . . We left our positions during a snowstorm and traveled all night across country unknown to us, to a destination which might be in enemy hands when we arrived. We were harassed by enemy artillery and patrols all night, and the night was bitter cold. We passed thru enemy lines during the night and reached our destination at day-light.

During the counterattack,

> Capt. Bartell's company was overrun by the enemy, but he rallied his men, took up new positions, and held on until the reserve company came up and

counterattacked. Capt. Comer's Co. was subjected to heavy and continued artillery fire, but he refused to let his men give way. . . . Several times the enemy surged up to his positions, only to be set back by casualties beyond what he could stand. Several times men in the several companies became rather panicky and wanted to leave their positions—some officers too—and it was only the leadership of these and others that prevented a rout, with terrible results. German officers captured were amazed at our resistance, since they knew we were an untried outfit.[38]

In the face of that December and January onslaught, small American units were cut off and surrounded but continued to fight. Pvt. Ormel Iverson Boyd ('45) had signed up for the enlisted reserve corps (ERC) in 1942 while a student at Tarleton State College (affiliated with Texas A&M), anticipating that he would be inducted as an engineering officer. That program, however, was disbanded, and by September, 1944, Private Boyd was in England, assigned to B Company, 393rd Regiment, 99th Infantry Division. On December 16, when his company was flanked by German troops in Belgium, Boyd found himself alone behind enemy lines. A German soldier suddenly appeared in the woods and fired at him, hitting his hand, destroying the trigger housing on his rifle, and knocking him to the ground. Thinking Boyd was dead, the German moved rapidly past him. Eventually Boyd located a wounded comrade and decided to stick by him until both could travel. Two days later, they both became prisoners of war.[39]

George A. Burt ('45), also in the enlisted reserve, left the A&M campus in June, 1943, for processing and training and by December was on duty along the Moselle River between Luxembourg and Germany. Pvt. William H. ("Bill") Huffman ('45) first saw combat at Hofen, Germany, on November 9, 1944, with the 395th Infantry Regiment, 99th Infantry Division. Wounded by shrapnel during the early days of the German attack in December, Huffman suffered a concussion in January, when a "screaming meemie" rocket shell struck near him. After surgery in Paris and some recuperation, he rejoined his division at Bruckenau, Germany, in July.

Pvt. Joseph Waymond ("Jake") Langston ('46) was trapped behind enemy lines in December. He managed to make his way back to Elsenborn Ridge just in time to be ordered, along with other survivors of the 394th's E and F Companies, to "create a diversion" as a part of the V Corps' counterattack. Later that month Langston was briefly hospitalized for trench foot and chronic diarrhea but by March was back with his company along the Rhine. Lt. Y. B. Johnson Jr. ('44), also with the 99th Division, despite being wounded, made it back to Elsenborn Ridge and helped hold the line long enough for the American forces to regroup. Pvt. Robert E. Maclin ('45), another ERC recruit, had also arrived in Germany with the 395th in November. His 2nd Battalion was near Elsenore when the Germans launched their offensive, and the unit was sent into the mêlée as reinforcements. Maclin survived the initial battles but was soon stricken by double pneumonia. He recovered in time to rejoin his unit for an attack across the Remagen bridge over the Rhine on March 11.[40]

In late December, during the fiercest fighting of the Battle of the Bulge, American defenders, reinforced by the 101st Airborne, held out in the pivotal town of Bastogne despite repeated demands to surrender. As the skies cleared on Christmas eve, American air strikes and a determined defense of key road intersections halted the German drive short of its first objective, the Meuse River. The Third Army, under Gen. George Patton, then broke through to relieve Bastogne. Patton later cited the effective job Gen. O. P. Weyland's fighter pilots had done in knocking out German positions and supply lines while covering the advance of the U.S. tanks. Weyland was then commanding the Eighth Air Force. Among the army air corps pilots in action over Bastogne was Aggie Capt. Andrew C. Sorelle Jr. ('42), a P-47 pilot who completed ninety-one missions and received the DSC, Silver Star, and other awards.[41]

On the ground during the Bulge were the infantry, artillery, and tank corps, including Lt. Col. Jack Barnes ('30), Lt. R. W. Gerlich ('40), Maj. Joe Slovak ('35), Capt. A. F. Moffitt ('39), Lt. Col. Herbert M. Mills ('39), Maj. J. Wayne Stark ('39), Lt. Col. R. P. Gregory ('32), Lt. Pete Frost ('42), Lt. James Wiley ('46; A. P. Wiley's brother), and Lt. William A. McKenzie ('44). During the month-long campaign American casualties exceeded 75,000, including POWs. Germany's losses approached 100,000. The big bulge in Allied lines made it the "Battle of the Bulge." By New Year's Day, 1945, the Wehrmacht was in full retreat, and by late January, American forces had recaptured the ground they had lost in the desperate German offensive.[42] But it had been a Pyrrhic victory.

The Allied push to recover that lost ground came at a high cost as every available man was rushed into the battle. For example, on Christmas day, Lt. Eli Whiteley and I Company, 15th Regiment, 3rd Infantry Division, went into action at Sigolsheim, France. Ordered to attack on December 26, the troops were unable to defeat the heavily fortified enemy. Whiteley's company commander was severely wounded, and 40 of I Company's 96 men were killed in the first attack. When headquarters made Whiteley acting company commander and ordered another attack at once, Whiteley protested that the attack would be a needless slaughter. The battalion commander threatened to replace him, but Whiteley told him he would kill the man who tried to relieve him. No replacement was sent. Assuming command, Whiteley reorganized his unit and quietly moved it into position under cover of night. At dawn and in the lead, Whiteley entered Sigolsheim and led a house-to-house raid. Although wounded in the arm and shoulder, he managed to clear the first house by himself, killing 2 defenders and capturing 5. After searching the next house, Whiteley used a bazooka to blast a hole in the third dwelling, killing 5 SS troops and capturing 12. Though he received a third wound from a shell fragment in his eye, he continued leading his men from house to house until German reinforcements

Lt. Eli L. Whiteley ('41).

forced him to evacuate. For his courage, aggressiveness, and leadership and for killing 9 Germans and capturing 23, Whiteley was presented the Medal of Honor by Pres. Harry S. Truman. The assault he spearheaded had cracked the core of enemy resistance and captured the village. Returning to College Station, Whiteley became a professor of agronomy and served on the A&M faculty until his retirement.[43]

In January, 1945, 2nd Lt. Heywood C. Clemons ('43), who had received his commission in May, 1943, and been held with reserve forces in England since November, 1944, arrived at the battlefront with the 302nd Field Artillery Battalion and fought his way into Germany. His battery fired the first artillery round into Germany (near Detweiler) in early February and crossed into the country under heavy fire. By March, Lieutenant Clemons and his "A" Battery had crossed the Rhine near Koblenz, where they began to observe firsthand the collapse of the German resistance.[44]

Many Texas Aggies fought in the Battle of the Bulge and were in the final drive into Germany, including Lt. Col. J. Earl Rudder, commander of the 109th Infantry Regiment. Rudder fought from D-day to V-E (Victory in Europe) Day and after the war achieved the rank of major general. Other veterans of the Bulge and the war in Europe were Maj. Jim H. McCoy ('40); Maj. Bert P. Ezell ('40) and Maj. James Hollingsworth, commander of the 2nd Battalion, 67th Armored Regi-

The 4th Armored Division, III Corps, moves toward besieged Bastogne, Belgium.

ment, 2nd Armored Division, and both with the 2nd Armored Division; Capt. Jack E. Golden; and Capt. Y. B. Johnson Jr. At higher echelons were Maj. Gen. Roderick R. Allen ('15), commander of the 12th Armored Division; and Gen. Andrew Bruce ('16; DSC), a pioneer of tank warfare in World War I.

Cpl. Samuel L. Jenkins ('46) received the Bronze Star for combat, and Lt. Mike Cokinos ('43) was awarded the Silver Star and the Purple Heart while serving as a forward observer for the 7th Infantry Regiment. Air force Maj. Gen. Robert B. Williams ('23) commanded the 1st Bomb Division of the Eighth Air Force. Lt. Jack Ilfrey continued to bring down the Wehrmacht fighters, totaling eight, while Maj. Glenn E. Duncan ('40) scored 19.5 kills, and Capt. Lewis W. Chick Jr. ('38) had six confirmed. During the first hours of the Battle of the Bulge, Lt. Col. James Earl Rudder, with his 3rd Battalion commander, Col. Jim McCoy, met the 5th Panzer Division on the Oure River—and turned it back. After rising to the rank of general, Rudder returned to Texas to serve as mayor of Brady and as state land commissioner before becoming president of Texas A&M University. Later, Rudder's comrade in arms, Colonel McCoy, also returned to Texas A&M—as commandant of the Corps of Cadets from 1967 until mid-1971.[45]

By January, 1945, Maj. James Hollingsworth had been in combat for more than three years while serving in eight countries on two continents. During that time he rose from platoon leader to battalion commander. In combat from the landing at D-day until he reached the Elbe River, Hollingsworth was wounded five times. Upon promotion to brigadier general, he became the most decorated general officer in the army. He was awarded three DSCs, four Distinguished Service Medals, four Silver Stars, three Legion of Merit medals, three DFCs, four Bronze Stars, and six Purple Hearts. Reflecting on his career, Hollingsworth captured the essence of the contribution made by the citizen soldier: "By the time I was twenty-five years old, I had commanded a force of more than three thousand men in battle. A battle is a real test of man. I felt that I had met the test of man in the face of enemy fire on the battlefield. I felt that maybe I owed something to my country by serving in the army—a responsibility to my country and to be involved in the training of young men. I don't know of any profession that offers a man who is interested in people an opportunity for leadership, an association with new people, training, and growth more than the army. It is an awesome responsibility."[46]

Among Aggie casualties in the Battle of the Bulge and in the Allied offensive across the Rhine into Germany was A&M's first two-time All-American football player (guard) and team captain, Capt. Joe Routt ('37), company commander. More than sixty members of the Aggie football teams from 1936 to 1941 served on active duty, including All-Americans Marshall Robnett ('40; at guard) and "Jarring" John Kimbrough ('40; halfback), along with team captains James H. Thomason ('41) and Tommie Vaughn ('41); Martin O. Ruby ('42), Marshall Spivey ('42); James Sterling ('42), C. J. Rogers ('43), and Elvis Simmons ('43).

Other A&M men who were killed in action in the European campaign included Lt. Jack Bailey ('41), Pvt. Monte W. Kaufman ('46), Pfc. Louden C. Doney III ('43), Pvt. Paul D. Chaney ('43), P-47 fighter pilot Lt. Robert E. Daw ('43), Pvt. Harry F. Goodloe ('39), and Lt. Foster L. Lemle ('42). Among the dead were Pfc. Herbert O. Koehler ('47), Capt. James F. House ('38), Lt. Jarvis O. Butler ('45), Lt. Joseph D. Longley ('45), and Pvt. John V. Cox Jr. ('47). Aerial gunner S.Sgt. Ward C. Gillespie ('46) died on his twenty-third mission over Germany, and Sgt. Lark W. Hertz ('45), a gunner, died on his twentieth mission, while navigator Lt. H. O. Borgfeld Jr. ('42) was shot down on his fifth mission. As the war neared its climax, Aggies killed in Europe included Lt. Alvin Cowling Jr. ('41), Lt. William G. Goodwin ('43), Pfc. Thomas R. Learn ('46), and Lt. Joe R. Clark Jr. ('43).[47]

Not since the time of Napoleon had the Rhine River been crossed by armies invading Germany. The key to the battle for the Rhineland was gaining control of the many bridges. While most of them were destroyed by the retreating Germans, in early March, the Ludendorff bridge at Remagen, although damaged, was still standing. On March 7, 1945, it was captured by the 9th Armored Division. The next day, Lt. James Posey Alford ('43), commanding a platoon of medium tanks, had reached midway on the span when he saw "a sleek, single-engine airplane coming at us low over the water. My thought was that the crazy pilot was going to fly under the bridge." But it was a Messerschmitt "Me-109G—with a bomb strapped to its belly that was nearly as long as the fuselage!" The pilot released the bomb, and it exploded in the river, throwing up a geyser of water. Antiaircraft gunners downed the plane, and Alford's tanks made it across. Those troops crossing, guarding, and repairing the Ludendorff bridge caught a glimpse into the future as the Germans used V-2 rockets, Messerschmitt ME-262 jet fighters, and frogmen in attempting to destroy the bridge. Nevertheless, the Americans held the bridgehead and quickly established sixty-two pontoon bridge crossings over the Rhine.[48]

Casualties in the last ten weeks of the war in Germany soared as stubborn resistance continued town by town. Among those killed in action were former A&M students Lt. Jimmie S. Knight ('43), pilot Lt. Marshall C. Dunn ('45), artillery battalion commander Lt. Col. Marshall A. Langley ('36), Lt. Paul G. Haines ('41), S.Sgt Gus T. Hodge ('46), Lt. Alfred R. Ehlers Jr. ('45), Lt. Donald H. Cooper 9'45), Pfc. Vick Clesi Jr. ('45), Sgt. Henry J. Canavespe ('45), Lt. Bryce C. Gibson Jr. ('45), Lt. Ernest W. Genthner ('46), Lt. James E. Connolly ('45; recipient of the Silver Star), Lt. Charles W. Carpenter ('39), and Capt. John E. Edge ('40). Captain Edge, who also held an MD degree from the Texas Medical School at Galveston, was on the front lines caring for wounded when he was killed.[49]

As the Allied offensive pressed into the German heartland, German fighter protection declined, and bomb runs over Berlin and the industrial centers intensified. On one such mission, while making a solo run on the rail yards at Berlin, a German ME-262 jet fighter came in so close to Capt. Roy McCaldin's bomber that "if I'd had a brick I could have hit him," McCaldin recalled. (McCaldin said that he was one of those Aggies who enrolled at Texas A&M in September, 1941, and finished eight years later.) Missing on the first attempt, the enemy jet came back for another run and blew off the right stabilizer of McCaldin's plane, shot up the right wing, and knocked out number three and four engines. Pilot McCaldin told the crew to "hang on" until they could reach the Russian lines east of the Oder River. They did—but barely. McCaldin was the last one to parachute out as the aircraft descended. McCaldin made it to the ground, got out of his parachute, and walked to a nearby road, where he found his radio operator sitting in a Russian's car. In time, McCaldin and several other Americans traveling with him arrived at the American embassy in Moscow.[50]

On April 12, as U.S. troops reached the Elbe River only one hundred miles from Berlin, Pres. Franklin D. Roosevelt, while visiting his Warm Springs,

Georgia, vacation home, died of a massive stroke. Harry S. Truman became the fifth vice president to become commander in chief upon the death of a sitting president. And there along the Elbe River, Lt. Albert ("Buck") Kotzebue ('45) and Frank W. Parent ('31) were two of the first Americans to cross the river and link up with the Russians. This marked the closest approach to Berlin by American army units before victory in Europe. Aggies on the Elbe staged a large celebratory Muster on April 21. The event chair and toastmaster was former cadet corps commander Durwood B. ("Woody") Varner ('40; later chancellor of the University of Nebraska). The festivities featured an old-fashioned Texas barbecue with all the trimmings. Those attending the Muster included Maj. Leo Bumgarner ('33), Maj. F. C. Smith ('37), Maj. Mark Hodges ('39), Lt. J. G. Fry ('39), Capt. Frank Pool ('40), Maj. F. A. Pierce ('40), and Capt. Joe M. Robinson ('38).

As the Allied troops halted their advance along a line that SHAEF considered to mark the completion of their mission to defeat Germany, the Soviet Red army continued forward and eventually took Berlin, Prague, and Vienna. Those final troop movements, it turned out, altered the balance of power in the region, resulted in Soviet domination of Central Europe, and contributed to the onset of the Cold War, which lasted for the next forty-five years.[51]

Among those for whom the muster was softly called on the Elbe was Jack Golden, whose "war bond" letter to his family in December gave a personalized view of the approaching end of the war. Golden was killed in action on April 15, 1945. In his last letter home from the battlefield, the twenty-three-year-old captain and decorated combat veteran seemed to be able to visualize the postwar world: "America . . . lacks sustained emotion in anything. Someday I will tell you why I think my children and possibly yours will have to fight again over this same ground I did and it will be a different and harder war. We have got to have military training in America for years and years to come. We have got to be so powerful that we can strike and strike hard in a very short time. We have got to build character, maybe I should say get hard and tough."[52]

Combat and casualties continued into early May, when emissaries of the German government, following the suicide of Adolf Hitler, signed an unconditional surrender in the old brick schoolhouse in Reims, France. Finally, General Eisenhower declared May 8 "V-E Day," and the official end of the war in Europe. The war in the Pacific, however, was far from over.[53] American forces worked their way slowly and at great cost across the vastness of the Pacific and through southeast Asia. The names of the islands and peninsulas they fought on have become a part of the American lexicon and a part of Texas A&M's military history and tradition.

Suggested Readings

Ambrose, Stephen. *Citizen Soldiers: The U.S. Army from the Normandy Beaches to the Bulge to the Surrender of Germany* (New York: Touchstone, 1998).

Cole, Hugh M. *The Ardennes: Battle of the Bulge* (Washington, D.C.: GPO, 1965).

Greenfield, Kent R. *American Strategy in World War II* (Malabar, Fla.: Krieger, 1963).

Lane, Ronald L. *Rudder's Rangers: The 2nd United States Ranger Battalion* (Manassas, Va.: Ranger Associates, 1979).

Mitchell, Johnny. *The Secret War of Captain Johnny Mitchell* (Houston: Pacesetter Press, 1976).

Ryan, Cornelius. *The Longest Day: June 6, 1944* (New York: Simon and Schuster, 1959).

———. *The Last Battle* (New York: Simon and Schuster, 1966).

Toland, John. *Battle: The Story of the Bulge* (New York: Random House, 1959).

Wiley, A. P., Jr. "War at Ground Level: The Experiences of a Combat Infantryman in Europe during World War II" (n.p., n.d.), 68 pp.

Over the South China Sea, B-24 bomber pilot Maj. Horace S. Carswell ('38) single-handedly attacked an enemy task force, severely damaging one ship before firing on a fully alerted fleet at only 600 feet above the ocean. He took direct hits and lost three engines. Nevertheless, he released his bombs and then flew the crippled aircraft over the shoreline. Carswell ordered his crew to bail out. One man's parachute, however, had been damaged in the attack, so Carswell decided to remain with him and attempt to land the plane. Unable to acquire altitude, however, he flew into a mountainside and burned. "Major Carswell gave his life in a supreme effort to save all members of his crew." He was posthumously awarded the Medal of Honor, and Carswell Air Force Base in Fort Worth was named in his honor.

11

WAR IN THE PACIFIC

The return to Corregidor and the final defeat of Japan was a bitter, bloody business. The mission took Americans and their Allies on an island-hopping, no-holds-barred, no-surrender campaign across the wide expanses of the Pacific and southeast Asia. By late spring of 1942, Japanese forces occupied territory in the Pacific ranging from the Aleutian Islands in the north through the Marshal and Gilbert Islands in the central Pacific to New Guinea and the Dutch East Indies in the south. On the Asian mainland they controlled Malaya and Burma and expanded their enclaves in China through Manchuria to the borders of the Soviet Union. The Allied counteroffensive hinged on regaining air and naval superiority across the vast expanses of the Pacific as well as attacking and securing strategic islands leading to the Japanese homeland. By 1943, the Pacific strategy had been modified to include bypassing and isolating selected strongly fortified Japanese positions.

Immediately after Pearl Harbor, the British and Americans created major theaters of operation for the Far East, which eventually became segmented into a North, Central, South, and Southwest Pacific theater; a China-Burma-India (CBI) theater, and a Southeast Asia command. In 1944, the war zones were restructured into two theaters: the Central Pacific, under Adm. Chester W. Nimitz, and the Southwest Pacific, under Gen. Douglas MacArthur. (See map on p. 83.)

Two great sea battles in the late spring of 1942 halted Japanese expansion. The Battle of Midway in the Central Pacific and the Battle of the Coral Sea in the South Pacific severely diminished Japan's air and naval power and gave the Allies the strategic initiative. In 1943, American troops expelled occupying forces from the Aleutians, dislodged the Japanese from Guadalcanal in the Solomon Islands, attacked enemy forces in New Guinea, and began the five-thousand-mile march to Tokyo by way of Burma, Kwajalein, Eniwetok, Saipan, Iwo Jima, Peleliu, the Philippines, Bougainville, New Georgia, Guam, Tarawa, and Okinawa, among other places. Pacific warfare proved to be one great octopus of a battle with many tentacles reaching throughout the entire area.

When Japanese forces landed on New Guinea in July, 1942, they were initially resisted by Australian units supported by native troops and New Zealanders with assistance from American engineering units. With reinforcements from the U.S. 32nd Infantry Division and the expanding presence of the Fifth Air Force, the Allies ultimately succeeded in halting the Japanese advance near Port Moresby on the southeast coast, turned back an invasion at Milne Bay in the south, and ousted the Japanese from their positions at Buna on the east. Col. Ernest D. Brockett Jr. ('34) left the oil fields of Odessa for military service in 1940 and fought in engagements at Lae, Finschafen, and Hollandia in New Guinea before going on to battles in Leyte and Mindoro. In the course of those actions, Brockett received numerous decorations, including the Legion of Merit.

Lt. Col. Everette E. Frazier ('32) also received the Legion of Merit for his work in New Guinea with the 875th Aviation Engineer Battalion. His outfit was composed of former career Buffalo Soldiers and African American recruits, who were responsible for the construction (and sometimes defense) of advanced airfields and fortifications, including a field at Tsili Tsili, west of Lae on the east coast, which became a particularly strategic field for fighter-escort refueling and rearming. During the course of the year, more than 12,000 Australian soldiers died on New Guinea, while American losses over a period of several months were 847 killed and 1,918 wounded. More than 2,900 men of the 32nd Division, which had been ill prepared and poorly trained for jungle warfare, were hospitalized with tropical diseases.[1]

In the spring and summer of 1943, the Combined Chiefs of Staff began to devise a new, comprehensive strategy for the defeat of Japan. The initial plan anticipated drives by U.S. forces on naval flotillas in a southwesterly direction toward the Philippines and due west from Hawaii across the central Pacific. Meanwhile, British and Chinese forces would thrust overland from India through Burma and China and also by sea from India via the Netherlands Indies, Singapore, and the Straits of Malacca into the South China Sea. The Solomon Islands, with New Georgia and its strategic airstrip at Munda, as well as nearby New Britain Island and its 100,000-man Japanese garrison at Rabaul, were primary objectives for the American forces in the Southwest Pacific. In the Central Pacific, the road to Tokyo lay through Tarawa and Makin in the Gilbert Islands and through Saipan and Guam in the Mariana Islands. As in North Africa and the European theater, Texas Aggies took part in combat and support operations in each engagement of the Pacific from Pearl Harbor to Hiroshima.

In June, 1943, the 43rd Infantry Division and the Marine Corps 4th Raider Battalion, supported by a naval task force, began the battle for New Georgia in the Solomons. Facing formidable opposition, they were later reinforced by troops from the 25th, 27th, and 37th Infantry Divisions. During that mission and related air and sea actions at New Guinea and New Britain, 1st Lt. John William Crow ('35) from Milford and Lt. Carl Bill Ehman ('43) from Houston were killed in action. Lt. Bobbie Livingston ('44), a Marine Corps fighter pilot who delivered a direct hit on a Japanese destroyer and won the Distinguished Flying Cross, survived the battles in the Southwest Pacific only to be killed during training exercises near El Centro, California, that same summer. Lt. Albert Dale Cotton ('41), a fighter pilot stationed aboard the *Saratoga*, fought in the New Georgia–New Guinea campaign but contracted a tropical disease and died at the close of the war in a hospital in Temple, Texas. American forces suffered some 1,000 killed and another 4,000 wounded in these early battles in the Solomons. By September, New Georgia and its strategic airstrip at Munda had been secured, but 2nd Lt. Thomas Ray Coffey ('43) from Sulphur Springs lost his life in the final days of battle, as surviving Japanese troops evacuated to nearby Kolombangara Island.[2]

Americans then landed almost six thousand troops of the 25th Infantry Division on unoccupied Vella Lavella island, fifty miles from Kolombangara, making the Japanese position on that island untenable and forcing the enemy to withdraw to Bougainville. Capt. L. G. Compton Jr. ('34) from Corsicana, a pilot with Eastern Airlines who had joined the air corps in March, 1942, was among those who provided air cover for the Vella Lavella invasion. After the 27th Infantry Division seized Kolombangara in October, the Americans next turned their attention to securing their flank with attacks on Makin and Tarawa in the Gilbert Islands and then focused on Japan's strongly fortified Bougainville Island in the Solomons.[3]

An Aggie who saw all of those actions from a unique perspective was Henry Bismark Ferguson ('32), who quit his job in oil exploration in 1942 to join the Marine Corps and his four younger brothers already in service. The Fergusons were one of three American families known to have had five sons in military service at the same time. One brother, Lt. George Ferguson, 3rd Infantry Division, fought in North Africa and was wounded in the invasions of Sicily and Italy. Brothers Robert and John were marines, while Charles was in the navy. All four of them fought in the Pacific theater, as did Henry, who served as an intelligence staff sergeant aboard Adm. William F. Halsey's Task Force 34 flagship, decoding enemy messages and disseminating misinformation designed to mislead and confuse the enemy.[4] As a result, the landings on Makin Island in the Gilberts, Choiseul in the Solomons, and Stirling and Mono in the Treasury Islands were partly designed to conceal the fact that Bougainville and Tarawa were the major Allied targets.

In 1942 and 1943, quick-striking, specially trained Marine Raider and parachute units were used as the primary tool for seizing smaller, less fortified islands. Maj. Jack Kenny Williams, a graduate of Emory and Henry College in Virginia, fought with the Marine Raiders and later led forces ashore on Saipan, where two Japanese bullets took him out of the war. Williams later served as president of Texas A&M University from 1970 to 1977 and was chancellor of the Texas A&M University system from 1977 to 1979.

Another Marine Raider was Cpl. Max E. Bergfeld Jr. ('46) from Seguin, Texas, who left the campus in January, 1942, to join the marines. He received basic and specialized commando training at Camp Elliott before being shipped out to the South Pacific to join the 3rd Marine Raider Battalion, 1st Marine Raider Regiment, on Guadalcanal. From there he was sent "to clear off a few small islands," including Bougainville, and then to Guam, where he was killed in action on July 27, 1944, "while performing as guard for a stretcher-bearer" carrying a wounded soldier away from the line of fire.[5]

By late 1943, it had become apparent that American forces were more likely to reach the coast of China across the Pacific before the British and Chinese armies could reach it by land. Given this assessment, American strategy began to focus on two lines of advance toward Japan: one across the Central Pacific via the Gilbert, Marshall, and Mariana Islands and the other through the Southwest Pacific by way of the north coast of New Guinea and thence to the southern Philippines. The Central Pacific campaign began in November, 1943, when Admiral Nimitz sent army and marine forces to the Gilbert Islands to seize bases that might support subsequent jumps into the more western Marshall Islands.

The invasion of Tarawa was assigned to the 2nd Marine Division, while the smaller and much less defended Makin Island went to the army's 27th Infantry Division. Landings on both islands began about November 20, and by November 23, Maj. Gen. Ralph C. Smith declared "Makin taken," with a loss of 64 men killed and 150 wounded. Tarawa was another story. There, despite a heavy preparatory naval bombardment, almost 5,000 Japanese defenders in entrenched positions (as opposed to the 800 defenders on Makin) met the invading marines with deadly artillery and automatic-weapons fire. In the first seventy hours of the assault, 980 marines and 29 sailors with the landing parties were killed. Among the attackers was marine Lt. Col. Raymond L. Murray ('35), who had recently received the Silver Star for action on Guadalcanal, earned another one on Tarawa, and won the Navy Cross on Saipan. The Japanese, characteristically, fought to the last man. Only 146 of the 4,690-man Japanese garrison surrendered.[6]

The battle for Bougainville also began in November, 1943. Until that time, Japanese fighters and bombers from Rabaul provided devastating air cover throughout the region and generally dominated the skies. The Fifth Air Force's task was to eliminate as much of Japan's air power as possible beforehand and then to provide air protection during the landings. Now, throughout October,

1943, from land bases on Guadalcanal and from carriers at sea, the navy and air corps launched concentrated air attacks against Japanese airfields and defenses on New Britain and neighboring islands.

From airfields in the Solomons, in late 1943, Jay Thorpe Robbins ('40) from Coolidge, Texas, flew a P-38 Lightning in support of a B-25 bombing mission over Rabaul. The attackers, badly outnumbered, were met by a "hornets' nest of Japanese fighters." With Japanese fighter planes overwhelming the American escort, the air battle, Robbins said, ranged at elevations from 200 to 20,000 feet. He shot down his first fighter at 300 feet, a second at 7,000, and made his third kill in a head-on attack at 15,000 feet. "I hit him dead center and he disintegrated." The fourth kill followed a near midair collision with a Japanese fighter. After a number of other "probable" kills and a malfunctioning engine, Robbins made his way back to an outlying Australian landing strip designated for emergencies. He emerged from the battle with numerous kills and a Distinguished Flying Cross. During those far-ranging October air battles, more than two hundred Japanese planes were destroyed. The enemy, however, was resourceful and unrelenting, and the battles continued.[7]

Landings by the 3rd and 9th Marine Regiments and the 2nd Marine Raider Battalion began on Bougainville on November 1. By midmonth the Japanese had been driven into the hills with substantial losses but remained powerful. Reinforced by the 37th Infantry Division and other units of XIV Corps, commanded by Maj. Gen. Oscar W. Griswold, almost 50,000 American troops were concentrated on Bougainville against 10,000–15,000 defenders by the end of December. Nevertheless, the Japanese, by no means overwhelmed, launched a final, desperate counterattack in March that failed, and by April the island was secure. On April 21, 1944, several dozen Texas Aggie warriors celebrated the close of the battle of Bougainville with a Muster.

In early 1944, combined army and navy forces under Nimitz landed well to the north on Kwajalein and Eniwetok Islands in the Marshalls. They hoped to use these as stepping-stones westward toward Japan through Saipan and Guam in the Marianas and from there to Iwo Jima and Okinawa. Brig. Gen. John T. Walker ('17), fresh from combat on Attu and Kiska in the Aleutians, commanded the 7th Infantry Division troops, who, with special forces and the 22nd Marine Regiment, overwhelmed the very lightly defended Kwajalein and Eniwetok Atolls. Walker was awarded the Navy Cross for his leadership during the assault on Eniwetok.[8]

American forces then headed for the Central Pacific with simultaneous air strikes on Saipan, Tinian, and Guam on June 11. This was followed by heavy naval bombardments of Saipan for more than three days, with landings by the 2nd Marine Division on the northern coast and by the 4th Marine Division on the south side of the island. Despite the fierce bombing and shelling, the marines took heavy casualties from the well-entrenched Japanese defenders, who, two

On April 21, 1944, several dozen Texas Aggies, with Maj. Gen. Oscar W. Griswold, commander of XIV Corps, celebrated the close of the Battle of Bougainville with a Muster. *Front row, left to right:* Capt. H. R. Gowan ('39), Estelline; Capt. W. C. Freeman ('40), Bryan; Capt. V. N. Burgess ('40), Dallas; Capt. J. B. Allen ('39), Hull; Maj. W. D. Bellamy ('33), Bryan; Pfc. W. H. Crawford Jr. ('43), Forney; Brig. Gen. William H. Arnold, St. Louis (guest); Capt. J. H. Campbell ('39), Midland; *center row, left to right:* Maj. Max. A. Mosesman ('36), Dallas; Col. M. F. O'Donnell, Phoenix, Arizona (guest); Lt. Col. James D. Edgar ('32), Cuero; Col. Hugh Milton ('24), State College, New Mexico; Maj. Gen. Oscar W. Griswold, Elko, Nevada (guest); Pfc. Leon H. Kainer ('46), Schulenberg; Maj. E. R. Poutra ('38), Houston; Maj. James J. Riley Jr. ('41), San Antonio; Maj. J. R. Dean ('31), Kilgore; *rear row, left to right:* Sgt. J. L. Bowman ('42), Victoria; Sgt. H. D. Calmelet ('46), Brenham; Pvt. R. T. Roznovak ('42), Taylor; Lt. C. J. Curlee ('40), Houston; Capt. H. M. Smith ('40), Lockhart; Lt. M. F. Bedner ('33), Chickasha, Oklahoma; Lt. S. J. Marwill ('43), Henderson; Cpl. John W. Watson ('45), Henderson; Pvt. D. K. Barret ('45), Comanche.

days after the landing, launched a furious counterattack using forty-four light tanks against the marines on the northern coast. Lt. Col. Raymond Murray ('35) had just seen action in Guadalcanal and Tarawa. Although he was wounded defending his battalion's command post, he continued to direct the action. For his leadership and bravery, Murray received the Navy Cross.[9]

As the battle raged on shore, two formidable Japanese carrier groups moved into the Philippine Sea off Saipan, determined to destroy the American carrier force and eliminate the invading forces on the island. One of the great naval and air battles of the war ensued: the Battle of the Philippine Sea. Lt. Clayton N.

DuVall ('42), with the 6th Fighter Squadron, Seventh Air Force, was killed in action over Saipan on June 24. That same month Lt. Ivy D. Kuykendall ('42) from Fruitvale, Texas, died in an air mission over the Gilbert Islands. The Japanese lost 330 aircraft and two carriers, including the Japanese carrier-flagship *Taiyo*, severely crippling the enemy's naval and air power and greatly enhancing the conditions for an invasion of Saipan and Guam. The U.S. Army's 165th and 106th Infantry Regiments of the 27th Division reinforced the marines. By October, resistance on Saipan had all but been eliminated, but the costs had been high. Again, Japanese soldiers fought to the death, with an estimated 20,000 killed on Saipan. More than 3,000 Americans died in combat, and another 10,992 were wounded or missing in action.[10]

The associated landing on Guam, which was delayed by the need to reinforce the marines on Saipan, began on July 21, 1944, and was led by the 77th Infantry Division, which had completed maneuvers in Louisiana in early 1943 before being transferred to Arizona for desert training. Maj. Gen. A. D. Bruce ('16) assumed command of the 77th in May, 1943, and after additional commando and amphibious training, the unit was sent to the Pacific theater. Amid the furious fighting on Guam, the attackers, General Bruce said, had to contend with mud, jungles, and tenacious, ever-present Japanese defenders. The 77th killed 2,741 of the enemy and took 36 prisoners while losing 267 men, with 876 wounded.[11]

Among the invading forces were the III and V Amphibious Corps of Fleet Marine Forces (FMF) Pacific. Marine Corps Brig. Gen. Victor A. Barraco ('15), after serving as provost marshal for Samoa and then chief of staff at San Diego for FMF Pacific, was a battalion commander in the assault on Guam. When the battle ended, he became provost marshal for Guam. During his service in the Pacific, Barraco earned numerous decorations, including the Legion of Merit, the Bronze Star, and a Navy Commendation Medal.[12]

Before combat fully ended on neighboring Saipan, the 500th Bomb Group arrived there, and Lt. Charles ("Chili") McClintock ('40) and other B-24 pilots from the group flew the first land-based mission over Tokyo on Thanksgiving day, 1944. The ability to regularly launch heavy bomber raids on Japan began to change the dynamics of the war. Subsequently, on April 21, 1945, thirty-nine Texas Aggies, including McClintock and Lts. Elwyn Shinn ('43) (who died during one of the first Japanese kamikaze attacks), Bill Barton ('45), Glenn McGouirk ('42), and Elvin ("Czech") Svoboda ('45) gathered to celebrate an Aggie Muster. The event took place in a rustic building that was specially constructed for the occasion and boasted an A&M logo and a Texas flag.[13]

In the summer of 1944, the reduction of Japanese naval and air strength in the south and central Pacific triggered a debate at the highest levels over MacArthur's proposal to finally "return to the Philippines." The navy preferred an assault against Formosa. In the path of either offensive lay Rabaul, New

Britain, but the Joint Chiefs decided an attack on that base would be too costly in terms of men, equipment, and time. They thus elected to encircle the fortress, neutralize it by air bombardment, and push on to a base in the Admiralty Islands, leaving Japanese defenders at Rabaul to "wither on the vine." The attack on the Admiralty Islands began on the last day of February, 1944, with 1st Cavalry Division landings on Los Negros Island aimed at securing an air base. An accompanying attack took place on Manus Island to provide an important navy base fronting on Seeadler Harbor. Both actions were essential to expanding regional operations against the Japanese strongholds.

The amphibious assaults on the Admiralties began with a high-risk reconnaissance landing to test Japanese strength and to secure, if possible, the Momote Airfield on Los Negros Island. Leading the assault was the 2nd Squadron, 5th Regiment, 1st Cavalry Division, and with them was 1st Lt. Sam E. Harris ('39) from Georgetown. Harris recalled that "We were outnumbered 4 to 1 but we managed to hold on until reinforcements arrived 3 days later. I was wounded during that campaign with a sniper's bullet through my left leg." A few weeks later, 1st Lt. Hugh D. Reich ('42) from Austin landed with a small reconnaissance group on a little island across Seeadler Harbor from Manus Island to select artillery emplacements in support of the planned amphibious assault of Manus Island. When the party was ambushed by Japanese troops and their Higgins boat sunk by mortar fire, Reich and the survivors swam in Seeadler Harbor for five hours before a PT boat chanced by and rescued them.[14]

As MacArthur's forces began leapfrogging up the northern coast of New Guinea toward the Admiralties, Capt. Thomas E. McCord ('40) from Kingsville, commanding A Company, 162nd Regiment, 41st Infantry Division, received an unusual assignment: "My reinforced company was deployed to Soepior Island, Dutch New Guinea, to aggressively patrol in search of Vice Admiral Senda, Japanese commander of Biak. One of my patrols was about to land on the north shore when it encountered a Japanese PT boat, manned by what we hastily identified as Japanese Marines. All patrol soldiers emptied their weapons, including rifles, light machine guns, and Browning automatic rifles, sinking the PT boat. 41st Division intelligence estimated that the boat was possibly evacuating Admiral Senda, who, to the best of my knowledge, was never accounted for. My battalion commander commended 'A' Company on its 'naval victory.'"

Serving with McCord in the 41st Division were Alfred E. Coffey ('39), executive officer of a battalion; Robert Trimble ('40) from Greenville, the division commander's aide-de-camp; and Merton E. Austin ('40) of Palestine, an artillery forward observer.[15]

During the summer of 1944, the Joint Chiefs of Staff (JCS) resolved the debate over whether the next major target should be Luzon in the Philippines or Formosa, off the coast of mainland China. Vice Adm. William F. Halsey Jr., commander in chief of the South Pacific area, concluded that the Philippines were more vulnerable than the coastal regions of China since Japanese air strength was unexpectedly weak over the islands and ground and naval activity had ebbed. On the basis of Halsey's report, MacArthur and Nimitz recommended to the Joint Chiefs that U.S. forces move against Leyte Island in the Philippines in October. The JCS approved the proposal, validating MacArthur's longstanding argument that American forces should recapture the Philippines at the earliest opportunity.[16]

The campaign to recapture the Philippines was preceded by attacks on Morotai and Peleliu Islands. In September, 28,000 American soldiers and marines landed on Morotai Island, located due south of the Philippines, and quickly routed the 500 defenders. With them was Maj. (later Brig. Gen.) Charles McQueen Taylor ('42), a liaison pilot for the artillery. Taylor earned the Silver Star, Air Medal, and other decorations in combat in the Philippines.

Also in September, the 1st Marine Division and the army's 81st Infantry Division attacked Peleliu in the Palau Islands group east of the southern Philippines. Among the marines was Harold ("Hagie") Warren Jones ('46) from Dallas, whose company spent its first night ashore in a defensive circle. When they pushed deeper into the jungle on the second day, Jones stepped out in front and was hit by machine-gun fire in the knee. After surgery performed on the island, he was scheduled to be sent back to the States. Instead, he slipped out of the hospital and returned to fight with his unit, only to be wounded in the same leg once more by shrapnel from a mortar round. Jones was treated and stayed in the battle.[17] On Peleliu, several thousand Japanese fought to the death and inflicted unexpectedly heavy casualties on the Americans. Nonetheless, these actions removed the final obstacle to the projected landings on Leyte and Luzon.

MacArthur's main assault at Leyte began on October 20, 1944, as four army divisions from Lt. Gen. Walter Krueger's Sixth Army landed abreast in the largest amphibious operation yet conducted in the Pacific. Vice Adm. Thomas C. Kincaid, who commanded MacArthur's Seventh Fleet, provided air and naval artillery support for the Seventh Amphibious Force. The Fifth Air Force, under Lt. Gen. George C. Kenney, gave land-based air support. As U.S. forces approached the Philippines, Japan began reinforcing its garrisons on Leyte and increased its land-based air strength in an effort to destroy Allied shipping in Leyte Gulf. Concurrently, most remaining Japanese surface vessels attempted to converge in Leyte Gulf to attack the invading fleet and destroy Allied shipping. The air-sea battles of Leyte Gulf were among the most critical of the Pacific campaign.[18]

The Leyte landings were made under the umbrella of the final great naval and air battles of the Pacific war. Kamikazes, Japan's special attack corps of pilots who flew their bomb-laden aircraft on suicidal missions, became a dangerous new element in naval combat. Beginning on October 23, the Japanese sent waves of aircraft against the American fleet, destroying the carrier *Princeton*, while American aviators concentrated on the Japanese superbattleship *Musashi* and succeeded in sinking it on October 24.

Lt. Sidney Caldwell Kimball ('41), commissioned as a navy ensign in April, 1942, died aboard the USS *Gambier Bay* when it was sunk during an engagement with enemy ships on October 25. The next day, October 26, Maj. Raymond Scott Evans ('36) from San Antonio was killed in air combat in the same area of the Philippine Sea. That night, Maj. Horace S. Carswell ('38), piloting a B-24 bomber on a solo reconnaissance mission over the South China Sea, discovered an enemy task force of twelve ships escorted by two or more destroyers and decided to attack. As the account at the beginning of this chapter relates, he did not survive that mission. During the air battles over Leyte and Luzon, Lt. Melvin G. Hass ('44) from Mission, Texas; Lt. James Edward Inglehart ('42) from Brenham; and Lt. (jg) H. B. Hales Jr. ('44) from Amarillo were all killed in action.[19]

Texas Aggies were also prominent among the two hundred thousand American troops of the Sixth Army, who landed on Leyte beginning on October 20. The 1st Cavalry Division, on the right of the four divisions assaulting the beaches, quickly seized the capital city of Tacloban. More than thirty Aggie officers, representing the classes from 1932 to 1945 (with five from the class of 1941 and twelve from the class of 1942), fought with the 1st Cavalry, most of them in the artillery branches. The anticipated Japanese counterattack was repulsed. After they pulled back, the Japanese continued a strong resistance with ambush their major tactic, while miserable weather bogged down the Allied advance, delayed airfield construction, curtailed air support, and allowed the Japanese to continue to ship reinforcements to the island. The clean-up was difficult, and costly.[20]

In early December, Gen. A. D. Bruce's 77th Infantry Division executed an amphibious envelopment of Leyte's west coast, and, by late December, the Sixth Army had secured the island's most important sections. During the last phase of the campaign, the 1st Cavalry Division drove south toward the western coast in an effort to close with the 7th and 77th Divisions, located to the south. There, Maj. W. A. ("Bill") Becker ('41), executive officer of the 61st Field Artillery Battalion, 1st Cavalry Division, had an interesting encounter: "We were moving our battalion to forward positions along the muddiest road in continued rain. Standing by the roadside as I passed was Major Clifford 'Mom' Simmang ['36], a favorite engineering prof at A&M. We exchanged a 'gig 'em' and a salute, and carried on. I ran across Aggies all along our path from Australia to Japan. After we got into new positions, Lt. Jim Sterling ['42] of Conway (right end on the 1939 A&M championship football team) spotted from an observation plane the remnants of a routed Japanese division fleeing to the coast seeking to be picked up and evacuated. Jim spent several hours and most of our ammunition supply attacking them—effectively."[21]

Combat and clean-up operations continued into the spring of 1945 under the

Maj. Horace S. Carswell Jr. ('38).

direction of Lt. Gen. Robert L. Eichelberger's Eighth Army. Generally preferring suicide, the Japanese refused to surrender and conversely took few prisoners.[22]

In December, 1944, the miserable plight of the Allied prisoners of war held by the Japanese worsened. As pressure on the Japanese defenders increased, they began to remove troops and war materials from the Philippines, as well as POWs (mainly survivors of Corregidor and Bataan). A major assembly point for transshipment was the Cabanatuan prison camp, deep in the interior of Luzon. In December, the *Oryoku Maru* left Luzon carrying war materials, wounded Japanese soldiers, and POWs to Japan to serve as forced laborers in the ports, steel mills, and mines as needed.

Executions, brutality, and starvation characterized POW life. Capt. Robley David Evans ('40), for example, survived Bataan and the Death March, only to spend the next three years in the Cabanatuan prison camp. His weight dropped from 190 to 100 pounds, and, like many others, he went blind from the lack of vitamin A and nutritious foods. The arrival of Red Cross food and supplements including liver extract, cod liver oil, and vitamins enabled Evans and some of the other POWs to eventually recover their sight. While Evans was held in the Philippines until he was liberated, other POWs intended for forced labor were packed into the holds of the *Oryoku Maru* and other unmarked transports such as the *Shinyo Maru*, *Enoura Maru*, and *Brazil Maru* for transfer to Japan amid filth and privation. Prisoners died on the *Enoura Maru* at the rate of four or five a day. On the other ships the toll was never recorded.[23]

On December 15, American war planes discovered the unmarked *Oryoku Maru* at sea and attacked. At least two hundred prisoners in the holds, including Corregidor survivor Capt. Cary M. Abney Jr. ('34) from Marshall, Texas, died in the first attack before the ship was abandoned. Another Corregidor survivor, marine Maj. Paul Armstrong Brown ('28) from Somerville and Galveston, made it to shore. There he was recaptured and taken to the Fukuoka Prison Camp on the island of Kyushu, Japan, where he died of disease in February, 1945. Capt. Sydney R. Greer ('35) from Tyler, who was taken prisoner on Mindanao in 1942 and transported to Japan, also died in an unidentified prison in February, 1945. Lt. Andy M. James Jr. ('41) from Dalhart was apparently killed when American aircraft attacked an unmarked Japanese transport on October 24, 1944. For many prisoners, however, the place and time of their death remain unknown.[24]

After the war, survivors of one POW transport organized the *Shinyo Maru* Survivors Association and provided information for a film production later shown at the Nimitz Museum in Fredericksburg, Texas. Some 84 men of the 750 aboard escaped the sinking freighter, but during the attack, the ship's holds were flooded, and many prisoners who were trying to climb out were machine-gunned by Japanese guards. Among the survivors was Maj. Rufus H. Rogers ('26), a teacher from Del Rio, Texas, who was called to active duty. Rogers earned a reputation in the Philippines POW encampment of "trying to look out for the benefit of men under his command, without regard to his own safety and well being." Rogers survived imprisonment and the war against over-whelming odds.[25]

While the battle for Leyte continued, MacArthur's forces moved on to Luzon, first seizing an air base on Mindoro to support the landings of four army divisions on the shores of Lingayen Gulf. As MacArthur poured reinforcements onto Luzon, the battle became one of the largest of the Pacific campaign. The landing, originally scheduled for November, 1944, was delayed in part because of the unexpected kamikaze attacks. In the meantime, furious air battles raged over Leyte and Luzon and continued from October through February.

During those air battles, Fifth Air Force pilots Lt. Albert B. Capt ('46) from San Antonio, flying a "Billy Mitchell" bomber, and Lt. James R. Collins Jr. ('45) from Gonzales, piloting a fighter, were shot down and killed over Leyte. Yeoman First Class Noah Horn ('38) from Lufkin died aboard the USS *Ticonderoga* when it was hit by a kamikaze. Lt. Ernest R. Alexander ('44) from Paris, Texas, ditched his Mustang on an island after a combat mission on February 26. He was taken prisoner, escaped, and was presumably recaptured and killed.

On January 8, the navy began heavy bombardment of the primary landing area at Lingayen on the east-central coast of Luzon, and on January 9, 1945, XIV Corps, spearheaded by the 40th and the 37th Infantry Divisions, made a largely unopposed initial landing, while I Corps encountered much tougher resistance. Inland, the resistance from almost two hundred fifty thousand Japanese defenders stiffened, especially as American forces moved toward the mountainous regions and began a drive on Manila, where new landings north and south of the city were conducted on January 29 and January 31. The Luzon landings have been characterized as the "longest and most difficult of the entire war," while the Lingayen landings alone "eclipsed in size [that is, in the volume of men and matériel] the invasion of North Africa, Sicily, and southern France."[26]

As the battle progressed, Gen. Walter Krueger ordered a daring rescue attempt of the remaining POWs in the infamous Cabanatuan prison camp, then located about twenty-five miles behind enemy lines. Based on the experiences of Lt. J. R. C. McGowen ('39), who led the first Alamo Scout mission on Los Negros, Alamo Scouts were sent to reconnoiter the prison camp. The rescue mission became the task of a reinforced company of the 6th Ranger Battalion. That special operation was a brilliant success: The Ranger force lost 2 killed and 1 wounded and killed more than 200 of the enemy. It also liberated 512 prisoners of war, including 100 disabled soldiers, who were transported out on carabao (water buffalo) carts. After the prisoners were brought to an evacuation hospital of the newly arrived 1st Cavalry Division at Guimba, they were treated, evacuated to Leyte, and then shipped back to the States.[27]

The 1st Cavalry Division was then given the high-priority mission of moving ahead of all of the other units to liberate the civilian internees and POWs at the Santo Tomás prison and seizing the seat of government (Malacanan Palace) in Manila. General MacArthur personally instructed the division commander, Maj. Gen. Verne Mudge, to "Go to Manila. Go around the Nips, bounce off the Nips, but go to Manila. Free the [3,700] internees at Santo Tomás. Take Malacanan Palace and the Legislative Building." When 1st Brigade commander Brig. Gen. William Chase was assigned the mission, he organized his "Flying Column" into three task forces, each to punch through separately to Manila as quickly as possible. The columns covered a remarkable 186 miles in three days, completely surprising the enemy and arriving at the front gate of the Santo Tomás camp on February 3. Simultaneously, the lead tank of the 8th Cavalry Task Force crashed through the gate at Santo Tomás University among cheers from the prisoners. With that task force was Capt. Jim Davis ('40), a fire-support coordinator who won the Silver Star for his performance. Also with them was Jim Sterling ('42) with "F" Troop, which peeled off to seize Malacanan Palace. Sterling wrote the following: "We were sent to Malacanan Palace; established security on the nearby Passig River; and spent a week in the 'White House of the Philippines.'"[28]

Another task force that also targeted the Santo Tomás prison camp included 1st Lt. Sam E. Harris ('39) from Burnet, Texas, and Capt. Hughes ("Buddy") Seewald ('42) of Amarillo and with the 5th Cavalry. After Seewald, who was commander of "G" Troop, was seriously wounded on the drive toward Manila, he was evacuated. He won a Silver Star and a promotion to major. For Seewald, the war was over.

The third column in the mission was led by the 44th Tank Battalion, which included 1st Cavalry's 302nd "eyes and ears" Reconnaissance Troop, commanded by Capt. Don H. Walton ('42) from El Paso. Shortly after the seizure of Santo Tomás, the 37th Infantry Division freed five hundred American prisoners of war at nearby Bilibid Prison. Among those rescued was Lt. Clifton Chamberlain ('40) from Marlin, who spent 999 days as a POW on Luzon and who lamented that, among other things, his guards took his Aggie ring from his finger. Finally, by early spring, American forces began moving into Manila, intending to seize it with minimal damage to the city, but heavy combat requiring artillery and air support erupted there and on Corregidor.[29]

After furious fighting, Corregidor fell to U.S. forces on March 2, and Manila surrendered on March 6, although fighting persisted as late as June, 1945. Even after the Philippines were considered secure, an estimated 250,000 Japanese soldiers remained at large, many of whom fought on tenaciously. Maj. Charles Benton Adams ('40), for example, a P-51 pilot, was killed on June 5 in a dive-bombing attack on a Japanese position in the mountains. In the past few months, Adams had earned the Air Medal and several oak-leaf clusters for his battles. Maj. Robert Balch ('39) with the 33rd Infantry Division had seen action in New Guinea and on Morotai. On June 8, Balch died of combat wounds he received two days earlier. Capt. Walter M. Hart ('42) from Gruver, Texas, was killed by machine-gun fire during a Japanese counterattack on May 28, 1945.[30] After securing the Philippines, the American forces began to move toward Japan and into ever fiercer battles at Iwo Jima, Okinawa, and Ie Shima.

As the Allies made spectacular advances in the Central and South Pacific campaigns, the war in Southeast Asia bogged down in a mire of conflicting national purposes. The United States hoped for great achievements on the Asiatic mainland but committed relatively few resources to that effort, depending instead on the British and Chinese to carry the main burden of the conflict. In early 1942, the United States sent Gen. Joseph Stilwell to the Far East to command American forces in China, Burma, and India and to serve as chief of staff and principal advisor to Chiang Kai-shek, the leader of Nationalist China and Allied commander in the China theater. Although General Stilwell's stated mission was "to assist in improving the efficiency of the Chinese army," the Japanese conquest of Burma had cut the last overland supply route to China and hampered American supply efforts. The only avenue was a long and difficult airlift from Assam, India, to Kunming, China, over the lower ranges of the Himalayas. Americans assumed responsibility for the airlift and worked with the Allies to reopen a land route to China, while establishing bases there for a force of B-29 Superfortresses. In the autumn of 1944, as Japanese armies were forced to focus more of their resources on the east coast of China, British and Chinese forces began advancing into north Burma, and by early 1945, the full route of the Ledo Road had been secured, even as American airlift capacity multiplied.

Japanese forces overran Burma and approached India in mid-1942, and Allied and American defenses in the region crumbled. Brig. Gen. William Donald Old ('24) oversaw the air evacuation of nearly five thousand sick and wounded troops from Burma, thereby preventing their capture, and became the key figure in the command structure of the USAAF in the CBI theater. Another Texas Aggie, Gen. Jerome J. Waters ('13) was sent to China in 1942 to organize a field-artillery school for Chinese armies that were being equipped as rapidly as possible with American artillery pieces. "Chindits," or "Special Forces," initially organized by British Brig. Orde Wingate, marched into Burma in 1943. A special "Galahad Force," the 5307th Composite Unit (Provisional) that the media called "Merrill's Marauders" for their new American commander, Brig. Gen. Frank D. Merrill, as well as a special air commando force, headed by Col. John Alison and Col. Philip Cochran, helped destabilize Japanese military control in the region. The Marauders and other units successfully began to undermine the Japanese forward positions by striking at supply depots, roads, bridges, and other vital spots behind enemy lines. These special forces, much like the Flying Tigers, helped stabilize the disintegrating military situation. Among the Marauders was Texas Aggie Capt. Newton Vincent Craig ('42) from Miami, Texas. In July, 1944, Craig died in an accident along the India border shortly before the Marauders were disbanded and absorbed by army and Marine Raider units. While the Marauders, Chinese, Indian, provincial, and irregular forces harried the Japanese in early 1944, the air corps, operating from bases on the India-Burma border, was particularly effective in providing the Chinese armies with arms and munitions. That assistance ultimately contributed significantly to the weakening of Japanese control on the mainland.[31]

Oversight for the air buildup became the primary responsibility of Alvin Roubal Luedecke ('32), who was deputy chief of air staff to the commanding general of army air forces in CBI from 1943 to 1946. Luedecke was promoted to brigadier general in 1944. Other Aggies involved in strengthening U.S. air power in the Pacific included Brig. Gen. William E. Farthing ('14), who commanded the Seventh Air Force Base Command in Hawaii in 1942; Maj. Gen. Howard C. Davidson ('11), who commanded the Tenth Air Force in Burma; and Maj. Gen. Edmond H. Leavey ('15), who attended Texas A&M for two years before transferring to West Point and ended his service in World War II as chief of staff for the armed services in the Western Pacific campaign. In June, 1944, Manning Eugene Tillery ('26) assumed command of the Fifth Air Service Area Command, which provided logistical support for the Fifth Air Force (New Guinea and the Philippines). After the close of the war, Brigadier General Tillery became CO of the Pacific Air Depot in Oahu, Hawaii. Air-combat readiness in the Pacific was also the responsibility of Brig. Gen. William L. Lee ('27), who organized and trained the Philippine air force between 1935 and 1938 before assuming command of the 49th Bomber Wing, Fifteenth Air Force.[32]

Although distant from the fighting front, other Texas A&M flag officers also made significant contributions to the war effort. Maj. Gen. Ralph H. Wooten ('16), for example, headed the U.S. Army Air Force Technical Training School at Boca Raton, Florida, and Maj. Gen. Robert Boyd Williams ('23) led the First Bomber Command at El Paso. After service with the Eighth Air Force in Great Britain, Williams commanded the Second Air Force at Colorado Springs, Colorado, which prepared pilots, personnel, and planes for action in the Pacific. Brig. Gen. John A. Warden ('08) helped train and reorganize the Quartermaster Corps, which would equip and feed the troops in combat in the Pacific and elsewhere. Warden served at Fort Frances E. Warren in Wyoming throughout the war. Rear Adm. Albert MacQueen Bledsoe, who attended Texas A&M in the fall of 1913 before going to Annapolis, served as director of enlisted personnel in the Bureau of Navy Personnel in Washington, D.C., from 1942 to 1944. Bledsoe played a major role in filling the navy's Pacific billets. In 1944, he assumed command of the USS *Denver* and won the Navy Cross and other commendations for his actions in the capture of Corregidor and the invasion of the Philippines.[33]

Admiral Nimitz had delayed the planned invasion of Iwo Jima and Okinawa from 1944 to 1945, primarily because the bulk of the navy's resources in the Pacific had to be shifted between the Central and Southwest Pacific theaters as they were interdependent operations. In addition, the war in the Pacific, for the most part, took second priority to the prosecution of the war in Europe. Given those limitations, the pace of the advance in the Pacific was all the more remarkable since, throughout 1944 and 1945, Allied forces took the offensive all through the Pacific and began the thrust toward the Japanese homeland.

On February 19, 1945, the 4th and 5th Divisions of the Marine Corps V Amphibious Corps led the landing assault on Iwo Jima. Despite massive air and naval bombardment, the defenders survived, and extremely heavy fighting and high casualties ensued. Lt. Benton H. Elliott ('41), one of two Texas Aggies who received a regular commission with the Marine Corps in 1941 and who had fought on Roi-Namur in the Marshall Islands and Saipan and Tinian in the Marianas, landed with the 14th Regiment, 4th Marine Division. By February 21, the marines had reached the base of Mount Suribachi, which was honeycombed with holes and caves and filled with Japanese defenders.

The progress up the mountain was slow and painful. Finally, a marine patrol neared the pinnacle and spontaneously hoisted a small American flag. This act became one of the most memorable moments and greatest morale boosters of World War II. Seaman Jesse C. Grady ('49), who joined the navy in 1942 and served in the Pacific aboard an LST landing craft until the end of the war, was there. Grady was also at Okinawa, Ie Shima, and elsewhere. He remembers best the morning of February 21, 1945. At sea for the past three days while landing

Sgt. William G. Harrell ('43).

marines, supplies, and reinforcements and removing the dead and wounded, Grady recalls that it was an electrifying moment when he saw the flag go up on Mount Suribachi. "The hair stood up on the nape of my neck."[34]

But the fighting intensified. Cpl. Philip Albert Davidson ('46) from Kirkwood, Missouri, died in action on February 22. One of his classmates, Cpl. Samuel David Hanks, from Snyder, Texas, was killed on February 23, and yet another classmate, Cpl. Monteith Talmadge Lincecum Jr., was killed a week later by a sniper while helping a wounded comrade. Lincecum had served with the Marine Parachute Regiment until that unit was disbanded. He fought on Iwo Jima as a flame-thrower operator with a demolition squadron.

On March 3, 1945, Sgt. William G. Harrell ('43) led an assault group attached to the 1st Battalion, 28th Marines, 5th Marine Division, against Japanese troops located in rugged terrain that was studded with caves and ravines. Just before dawn, the enemy infiltrated the 1st Battalion's position, and Sergeant Harrell killed two of the enemy at close range. The attack continued. Harrell lost his left hand and was wounded in the thigh. Unable to reload his carbine, he drew his pistol and killed an enemy officer who was about to strike with a saber. He then shot two more enemy soldiers who placed a grenade near his head and managed to push the grenade toward another charging Japanese soldier, who was killed. At dawn, the medics extracted him, still alive, from a mound of twelve enemy dead. Harrell had lost his other hand as well. He was awarded the Medal of

Honor for "exceptional valor and indomitable fighting spirit against almost insurmountable odds."[35]

On Iwo Jima that same day, Pfc. Jack S. Lipscomb ('47) from Palacios died in combat. Lipscomb, who enlisted as a freshman in 1944, had fought on Guam for seven months before landing on Iwo Jima. His brother, Ens. John W. Lipscomb Jr. ('44) was aboard ship in the Philippine Sea. Another Aggie casualty that day on Iwo Jima was Lt. Charles E. Harrington Jr. ('44) from Plano, who got married and then joined the marines at the close of his senior year at Texas A&M. About March 5, Japanese defenders launched a massive banzai charge against the marines, which was broken but entailed serious losses. Iwo Jima, the costliest battle in Marine Corps history, witnessed 6,821 killed and more than 19,000 wounded, while almost the entire 20,000-man Japanese garrison perished.[36]

Before mopping-up operations ended on Leyte, General Bruce's 77th Infantry Division received orders to land at Kerama Rhetto, a group of small islands twenty miles west of Okinawa, to secure a protected anchorage and a seaplane base for operations against Okinawa. During the preparations for the invasions, Japanese kamikazes struck Naval Task Force 58, which was bombing Kyushu, Japan, and supporting the landings on Kerama Rhetto and Okinawa. The carriers *Intrepid* and *Yorktown* were damaged, the *Wasp* severely impaired, and the *Franklin* disabled. Lt. William Perry Brown ('46) shot down four Japanese bombers during the air battles near Okinawa and received the Navy Cross, the DFC, and the Air Medal. Lt. Charles M. Nettles ('45) from Alexandria, Louisiana, flying with Marine Squadron VMF-221, provided fighter-bomber air support for the landings on Iwo Jima and Okinawa and received the DFC.[37]

Navy Lt. Joe R. Spiller Jr. ('41) of Houston, division officer of the aircraft maintenance division on the USS *Intrepid*, recalled the battles:

One day we were at general quarters fighting off a squadron of Japanese planes. Our 5-inch guns and 40mm pom-poms were repelling the attack when I saw one of the enemy planes get hit. With fire and smoke trailing from the fuselage, it crashed into the sea. That same day one of our planes was hit. The pilot tried to land aboard, but crashed into the after gun turret and the plane exploded, killing the pilot and a number of men on deck. The day ended as we attended our first burial at sea.

Another time at general quarters I happened to be in the Air Office when one of the officers in my division came in. He warned me that he had a peculiar feeling that I should get out of there. . . . He insisted, "I mean NOW!". . . I had started up the ladder to the flight deck when I heard a loud crash followed by an explosion. It was a Japanese Kamikaze carrying a 500-pound bomb. It had crashed through the flight deck and right through the Air Office where I had been less than a minute before. I had not been aware of God's presence on that ship before, but I knew at that moment He was not only watching over me; He was also protecting me![38]

During those battles the *Intrepid*'s planes played a major role in sinking the *Ya-mato*, Japan's largest battleship. On March 26, the 77th landed successfully on Kerama Rhetto, and the surprised garrison was quickly overwhelmed. Since Japanese soldiers and many among the civilian populations chose suicide rather than surrender, few prisoners were taken.[39]

Okinawa took a heavy toll on the men of Texas A&M, most of them young and now from the classes of 1945 and 1946. They had entered service in 1943 and 1944. The newly formed Tenth Army, commanded by Lt. Gen. Simon Bolivar Buckner, including the III Marine Amphibious Corps (1st and 6th Marine Divisions), the Army XXIV Corps (7th and 96th Divisions), and the 2nd Marine Division, struck at three different landing areas. With the 77th providing backup, the invasion of Okinawa began on April 1. Brig. Gen. Claudius Easley ('16) from Waco, Texas, assistant commander of the 96th Division, was among the first ashore. Radioman Third Class Calvin Floyd Ballard ('46) of Denton, Texas, died the next day aboard the USS *Dickerson* (APD 21), which was sunk while supporting the landing operations. Once the beachheads were established and the troops began to move inland, the battle intensified. Lt. Charles Glynn Ray Jr. ('42) from San Antonio, who fought with the 96th on Leyte before participating in the invasion of Okinawa, was killed on April 9. Sgt. Cecil Martin Holekamp ('45) from Junction, who had received the Bronze Star and was wounded during heroic action on Leyte, was killed leading his machine-gun section in an attack on Kakazu ridge. "He was a good soldier," his buddies wrote the family.[40]

During the early phase of the battle for Okinawa, General Buckner decided to land the 77th Division on Ie Shima Island adjacent to the northeast end of Okinawa. Ie Shima had an airfield and strongly fortified defenses on a 640-foot-high hill. On April 16, Gen. A. D. Bruce sent the 305th Infantry ashore on the southern coast near the town of Ie Shima, while the 306th landed on the western beaches closer to the airport. While the 306th encountered only light resistance, the 305th ran into heavy enemy fire on the beach front and were then struck by a furious counterattack. Bruce rushed in reinforcements, and, after a six-day battle, the island was secured, with 239 men killed, 897 wounded, and 19 missing. The Japanese had 4,794 killed, with only 149 taken prisoner. Among those who died on Ie Shima was one of America's best-known war correspondents and journalists, Ernie Pyle. The men of the 77th erected a marker on the spot where he fell: "On this spot the 77th Infantry Division lost a buddy, Ernie Pyle, 18 April 1945."[41] Ie Shima subsequently became an important bomber base for direct attacks on the Japanese homeland.

Meanwhile, the casualty list on Okinawa lengthened. Capt. Joe Benjamin Guerra ('38) from Carrizo Springs; Pvt. James Harold Henry ('47) from Crystal Springs, Mississippi; Lt. William Bryant Caraway Jr. ('43) from Weatherford; Lt. Jesse Lee Brown ('39) from Santa Anna; Pvt. Miles Joseph Luster ('46) from Clarksdale, Mississippi, a veterinary medicine student in the army student training program at Texas A&M; Pvt. John Galen Lawrence ('46) from Flat, who had been doing graduate work at Texas A&M; and S.Sgt. Ben Davis Cannan Jr. ('41), a machine gunner and navigator with a marine dive-bomber squadron all died in combat on Okinawa in April and May, 1945. Cpl. George Henry King ('46) from Seguin, with the 4th Marine Regiment, 6th Marine Division, fell in the assault against entrenched Japanese positions, which were "thick with guns" that poured concentrated fire onto the Sugar Loaf Hill attackers on May 21.[42] The sixty-mile-long, two-mile-wide island was occupied by 110,000 Japanese defenders who fought to the death.

Within a twenty-four hour period on June 18 and 19, Lt. Gen. Simon Bolivar Buckner Jr., Tenth Army commander, and Brig. Gen. Claudius M. Easley ('16), with the 96th Infantry Division, were killed in combat on Okinawa. Easley, who had carried out border-patrol duties along the Rio Grande in 1916 and served in the Philippines in the 1920s, was attempting to outflank a Japanese machine gunner by crawling up to the summit of a hill, where he could better direct fire. Another machine gunner, whom he had not seen, got him. Easley provided exemplary leadership on the front lines in a "setting of bursting mortars and flying bullets."[43]

Other Aggie casualties at Okinawa included Pvt. Phillip Francis Schaefer ('43), who joined the marines in 1940 and was serving on Samoa when war was declared. Seaman First Class John Batiste Roemer ('48) had only a brief time on campus before joining the navy. Roemer was killed when the USS *Pennsylvania* was torpedoed by a Japanese plane that had slipped through the radar. During this action, Emil Joe Chromcak ('50), fire-control man third class, was topside on the USS *Columbia*, a light cruiser, which was about 1,000 yards away. Chromcak, who left Schulenburg high school at midterm in 1944 to "join the Navy and fight the Japanese," enrolled at Texas A&M in 1947. After graduation in 1950, he was recalled to active duty for the Korean War. Lt. Ransom D. Kenny Jr. ('42), who had fought at New Guinea, Leyte, Manila, and Iwo Jima, was shot down and killed on a photo reconnaissance mission, and Lt. Roger Eugene Edwards ('46) died when both engines of his plane stalled on takeoff.[44]

In May and June, Japanese counterattacks and heavy rains impeded progress. Shuri, Okinawa's second largest city, was virtually destroyed before Japanese defenders finally withdrew. Finally, by mid-June, organized resistance had crumbled, but the disorganized Japanese units continued to fight. Ultimately, after three months Okinawa was deemed secure—but at horrendous costs. Almost 110,000 Japanese soldiers and an estimated 80,000 civilians had died, while more than 12,500 U.S. servicemen were killed or missing in action; another 37,000 were wounded.[45] Of the 12,500 who died, 5,000 were victims of the kamikazes—the greatest number lost in a single battle. More ominously, the battle for Okinawa offered a preview of the unspeakable toll that would be involved in an invasion of the Japanese mainland.

But the war appeared to have a long way to go. Although the Japanese mainland was now under direct naval attack and being heavily bombed by B-29s, Japan's ability to wage war on its own terrain was unimpaired. The examples of Peleliu, Manila, Iwo Jima, Guam, Ie Shima, and Okinawa suggested that invading Japan would be more expensive in men and matériel than all of the Pacific War thus far. Military planners began working on Operation Olympic and decided to begin with a massive bombing campaign of the Japanese mainland from land and sea, focusing on the strategic cities and Tokyo, while tentatively planning an invasion of the southernmost island, Kyushu, for November, 1945. This would be followed by an invasion of the mainland (Operation Coronet) in the spring of 1946.[46] Estimates at that time indicated that an assault on the Japanese homeland could cost the Allies one million lives or more.

A leading architect of the air offensive that sought to pulverize Japan into submission was Col. Carl R. Storrie ('28), commander of the 314th Bombardment Wing, based on Guam. He planned and personally tested a new low-level bombing technique that inflicted tremendous destruction in urban areas much more efficiently than traditional high-altitude random drops. To test his theory, Colonel Storrie flew a B-29 in a single-plane, low-level, night incendiary-bomb attack over Nagoya, Japan, in late 1944 and remained over the target for almost an hour, taking photographs to provide evidence of the technique's effectiveness. Subsequent bombing raids over Japan through early 1945 caused tremendous damage to strategic urban centers such as Kobe, Osaka, Nagoya, Nagasaki, Hiroshima, and Tokyo. Storrie received a cluster to his Silver Star for his work on the new aerial bombardment tactic. Over those same cities, 2nd Lt. Shelton H. Wagner ('44) made seven bomb runs flying a "new" B-29.[47] Although more effective, low-level bombing was considerably more dangerous.

Many Texas Aggies flew in raids on the Japanese homeland between February and July, 1945, and many were killed in action. Lt. Otis Forest Lowry ('42) from Quanah was commanding a B-29 Superfortress when he was shot down during a raid over Ota, Japan, on February 10, 1945. Lt. Richard Lanier Haxthausen ('44), a fighter pilot, died in a crash in Hawaii on February 23. First Officer Frank G. Albritton, a navigator on a B-29, was reported missing in action after a raid over Nagoya on March 25. Maj. John Charles Conly ('38) died in a crash landing after a Tokyo raid in March. During a previous mission, in an attempt to keep the plane flying, Conly and his navigator were trying to jettison equipment through the bomb bay after being hit by antiaircraft fire when some of the gear jammed the open doors. Conly lowered himself into the bomb bay and kicked the obstruction loose, allowing the doors to close. Sgt. Rex W. Hamilton ('42) from Andrews died when his bomber was being transferred from Tarawa to Los Negros in April. And as a reminder that the war was not at all confined to the Pacific Ocean, Capt. Walter J. Clemans ('40) died in April, when the troop transport he was piloting crashed into the Himalayas. Lt. Leonard Gage Larsen ('39), who left the A&M campus in 1940 to serve with the

Royal Canadian Air Force through June 1944, was transferred to the U.S. Army Air Corps. Flying with his bomber group out of Attu, he died on May 11, 1945, during a mission over Paramushiro, Japan. Among his decorations were the Canadian Star, a King's Commendation, and the DFC.[48]

On May 4, 1st Lt. John P. Bradley ('39), assigned to the aviation engineers (and who completed his education at West Point), died in combat. On May 25, Lt. Henry W. Heitmann III ('41), flight engineer of a B-29, died in a bombing raid over Tokyo. Heitmann had already completed 29 missions during his first year in the Pacific theater and held the Distinguished Flying Cross and other awards. Lt. Lawrence Smith Gready Jr. ('41) was killed in a plane crash near Rangoon, Burma, in May, after more than 100 missions with the 1st Combat Cargo Group in India.[49] The bombing missions and the casualties increased in June and July. Table 8 lists a number of the Texas Aggies who died in air combat during those months.

In addition to inflicting heavy damage on major Japanese industrial cities, American bombers began to hit smaller industrial sites in June and July. Japan had been badly battered by the heavy bombing, but there was no immediate hope that Japan might surrender and little evidence of a foreseeable end to the war in the Pacific. Millions of Allied troops, sailors, and aviators were preparing for Operation Olympic Coronet, the invasion of the Japanese mainland.

However, there was a resolution to the war in the making. On August 6, 1945, a lone American B-29 dropped an atomic bomb on Hiroshima. Three days later another was dropped on Nagasaki, while a massive Soviet offensive overran Manchuria. The next day Japan sued for peace. Japan had 1.6 million ground troops in the homeland and another 3 million under arms and deployed throughout areas of the Pacific and Asia that were still under Japanese control. Much of East Asia was still under Japanese domination when the war ended on August 15.

TABLE 8. Texas Aggies Who Died in Air Combat in June and July, 1945

Name and Class Year	Hometown	Date	Location
F/O Albert Campbell Deutsch Jr. ('46)	San Antonio	June 5	Philippines
Lt. Edward Allen Gripp Jr. ('44)	Port Arthur	June 10	Tokyo
Lt. Paul Howard Damrel ('42)	Pineland	June 12	Not reported
Lt. Paul Clifford Crouch ('44)	Barstow	June 21	SW Pacific
Lt. Leslie A. Evans Jr. ('45)	Wichita Falls	June 22	Kure, Japan
Lt. Harold T. Cobb ('44)	Gilmer	June 26	Japan
ART 1/c Jack Coogan Cameron ('44)	McKinney	June 26	Yellow Sea
F/O Charles Leroy Dickens ('45)		July 5	Over China
Lt. Weldon W. Dyess ('44)	Bryan	July 31	Nagasaki

A number of Texas Aggies witnessed the epic closing events of World War II. Among them was Lt. Charles ("Chili") McClintock from San Antonio. On August 6, 1945, while returning to base following a mission over Honshu, Japan, McClintock saw a huge, dark mushroom cloud off to the left of his aircraft. The crew were later informed that an atomic bomb had been dropped over Hiroshima. One Texas Aggie was directly involved in the events that led to the bombing of Hiroshima on August 6 and Nagasaki on August 9. Harry Igo ('41) from Clarksville joined the army air force after graduation and went to war as a C-54 cargo pilot. On July 25, 1945, he and another C-54 crew received a cargo from the chief of security of the Manhattan Project that they were ordered to deliver, in separate aircraft, to Hamilton Field, California. Unknown to them at the time, aboard each plane were small U-235 nuclear components. On July 26, they left Hamilton Field for Hickam Field in Honolulu, and from there they flew to Guam, where the atomic bomb was assembled. Igo had no idea whatsoever, he later said, of the part he would play in ending World War II.[50]

Thomas C. Cartwright ('54) just missed being on the receiving end of the Hiroshima bomb. In late July, following a bombing raid over Kure, he bailed out of his stricken airplane, the "Lucky Lady," near Hiroshima. Taken prisoner, he was sent into Hiroshima, where he was interrogated on July 30. Following the last aggressive questioning on July 31, he was put on a train for Tokyo. Six fellow crewmen from the "Lucky Lady" and at least four other American POWs known to be in Hiroshima died on August 6. Cartwright survived and was liberated at the end of the war.[51]

Flight leader Lt. Richard ("Rip") Collins ('45), with the 40th Fighter Squadron operating from Okinawa, was in the air near Hiroshima on August 9, providing escort to a crippled B-24. At 11:02 A.M. Collins "saw in the distance [over Nagasaki] an extremely bright flashing fireball, rising up through a cloud cover, rapidly growing in size." The "multi-colored boiling, growing, color-changing ball of fire" disappeared after only a few seconds, and "a tall, irregular stove pipe shape" began to reach to the heavens.[52] What he had just witnessed was, in effect, the end of World War II.

The war ended immediately after the bombing of Nagasaki, even though most of the Japanese military officers wanted to continue the fight. At noon on August 15, Emperor Hirohito accepted the Americans' terms of surrender "to effect a settlement of the present situation." By the end of the month American troops had begun occupying air and sea bases in Japan. The formal surrender was signed aboard the USS *Missouri* on September 2, 1945, by Gen. Douglas MacArthur and Adm. Chester Nimitz for the United States and by representatives of each of the Allied powers. Col. Tom Dooley ('35), aide-de-camp to Lt. Gen. Jonathan Wainwright at Corregidor in 1942, was chosen to witness the surrender aboard the *Missouri*. Also present was Col. Myron J. Conway ('17) with the adjutant general's department. Almost at the moment of signing, major elements of the 1st Cavalry Division, including many Texas Aggies who were to land and assist in the occupation of Tokyo, sailed into Tokyo Bay past the battleship *Missouri* while listening to the broadcast of the ceremony. The following day, September 3, in Baguio, Luzon, in the Philippine Islands, General Wainwright and Maj. Gen. Edmond H. Leavey ('15) signed documents formally accepting the surrender of the Philippines to the United States.[53]

On September 8, General MacArthur made his official entry into the city escorted by a squadron of the 7th Cavalry and the 302nd Reconnaissance Troop commanded by Capt. Don H. Walton ('42). "On the sides of his scout car was emblazoned *We've Never Been Licked*; flying from his radio antenna was the Texas flag."[54] Nothing could better symbolize the fact for Texas Aggies in military service that the war was over.

Suggested Readings

Bond, Charles R., Jr., and Terry A. Anderson. *A Flying Tiger's Diary* (College Station: Texas A&M University Press, 1984).

Feifer, George. *The Battle of Okinawa: The Blood and the Bomb* (Guilford, Conn.: Lyons Press, 1992, 2001).

Gailey, Harry A. *The War in the Pacific: From Pearl Harbor to Tokyo Bay* (Novato, Calif.: Presidio Press, 1995).

O'Donnell, Patrick K. *Into the Rising Sun* (New York: Free Press, 2002).

Owens, William A. *Eye-Deep in Hell: A Memoir of the Liberation of the Philippines, 1944–1945* (Dallas: Southern Methodist University Press, 1989).

Prefer, Nathan N. *Vinegar Joe's War: Stillwell's Campaign for Burma* (Novato, Calif.: Presidio Press, 2000).

Sides, Hampton. *Ghost Soldiers: The Forgotten Epic Story of World War II's Most Dramatic Mission* (New York: Doubleday, 2001).

Wright, B. C. *The First Cavalry Division in World War II* (Tokyo: Toppan Printing, 1947).

Of the more than 20,000 Aggies in combat during World War II, 953 died in combat, thousands were wounded, scores became POWs, 7 received the Congressional Medal of Honor, 10 were aerial fighter aces, some 14,000 served as officers, and 29 reached the rank of general officer during the war. Texas A&M had made a significant and remarkable contribution to the war effort, and now, for those returning from war, it was time to start living again.

THE IMPACT OF PEACE

The world, the United States, and Texas A&M would never again be as they had been before the war. As the armed services rapidly and sometimes chaotically demobilized and the soldiers came marching home, many in the army, navy, and marines remained on active duty both abroad and in the States, performing the considerable and diverse duties related to peace, reconstruction, and military occupation. Many of those who returned to civilian life remained on call, on active or inactive reserve status, citizen soldiers who were instantly available for war if needed. Some who returned to civilian life had difficulty finding their personal peace. They "alerted" when an airplane flew overhead; they slept with a pistol under their pillow; they took cover when an automobile backfired; they were, commented Brig. Gen. Kay Halsell II ('35), simply "tired and worn out."[1] It took time for peace to become the new reality, and by the time it did, the reality was already frayed. Hardly had the old war ended when a new kind of war— a Cold War—began to take form.

While the laying down of arms and the end of combat spread spontaneously throughout Europe upon the surrender of the Axis powers on May 8, 1945, tensions were already developing between the USSR and the western Allies. Two weeks earlier, peace had been confirmed by the first linkup of American and Russian armies along the Elbe River, a connection established by a Texas Aggie, Lt. Albert ("Buck") Kotzebue ('45). Under orders from the commander of the 273rd Infantry Regiment, Kotzebue set out with seven jeeps and a twenty-seven-man patrol from the American lines near Trebsen, Germany, to contact Russia's Red Army, which was approaching from the east. Initially they encountered seventy-five demoralized German soldiers, took their arms, and sent them back to Trebsen. Then they found a hospital full of Allied prisoners of war who

Lt. Albert L. ("Buck") Kotzebue ('45), heading a twenty-seven-man patrol, made the first contact with Russian armies approaching from the east.

were too ill to be moved but who both cheered and cried when the Americans entered, for they knew they were finally free. Kotzebue's column next entered Kühren, a town full of armed German soldiers who offered no resistance, and they gave chase to a fleeing German officer in a staff car. The patrol fired at the escaping car but were unable to bring the fugitive to a halt. After spending the night in Kühren, Kotzebue's patrol reached the banks of the Elbe and spotted Russians on the other side.[2]

Kotzebue was eager to make contact with the Russian soldiers not only because he was under orders to do so but also because he felt a personal connection with them. One of his ancestors had been a playwright in the court of Empress Catherine the Great; yet another relative was a famed explorer who discovered Kotzebue Sound on the northwest coast of Alaska. After commandeering a sailboat to cross the Elbe, Lieutenant Kotzebue explained that his mission was to bring the Russian and American commanding officers together. The Soviet officers, including Maj. Gen. Vladimir Rusakov, returned with Kotzebue's patrol and soon arrived in Mühlberg, where a banquet table had been set. The celebrations began. "Everyone was in the festive 'Spirit of the Elbe,' a spirit of comradeship, mutual sacrifice, happiness, and relief that the war would soon be at an end. . . . We toasted the late President Roosevelt, President Truman, Prime Minister Churchill, Marshal Stalin, and 'everlasting friendship' between us all."[3]

Peace came more slowly and sometimes reluctant in some areas of the Pacific and Far East following the formal signing of the peace agreements aboard the USS *Missouri* in Tokyo Bay and Manila, respectively, on September 2 and 3, 1945. There was a great sense of unease when advance U.S. units, including nearly thirty Texas Aggies with the 1st Cavalry Division, moved into Yokohama, Japan, to disarm the resident quarter-million-man Japanese army that could fight, should it choose to do so.[4] But they did not resist, and the occupation of Japan proceeded peaceably.

Ben R. Reynolds Jr. ('46) from Houston was among those who arrived in Yokohama and Tokyo soon after the close of hostilities. Scheduled to graduate in 1946, Reynolds was hurried into service as a second lieutenant in July, 1945, and sent to Manila. Assigned to Gen. Douglas MacArthur's staff at the general headquarters of the U.S. Army Forces, Pacific (GHQ-AFPAC), Reynolds remained with the group when it transferred to Japan in October. Yokohama and Tokyo, he said, were "totally bombed-out cities." MacArthur lived in the American embassy and had his office in the Kiechi Building across the moat from the emperor's palace. "The Japanese were friendly and accepted us," said Reynolds, who helped organize the American League of Japan baseball team in Tokyo, which proved to be an important peace initiative. Then, in September, 1946, when Reynolds had earned enough "points" to return home, he was separated from the army as an infantry first lieutenant. At the time, he was all of twenty-one years of age.[5]

John Allen Ater ('47), who began his studies at Texas A&M in 1943, joined the navy as a seaman first class in July, 1945, mustered out in 1947, was commissioned as a lieutenant (jg) in the navy, and returned to A&M to complete his studies in chemical engineering. Lt. Col. Charles F. Girand ('31), who had earned the Silver Star and Bronze Star during the Battle of the Bulge, made the transition from war to peace as commanding officer of a POW camp near Bretzenheim, Germany. The camp originally held almost one hundred thousand prisoners and was decommissioned in July, 1945, after peace settled upon the land. Girand then became the military governor of the city of Karlsruhe, Germany. Similarly, Lt. James E. Wiley, who left the campus for combat in New Guinea in 1944, commanded a POW compound there at the close of the war. In 1946, he returned to Texas A&M to complete his studies in civil engineering. Lt. Col. (later Brig. Gen.) Robert M. Williams ('38) from Greenville, Texas, remained on active duty and returned to Texas to head the personnel section of the Fourth Army's headquarters at Fort Sam Houston. Marine Sgt. William Harrell, who, as chapter 11 notes, lost both hands during a fierce battle on Iwo Jima and won the Medal of Honor, also returned to Texas after the war to serve as chief of the prosthetic and sensory aids service of the Veterans' Administration's regional office in San Antonio.[6]

As thousands of Texas Aggies remained at their duty stations around the world during the transition from war to peace, the hazards of military service continued to exact a toll. Lt. Benjamin Barton Isbell Jr. ('45), for example, served in the China-Burma-India theater and was killed in the crash of an army transport C-54 while returning to the States. David Allen Harris ('47), seaman first class from Houston, died in the National Naval Medical Center of an illness he acquired while on active duty. Lt. Charles Eldridge Harrell Jr. ('45) from Dallas, commissioned a second lieutenant in the Marine Corps, was killed in a flight-training accident in Deland, Florida. Lt. Taswell Fielding Hackler ('45) from Dallas, a squadron operations officer with the 340th Fighter Squadron in Osaka, Japan, died in an aircraft accident in late 1945, as did Lt. William Gonzalez ('44) from Houston, who was killed in a B-17 crash near Alexandria, Louisiana. Capt. Charles L. Hynds ('42) from Waco, who had logged more than 5,400 hours of flying time, was also killed in 1945 in an aircraft accident in the States. Lt. William S. Gordon ('43) from San Antonio died on Mindanao following the accidental discharge of another soldier's rifle. George Stevens Gay ('38) from Asherton, Texas, died in September, 1947, of a tropical fever he contracted while serving with the 3rd Marine Division in combat on Guam. Robert G. Dunphy ('43) was killed when his C-47 crashed into the waters of Cook Inlet near Fort Richardson, Alaska, in September, 1949.[7]

The end of combat failed to entirely stem the flow of letters, telegrams, and memoranda to the mothers, fathers, spouses, and relatives back home from the War Department. Gold stars continued to be placed in homes denoting Aggies "declared dead after being reported missing in action" and "killed in action. No other details received." And there were those who might have been at the front but who died stateside in the service of their country, such as Flying Cadet Duke W. Harrison Jr. ('40), who was killed in flight training, and Lt. Charles L. Babcock Jr. ('43), a D-day veteran with Patton's Third Army, who had returned to the States and was killed in a jeep accident near Camp Gruber, Oklahoma.[8]

The story of the return of Texas Aggie war veterans to the A&M campus offers a glimpse of the postwar dynamics sweeping the United States. Jim Carroll of the *Houston Press* captured this in a special series published in April, 1946, just as the return was beginning:

> Unsung heroes are everywhere among the 2,541 returned veterans on the A.& M. College campus. And if they have their way, they'll remain unsung.
>
> They are the boys who didn't make the headlines during the war.
>
> They weren't the first to contact the Russians. They weren't aces. They didn't get the publicity and honors. They just fought hard as small cogs in America's mighty military machine. Many were wounded. Many suffered less glamorous hurts, for it takes a great deal of all sorts of misery to make a global war. Many were decorated "for merit," not heroics.
>
> All of them did their jobs to the best of an Aggie's ability, which is all the way.
>
> Each is tremendously proud of the accomplishments of his individual group in the war, whether ferrying supplies over oceans or building bridges out in front of foot soldiers with Japs or Jerries taking dead aim on them as they worked. . . . They fought as a team.[9]

At the close of the war, most of the veterans, including Texas Aggies, simply wanted to come home and resume a "normal" civilian life—a life that they had never really known as adults. They wanted to finish their education, get married, start families, and go to work. Those aspirations were greatly facilitated in 1944, when Congress passed the Serviceman's Readjustment Act, better known as the GI Bill of Rights. This legislation provided educational grants and loans for returning veterans, as well as low-interest mortgages for housing, loans to enable veterans to establish new businesses, and the right to return to their prewar jobs. As a result, more Americans than ever before were able to obtain a college education, thus creating one of the world's largest trained, educated, and skilled labor forces. In the ten years following World War II, almost ten million veterans received tuition and training benefits under the bill. By 1947 and 1948, almost half of all students enrolled in colleges and universities were funded by the GI Bill. Indirectly, the bill subsidized the creation of suburban America, helped create a broad new tier of small business enterprises, and introduced an era of prosperity unequaled in American history.

Enrollments at Texas A&M rose from an average of 2,000 students during the period from 1943 to 1945 to 2,718 in January, 1946. Then, during the 1946–1947 academic year, beginning in September, enrollments more than tripled to nearly 8,700. More than half of those were returning veterans, many of whom were married. The administrators converted two dormitories, Hart and Walton Halls, along with cooperative (or project) housing facilities built during the Depression, into married-student quarters and began building family dwelling units under Federal Public Housing Authority contracts. In addition, some students moved trailers onto the campus, and local families opened their homes to married and single students.[10]

These students were veterans, mostly still young, but mature and experienced, with a knowledge far beyond their years. Their return was a story of war and a search for a personal peace. Among them was James M. McGraw from Fort Worth, aviation ordnance man third class, who had served aboard the USS *Enterprise* for two and a half years and fought the sea battles in the Philippines. In a torpedo attack on a Japanese battleship, his plane caught flak. As he told the story to a new acquaintance on campus, "The 21-year-old veterinary medicine student patted his left leg," hitched up his trousers, and revealed an artificial limb. Gene Howard ('45) from Wichita Falls returned to the campus after flying twenty-six bombing missions from England with the Eighth Air Force. He described his combat missions as a "milk run," in sharp contrast to his flight training, during which a wing fell off of his trainer over Tulsa. E. L. Byrd ('42) returned after three years of combat in North Africa, Sicily, Anzio, and southern France with a promotion to captain and a Bronze Star, about which he said, "It's funny about the military. They tell you to do something you should do, then if you do it, they give you a decoration." Now he was studying mechanical engineering and living in a project house on campus with his wife.[11]

Twenty-three-year-old Lt. Don ("Rocky") Sullivan ('50) from Winnsboro had flown thirty-one missions in a *Liberator* bomber, which earned him the Distinguished Flying Cross. J. B. Coolidge ('44), from Houston and also twenty-three, was a technical sergeant with the 106th Infantry Division during the Battle of the Bulge. His unit had crossed the Remagen Bridge with the 9th Armored Division. However, the worse thing that happened to him personally, he insisted, was when a guy in a truck threw a shell case out and hit him in the head. Many veterans resorted to such humor when queried about their experiences. Sam R. Nesbit from Dallas, who enrolled in management engineering, was also in the Battle of the Bulge with the 75th Infantry Division, sometimes referred to as the "diaper division" because it was composed of mostly eighteen-year-olds hastily called into service from the U.S. Army Specialist Training Program (ASTP). After surviving the Bulge and crossing the Rhine River unscathed, Nesbit had trouble getting an apartment in Bryan or College Station.[12]

Lt. E. J. Creider from Pittsburgh, Pennsylvania, and Lt. W. C. Abbey from Houston brought a trailer and located it in "trailer town," adjoining the north wall of Kyle Field. Both were air force veterans: Creider had served in the Fifteenth Air Force, and Abbey in the Eighth. Abbey flew twenty-six bombing missions out of England, while Creider was based in North Africa and Italy. Creider accused Abbey of being a "glory boy," arguing (as a crewman from the Fifteenth) that the Eighth Air Force had gotten a lot more publicity than it deserved. Their neighbors in trailer town included Lt. Joe Snow, who fought with the army engineers in Europe, and Abbey's brother-in-law, R. A. Smith, who had been a yeoman second class aboard a gunboat during the invasion of Okinawa, among other colorful experiences.[13]

T/Sgt. T. P. McKnight from Quitman, Texas, flew more than fifty-five bombing missions as top turret gunner on a B-17 over targets such as Ploesti, Rumania, and in support of the Normandy invasion. He earned the Distinguished Flying Cross and six battle stars on his Eastern Theater of Operations ribbon. In addition, McKnight was awarded the DFC after antiaircraft fire knocked out his plane's electrical system over Rumania, and in desperation he used bomb arming wires to effect repairs. His ingenuity worked, and his plane was able to rejoin the formation. McKnight returned to Texas A&M after the war to prepare for admission to law school. Travis Joel Smith from Wichita Falls, then twenty-four years old, had spent the past four years of his life in a Japanese prison on Java. A member of the class of 1941, he had entered service with the 36th Division in 1940 and was with the "Lost Battalion" when Japanese forces overran Southeast Asia. Wanting to forget the past, Smith declined to list his record of military service when enrolling at Texas A&M in 1946.[14]

Four Texas Aggies who returned from very disparate global battlefields moved into the four adjoining apartments of project house number one with their wives in January, 1946: Capt. A. J. Praeger from Big Spring, who served in North Africa and Europe with the Quartermaster Corps; Lt. D. L. Read from Fort Worth, who was in England with the Eighth Air Force; S.Sgt. B. R. Greer from Burnett, who fought in the infantry in the Southwest Pacific and mainly in the Marianas; and Lt. A. R. Crews from San Angelo, who was first stationed in Greenland and then transferred to the army air force to fly twenty-five bombing missions over Europe.[15]

John F. Roganac, an "old man" at age twenty-six, joined the air force early in the war, attended seven different air training schools, and finally saw combat as a bombardier and navigator on a B-25 flying out of Corsica with the Twelfth Air Force. His plane was nearly hit by a bomb that was dropped from a plane flying above his formation. "Did the bomb explode?" he was asked. "Naw," he replied, "it was full of propaganda, not powder. Printed matter for the French, but it dern near wrecked our plane." After twenty-three-year-old A. L. Akins from Franklin, Texas, spent twenty-three months of his life in combat as a marine in the Pacific, he said he hadn't done anything "special." However, he had fought on Eniwetok, Okinawa, and Ie Shima—and was nearby when Ernie Pyle was killed. "There were no decorations," he said, "just hard work." His roommate, K. C. Martin, then twenty years old, also confessed to "not doing much" while serving as a pharmacist's mate third-class corpsman with the marines. That "not much" included a Silver Star for rescuing a wounded marine under fire on Iwo Jima.[16]

Four other Aggies "shooting the bull" before going to class included Lt. Stewart E. Cartwright ('44) from Dallas, Sgt. Y. C. Grimland ('49) from Waco,

Lt. George R. Brauchle ('44) of Pleasanton, and Lt. James E. Melson ('44) from Mount Vernon. Cartwright served with a Corps of Engineers maintenance outfit in England and France; Grimland was with the 36th Division from Salerno through Cassino, except for an interval in a troop hospital while waiting for bits of shrapnel to exit his body. He recalled one day on the front when the "meat wagon" was being loaded: "It was rough that day. Corporals became company commanders just like that," he said, snapping his fingers. Brauchle served as a forward artillery observer for the 276th Armored Battalion, 11th Armored Division, of Patton's Third Army. Melson's combat tour with the 11th was cut short near Rheims, France, when his jeep overturned; he spent a year in a hospital while recovering.[17] To paraphrase Stephen Ambrose in his World War II histories, they were young and had been soldiers.

After those ordeals, college life could never be "normal" for many returning veterans. For example, Lt. (jg) Frank Wagenhauser and his roommate, Lt. Raymond Hawthorne, both twenty-two years old and from Dallas, had spent the past three years of their lives in combat in the Pacific. Wagenhauser had flown a C-54 cargo plane across the Aleutians and into Siberia from bases at various islands, including Adak. Hawthorne had served with a mortar battalion on Peleliu and other assault landings, earning the Bronze Star and the Purple Heart.[18] Civilian life for Wagenhauser and Hawthorne and most of the returning veterans was serious business, and they were determined to get on with it.

In 1946, to assist the large influx of veterans, the Texas A&M faculty and staff began a 7:00 A.M. to 6:00 P.M. workday for five and a half days a week and scheduled additional evening classes for graduate students. The pressure on students, faculty, staff, and facilities was extreme. In late spring of 1946, Texas A&M obtained the use of Bryan Army Air Base as it was being deactivated. It was well that they did. Many student veterans, unable to find housing on the campus or in the community, had simply taken squatters' initiative and moved into vacant housing at the air base. No one challenged them. By the fall semester, Texas A&M's "annex" became fully operational, and in 1947, the administration converted the site into an exclusively freshman division with an enrollment of about 1,500 students.[19]

To better handle the special needs of a predominantly veteran enrollment and to help rebuild the war-drained cadet corps, Texas A&M's administrators sought out some of their own. Durward B. Varner ('40), a veteran from Cottonwood, became the first dean of men. Lt. Col. Bennie Zinn ('26) was assigned as veterans' service officer. They were recruited to help accommodate the large number of returning noncorps veterans.[20]

In 1946, to restore the cadet corps, Aggie officers who had recently returned from combat were assigned as assistant professors of military science and tactics, including army Lt. Col. William A. Becker ('41) from Kaufman, Maj. John Cook ('39) from Carrizo Springs, Lt. Col. L. E. Garret ('39) from Pitts-

Victory Muster, 1946, with Gen. Dwight D. Eisenhower as the principal speaker. To his right is Col. Olin E. Teague ('32).

burgh, Texas, and air force Lt. Col. Dexter Hodge ('39) from Pledger. These officers and the commandants under whom they served, Col. Guy S. Meloy (who became a four-star general) and Col. Hayden L. Boatner (Stilwell's chief of staff in Burma, who later became a two-star general), knew well what it took to produce leaders.[21]

Student veterans, some of whom had been commissioned in the service, were exempt from mandatory participation in the corps, and most chose not to join. A significant number, however, elected to enroll in the ROTC program to prepare themselves to serve as officers if needed in the future.

In April, 1946, Texas Aggies held their Muster on campus in common with other Aggies still in service around the world. In one of his first major postwar public appearances, Gen. Dwight D. Eisenhower, now army chief of staff, presented the address for the victory homecoming Muster. In his tribute, General Eisenhower expressed his lasting gratitude to the Texas Aggies for their contributions to the war effort. Texas Aggies, he said, "lived up to the ideals and principles inculcated in their days on the campus."[22] Meanwhile, Aggie Musters in 1946 and for most years thereafter, as it turned out, continued to be global affairs.

"Somewhere in India," at a place identified only by their APO number, four

Aggies held a Muster: Lt. Col. Joseph D. Tomkins ('25), Capt. Ralph R. Thomas ('21), 1st Lt. Robert J. Cook ('40), and 1st Lt. Kenneth R. Jahns ('43).[23] Eleven Aggies in Calcutta, India, less reticent about their location, each anted up $3.43 to send back to College Station as a contribution to the Texas A&M Development Fund. They were as follows:

Name	Hometown
Maj. Max McCullar ('40)	Kingsville
Thomas M. Smith ('32)	Victoria
Capt. H. Albert Stroebele ('42)	Marshall
1st Lt. Billy C. Sanders ('44)	Dublin
1st Lt. Charles L. Taggart ('44)	Dallas
1st Lt. Henry F. O'Lexa ('45)	Houston
1st Lt. Henry Wahrmund ('44)	San Antonio
1st Lt. Donald Weihs ('45)	Sherman
1st Lt. James E. Gardner ('45)	Abilene
Pvt. Alvin R. Rees ('47)	San Antonio
1st Lt. Ben B. Isbell ('45)	Collierville, Tenn.

Several Aggies in Calcutta could not make Muster, including Capt. Thomas A. Head ('43) and 1st Lt. Jack Metcalf ('45), who had duty that evening. Two others, 1st Lt. Melvin R. Mirick ('42) and 1st Lt. Floyd Ellis ('45) were aboard ship in the harbor at Calcutta, waiting to start the long journey home. During the past few months, Max McCullar had commented, "Dozens of Aggies had passed through Calcutta on the way home, and now the few of us who are left aren't far behind."[24]

Those sentiments were shared by Aggies on Okinawa. In April, 1946, 1st Lt. Neil S. Madeley ('44), secretary-treasurer of the Okinawa A&M Club, wrote that "All of us are getting awful eager to get back to the States and even more eager to get back to Texas." He added that he hoped there would be room at Texas A&M for all of them in the fall semester.[25]

Quite a few Aggies remained on Okinawa, including Brig. Gen. William D. Old ('24), who had spent much of the war as commander of the 54th Troop Carrier Wing in Burma and now commanded the Fourth Air Service Area Command. Many Aggies on Okinawa were men from the classes of 1944 and 1945 who had ended their studies abruptly, received commissions, and been rushed off to the Pacific in anticipation of the coming invasion of Japan, an event that happily did not occur.

The "old" men on Okinawa included Maj. James M. Hamblin ('40) from Paris, Texas; 1st Lt. William E. Blair ('41) from Dallas (army air force); Albert W. ("Bert") Reynolds Jr. ('42) from Bryan; and 1st Lt. Thomas L. Jones ('42) from

Cisco. Those from the class of 1943 included Lt. Francis X. Fallwell of Dallas; Lt. Haskell L. Miracle of Wills Point; Capt. E. G. Bailey from Dexter, Missouri, and with the Veterinary Corps; and 1st Lt. J. H. Barrett from Beaumont. The "young guys" included the following:[26]

Class of 1944

1st Lt. Neil S. Madeley, Harlingen, AAF
2nd Lt. L. E. Dorley, Hamilton
1st Lt. Paul I. Bearden, Coleman, QMC
1st Lt. Edward E. Armstrong, Amarillo, AAF
1st Lt. Seymour B. Shwiff, Galveston
1st Lt. Richard H. Phillips, Dallas, Infantry

Class of 1945

1st Lt. Ben M. D. Newsom, Lufkin, AAF
1st Lt. Hector H. Mendieta, Bruni, CE
1st Lt. Robert W. Davies, Fort Worth
1st Lt. Glenn E. Tanner, Beaumont, AF
1st Lt. George C. Westervelt Jr., Corpus Christi
1st Lt. R. K. Williams, Midland, Cavalry

The Corregidor Muster, which commemorated those Aggies under Gen. George F. Moore ('08) who fought and died or were taken prisoner following their heroic defense, has become the most celebrated of all Aggie Musters.

In Tacloban, on Leyte in the Philippine Islands, a number of Aggies, mostly freshly minted lieutenants who were "not yet eligible for readjustment to Texas" and who could not get to Corregidor for the "big event," held their own Muster. Those present were R. R. ("Doc") Norton ('42) from Modesto, California; Jim Bamhart ('45) from San Antonio; L. H. ("Long Tom") King ('45) from McAllen; "Cy" Hogan ('45), Beaumont; J. L. ("Pat") Collier ('44), Harlingen; J. T. ("Johnny") Kantz ('39); Joe Mertz ('45), San Angelo; George Hughes ('47), San Angelo; R. D. ("Dick") Hembree ('47), Ballinger; R. C. ("Sparky") Adams ('42), Killeen; S. P. ("Sandy") Brown ('44), Beaumont; and Schuyler Kuykendall ('45) from Bonham. After their meeting, they spent the remainder of the day swimming and surfing in Leyte Gulf. It beat making war.

Among the seventy-six Texas Aggies who celebrated their 1946 Muster at the Imperial Hotel in Tokyo were speakers Maj. Gen. P. W. Clarkson ('15) from San Antonio, deputy chief of staff, GHQ, supreme commander of the Allied Powers; Maj. Daniel C. Imboden ('12) from San Luis Obispo, California, executive officer for the press division of the GHQ, supreme commander of the Allied

Corregidor Muster, 1946.

Powers; toastmaster Lt. Col. Gus A. Schattenberg ('27) from San Antonio, GHQ, Air Force Pacific; Col. I. G. Walker, instructor at Texas A&M between 1928 and 1932; and Capt. H. B. Gibson ('43), also from San Antonio, assigned to the 836th Engineer Aviation Battalion. The highlight of the event was "choice Texas steaks." Table 9 lists those who attended the Tokyo Muster.

Although the Muster turnout in Paris was disappointing, chiefly because Maj. Homer Fry ('17) and 1st Lt. Jack J. Keith ('44) were away and unable to organize things, they, along with 1st Lt. John H. Evans ('44) and 1st Lt. George H. Morris ('45), nevertheless toasted the Aggies in enough champagne to compensate for those who could not attend. The twenty-one Aggies who gathered in Munich, Germany, included 2nd Lt. Leslie G. Deny, 1st Lt. Joe B. Stewart, 2nd Lt. Clarence C. Burt, Capt. Alfred A. Baeucble, 1st Lt. E. A. Gordon, 1st Lt. Bobbie Stephens, and Lt. George W. ("Hap") Russell—all of the class of 1943. The class of 1944 was represented by 1st Lt. Carroll N. Morris, 1st Lt. C. J. Haralson, and Capt. Sid V. Smith. Three Aggies from the class of 1942 were 1st Lt. Leslie E. York, Capt. Vladimer J. Hornak, and 1st Lt. J. B. Carothers; the three from 1947 were Pfc. Milton L. King, Sgt. Jimmy W. Roach, and Cpl. Harold Golman; the lone Aggie from the class of 1948 was Cpl. Claude Robbin. The real old-timers were Maj. Fred E. Wilson ('29) and Capt. Ray S. Bartholomew ('27).[27]

Quite a few "old Ags" also gathered in San Juan, Puerto Rico, in April, 1946, to help celebrate peace. Among them were Col. William R. Irvin ('08), Lt. Col. Charles M. Webb Jr. ('27), Ulmont S. Allison ('27), Capt. Hugh R. Primm ('37), Capt. James G. Schoultz Jr. ('40), and a "new Ag," Lt. Horace B. Williams ('45). By the summer of 1946, many Aggies who had participated in the April Musters around the world were either back home or on the way.[28]

TABLE 9. Texas Aggies Who Attended the Tokyo Muster

Name, Class Year, Hometown

Capt. H. B. Gibson ('43), San Antonio	Harney Estes Jr. ('33), San Antonio
Maj. Daniel C. Imboden ('12), San Luis Obispo, Calif.	J. R. ("Bob") Latimer ('44), Fort Worth
Maj. Gen. P. W. Clarkson ('15), San Antonio	1st Lt. W. P. Kincy ('44), Fort Worth
Capt. Marche P. Sirick ('43), Strawn	1st Lt. E. L. McKinney ('44), Jacksonville
Capt. Robert M. Logan ('40)	1st Lt. J. C. Jagers ('45), Big Lake
Lt. William S. Potter ('44), Houston	2nd Lt. C. M. Cope ('46), Weatherford
Lt. Roy K. Nelson ('44), Houston	1st Lt. Roscoe R. Baldwin ('45), Kilgore
Lt. Joseph Paulekas ('45), Lawrence, Mass.	T/S H. M. Sorrels ('47), College Station
Lt. Fred Pochyla ('45), Waco	1st Lt. B. J. McDaniel ('45)
Lt. Harrold A. Osterholm ('43), Texas City	S.Sgt. O. M. Henry ('48)
Lt. Milton R. Thompson ('43), Dallas	Lt. George M. Wunderlick ('44), Dallas
Lt. R. C. Atkins ('43), Dallas	Lt. William R. Johnson ('43), Palestine
Lt. A. W. Wagner Jr. ('43), Houston	Lt. Robert L. Welch ('45), Palestine
Lt. A. B. Herod Jr. ('43), Houston	Lt. W. H. Culver ('45), Lampasas
Lt. Charles N. Adams ('45), Newton	Lt. Ben R. Reynolds ('46), Houston
Lt. Marvin F. Miller ('45), Florence	Lt. Harry O. Kunkel ('43), Olney
Lt. R. R. Anderson ('46), Gatesville	Lt. Bob Frymire ('45), Dallas
Capt. C. C. Mitchell ('44), Fort Worth	Lt. H. A. Pimlott ('43)
Lt. W. R. Marshall ('44), Dallas	Lt. J. H. Heir ('43), Wills Point
Lt. H. P. Shoulin ('45), San Antonio	Sgt. Don E. McInturff ('48), Lubbock
Lt. Jack F. Brown ('46), San Antonio	S.Sgt. Homer L. Faulkner ('45), Bellevue
Lt. E. A. Baetz ('47), San Antonio	QM 3/c Paul E. Webster ('48), Tyler
Lt. C. E. Crosslin ('44), Shreveport, La.	Lt. Gibney Kendrick Jr. ('46), Houston
Lt. Sylvan E. Ray ('43), Dallas	Lt. R. H. Rodgers ('43), Mineola
Lt. Frank A. Hollingshead Jr. ('45), College Station	Lt. R. M. Mullinix ('43), San Benito
Capt. Robert A. Greenhalgh ('39), Greenville	Capt. J. A. Bauml ('43), San Antonio
1st Lt. John M. Stout ('44), Fort Worth	Lt. George R. Thenn Jr. ('43), Dallas
Charles J. Rich ('45), San Antonio	Lt. H. N. Pranglin ('43), Pearsall
James R. Noblitt ('44), Dallas	Lt. John H. Lindsey ('44), Houston
John W. Reagan ('44), Kerrville	Capt. John M. Lawrence III ('43), Bryan
Lt. Joseph R. Hoover ('45), El Paso	Lt. Col. Gus A. Schattenberg ('27), San Antonio
Lt. Tom Rogers ('43), Colorado City	Lt. W. L. Beckman Jr. ('42), Baytown
Lt. Victor Lehmberg ('45), Mason	Capt. Roy E. Burnett Jr. ('42), Goose Creek
Bruce McCammon ('45), Dallas	Lt. Harold G. Freedman ('47), Dallas
Sgt. Joseph C. Cain ('41), Houston	Lt. George G. Galloway ('46), Livingston
Maj. Martin M. Daugherty ('16), Alpine	Lt. Donald S. Sandelin, St. Clair Shores, Mich.
Lt. Wm. H. Ogan ('44), Kansas City, Kans.	

"Last night, through the efforts of Major D.C. Imboden, class of 1912, and myself, we held a Muster at the Imperial Hotel in Tokyo. It was gotten up on short notice, without adequate opportunity for publication, but much to our embarrassment, with regard to food and liquid refreshments and space, some 65 Aggies attended. [Lt. Col.] Gus Shattenberger, class of '23, acted as toastmaster. I consider that it was a very successful meeting." Maj. Gen. P. W. Clarkson ('15), GHQ, deputy chief of staff, supreme commander of the Allied Powers, to E. E. McQuillen, April 22, 1946.

As powerful forces began to affect all of American society after World War II, Texas A&M was able to accommodate and even embrace change without really altering its central character. As in the past, the school retained a unique environment for training its students with an unparalleled spirit of leadership: "leadership," as Gen. Omar Bradley told the graduating class of 1950, "in the pursuits of peace, and if it comes to war, leadership in battle."[29]

By the close of the 1950–1951 academic year, most of the World War II veterans had returned to the duties, obligations, and pleasures of civilian life—as business people, farmers, ranchers, engineers, veterinarians, teachers, doctors, and lawyers. At the same time, many Aggie veterans of World War II had remained on active duty and made the transition from the heat of combat to the deadly chill of the Cold War. Some of these veterans soon joined the ranks of Texas A&M's flag officers, while many other returning Aggie veterans became, or reassumed, the dual role of citizens and soldiers, as active members of the army, air force, or navy reserves, or the Texas Army or Air National Guard.

After the close of World War II, participation in the ready reserves became an increasingly important avenue for continuing military service. Lt. Kay Halsell II, for example, who had served with the National Guard before the war, returned to those duties after the war. After graduation, he served in the National Guard and in April, 1941, began a one-year tour of active duty with the 7th Infantry Division's artillery school at Fort Ord, California. Following the attack on Pearl Harbor, Halsell began active duty as an artillery training officer and later moved to antitank warfare. He also helped train units for amphibious assaults in the Pacific. In 1944, he went to the South Pacific to help prepare the 1st Cavalry and the 43rd Infantry Division for the return to the Philippines. After returning to Texas in 1946, Halsell accepted a temporary appointment with the Texas National Guard as a captain in an engineer battalion that was just being organized. He ended his military career in the Texas National Guard as a brigadier general, having spent forty years primarily training citizens for the role of combat soldiers.[30]

A unique end-of-war experience was that of Kyle L. Riddle ('31). After he earned his "wings" and commission in 1939, he was sent to Panama when the war began to command a squadron of P-36 fighter planes, which soon converted to P-40s. In 1942, Riddle was transferred to the Fourth Fighter Command on the West Coast, where he trained pilots in P-38 Lightnings. In May, 1944, Lieutenant Colonel Riddle went to England to command a fighter squadron that flew escort during the intensified bombing raids preparatory to the invasion of Europe. In August, 1944, while serving as squadron leader, Riddle was hit by flak over northern France during an attack on a railroad yard. Although his plane was in flames, he landed in a field and was promptly assisted by the French underground, who had him back to his base in England within ten days.[31]

During those critical ten days, American forces were rapidly advancing toward Germany and the village in which Riddle was hiding, and he was soon liberated. Riddle recalls feeling immeasurable "happiness . . . and relief." By August, he had returned to combat and in October resumed command of his fighter group, which by now was flying P-51 Mustangs. Fighter-escort duty now shifted to the interior of Germany, where the primary threat was from anti-aircraft fire rather than from enemy fighter planes. On one of those missions, in early May, 1945, on the eve of Germany's surrender, Riddle's fighter escorts had a strange encounter: "As we approached the target from the north, we were out ahead of the box of bombers. I looked out ahead, about eleven o'clock to me, and maybe five hundred, seven hundred feet above me was this lone aircraft. It first looked like a P-38. That didn't make sense, because there were no P-38s flying except for reconnaissance. . . . The British had a Mosquito that looked somewhat like it, except for the twin tails." As the aircraft approached, Riddle saw muzzle flashes from its nose: The plane was attacking. Riddle's escort group armed their guns and attacked the intruder, which, they discovered, had "red stars all over it." The attack could have been an incident of "friendly fire," an anomaly, or a premonition of things to come.[32]

Colonel Riddle returned to the States in November, 1946, and was sent to Greece in 1949 with a joint U.S. military aid group, providing assistance to the Greek government, which was then at the close of a long, bitter civil war against Communist insurgents. In 1959, when Riddle returned to France to assume command of the 66th Tactical Reconnaissance Wing, based at Laon Air Base, he revisited the family that had sheltered him at the end of World War II. They returned to him the flight suit, shirt, and trousers he had worn when shot down.[33]

Like Riddle, Frederick H. Weston ('29) from San Antonio had walked out of college and into the Great Depression. In 1932, he had then been commissioned as a second lieutenant in the cavalry. After a brief period of training, Weston returned to civilian life to coach for several years before accepting a Regular Army commission for assignment to the Civilian Conservation Corps (CCC). In 1940, he was transferred for training with the 1st Cavalry Division; an anticipated one-year tour turned into six years of wartime active duty, with assignments as special services officer at posts ranging from North Africa and Europe to Alaska and Burma. After the war Colonel Weston thought about retirement but was "coerced," he recalled, into taking command and helping organize the Texas National Guard's 112th Armored Cavalry Regiment. He retired from the Texas National Guard as a major general in October, 1967.[34]

Clarence A. Wilson ('38) from Hondo graduated with a degree in aeronautical engineering and, after several temporary jobs in construction, decided to join the army. Wilson enrolled for special courses at Camp Bullis and, after completing the military requirements, received a commission in June, 1941. Upon arriving in North Africa in November, Wilson, then a captain, began preparing for the invasion of Sicily and Italy. His outfit, the 594th Signal Aircraft Warning Battalion, did not take part in the invasion of Sicily but went instead to Italy, where Wilson ended the war.[35]

When Wilson returned to Texas and civilian life, he decided to stay in the air force reserve. The Texas National Guard had a history and was much more structured than the U.S. Army Reserves (USAR) in 1946; it took time to build the latter into an effective military component. In 1950, Wilson became the supply officer for the 141st Infantry, 36th Division, in the Texas National Guard and played a key role in organizing disaster relief for Hurricanes Carla and Beulah on the Gulf Coast. Later he helped prepare the 36th Infantry Brigade to go to Vietnam (which did not happen) and in 1969 was promoted to brigadier general and commander of that unit. The National Guard, he concluded when he retired in 1972, "was a hell of a good outfit" and remained combat ready. "There is a lot of patriotism in the Guard, a hell of a lot. Most of the people believe in Texas, and they believe in the army, the country, apple pie, and a mother's love."[36]

Joe G. Hanover ('40), who ended his reserve military career as a brigadier general in command of the 420th Engineer Brigade, was among those who helped build that postwar reserve organization. He grew up on a family farm in McGregor, completed his engineering studies in 1940, and worked for a time with the Texas Highway Department. In February, 1941, he was called to active duty with the 54th Coast Artillery and served on both the East and West Coasts until he joined the 519th Engineering Maintenance Division. Hanover was then sent to Europe as a company commander and debarked at Le Havre, France, in February, 1944. Later his unit became involved primarily in assisting with the movement of troops back to the States.[37]

On his return to Texas in 1946, Hanover remained in the army reserves, which he found disorganized and unfocused. By the late 1940s things had improved, which is fortunate because "the Korean War was right around the corner." Hanover helped organize the 420th Engineer Brigade, one of four existing in the United States. This unit was designed to provide the technical knowledge, skills, and resources required to complete major engineering tasks, such as the construction of everything from roads and bridges to buildings and fortifications. Hanover retired as a district engineer of the Texas Highway Department and completed his reserve duty at the rank of brigadier general.[38]

After World War II large numbers of Texas Aggie veterans continued a military affiliation by either remaining on active duty, joining active and inactive reserve units, or becoming members of the Texas National Guard. Nationwide, the result was that, by 1950, despite demobilization and a drastic downsizing of the armed forces, the United States had a cadre of combat-ready officers and troops available for service. This group could become the nucleus of an expanded modern army, should the need arise—and it soon did.

Peace became both elusive and fragile as the Allied victory over the Axis powers invoked major compromises and potential conflicts. Foremost was the partition of Germany into four military-occupation zones, each of which was governed individually by France, Great Britain, the United States, and the Soviet Union, pending return to self-government. The practical result was the division of Germany into east and west zones, with the eastern section governed by the communist Soviet Union and the western sectors by the democratic Allied Powers.

Germany's former capital city, Berlin, seventy-five miles inside the Russian sector, was itself divided into an eastern sector under the control of the Soviet Union and the remainder under Allied authority. Also, even before combat ceased, the Soviet Union began to impose communist governments on the territories it controlled, while the western Allies sought to check Soviet expansion and establish democratic governments in the occupied nations. By the end of 1949, as peace appeared to be evaporating, the United States and its allies were preparing for a ground and possibly nuclear war with China and Russia and their communist satellites.

Suggested Readings

Ambrose, Stephen E. *Rise to Globalism: American Foreign Policy since 1938*, 5th ed. (New York: Penguin Books, 1988).

Brands, H. W., Jr. *The Devil We Knew: Americans and the Cold War* (New York: Oxford University Press, 1993).

Harris, Seymour E. *The European Recovery Program* (Cambridge: Harvard University Press, 1948).

LeFeber, Walter. *America, Russia, and the Cold War, 1945–1980*, 7th ed. (New York: McGraw-Hill, 1993).

McCullough, David G. *Truman* (New York: Simon and Schuster, 1992).

Miller, Roger G. *To Save a City: The Berlin Airlift, 1948–1949* (College Station: Texas A&M University Press, 2001).

Four-star general Bernard Schriever ('31) flew more than sixty-three combat missions in B-17s and B-25s and served as commander of advance headquarters for the Far East Air Service during World War II. He later organized the air force program that built America's Atlas, Titan, and Minuteman booster and missile systems, which constituted a key element of the National Aeronautics and Space Administration (NASA). In 1998, Falcon Air Force Base in Colorado was renamed in Schriever's honor.

THE COLD WAR

"Being completely surrounded by not-too-friendly forces isn't so good on the nerves," 1st Lt. Robert M. Shuffler ('43) wrote in April, 1946, from Berlin.[1] There, Americans troops had begun to witness the transformation of the warm Soviet-American meetings and greetings that had ended World War II into what soon became known as the Cold War, a protracted confrontation between East and West. Shuffler was one of many Texas Aggies with the American occupation forces in the divided city of Berlin (table 10).

The situation in Berlin became increasingly tense as what Prime Minister Winston Churchill referred to in 1946 as an "iron curtain" fell across Europe. In 1947, the United States adopted the Truman Doctrine, which committed the nation to the military, diplomatic, and economic containment of communism. Congress approved the Marshall Plan, which provided American economic assistance to help reduce "hunger, poverty, desperation, and chaos" and to restore the economic welfare and independence of nations under threat of communist aggression.

On June 23, 1948, the Soviet Union clamped a tight blockade around the western sectors of Berlin. Pres. Harry S. Truman responded by sending cargo planes, rather than armored divisions, into the city. Within a year, round-the-clock relief flights by C-54s had packed in about 2.5 million tons of food and supplies to the beleaguered residents and military personnel isolated behind Soviet military lines. Lt. Edwin Glazener ('45), who earned his MD while in the military, and thousands of other personnel assisted in the "Berlin airlift." Glazener later said that he did not want anyone to think "I equate being in the Airlift with being in the fighting," but this mission took the United States to the precipice of combat. Among those managing the Berlin airlift's logistical

TABLE 10. Texas Aggies in West Berlin, 1946

Name and Class Year	Post	Hometown
1st Lt. Joe Biry ('45)	HQ Co., 3rd Bn., 3rd Infantry	D'Hanis, Tex.
1st Lt. E. H. Cook ('45)	303rd Engineer Bn., 78th Infantry	Ardmore, Okla.
Pfc. F. M. Floyd ('47)	Co. B, 3110th Sig. Sv. Bn.	
1st Lt. B. W. Frierson ('45)	HQ Command, OMGUS*	
Capt. O. C. Hope ('42)	1st Armored Co., OMGUS*	
Pfc. J. B. Jones ('47)	HQ Co., 3110th Sig. Sv. Bn.	Ranger, Tex.
1st Lt. Jack D. King ('44)	252nd Engineer Combat Bn.	Texarkana, Tex.
Pfc. E. S. Mayer Jr. ('47)	3712th QM Truck Co., OMGUS*	Sonora, Tex.
1st Lt. Leslie Peden ('43)	B Co., 1st Bn., 3rd Inf.	
1st Lt. H. W. Saunders ('44)	1151st Engineer Combat Bn.	Abilene, Tex.
W. G. Waggener ('44)	POW and Displaced Persons Division, OMGUS*	

*OMGUS Occupation Military Government, United States

supply effort was Brig. Gen. John M. Kenderdine ('34) from Fort Worth, Texas, who helped organize the joint military defense supply agency.[2]

In 1949, ten European nations, along with the United States and Canada, organized the North Atlantic Treaty Organization, which was committed to the defense of each of its members. Also at this time, the Chinese government of Chiang Kai-shek lost its war with communist forces led by Mao Tse Tung and retreated to the island of Formosa. By the end of 1949, the United States and its NATO allies appeared poised on the brink of a new and greater world war against China, Russia, and their communist satellites. The peace and national security that Americans had bought at so great a sacrifice appeared in jeopardy. In September, 1949, in a direct challenge to U.S. security, Russia exploded an atomic warhead, and over the next decade the wire fence dividing Berlin between the East and West became a wall.

The Cold War, an ideological and economic conflict laced with unending diplomatic confrontations and the threat of nuclear war on a global scale, was intermittently shattered by civil, regional, and border wars and military actions. Behind the iron curtain, in the words of President Truman, "lay the capitals of the ancient states of central and eastern Europe" under the domination of the Soviet Union and the communist system. There, he said, a way of life based upon the will of the minority was being imposed upon the majority through "terror and oppression, a controlled press and radio, fixed elections, and the suppression of personal freedoms." The Truman Doctrine stated America's intent to assist free peoples in resisting subjugation by armed minorities or outside forces, while the Marshall Plan committed first $17 billion and then, by

1960, $60 billion to assist Western Europe and Great Britain in economic recovery and to thwart communist subversion. Under NATO's unified military, the United States began to rebuild the armies it had so recently dismantled and to strengthen its forces stationed in Europe.

At home, educational advancement, coupled with active military training and reserve duty, became a significant part of the "arsenal of peace." For example, air force Sgts. Abraham L. Richmond from Jefferson; John C. Diebel from Elgin; and Willie A. Crabtree from Gladewater all enlisted in the air corps in 1945 and served in Germany during the inception of the Cold War. Diebel was in an intelligence division at Wiesbaden; Richmond was attached to Rhein-Main Air Force Base servicing airlift transports; and Crabtree was located at a nearby remote-communications station. All three returned to Texas A&M in 1949, graduated with the class of 1953, and received commissions in the air force. In like manner, Robert H. ("Bones") Allen ('51) finished high school in Houston in 1946, joined the army, and served in Japan as a private first class with the military police before returning to Texas A&M in 1948 to complete his education under the GI Bill, as did so many other young men.[3]

Similarly, Eivind H. Johansen ('50) enlisted in the army in June, 1945, following his graduation from high school in Port Arthur, Texas. He then left the army in January, 1947, at the rank of staff sergeant, to enroll at Texas A&M. After his graduation in June, 1950, 2nd Lt. Johansen returned to duty and to Germany with the 5th Field Artillery Battalion, 1st Infantry Division. By the time he retired from the armed services as commanding general of the U.S. Army Aviation Systems Command, Lieutenant General Johansen had served in diverse places such as Berlin, Korea, and Vietnam and was awarded the Legion of Merit, Bronze Star, and numerous other citations.[4]

In the initial three years of the Cold War, 1946–1949, which witnessed a rising confrontation between the western Allies and their former Soviet comrades, the fragile postwar peace in the Far East also disintegrated. When the war ended, large numbers of American soldiers were in China supporting the Nationalist Chinese. Texas Aggie soldiers in Shanghai, China, in April, 1946, included Capt. Homer E. Pace ('43), CID agent Henry F. Potthast ('38), Sgt. James C. Crow ('42), and Lt. John F. Whilden ('43). Also there from the class of 1944 were Lts. Frank R. Nye, Paul T. Goins, Robert Buniva, and Gordon W. Hurd, while Lts. Eugene R. Dillon, Alvin B. Wooten, and Hugh O. Walker Jr., class of 1945, and Lt. Barton B. Wallace Jr. ('47) and Seaman 1/c Weldon R. Holbrooks ('48) were also on hand. Other Aggies with the American forces in Chungking, China, included Capt. Alexander ("Doc") Munson ('43), Lt. Ed Rollman ('44), assigned to the 1st Cavalry Division headquartered in Tokyo, Sgt. Nick Sabonovich ('45), and Lt. William A. ("Kizer") Wright ('44).[5] Although most of the American troops were withdrawn from China by the close of 1946, many remained until 1949, when the Nationalist Chinese armies were driven from the mainland to Formosa by the Communist Peoples' Liberation Army, led by Mao Tse Tung, Lin Piao, and others. Subsequently, in February, 1950, the Soviet Union and Communist China signed a treaty of alliance, which increased the threat of global conflict.

A steady flow of former Texas A&M students continued to enter the military services, and many of those soon saw combat in northeast Asia, on the Korean peninsula, which had been divided into two sectors at the end of World War II, and in the southeast in Indochina. After the war, Korea north of the 38th parallel came under the administrative and military control of the Soviet Union, while the south came under U.S. occupation. Although both major powers withdrew most of their forces in 1948, by 1950, mounting border tensions along the 38th parallel evolved into armed combat. American troops, including many Texas Aggies, began to fight in a war that was never declared and never formally ended. Former students served in the front lines of Korea for most of the next half-century. War also erupted in Indochina, where, following Japanese withdrawal, French troops reoccupied their old colony in 1946. In 1948, a long war with Communist insurgents began, a war that led to French withdrawal in 1956 and the division of Indochina into North and South Vietnam, Cambodia (formerly Kampuchea), and Laos—a failed solution that too soon led to American combat in the region.

While the Korean War (1950–1953) and the Vietnam War (1965–1973) saw hundreds of thousands of Americans engaged in combat, the Cold War involved millions more in defense-related assignments all over the world. Conscription, which started under the Selective Service Act of 1940, continued in some form until 1973. Many students who were enrolled in colleges or universities with ROTC programs were enticed into service with the promise of a commission and associated benefits. Texas A&M graduates continued their strong historic commitment to the military with roughly seventy-five percent serving some time on active duty between 1946 and 1970. In addition to being posted in Korea and Vietnam, many of them participated in military encounters such as in the South Pacific at Quemoy and Matsu Islands (1958–1963), the Congo (1960–1962), Laos (1961–1962), Cuba (1962–1963), the Dominican Republic (1965–1966), the Persian Gulf (1987–1995), Panama (1989–1990), and Kosovo (1999).

As an example, eighty-six percent (516 of the 600 graduates) of the class of 1953 served in the military, mostly for two-year tours, with initial assignments typically at basic branch schools. Of those, 114 became career officers. Infantry officers went to Fort Benning, Georgia; artillery officers to Fort Sill, Oklahoma, or Fort Bliss, Texas; and those in armor, to Fort Knox, Kentucky, and Fort Hood, Texas. Signal Corps personnel usually trained at Fort Monmouth, New Jersey, or Fort Gordon, Georgia, and engineers at Fort Belvoir, Virginia (Fort Leonard Wood, Missouri, after 1988). Some officers were sent to parachute training or "jump school" at Fort Benning, and others to Ranger schools at various sites. Subsequent duty assignments varied widely, ranging from Fort

Bragg's 82nd Airborne Division and Fort Hood's 1st and 4th Armored Divisions to duty in Germany, Japan, Korea, Panama, or Alaska to the Army Security Agency in locations scattered around the world.[6]

Noncombat duty assignments during the Cold War were usually challenging and significant for the preservation of peace. Some were dangerous. Air Force Capt. Lester L. Lackey ('52) went down in his RB-57F Canberra reconnaissance plane in the Black Sea near Soviet territorial waters on December 14, 1965, and was never seen again. Many Aggies of this era spent their tour of active duty in Germany, where the United States and NATO allies maintained a strong military presence as a deterrent to a Soviet attack or invasion. Among them from the class of 1953 were Joe B. Mattei, Alton R. Stoddard, Ronald C. Stinson Jr., Spencer Buchanan, Arthur M. Heath, Raymond Marlow, Lee J. Phillips Jr., A. Earl Massengale Jr., Jack K. Reynolds, and Bob Dawson, as well as Arno Becker, Charles H. Pluennecke, Lester L. Brawner, Kenneth M. Jones, Clarence Earl Beavers III, Edwin H. Cooper, Frank M. Foster, and Glenn Black. On the opposite side of the globe, in Japan, air force Lt. Willard Sholar got caught in a snowstorm at a radar installation on a mountain top. He discovered later that the rescue helicopter was flown by a classmate, Charles Adolph Pinson, who became a career air force officer. Charlie Burgess, whose first assignment was with the 711th AC&W Squadron in Alaska, also remained in service. While on active duty on Guam in March, 1947, James W. McDonald, who joined the navy in 1946 as a yeoman first class, participated in the capture of several Japanese soldiers who had been in hiding since the surrender of Japan. Another Aggie who had an unusual Alaska assignment was Tommy Dunagan, a zoologist who spent three years at the Arctic Aeromedical Laboratory.[7]

Many Texas Aggies served in the air force, some in surveillance and reconnaissance, others in engineering and support, and many in combat. Lt. Col. Dean D. Duncan ('53) spent most of his twenty years of active duty as an engineering officer, including three years as an instructor at Texas A&M. A classmate, Lt. Col. Bethel Q. ("Buck") Evans was a master navigator on heavy aircraft with more than 220 combat missions in RF-4s in Vietnam, where he won the Distinguished Flying Cross with twelve oak-leaf clusters. Other classmates and recipients of the DFC included Lt. Col. Maurice W. Miller, a navigator with more than 1,000 combat missions, while Col. Alvin L. Langford was a pilot whose twenty-seven years in service included assignments as a squadron and base commander. Lt. Col. Max L. Templin, recipient of the DFC, Silver Star, and Bronze Star, saw duty as a fighter pilot and squadron commander in Europe and Vietnam. Col. James H. ("Jim") Thomas ('53) spent most of his service in maintenance and logistics and retired after twenty-six years as deputy commander for maintenance of the C-130 air fleet.[8]

During his air force career, Col. Ted L. Skeans ('53) was assigned to KC-135 refueling tanker units. On a mission in May, 1964, he refueled Maj. John O. Barrett ('53) on an 8,028-nautical-mile flight piloting a B-58 Hustler bomber that set a world speed record of eight hours and thirty-five minutes, averaging about 1,000 miles per hour. Only years later did Skeans and Barrett learn about their having "connected" over the Pacific. The service record of the 1953 graduates looked much like that of other Texas A&M classes of this period. Sixteen members of the class died in service, ten of them in aircraft accidents, reflecting the substantial number of pilots and aviators from that class.[9]

By 2004 (from classes up to 1976), the Texas A&M Corps of Cadets had produced 226 officers of flag rank, beginning with Maj. Gen. Bennet Puryear (U.S. Army) from the class of 1906 to Brig. Gen. Robert C. Williams (U.S. Public Health Service) of the class of 1976. Nearly every class produced an admiral or a general, and seventeen classes supplied five or more, with the class of 1962 leading with eleven (table 11).

That record reflects the continuing and intense commitment to military service by former students of Texas A&M during the Cold War and the years following it. Most officers and enlisted personnel from this era served their assigned two or three years of active duty and then resumed an active or inactive affiliation with a National Guard or reserve unit. Maintenance and training of combat-ready reserve forces was a critical component of post–World War II military strategy, and thousands of soldiers returning from active duty continued to serve in the ready or standby reserves. On occasion they were recalled to active duty when needed to meet a new crisis.

The Texas National Guard, for example, which was initially composed largely of World War II veterans, was one of the first reserve units called to active duty for the Korean War. Otto G. Tumlinson ('17) fought the Germans in World War I and World War II and, when discharged in 1945, remained in the air force active reserves until retiring as a colonel in 1955. After Col. John Michael Braun ('71) served as an instructor pilot and flight examiner with the German Air Force between 1972 and 1977, he returned to Texas to serve twenty-three years with the U.S. Army National Guard. He was later called to seven months of active duty in Bosnia as part of NATO's peacekeeping forces in 1990 and 1991. Similarly, Lt. Cdr. Jim R. Pack ('66) from Waco served on active duty in the navy from 1966 to 1970 and spent the next thirty years with the navy reserves as a communications officer. In 1954 and 1955, 1st Lt. Jim Carroll McReynolds ('53) from Dawson, Texas, was "on the line" in Korea and then remained in the active reserve until 1973. Cmdr. Timothy Dring ('75) from Staten Island, New York, began his naval service in 1975 and spent most of his years in active-duty training and readying naval reserve units for possible activation. Brig. Gen. Joe M. Ernst ('67) became commander of the 125th Army Reserve Command headquartered in Nashville, Tennessee, in 1994.[10]

Many Texas Aggies served on the faculties of the military academies. One of the most notable was Maj. Gen. Patrick K. Gamble ('67), who became commandant of cadets at the U.S. Air Force Academy. In the Cold War era, supply

TABLE 11. Texas Aggies Who Have Achieved Flag Rank in the Military

General/Admiral

Otto P. Weyland ('23) USAF

Bernard A. Schriever ('31) USAF

Jerome L. Johnson ('56) USN

Joseph W. Ashy ('62) USAF

Patrick K. Gamble ('67) USAF

Hal M. Hornburg ('68) USAF

Veerapun Putamanonda ('69) RTA

Teed M. Moseley ('71) USAF
   (Chief of Staff)

Lieutenant General/Vice Admiral

Andrew D. Bruce ('16) USA

John T. Walker ('17) USMC

Ion M. Bethel ('25) USMC

Robert W. Colglazier ('25) USAR

Harry H. Critz ('34) USA

Ormond R. Simpson ('36) USMC

Woodrow W. Vaughan ('39) USA

James F. Hollingsworth ('40) USA

Herron M. Maples ('40) USA

Jay T. Robbins ('40) USAF

John H. Miller ('46) USMC

Eivind H. Johansen ('50) USA

Herman O. Thomson ('51) USAF

Richard T. Gaskill ('52) USN

Kenneth E. Lewi ('52) USA

James S. Cassity Jr. ('57) USAF

Melvin F. Chubb Jr. ('62) USAF

David B. Robinson ('62) USN

James T. Scott ('64) USA

Herbert A. Browne ('65) USN

Theodore G. Stroup ('65) USA

John A. Van Alstyne ('66) USA

Leonard D. Holder Jr. ('66) USA

Donald L. Peterson ('66) USAF

Randolph W. House ('67) USA

John B. Sylvester ('67) USA

Gerald F. Perryman Jr. ('70) USAF

Patrick P. Caruana ('72) USAF

Joseph F. Weber ('72) USMC

William F. Fraser III ('74) USAF

Lloyd S. Utterback ('75) USAF

Alfred G. Harms Jr. ('78) USN

Major General/Rear Admiral

Bennet Puryear ('06) USA

George F. Moore ('08) USA

Howard C. Davidson ('11) USAF

William E. Farthing ('14) USAF

Roderick R. Allen ('15) USA

Percy W. Clarkson ('15) USA

Edmond H. Leavey ('15) USA

Ralph H. Wooten ('16) USAF

Albert M. Bledsoe ('17) USN

Harry H. Johnson ('17) USA

Herman M. Ainsworth ('19) USA

Jim Dan Hill ('21) USA

Gerald Bogle ('23) USN

Robert B. Williams ('23) USAF

William D. Old ('24) USAF

Manning E. Tillery ('26) USAF

William L. Kennedy ('28 USAF

George P. Munson Jr. ('28) USAR

Stuart S. Hoff ('29) USA

Benjamin H. Pochyla ('29) USA

Frederick H. Weston ('29) TANG

Alvin R. Luedecke ('32) USAF

James Earl Rudder ('32) USAR

John H. White ('32) USAF

Robert F. Worden ('33) USAF

Bruno A. Hochmuth ('35) USMC

Raymond A. Moore ('35) USN

Raymond L. Murray ('35) USMC

Wood B. Kyle ('36) USMC

Robert L. Pou Jr. ('37) TANG

Andrew P. Rollins Jr. ('39) USA

John H. Buckner ('40) USAF

Homer S. Hill ('40) USMC

William A. Becker ('41) USA

George L. Cassell ('41) USN

Otto E. Scherz ('42) TANG

Harold C. Teubner ('42) USAF

Harold B. Gibson ('43) USA

Tom E. Marchbanks ('43) USAF

Homer D. Smith ('43) USA

Merton D. Van Orden ('43) USN

Wesley E. Peel ('46) USA

William L. Webb Jr. ('46) USA

Guy H. Goddard ('47) USAF

Charles R. Bond Jr. ('49) USAF

Robert E. Crosser ('49) USAR

Charles I. McGinnis ('49) USA

James L. Brown ('50) USAF

Glenn H. Kothmann ('50) TANG

Waymond C. Nutt ('51) USAF

Howard H. Haynes ('52) USN

Charles H. Kone ('52) TANG

John H. Storrie ('52) USAF

James W. Taylor ('52) USAF

William R. Wray ('52) USA

Dionel E. Aviles ('53) USAR

Charles R. Cargill ('53) USAFR

Harry V. Steel Jr. ('53) TANG

G. J. Wilson Jr. ('53) USAR

Thomas G. Darling ('54) USAF

George H. Akin ('56) USA

Don O. Daniel ('56) TANG

Thomas R. Olsen ('56) USAF

Paul L. Greenberg ('58) USA

Sam C. Turk ('58) TANG

Ira E. Scott ('59) TSG

James R. Taylor ('59) USA

Richard A. Box ('61) TSG

Robert Smith III ('61) USNR

Darrel P. Baker ('62) TANG

John J. Closner III ('62) USAFR

Jay T. Edwards III ('62) USAF

Charles W. McClain Jr. ('62) USA

Walter B. Moore ('62) USA

Gerald H. Putman ('62) USA

Jay D. Blume Jr. ('63) USAF

Billy G. McCoy ('63) USAF

Hiram H. Burr Jr. ('65) USAF

Marvin Ted Hopgood ('65) USMC

James M. Hurley ('65) USAF

John E. Simek ('65) USAR

Alvin W. Jones ('66) USAR

Frank D. Watson ('66) USAFR

Jeffrey L. Chesbrough ('67) USAF

Joe M. Ernst ('67) USAR

Richard L. Engel ('68) USAF

Michael C. Kostelnik ('68) USAF

William W. Pickavance Jr. ('68) USN

Kenneth W. Hess ('69) USAF

Wilbert D. Pearson Jr. ('69) USAF

Michael H. Taylor ('72) TXARNG

William H. McCoy Jr. ('73) USA

James W. Robinson ('75) TSG

Brigadier General/Rear Admiral (lower)

Douglas B. Netherwood ('08) USA

John A. Warden ('08) USA

William C. Crane Jr. ('10) USA

John F. Davis ('11) USA

Oscar B. Abbott ('13) USA

Eugene A. Eversberg ('13) USAR

Jerome J. Waters ('13) USA

Robert R. Neyland Jr. ('14) USA

Victor A. Barraco ('15) USMC

Claudius M. Easley ('16) USA

Durant S. Buchanan ('17) USMC

Walter T. H. Galliford ('17) USMC

Nat S. Perrine ('17) USA

George H. Beverly ('19) USAF

Paul L. Neal ('19) USA

John T. Pierce ('19) USA

Arthur B. Knickerbocker ('21) TANG

Cranford C. Warden ('21) USA

Aubry L. Moore ('23) USAF

Spencer J. Buchanan ('25) USAR

William R. Frederick ('25) USA
Richard J. Werner ('25) USA
William L. Lee ('27) USAF
James P. Newberry ('27) USAF
Charles S. Hays ('32) USA
Travis M. Hetherington ('32) USAF
John A. Hilger ('32) USAF
Graber Kidwell ('32) USAR
John M. Kenderdine ('34) USA
Odell M. Conoley ('35) USMC
Kay Halsell II ('35) TANG
Clifford M. Simmang ('36) USAR
Carter C. Speed ('36) USA
Jack T. Brown ('37) TANG
Kyle L. Riddle ('37) USAF
Theodore H. Andrews ('38) USA
David L. Hill ('38) TANG
Robert M. Williams ('38) USA
Clarence A. Wilson ('38) USAR
O. D. Butler ('39) USAR
Andrew W. Rogers ('39) AUS
Joe G. Hanover ('40) AUS
Thomas F. McCord ('40) USA
George P. Cole ('41) USAF
Hubert O. Johnson ('41) USAF
Seaborn J. Buckalew Jr. ('42) USA
Charles M. Taylor Jr. ('42) Calif. ANG
Victor H. Thompson Jr. ('42) USAF
Mike P. Cokinos ('43) USAR
Charles V. L. Elia ('43) USA
Jack N. Kraras ('43) USA
Guy M. Townsend ('43) USAF
George W. Connell ('45) USA
Irby B. Jarvis Jr. ('45) USAF
Joseph E. Wesp ('45) USAF
Allen D. Rooke Jr. ('46) USA
David O. Williams ('46) USAF
Thomas G. Murnane ('47) USA
Carl D. McIntosh ('48) USAR
Robert M. Mullens ('48) USA
John D. Roper ('48) USAF
Billy M. Vaughn ('49) USA
Walter O. Bachus ('50) USA
Wilman D. Barnes ('51) USA
Keith L. Hargrove ('51) USAR
Frank A. Ramsey ('51) USA
Walter J. Dingler ('52) TANG

Louis L. Stuart Jr. ('52) USAR
Robert C. Beyer ('53) USA
George R. Harper ('53) TANG
Robert O. Petty ('53) USAF
John J. Roark ('53) TANG
Charles M. Scott ('53) Arizona ANG
Donald J. Johnson ('55) TSG
Woodrow A. Free ('56) USAR
Dennis A. Wilkie ('56) USA
Donald L. Moore ('57) USAF
Paul L. Carroll Jr. ('58) Calif. Air NG
James E. Freytag ('59) USAF
John Serur ('59) USAF
Charles R. Weaver ('59) TSG
Ed. Y. Hall ('60) SCSG
Kenneth F. Keller ('60) USAF
Edmond S. Solymosy ('60) USA
Malcolm Bolton ('61) USAF
Don M. Ogg ('61) TANG
Jimmy L. Cash ('62) USAF
Michael M. Schneider ('62) USA
John A. Hedrick ('63) USA
Ronald D. Gray ('64) USAF
George E. Chapman ('65) USAF
Manuel A. Guzman ('65) PRANG
Lee V. Greer ('67) USAF
Stephen D. Korenek ('68) Alaska ANG
Thomas S. Bailey ('69) USAF
James M. Richards III ('69) USAF
Robert T. Howard ('70) USA
Michael H. Taylor ('70) TANG
Henry J. Osterman ('72) USAR
Robert L. Herndon ('73) USA
Darren G. Owens ('73) TANG
Louis W. Weber ('75) USA
Randolph D. Alles ('76) USMC
Robert C. Williams ('76) USPHS
Harold B. Bunch ('76) USA
Floyd F. Carpenter ('77) USA
David A. Rubenstein ('77) USA
Michael B. Cates ('79) VMC
Joe E. Ramirez Jr. ('79) USA
James W. Hyatt ('80) USAF
Jennifer Napper ('82) USA
Meredith W. B. Temple ('85) USA
Tommie G. Smith ('01) USA

Air NG	Air National Guard	USAF	U.S. Air Force
ANG	Army National Guard	USAFR	U.S. Air Force Reserve
AUS	Army of the United States	USAR	U.S. Army Reserve
PRANG	Puerto Rico Army National Guard	USMC	U.S. Marine Corps
RTA	Royal Thailand Army	USN	U.S. Navy
SCSG	South Carolina State Guard	USNR	U.S. Naval Reserve
TANG	Texas Air National Guard	USPHS	U.S. Public Health Service
TSG	Texas State Guard	VMC	Veterinary Medical College
USA	U.S. Army		

Note: Ranks are from records of the Association of Former Students, as of 2005.

and logistics operations became increasingly specialized and complex. These functions were under the surveillance of officers such as Maj. Gen. Lee V. Greer ('67), who retired in 1990 after commanding the U.S. Air Force Materiel Command in Sacramento, California.[11]

As the years following World War II passed, the need for smaller, more efficient, and specialized military or combat missions increased. Reserve and National Guard units and the continuing service of the citizen soldiers, sailors, and aviators became more integral to the mission and success of army, navy, air force, and Marine Corps plans and operations.

Like the early Texas militiamen, who personified the concept of a citizen soldier, Texas Aggies in military service came from different backgrounds and contributed to national defense in diverse ways. Air force Maj. Gen. Jay T. Edwards III ('62), a graduate of the U.S. Military Academy, received his master's degree in aeronautical engineering at Texas A&M. While on active duty he directed advance research programs at the U.S. Air Force Flight Dynamics Laboratory. Another leader in advanced weapons development, Lt. Gen. Melvin F. ("Nick") Chubb Jr. ('62), was head of the electronic system division of the U.S. Air Force System Command when he retired from active duty in 1988. During his career Chubb managed the acquisition of strategic aeronautical systems such as the B-52 weapons system improvement, B-1 weapons research and development, and air-launched and cruise missile programs. A command pilot with more than five hundred combat missions, Chubb earned the Distinguished Flying Cross, Purple Heart, and other awards.[12]

Maj. Gen. Bill McClain ('62) spent most of his army career in media relations and concluded his service as U.S. Army Chief of Public Affairs. Maj. Gen. W. Bruce Moore ('62) helped significantly in developing assault-helicopter tactics in actions ranging from Vietnam to Somalia. Maj. Gen. John J. Closner III ('62) served in Vietnam, Operation Desert Storm, and Bosnia, ending his service as chief of the U.S. Air Force Reserve. Army Brig. Gen. Michael M. Schneider ('62) retired in May, 1993, as head of the U.S. Army Foreign Intelligence Command after a thirty-year military career.[13] These personal histories show how the ready reserves embodied the citizen-soldier ideal while providing access to a large, diverse, and technically trained pool of military personnel.

Among those who contributed to the readiness of the air force reserves were Maj. Gen. Charles R. ("Chuck") Cargill ('53) and Brig. Gen. John J. Roark ('53), both of whom achieved their flag rank as members of the reserves. Cargill's assignments included the post of mobilization assistant to the commander of the U.S. Air Reserve Personnel Center. Roark headed the Civil Engineering Squadron's 136th Air Refueling Wing and later was deputy commanding general of the Texas Air National Guard. Other flag officers included Maj. Gen. Harry V. Steel Jr., who commanded the 1st Battalion, 141st Infantry Division, for five years before assuming command of the Base Units Command, Texas Army National Guard. Brig. Gen. George R. Harper ('53) headed the 71st Airborne Brigade, Texas National Guard, and Maj. Gen. Guilford J. Wilson ('53) was deputy commanding general for army support forces before he became commanding general, 75th Maneuver Area Command. Brig. Gen. Charles M. Scott Jr. ('53), with the U.S. Army National Guard, served on active duty in the 82nd Airborne Division and later the 153rd Field Artillery Brigade. After leaving active duty Scott became assistant adjutant general for the Arizona Army National Guard. Maj. Gen. Dionel E. Aviles left active duty on Guam and in the Marianas Islands to return to reserve duty with the 420th Engineer Brigade in Bryan, Texas. Eventually he became commanding general of the 75th Maneuver Area Command.[14]

In addition to the Texas Aggies serving in the air force reserves and on active flight duty during the Cold War years, many Aggies also helped make that flight possible. Numerous A&M engineering graduates, for example, spent much of their professional career in the aerospace industry, for example, with General Dynamics Corporation in Fort Worth, which designed, produced, and marketed the extremely effective F-16 Multirole Fighter; Boeing, which built the B-52 Stratofortress or B-47 Stratojet; McDonnell-Douglas, which developed aircraft such as the navy's A3D and F4D; or Lockheed-Martin, which manufactured planes such as the C-130 and U-2 reconnaissance aircraft. When General Dynamic's F-16 was introduced, A. Dwain Mayfield ('59) was director of domestic marketing for that company. Capt. Wayne C. Edwards ('72), Maj. Tom J. McKnight ('67), and Lt. Col. Sam Holmes ('60) were members of the 388th Tactical Fighter Wing, the first unit to receive combat-ready F-16s.[15]

Military readiness and training, as well as overt regional combat in places such as Korea and Vietnam, were deterrents to the outbreak of global conflicts and catastrophic warfare. Readiness required a broad spectrum of personnel and talents. Texas Aggies in the Cold War served in many diverse capacities in all of the services, including space. Brig. Gen. Seaborn J. Buckalew ('42), for example, became military adjutant general for Alaska in 1971. Brig. Gen. Frank A. Ramsey ('51), appointed chief of the U.S. Army Veterinary Corps in 1980, succeeded Brig. Gen. Charles Van Loan Elia ('43), who had accepted those duties in

1972. And Texas Congressman Olin E. Teague ('32) headed the Congressional Committee on Manned Space Flight.[16]

Maj. Gen. Homer D. Smith Jr. ('43) completed his thirty-six years in the army, including service in France, England, and Germany during World War II, as commander of the 7th Infantry Division in Korea. After "retiring," he became director of logistics for NATO's international staff and helped ensure that NATO's military forces were in a constant state of preparedness. While fewer Texas Aggies were in the navy than in the army and air force during the Cold War era, one of those, Capt. Foster S. ("Tooter") Teague ('56), assumed command of the 80,000-ton aircraft carrier USS *Kitty Hawk*, with a crew of 5,200 men and a fleet of ninety tactical aircraft.[17]

Preparedness also went beyond strictly military matters. Thus, at least one Texas Aggie, Bill Libby ('58) from Dumas, served as an army chaplain. Libby's service included assignments with the 24th Infantry Division in Germany and the 101st Airborne Division in Tennessee. He confessed that he lived in not only "a world where evil and suffering in all their forms are obvious" but also "a world of infinite possibilities if only we harness our resources."[18]

Indeed, the Cold War was rife with new technologies and new ideas, particularly in communications, electronics, radar, nuclear energy, supersonic flight, and space. Brig. Gen. Travis Monroe Hetherington ('32) helped pioneer the army air corps' radio and radar training programs before and during World War II and later served in Washington, D.C., as deputy director of the National Security Agency. One of his contemporaries at Texas A&M, Maj. Gen. Benjamin H. Pochyla ('29) from Tucson, Arizona, became a specialist in electronic warfare and retired as commanding general, U.S. Army Electronic Proving Ground, Fort Huachuca, Arizona.[19]

James M. Sharp ('40) from Denison, who completed his undergraduate studies in physics and mathematics at Texas A&M before completing his doctorate, served with the U.S. Army Signal Aircraft Warning Service in the Philippines and New Guinea during World War II, utilizing radar and radio technology. After a brief stint in civilian life, Sharp joined the Air Force Special Weapons Center (AFSWAP) in New Mexico in nuclear testing and development work relating primarily to the hydrogen bomb. After leaving defense-related research in 1954, Sharp began a successful career with public and private research institutes in Texas.[20]

Air force Lt. Charles H. Robison ('59), a chemical engineering graduate, also made significant contributions to nuclear research. After advanced studies in nuclear engineering, he was sent to the Air Force Special Weapons Center in New Mexico before completing a doctorate in nuclear engineering at the University of California–Davis. During his military career Robison conducted research on controlled nuclear fusion at the Lawrence Radiation Laboratory in Livermore, California, and taught nuclear engineering at the U.S. Air Force Academy in Colorado Springs.[21]

Many who served with the armed forces often continued that service in affiliations with government agencies, research institutes, and industry. Alvin R. Luedecke began his military service in flight operations and served in the diplomatic corps as an attaché, in air intelligence, and in nuclear energy and space. After the war he was general manager of the Atomic Energy Commission and deputy director of the (NASA) California Institute of Technology's Jet Propulsion Laboratory. Luedecke completed his career of service as acting president of Texas A&M University (March–November, 1970). Luedecke attributed his successful management of these technical programs to a strong basic engineering education, "plus a good background in English and law."[22]

Bernard Schriever, who achieved the rank of four-star general, was the foremost American military pioneer in defense and space flight. Born in Bremen, Germany, in 1910, Schriever moved with his family to New Braunfels, Texas, in 1917. After graduation from Texas A&M in 1931 with a degree in structural engineering, he received a commission in the army and enrolled in flight school at Randolph Field in San Antonio. Following tours of active duty in California and the Canal Zone, Schriever took a one-year stint as a commercial pilot in 1938, then returned to the air corps as a test pilot at Wright Field, Ohio. The air corps sent him to Stanford University for a master's degree in mechanical engineering. When war came, he was sent to the 19th Bomb Group in the South Pacific, where he flew more than sixty-three combat missions in B-17s and B-25s, earning the Legion of Merit, Air Medal, and a Purple Heart. In 1944, Schriever assumed command of advance headquarters for the Far East Air Service, which provided oversight for combat-support operations from bases in New Guinea, Leyte, Manila, and Okinawa.[23]

Despite that distinguished career, Schriever's most significant contributions came in the areas of Cold War advanced missile systems and space flight. After the war, he spent eight years in flight studies and development programs with the air force before being assigned to organize and head what was first called the air force's "Western Development Division." On June 1, 1957, that became the Ballistic Missile Division, an organization that paralleled the work of the army's Ballistic Missile Agency, which was headed by Wernher von Braun. In October, 1957, the military's somewhat belated entry into ICBM (intercontinental ballistic missile) and space flight development was galvanized by the Soviet Union's successful launch of Sputnik I, the first orbital space vehicle. Missile development—and space—became top priorities.

Under Schriever's management, the air force developed an organization that utilized private contractors in collaboration with scientists, research laboratories, and industry. It succeeded in building and testing some of America's most successful rocket programs, including the Atlas, Titan, and Minuteman booster and missile systems, which, with army and navy systems, provided the technical underpinning for the National Aeronautics and Space Administration, which was created by Congress as the civilian centerpiece for the development

Gen. Bernard A. Schriever ('31).

of American space technology. In recognition of Schriever's contributions to flight, in June, 1998, the air force renamed Falcon Air Force Base in Colorado Schriever Air Force Base.[24]

Management, Bernard Schriever argued forcefully and convincingly, was a critical and integral part of national security: "This rapid advance in military technology since World War II is a measure of the enormously increased requirements of national security. Military strength has long been heavily dependent on science and engineering; today, [in] the space age, technological superiority is the cornerstone of national survival."[25] As the Cold War fused engineering, science, and technology with military preparedness and combat in a way no war had ever done, Texas A&M's expertise in science and engineering and its military training programs and past war experiences enabled it to make unique contributions to national security.

Among those who played significant roles in new-weapons development was Maj. Gen. Michael C. Kostelnik ('68), who retired as commander of the Air Armament Center, Air Force Materiel Command, located at Eglin Air Force Base in Florida. The center was responsible for developing, testing, acquiring, and deploying air-delivered weapons. During his service Kostelnik also commanded the U.S. Air Force Test Pilot School and completed his military career as a deputy associate administrator for NASA's international space station and space shuttle programs. Among the Aggie test pilots who pushed the limits of flight was Tommie D. ("Doug") Benefield ('49), who died on a low-level test of a B-1A bomber. Jerry Reed ('60) spent two years with the Army Aviation Materiel Command working on projects to improve fire-control systems. Reed later returned to the Army Aviation Materiel Laboratory as a civilian to continue the same kind of work, including the development of electronic countermeasures. Similarly, Douglas R. DeCluitt ('57), a Nike-guided-missile officer while on active duty, returned to civilian life with Texas Instruments, where he helped develop and improve the integrated-circuit systems for the Minuteman missiles and in time served as a regent of Texas A&M University.[26]

Despite its civilian orientation, NASA closely complemented army, navy, and air force space and missile defense studies and programs, especially as competition in space and missile development took center stage in the Cold War. Indeed, the hallmark of the Cold War was its contribution to spectacular advances in supersonic and hypersonic flight, with related advances in weapons systems—and in space. As NASA took humans into space and to the moon, military and test pilots were taking aviation to the very edge of space. Among those pioneers was Col. Robert L. Stephens ('43), who spent his postwar military career as an air force test pilot. On May 1, 1965, he set the world speed record for an aircraft at 2,070 miles per hour (more than three times the speed of sound) and established the sustained-altitude record of 80,257 feet flying a delta-winged YF-12A advanced interceptor. Fifteen years later, in 1980, Lt. Col. Larry M. Jordan ('68) set a B-1B flight-endurance record of twenty-one hours and forty minutes. Robert C. Barlow ('56) completed pilot training at Laredo Air Force Base in September, 1958, taught for several years at the U.S. Air Force Academy, served in Vietnam, where he earned the DFC and Air Medal, and then became chief of academics for experimental test pilots at the Aerospace Research Pilot School. Barlow inherited his affinity for flight from his father, Howard W. Barlow, who designed racing aircraft in the 1930s and helped establish Texas A&M's Department of Aeronautical Engineering in the 1940s.[27] That enthusiasm was nurtured by Texas A&M's post–World War II engineering, science, and military cultures.

Others who were prominently involved in the development of NASA's space programs were Aaron Cohen ('52), Gerald D. ("Gerry") Griffin ('56), from Athens, Texas, and Edward ("Pete") Aldrich ('60). Cohen earned his degree in electrical engineering, was commissioned in the army after graduation, and, after completing his tour of active duty, worked with RCA and General Dynamics as a senior research engineer. In 1962, he joined the Manned Spacecraft (Johnson Space) Center in Houston and managed the command and service modules offices of the Apollo spacecraft program from 1969 to 1972. Then, for the next ten years, Cohen headed the Space Shuttle Orbiter Project Office. In October, 1986, he became director of NASA's Johnson Space Center. When he retired from NASA, Cohen joined the Texas A&M University faculty.[28]

A managing engineer, Cohen defined space-project management as a creative process aimed at optimizing the use of given technological and material resources. Johnson Space Center's end product, he said, "is putting men and women into space, keeping them alive and productive while they're there and returning them safely to Earth. We design, develop and operate manned space-craft and train the crews that use them. We conduct scientific and medical experiments that help us understand how space affects our astronauts and spacecraft."[29]

Activities in space require intensive activity, careful scheduling, constant testing and evaluation, cost controls, and relentless attention to detail. It is the kind of work environment that has attracted engineers and Texas Aggies such as Gerry Griffin and Larry Griffin. Gerry Griffin, an aeronautical engineer, received his air force commission as a second lieutenant in 1956. He served as a weapons systems officer for F-89 Scorpion and F-101B Voodoo aircraft until 1960, when he joined Lockheed Missile and Space Company as a missile sys-tems engineer assigned primarily to the Air Force Satellite Test Center. After that, he worked for General Dynamics on research and engineering tasks involving spacecraft guidance and control systems for NASA and the air force. Griffin then transferred to NASA's Mission Control Center at Johnson Space Center. There he was a flight controller for the entire two-person Gemini pro-gram, which followed the pioneering Mercury flights, which sent John Glenn Jr. on America's first orbital space flight. Mercury prepared the way for the his-toric Apollo lunar program, for which Griffin served as flight director from 1968 to 1973, managing the Apollo 12, 15, and 17 lunar landing and exploration missions.[30]

Later, as head of external relations, Griffin became a key spokesperson for NASA and, in 1982, returned to Johnson Space Center as its director. After re-tirement in 1984, he and his twin brother, Larry D. Griffin ('56), who had spent his career with the air force in space and supersonic flight programs, set world speed records for flights in a Class C-1b aircraft, an improved Piper Cub.[31]

Another of the early Texas Aggie space pioneers, Edward Aldrich from Hous-ton, completed his studies in aeronautical engineering first at Texas A&M and then Georgia Tech and became manager of the missile and space division for Douglas Aircraft Company. In 1967, Aldrich first became deputy assistant sec-retary for strategic defense and strategic programs and then became director of planning and evaluation. He also headed the National Reconnaissance Office, which oversaw satellite intelligence activities. Aldrich strongly influenced NASA and the Department of Defense in modifying the Titan II and Titan IV missile programs, as well as the production of the Atlas II and Delta II expend-able launch vehicles. He was scheduled to fly aboard a shuttle as a payload spe-cialist in July, 1986, but the flight was canceled following the loss of *Challenger*. During his career, Aldrich served variously as secretary of the air force and pres-ident of both McDonnell-Douglas Electronic Systems Company and the Aerospace Corporation, the latter a nonprofit business operating a federally funded research and development center for the Department of Defense.[32]

Many Texas Aggies subsequently pursued air force and NASA careers and made major contributions to national defense and flight programs. The pioneering efforts of former students such as Bernard Schriever, Alvin Luedecke, Aaron Cohen, Gerry Griffin, Larry Griffin, and Pete Aldrich greatly enriched the university's aerospace programs and subsequently helped channel Texas Aggies into flight and space studies. In 1985, Texas A&M organized a space research center that, in turn, led to the organization of the Texas Space Grant Consortium, which included twenty-one state universities, eighteen Texas aerospace corporations, and two state agencies. Texas Congressman Olin E. Teague ('32) also played a major role in the inception and development of the nation's space flight programs, first as head of a congressional subcommittee on scientific research and development and then as a member of the House Committee on Science and Astronautics and head of the Subcommittee on Manned Space Flight.[33]

The Cold War occupied America and the global community throughout most of the post–World War II era to the eve of the twenty-first century. A multidimensional phenomenon, it involved ideological and economic warfare between different factions of a divided world. It was highlighted by competition in space and technological warfare between the Soviet Union and its satellites and the United States and its Western allies. It engaged American society across a broad spectrum and necessitated as never before a state of military preparedness. The Cold War required the maintenance of a large standing army and the deployment of American troops and armaments at contact points throughout the world. It thus also necessitated the supplementation and support of those forces with a large, diverse, and technically skilled pool of ready reserve personnel. Texas A&M made significant contributions by providing trained men and women for the armed services who, because of their predominant background in agriculture, engineering, and the sciences, possessed the special knowledge required for modern, technological warfare. Perhaps most importantly throughout the Cold War era as in the past, Texas A&M provided "leadership in the pursuits of peace, and if it came to war, leadership in battle."[34]

The battle in Korea was very soon joined. On June 25, 1950, the North Korean People's Army struck the Republic of Korea's meager defense forces along the 38th parallel. Four days later, South Korea's capital, Seoul, fell to the invading armies, who rapidly pushed southward. Also, on June 25, the UN Security Council recommended assistance to the Republic of Korea "as may be necessary to repel the armed attack and to restore international peace and security in the area." On that day, Pres. Harry S. Truman directed Gen. Douglas MacArthur and American forces in Japan and elsewhere in the Pacific to provide the armies with air and naval support. By early July, American soldiers had joined the Army of the

Republic of Korea and were clinging to a small defensive perimeter around Pusan that represented the only remnant of what had recently been the Republic of Korea.[35]

Suggested Readings

Ambrose, Stephen E. *Eisenhower*, 2 vols. (New York: Simon and Schuster, 1983–1984).

Brands, H. W., Jr. *The Devil We Knew: Americans and the Cold War* (New York: Oxford University Press, 1993).

Clowse, Barbara B. *Brainpower for the Cold War: The Sputnik Crisis and National Defense Education Act of 1958* (Westport, Conn.: Greenwood Press, 1981).

Divine, Robert. *Eisenhower and the Cold War* (New York: Oxford University Press, 1981).

LeFeber, Walter. *America, Russia, and the Cold War, 1945–1980*, 7th ed. (New York: McGraw-Hill, 1993).

Leslie, Stuart W. *The Cold War and American Science: The Military-Industrial-Academic Complex at MIT and Stanford* (New York: Columbia University Press, 1993).

McCoy, Donald R. *The Presidency of Harry S. Truman* (Lawrence: University Press of Kansas, 1984).

Olson, Keith W. *The GI Bill, the Veterans, and the Colleges* (Lexington: University Press of Kentucky, 1974).

When the 5th Marine Regiment was cut off at the Chosin Reservoir, Lt. Col. Raymond L. Murray ('35) organized a withdrawal, sending this note to all of his units: "From C.O. 5th Marines. All hands make sure every shot counts. . . . Gentlemen, we are going out of here. And we're going out like Marines. We are sticking together and we are taking our dead and wounded and our equipment. Are there any questions?" The 5th and 7th Marines sustained more than 1,800 casualties. Best reports indicated that the enemy suffered more than 37,000 casualties.

14

KOREA THE FORGOTTEN WAR

Almost two thousand Texas Aggies served in Korea during the "Forgotten War," and sixty-three died in combat or war-related accidents. Numerous Aggies received the Silver Star for gallantry in action; others received the Distinguished Service Cross and the Distinguished Flying Cross. They fought at places referred to as Pork Chop Hill, Heartbreak Ridge, Bloody Ridge, Smoke Valley, the Pusan Perimeter, Luke's Castle, Hill 812, Hill 854, and Triangle Hill. They flew thousands of combat missions into MiG Alley and elsewhere from Kimpo Air Base and carriers at sea. "Aggies were everywhere," reported 2nd Lt. Robert L. ("Bob") Middleton ('51) of the 3rd Battalion, 160th Infantry Regiment, 40th Infantry Division, who headed a fifty-five-man platoon on Heartbreak Ridge.[1]

Among them were Lt. Tommy Splittgerber ('49), a former yell leader attached to the 40th G2 (Intelligence) Division in Korea, and Lt. Ken Schaake ('51), who headed a platoon of five M-26 tanks assigned to the 40th Infantry Division. There too were Capt. James V. Proffitt Jr. ('46) and Donald Jones with the 35th Squadron, 8th Fighter Bomber Group, Lt. Helmut Quiram ('49), an air force maintenance officer stationed in Taegu, and hundreds of others, including Maj. Fred Dollar ('44), who had helped supply the troops landing on Omaha Beach in World War II and now worked sixteen-hour days trying to keep the troops fed in Korea. Lieutenant Colonel Dollar retired from the army in 1965 and returned to Texas A&M to keep the Aggies fed, which he did in fine form. Providing backup in the States were thousands more, such as Lt. John W. ("Shotgun") Schattenberg ('46), an air force nuclear weapons officer at Los Alamos, New Mexico, and Anderson ("Andy") J. Walters ('46) and his brother, Fred A. Walters ('50), who was killed when his F-86D engine exploded on takeoff from Eglin Air Force Base in Florida.[2]

Although the United States, for the most part, remained focused on aid, armaments, and the defense of Europe during the Cold War, combat involving U.S. forces erupted in Korea in June, 1950. Texas Aggies were there at the beginning and remained on duty in Korea after the cessation of hostilities and for the rest of the century. It is estimated that 54,246 men with U.S. forces died in Korean-related service.[3] Even after nominal peace (not victory) was achieved in Korea and then in Vietnam, the immediacy of combat remained ever present in Southeast Asia into the twenty-first century.

In December, 1943, Allied leaders decided at the World War II Cairo conference that, upon the close of the war and the expulsion of the occupying Japanese forces, Korea would be "in due course" a free and independent nation. Following Japan's surrender, President Truman suggested to the Soviets that the United States supervise the surrender of Japanese forces below the 38th parallel—an imaginary line selected randomly by American officers from a *National Geographic* foldout map as the strip that only roughly, in geographic terms, divides the peninsula—while the Soviets would manage the surrender above this parallel. The 550-mile-long Korean peninsula, jutting out of the Chinese mainland and about twice the size of the state of Mississippi, is a raw, mountainous landscape with less than 20 percent of arable land. Historically, with two-thirds of the population living below the 38th parallel, the north depended upon the south for most of its food and production goods, while the south obtained its raw materials and electrical power from plants constructed by the Japanese in the north. Free elections brought an aging pro-American, Princeton-educated Korean, Syngman Rhee, to the presidency of the Republic of Korea, which officially came into being on August 15, 1948.

The United States, already removing its troops from the Philippines, the South Pacific, and Southeast Asia, completed its withdrawal of most of the ground troops from Korea in late June, 1949, leaving behind only a small cadre, the U.S. Military Advisory Group (KMAG), to assist President Rhee and the South Korean army (ROK). Poorly equipped and led, the South Korean army was little more than a national guard force, prone to rotate duty based on the planting and harvest seasons. Thus, Korea provided the Soviet Union and its Chinese communist allies a prime regional target in Southeast Asia, and Korea became a litmus test of how the United States might react to such aggression.[4]

Chinese communists and the Soviet Union quickly refused to recognize Syngman Rhee's elected pro-Western government. Following the expulsion of Chiang Kai-shek's government and armies from mainland China in 1950, the Soviets and the new People's Republic of China installed a communist government in North Korea, with Kim Il Sung as president. Then, following the election of Rhee and the departure of U.S. forces from the Korean peninsula, China's chairman Mao Tse-tung ordered the 28,000 North Korean troops who had served in the Chinese army to return to North Korea for service with the North Korean

People's Army (KPA). With additional recruits, these battle-hardened veterans composed the core of eight divisions of the North Korean army's new 150,000-man communist force, including 89,000 well-trained and equipped combat troops. Concurrently, in 1950, the army of the Republic of South Korea was composed of four divisions, totaling about 65,000 troops, of which only one division was stationed on the border and possibly combat ready.[5]

The theoretically neutral boundary separating the two halves of the Korean peninsula was (and is today) a virtual no-man's land. However, in early 1950, North Korea began probing south of the 38th parallel with armed incursions. Viewed at the time as isolated cases, the intrusions appeared to be nothing more than harassment by small patrols. There was no sense of an imminent military threat, and the South Korean military persisted in being lax in its vigilance, generally maintaining a low state of preparedness. Despite recurrent rumors of a major invasion, U.S. intelligence informed South Korea and Gen. Douglas MacArthur, commander of American forces in the region and proconsul for the United States' occupation of Japan, that only a remote possibility existed of a serious attack on South Korea from the north. Unfortunately, the rumors proved much more accurate than the intelligence.[6]

On June 25, 1950, the North Korean army, 90,000 strong with more than 150 Russian-built T-34 tanks, drove southward, smashing across the border along a forty-mile front north of Seoul. Soviet military advisors had developed and written the extensive battle plan with operating orders translated from Russian into Korean. The attack called for an invasion directed at the capture of the capital city, associated with a thrust that would at the same time cut off and isolate the weak South Korean divisions stationed near the demilitarized zone (DMZ). The fall of Seoul was to be followed immediately by a major drive to the port of Pusan, on the far south end of the peninsula. Soviet planners believed that South Korea could be seized before its armies could regroup and before the United States could send combat forces in to assist. Indeed, caught by surprise, South Korea came perilously close to being extinguished within weeks of the initial attack.

The day of the North Korean onslaught, President Truman immediately ordered American forces in the Pacific to the defense of South Korea: "What is developing in Korea seems to me like a repetition on a larger scale of what happened in Berlin, The Reds are probing for weaknesses in our armor. We must meet their threat without getting embroiled in a worldwide war."[7] At the same time, the UN Security Council recommended armed assistance to the Republic of Korea "as may be necessary to repel the armed attack and to restore international peace and security in the area." On June 30, without asking for the traditional declaration of war from Congress, as commander in chief of the armed forces, President Truman committed U.S. combat troops to Korea.

Gen. Douglas MacArthur was given command of American forces. Truman authorized a sea blockade of the Korean coast and the use of American air power in South Korea to help halt the ground attack. He also approved the bombing of North Korea. Congress concurred by authorizing the call to active duty of all reserve components for up to twenty-one months and, through Public Law 590, extended the draft until July 9, 1951. Troops on occupation duty in Japan were immediately available for service in Korea, while back in the States, the Texas, Louisiana, and California National Guard units were among the first of many to be summoned. Fielding questions from the Washington media, Truman termed the conflict "merely a police action taken up to help the United Nations," while, in fact, he had obligated the full resources of the American armed forces to war in Korea. Gen. Omar Bradley, chair of the Joint Chiefs of Staff, reflected the opinion of many in the armed forces and among the American public who were so focused on the defense of Europe that the distant conflict in Korea promised to be "the wrong war, in the wrong place, at the wrong time, with the wrong enemy."[8]

It was definitely "the wrong time." By 1950, American forces worldwide were being demobilized. Most of the military units were considerably under strength, and many at overseas posts were effectively no more than a garrison force on R&R. Total army personnel had been slashed by 75 percent from troop levels existing at the close of World War II. The Marine Corps, which numbered half a million soldiers in 1946, had been slashed to 86,000. The air force had shrunk from 248 to only 2 combat-ready groups, declining in size from the days of the army air force (AAF), numbering 2,253,600 men on V-J Day, to about 300,000 in mid-1947.

Given the stringent congressional budget cuts for defense, the air force could ill afford new aircraft or even the replacement and maintenance of existing equipment. Weapon replacements and logistical support had deteriorated everywhere. Most of the U.S. naval strength had been reduced to decommissioned hulks floating in vast coastal "mothball fleets." Cuts to the military budget had been drastic. Morale was low throughout the armed services. For example, then air force Lt. John A. Adams, returning stateside from Okinawa in April, 1950, recalled a very "unsettled environment—pilots of all grade were being reduced in rank and hundreds of rated pilots were discharged out of the air force, morale was indeed low during the 1949–1950 period."[9]

President Truman had been briefed on the poor state of the military as early as April, 1950, yet he and his advisors assumed that, despite Russia's explosion of an atomic warhead in 1949, the U.S. monopoly on the global nuclear arsenal was enough of a deterrent to halt communist expansion. In reality, the administration's policy of worldwide "containment" and "nuclear deterrence" of communism was little more than a bluff played without a strong, well-trained, conventional force.[10] Furthermore, due to the swiftness of the events in Korea, neither Washington nor American observers in Tokyo had a complete understanding of the magnitude of the crises. Korea became a fierce and frustrating conflict that was complicated in the early months of the war by the seeming overconfidence of both the military and the politicians, resulting in many strategic blunders and a tremendous loss of life in the early stages of the war.[11]

The dynamics of the Korean conflict suggest the following five dominant phases and chronological sequence of the war:

June 25 to September 14, 1950: initial North Korean invasion, capture of Seoul, and U.S. withdrawal to the Pusan (Naktong) Perimeter; Gen. Walton Walker in command of the U.S. Eighth Army

September 15 to November 25, 1950: landing at Inchon under the command of General MacArthur; recapture of Seoul; subsequent drive of U.S. and UN forces to the Yalu River

November 25, 1950, to January 24, 1951: massive invasion by Chinese communists into Korea, pushing the UN back to the south; second loss of Seoul on January 4, 1951; Gen. Matthew Ridgway in overall command following the accidental death of General Walker

January 24 to November 12, 1951: enemy pushed back northward to the 38th parallel; air war in MiG Alley; relief of General MacArthur by Truman in April; replacement of MacArthur first by Ridgway and then Lt. Gen. James A. Van Fleet; beginning of armistice talks on July 10, 1951

November 13, 1951, to July 27, 1953: continuation of armistice talks as fighting and local attacks continue; final major offensive attempt by communists in June, 1953; prisoner exchange is key issue prior to signing of armistice on July 27, 1953; little or no change in the boundary line (4 miles wide and 155 miles long) in place prior to June 25, 1950[12]

The first stage of the multifaceted war involved primarily a defensive delaying action from June 25 through mid-September, 1950, by remnants of the ROK and newly arriving American troops. Seoul fell to invading forces before the first contingent of U.S. troops from Japan arrived on July 1. When they arrived in Korea, they found a confused ROK army in full retreat toward Pusan. To compound the situation, equipment sent with the U.S. troops was often old or worn out, radios were inoperative, and many of the weapons were not functional. Some were even obsolete. Water-cooled .50-cal. machine guns of World War I vintage failed to function in the subzero temperatures later encountered in Korea. Even the World War II–era lightweight antitank bazookas (M-1 2.36-inch launcher), for example, were nearly useless against the well-armored Soviet-made T-34 tanks. But America's strategists had determined that antitank weapons were not needed in Korea because that terrain, like the famed Ardennes region in the Battle of the Bulge, was deemed not to be "tank country."[13]

Former Texas A&M commandant (1946–1948) Col. Guy S. Meloy Jr. (West Point, '27), who completed the National War College in 1949 following his tour

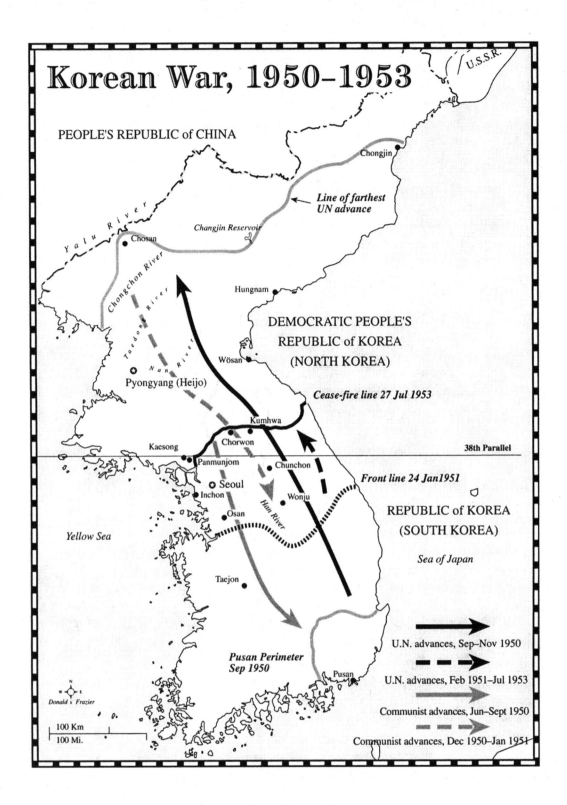

Korean War, 1950–1953

PEOPLE'S REPUBLIC of CHINA

U.S.S.R.

Chongjin

Line of farthest UN advance

Yalu River

Changjin Reservoir

Chosan

Chongchon River

Taedong River

Hungnam

DEMOCRATIC PEOPLE'S REPUBLIC of KOREA (NORTH KOREA)

Wösan

Nam River

Pyongyang (Heijo)

Cease-fire line 27 Jul 1953

Kumhwa

Kaesong

Chorwon

Panmunjom

38th Parallel

Chunchon

Seoul

Inchon

Wonju

Front line 24 Jan1951

Han River

Osan

REPUBLIC of KOREA (SOUTH KOREA)

Yellow Sea

Sea of Japan

Taejon

Pusan Perimeter Sep 1950

Pusan

U.N. advances, Sep–Nov 1950

U.N. advances, Feb 1951–Jul 1953

Communist advances, Jun–Sept 1950

Communist advances, Dec 1950–Jan 1951

Donald s Frazier

100 Km
100 Mi.

in Aggieland, was among the first American combat commanders to arrive in Korea. He was sent to Japan and placed in command of the 19th Infantry Regiment, 24th Division. With only a few days' advance notice he was ordered to prepare his regiment for deployment to Korea. Meloy had a reputation as a strong disciplinarian and, while at Texas A&M, made significant adjustments to the post–World War II Corps of Cadets.[14] However, when Meloy arrived in Korea in early July, 1950, his unit was understrength with 2,276 green troops, few of whom had combat experience. Moreover, their equipment and clothing were generally unsuited for the terrain and the freezing winters. The cold, mountains, rivers, and terrain were formidable elements of the military campaign, as were the enemy.

The 19th Infantry was rushed into battle on July 12, only a week after the first U.S. ground action at Osan, south of Seoul. Elements of the 24th Infantry Division soon arrived by air and sea from Japan and were joined by units from the 1st Cavalry Division and the 25th Infantry Division. By mid-July, there were approximately eighteen thousand American troops in the country, but they had had little time to properly prepare for war. What training occurred came during the course of deployment. At the Taep'yong-ni crossing on the Kum River, south of the capital, Meloy's unit dug in to defend the bridge across the river and halt the enemy's advance. There, too, Maj. John M. Cook ('39) from Carrizo Springs and 1st Lt. Stanley Tabor ('45), with the 19th Regiment, 24th Infantry Division, fought to stall the North Koreans' advance. The first firefight came on July 5. American and South Korean forces were "outmanned and outgunned—our antitank weapons bounced off their tanks."[15]

On July 15, the enemy attacked in force. Heavily outnumbered, the defenders were outflanked, surrounded, and cut off. As the North Korean Peoples' Army (NKPA) broke through the lines, Colonel Meloy, in an effort to protect the command post, hastily organized a counterattack with the walking wounded, cooks, drivers, headquarters clerks, and mechanics attacking behind two lightly armored vehicles. At the same time, Major Cook, who had served in World War II as a paratrooper in the Philippine campaign, organized his men for a counterattack and succeeded in knocking out several of the enemy positions with hand grenades until they were finally overwhelmed by sheer numbers. Cook, the first Texas Aggie to be killed in the Korean War, died in hand-to-hand combat on July 16, 1950, having killed one attacker with his pistol and another with his bayonet.

The Americans' counterattack slowed the North Korean onslaught but only for a moment. During the battle, Colonel Meloy was badly wounded and, in the confusion, left for dead on the battlefield. After a rally by the U.S. troops, Meloy and the other wounded were collected and evacuated just before the enemy began a final, decisive counterattack. On July 26, First Lieutenant Tabor was killed in action during the final engagements while attempting to help his injured commanding general, Maj. Gen. William F. Dean, escape capture. Lt. Earl

M. Seay ('44) and Lt. Robert H. Wood ('49) both died in the battle at Taejon. In the air over the battlefield, USAF F-80 pilot Lt. Leon W. Pollard Jr. ('47), first listed as missing in action, was later confirmed KIA. Tabor and Cook each received the Silver Star posthumously.

For his leadership and heroism under fire, Colonel Meloy was awarded the Silver Star and the DSC. Following that engagement, in a letter to A&M commandant Col. Hayden L. Boatner (1948–1951), Meloy stressed the need for well-trained officers. Korea was going to be a long fight, he believed. Subsequently, Colonel Meloy, recovered from his wounds, rose to the rank of four-star general and returned to Korea in 1961 as commander of both the Eighth Army and the UN Command. Although not a former student, Colonel Meloy was one of the most ardent supporters of Texas A&M's Corps of Cadets and military training program.[16]

Between July and September, 1950, U.S. and ROK troops were relentlessly pressured toward the southern tip of the Korean peninsula into what appeared to be a "final" defensive perimeter around Pusan, where the Eighth Army, under Lt. Gen. Walton H. Walker, desperately tried to regroup. The U.S. 2nd Infantry Division from Fort Lewis, Washington, as well as the First Provisional Marine Brigade from Camp Pendleton, were rushed to the Pusan Perimeter to help stabilize the lines, as was the British 27th Infantry Brigade from Hong Kong.

Back in the States, in early August, Congress removed the limits imposed on the size of the army, and President Truman immediately ordered an increase in strength to 1,081,000. Nearly 8,000 reserve captains and lieutenants were ordered to report at once to involuntary active duty as the troops already in Korea fought for survival. Aggies were among those reservists called to arms, and others were already in combat. The battles along the Pusan Perimeter in late summer and early fall of 1950 resulted in the deaths of Lt. Frederick P. Forste ('48), Pfc. Aubrey W. Pollard ('51), and Lt. Cecil E. Newman Jr. ('52), among others. Despite astounding initial successes, the enemy attack began to stall as the North Korean forces outran their supply lines. The brief pause from the relentless pressure finally allowed U.S. and UN forces to regroup and resupply. Moreover, Gen. Douglas MacArthur and his staff formulated a bold maneuver designed to save UN forces at Pusan and to bring the war home to the enemy.[17]

MacArthur planned a daring landing behind enemy lines at Inchon, Korea's second largest port, located far to the north of Pusan, near Seoul and the 38th parallel. Despite opposition from the Joint Chiefs of Staff in Washington, D.C., MacArthur nevertheless gained last-minute approval from President Truman for the execution of this flanking operation. While the risks were enormous, a successful landing would force the enemy to fight on two fronts and reduce pressure on the defenders at Pusan. For five weeks U.S. and Korean spies reconnoitered the landing site and enemy gun placements and devised the tactics that would most quickly seize the port.[18]

The greatest concern was the tide at Inchon, which varied from 29 to 36 feet.

The landing, code-named Operation Chromite (calculated as a 5,000-to-1 "gamble" by Gen. Matthew Ridgway, if not conducted at precisely the right moment), would encounter massive mudflats that would strand the assault craft and mire men and equipment waste deep in mud. MacArthur assembled the 5th Marine Regiment's 1st Battalion, the 1st Marine Division, and elements of the 7th Infantry Division for the planned landing. When the strategy was conceived, the 1st Marine Division was a "shell force" of fewer than 3,500 men and was hastily brought up to strength with the addition of personnel from the 2nd Marine Division, Organized Reserve, and the Marine Corps Reserve. On August 7, the 1st Marines, with somewhat more than 17,000 men, was activated under Maj. Gen. Oliver P. Smith from Menard, Texas, while Col. Lewis B. ("Chesty") Puller, who had commanded the marine barracks at Pearl Harbor during the opening shots of World War II, was regimental commander. The 1st Marines began boarding ships at San Diego on August 8 and were on the scene at Inchon by mid-September. The 7th Infantry Division, based in Japan, was at half-strength, and its force was supplemented by the addition of about 8,600 untrained Korean augmentation troops (KATUSA). Thus, the Inchon landing was, by any measure, a daring and desperate action.[19]

Leading the attack would be the 5th Marine Regiment's 1st Battalion, commanded by Lt. Col. Raymond L. Murray ('35), then thirty-seven and a veteran of World War II Pacific warfare. During World War II Colonel Murray was awarded his first Silver Star at Guadalcanal and his second during the landing at Tarawa. While serving as a unit commander on Saipan, he won the Navy Cross for his heroism when, during an engagement, although seriously wounded, he defended his command post and continued to direct his battalion in an assault. For this bravery, author Leon Uris, a member of Murray's unit, modeled Murray as the fictitious commander "Highpockets" of the 2nd Battalion, 6th Marines, in the famous World War II novel Battle Cry. At Inchon, Murray and his men faced yet another challenge.[20]

Marine and army units were quietly moved from the Pusan area (notwithstanding the interference of two typhoons) and shipped to staging points off the west coast of the peninsula. Operation Chromite began in mid-September. At 0633 on September 15, 1950, dodging an extensive enemy minefield in narrow Flying Fish Channel at high tide, Colonel Murray's 5th Marine Regiment landed on the well-fortified Island of Wolmi-do (which translates roughly as "Moontip"), in the mouth of the port of Inchon following naval bombardments and carrier-based air attacks on defenses there and at Inchon. The marines quickly scaled the twelve-foot seawall and moved inland, clearing out the North Korean garrison and capturing the small island without suffering a single fatality. Following one of the most successful amphibious landings in the history of warfare, an elated MacArthur came ashore on September 17 and presented Murray his third silver star.[21]

Among the reserves recalled to active duty to fill out the ranks of the 1st

Marine Division, which landed at Chosin just south of Wolmi-do, was 2nd Lt. John H. Miller ('46) from Axtel, Texas. He was a WW II veteran who left A&M in 1943 to join the marines and saw combat on Okinawa and in the Marshall Islands. In 1946, he returned to the A&M campus and completed his degree in 1949. Miller then went on to a marine platoon leaders' class at Quantico, Virginia, an insurance policy that meant that, if he had to go back to war, he would go as an officer. Miller then went through officer's training. Only two weeks after he completed the course, the Korean war began. He was with the first wave of marines ashore at Inchon. After the capture of Seoul, Miller was extracted from the area for a winter invasion with the 3rd Battalion, 1st Marine Division, on the east coast as American and ROK forces streamed northward toward the Yalu River.[22]

Marine and army assault troops, including army Lt. Thomas R. Parsons ('49), later commandant at Texas A&M, moved from Inchon eastward toward Seoul, first capturing the Kimpo Air Base and then, on September 27, crossing the Han River to liberate the besieged capital. MacArthur, extremely pleased with the success of the landing, began moving his armies aggressively northward to cross the 38th parallel against the NKPA. Kimpo Air Base (K-14), despite its short 5,000-foot runway, was converted into a major fighter base. Thirty miles south of Kimpo K-14, another fighter base, K-13, helped maintain air superiority over North and South Korea, a superiority that was constantly challenged by enemy aircraft flying out of North Korean and eventually Manchurian air bases.[23]

As the Inchon landings progressed, in the south the Eighth Army, under General Walker and after meeting fierce resistance, broke out of its defensive perimeter at Pusan about September 22 and began the drive northward, with North Korean armies in full flight and disarray. By the end of September, the Pusan and Inchon forces linked up at Osan, site of the American troops' first battle in Korea. MacArthur's Inchon landing was a military masterpiece and struck a tremendous psychological blow to the NKPA. For a time the tide of war in Korea had turned in favor of U.S. and UN forces.[24]

Indeed, having seemingly reestablished military control of the south, policy makers in Washington felt that the time was right to clean up the "Korean problem," that is, to permanently depose the North Korean government of Kim Il Sung, push the communists out, and reassert American power by reuniting the two divided Koreas as one nation, sending a clear message to communists—North Korean, Chinese, and Russian—that the United States and the United Nations would not tolerate naked aggression. Thus, on October 7, 1950, the UN General Assembly passed a resolution authorizing UN troops to move north of the 38th in order to establish a unified Korea. The overwhelming success of Inchon had accelerated the UN's determination to seek a "total victory." The previously mentioned landing of Second Lieutenant Miller and the 3rd Battal-

"It was cold as hell, twenty degrees below zero!" was 2nd Lt. John H.
Miller's emphatic description of the landing at Wonsan, Korea.

ion, 1st Marine Division, on the east coast at Wonsan was largely, Miller recalled,
"an administrative landing" because ROK forces had moved into the area as
the marines were coming ashore. But the battle had only begun. Miller's unit
quickly moved west toward Pyongyang and then headed north toward the
Chosin Reservoir. Among other things, he remembers, "it was cold as hell,
twenty degrees below zero!" Two weeks later, following a meeting of President
Truman and General MacArthur at Wake Island, as American and UN forces
moved rapidly through North Korea, the 1st Cavalry Division seized the northern capital of P'yongyang. For a short time the war seemed near an end and
Korea on the verge of becoming a reunited, democratic nation.[25]

Through late October, 1950, army and marine units drove northward through
Korea with lead elements of the U.S. Army, reaching the Yalu River on the Chinese border just before Thanksgiving. Then Lt. Tom Parsons was among the
first to arrive at the Yalu. He recalled that, upon reaching the river, his entire unit
lined up and relieved themselves in the water. With virtually all of North Korea
now in the UN's hands, the rapid push to the Chinese border appeared to have
been a strategically decisive action that would bring an end to the short-lived

war. Indeed, to commemorate the march to the Yalu, General MacArthur flew to Korea from his headquarters in Tokyo, where he announced to the press that "I hope to get the boys home for Christmas."[26] However, it was not to be.

Shortly after consuming a still-frozen Thanksgiving meal, Tom Parsons and his unit and the UN forces arrayed along the northern border with China were shocked as a massive Red Chinese army, some 300,000 communist Chinese forces (CCF) troops with Soviet air support, poured across the Yalu River into North Korea. In retrospect, the Inchon landing and rapid transit across North Korea were the events that caused Mao and the Chinese Politburo to agree to a military intervention in Korea. Soviet marshal Joseph Stalin strongly encouraged the attack by stating that the Americans were a clear threat to China despite their professed intentions of halting at the Yalu, and he thus offered Soviet assistance to China, including armor, artillery, planes, and military advisors. Even though Truman assured the Chinese via a press conference on November 15 that the United States had no plans whatsoever to enter China but sought only peace and a reunited Korea, the president's statement fell on deaf ears. CCF objectives were to isolate and eliminate American forces in North Korea and then reestablish communist control over both the North and the South.[27]

Most of the American and UN troops were able to fall back and escape entrapment by the overwhelming Chinese armies. Some army and marine units, however, were not so fortunate. In the north-central part of North Korea, U.S. Marines and a contingent of army troops had pushed to the Chosin Reservoir by mid-November. A bitterly cold winter, reported to be the coldest in more than a hundred years, had already blanketed the region in snow and ice. The lead element of the troops deployed at Chosin included Colonel Murray's 5th Marines, who dug in west of the reservoir at a small hamlet named Yudam-ni. On the eastern slopes of the reservoir, elements of the 7th Army Division known as "Task Force Faith" took up positions. South of these locations, marines, including Lieutenant Miller and elements of the 1st Division, were thinly stretched throughout a string of small villages and mountain passes, including Chinhung-ni, Koto-ri, Hagaru-ri, Toktong Pass, Sudong, and Funchlin Pass. Although overextended, Chinese general Sung Shin-lun planned to divide and destroy the Americans piecemeal as the U.S. Marines thinned their lines over thirty miles of winding dirt roads. With whipping high winds, called the "Siberian Express," overcast skies, and temperatures dropping to more than twenty degrees below zero by late November (and seldom above zero during the day), the marines entered into one of the epic battles in the annals of the corps.[28]

As U.S. forces sought to reestablish their lines, on November 13, 1950, Lt. Walter N. Higgins ('48), with "Puerto Rico's Fighting 65th Infantry," led a motorized patrol that was searching for the location of the enemy's forces. Near the village of Handongson, Higgins's patrol encountered intense fire from enemy forces entrenched on a high ridge. As his troops scattered for secure positions, Higgins ran straight toward the enemy, firing his automatic weapon, killing two, wounding others, and forcing the opposing forces to "run for their life." Higgins thus extracted his men from a dangerous situation and received the Silver Star for his action. Before he could receive the award, however, he died—on January 21, 1951, when, during a grenade practice by South Korean troops behind combat lines, an ROK soldier dropped a live grenade among the trainees. Higgins grabbed the grenade in an attempt to throw it out of danger, but it exploded before he could release it, thus giving his life for his comrades.[29]

By nightfall on November 27, about 8,200 Marines of the 5th and 7th Regiments were dug in on the west side of Chosin. On the eastern slopes of the reservoir, the army, with 3,000 troops, were quickly outflanked and surrounded by more than 70,000 veteran Chinese soldiers. South of the two positions were about 5,000 marines and GIs strung out along the southern approach to the reservoir. The Chinese assault was overwhelming. Thousands of CCF troops slipped through the marine and army lines. The battle ranged in all directions. Forced from his command post, Murray set up a temporary headquarters in an empty field in order to stay in touch with his three battalions. After sixteen hours of combat, the 5th Marines gained only about 1,500 yards to the southeast. Casualties mounted, and the enemy had cut the road to Murray's rear. "I realized we were in a serious predicament," Colonel Murray recalled. "We were being hit from all sides in considerable strength. . . . I figured we were finished." Although running low on ammunition, the command veteran took a moment to send a brief note to all of his units: "From: C.O. 5th Marines. All hands make sure every shot counts."[30]

After three days, few outside of the immediate battle area were aware of the dire straits in which the embattled units found themselves. The cold weather caused the automatic weapons to work sluggishly; the carbine was a great disappointment because of its weak stopping power; grenades failed to explode; mortar tubes cracked; short rounds proved a constant hazard to friendly forces; blood plasma froze solid; and the bitter cold froze fuel oil for the stoves.

Murray sought to regroup his marines for a withdrawal back down the road toward Hagaru-ri by way of the Toktong Pass while still engaged with the enemy—a perilous operation. The path formed a narrow shooting gallery, with the marines as the "sitting ducks." Marine and air force air cover operating at treetop level under the direction of ground observers was able to save the units from total annihilation. Despite being surrounded by at least six Chinese communist divisions in the Chosin sector, the marines were not used to retreating, which caused 1st Marine Division commander Maj. Gen. O. P. Smith to remark, "Retreat? Hell! We're just attacking in another direction."[31]

Murray, knowing nothing like this had ever happened to the marines before, echoed his commander's orders in briefing his tired soldiers: "Gentlemen, we are going out of here. And we're going out like Marines. We are sticking together and we are taking our dead and wounded and our equipment. Are there any questions?"[32] With the temperature near twenty degrees below zero and the Chinese in positions on the high ground as well as in ditches on all sides, the units ran the gauntlet southward. By November 30, the marines and GIs had gained a momentary degree of safety near Hagaru-ri, but the battle was not over. In one of the bloodiest fighting withdrawals in military history the United States suffered more than 7,500 killed and wounded. The 5th and 7th Marines alone sustained more than 1,800 casualties. Best reports indicated that the enemy experienced more than 37,000 casualties. Shortly after extracting their units to Hagaru-ri, Colonel Murray and Col. Homer Litzenberg, CO of the 7th Marines, found little time for rest. They were both presented the Distinguished Service Cross in the blowing snowstorm. Once they had the DSC in hand they were given orders to again regroup and launch an attack against the enemy-infested hills. However, the final breakout from Chosin did not occur until December 10.[33]

Later, reflecting on the battles of the Chosin Reservoir, Brig. Gen. Ray L. Murray commented that "American soldiers are far superior to Koreans and Chinese in fighting ability and adaptability to difficult circumstances, they will retain positions and fight to the finish under heavy fire which seemingly no human could withstand." However, it all meant that potential defeat and desperation had replaced the euphoria generated by the hope of a quick victory in Korea. The CCF drove the UN forces from northeastern Korea, and no American or UN troops ever returned there. The retreating Americans and ROK troops were pushed out of the north to Hamhung on the Sea of Japan, where they were evacuated on ships.[34]

On December 23, 1950, Lt. Gen. Matthew Ridgway was sent to Korea to assume command of the shattered Eighth Army. He arrived just as the communists launched their third great offensive. Among those who died in combat in late January, 1951, was Texas A&M's first four-year football letterman, Lt. Walter Norton ("Country") Higgins ('48). Lt. John Miller ('46) was wounded three times during the withdrawal of his marine regiment; the third facial wound sent him to a hospital in Tokyo, and for a full year he was hospitalized in Corpus Christi, Texas. He recovered and was promoted to first lieutenant. Miller returned to fight again—in Vietnam—and eventually retired after more than thirty years of service as a lieutenant general of the USMC.[35]

After falling back under the initial impact of the attack, Ridgway began to gain a slight edge as a result of air cover from the air force and navy. As a result, communist troops began to travel and fight at night in order to avoid detection from the air. Combat became increasingly sudden and brutal. The enemy offensive was relentless, but once again the inability of the Chinese forces to maintain their overextended supply lines began to give the UN forces an advantage. The Americans were able to gradually bring the troop level of the combat units to full strength. Moreover, U.S. troops arriving in Korea included more and more combat-experienced veterans of World War II.

Texas A&M vets returning to active duty in Korea included James D. Eiland ('40), who commanded Kimpo Air Force Base near Seoul; Victor M. Wallace ('38), who fought in Patton's army during the battle of the Rhineland and served on MacArthur's staff in Korea; and pilots James E. Thompson ('38), Robert G. Lowrie ('40), Jim B. Sharp ('44), Leslie G. Tingle ('47), Thomas C. Hogan ('45), Albert M. Billingsley ('43), Erwin F. Burnett ('41), Maury W. Curtis ('42), Robert A. Epstein ('44), McRae W. Hill ('42), Lesley V. Strandman ('43), and Garland A. Powers ('45), as well as air force chaplain Mickey T. Edwards ('43). Others included army officers Kenneth C. Bresnen ('43), Charles E. Wright ('47), and navy veteran Manfred W. Gerhardt ('46).[36]

Among the new officers arriving for combat from Texas A&M were Lts. John E. Orr, George E. Harris, Fred L. Maxwell, Charles Harris, and Thomas H. Price, all from the class of 1949. Capt. Walton Perrire Jr. and Lts. Jack Turcotte, George Rodgers, Robert L. Hedrick, Clarke C. Monroe, Harold C. Byler Jr., J. Williams, Raymond W. Bonsall, William A Broussard, Robert Carlson, Eugene J. Hogan, Eugene W. Robbins, Hugh C. Behrens, Gerald Atmar, Edwin L. Hazenbuehler, John H. Ludwig, Jack Tomkins, and Donald H. Hooten, all from the class of 1950, went into combat.[37]

By the spring of 1951, as existing units were brought to full strength and new, well-equipped ground and air units arrived, the initiative gradually returned to the United States and its UN allies. On March 14, 1951, Seoul changed hands for the fourth time in nine months as the U.S. Eighth Army recaptured the capital. In nearby Chino-Ni, in early April, the 2nd Battalion, 21st Infantry Regiment, sought to dislodge an enemy force entrenched on "Hill 1010." The attack was stopped cold by a heavy concentration of small-arms fire and grenades from the enemy. When an enemy machine gun then opened up on the flanks, almost forcing the attackers to withdraw, Lt. Billy M. Vaughn ('49) led a group of riflemen in a ferocious charge against the emplacement and eliminated it, removing a serious threat to the security of the battalion and contributing significantly to the success of the mission. Vaughn received the Silver Star for this action. That same month, April, 1951, President Truman relieved General MacArthur of the command of the American armies in Korea and replaced him with Lt. Gen. Matthew B. Ridgway.[38]

The first half of 1951 was marked by bloody seesaw battles along the Han River north to the 38th parallel. In May and June, U.S. and UN forces lost 39,000 men (KIA), while the communist armies suffered an estimated 85,000 battle deaths. Under the impact of those losses, Chairman Mao Tse-tung began to modify China's war objectives from seeking to unify the two Koreas under a single communist government to preserving North Korea as a communist state. At the same time, the United States became increasingly reconciled to the idea of preserving the independence and integrity of the Republic of South Korea as opposed to reuniting both north and south under a free, elected government. In addition, both China and the United States began to perceive that a cease-fire or limited war might better achieve each country's objectives. Thus, in mid-July, 1951, Chinese and American representatives at Kaesong began to discuss the possibility of a cessation of hostilities. Indeed, a halt to combat was intermittently agreed to but invariably violated.[39] In October, truce talks were moved to Panmunjom, and the Korean war entered a new dimension.

By the fall of 1951, large numbers of new troops began to arrive in Korea from the United States, including draftees who had been called to duty after June, 1950, as well as a considerable number of newly minted officers, including many from the Texas A&M class of 1951. Of the 574 senior corps members of the class of 1951, 440 second lieutenants were commissioned. Of those, 239 were assigned to eleven different branches of the army, while 201 went to the air force. Officers who were appointed to infantry, artillery, and armored divisions left Texas A&M within weeks of graduation to attend basic and branch training, and most of those arrived in Korea by late fall or early 1952. Because air force flight training took longer, most of the pilots were not ready for combat until July, 1952. Troops arriving in Korea in the fall of 1951 and thereafter were for the most part younger and less experienced than their predecessors.[40] Nevertheless, they learned fast.

The harsh winter of late 1951 and the repeated attacks by the communist forces took a high toll on both the ground and air operations. Among Texas Aggies killed in action during this period were Lt. Joe R. Allison ('46), a World War II veteran. In October, Allison was with the 1st Cavalry Division at the time of his death. He was awarded the Silver Star and Bronze Star. Lt. Mondal R. Ammons ('53), a marine with the 1st Tank Battalion, died in action on Heartbreak Ridge. Lt. Peter H. Bowden ('43), a tank platoon commander with the 1st Cavalry, died in combat at Kaesong. Lt. Edgar B. Gray ('47), who earned the Distinguished Flying Cross, was killed in action on December 14, shortly before he was to be rotated to the States. During World War II Gray, who had been too young for military duty, served in the Merchant Marines. Capt. William S. McCarson ('43) was awarded the Bronze Star. Capt. James G. Willis Jr. ('41) was killed when his fighter crashed into a mountain following an air strike. Lt. (jg) Beau R. Wilson died in an F-4U training accident. Concerned about the harsh conditions of combat and the rising casualties in Korea and aware of the large number of new Aggie officers already in Korea and soon to arrive, former corps commandant Brig. Gen. Haydon L. Boatner, assistant division commander, 2nd Infantry, wrote to the Military Department at Texas A&M, urging the staff and cadets to "be prepared and train hard. This type of warfare is a special one. There is none harder on our young combat officers and men. . . . The military character of our Officer Corps remains the keystone of its effectiveness."[41]

Lt. Wilman D. ("Pusher") Barnes ('51) and Lt. Thomas Harvey Royder III ('51) were among the troops who reached their assigned units with the 25th Infantry Division along the front lines in September, 1952, as UN and Chinese forces jockeyed for position along a front roughly in line with the 38th parallel. In September and October, marines and the 2nd Infantry Division fought for the higher ground and particularly for Heartbreak Ridge and Bloody Ridge in the vicinity of the Punchbowl (a huge circular valley enclosed by ragged peaks 1,000–2,000 feet high on the western slope of the Taeboek Mountains), while five divisions of I Corps, including the 3rd and 25th Infantry Divisions, the 1st Cavalry Division (in the center of the advance), and the ROK 5th and 7th Divisions, moved northward from Seoul, clearing resistance and protecting the flank of the IX and X Corps operating just north of the 38th parallel.[42]

Lieutenant Royder later recounted his first day—September 2, 1952—with his new outfit, Company B, 14th Infantry Regiment, on the western side of Heartbreak Ridge. At daybreak in this "Land of the Morning Calm," everything was clear and still. A forward artillery observer, Royder checked out neighboring locations for enemy activity and overheard an animated discussion led by a sergeant from Dallas who was cleaning his .45-cal. pistol when an incoming artillery round smashed into the hill behind them. Royder's unit began to catch rounds at about ten-minute intervals. The sergeant from Dallas was accidentally wounded by his own pistol and was placed in a basket to be airlifted by helicopter out of the area—when an enemy shell landed directly on the basket. Enemy fire came in all day and all night, with "so many rounds landing that their individuality was lost in a continuous roar." Royder's 105-mm howitzers responded in kind.[43] It was a long night—and promised to be a long war.

Meanwhile, Royder's classmate, "Pusher" Barnes with the 27th Infantry Regiment (the "Wolfhounds"), came into combat as a rifle platoon leader and rapidly progressed to the position of rifle company commander. Barnes, who has emphasized that he never did anything "heroic" in his thirty years of service to the country, nevertheless participated in several combat patrols, where he never engaged in close combat, he said, but frequently dodged enemy mortar and artillery shells. Barnes returned to Korea in the 1970s' "peace-keeping" era as assistant division commander (ADC) of the 2nd Infantry Division and retired from the army in 1981 as a brigadier general. He received the Distinguished Service Medal.[44] It is the commitment and the constancy of service to their country, as exemplified by Barnes and so many others, that has served the nation so well in times of war.

By the close of 1951, the style of warfare on the ground and in the air had begun to change markedly from that of the first year and a half. On the ground, mass frontal attacks and counterattacks by the army gave way to probing, small-scale assaults from entrenched positions along a line ranging across the Korean peninsula near the 38th parallel. In the air, the enemy's introduction of the very maneuverable and advanced MiG-15 aircraft challenged American air dominance. The United States for the most part had relied on World War II–era B-26s, P-51s, F-82s, a few B-29s, and seven operational F-80 "Shooting Star" jet fighters. The navy contributed carrier-based Skyraiders and Corsairs.[45]

Now U.S. and UN air dominance evaporated. Korea became the first war in which air-to-air jet combat revolutionized air warfare. The MiG-15 was a sleek, single-engine fighter that could turn faster and fly higher than the American F-80 or F-86 Sabres. For the most part, though, American pilots were better trained than their Chinese and North Korean counterparts and were able to more than match the enemy in air-to-air combat. A great disadvantage in American air operations was that the MiG and other North Korean and Chinese aircraft were able to launch their attacks over the Koreas and then hide in the remote safety of Manchuria and mainland China—territories that were off limits to U.S. and UN air raids. Also, it soon became clear that Russian advisors and sometimes even Russian pilots were directing the air war over Korea. Soviet pilots flew numerous missions into the northwest corner of Korea, better known as MiG Alley. While the numbers vary, after the war, the USAF listed 818 MiG kills and the loss of 103 Sabres.[46]

Selected Readings

Appleman, Roy E. *East of Chosin: Entrapment and Breakout in Korea, 1950* (College Station: Texas A&M University Press, 1987).

———. *Ridgway Duels for Korea* (College Station: Texas A&M University Press, 1990).

Bruning, John R. *Crimson Sky: The Air Battle for Korea* (Dulles, Va.: Brassey's, 2000).

Crane, Conrad C. *American Airpower Strategy in Korea: 1950–1953* (Lawrence: University of Kansas Press, 2000).

Futrell, Robert F. *The United States Air Force in Korea 1950–1953* (Washington, D.C: GPO, 1983).

Hallion, Richard. *The Naval Air War in Korea* (Baltimore: Nautical and Aviation Publishing, 1986).

Hinshaw, Arned L. *Heartbreak Ridge: Korea, 1951* (New York: Praeger, 1989).

Russ, Martin. *Breakout: The Chosin Reservoir Campaign* (New York: Penguin: 2000).

Toland, John. *In Mortal Combat: Korea, 1950–1953* (New York: William Morrow, 1991).

Zhang, Xiaoming. *Red Wings over the Yalu: China, the Soviet Union, and the Air War in Korea* (College Station: Texas A&M University Press, 2002).

In Korea, Gen. O. P. ("Opie") Weyland ('25) conceived and perfected air war plans that changed the nature of air-to-air and air-to-ground combat. The new technique demanded close interaction and support among air force, army, and navy combatants.

FROM KOREA TO VIETNAM AN END AND A NEW BEGINNING

The war in Korea became something of a self-imposed stalemate between 1951 and 1953, along lines hauntingly close to where the war had begun. Best characterized as "thrust and counterthrust," combat—in the air, on the ground, and at the negotiating tables at Kaesong and Panmunjom—continued. Combatants fought and jockeyed for advantage and position as opposed to victory.[1] But the war remained, under whatever terms and conditions, a war with all of the death, destruction, hardship, and heroism anyone could imagine.

In early 1952, Gen. O. P. Weyland became commander of the UN's air operations in Korea. An "airman's airman," Weyland had earned a sterling reputation as a young brigadier general during the 1944 campaign across Europe following the Normandy landing. As commander of the 19th Tactical Air Command (TAC), operating in cooperation with General Patton's Third Army, Weyland helped set the standards for future air-land teamwork.[2] After World War II, he was a key planner in the development of the strategic role of the newly created U.S. Air Force.[3]

In Korea Weyland was the major architect of the air war plans that revolutionized air-to-air and air-to-ground combat. The new technique that became known as "air pressure strategy " called for the air force, army, and navy to work in concert. In spite of having to use obsolete maps and old World War II equipment, Weyland envisioned an air war that would utilize the most advanced technology, including the strategic use of precision radar bombing and the coordination of close air tactics to support ground troops at night as well as in daylight, coupled with better air crew training to address the increased demands of the battlefield in the jet age. A vocal and demonstrative leader, as was his associate, Strategic Air Command's (SAC) Gen. Curtis LeMay, Weyland flew numerous combat missions to the Yalu in order to test his theories about air

Gen. Otto P. ("Opie") Weyland ('23).

combat. He also wanted to further emphasize the importance of participating ("we're all in it together") and of maintaining high morale at every level of an effective fighting force. His leadership and personal interaction with the troops in Korea included an April, 1953, Muster address to a gathering of more than 125 Aggies at K-55 airbase. In 1954, following the close of hostilities in Korea, Weyland was promoted to four-star general in command of all U.S. tactical air forces worldwide.[4]

Lt. Richard R. ("Dick") Tumlinson ('51) has provided an interesting commentary on the air war in Korea from the perspective of an airman literally at ground level. Tumlinson arrived at K-13 air base in Suwon, Korea, southwest of Seoul, in December, 1952, as maintenance officer for the 51st Fighter Interceptor Group headquarters. The job, he said, was not the technically challenging experience he had expected, but Suwon K-13 was an exciting place: "The 51st Fighter Interceptor Wing, along with the 4th Fighter Interceptor Wing operating from K-14 at Kimpo Air Base near Seoul were flying F-86s and engaging the North Korean and Chinese MiG-15s over 'MiG Alley' south of the Yalu River on a daily basis. Their job was to keep the MiGs off of our bombers and fighter-bombers during their missions. Our imperative on the ground was to get as many of our planes ready for the next mission as possible from our three squadrons, the 16th, the 25th, and the 39th. And, once our planes were off, we sweated them out until they returned." Tumlinson reported that the American fighter pilots, despite the MiG's aerodynamic superiority, consistently shot down more MiG aircraft for each F-86 lost. He counted an "official tally" at war's end of seven MiGs downed for each American jet lost in combat. A number of the air force officers associated with Tumlinson included Texas Aggies 1st Lt. Ed Hatzenbuehler ('50) with the 39th Fighter Interceptor Group, 1st Lt. Hugh Scott ('51), a maintenance officer with the 4th Fighter Interceptor Group, 1st. Lt. Frank D. Frazier ('51), and 1st Lt. Frank Thurmond ('51), "who was in the Support Group on the other side of K-13." His role, Tumlinson said, "was pretty hum-drum compared to those of the fighter pilots." Nevertheless, there were exciting moments, such as the time he was sent to Cho-do Island off the coast of North Korea to see if an F-86 that had landed on the beach in an emergency could be salvaged and flown off the island. Cho-do served two important functions in the air war over Korea. It was a significant part of General Weyland's air pressure strategy in that it served as a radar base used to guide fighters and bombers to their targets, and secondly, it was an important post for rescue operations of pilots downed off the coast of North Korea.[5]

One of Tumlinson's classmates, 1st Lt. Bert Beecroft, arrived at neighboring Kimpo Air Base north of Seoul in late March, 1953. In a sense, Beecroft's journey to Korea began in 1947 at the former Bryan Air Force Base, where he spent his freshman year at Texas A&M. Following graduation in 1951, he was commissioned in the air force and began flight training in Mississippi in World War II–vintage T-6Ds. Following that phase he transferred back to Bryan Air Force Base, now reactivated, flying a T-28A, which boasted 900 horsepower and "big two-bladed propellers." Then Beecroft began training in the air force's first jet trainer, the T-33, near Orlando, Florida: "The first flight in a jet was quite an experience. The most impressive thing about the first jet flight was how quiet it was and the only noise was the pilot's breathing in the oxygen masks. The oxygen valves in the masks made a whistle when the pilots breathed. The engine noise was behind the jet and could not be heard from the cockpit when in flight." That T-33, he recalled, could fly 350 mph and climb to 20,000 feet in a few minutes; moreover, the cabin was pressurized and air conditioned. Following training, Beecroft received his wings and went to Nellis Air Force Base near Las Vegas, Nevada, where he was introduced to the F-86 Sabre jet, "which was the finest airplane in the world at that time and some believe it still is."[6] Among the attributes of the North American F-86 was a 707-mph speed with an attainable altitude of 54,600 feet. The F-86 Sabre jet was now ready for combat in Korea.

After a thirty-six-hour flight to Japan and then on to Seoul, Beecroft arrived in Kimpo late at night and was given a cot in transit quarters: "Soon after I went to sleep I was awakened by one of the loudest noises I had ever heard. Right next to the building I was in there was a gun emplacement with what was called a 'quad 50' gun and crew. Some North Korean plane was bombing our base. The quad 50 opened up and the four 50-caliber machine guns all fired at once. Out the window I could see searchlights and tracers of what seemed a hundred different guns."[7]

Beecroft was one of the "new sports" assigned to the 335th Fighter Interceptor Squadron, 4th Fighter Interception Group, 4th Fighter Interception Wing, Fifth Air Force, USAF Far East. Their job was to maintain air superiority over all of North and South Korea during daylight hours. It was not an easy assignment. The MiGs were tough competitors for the F-86 and flew out of Manchuria, which was off limits to UN attack. Early in the war, one of the F-86 squadrons' major jobs was to protect the large slow-moving, four-engine, World War II–era B-29 Stratofortress bombers from attack by the much faster MiGs. Despite the admirable efforts of the fighter escorts, there was, nonetheless, a shocking loss of B-29s. Later, the B-29s flew mostly at night.

On Beecroft's first combat mission over P'yongyang, the capitol of North Korea, "anti-aircraft guns started shooting at us with some mighty big guns. . . . When the flak first started, all I could think was, 'Why are you trying to kill me? . . . I'm a good guy.'" He soon became a veteran. On one mission over the Yalu, flying screen on a bombing run, Beecroft recalled that the MiGs that often flew 15,000 feet above the F-86s decided to come down and hit the fighter bombers. Beecroft's fighter went after the MiGs. In the ensuing combat, he was hit by flak but maintained formation and made it back to base. His skill and bravery on that mission earned him an Air Medal.[8]

The use of more experienced Russian pilots in MiG Alley, plus the MiGs' ability to avoid pursuit by simply crossing the nearby borders into China and Manchuria, put U.S. pilots at a distinct disadvantage. Moreover, "We quickly found out the Russians were damned better pilots than the Chinese," recalled F-86 pilot Lt. Waymond Nutt ('51), who retired a major general. Nutt and other Texas Aggie pilots credited with many missions and MiG kills included:

AGGIE AIR WAR STATISTICS, 1950–1953[9]

Name and Class	Missions	MiG Kills
1st Lt. Waymond Nutt ('51)	86	1
1st Lt. Doyce L. Aaron ('51)	100	
1st Lt. James V. Proffitt ('47)	100	
1st Lt. Bill McCord ('49)	100	
1st Lt. Randolph W. Backer ('49)	100	
1st Lt. Frank D. Frazier ('51)		1.5
1st Lt. Edwin J. Hatzenbuehler ('50)		.5 kill credited
1st Lt. Raymond A. Kinsey ('50)		1 damaged
1st Lt. John H. Ludwig ('50)		.5 kill credited
1st Lt. Jerry K. Deason ('50)		1 damaged
1st Lt. Albert W. Beerwinkle ('53)		1
1st Lt. Donald H. Hooten ('51)		1

Of the preceding group, 1st Lt. Randolph Backer earned the Distinguished Flying Cross.

As part of the Russians' effort to keep secret the fact that Soviet pilots were flying air-to-air combat missions in Korea, Premier Joseph Stalin issued a direct order that no Russian pilot was to allow himself to be captured.[10] Another disadvantage was that the F-86s deployed to Korea were outnumbered 6 to 1. The Joint Chiefs of Staff gave priority to the maintenance of larger numbers of F-86s in Europe and in the United States. This, coupled with the relatively slow production rate of eleven new fighters per month and maintenance problems with the existing fleet, meant that replacements and new aircraft were scarce. Nevertheless, despite the altitude advantage, the MiG's greater maneuverability, and the fact that the F-86s were outnumbered, American fighter pilots downed a total of 818 MiGs during the war, with a kill ratio of 8 to 1.[11]

In January, 1953, 1st Lt. J. L. McFarling Jr. ('51), a navigator on a B-26 with the 17th Bomb Wing, Fifth Air Force, reached Pusan. By June, he and his crew had accumulated 232 combat hours in the air, most of those on "full-moon missions" over North Korean rail lines and depots. During a mission on April 1, McFarling flew as navigator and bombardier, and his crew executed five bombing attacks and four strafing passes on an enemy train and rail bridge in the face of intense enemy fire, destroying the bridge and vital enemy supplies. McFarling received the Distinguished Flying Cross for this extraordinary achievement. He served again in Vietnam and Thailand and retired as a lieutenant colonel in 1971.[12]

In May, 1953, 1st Lt. Dare K. Keelan ('51) arrived at Kadena Air Force Base on the island of Okinawa and began flying his B-29 in scheduled night missions over Korea in June. Heavy losses from enemy fighters caused the shift to night bombing. American pilots were by then using a sophisticated new short-range navigational system (SHORAN) and were supported by a night fighter "cap" over the bomb group. These innovations reduced losses significantly and improved targeting. Keelan said that before the truce was announced in July, 1953, he and his crew flew "nine successful night missions hitting primary targets, no aborted flights, no direct MiG attacks, [and] no direct hits by anti-aircraft fire." By December, Keelan was on the way home.[13]

In 1951, 2nd Lts. Frederick P. Henry and Winston A. McKenzie graduated from A&M. Both flew more than fifty missions in Korea in a matter of months in 1953, and both earned the Distinguished Flying Cross. Piloting an F-84G on one of his missions, Henry tried to follow the instructions for taking gun-camera pictures during a bombing run. On one mission he thought he had tied in his gun switch and camera so that, when he pulled the gun trigger, the camera would operate, but he ended up making a run straight into heavy flak doing nothing but taking pictures. The "hot rounds" coming at him "appeared to me to be glowing golf balls." He finally got his bombs released, and on all future runs he had his guns ready to fire "and to hell with the pictures." Henry lived to fight again another day—in Vietnam, where he chalked up seventy-three combat missions as an aircraft commander flying B-52s out of Guam, Okinawa, and Thailand. McKenzie, with the Third Bomber Wing, completed fifty night missions in less than four months as bombardier and navigator on a B-26, earning the DFC and an earlier-than-usual rotation out of Korea to get back home "to my beautiful new wife," whom he had wed only weeks before being shipped overseas.[14]

On one of the last B-29 bombing missions over North Korea, 1st Lt. Robert L. Pierson ('51), the navigator for the night mission, and all but one of the thirteen-man crew perished in an emergency landing attempt at 0315 hours on July 7, 1953. Instrument failures forced the crew to overfly their primary target and bomb a secondary frontline support target. However, the run took more fuel than anticipated. Forced to attempt a landing at an emergency airfield (K-3 near P'Ohang) in the dark and unfamiliar terrain, the pilot missed the first approach and ran out of fuel on the go-around. A wing then caught a hill, and the plane cartwheeled and crashed. The tail gunner was the only survivor.[15] Accidents from low fuel, radar and equipment failures, missed approaches, and inclement weather exacted a heavy toll on air operations.

Despite the relative successes of the UN forces in the skies south of the Yalu River, North Korea and China challenged UN air control until the final hours of combat. As in the air, the virtually incessant ground combat between 1951 and 1953 ended as it had begun—in a strategic stalemate despite the energy, initiatives, sacrifices, and lives lost.

On a hundred hills the ground battle in Korea dragged on through 1952 and into early 1953. Most of the high points in the terrain were given numbers such as "Hill 702," based on their elevation. Some of them were given names such as Heartbreak Ridge, Bloody Ridge, Yoke Ridge, Turks Ridge, Bayonet Hill, Punchbowl, Jamestown Line, and Bunker Hill. Lt. Wescomb R. Jones ('51), gunnery officer for the fire direction center, which provided support for ROK and U.S. forces and focused on the segment of Sniper's Ridge called Pin-Point Hill, spent his tour launching "insane comets that dashed themselves with a terrifying roar against the Chinese hills."[16] Aggie men fought and died at many of these locations as the rough terrain changed hands repeatedly.

In Seoul, 2nd Lt. Robert Middleton ('51) arrived with a loaded .45-cal. automatic pistol and a cylinder of top-secret documents addressed to Eighth Army headquarters chained to his wrist. At headquarters he was relieved of his documents, allowed to keep his pistol, and sent on his way to be a platoon leader in Company K, 40th Infantry Division, 160th Infantry Regiment, 3rd Battalion—on Heartbreak Ridge. A freshly commissioned officer, he was, like so many others, "a young small town boy suddenly put in charge of 55 men, at least half of whom were older than me, and all hoping and praying that this kid would make the right decisions and not botch things up and get us all killed." Middleton's 55-man platoon and the attached five M-26 tanks helped defend the westward slope and were "constantly under fire." His platoon was a fairly typical "international platoon" that included men from Cuba, Puerto Rico, Mexico, Canada, and the United States, as well as KATUSAs (Koreans attached to the U.S. Army), who had been sent to fill out shortages in the ranks of the 40th Infantry. "The line was manned in shifts 24 hours a day with particular emphasis at night. We were usually up all night and tried to rest during the day."[17]

During one of the regular night "nursery" patrols (that is, a patrol that guarded the perimeter at night while the troops theoretically slept), one man turned up missing. Two days later, on a ridge some two thousand yards from their positions, the men of King Company saw a body "staked out high on the ridge with his helmet on a stick beside him." It was their missing man. "It was the worst display of arrogance," Middleton recalled, and everyone was "devastated, mad as hell, and appalled that members of the same human race as ourselves" could do such a thing. Heartbreak Ridge was appropriately named, and war was indeed hell. There were numerous "incidents," many encounters, and many casualties. He would have been one of those KIA, Middleton thought, but for the quick action of a classmate, Lt. Ken Schaake, whose tank fire enabled Middleton's platoon to extract itself from being entrapped by an overwhelming enemy force.[18]

In that action, Middleton withdrew his patrol to a position that forced the enemy to expose itself. Without regard for his personal safety, he then "continually exposed himself to the murderous enemy fire in order to direct the fire of his own patrol and that of supporting weapons," including Schaake's tanks. When one of the members of his patrol was killed, Middleton courageously moved forward to retrieve him, killed two enemy soldiers who attacked him, and after giving orders to his patrol to withdraw, he remained at the rear to provide covering fire and to assist in the evacuation of the killed and wounded. For this heroism Middleton was awarded the Silver Star and the Korean Service Medal with three campaign stars. His unit was eventually rotated out of combat and assigned to Koje-do Island prison to quell riots.[19]

One of Middleton's classmates, 2nd Lt. L. D. ("Pete") Ross ('51), a platoon leader of B Company, 2nd Chemical Mortar Battalion, was also in action along the static front. With his platoon, Ross moved toward enemy positions to better observe and direct mortar fire. In doing so, they came under intense mortar fire. One soldier was wounded, and the others scattered for cover. Ross "unhesitatingly moved forward, disregarding the extreme personal hazard, to actively assist in evacuating the wounded soldier." The man was saved, and Ross received the Silver Star for his action.[20]

Lt. Dudley J. Hughes ('51) and his twin brother, Daniel, also of the class of 1951, both arrived on the eastern front in Korea for duty as artillery officers with

Left to right: Lt. Ken Schaake ('51) and Lt. Bob Middleton ('51) at platoon command post, Mungdung Ni Valley, Korea, 1952.

the 45th Infantry Division in December, 1952. It was bitterly cold. Dudley went to A Battery, 145th AAA (Antiaircraft Artillery) AW Battalion, while Daniel went to D Battery. Their job was to direct the fire of quad-50 antiaircraft weapons mounted on half-track M-16s. It was a devastating weapon, Hughes noted. "Four 50-caliber machine guns could be fired alternately or together, spewing out murderous streams of 'armor piercing incendiary (API) miniature projectiles.'" Confronting the 45th Infantry and two regiments of the South Korean 12th ROK Division, which had come in to relieve units of the 45th Division, were two heavily entrenched North Korean corps. Dudley Hughes, who had taken courses in surveying at Texas A&M, figured out a way to use the quad-50s much as one would use artillery pieces, "figuring the angle of elevation and azimuth to set on the guns so that they could fire at targets unseen, even at night." In the early morning of January 12, in the battle for Hill 854, the targeting system for the quad-50s proved deadly and effective. As the enemy attacked over a pass to take the hill, they were hit by a "wall of fire" from the quad-50s using preset targeting data. It was a major attack, and the enemy was repulsed by the quad-50s and an ROK infantry counterattack. The same thing happened again in February, 1953, when a North Korean battalion of more than seven hundred men charged down the ridge toward Hughes's fortifications on Hill 812, only to run into a withering hail of quad-50 fire. Despite the heavy firing, the North Korean attackers fought their way down the ridge to within fifty yards of the ROK positions. When the ROK counterattacked, "the North Koreans had to retreat through the 50-caliber inferno again to reach their lines." Soon after that battle, Dan Hughes, Dudley Hughes, and their platoons were moved ten miles west to the east flank of Heartbreak Ridge. During their tour the shelling and the threat of attack never ceased. Before they were rotated out of the front lines, both had spent almost a year under fire and were glad to be leaving Korea.[21]

In a related engagement on January 28 near Su-Dong, Korea, 1st Lt. Gilliam P. Reddell Jr. ('51), a forward observer from Texas City, Texas, was calling fire on enemy positions when the enemy infiltrated his observation post from the rear. Reddell temporarily drove the troops back with "a withering fire" from his carbine, then requested artillery fire close to his own position. He then returned and, in hand-to-hand combat, helped drive the enemy away from the rear trenches and the top of his observation bunker. He then returned to his post once again to direct close fire upon the enemy's machine-gun positions, finally forcing their withdrawal. Reddell was awarded the Silver Star for gallantry in action.[22]

Although other UN coalition forces were engaged, American military personnel from the army, air force, navy, and Marine Corps were involved in more than 90 percent of all ground and air actions in Korea. Texas Aggies participated in most of these encounters, and many died in Korea in service of their country. Only days apart, Lt. James R. Holland ('50) and Lt. William C. Knapp ('44) were lost in combat. Lieutenant Holland died in action on October 8, 1952. A letter from his mother to Dick Hervey at the Association of Former Students reads as follows: "We received a letter from the commanding officer of the 7th Div. confirming his death, but it is unbelievable. We noticed in James' returned bank checks that he had sent your Association of Former Students a gift. Probably the last thing he did as it was dated about the time of his death. This was so like him, even from the battle front to remember. . . . He loved his school very much."[23]

Lieutenant Knapp, a World War II veteran, left his job as director of the Agricultural Experiment Station in Lufkin, Texas, to return to active duty. He died rallying his men in a counterattack during a furious battle at Triangle Hill on October 18, 1952. The citation for his Distinguished Service Cross reads as follows: "He led his men through mortar and artillery fire and kept them moving. When he got to the top of the hill there were no trenches to take cover in and the Chinese in bunkers had to be flushed out. He kept moving among his men, directing them, giving them encouragement. And when the objective was secured he had the men dig in to get set for the counterattack. The way he could talk to you could make a fighting soldier out of anyone."[24]

Among the numerous Texas Aggie veterans of World War II who also served in Korea were Maj. William F. Graves ('45), Capt. Leonard D. Holder ('42), Maj.

Herbert W. Hartung ('37), Capt. John D. Yowell ('40), Lt. Gen. James F. Hollingsworth ('40), who commanded I Corps, and Lt. George E. Hill ('49). Hill, for example, fought with the 65th Infantry Regiment during the desperate days of December, 1951, through the spring of 1952, when he became unwell. He was hospitalized but rejected the doctor's opinion that he was too sick to return to the front. Hill rejoined his unit and, after an engagement in June, became critically ill and died before he could be evacuated to Seoul.

Other World War II veterans who returned to fight in Korea included Lt. Col Edgar B. Warner ('40), Lt. Col. Jerry F. Dunn ('41), Capt. Thomas Stanford ('41), Maj. Richard J. Titley ('42), Capt. John B. Wise ('40), Maj. William C. Carter ('42), Lt. Col. John L. Carson ('41), Capt. Mark L. Browne Jr. ('44), Col. Harry N. Shea ('37), and F-86 pilot George G. Greenwall ('45), who was reported lost in action over Anju, Korea, on May 15, 1952. For these men, as for so many Americans returning home from war, a normal civilian life was more illusion than reality. For many, there would be no return from Korea.

During the war, Aggies from the class of 1925 through the class of 1957 served either in Korea proper, Japan, or the South Pacific. Contributing significantly to the war effort in disparate roles were Lt. Jack Herman Levine ('44) with the Dental Corps and Jes D. McIver ('51) with the 13th Engineer Combat Battalion, 7th Infantry Division. Almost fifty years after attempting to locate a "digging noise" on one of the northern outposts, McIver, while on a "revisit" to South Korea, discovered a North Korean tunnel in the area he had been searching. Aviation electrician Robert E. Thompson ('57) served with the Military Air Transport Service (MATS), which provided a direct supply link to Korea from Hickam Field, Honolulu, throughout the Korean War. Hundreds of other Texas Aggies served stateside in support of the combat forces, including, to mention a few, Lts. Wilbur Lippman, Jack Holland, Hal Jonsson, Charles McNeil, and Francis Otken, all of the class of 1951. By early 1953, more than 1,500,000 men were in uniform scattered through twenty combat divisions and eighteen separate regiments or regimental combat teams. Nearly 48,000 reserve officers had been recalled to active duty. The war cost America 54,246 lives and more than 100,000 wounded. An estimated 1,900 Texas Aggies served in Korea, and 62 former students died in combat or war-related accidents. Sixty percent of those were killed in action. Most of those former students came from the classes of 1949, 1950, 1951, and 1952. The main cause of noncombat deaths was training accidents, and most of those involved plane crashes.[25]

Many of those who served in Korea—such as infantry Lt. Joseph B. Murphy ('50), who earned four Bronze Stars, four Purple Hearts, and the Legion of Merit and retired as a colonel—continued in the service of their country in places such as Vietnam, Germany, Japan, and other spots around the globe. Many returned for one or more additional tours of duty in Korea.[26] Lt. Gen. James F. Hollingsworth ('40), a much decorated veteran of campaigns in North Africa, Europe in WWII, and in Vietnam, was assigned to Korea in the early 1970s. He commanded the U.S. Army I Corps with twelve Korean divisions under his operational control.

The making of peace during the course of almost three years of combat was a tenuous process. And when it came, that peace was more of an institutionalized stalemate than a resolution to a problem. During the later discussions at Panmunjom, a key issue dealt with the status and return of prisoners. The United States wanted the return of all American and allied POWs and a full accounting of all POWs and MIAs. The communists, the American negotiators believed, wanted only propaganda. A key point of contention had to do with the Red Chinese and North Korean POWs at the island prison of Koje-do on the southern tip of the peninsula. There, some sixty thousand enemy POWs were in constant revolt and riot, a problem that was finally solved by former Texas A&M commandant Brig. Gen. Haydon L. ("the Bull") Boatner, who was sent to take command of the riot-torn camp.[27]

Having graduated number one in his West Point class, Boatner, who was fluent in Mandarin, had served in Tientsin, China, in 1928, and in World War II was deputy to Gen. Joseph ("Vinegar Joe") Stillwell in Burma. When Boatner arrived at Koje-do, he lined up his tanks with the guns facing the POW camp, personally faced down a POW mob, and restored order.[28] In July, 1953, a truce, not really peace, ensued in Korea. First Lt. Jack D. Gressett ('52) remembers that month very well because that is when he arrived on the front with Battery A, 63rd Field Artillery, 24th Division. The year following, when 1st Lt. Edward E. Thomas ('53) began his duties near Pusan with the 296th Transportation Battalion, the continuation of the war was always imminent.[29] And so it remained for many years.

The Aggie presence in Korea was recorded in part by the large number of combat decorations awarded during the course of the war (table 12).

Yet the final and more definitive evidence of participation is given by those who died in the service of their country (tables 13 and 14).

Although combat in Korea technically ended in July, 1953, and though, by the spring of 1954, the American military presence in Korea had dwindled sharply, war for the United States never really ended in Asia; it just shifted farther south. There, in what had been French Indochina, which comprises the present-day states of Cambodia, Laos, and Vietnam, the defeat of the Japanese resulted in the reoccupation of its colonial territories by France under a UN mandate that provided for the independence and self-government of those countries. During World War II, a communist resistance force (Viet Minh), headed by Ho Chi Minh, actively assisted the United States and its allies in the war against Japan. Once the Japanese left and the French resumed control, the Viet Minh began to actively resist and oppose French domination. In the process, the Viet Minh created a regular military "liberation army," and, together with other resistance groups, waged intermittent guerrilla warfare. Open war began at the end of 1946, and on May 7, 1954, following a wide-ranging, hit-and-run campaign and

TABLE 12 Combat Decorations Awarded to Texas A&M Soldiers in the Korean War

Decoration

Silver Star Recipients

Lt. Col. Raymond L. Murray ('35)	Lt. Billy M. Vaughn ('49)
Maj. John M. Cook ('39)	Lt. Jerry L. King ('51)
Lt. Stanley Tabor ('45)	Lt. Bob Middleton ('51)
Lt. Joe R. Allison ('46)	Lt. Gilliam P. Reddell Jr. ('51)
Lt. David R. Blakelock ('46)	Lt. David A. Rives ('51)
Lt. James Callan ('46)	Lt. L. D. Pete Ross ('51)
Lt. Walter N. Higgins ('48)	

Bronze Star Recipients

Maj. Herbert W. Hartung ('37)	Lt. Homer Finch ('51)
Capt. John D. Yowell ('40)	Lt. Earl Gilmore ('51)
Capt. William S. McCarson ('43)	Lt. Dan Hughes ('51)
Maj. William F. Graves ('45)	Lt. Westcomb R. Jones ('51)
Lt. Joseph B. Murphy ('50)	Lt. David Leavitt ('51)
Lt. Kenneth Schaake ('51)	Lt. Charles Ruble ('51)
Lt. Bruce H. Morisse ('50)	Lt. John Jennings ('51)
Capt. Francis P. Robles ('45)	Lt. William Fockelmann ('51)
Maj. Fred W. Dollar ('45)	Lt. Wilman D. Barnes ('51)
Lt. Roy L. Garner ('49)	Lt. Ralph Bass ('51)
Lt. Ben E. Solomon ('50)	Lt. Charles A. Chambers ('51)
Lt. Robert W. Coglazier III ('49)	Lt. Edwin Clark Edwards ('51)
Capt. William R. Thomas ('49)	Lt. John Paul Thomas ('51)
Lt. Bob Gebert ('51)	Capt. Leonard D. Holder ('42)
Lt. Col. James M. Hamblin ('40)	Lt. William C. Knapp ('44)
Lt. Dudley J. Hughes ('51)	Lt. George E. Hill ('49)
Lt. James J. Cain ('51)	

Purple Heart Recipients

Lt. Jack W. Birkner ('51)	Lt. Donald P. ("Doggie") McClure ('50)
Lt. Gerald Atmar ('50) (rescued from the field of battle by his ROK advisor/ interpreter)	Lt. Gillam P. Reddell ('51)
	Lt. William J. Dunlap ('51)
Lt. Joe H. Nagy ('49)	Lt. Joe Murphy ('51)

Distinguished Flying Cross Recipients

Lt. Edgar B. Gray ('47)	Lt. Fredrick Henry ('51)
Lt. Richard L. Goodwin ('51)	Lt. J. L. McFarling Jr. ('51)
Lt. Albert W. Beerwinkle ('53)	Lt. Ray Falke ('51)
Lt. Knox T. Johnston ('48)	Lt. Winston A. McKenzie ('51)
Lt. Randolph W. Backer ('49)	Lt. Fredrick F. Nye III ('51)

TABLE 13. Texas A&M Korean War Deaths June, 1950–July, 1953

Name and Class	Branch	Death	Date	Where	Comments
Col. Charles S. Ware ('25)	Army	Illness	Apr. 3, 1952	Dep. Chief of Staff, IX Corps	WWII
Lt. Col. Jess E. Evans ('38)	Army	POW**	Nov. 27, 1950		Died in captivity
Maj. John M. Cook ('39)	Army	KIA	July 16, 1950	Kum River, Korea, 19th Inf. Div.	WWII: SS, PH
Maj. Harvey H. Storms ('39)	Army	MIA*	Dec. 1, 1950		Presumed dead
Capt. Sidney C. Hill ('40)	Air Force	Training	Jan., 1953	Harmon AFB, Newfoundland	
Capt. James G. Willis Jr. ('41)	Air Force	KIA	Sept. 3, 1951	Plane crash in Korea	
Capt. Rupert J. Costlow ('42)	Air Force	Training	Feb. 18, 1952	FAC plane crash, Korea	
Maj. Edwin J. Herman ('42)	Marines	MIA*	June 2, 1952	Unknown	
Lt. Peter H. Bowden ('43)	Army	KIA	Oct. 4, 1951	Kaesong, Korea	1st Cav. Div.
Lt. John A. Mercer ('43)	Army	KIA	Aug. 8, 1950	5th Com. Reg.	WWII
Capt. William S. McCarson ('43)	Marines	KIA	Dec. 6, 1951		Jet pilot, BS
Lt. William C. Knapp ('44)	Army	KIA	Oct. 18, 1952	Kumhwa at Triangle Hill, Korea	7th Inf., WWII, DSC
Lt. Earl M. Seay ('44)	Army	KIA	July 24, 1950		1st Cav. Div., 82nd Fld. Art.
Maj. Maurice H. Smith ('44)	Air Force	Training	May 1, 1951	T-33 crash, Japan	33 missions
Lt. Gerald M. Camp ('45)	Army	KIA	May 15, 1951	38th Inf. Reg.	WWII
Capt. James L. Garrison Jr. ('45)	Marines	POW**	Feb. 14, 1953		WWII Corsair pilot, squad leader
Capt. Will H. Gordon Jr. ('45)	Army	KIA	June 16, 1952	Unknown	
Capt. George G. Greenwell ('45)	Air Force	MIA*	May 15, 1952	Over Auju, Korea	
Lt. Robert S. Roberts ('45)	Army	KIA	Sept. 5, 1950	7th Cav Inf.	WWII; in Korea only ten days
Lt. Stanley E. Tabor ('45)	Army	POW**	July 20, 1950	Taejon, Korea, 24th Inf. Div.	WWII: SS
Lt. Joe R. Allison ('46)	Army	KIA	Oct. 4, 1951	1st Cav. Div.	WWII: SS, BS

(continued)

TABLE 13 (continued)

Name and Class	Branch	Death	Date	Where	Comments
Lt. David R. Blakelock ('46)	Army	KIA	Oct. 19, 1950	1st Cav. Div.	WWII: SS, BS,
Capt. William P. Brown ('46)	Marines	KIA	Feb., 1952		WWII: NC, DFC, ace
Lt. James Callan III ('46)	Marines	KIA	June 14, 1951	Honjon-ni	DFC, AM, SS
Lt. Cecil E. Newman Jr. ('46)	Army	KIA	Aug. 15, 1950	5th Com. Reg.	1st Cav. Div.
Lt. Edgar B. Gray ('47)	Air Force	MIA*	Dec. 14, 1951	F-80 crash	WWII: DFC; 86 missions,
Lt. Leon W. Pollard Jr. ('47)	Air Force	MIA*	July 9, 1950	F-80 crash	
Lt. Cornelius C. Duyf ('48)	Army	KIA	Mar. 24, 1953	7th Inf. Div.	
Lt. Frederick P. Forste ('48)	Army	KIA	Sept. 2, 1950	2nd Inf. Div.	
Lt. John F. Helm ('48)	Air Force	KIA	July 9, 1953	6149th Tac. Sqdn.	41 missions
Lt. Walter N. Higgins ('48)	Army	KIA	Jan. 21, 1951	Korea	SS; football letterman '44, '45, '46, '47
Lt. Jack K. Laughlin ('48)	Army	KIA	Feb. 19, 1951	Unknown	
Lt. A. Stuart MacFarlane ('48)	Marines	MIA*	Oct. 1, 1950	Unknown	31st Inf. Reg.
Lt. Charles W. Mitchell ('48)	Air Force	Training	Unknown	Plane crash, Sumter, S.C.	
Pvt. Milton L. Cagle ('49)	Army	KIA	Apr. 8, 1953	23rd Inf. Reg.	
Lt. George E. Hill ('49)	Army	Illness	June 12, 1952	Seoul, Korea	WWII: BS
Lt. Alexander Ortiz ('49)	Air Force	Training	Oct. 11, 1952	Jet crash, St. Cloud, Fla.	
Lt. Lynn B. Whitsett ('49)	Marines	KIA	Unknown	Unknown	
Lt. (jg) Beau R. Wilson ('49)	Navy	Training	Nov. 28, 1951	F-4U plane crash	
Lt. Robert H. Wood ('49)	Army	KIA	July 30, 1950	7th Cav., 1st Cav. Div.	
Lt. Mabry E. Cain ('50)	Army	KIA	Sept. 23, 1950	8th Cav.	
Lt. Frank T. Davidson ('50)	Army	KIA	Jan. 25, 1953	7th Inf. Div.	
Jerry Deason ('50)	Army	Training	Unknown	Plane crash, Denison, Tex.	

Name	Branch	Status	Date	Location	Notes
Lt. Don R. Eberhardt ('50)	Air Force	Training	Unknown	Plane crash, Waco, Tex.	
Lt. James R. Holland Jr. ('50)	Army	KIA	Oct. 8, 1952	7th Div.	
Lt. Gordon D. Leesch ('50)	Army	KIA	Sept. 19, 1951	Songnaedong, North Korea	
Capt. Gene R. Mauldin ('50)	Army	KIA	Oct. 4, 1952	Unknown	
Lt. William Rodenberry ('50)	Air Force	Training	Unknown	Train crash, Arizona	
Lt. Kenneth G. Rogers ('50)	Army	KIA	Apr. 11, 1953	32nd Inf. Reg.	
Lt. Fred A. Walters ('50)	Air Force	Training	Jan. 20, 1953	F-84G crash, Ft. Dix, NJ	
Lt. Paul C. Coffin Jr. ('51)	Army	KIA	Oct. 8, 1952	278th Inf., 46th Div.	
Lt. Autrey W. Frederick ('51)	Air Force	MIA*	Mar. 31, 1953	Died while missing	
Lt. Weldon D. Gardner ('51)	Air Force	KIA	May 30, 1953	F-84 bomber	9 missions
Lt. Jerry Jackson Jr. ('51)	Army	KIA	Apr. 17, 1953	Unknown	
Lt. Jimmie D. Lester('51)	Marines	KIA	Jan. 30, 1952	F9F-5 plane crash	
Lt. Robert L. Pierson ('51)	Air Force	KIA	July 7, 1953	Plane crash, Korea	
Pfc. Aubrey W. Pollard ('51)	Army	KIA	Sept. 19, 1950	5th Com. Reg.	
Lt. David A. Rives ('51)	Army	MIA*	June 12, 1952	Chowan	SS
Lt. Lewis E. Jobe ('52)	Army	MIA*	July 8, 1953	Pork Chop Hill, Korea	
Lt. Sterling R. Peterson ('52)	Air Force	Training	Jan. 4, 1954	Korea	Plane crash, Hawaii
Lt. Alford F. Summy ('52)	Air Force	Training	Oct. 5, 1952	Plane crash, Ft. Sill, Okla.	
Lt. Mondal R. Ammons ('53)	Marines	KIA	Oct. 17, 1951	Heartbreak Ridge, Korea	1st Marine Div.

AM	Air Medal	SS	Silver Star
BS	Bronze Star	MIA	Missing in action
DFC	Distinguished Flying Cross	KIA	Killed in action
DSC	Distinguished Service Cross	POW	Prisoner of war
NC	Navy Cross	*	Declared dead while missing (MIA)
PH	Purple Heart	**	Declared dead while captured (POW)

TABLE 14. Profile of Texas A&M Men Lost during the Korean War, 1951–1953

Army	35	KIA	37
Marines	8	MIA and KIA	9
Air Force	19	POW	3
Navy	1	Training	12
		Illness	2

relentless guerrilla war supported by an overwhelmingly hostile civilian population, France surrendered its forces at its garrison at Dien Bien Phu, leaving control of Vietnam and possibly all of French Indochina to the communists.[30]

Under the Geneva Accords approved by the United Nations, Vietnam, just like Korea, was divided into two states, with the territory north of the 17th parallel designated the Democratic Republic of Vietnam under the leadership of Ho Chi Minh, while the south became the Republic of Vietnam (RVN) with a titular emperor, Bao Dai, and a prime minister, Ngo Dinh Diem, a former French colonial administrator. Very quickly, the Viet Minh seized the opportunity to infiltrate the south, undermine the government of the RVN, and incite armed rebellion by the Viet Minh and their communist sympathizers in the south against the government of Diem.[31]

The United States and Southeast Asia Treaty Organization (SEATO) members, locked in the Cold War struggle with the Soviet Union and China, feared that the loss of Vietnam would create a "domino effect" that would inevitably lead to the loss of all of Southeast Asia and beyond. The Eisenhower administration believed that it was within the scope of SEATO to increase the presence of American military advisors in Southeast Asia. While Cambodia, Thailand, Laos, Burma, and Malaysia were all of immediate concern, the United States reasoned as early as 1956 that the line must be drawn in Vietnam. In the interest of providing assistance to the government of South Vietnam and helping to check the possibility of communist intervention, the United States created the U.S. Military Assistance Advisory Group Vietnam (MAAG) to "advise" the South Vietnamese military. An initial group of 342 American advisors were sent to Vietnam at the request of that government in 1955. By the late 1950s, military advisors by the dozens, but seldom in groups of more than 100 at any one time, were on "counterinsurgency" duty in Vietnam and Thailand.[32]

Selected Readings

Appleman, Roy E. *East of Chosin: Entrapment and Breakout in Korea, 1950* (College Station: Texas A&M University Press, 1987).

———. *Ridgway Duels for Korea* (College Station: Texas A&M University Press, 1990).

Bruning, John R. *Crimson Sky: The Air Battle for Korea* (Dulles, Va.: Brassey's, 2000).

Crane, Conrad C. *American Airpower Strategy in Korea: 1950–1953* (Lawrence: University of Kansas Press, 2000).

Futrell, Robert F. *The United States Air Force in Korea 1950–1953* (Washington, D.C: GPO, 1983).

Hallion, Richard. *The Naval Air War in Korea* (Baltimore: Nautical and Aviation Publishing, 1986).

Hinshaw, Arned L. *Heartbreak Ridge: Korea, 1951* (New York: Praeger, 1989).

Russ, Martin. *Breakout: The Chosin Reservoir Campaign* (New York: Penguin: 2000).

Toland, John. *In Mortal Combat: Korea, 1950–1953* (New York: William Morrow, 1991).

Zhang, Xiaoming. *Red Wings over the Yalu: China, the Soviet Union, and the Air War in Korea* (College Station: Texas A&M University Press, 2002).

16

Of the twenty Aggies who went down in enemy territory in Vietnam, only four, all F-105 pilots and all captured between late 1965 and early 1967 during the height of the air war over North Vietnam, were held as POWs by the North Vietnamese. One of those, Lt. James E. Ray ('63), was held captive for six years and nine months. Recalling the weeks of torture, sleep deprivation, and solitary confinement and reflecting on his experiences, Jim Ray said, "The Corps of Cadets teaches you to recognize what is legitimate and what isn't. If it wasn't, you learned to retaliate or resist while at the same time keeping a sense of honor, integrity, and respect. You learn unity, loyalty, and teamwork against an oppressor."

VIETNAM EYE OF THE DRAGON

Experiences in Korea strongly influenced American military actions and reactions in Vietnam. There, as in Korea, the omnipresence of potential Chinese involvement "paralyzed our strategic thinking" and greatly affected decisions on the objectives and limits of war. The United States' overall objective was to halt further communist expansion in Southeast Asia and to aid the Republic of South Vietnam in pursuit of that goal. Thus, for example, Maj. Mebane G. Stafford ('49) arrived in South Vietnam in 1958, just as the Viet Minh had begun to step up the level of infiltration and the frequency of attacks on positions held by the Army of the Republic of Vietnam (ARVN). Stafford's job, and that of most of those who arrived early on the scene, was to help train and equip the ARVN infantry for combat. That meant, in part, upgrading it from the weapons of World War I and II vintage they were using and also reoutfitting and instructing the infantry in the use of the M-16 rifle. The second priority of the U.S. military advisors was to improve intelligence-gathering capabilities.[1]

U.S. military assistance to South Vietnam was severely curtailed by congressional budget cuts that directly affected the resources of the Department of Defense. For a number of years, congressional budget cuts, which particularly affected the classes of 1957–1959, were translated by the Department of Defense into reduced active duty for newly commissioned officers—at Texas A&M and elsewhere. Thus, 2nd Lts. Myron Gantt and J. Rhea McLarry ('57) and many others found their two-year, active-duty obligation reduced to six months—with a six-year reserve-duty requirement. As Gantt explained, they were nonetheless, in perhaps the best "twelfth man tradition," on call and ready to serve. Meanwhile, the situation in South Vietnam became increasingly critical.

In mid-1959, the North Vietnamese began the first large-scale wave of steady infiltration of personnel and weapons down the Ho Chi Minh Trail (a thousand-mile-long network roughly paralleling the Vietnam-Cambodian-Laos border). In response, and following the election of Pres. John Kennedy in November, 1960, congressional appropriations for defense—and subsequently the number of American "advisors" in Vietnam—was gradually increased. In December, 1961, President Kennedy responded to an "urgent appeal" from South Vietnam for immediate military assistance, and by year's end, three thousand American personnel were "in country."[2]

Concurrently, the domino effect seemed to be operating as Thailand came under increasing pressure from communist insurgents located on the border with Laos. In May, 1962, responding to a Thai-Laotian crisis, the United States dispatched the 3rd Marine Expeditionary Brigade, Joint Task Force 116, from Okinawa to Thailand under the command of Brig. Gen. Ormond R. Simpson ('36). Its job was to help stabilize the Thai government and halt any insurgency from the north. Then, in February, 1963, in response to the growing pressures in Vietnam and Southeast Asia, the United States created a new command structure to oversee military assistance to the region, styled the U.S. Military Assistance Command, Vietnam (MACV), under the authority of a four-star army general, Paul D. Harkins. By late 1963, the United States had almost seventeen thousand ground troops committed in South Vietnam. That year in June, the first known combat death of a Texas Aggie in Vietnam occurred when the T-28 flown by air force Lt. Condon H. Terry Jr. ('56) was shot down by ground fire.[3] The United States began sending additional troops into South Vietnam.

The 650 "advisors" present in 1959 grew slowly to 23,300 by 1964, with the troops increasingly assuming combat roles—by necessity, not by choice. Many of the new second lieutenants who were being assigned advisor and combat roles in South Vietnam were recent graduates of Texas A&M. Officer production at A&M during the late 1950s and early 1960s averaged about 300 newly commissioned second lieutenants annually. Each year about half of those entered the army, 120–135 joined the air force, and 5–10 entered the Marine Corps via the Platoon Leaders Program (PLC), and a small number entered the officer-production program in the U.S. Navy. During these years, Texas A&M's president, Lt. Gen. James Earl Rudder, who had led his Rangers ashore at Normandy, impressed upon his students an awareness of their obligation to serve their country. Over the next few years more and more Texas Aggies began their active-duty tours in South Vietnam. By December, 1965, more than 184,000 American troops were stationed in "Nam." The next year the numbers rose to more than 485,000, and in 1966, Pres. Lyndon B. Johnson sent President Rudder on a special fact-finding mission to South Vietnam.[4] There he found, among other things, numerous former Texas A&M students, including Capt. Thomas R. Hargrove ('66), who spent most of his service on special assignment in Central America, the Philippines, and Southeast Asia. He later described Texas A&M

graduates of the 1950s' and 1960s' vintage as "steeped in tradition, mostly military and macho. The A&M Corps of Cadets was far more army than the real army. . . . And A&M prided itself in being Old Army."[5] Hargrove, as did other former students of Texas A&M, became deeply engaged early in the American military presence in Vietnam.

The terrain in Vietnam was much like that fought over in Korea, minus the bone-chilling subzero weather. Jungle, rough terrain that provided cover for the enemy above and below ground level, and small hamlets that not infrequently supported the Viet Minh broadly characterized the Indochinese combat environment. But there were differences in the style of combat. As in Korea, the war in Vietnam became an incessantly long conflict, referred to by one author as the "25-year war," and, more so than Korea, it evolved as an unwinnable war, given the constraints on military actions and the rising tide of public opposition. Although a few Americans became involved in military roles in Vietnam as early as 1955, the most intense combat phase lasted fully a decade, from 1963 through 1973, and, when the fighting ended, the war was not really over. During that decade, American troops were generally rotated into and out of Vietnam for tours of duty spanning 12 months (13 months for the marines). Many of them, such as Maj. James C. Smith II (who held an MS in civil engineering, '70, and a PhD in engineering,' 76), served more than one tour of duty.[6]

For example, Lt. Col. Donald R. ("Buck") Henderson ('62), recipient of three Bronze Stars, was in country for thirty-one months. Others serving two or more tours included Brig. Gen. Billy M. Vaughn ('48; Combat Infantry Badge, Silver Star, and DFC), Col. Jerry M. Lowrance ('62), Capt. Louis McDonald, Col. William R. Swan ('52), Maj. Kenneth Cooper ('52), Capt. Jay Bisbey ('59; DFC), Capt. Frank Muller ('65; Bronze and Silver Stars), and Capt. William A. Beasley ('58). Also there were Maj. (later Brig. Gen.) Edmond S. Solymosy and Maj. Jarrell H. Gibbs, both of the class of 1960, and Capt. Donald J. Stevenson ('66), who served with the 321st Field Artillery. While flying with the 615th Tactical Fighter Squadron from Phan Rang Air Base, Col. (later Maj. Gen.) Thomas R. Olsen flew 301 combat missions between 1967 and 1968, while Marine Corps pilot Capt. Michael L. Richardson ('65) flew 300 combat missions in his A-4 and F-4 fighters, and Col. John A. Adams flew 225.[7]

Capt. Byron Stone ('60), a member of Company A ("Animal") in the Corps of Cadets, volunteered for Vietnam and completed Ranger School before heading overseas. After his first tour, Stone volunteered for another, telling his parents that "he liked the people and had an important job to do." Stone returned to be an advisor to a Vietnamese Ranger battalion in Kein Hoa province, forty-five miles from Saigon. On August 23, 1964, while accompanying an ARVN unit of 250 troops, Stone and three other American officers were caught in a Viet Cong (VC) ambush. For nearly two hours and in rough terrain, Stone and the troops fought but were overcome. In presenting the Distinguished Service Cross posthumously to Stone's mother, Maj. James P. McKnight, his former commander, read the following citation:

> Captain Stone was serving as an advisor to a battalion when suddenly ambushed by hostile elements. Undaunted by the extremely heavy enemy gun fire, Capt. Stone completely disregarded his own personal safety and bravely exposed himself to the full force of the violent enemy attack to cover the withdrawal of the friendly troops. During the ensuing battle in which the enemy launched several assaults, he remained in an exposed position to repel the enemy. Although the intensity of the enemy gun fire increased, he demonstrated fortitude and perseverance by holding his position for one hour and 40 minutes while annihilating a great number of enemy troops. Despite the overwhelming onslaught he continued his courageous efforts until mortally wounded. Capt. Stone's conspicuous gallantry and extraordinary heroic actions are in the highest traditions of the U.S. Army and reflect great credit upon himself and the military service.[8]

On August 25, 1964, Gen. William Westmoreland attended a memorial service for Captain Stone and the three other U.S. Army officers in the U.S. Air Force Chapel at Tan Son Nhut. At the service Stone was posthumously awarded the Vietnamese Gallantry Medal and the Vietnamese National Order Medal, Fifth Class. As his close friend Len Layne ('59) noted, "When Taps sounded, Captain Stone's burial would bring the total number to 185 Americans killed in action in Vietnam."

One irony is that Stone and all the others who were killed in action through 1965 were listed as "nonbattle" deaths inasmuch as the conflict in Vietnam was not at the time recognized as a "war or battle," despite the fact that Congress had approved the Southeast Asia Resolution (better known as the Gulf of Tonkin Resolution) on August 7, 1964. That declaration authorized President Johnson "to take all necessary measures to repel any armed attack against the forces of the United States and to take all necessary steps including the use of armed forces to assist South Vietnam and any SEATO member nations." After numerous complaints, the policy was changed to properly classify those killed in action as deaths incurred in war. By the end of 1964, some 25,000 American advisors were in Southeast Asia, while, by the close of 1965, almost 200,000 American troops were in Vietnam. The toll of those killed in action began to rise precipitously from several hundred a year to thousands.[9] The action in Southeast Asia had become a war.

For most of those in battle, the primary issues are defeat of the enemy and personal survival. Air force Col. James M. Morgan ('64) had two tours in Southeast Asia, the first flying RF-4Cs at Tan Son Nhut, followed by a stint flying the RF-8G aboard the USS *Midway*, located on "Yankee Station" in the Gulf of Tonkin. Other Texas Aggie naval aviators included A-7D pilot Robert L. Keeney

('71) and F-8 Crusader pilot Joseph R. ("Gail") Baily ('73), who made one of the first raids into the heavy surface-to-air missile (SAM) defenses of North Vietnam on August 5, 1964.[10]

A bombing campaign in South Vietnam, named Arc Light, in support of ARVN troops on the ground seeking to block key supply routes from China through North Vietnam and down the Ho Chi Minh Trail began on February 25, 1965, and continued through 1970. Air strikes in North Vietnam, called Operation Rolling Thunder, soon followed. Due to tensions with Japan, B-52 bombing missions could not be launched from Okinawa, which required them to fly an extra 2,500 miles from Guam. Former A&M commandant of cadets Maj. Gen. Thomas Darling ('54) flew forty-six combat missions in the fall of 1966 and recalled, "After an early morning takeoff from Guam it was a twelve-hour round trip (about 5,000 miles) to targets in Vietnam. We came in over the South China Sea and a couple of times bombed targets in Laos."[11]

Beginning early in 1965, Viet Cong forces, reinforced by the North Vietnamese Army (NVA), opened a series of offensives. A complete NVA division was deployed to the central highlands, and the ARVN began to crumble. President Johnson concluded that combat troops had to be introduced in order to prevent the fall of South Vietnam to communist forces. In March, two battalions of marines were sent ashore to defend the port at Da Nang, and in May, the 173rd Airborne Brigade was deployed to Saigon. The air force brought in more fighters and bombers, and the Seventh Fleet began to assist with coastal patrols. Next, the 1st Brigade, 101st Airborne Division, arrived at Qui Nhon, in the geographic center of South Vietnam, to prepare for the arrival of the 1st Air Cavalry Division, which fought the first engagement with an NVA division at Ia Drang in November.[12]

Viet Cong and NVA combat tactics were not fully absorbed until years of fighting had passed. Vietnam differed from Korea. Combat in Vietnam in some respects reflected early American frontier warfare. The battle of Ia Drang in November, 1965, for example, is chronicled by the U.S. commander of the action, Col. Harold G. Moore, in his epoch *We Were Soldiers Once . . . and Young*. Aggies at the engagement included Lt. D. P. ("Pat") Payne ('65), reconnaissance platoon leader, Delta Company, 7th Cavalry, who defended the "Albany" perimeter and went on to serve two tours in Vietnam: "For that first hour or two, it was belly-to-belly and man-to-man. It didn't make any difference if you were a major, captain, sergeant, or private; we were all standing shoulder to shoulder, shooting it out with the NVA. I can hear the cry 'Here they come!' and we would all rise up and cut loose. There was fear in the air, but I never sensed panic. In one respect, you could think of it as the Little Bighorn; we were surrounded, with our packs in front of us, shooting it out."[13]

The NVA fled to safe havens across the Cambodian border, and for much of the duration of the war, U.S. forces were unable to encircle and destroy the enemy forces because of "foreign" sanctuaries. Moreover, U.S. ground operations were restricted to South Vietnam. Invasion of North Vietnam's home territory and that of the Laotian and Cambodian insurgent allies was not permitted. These parameters defined the unique military character of the Vietnam War.[14]

In November, 1966, Capt. Boyce A. Cates ('62) was flying reconnaissance for a search-and-destroy operation conducted largely by ARVN troops on a waterway in Kien Tuong province in the Mekong Delta. The troops in airboats came under intense fire from an advancing Viet Cong force. Cates made repeated low-level rocket attacks on the enemy while helping reorganize the ARVN forces. During the same engagement, he returned to provide protective fire for another boat in distress and under attack and fought "two hours of endless action," which ended with the return of the boat and its surviving soldier to friendly hands. Cates received the Silver Star for his brave actions. In a similar engagement the following spring, in 1967, Captain Cates was flying aerial support for a Special Forces Group in the same area on another search-and-destroy operation when the VC attacked and pinned down the U.S. advisor and his Vietnamese troops. Cates attacked the enemy forces in several rocket-firing passes, holding his fire until almost point-blank range in order to bring accurate fire on the enemy. Because of his courageous actions, a large friendly force was saved, and thirty-five Viet Cong were killed. Capt. Boyce A. Cates earned the DFC for that action. While in Vietnam, he received the DFC, Silver Star, the Purple Heart, and a total of forty-nine Air Medals representing 1,233 hours of air combat. Captain Cates continued flying after the war—with Delta Airlines.[15]

Throughout 1966, pressure from the VC forces continued to escalate. Lts. Jerome Rektorik and Frank Muller, who graduated from A&M in 1965 (friends and formerly 1st Brigade commander and student body president, respectively), were quickly immersed in combat when they arrived in Vietnam that year, and both earned the Bronze Star in fierce fighting. In subsequent action Lieutenant Muller received the Silver Star. That same season, their friend and classmate Lt. Neil Keltner (corps commander in 1965), a platoon leader with the 11th Cavalry, was ambushed with his platoon along a highway near Xuan Loc. Keltner extricated his platoon and drove off the attackers. For his deeds he earned the Distinguished Service Cross.[16]

Near Phu Loi, south of Da Nang, Maj. Frederick H. Mitchell ('54) was serving as the operations officer for the ARVN 2nd Battalion, 2nd Infantry, when two of the battalion's companies, located on the perimeter, were suddenly struck by numerically superior VC forces. Mitchell moved to the center of the battle area and, making contact with an aerial observer while under intense enemy fire, coordinated the maneuver and deployment of ground troops. He ultimately gained control of the battlefield, and his troops routed the enemy forces, earning him the Silver Star.[17]

A turning point in the war occurred in 1967. President Johnson, who became president and commander in chief following the assassination of John F. Kennedy, directed MACV commander, Gen. William Westmoreland, to move with haste to consolidate control over South Vietnam. To facilitate this objective, Johnson committed additional troops. Gen. William A. Becker ('41), assistant commander, 1st Air Cavalry Division in Vietnam, has provided a brief overview of the distinctive characteristics and strategy of the Vietnam War:[18]

General Westmoreland assembled a military force of more than 500,000 U.S. personnel organized into four subordinate commands, including the U.S. Army, Vietnam; Third Marine Amphibious Force; Seventh U.S. Air Force; and U.S. Naval Force, Vietnam (for coastal and river operations). The U.S. Navy Seventh Fleet supported the MACV but operated the Pacific Command, Hawaii. Allied forces of about 70,000, consisting mainly of Australian, New Zealand, and South Vietnamese troops, were deployed. The regular armed forces of Vietnam (ARFVN) built up to about a half-million. There were also as many soldiers in regional and popular (local security-type) forces.

U.S. military advisors were assigned to Vietnamese units down to battalion level and equivalent. Their role—to develop leadership throughout the Vietnamese forces—was difficult. The advisors were the unsung heroes of the Vietnam War. Logistic buildup to support the major forces was a great challenge to General Westmoreland's command. U.S. troops arriving in Vietnam moved first to occupy and secure key positions and existing U.S. installations. Then they began preparing a logistical base for whatever troops might be needed later. The only major port, Saigon, was clogged with shipping; only Tan San Nhut airport outside Saigon could handle jet traffic; the only major railroad had ceased to function; and use of the roads was minimal at best. Ports, warehouses, cantonments, airfields, maintenance facilities, communications—all had to be built where there was at first almost nothing. In this war Aggies of all military services, branches, and skills found plenty to do in these civil undertakings. And they stepped up to the tasks.

Despite the buildup of American forces in 1967, enemy pressure increased as a prelude to a massive attack in the spring of 1968 during the Vietnamese festival known as Tet, when fighting traditionally halted. Maj. Gen. Bruno A. Hochmuth ('35), commander of the 3rd Marine Division, was the highest-ranking officer killed in Vietnam. He died in action at Hue on November 13, 1967, as the initial Tet offensive began. Marine Corps officers in Vietnam with a Texas Aggie background participated in the first landing of marines at Da Nang on March 8, 1965, and continued to fight for the next several years. Lt. Gen. Ormond R. Simpson commanded the 1st Marine Division at Da Nang (1968–1969). Simpson, a recipient of the Distinguished Service Medal (DSM), later became associate vice president of Texas A&M, and the corps' drill field is named for him. His classmate Maj. Gen. Wood B. Kyle ('36) commanded the 3rd Marine Division

(1966–1967). Other marines in action included Lts. Jim Armstrong ('64) of Weatherford and Thomas Rodriquez Jr. ('64) of Laredo, as well as then Capt. Rick MacPherson ('63), Capt. Ted Hopgood ('65; Texas A&M commandant, 1996–2002), and 2nd Lt. Richard L. Daerr Jr. ('66).[19]

In May, 1967, Daerr's platoon (with Company L, 3rd Battalion, 3rd Marine Division), operating near Da Nang, took the point in an attempt to rescue a rifle company surrounded by enemy forces. His unit was ambushed, and enemy troops cut them off from behind. His men at the front of the attack were killed or wounded in the initial assault. Daerr quickly set up a fire base and pulled the injured to safe ground. He then led an assault under intense enemy fire to try to break through to the encircled rifle company. On the third attempt, his radio operator was knocked senseless by an enemy bullet, and Daerr pulled him back to safety. At daybreak, he directed mortar fire on enemy positions and then led his platoon in a charge using small arms, bayonets, and grenades, forcing the enemy to withdraw and enabling his men to collect the dead and wounded. They were finally able to make contact with the rifle company they were sent to relieve. Lieutenant Daerr received the Silver Star.[20]

At the end of that difficult year, on December 21, 1967, Maj. Jerry O. Robinette ('54) commanded an F-4C aircraft on a highly classified, low-level mission over North Vietnam at night. "Success of the mission depended on very precise high speed navigation at very low altitude over mountainous terrain and in an area of known heavy enemy defenses. Despite enemy 85 mm anti-aircraft fire, marginal weather conditions, and the need to navigate at high speed and low altitudes through clouds, the mission was completed and had a [still undisclosed] direct affect on future tactics and political/military decisions." Robinette received the Silver Star.[21]

A considerable number of Texas A&M officers served in South Vietnam as advisors to the RVN army, navy, and air force. Lt. Franklyn Supercinski ('64), for example, served as an advisor from 1965 to 1967 in Bac Lieu province with the Phoenix Program, whose mission was to identify, locate, and neutralize members of the command and operational structure of the Viet Cong. Lt. Charles F. Wetherbee ('66) was with the vehicles and weapons components branch at Long Binh. Maj. Donald Soland ('59), who had been the senior advisor to the 35th Vietnamese Ranger Battalion in 1956 and 1966, returned to Vietnam for another tour with the 173rd Airborne in 1969, while Capt. Manley Jones ('59) served two tours with Special Forces.[22]

By late 1967, despite more than 460,000 U.S. troops in Vietnam, the initiative seemed to be shifting to favor the enemy. Capt. William C. Hearne ('63), for example, arrived in Vietnam in August, 1967, and took command of Bravo Company, 1st Battalion, 2nd Infantry of the 1st Infantry Division. In December, his company was operating in an area along the Cambodian border known as the Bo Duc/Bu Dop region, where there seemed to be a massive enemy infiltration. The battalion had positioned itself so as to block the passes from Cambodia into

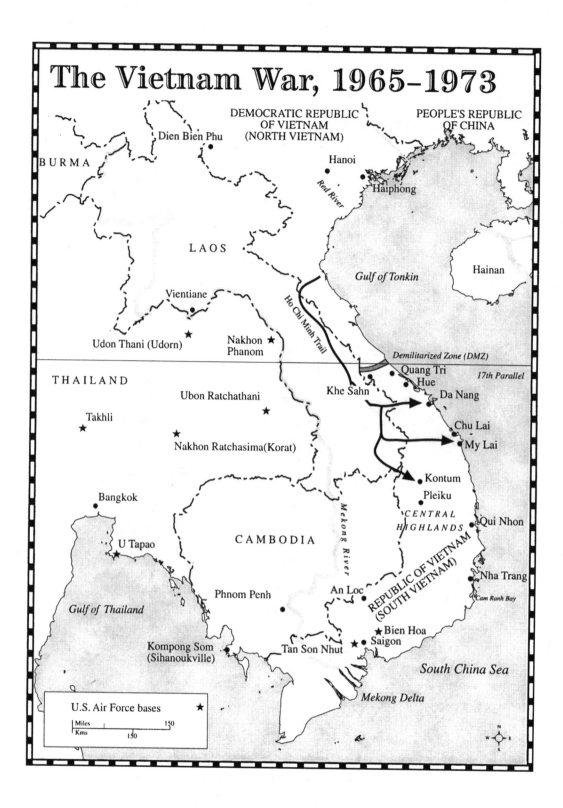

The Vietnam War, 1965–1973

DEMOCRATIC REPUBLIC
OF VIETNAM
(NORTH VIETNAM)

PEOPLE'S REPUBLIC
OF CHINA

Dien Bien Phu

BURMA

Hanoi

Red River

Haiphong

LAOS

Gulf of Tonkin

Hainan

Vientiane

Ho Chi Minh Trail

Udon Thani (Udorn)   ★

Nakhon
Phanom   ★

Demilitarized Zone (DMZ)

Quang Tri

17th Parallel

THAILAND

Ubon Ratchathani   ★

Khe Sahn

Hue

Da Nang

Takhli   ★

Chu Lai

★

My Lai

Nakhon Ratchasima(Korat)

Kontum

Bangkok

Pleiku

*CENTRAL
HIGHLANDS*

Qui Nhon

U Tapao   ★

CAMBODIA

Mekong River

Phnom Penh

An Loc

REPUBLIC OF VIETNAM
(SOUTH VIETNAM)

Nha Trang

Cam Ranh Bay

Kompong Som
(Sihanoukville)

Tan Son Nhut   ★

★ Bien Hoa
Saigon

South China Sea

Gulf of Thailand

Mekong Delta

U.S. Air Force bases   ★

| Miles | 150 |
| Kms | 150 |

South Vietnam. On the night of December 7, waves of assaulting VC struck the battalion's positions. After a four-hour battle the attackers were finally repulsed by razor-sharp "beehive" artillery rounds fired from within the defensive perimeter. At the height of the battle, medevac helicopters were called in to pick up the wounded. In helping to load the injured, Hearne, "with complete disregard for his own safety exposed himself to hostile fire." Soon afterward, during a heavy mortar attack, he remained in the open in order to command his unit and direct the fire until the enemy had been beaten back. Hearne earned the Silver Star. At a time when the average company commander survived for only two and a half months before being killed, wounded, or relieved, Hearne attributed his success and longevity as a company commander in Vietnam in part to his three-year assignment in Panama, where he went through jungle warfare school "two or three times," to his basic and airborne training, and to having graduated from Texas A&M.[23]

By 1967, concerns that the war was not going well were growing. Army Capt. Paul E. Dresser ('64), who served as corps commander, for example, described the war as "a hell of a war." When truces occurred, all they meant was that the U.S. forces could not initiate offensive actions, while the enemy could and did. Capt. Jay Bisbey ('59), pilot of a twin-engine army Mohawk and the recipient of the DSC and Purple Heart, said, "You can't dwell on getting shot at each day," but it could happen if "we just poked our nose in where we shouldn't have." Capt. Dick Beal ('62), with the 14th Infantry, after a battle in the central highlands, received the Silver Star for conspicuous gallantry while moving the wounded and dead to an evacuation zone. Navy Lt. Marvin J. Girouard ('61), serving with an amphibious strike and counterinsurgency team known as the "Beach Jumpers," was at Da Nang when the marines landed and participated in reconnaissance and rescue actions. After flying missions day after day, two marine helicopters crashed, and Girouard took a detail of sailors to the crash site "to save what we could. Sometimes there is nothing you can do." Sometimes there was something you could do but were better off not doing. Thus, Capt. John F. Erskine ('60), an engineer serving with the Green Berets at a medical station near Da Nang, complained that the Viet Cong had a "sniper on the main road between two of our medical stations. We could wipe him out anytime we want, but we don't. He is such a sorry shot we don't worry about him. If we took him out of action, he would be replaced—maybe with someone better."[24]

Nonetheless, Capt. Pat Resley ('58) was very optimistic. He thought the United States was making "tremendous gains" but still had "miles to go in the military effort." Second Lt. Harold Brent ('63) appreciated most of all those rare nights when he could sleep "warm and dry" and found few moments when the threat of attack did not seem imminent. At Sunday mass, for example, he noted that the altar "is maybe an ammunition box and the vestments are made of camouflage material and you have your rifle handy in case of attack." Lt. Neil Keltner

('65), who followed Paul Dresser as corps commander and was the nation's outstanding ROTC graduate for that year, commanded a platoon with the 11th Armored Cavalry. His unit, "while on a convoy escort mission, was ambushed by two battalions of VC. I lost three men, but the VC lost over 100 plus a few weapons. My PC [personnel carrier] was hit by recoilless rifle fire, grenades, and machine gun fire, but somehow we survived." Keltner fought the good fight, and his platoon held off superior enemy forces, for which Keltner received the nation's second-highest award for valor, the Distinguished Service Cross, and the Purple Heart. Those battles in 1967 and particularly the battle of Bo Duc/Bu Dop were but precursors of the massive Tet offensives launched by the Viet Cong and NVA against one hundred targeted areas, including Saigon and the ancient towns of Hue and Khe Sanh beginning in January, 1968. That action dramatically altered public opinion and support for the war in the United States.[25]

As the year 1967 came to an end, the war in Vietnam had cost the United States almost 16,000 killed and 100,000 wounded, with roughly 60 percent of those U.S. Army losses—numbers that would be substantially increased by the North Vietnamese Tet offensive. At the height of that action, on May 17, 1968, marine Capt. Thomas H. Ralph Jr. ('62) from Clifton, Texas, led India Company, 3rd Battalion, 27th Marine Regiment, "on patrol in an area which higher command had neglected for some time. At approximately 1 A.M., India Company, with 146 Marines, ran headlong into a North Vietnamese regiment with an estimated 2,000 plus men. . . . It was brutal, but the company did what Marines (and every serviceman in Vietnam) have always done—fought with everything they had. . . . Tom was all over the field, directing, comforting, fighting, leading. He was always at the weakest point, shoring it up. Somewhere close to 1 P.M. a bullet creased my head over my left eye. I did not fall but stood unconscious in the line of fire. From I don't know where, Tom ran to me, knocked me down, and attempted to drag me to some cover. The bullets that killed him were meant for me."[26]

There is more to this story. Lt. Charles E. Burge ('65) had bumped into his old campus mentor and former Aggie yell leader, Tom Ralph, at Camp Lejeune, North Carolina, in 1966. Ralph told Burge that he was leaving the Marine Corps and signing up for civilian employment with Brown and Root. Two years later, Burge, just returned from Vietnam, encountered Ralph again, this time at El Toro Air Station in California, where the 27th Marine Regiment was boarding planes bound for Vietnam. Ralph explained to Burge that "the reason he had come back into the Marine Corps was that he felt he had let everybody down by getting out and we had all gone to Vietnam and served. He felt like he had shrugged [off] his duties."[27]

U.S. efforts to observe and control the heavy influx of North Vietnamese into the south had begun as early as 1966. In one action near the Cambodian border, Capt. Harold J. Wunsch ('60), commanding Company C, 1st Battalion, 5th Cavalry, suddenly came under heavy attack by superior forces. Wunsch organized his company into good defensive positions and, moving continuously within his perimeters, personally directed fire on the enemy, continuing to do so even after being wounded. His company maintained its resistance until the enemy withdrew. Wunsch received the Silver Star and the Purple Heart. As enemy pressure increased, Capt. Jack Teague ('59), the son of Congressman Olin E. Teague ('32) and dubbed the "spy on Uncle Ho's trail," was part of a special unit in Laos operating from about 1966 through 1968 with a guerrilla band that monitored enemy activity along the Ho Chi Minh Trail.[28] With Tet, however, the flow of enemy forces became a torrent.

Although American and ARVN forces moved rapidly to stem the Tet offensive and defeat it, the perception grew in the United States and in much of the world that the United States could not win in Vietnam because U.S. forces could not control insurgency at the grassroots and hamlet level. Discontent with the war soared on the home front, giving the VC fresh resolve. Lyndon Johnson was influenced to step down as a presidential candidate in March, 1968, and this precipitated the beginning of peace negotiations in Paris, which were similar in character to those conducted in Korea in that combat continued as talks progressed or digressed.

Thus, in April, 1968, Maj. Clarence H. Woliver Jr. ('54), commanding three UH-1 gunships, fought intensely and without restraint in the successful rescue of eight downed helicopter crew members in a "particularly hostile area west of Da Nang." Woliver even made dry runs to attract enemy fire after his own ammunition was exhausted. He received the Silver Star for that action. Woliver ended his career as commander of Fort Sam Houston in San Antonio, having received two Legion of Merit medals, the Distinguished Flying Cross, three Purple Hearts, and other awards.[29] In June, 1968, Gen. Creighton Abrams assumed overall MACV command. Shortly thereafter, Richard Nixon was elected president on a promise to gradually withdraw troops and to turn the war over to South Vietnam, a process referred to as the "Vietnamization" of the war effort.

From 1968 through 1973, Texas A&M men were prominent in Vietnam among the general officers as well as in the ranks of junior officers. Brig. Gen. Andrew P. Rollins ('39) won the Silver Star in action near Bong Son. Other Aggie generals at war included Brig. Gen William A. Becker ('41), who had begun his career with the 1st Cavalry on horseback and now fought from a Huey helicopter. Becker was twice awarded the Distinguished Service Medal. With him in Vietnam were Lt. Gen. Herron N. Maples ('40), Brig. Gen. Robert M. Mullens ('48; 1968–1969 MACV G-3), Brig. Gen. James R. Taylor ('59), and Lt. Gen. Leonard D. Holder Jr. ('66), who earned three Bronze Stars with the "V" device for valor, plus other Meritorious Service Medals. Scattered through the ranks were Lt. Thomas M. Jackson ('66), Lt. Tom Striegler ('67), and Col. Donald Burton ('56; corps commandant, 1982–1986). Pvt. James Thurmond ('69) was drafted and went to Vietnam as an infantryman with 7/17 Air Cavalry in the central highlands: "My first executive officer was Capt. Lester C. Helmke ['62; DFC] from New Braunfels. I was a PFC, but he dropped handles with me (called me by first name) when we were visiting one on one."[30]

Combat seemed constant, and victory and peace elusive. For example, Col. James Woodall ('50), who later served as Texas A&M's commandant of cadets, 1977–1982, was 1st Battalion commander with the 173rd Airborne Brigade in February, 1969, when his convoy was ambushed by a company-sized enemy force using automatic weapons and rockets. Woodall rushed to the site of the action, spotted two enemy soldiers armed with a rocket-propelled grenade (RPG) launcher, and led an attack on the position, killing the enemy soldiers and seizing their weapons. He then organized a platoon of popular forces, directed them in another assault on the enemy's machine-gun positions, and led the pursuit of the retreating enemy forces. "His actions caused the enemy to flee and fail in its mission" and earned Colonel Woodall the Silver Star.[31]

Capt. Eddie Joe Davis ('67) and Capt. Hector Gutierrez ('69), former cadet corps commanders, fought in Nam, as did infantry Capt. Rick Beal ('62), Maj. Richard Biond ('60), navy Lt. Marvin J. Girourd ('61), Green Beret Capt. John F. Erskine ('60), and Lt. Pat Resley ('58). Lt. Harold Brent ('63), with the 173rd Airborne, fought in Vietnam as did Lt. Allan N. Pritchard ('63), Maj. Milton R. Roberts ('58), Col. Fred A. Moser Jr. ('44), Capt. Richard E. Nagy ('61), Capt. William P. Cherry ('63), Lt. Robert W. Thomas ('64), Capt. Dan Davis ('58), Capt. Hugh M. Davidson ('60), Lt. Paul A. Busch Jr. ('63), Lt. James R. Arnold ('61), Maj. Ralph C. Dresser ('52), and Lt. Lonnie D. Lewis ('65), among others. Also awarded the DFC were Maj. William R. Swan ('56), Capt. John B. Ferrata Jr. ('57), Lt. Col. Donald L. Zedler ('43), and Capt. Walter B. Moore ('62).[32]

Each soldier's experience in war is a unique, personal experience. That was certainly true of Maj. Arthur W. Noll ('51). Major Noll received the Bronze Star, Silver Star, Air Medal, and a Purple Heart for acts of exceptional bravery between November, 1969, and April, 1970, in the Dak Saeng area and during the height of the Tet offensive. In March, 1970, the ARVN 1st Battalion, 42nd Infantry Regiment, for whom Major Noll was senior advisor, came under intense fire from enemy forces. Noll immediately moved to the side of the ARVN commander and assisted in the deployment of forces and the adjustment of artillery fire on the enemy's positions, neutralizing them and greatly reducing casualties to the ARVN troops. Then, in April, the ARVN battalion command post was again attacked by overwhelming forces. Noll left his bunker to go to a forward position, where he called in and directed gunship support and helped repulse six distinct attacks on the battalion. The unit was then encircled by enemy forces and attacked for four days. On the final day, the enemy launched an assault that overran the battalion's positions. Noll fought the enemy in hand-to-hand combat, was wounded by shrapnel, and, refusing aid and in the face of unrelenting fire, led the remaining forces out of the encirclement. During the breakout, helicopters came in for a pickup as the small troop entered a clearing. The choppers succeeded in evacuating four U.S. and nine ARVN wounded "while bullets ripped the aircraft and sent metal and Plexiglas debris everywhere." Even after reaching the "safety" of the Special Forces Compound and under the umbrella of protective air cover, the battalion continued to be attacked.[33]

"Front lines" ceased to exist as the warfare extended throughout the jungles, villages, and cities of South Vietnam, making the air-ground warfare that had been developed in Korea even more applicable. The type of warfare was honed to a fine art in Vietnam, thanks in good measure to the UH-1B helicopter, officially styled the "Iroquois" but dubbed the "Huey" by the troops. The Huey became the centerpiece of the "airmobile division" and enabled the infantry, or "air cavalry," to make a "quantum jump" in both tactics and techniques, as Gen. Bruce Palmer put it. It made it possible "to integrate the air vehicle into the ground combat unit, substituting in some cases directly for ground vehicles, so that all fire and maneuver and mobility elements come under the same commander."[34]

One of the most decorated Aggies in the Vietnam War, Capt. Robert L. ("Bob") Acklen Jr. ('63), served thirty-two months in Vietnam as a helicopter pilot and infantry company commander. Awarded more than 60 decorations—17 for valor in combat—he left the fighting in Vietnam only after suffering a broken back in a helicopter crash. Perhaps the most decorated Aggie of all time, Acklen was awarded the Silver Star, 6 Bronze Stars (4 for valor), 40 Air Medals, 4 Army Commendation Medals (3 for valor), the Purple Heart, and 3 Vietnamese Crosses for gallantry. He simply never quit. After recovering from his injuries, Acklen became an Army Ranger and served in Korea.[35]

Col. Billy M. Vaughn ('48), a veteran of Korea, was a master at air combat control. In December, 1970, an air cavalry rifle platoon with the 1st Air Cavalry Division fell into "heavy contact" with an enemy force. Vaughn flew to the scene and took control of a chaotic situation on the ground and in the air, directing field artillery fire and aerial evacuations and designating target areas. When helicopters could not extract the wounded members of an aero-rifle unit from the battle zone, Vaughn sent rappel-qualified engineers to remove the wounded and bring in supplies and reinforcements. His outstanding flying ability and rapid organization of the air-ground war enabled the U.S. forces to complete their mission. Vaughn received the DFC.[36]

Hundreds of Aggies, as officers, warrant officers, and crew members, fought in Vietnam on helicopter combat teams engaged in moving troops and providing close air support during combat. Among the helicopter pilots was Lt. Randy House ('67; later Lieutenant General House), who earned the DSM, Silver Star, and four DFCs. A wounded Lt. Larry C. Kennemer ('66) was pictured on the January 1, 1968, cover of *Newsweek* magazine following the battle of Dak To in the highlands north of Pleiku. Gunship pilot Jeff Murray ('73), assigned to the 281st Assault Helicopter Company and a member of a top-secret Special Forces recon unit code-named "Project Delta," remembers this: "Whenever we flew a Delta mission we wore no rank and left our wallets in the tent. We moved all over I Corps and lived wherever we were told to pitch a few tents. We opened the Ashau Valley in 1969, where US troops had not been in almost a year, losing three Hueys—a pilot and at least two delta recon teams simply vanished."[37]

One of the unique functions of the military in Vietnam at the time was to recruit, even as combat progressed, popular support in the countryside and to win the hearts and minds of the people in support of the American and SEATO goals. These roles were often conflicting, explained Capt. Thomas R. Hargrove, who, on one hand, worked with the Civil Operations and Revolutionary Development Support (CORDS) program in the Mekong Delta, helping farmers to produce more rice. However, in order to protect a village from the VC, Hargrove almost routinely had to call in B-52s on the same farms he was helping to develop. Capt. Ed. Y. Hall ('60), an advisor with a civil action unit known as "Team 100" at Can Gio village, noted, "Six of us were sort of like the Peace Corps but we were way out there, alone, on a limb a long way from the flag pole at great risk—we thought of ourselves as the 'armed Peace Corps'—we got to shoot back!" Similarly, in Vietnam's delta region, Lt. Ray Harris Jr. ('65), with the Medical Supply Corps, which was working with the U.S. Agency for International Development to staff and supply provincial hospitals, was much more involved in the business of peace than in the business of war.[38] It was, as Captain Hargrove observed, a sometimes conflicting role.

Two Aggie classmates, Cmdr. F. S. ("Tooter") Teague ('56), a squadron commander, and Lt. Cdr. Jerry B. ("Devil") Houston ('56), a squadron operations officer, racked up a number of firsts as members of Fighter Squadron 51, the "Screaming Eagles," stationed aboard the USS *Coral Sea*. Both former residents of famed (sometimes infamous) Hart Hall on the A&M campus completed four combat cruises. Each of them flew more than 350 combat missions, earning the Silver Star. Both were former members of the Texas Aggie football team, and both were MiG killers. Houston downed a MiG-17 after a hair-raising dogfight on May 6, 1972.[39] Then, in June, Teague shot down a MiG. Reflecting on these kills, Houston stated, "You train all your life for that one fight, then when it happens you know you're ready and you'll win." Teague added, "You are only afraid you won't do well, but training, lifetime training, at school, on the football field and in the air pays off—you'll win."[40] But the air war was not limited to just dogfights with MiGs.

Conventional tactical air missions, such as the night attack led by forward air controller (FAC) Maj. Frederick F. Nye III ('51) in May, 1969, on a North Vietnamese storage complex, remained an integral part of air combat. In this instance, the assault made against a well-fortified complex resulted in a "significant loss of vitally needed supplies by the hostile forces" and earned Nye the Distinguished Flying Cross. Maj. Frederick P. Henry ('51; DFC), a seasoned

Korean war combat pilot, chalked up seventy-three Arc Light missions as a B-52 commander flying from Guam, Okinawa, and Thailand in 1969 and 1970, following the flight paths of General Darling and others, which were established as early as 1965.[41]

Aggies fought in air combat over Southeast Asia, Vietnam, Cambodia, Thailand, and Laos and flew long-range missions from remote bases in the Philippines and Guam. During World War II each pilot normally flew approximately 25 missions. In Korea the norm was 100, while in Vietnam pilots with multiple tours not infrequently racked up hundreds of missions.[42] As a young officer, Lt. Patrick K. Gamble ('67; later a four-star general) flew 394 combat missions in the slow-moving O-1 "Bird Dog," earning the DFC, 2 DSMs, and 14 Air Medals. Col. Robert E. Marshall ('60) flew 300 defoliation missions during Operation Ranch Hand, and Capt. Windol C. Weaver ('63), the recipient of the DFC and 24 Air Medals, flew 524 missions, most of them as a forward air controller. Capt. Joe H. Hughes ('60) of Henderson flew 377 missions in an O-1 Bird Dog and was awarded the Silver Star, two DFCs, and 14 Air Medals. F-4 pilot Col. Antony ("Shady") Groves ('68) had 388 missions. Texas A&M's All-Southwest Conference quarterback in 1953, Maj. Don E. Ellis ('54) flew around 300 missions in the A-37 out of Bien Hoa AFB with the 604th Special Operations Squadron. Other Aggie pilots who flew hundreds of missions included Lt. Wilbert D. Pearson Jr. ('69; 364 missions and three DFCs), F-100 pilot Capt. Samuel H. Holmes ('60) with 215 missions, Capt. Andres Tijerina ('67; DFC), Capt. Michael L. Richardson ('65), and Capt. Michael M. Marlow ('64).[43]

By the end of 1968, the U.S. Air Force had dropped more bombs on Vietnam than the total amount of ordinance dropped by the Allied powers on the Axis nations during World War II. Between mid-1965 and August, 1973, some 126,615 sorties were launched over North Vietnam, with the loss of 29 B-52s, 17 to hostile fire. In order to open up ground targets and expose enemy concentrations, the defoliation objective of Operation Ranch Hand was concentrated primarily in the Mekong Delta. Heavily loaded C-123s, operating out of Binh Thuy Air Base, had to come into their target areas "low and slow," according to Maj. Ralph C. Dresser ('52; recipient of two Silver Stars), much to the hazard of the pilots and crews. Other pilots and crews operating from bases in Thailand attacked Hanoi and strategic targets in the north. Among the pilots flying from bases at Takhli, Udorn, U Tapao, and Korat, Thailand, were then Maj. James B. Killebrew ('48), Lt. Dennis L. Graham ('63; DFC and Silver Star), Col. Waymond C. Nutt, and Capts. Alton Meyer ('60) and James E. Ray ('63). Their F-111s and F-105s brought the war to "downtown" Hanoi.[44] And sometimes the demons of war reciprocated.

Larry J. Hubbard ('75), chief reactor auxiliary operator on the carrier USS *Enterprise*, vividly recalls the flight-deck fire of January 14, 1969: "I was in the Number 1 Reactor room when the alarm sounded followed by the words 'This is not a drill! This is not a drill! Fire out of control on the flight deck. . . . Bombs and missiles [were] going off aft on flight deck.'"[45] Fortunately, the fire was soon extinguished.

Throughout the war, wherever they were in Southeast Asia, Texas A&M's former students usually celebrated their April 21 Aggie Muster. At least forty such Musters were held between 1967 and 1972 at bases and outposts across Vietnam. Attending the 1967 Saigon Muster, for example, were Lt. Mike Laughlin ('65) and Lt. Col. C. J. Clarke ('41). Some planned Musters were interrupted by combat, as in the battle of Khe Sanh in early 1968, where some 2,700 B-52 sorties dropped 110,000 tons of bombs.

On April 21, 1970, a group of F-4 Texas Aggie pilots with the 8th Tactical Fighter Wing, known as the "Wolfpack," stationed at Ubon Royal Thai Air Base in southeast Thailand, staged one of the most unique and daring Musters ever held by former students. Lt. Col. Robert K. Bell ('53) and fellow officers Lt. Ernie Petrash ('67), Capt. William L. Klutz ('65), Lt. Lou Obdyke ('67), Capt. Al Rutyna ('65), and Lt. Tom McKnight ('67) planned and flew a three-plane mission against a well-defended bridge in southern Laos along the Ho Chi Minh Trail in an area known as the "Steel Tiger." This all-Aggie mission was provided with maintenance and ground support by fellow Texas Aggies Maj. Jim Earl ('53), Maj. James W. ("Jake") Allbritton ('54), and Capt. Lynn Dobias ('62). The preflight weather briefing was given by Capt. Gale Gabbert ('68). Circling the target was FAC pilot Capt. Herbert E. Pounds Jr. ('65) in his OV-10 "Bronco." Pounds marked the target bridge with a smoke rocket and radioed the Aggie attackers to "hit my smoke." They eliminated the target, and all returned to the Ubon Officers' Club for a formal dinner, Muster gathering, and roll call of the absent. The three pilots and their three "backseaters" collectively amassed 1,401 combat mission and sixteen DFCs.[46]

That year, too, the I Corps Muster in Da Nang, chaired by Col. Homer D. Smith ('43), was attended by twenty-eight A&M men representing the classes of 1943 to 1968. Other memorable Vietnam-related Musters were those on the Texas A&M campus in 1972, 1973, 1974, and 1977. Lt. Larry B. Kirk ('66), who lost both legs and an arm after stepping on a land mine in Vietnam in 1968, gave the 1972 Campus Muster address. In 1973, former POW James E. Ray ('63) recounted his 7-year POW experience. Four years later he returned to comment on the importance of maintaining high standards and firm meaningful discipline. At a 1996 dedication, Ray noted that "Whenever danger calls . . . Aggies like these [eleven members of the class of 1969 who died in Vietnam] respond, 'Here am I. Send me.'" In 1974, the speaker was former Marine Corps Force Reconnaissance veteran Sheldon J. Best ('63).[47]

Meanwhile, combat conditions in Vietnam became increasingly difficult and desperate. On the night of September 16, 1972, Capt. Richard L. Poling ('69), on his 105th combat mission with his copilot, Joseph Personnett, fought at treetop level in their twin-seat CV-10 during a monsoon storm at Mo Doc to

The men of the Aggie Muster flight stand before one of their F-4D Phantom II jet fighters prior to mission launch. Left to right are 1st Lt. Ernie Petrash ('67), Capt. Bill Klutz ('65), Lt. Col. Bob Bell ('53), 1st Lt. Lou Obdyke ('67), Capt. Al Rutyna ('65), and 1st Lt. Tom McKnight ('67).

save an outnumbered army unit surrounded by NVA: "The situation became so desperate that the ground commander requested friendly artillery to fire on his position. Providing support, Poling and Personnett during the remainder of the night strafed and rocketed enemy muzzle flashes, directed Navy and ARVN artillery, and marked targets for the Navy A-7s that arrived as the weather cleared. Only after making eight low-level passes and taking many direct hits did the enemy stop their attacks. On the last pass the rudder and right engine was shot out resulting in a low level bailout. Surrounded by enemy forces, they evaded capture and were eventually evacuated."[48] The army ground commander later counted 265 enemy bodies on the perimeter. The U.S. and ARVN troops had been saved from annihilation. For extraordinary heroism both men were awarded the Distinguished Flying Cross, the second highest award for valor.

Combat sometimes spilled outside of the legally defined parameters. Despite UN conventions and congressional bans and limits on combat outside of Vietnam, special-operations forces sometimes became engaged in clandestine encounters with enemy ground forces in the neighboring nations of Laos, Cambodia, and Thailand. Those confrontations were seldom reported in the news, and, indeed, there was often no official accounting of the incidents. This also meant that military personnel who became engaged in "forbidden" or covert actions often failed to be tallied as combat casualties. Half of the twenty Texas Aggies listed as MIAs were lost in Laos. None of those lost in Laos ever returned alive. Former Aggie yell leader and Ranger Capt. Joe Bush ('68) of Temple, a U.S. Army attaché to the embassy, was killed in action during a late-night NVA "sapper," or enemy infiltration attack, at Muong Soui airfield in Laos in 1969. However, his death was never officially reported.[49]

Col. John B. Ferrata Jr. ('57) spent much of the Vietnam War on a covert mission in Thailand to train Thai and Laotian pilots in unmarked T-28s so that they could help control illicit traffic by North Vietnamese forces on the Ho Chi Minh Trail. Those specially trained air commandos played a major role in countering the Tet offensive and specifically in the battle of Khe Sanh. Later on, Ferrata received the Distinguished Flying Cross for an "unarmed photographic reconnaissance mission over hostile territory" under extremely adverse weather conditions.[50] Capt. Donald Luna ('60), Capt. Gregg Hartness ('60), and Capt. John R. Baldridge ('68) were all shot down on FAC missions in Laos, as was CH-53 helicopter pilot Albert Tijerina ('65), who had been head drum major of the Texas Aggie band. All were reported MIA and finally presumed KIA. Only nine Americans were returned as prisoners from Laos. Special operations, Ho Chi Minh Trail interdiction activities, and support of local friendly troops by American military and diplomatic interests continued throughout the war despite a congressional ban on the use of ground-support troops in these off-limit areas. Only in 2002, after the actions of the "night rustics" along the Cambodian border were declassified, did Col. Larry L. Landtroop ('67) receive the DFC (first oak-leaf cluster) for combat action near Phnom Penh on January 22, 1971.[51]

One of the most vexing chapters of the Vietnam War had to do with the handling of POW and MIA personnel by enemy forces. By the end of the conflict, more than 2,000 Americans had been listed as missing in action and/or taken prisoner. A total of 591 were known to be held captive and were returned as of early 1973. Most of Texas A&M's POWs and MIAs were pilots. Four F-105 pilots were captured between late 1965 and early 1967 and held as POWs by the North Vietnamese; they were returned in 1973. Capt. Robert N. Daughtrey ('55) remained a POW for seven years and six months; Lt. James E. Ray, for six years and nine months; Capt. Alton B. Meyer ('60), for six years; and Capt. John C. Blevins ('61), for six years and six months. All were tortured by the enemy, and most were imprisoned at the infamous Hoa-Lo Prison—referred to as the "Hanoi Hilton." As fate would have it, Meyer and Blevins were prison roommates for a brief time.[52]

None of the Aggie pilots who were shot down after July, 1967, were reported

TABLE 15. Texas A&M Former Students: MIA Status

Date MIA	Date KIA	Name	Class	Service	Aircraft	Location
Apr. 22, '69	**	Lt. Col. Walter S. Van Cleave	'48	USAF		Laos
Jan. 26, '69	June 8, '78	Maj. William E. Campbell	'52	USAF	F-4	Laos
Aug. 25, '67	May 16, '73	Maj. William O. Fuller	'57	USAF	F-4C	NVN
Mar. 27, '72	July 25, '78	Lt. C. Irving B. Ramsower	'57	USAF	C-130	Laos
July 1, '67	**	Lt. Cmdr. Robert D. Johnson	'58	USN		SVN
Dec. 11, '65	++	Capt. George P. McKnight	'58	USAF	Unknown	SVN
Nov. 26, 68	July 1, '80	Capt. Gregg Hartness	'60	USAF	O-2A FAC	Laos
Feb. 1, '69	Nov. 29, '78	Capt. Donald A. Luna	'60	USAF	O-2A FAC	Laos
Jan. 5, '68	++	Capt. William E. Jones	'62	USAF	F-105	NVN
Jan. 26, '68	Nov. 26, '73	Lt. Michael E. Dunn	'63	USN	Unknown	NVN
Mar. 28, '68	Feb. 15, '74	Capt. Dennis L. Graham	'63	USAF	F-111A	NVN
May 8, '69	Apr. 17, '79	Lt. Henry G. Mundt II	'64	USAF	F-4C	Laos
Dec. 30, '67	May 13, '73	Capt. Murray L. Wortham	'65	USAF	F-4C	Laos
Jan. 17, '68	May 5, '78	Lt. C. Robert F. Wilke	'65	USAF	A-1E	NVN
Mar. 1, '69	Mar. 1, '71	Lt. Clyde W. Campbell	'66	USAF	A-1E	Laos
Dec. 20, '69	++	Capt. Carl E. Long	'66	USMC	CV-10	SVN
Apr. 5, '68	++	Lt. Donald J. Matocha	'66	USMC		SVN
June 13, '69	June 20, '78	Lt. Neal C. Ward	'67	USAF	A-1H	Laos
Nov. 20, '69	July, '73	Lt. John R. Baldridge Jr.	'68	USAF	O-2A FAC	Laos
Dec. 27, '72	Sept. 5, '78	Capt. Ronald W. Forrester	'69	USMC	AD-6	NVN

++ Body recovered
** KIA, body not recovered
NVN North Viet Nam
SVN South Viet Nam

by communist forces to have been captured, held as prisoners, or otherwise accounted for in any way, and those names were added to a growing MIA roster (see table 15). Those known to be in captivity as well as the MIAs were not forgotten. Efforts from College Station to Washington and across the nation were launched to pressure the communists to identify and arrange for the release of the prisoners. At the national level, former astronaut Col. Frank Borman and businessman and one-time presidential candidate Ross Perot of Dallas as well as Joe Dan Boyd ('57) undertook a special mission in 1973 to North Vietnam with the approval of Pres. Richard Nixon to seek a full accounting of MIAs and an early release of all POWs.[53]

In addition to the negotiating efforts led by Perot, Texas A&M students and former students, along with wives and families of the POWs and MIAs, launched an extensive information and writing campaign to Washington, Hanoi, and Paris, seeking information and a release of the prisoners. Among those who were most active were Mrs. Bobbie Meyer, Mrs. Mary Ward, Capt.

Nick Maselli ('71), Lt. Audley W. Downs ('72), Maj. Worth Blake ('54), Lt. Col. Jerry O. Robinette ('54), and Ben H. Allen ('56). Allen was one of the founders of the Red River Fighter Pilots Association, whose membership included many pilots who had flown in harm's way in North Vietnam.[54]

The POW-MIA campaign was highlighted by full-page ads nationwide. The March, 1971, *Texas Aggie* asked, "But when are they coming home?" and featured a photograph of Maj. Robert N. Daughtrey as a prisoner of war. In mid-1971, families and friends of the Aggie POWs and MIAs, led by Jack W. Cumpton ('59), president of the Bryan–College Station Jaycees; Larry Locke ('63), president of the Brazos County A&M Club; Jim Jett ('66) and Connie Eckard ('55), representing the Association of Former Students; and Texas A&M student body president Kent Caperton ('71), organized project "On to Paris," which raised funds to send a delegation of Texas Aggies to the Paris peace talks, where they could better urge a full accounting and release of all POWs.[55]

The beginning of the end of America's involvement in Indochina came in the early 1970s, as U.S. ground troops and advisors were gradually withdrawn. South Vietnamese armed forces totaled about one million troops and were thought to be capable of making the transition to the Vietnamization phase. Bases, equipment, and training were being turned over to the ARVN, while American forces moved from a combat role to one of providing specialized ground advisors and air support. MACV envisioned no geographical expansion of the war (with the exception of continued covert activity in Cambodia and Laos) and assumed that the status quo could be maintained by an exclusively defensive posture instead. The first test of this shift in U.S. and ARVN roles came in early 1971.[56]

In February, 1971, the ARVN launched the Lam Son 719 offensive into Laos across from the DMZ. The objective was to neutralize the area around Tchepone, thirty-five miles inside the border, and disrupt a key staging area of the Ho Chi Minh Trail. The results on the ground were mixed. Bad weather and inadequate air cover gave the enemy the advantage. The United States suffered heavy helicopter losses: Hostile fire downed 118 army Hueys. In the confusion, the ARVN abandoned much of its equipment.[57]

Within a year of the beginning of the Vietnamization program, the North Vietnamese had regrouped, rearmed, and increased their strength and then launched a three-pronged Easter, 1972, offensive. Crossing over from Laos, the first wave of the NVA targeted an area south of the DMZ near Quang Tri-Hue. The second target was the Kontum-Pleiku area, and the third strike was against III Corps along Highway 13 at An Loc and Loc Ninh. At An Loc, beginning in mid-April, 1972, two dozen U.S. Army advisors and 3,000 ARVN fought to repel repeated attacks by three NVA divisions, totaling some 36,000 troops during a sixty-six-day siege. Capt. James Willbanks ('69), an advisor with a task force attached to the 5th Infantry Division (ARVN), fought in those desperate actions and was the recipient of the Silver Star and his second Purple Heart. Maj. Frank

Muller, with several years of combat already behind him, earned the Silver Star when he completed a daring night rescue of a downed helicopter pilot and a gunner.[58]

The goal of the NVA was to quickly overrun An Loc and move down Highway 13 to Saigon. The overall commander of Third Regional Assistance Command (TRAC) was Maj. Gen. James F. Hollingsworth ('40). Intelligence provided Hollingsworth with some foreknowledge, and he quickly realized a major attack was in the offing. Using well-armed regular NVA troops equipped with Soviet-made T-54 tanks and 130-mm howitzers (along with U.S.-made 105-mm and 155-mm howitzers captured from the ARVN during Lom Son 719), the enemy shelled An Loc and breached the town's northern perimeters. An armada of air-ground support aircraft, including fixed-wing A-6s, A-7s, F-4s, A-37s (close-air-support fighters), and AC-119K Stingers and AC-130 gunships, along with army Cobra attack helicopters, was called in and helped stymie the NVA assault. Col. Chuck Holt ('69), a TDY C-130 pilot assigned to Tan Son Nhut AFB in Saigon, recalled the many attempts to resupply An Loc during the combat: "We had to drop our loads on a soccer field in very heavy enemy fire. It was a real mess. We tried to come in low and later high, all the drops were at night. We lost four 130s and three crews."[59]

Lt. Robert V. ("Vic") Reid ('70) flew as the navigator on an AC-130 Spectre gunship carrying a crew of fifteen into the An Loc battles in June, 1972. On one mission they discovered an NVA truck in an open area in the Ashau Valley of South Vietnam. The crew attacked with 40-mm cannon but were met by extremely heavy and accurate antiaircraft fire and finally were hit by an SA-7 "Strella" heat-seeking missile. The right wing of their aircraft was blown away. As the aircraft spiraled down toward the jungle, Reid and most of the crew bailed out at a very low altitude. Despite a partially opened chute and a five-inch hole in the top of his left boot, Reid made it to the ground. NVA troops soon swarmed nearby, searching for the wreckage and survivors. Reid buried his identification, including photos of his wife and daughter (and his Aggie ring), so that, if taken prisoner, that information could not be used against him. He was able to make radio contact with rescue units, and, during the rescue attempt, several aircraft were shot down by the enemy. Reid finally made it to a rescue device lowered from a helicopter to within twenty yards of his location. He dug up his pictures and ring, raced for the lifeline, and made it back to his base and the hospital. He soon returned to duty and completed a total of 125 aerial-combat missions before returning to the United States in March, 1973. Reid retired from the air force as a colonel in 1997.[60]

In addition to the gunships and close air support, General Hollingsworth was given direct control over the B-52 strikes. He called in wave after wave of bomb runs on the attacking enemy forces, each bomber dropping 108 MK-82 five-hundred-pound bombs on the NVA staging areas northwest of the city. Thanks to the air support, the defenders held An Loc. While the Nixon administration declared the "victory" at An Loc a success for the Vietnamization policy, the reality was that the attack was checked only because of the overwhelming and persistent use of U.S. air support. In a detailed study of what came to be the last major battle of the war, James Willbanks notes in his monograph on the An Loc battle that "American air power and the performance of the U.S. advisors on the ground meant the difference between victory and defeat." Both Nixon's Secretary of State, Henry Kissinger, and General Hollingsworth fully agreed that the tactical use of B-52s disrupted the NVA's ability to stage sustainable operations.[61] The battle of An Loc permanently changed the character of air-ground combat, but it did not at all prove the success of Vietnamization.

Nevertheless, in the months following An Loc, the MACV drafted plans to completely phase American ground troops out of Vietnam. Back home, it was the popular thing to do. For many Americans, Vietnamization meant leaving the war to the Vietnamese and "getting the hell out of there." During the 1960s, college campuses across the nation had experienced antiwar demonstrations and rallies. Major disruptions and some violence occurred at seventy-three colleges and universities nationwide, and some institutions were forced to suspend classes and operations for short periods of time. Texas A&M seemed exempt from these tribulations. Support for the war effort remained very high across the campus. Around the country, however, enrollments in the Reserve Officers Training Corps dropped from 191,749 in 1966 to 72,459 in 1973. This was a vital statistic inasmuch as the ROTC produced more than half of all officers on duty in Vietnam.[62]

Texas A&M sustained its active commissioning program throughout the "Vietnam decade" from 1962 to 1973. During those years, more than four thousand Aggies were commissioned on campus, and scores more obtained commissions via Officer Candidate School (OCS) and Officer Training School (OTS) programs in the various armed services. A representative army recruiting letter mailed to the parents of entering first-year students at Texas A&M noted that by joining ROTC "your son will fulfill his military obligation as an officer . . . receive $50 per month as a cadet . . . and the management experience will be an asset throughout the remainder of his life." What this meant was that, in Vietnam, as in Korea, "Aggies were everywhere" and perhaps in disproportionately large numbers due to the reduced production of ROTC officers in other institutions. Texas A&M, however, sustained and even increased its annual production of officers. Moreover, while certainly the larger proportion of Texas A&M officers returned to civilian employment after the close of hostilities in Vietnam and to life in the inactive and ready reserves, many of them remained in the military and soon began to fill the levels of higher-ranking and general officers. In the three decades following the cessation of combat in Vietnam, more than fifty former students of Texas A&M became flag and general officers. The class of 1962 produced eleven generals; the class of 1965, seven; and the classes of 1963, 1966, 1967, and 1968 each had five general officers.[63]

By 1973, if not before, Vietnamization had come to mean the withdrawal of American forces from combat in Vietnam. In December, 1972, as a final strategic action in that process, the United States initiated a massive bombing campaign of North Vietnam in order to destroy North Vietnamese supplies and resources and to undermine the NVA's determination to continue the war against South Vietnam. To be sure, the bombing campaign had a more immediate diplomatic objective, that is, to force or encourage North Vietnam to close the negotiations in Paris and accept an immediate cease-fire, which did occur.[64] Subsequently, in January, 1973, the Pentagon announced an end to the draft calls. That meant an end to the war and, it was hoped, to public discontent. In retrospect, however, the end of the draft calls may have been premature, and the massive bombing initiatives too late.

As early as 1968, Congressman William O. Cowger ('43) became deeply concerned that the troops fighting in Vietnam had been handicapped for too long: "We have literally been fighting an off-limits part-time conflict. Some 90 percent of the war-making industrial complex of North Vietnam has not been bombed, 75 percent of the air defenses are off limits to our flyers, almost 70 percent of the military facilities are forbidden targets."[65] As public and political support for the war effort waned over the next few years, those constraints increased rather than diminished.

Some years after the close of the combat in Vietnam, Gen. Ormond R. Simpson, a World War II veteran, member of General MacArthur's staff, regimental commander in Korea, commander of the Thailand expedition in May, 1962, and marine division commander at Da Nang in 1969, confirmed the concerns raised by Congressman Cowger:

The one big lesson of the war, the one that this country must burn into its soul is, do not enter a war unless you plan to win it. And by winning it I mean doing the things that are necessary to win the war. Our country, or at least our national leaders, never made the conscious decision—they said they wanted to win the war—but they never did the things that had to be done to win that war. By the time I arrived in Vietnam in 1969, knowing the temper of the country and the thinking of the national leaders, in retrospect, it was obvious to me that the war was not winnable in 1969.

We lost the war because we incremented our force against all the principles of war, we incremented our force and gave the enemy time to build up in opposition to our buildup. We did it over a prolonged period of time. We were too timid. We did not have the courage nor the will to actually invade North Vietnam, which was the seat of the enemy. The Viet Cong were not the problem, the NVA was our problem. The NVA denied up until 1972 that they were ever there, but, of course, everybody in the world knew they were there. So, we should have gone where we could have fought them on their ground. And with our superior fire power, we could have won.[66]

More than three million U.S. troops served in Vietnam from 1960 through the formal cease-fire signed in Paris on January 23, 1973, and some U.S. forces remained in Indochina as late as mid-1975. The wall at the Vietnam Memorial in Washington, D.C., is a simple but striking reminder of the Vietnam conflict, which cost more than 56,000 lives, some 46,000 of which were lost in battle.

TEXAS A&M UNIVERSITY FORMER STUDENTS
KILLED IN ACTION IN SOUTHEAST ASIA

Maj. Gen. Bruno A. Hochmuth ('35)
Col. Leonard D. Hodler ('42)
Lt. Col. John S. Bonner ('44)
Lt. Col. Walter VanCleave ('48)
Lt. Col. Edward L. Williams ('49)
Lt. Col. Elden Golden ('50)
Sgt. Graham H. Howison ('51)
Col. William E. Campbell ('52)
Capt. Royal Clifton Fisher ('52)
Maj. Teddy J. Tomchesson ('52)
Capt. Johnnie L. Garner ('53)
Capt. Heriberto A. Garcia ('54)
Capt. Russell W. Condon ('55)
Maj. Hadley Foster ('55)
Capt. Richard E. Steel ('55)
Capt. Dalton M. Estein ('56)
Maj. John M. Kessinger ('56)
Capt. Ernest McFeron ('56)
Capt. Condon H. Terry Jr. ('56)
Maj. William O. Fuller ('57)
Capt. Charles C. Jones ('57)
Maj. Tedd M. Lewis ('57)
Capt. Foy Manion Mathis ('57)
Lt. Col. Irving B. Ramsower II ('57)
Capt. James C. Caston ('58)
Capt. Don Thomas Elledge ('58)
Lt. Cdr. Robert D. Johnson ('58)
Capt. George P. McKnight ('58)
Capt. Donald D. Blair ('59)
Maj. Allen G. Goehring ('59)
Capt. Donald Rey Hawley ('59)
John F. Martin ('59)
Maj. Allan L. Smith ('59)

Lt. Ronald D. Stewart ('59)
Lt. Billy J. Coley ('60)
Capt. William F. Cordell Jr. ('60)
Col. Greg Hartness ('60)
Capt. Floyd W. Kaase ('60)
Lt. Col. Donald A. Luna ('60)
Capt. Byron C. Stone ('60)
Maj. James M. Vrba Jr. ('60)
Lt. James C. Thigpin ('61)
Capt. Gerald J. Walla ('61)
Capt. Gregory K. Whitehouse ('61)
Maj. William E. Jones ('62)
Capt. Thomas H. Ralph Jr. ('62)
Lt. James L. Reed ('62)
Capt. Ralph B. Walker II ('62)
Capt. Charles F. Allen II ('63)
Donnie Ray Dehart ('63)
Lt. Michael E. Dunn ('63)
Capt. Dennis L. Graham ('63)
Lt. George Gutierrez Jr. ('63)
Lt. James R. Hottenroth ('64)
Capt. George L. Hubler ('64)
Lt. Colin E. Lamb ('64)
Capt. Thomas A. McAdams ('64)
Capt. Henry G. Mundt II ('64)
Lt. John B. Price ('64)
Warrant Officer Wesley W. Carroll III ('65)
Lt. John C. Dougherty ('65)
Lt. John R. Hernandez ('65)
Capt. Charles D. Jageler ('65)
Capt. Julius J. Jahns ('65)
Cpl. Richard A. Oman ('65)

Lt. José C. Santos ('65)

Lt. Victor H. Thompson III ('65)

Capt. Albert A. Tijerina Jr. ('65)

Lt. R. Bryson Vann ('65)

Col. Robert F. Wilke ('65)

Maj. Murray L. Wortham ('65)

Capt. Jack Patrick Blake ('66)

Capt. Joseph K. Bush Jr. ('66)

Lt. Michael R. Callaway ('66)

Lt. Clyde W. Campbell ('66)

Lt. James A. Dimock ('66)

Sgt. Larry K. Kaiser ('66)

Capt. Carl E. Long ('66)

Lt. Donald J. Matocha ('66)

Lt. James E. Neely ('66)

Capt. Eugene C. Oates III ('66)

Lt. Stephen R. Tubre ('66)

Maj. Elbert A. Welsh ('66)

Sgt. John T. Whitson ('66)

Lt. Layne Hale Connevey ('67)

Cpl. Converse R. Lewis III ('67)

Lt. John E. Russell ('67)

Lt. Andrew D. Smith ('67)

Capt. Neal C. Ward ('67)

Lt. Marvin S. Arthington ('68)

Capt. John Baldridge Jr. ('68)

Cpl. Tom M. Boyd III ('68)

Lt. James M. Butler ('68)

Lt. Richard E. Harlan ('68)

Capt. Steven B. Johnston ('68)

Capt. James E. Morton Jr. ('68)

Lt. Michael D. Noonan ('68)

Lt. Kevin A. Rinard ('68)

Lt. Rayburn L. Smith III ('68)

Lt. George T. Taff Jr. ('68)

Sp5 James Ned Woolley ('68)

Lt. James H. Cartwright ('69)

Sgt. Jeffrey E. Cowley ('69)

Capt. Ronald W. Forrester ('69)

Lt. Robert H. Johnson ('69)

Sp4 Sanderfierd Jones ('69)

Pfc. Bill Kildare ('69)

Capt. Walter S. Mullen ('69)

Lt. Vincent C. Anderson ('70)

Chief Warrant Officer Phillip R. Pannell ('72)

Suggested Readings: Books on Vietnam by Former Students of Texas A&M

Adams, John A. *The Noise Never Dies: Tan Son Nhut, 1970–1971* (College Station, Tex.: Intaglio Press, 2003).

Eschmann, Karl J. ('71) *Linebacker: The Untold Story of Air Raids over North Vietnam* (New York: Ivy Books, 1989).

Hall, Edward Y. ('60) *Valley of the Shadow* (Spartanburg, S.C.: Honoribus Press, 1986).

Hargrove, Thomas R. ('66) *A Dragon Lives Forever: War and Rice in Vietnam's Mekong Delta, 1969–1991, and Beyond* (New York: Ivy Books, 1994).

Lanning, Michael Lee. ('68) *The Only War We Had: A Platoon Leader's Journal of Vietnam* (New York: Ivy Books, 1994).

Willbanks, James H. ('69) *Thiet Giap! The Battle of An Loc, April 1972* (Fort Leavenworth, Kans.: U.S. Army Command and General Staff College, 1993).

———. *Abandoning Vietnam: How America Left and South Vietnam Lost Its War* (Lawrence: University of Kansas Press, 2004).

———. *Vietnamization* (Manhattan: Kansas State University Press, 2004).

A GLOBAL COMMITMENT

Two years after the Paris peace agreement in January, 1973, and the withdrawal
of U.S. troops from Vietnam, North Vietnamese armies struck South Vietnam,
seized the capital city, Saigon, renaming it "Ho Chi Minh City," and then reunited the country with communist North Vietnam. The war, if it had not been
so before, was then irrevocably lost. The United States began to extricate troops
and civilian friends from neighboring Cambodia as the communist Khmer
Rouge seized power there. Lt. Col. Robert Lee Keeney ('71) clearly remembers
each of the missions he flew in his A-7D single-seat attack jet against the Khmer
Rouge, including those in the last month of the air war over Cambodia in 1973.
The "K.R. was terrorizing Cambodia—a preview of their genocide over the next
few years."[1] Concurrently, the communist Pathet Lao completed its takeover of
Laos. Along the 38th parallel dividing North and South Korea, American troops
and advisors maintained a presence and were on alert for most of the remainder
of the century. The repercussions of the war in Vietnam were great and often
complex and continued to unfold until the turn of the millennium.

An immediate result was the return of POWs. Robert N. Daughtrey ('55),
Alton B. Meyer ('60), John C. Blevins ('61), and James Earl Ray ('63) came home.
Col. Donald E. Ellis ('54), with 333 combat missions under his belt in Vietnam,
was assigned to Randolph Air Force Base to command the 560th Flying Training Squadron (FTS). That unit had been selected to conduct requalification
training for returning Vietnam POW pilots who wanted to requalify in jet aircraft. For the next thirty-one years Colonel Ellis and the FTS celebrated the
anniversary of the release of POWs from captivity with a formal dinner. More
than forty former POWs joined him for the thirty-first celebration in 2004.[2]
Nevertheless, there was an undercurrent of protest against the Vietnam War in
particular and war in general.

"Vietnam cost the nation the draft" and contributed significantly to the changing structure and character of the armed forces and ultimately to the way Americans would wage war, believed Brig. Gen. James R. Taylor ('59), then chief of staff at Fort Hood, where almost forty thousand soldiers were being trained for the 1st Cavalry, the 2nd Armored Division, and the 13th Support Command. Taylor commanded a battalion of the 9th Infantry Division in Vietnam, which did what it was supposed to do without suffering too many casualties. However, Taylor was not satisfied with his service in Vietnam "other than in a narrow tactical sense. . . . [We tried] search and destroy, . . . we had the fortified hamlet phase," and "we tried pacification and Vietnamization." Nonetheless, "[e]ventually, the realities of the political situation at home coupled with what could be seen day in and day out, night in and night out on your TV set brought that war to an end."[3]

Americans continued to struggle with the old idea that "once we have fixed the outside world it ought to have the good grace to stay fixed."[4] Americans fought the Spanish-American War to "bring peace to this blood-smitten land." At the end of World War I, they thought they had just "made the world safe for democracy." They believed that the defeat of the Axis powers meant peace for all time. They thought that the settlement of the conflict in Korea would restore stability and ensure peace, and in 1973, they believed that America had done all it could and should do to restore peace and maintain the territorial integrity of South Vietnam.

As part of the closure on the war, in 1973, Congress eliminated the draft for military service that had been in effect since 1940, while retaining the selective-service requirement for a national system of registration that would provide the necessary information, should conscription need to be reinstated in the event of a national emergency. The creation of an all-volunteer force markedly changed the composition of the military. In one sense it reinstated the basic system that had always existed, that is, a U.S. defense system that depended on volunteers—in the militia tradition.

But the combat waged in Korea and Vietnam and the numerous Cold War military encounters and expeditions since the close of World War II had made it clear that preparation and readiness had become an increasingly critical element of modern warfare. Modern war no longer gave the United States the time and luxury of converting from peacetime to war production or of recruiting and training civilians for combat. The United States needed to be ready to fight the day a war began. As General Taylor explained it, "while we still have the same worldwide interests and requirements to support our allies, we no longer have that 1–2 year period of time where we can gear up once a conflict has started. We are trying to train our soldiers to fight a 3-day war—the day the war starts, the day we fight the war, and the day after the war."[5] The likelihood that there would ever be a three-day war seemed remote, but the atomic age made the possibility that a war might be decided on the first day increasingly plausible.

As never before, the United States now needed to maintain a more effective, combat-ready, well-trained standing army, one that knew how to utilize the most advanced technology and weaponry—albeit a volunteer army. Special forces, special weapons, surveillance, and preemptive operations became increasingly important. Moreover, in the post–World War II era and now, after Vietnam, American military forces had to sustain a global presence in order to maintain national security. Military operations abroad occurred in almost every year from 1974 to 2004 and ranged from Cambodia in Southeast Asia to the Indian Ocean, Africa, the Baltics, and Central and South America. All of this helps explain the very diverse tasks and the geographically scattered areas of the world in which the men and women of Texas A&M served during the last quarter of the twentieth century.

In the context of intermittent conflicts and America's global presence, planning, diplomacy, and disarmament became increasingly critical to the preservation of peace and the prevention of a major war. For example, during the Vietnam War, Edward C. ("Pete") Aldrich ('60) headed the Pentagon's Office of Strategic Defense. After the war, he went on to become undersecretary of the air force and then secretary in 1986. During his policy and planning years, Aldrich served as a resource and an advisor for arms-limitations conferences and diplomacy that sought to preserve global peace through military, missile, and nuclear agreements between the United States, the Soviet Union, and other major world powers.[6] The business of maintaining peace kept American military forces constantly occupied from the close of World War II through the remainder of the twentieth century (table 16).

A fast response to global crises also helped ensure peace and usually depended upon having ready access to information. That, in part, meant data automation for the military services. Brig. Gen. Donald L. Moore ('57) from Borger, Texas, for example, began his career as a KC-135 Stratotanker pilot and then served in Vietnam as director of operations for the Seventh Air Force at Tan Son Nhut Air Base. He then spent most of his military career in communications, where he pioneered in the integration of air force communications with data-automation systems. One of Moore's classmates, Lt. Gen. James S. Cassity Jr., led the European Information Systems Division of the Communications Command. He then served as deputy chief of staff for systems integration, logistics, and support for the North American Aerospace Defense Command. In 1989, Cassity was selected as director of command, control, and communications systems in Washington, D.C., a post that rotated every two years among the three branches of military service.[7]

Rapid response and deployment also meant having the logistics to support combat or other actions whenever and wherever they might occur. In 1977, Lt. Gen. Eivind H. ("Ivy") Johansen ('50), whose military career was spent in key logistics assignments throughout the world, became the army's deputy chief

TABLE 16. Military Engagements, 1945–2000

Campaign or Expedition	Inclusive Dates
Navy Occupation of Trieste	May, 1945–October, 1954
Navy Occupation of Austria	May, 1945–October, 1955
Army Occupation of Austria	May, 1945–July, 1955
Army Occupation of Germany	May, 1945–May, 1955
Army Occupation of Berlin	May, 1945–October, 1990
Units of the Sixth Fleet (Navy)	May, 1945–October, 1955
Army Occupation of Japan	September, 1945–April, 1952
Chinese Service Medal	September, 1945–April, 1957
Korean Service	June, 1950–July, 1954
Lebanon	July, 1958–November, 1958
Quemoy and Matsu Islands	August, 1958–June, 1963
Taiwan Straits	August, 1958–June, 1959
Vietnam (including Thailand)	July, 1958–July, 1965
Congo	July, 1960–September, 1962
Laos	April, 1961–October, 1962
Berlin	August, 1961–June, 1963
Thailand	May, 1962–August, 1962
Cuba	October, 1962–June, 1963
Congo	November, 1964
Vietnam Service	July, 1965–March, 1973
Korea	October, 1966–June, 1974
Cambodia	March, 1973–August, 1973
Cambodia Evacuation	April, 1975–April, 1975
Mayaguez Operation	May 15, 1975
Iranian/Yemen/Indian Ocean	December, 1978–June, 1979
Indian Ocean/Iran (N/MC)	November, 1979–October, 1981
Panama	April, 1980–December, 1986
El Salvador	January, 1981–February, 1992
Lebanon	August, 1982–December, 1987
Grenada (Operation Urgent Fury)	October, 1983–November, 1983
Libyan Area	January, 1986–June, 1986
Persian Gulf (Operation Earnest Will)	July, 1987–August, 1990
Panama (Operation Just Cause)	December, 1989–January, 1990
Southwest Asia (Desert Shield/Desert Storm)	August, 1990–November, 1995
Somalia (Operation Restore Hope)	December, 1992–March, 1995
Rwanda (Operation Distant Runner)	April, 1994–April, 1994
Haiti (Operation Uphold Democracy)	September, 1994–March, 1995
Persian Gulf (Operation Southern Watch)	December, 1995–
Persian Gulf (Operation Intercept)	December, 1995–
Persian Gulf (Operation Vigilant Sentinel)	December, 1995–February, 1997
Iraq (Operation Northern Watch)	January, 1997–

(continued)

TABLE 16 (continued)

Campaign or Expedition	Inclusive Dates
Persian Gulf (Operation Desert Thunder)	November, 1998–December, 1998
Persian Gulf (Operation Desert Fox)	December, 1998
Kosovo (various operations)	March, 1999–November, 1999

Source: Department of Labor, Office of Veteran's Employment and Training.
Note: World War II Service is recognized by Congress as extending from December 7, 1941, through April 28, 1952.

of staff for logistics in Washington, D.C., and managed the army's worldwide logistics organizations and systems.

That kind of responsibility was shared by Maj. Gen. Waymond C. Nutt ('51), who, after service as a combat jet fighter pilot, became an air force logistician. Following the Vietnam War, Nutt served as deputy chief of staff for logistics in Europe before assuming command of the San Antonio Air Logistics Center at Kelly Air Force Base in 1982. There he had primary responsibility for repair and maintenance support of most of the air fleet ranging from reciprocating engines for cargo and transport aircraft to jet engines for F-15s and F-16s.[8] One of the lessons learned in Korea and Vietnam was that aircraft that were grounded for lack of a replacement engine (as many were) could be very costly.

Being ready for combat on the first day of a war also meant having aircraft, ships, and submarines to deliver an attack or respond virtually anywhere. Throughout the post-Vietnam era, many Texas Aggies, such as navy Capt. Foster S. ("Tooter") Teague ('56), commanded strategic elements of the U.S. military strike forces. Teague, who flew 350 combat missions over North Vietnam and who had earned two Silver Stars, six Distinguished Flying Crosses, and the Purple Heart as a naval pilot, commanded the USS Kawishiwi for several years before being transferred to command the aircraft carrier USS Kitty Hawk in 1977. In 1981, the Kitty Hawk and its 5,600-member crew and 95 aircraft moved into the Indian Ocean for patrol and to "carry the flag" into major ports in the Philippines, Singapore, Korea, Sri Lanka, and Australia. With Teague aboard the Kitty Hawk were Lt. Dave Lewis ('76), Lt. Tom Harger ('70), marine Capt. Mike O'Neal ('75), and Lt. Tom Glaser ('65).[9]

Some years later Capt. William W. ("Bear") Pickavance Jr. ('68) from Ft. Worth followed Captain Teague to the bridge of the Kitty Hawk when he assumed command in June, 1993. The Kitty Hawk was sent on a high-alert cruise into the Persian Gulf, where U.S. forces had recently repelled invading Iraqi forces from Kuwait. There, American forces and naval units had been on almost uninterrupted patrol since 1987 (see table 16). Pickavance began his naval career flying the A-7 A/B Corsair from the USS Midway and later was executive officer of the aircraft carrier USS *Constellation* before commanding the USS *Mars* and then the *Kitty Hawk*. His decorations included the Distinguished Flying Cross and the Legion of Merit.[10]

A number of Texas Aggies were also at sea and on patrol in undisclosed locations aboard America's fleet of nuclear submarines. The USS *Michigan* was commanded by Capt. Bernard D. ("Dan") Greeson ('76), who graduated from the U.S. Naval Academy and then earned his master's degree in ocean engineering at Texas A&M. The *Michigan* was one of America's most advanced Trident missile submarines. While at sea, its location was classified; the sub neither sent nor returned communications.[11] As were the *Kitty Hawk* and other ships on patrol, the nuclear-powered Trident-class submarines were powerful deterrents to attacks on American territories.

Navy Lt. Cmdr. Michael R. ("Ollie") Oliver ('72) from El Paso and Lt. Cmdr. Darrel Westbrook ('80) from Houston also served aboard nuclear submarines and, during one tour, were officers on the same boat. Oliver became the executive officer aboard the USS *Parche* (SSN 683), "a front-line, fast-attack submarine," while Westbrook was in charge of the maintenance and repair of the sub's nuclear-reactor plant.[12]

Another nuclear-powered submarine was the USS *Drum*, whose primary "mission was to ferret out enemy submarines without being detected and to fire the navy's latest missiles and torpedoes to destroy enemy targets." Navy Lt. James E. Mayer ('78), an electrical engineer from Friendswood, served as an electrical and communications officer aboard the *Drum* for a number of years. Mayer completed his degree in nuclear engineering and was promptly assigned to the nuclear submarine fleet. "Where else could a guy who's been just a few years out of college run a nuclear power plant?" he exclaimed. His duty took him to ports in the Philippines, Guam, Hong Kong, Japan, and other places. However, the sub's schedules and destinations often changed within "a minute's notice. . . . The Navy's got a job to do, a very important job, and we've got to do it," Mayer explained.[13]

Adm. Jerome L. ("Jerry") Johnson ('56) would be one of the first to agree with Mayer. In 1988, Vice Admiral Johnson assumed command of the U.S. Second Fleet, Joint Task Force 120, and NATO's Striking Fleet Atlantic. This unit was one of the most powerful battle groups of the U.S. Navy and provided security for 38 million square miles of ocean in the Atlantic theater. Johnson had previously commanded Carrier Group Four, NATO's Carrier Striking Force, and served in the office of the chief of naval operations and with the secretary of the navy. In May, 1990, Johnson was promoted to admiral and vice chief of naval operations and became the third Texas A&M graduate to attain four-star rank.[14]

Two years earlier, in 1988, Capt. Ann Sanborn ('79) became the first American woman to captain a merchant ship, the *Texas Clipper*, Texas A&M's maritime training ship, and in this capacity she helped train Texas Aggies for command responsibilities at sea.[15]

Carrier and land-based long-range fighter and bomber aircraft located at strategic bases or positions around the globe were also powerful elements in the preservation of world peace. As in previous wars, Texas Aggies continued to serve prominently as pilots and air unit commanders in the post–Vietnam War era. Near the close of the century, Col. William Fraser ('74) assumed command of Barksdale Air Force Base, a home of the Second Bomb Wing of the Strategic Air Command (SAC). After graduation, Fraser joined the air force, completed pilot training, became a pilot training instructor, and later became aircraft commander and chief of staff for SAC at Offutt Air Force Base in Nebraska. "Training is important," Fraser emphasized. "We owe it to our country for [our troops] to get the right training. We must be mission oriented, mission focused. The world is still a dangerous place." [16]

Among those who helped make it less so was Capt. Wayne Edwards ('72), who became one of the air force's most proficient fighter pilots. In 1981, as part of the air force training and readiness exercises, Edwards flew with the 388th Tactical Fighter Wing in the British Royal Air Force Strike Command's tactical bombing competition. His F-16 Fighting Falcon team achieved top honors while competing against British and other U.S. participants.[17]

One of Edwards's classmates, James R. ("Rick") Perry ('72), a yell leader during his undergraduate years at Texas A&M, began his career of service as an air force second lieutenant. During his five years of military service, he flew C-130 tactical airlift aircraft in the United States, Europe, South America, and the Middle East. Captain Perry returned to farming and ranching in 1982 and in 1984 began a six-year term in the Texas House of Representatives. From 1990 to 1998, he served as Texas commissioner of agriculture, and in 1998, he was elected lieutenant governor of Texas. Perry became governor of Texas in 2000, replacing George W. Bush, and was elected governor in 2002. He characterized his Corps of Cadet training and military experiences as critical milestones in his life of service.[18] During Perry's military service, he, as did so many other Texas Aggies, helped maintain America's readiness in the air.

In the 1980s, two Texas Aggies were among those who headed navy and marine FA-18 "Hornet" training operations in California. Cmdr. Bill Pickavance and marine Lt. Col. Bob ("Mad Dog") Maddocks ('69) were respectively the CO and executive officer for Strike Fighter Squadron 125, the largest joint combat-readiness training squadron in the U.S. Pacific Fleet's Naval Air Force. As part of NATO's combat-readiness efforts, the squadron trained pilots and maintenance technicians, including navy and marine personnel, as well as crews from the Canadian Armed Forces, Royal Australian Air Force, and Spanish Air Force. Navy Attack Squadron 122, a light attack fleet pilot-replacement squadron for the A7E Corsair II carrier-based attack jet, also based in California, was another significant component of the Pacific fleet's naval air force. At the close of the 1980s, Texas Aggie members of Attack Squadron 122 included Lt. Joseph A. Cooper ('81), Lt. (jg) Jon T. Ross ('86), Lt. (jg) Kevin L. Duggan ('85), Lt. (jg) Lisa E. Lehman ('85), Lt. Byron L. Wright ('83), and Lt. Gary T. Harper ('80).[19]

Two air force squadrons, both under the command of Texas Aggies, were activated at the close of the 1980s as trouble began to develop in the Persian Gulf and in Panama. The 98th Bombardment Squadron and the 99th Fighter Squadron, located at Williams Air Force Base in Arizona, were reactivated, with Lt. Col. William G. Fuller Jr. ('70) in command of the 98th Training Squadron, which was outfitted with T-37 jet trainers. One of Fuller's classmates, Lt. Col. Johnny Jarnagin ('70), commanded the 99th Squadron, which was equipped with T-38 supersonic jet trainers. It was probable, noted the *Texas Aggie*, that "this could be the first time in history that two classmates have assumed command of squadrons in the same wing on the same day."[20] Cold War and post–Vietnam War planning held that readiness for combat was the strongest deterrent to war.

At ceremonies at Ramstein Air Force Base, Germany, evidence of that readiness was the award given to U.S. Air Force Capt. Jeffrey D. Gardner ('82) in 1988 as the outstanding air controller in the U.S. Air Force–Europe. As command post training officer and emergency actions officer for the 81st Tactical Fighter Wing based in England, Gardner developed a "quick reaction checklist monitor," rewrote emergency procedures for handling top-secret and NATO information, and revised training tests and practices, resulting in markedly enhanced performance. He also improved computer programming and utilization in the training curriculum. Those developments were soon adopted by other bases under U.S. Air Force–Europe command and resulted in increased combat readiness.[21]

Readiness also meant having appropriate and maintained air bases and troop facilities available as needed. For example, 2nd Lt. Charles D. McMullan ('58), an architectural engineer, began his air force career as a special projects officer and instructor at the U.S. Air Force Civil Engineering School at Wright-Patterson Air Force Base. He then spent three years at Clark Air Force Base in the Philippines in charge of housing projects. McMullan also devised runway improvements for bases in Thailand, provided oversight for the operation of power plants located throughout Southeast Asia, helped design air defense programs, and supervised the construction of aircraft facilities at Kunsan, Korea. Later he spent three years at Eielson Air Force Base, Alaska, where he was chief of engineering and construction with the 5010th Civil Engineering Squadron. McMullan retired from the air force as a lieutenant colonel in 1979 and returned to Texas A&M for a second career in the Department of Construction Science.[22]

The armed services were also required to be ready for biological and chemical warfare. Col. Pat ("Callaghan") Nossov (DVM; '81) contributed to that readiness through her research and work with the army veterinary corps. Colonel Nossov became director of lab animal research at the Walter Reed Army Institute of Research, while her Aggie husband, Col. Robert Nossov ('76), was assigned to the U.S. Army Test and Evaluation Command. When both of their fathers retired as colonels in the army, the two generations of Nossovs had compiled one hundred years of military service.[23]

An important element of air combat readiness was also the availability of well-trained reserve pilots who were ready for active duty. Among those who made particularly significant contributions to ready reserve air training was Charles R. ("Chuck") Cargill ('53), who was promoted to the rank of major general in 1986 while serving as mobilization assistant to the commander of Air University, Maxwell Air Force Base, Alabama. Similarly, while in the air force reserves in 1987, John J. Closner ('62) led the first F-16 unit, the 419th Tactical Fighter Wing based at Hill Air Force Base in Utah. Under his leadership the wing won the "Gunsmoke" championship and other awards in a worldwide fighter olympics similar to the tactical bombing competition mentioned earlier in this chapter. Later Closner commanded the Tenth Air Force at Bergstrom Air Force Base and was selected as chief of the air force reserves as a major general. In 1989, Maj. Waymond ("Wayne") Nutt ('75) led his air national guard 169th Tactical Fighter Group to the world championship in the Gunsmoke competition at Nellis AFB, Nevada. After leaving active duty, Nutt, the son of retired Maj. Gen. Waymond C. Nutt ('51), became a pilot with American Airlines and remained flight and combat ready with the active reserve.[24]

Maj. Gen. Thomas R. Olsen ('56) flew 301 combat missions in Vietnam with the 615th Tactical Fighter Squadron and later commanded the 391st Tactical Fighter Squadron. After several years in the States and graduation from the Air War College in 1975, Olsen returned to the Pacific as vice commander of the 314th Air Division in Seoul, South Korea. From there he went to Japan as the Fifth Air Force's deputy chief of staff for operations, returned to Korea to command the 51st Tactical Fighter Wing, and completed his military career with a war in the Persian Gulf.[25] As General Olsen's post–Vietnam War career indicates, preparedness meant having a global air-power presence.

Adequate preparation also meant having effective training and support programs and facilities for service commands around the world. Among those who contributed to that readiness on the home front in the 1980s was Assistant Secretary of the Army Robert W. Page ('48), who directed the activities of the U.S. Army Corps of Engineers in the United States and abroad. Page had served in the Pacific theater with the navy, earned his degree in architectural engineering after World War II, and worked for a time with the Central Intelligence Agency. Col. William R. Andrews Jr. ('63) also accepted numerous assignments with the Corps of Engineers and, in 1982, became commander of the Omaha (Nebraska)

District. One of his jobs was to assist in the design and construction of facilities needed to support the air-launched cruise-missile weapons systems installed on B-52 aircraft. Earlier, Andrews served with the 82nd Airborne Division in the Dominican Republic and the 46th Engineer Battalion in Vietnam, and he commanded the 2nd Engineer Battalion in Korea. Col. Clarence H. Woliver Jr. ('54), who also had previous service in Korea and commanded an aerial-rocket artillery unit with the 1st Cavalry Division in Vietnam, was executive officer of the aviation school at Fort Rucker, Alabama, before assuming command of Fort McPherson, Georgia, and then Fort Sam Houston, San Antonio, in the 1980s.[26]

Since Korea and Vietnam, one of the major infantry attack vehicles had been the helicopter. Then, in the 1980s, the helicopter began to be adapted and enhanced for air-to-air combat. Contributing to this transition was Maj. Gary A. Sharon ('71), a project officer and test pilot for the BK-117 helicopter—the first of its kind. Sharon's tests, including loops, rolls, lazy eights, and other maneuvers, helped establish the engineering design data for improving the maneuverability of future generations of army helicopters. At the time, his commanding officer at Edwards Air Force Base, California, was another Aggie, Col. Alan R. Todd ('57), commander of flight activity.[27]

Among the newer, unique, special-purpose aircraft was the Harrier "jump jet," which Capt. Michael W. Watkins ('77) piloted. The Harrier could hover a few feet above the ground and then climb rapidly at high speeds. Navy Lt. George A. Mason Jr. ('81) and Lt. (jg) Steven L. Spicer ('83) flew the TA-4 Skyhawk attack helicopters, and USAF Reserve Maj. Steven D. Higgs ('73) flew the A-10 Warthog with the 46th Tactical Fighter Squadron. The Warthog was a highly maneuverable close-air-support aircraft that carried a 30-mm gun and protective armor for its pilot. Higgs and air force pilots Carleton R. Walker, Glen R. Cernik, William Carl Collins, and David Wayne Young, all of the class of 1973, became career airline pilots after completing their active duty.[28]

Distinctive among the new-era combat aircraft were the tilt-rotor aircraft such as the V-22 Osprey, which was first assigned to navy and marine air units. The V-22 could take off and land vertically like a helicopter, but, in standard flight, it converted into a conventional turboprop airplane, which gave it the versatility of a helicopter and the speed of a ground-support fighter aircraft. Flight tests on a prototype XV-15 began in the early 1980s, and among those conducting the tests were marine Capt. William J. ("Bill") Wainwright ('83) and Bell helicopter test pilot Roy C. Hopkins ('68), a former marine pilot who flew a Cobra gunship in Vietnam before joining Bell.[29] They played a dangerous and critical role in maintaining a technological edge over potential enemy forces.

Two other exceptional aircraft added to the American air arsenal near the close of the twentieth century were the ER-2, the descendant of the U-2 "spy plane," and the Stealth B-2 bomber. The U-2 became "widely known in the 1950s when Francis Gary Powers, a civilian pilot employed by the Central Intelligence

Agency, was shot down during a reconnaissance mission over the Soviet Union." That incident brought the East and West perilously close to a nuclear confrontation but was finally resolved when Powers was exchanged for a Russian KGB agent. The U-2's successor, the ER-2, was considerably larger than the U-2 and had a range that exceeded three thousand nautical miles and was capable of eight-hour flights without refueling. The ER-2 cruised at altitudes above 80,000 feet and used imaging sensors to collect surveillance data. In 1989, only four pilots were qualified to fly the ER-2, and two of those were graduates of Texas A&M. One was James Barrilleaux ('64) from Houston, who flew air force F-4 Phantom jets in Southeast Asia in the 1960s and 1970s. Barrilleaux returned from combat to serve as a flight instructor and then volunteered for the U-2 flight program in 1974. He retired from the air force in 1986 and joined NASA as an ER-2 pilot. Gardner Doyle Krumrey ('62) completed pilot training and spent tours with the Strategic Air Command in Oklahoma, Thailand, and Korea before becoming a U-2 and then an ER-2 pilot. Both Barrilleaux and Krumrey were recipients of the Distinguished Flying Cross and other awards.[30]

The Stealth bomber, a high-speed, high-altitude, radar-evading attack bomber designed to replace the aging B-52, was flight-tested for the first time on July 17, 1989, from a takeoff at Palmdale, California, by Northrop test pilot Bruce Hinds and air force Col. Richard S. Couch ('68), an electrical engineer from Texarkana, Arkansas. Couch commanded the 6510th Test Group at the U.S. Air Force Flight Test Center, Edwards Air Force Base, California. Couch and Hinds put the plane through a two-hour test run and concluded that it was "very nimble" in flight and "rock steady" on landing. The landing was so smooth, Couch said, that he had to ask the tower whether he were on the ground. When Couch took off on the test flight, his wife, Ann, was asked whether he had any special rituals or lucky charms he used. "He has on his A&M underwear," she replied. He flew 199 combat missions in Vietnam, Laos, and Cambodia before beginning test-pilot training in 1975. The Stealth entered production in the range of $1 billion for each aircraft, which brought about reductions in the number of aircraft that actually entered service. However, it did achieve the design requirements for an "advanced technology bomber" and became a centerpiece of American air power.[31]

Cruise missile systems and aircraft such as the ER-2 and Stealth bombers meant that future warfare verged on space. Systems previously considered "aeronautical" became "aerospace." Pilots often became astronauts. The line between flight and space became obscured. In the closing decades of the twentieth century, many Texas Aggies operated on the perimeters of aerospace. They served as members of the armed forces, NASA engineers, scientists, astronauts, and often production engineers with aerospace companies that supplied the military or NASA with supersonic and hypersonic aerospace craft and space vehicles. Among them, for example, was Capt. Joe Squatrito ('79) from San

Antonio, a computer science graduate and air force officer assigned to NASA's Johnson Space Center (JSC) to train military shuttle ground-operation crews for space operations. His job was to help maintain the five computers aboard the space shuttle and the linkages with the mission-control room and to assist in pilot computer training. While NASA's space-flight programs were distinctly civilian oriented, they also had very clear defense ramifications. "Why do we need to be in space?" Squatrito asked. "Think about why we have a national defense—it's to defend the things we believe in and the security of this country. Think about our communications satellites. We depend on them, and we need to defend them."[32]

As chapter 13 points out, many Texas Aggies helped the armed forces, NASA, and the nation extend its reach from air into space and then helped make the transition from the Apollo lunar missions to the space shuttle. Similarly, those Aggies and other former students contributed significantly to the transition from the Cold War to a new era of Russian and international cooperation. Space exploration brought about many contributions to conventional flight and communications, as well as to national defense. Texas Aggies, following in the tradition set by Johnson Space Center directors such as Aaron Cohen ('52) and Gerald D. Griffin ('56) were very involved in NASA and military-related space programs. Bryan P. Austin ('81) from League City, Texas, joined the Johnson Space Center immediately following his graduation and began training shuttle flight crews and flight controllers in data-processing systems and navigation. He estimated that, by the year 2000, almost 15 percent of the combined contractor and civil service work force (or armed-services-affiliated associates) at JSC were Texas Aggies. Austin headed Johnson Space Center's shuttle mission simulator team in 1987 and became a flight director in 1993. By 2002, he had served as the orbit flight director on sixteen shuttle missions and was the lead flight director on four of those.[33]

The first Aggie to achieve astronaut status was air force Maj. William A. Pailes (MS in computer science at Texas A&M in 1981 and a U.S. Air Force Academy graduate), who made his first flight aboard the shuttle as a payload specialist in 1985. Alan L. ("Lee") Briscoe ('68) from Houston began his NASA career as a communications officer for the Apollo, Skylab, and space shuttle missions and became a flight director in 1984. He directed the reentry on seven missions and managed the orbital flight for four others. In 1991, he became deputy manager of space shuttle operations and the next year was chief of the flight director office. In 1998, Briscoe became deputy director of Johnson Space Center. After almost a decade of work in guidance and navigation control systems, John P. Shannon ('87), also from Houston, became a flight director in 1995. By 2002, he had participated in twenty-three shuttle flights and specialized as an ascent/ entry flight director. Other JSC Aggie flight directors over the years have included Matthew R. Abbott ('85), Richard D. ("Rich") Jackson ('80), John M.

Curry ('87), and Paul S. Hill ('84), who transferred to NASA from the air force, where he had worked in missile launch detection. Bryan Lunney ('89), a NASA flight director, followed a NASA career in the footsteps of his father, Glynn Lunney, who was a flight director on early Gemini and Apollo missions. J. Stephen ("Steve") Stitch ('87) from Austin became an expert in low-earth-orbital decay, served as orbit flight dynamics officer for twenty-one missions, and managed fifteen rendezvous flights, including five Mir missions, among them the historic rendezvous between American astronauts and Russian cosmonauts.[34]

On one shuttle flight (STS-109) sent to service the Hubble space telescope in March, 2002, most of the flight control personnel were Texas Aggies, including Bryan Austin, who was lead flight director. With him were John Shannon ('87), who managed the ascent and entry; Dana J. Weigel ('93), who supervised the extravehicular activities (EVA); and Cori L. (Hembree) Kerr ('90), who was the lead propulsion officer. Her brother, Roger M. ("Mike") Hembree ('88), was also a flight controller. Stephen ("Steve") R. Walker ('65) served as the rendezvous officer, and Sotirios Liolios ('94) from Kavala, Greece, was in charge of crew team mission training. Having launched on March 1, the day before Texas Independence Day, the mission succeeded in upgrading the telescope with a new camera, power supplies, and solar arrays, thus enabling the capture of more spectacular pictures of deep space.[35]

Perhaps nothing so conspicuously signaled the demise of the Cold War as did the Mir missions and the assembly of an international space station in orbit, which project was begun in 2001. Indicative of that new Soviet-American détente, in June, 2000, NASA sent astronauts Michael E. Fossum ('80) and Steven R. Swanson ('98) to Star City, Russia's space center, for water survival training in the Black Sea with Russian Soyuz cosmonauts who were preparing for flights to the international space station.[36]

Although the Apollo lunar exploration, moon walks, rover journeys on the moon, and shuttle activities attracted some media attention and the public's imagination, global peace and national security issues still remained. In the Middle East, the Camp David accords, brokered by the United States in 1978, brought a short-lived hope of peace between Israel and its Arab neighbors. The imminent threat of war and the ever-present possibility of nuclear holocaust stood in sharp contrast to the progress that was occurring in expanding world trade and space exploration. Impending war and terrorism conflicted with the remarkable technological and economic revolution going on in the United States and major world economies. The threat of catastrophic warfare, however, began to force a reconciliation and a détente between the United States and the Soviet Union and eventually between the United States and China.

Close to American shores, Cuba remained beholden to the Soviet Union and provided assistance in the overthrow of the pro-American government of Nicaragua, which encouraged revolution in El Salvador and unrest in Panama and throughout Central and South America. Military coups in Afghanistan triggered a Russian invasion of that country in 1979, thus renewing the threat of confrontations between the Soviet Union and the United States. African nations, freed from the yoke of empire after World War II, vacillated between Soviet and American overtures and fell prey to ancient tribal warfare.

Perhaps nothing so well illustrates the tumult and chaos of many of the African nations and the diverse and often unique peace-keeping duties performed by military personnel as the experiences of Robert R. Gosney ('54) from Belton, Texas. An offensive guard and linebacker on the A&M football team, Gosney entered military service after graduation. In 1973, after completing special training with a group of officers from every branch of the armed forces, as well as from the U.S. State Department, the CIA, and the Coast Guard, Gosney was assigned as chief of the military mission in Monrovia, Liberia. His job was to help train the Liberian military and to advise the president of Liberia, William Richard Tolbert. Liberia was critical of America's Cold War interests because the United States operated an important submarine-navigation system and electronic intelligence-gathering systems from that country. However, Liberia was tightly controlled by a small group who dominated a very large tribal majority. On one occasion, when a sudden hike in rice prices sparked riots and massive protests by tribal leaders, President Tolbert asked Gosney to take command of the armed forces and restore order. Gosney obtained approval from the U.S. State Department, assumed command of the army, and, in a massive show of force, concentrated the army in the capital city. "Within two days, all the rioting had stopped. The people had gone back up to their villages."[37]

Commenting on the incident, Robert P. Smith, U.S. ambassador to Liberia, said that "Col. Gosney is one of the finest army officers I've ever encountered. He did a superb job and saved many lives." Nevertheless, Gosney advised Tolbert that, if he did not implement reforms, he would suffer a coup. The rebellion soon occurred, and again, to help forestall total anarchy, Gosney helped the coup's leaders, including the new president, Samuel Doe, organize their new government. Gosney soon left the country for other assignments, but Doe implemented another authoritarian regime, and, after a decade of power, he too was violently deposed.[38] In 2003, American military advisors and UN troops were again involved in rescue-and-assistance missions in Liberia.

In North Africa and the Middle East, continuing conflicts between Israel, its Arab neighbors, and the Palestinian Liberation Organization (PLO) kept the region on the brink of war. In 1979, even as Russia and the United States jousted over Russian control in Afghanistan, in neighboring Iran a revolution led by Iranian fundamentalists under Ayatollah Ruholla Khomeini forced the collapse of the pro–U.S. government of Shah Mohammed Reza Pahlavi. Iranian mobs stormed the U.S. embassy and seized American hostages. A nighttime helicopter rescue mission staged by American special forces failed to achieve its objective. In June, 1982, Israel invaded Lebanon in an effort to destroy the PLO. The United States responded by sending marines into Beirut, Lebanon, in an effort to promote stability.

In October, 1983, a terrorist bombing of a marine barracks in Beirut killed 241 American marines, and terrorism increasingly became a global threat. Subsequently, in 1986, the United States struck a blow against international terrorism by bombing targets in Libya, where Muammar Qaddafi was believed to be fueling terrorism. Meanwhile, open warfare between Iran and Iraq threatened to embroil the United States, the Soviet Union, and the entire Middle East. Fortunately, conflicts over the Middle East between the United States and the Soviet Union were averted with the election of Mikhail Gorbachev as general secretary of the Soviet Communist Party. Eventually, glasnost ("openness") and cooperation began to replace confrontation. Over the next five years, revolutionary events transformed the Soviet Union and Europe and brought an end to the Cold War era of Soviet-American confrontation.

In March, 1989, the Soviet Union held free elections, which resulted in the end of the Communist Party's control. In June, Poland held free elections and repudiated communist control. Democratic elections and reforms in Hungary, Czechoslovakia, Bulgaria, Romania, and East Germany gradually ended communist domination. The Berlin Wall separating East and West Germany, communist and free nations, was literally torn down by exuberant Berliners, and Germany became one nation once again. Navy Cmdr. Allen Bettisworth ('75), whose military service spanned the Cold War from 1975 to 1995, remembers the collapse of the Berlin Wall as his most memorable military experience.[39]

Although the end of the Cold War greatly lessened the threat of nuclear holocaust and world war, it nonetheless failed to bring world peace and did not diminish the need for the United States to be ready for war at any time and in any place. "Economic competition, ethnic hatreds, and regional struggles for power seemed to replace the old ideological divide between the United States and the Soviet Union as the fulcrum of international conflict."[40] On August 2, 1990, Iraqi armies swept into tiny, oil-rich Kuwait, deposing the government and annexing it to Iraq. The action threatened to plunge the entire Middle East into war and immediately disrupted vital Western oil supplies. American forces responded with Operation Desert Shield, which sought to stabilize the situation there and protect Saudi Arabia from possible Iraqi attack by mobilizing a large military force in the area. Following failed diplomatic negotiations, the United States launched Operation Desert Storm to remove the Iraqi invaders from Kuwait.

Suggested Readings

Ambrose, Stephen E. *Rise to Globalism: American Foreign Policy since 1938*, 5th ed. (New York: Penguin Books, 1988).

Deac, Wilfred P. *Road to the Killing Fields: The Cambodian War of 1970–1975* (College Station: Texas A&M University Press, 1997).

Dethloff, Henry C. *The United States and the Global Economy since 1945* (New York: Harcourt, Brace, 1997).

Gaddis, John L. *The United States and the End of the Cold War: Implications, Reconsiderations, Provocations* (New York: Oxford University Press, 1992).

Quinn, Frederick. *Democracy at Dawn: Notes from Poland and Points East* (College Station: Texas A&M University Press, 1998).

Rubin, Barry. *Paved with Good Intentions: The American Experience and Iran* (New York: Oxford University Press, 1980).

Maj. Gen. Thomas R. Olsen ('56), deputy commander of the U.S. Central Command Air Forces (CENTAF) during Operation Desert Storm, said he never really had a feeling for how many Aggies were stationed in the Middle East during the war, "but I would meet them most everywhere that I went. We had several working at our CENTAF headquarters . . . from various other air force commands, the army, marines, and navy."
—Jerry C. Cooper

Ours has always been an army like no other, because our soldiers reflect a society unlike any other. They are pitiless when confronted by armed enemy fighters and yet full of compassion for civilians and even defeated enemies.
—Jim Lacey, "The Men Who Won the War"

DESERT STORM IRAQI FREEDOM

On Thursday, August 2, 1990, Iraqi tanks, troops, and helicopters poured across Iraq's southern border into tiny, oil-rich Kuwait. Iraqi troops met minimal resistance and, after only twelve hours, seized control of the entire nation. That same day, the UN Security Council, meeting in New York, demanded Iraq's immediate withdrawal. Iraq, under the rule of Saddam Hussein, declined. On August 6, the UN Security Council declared an economic embargo and halted Iraqi imports and oil exports. Iraq was unfazed. Then Pres. George H. W. Bush, seeking to increase the diplomatic and economic pressure on Iraq and further encourage a withdrawal, began requesting international support for an armed coalition to be led by U.S. troops that could, if necessary, force an Iraqi withdrawal. As a part of this initiative and to help protect Saudi Arabia and other neighboring states from attack, on August 7, President Bush ordered the deployment of U.S. forces to the Persian Gulf. Within hours of the commander in chief's deployment order, Maj. Chuck Friesenhan ('74) from Castroville, Texas, and hundreds of others on active duty and in the reserves began the move to the Persian Gulf, followed by thousands and soon tens of thousands more.[1]

On August 7, Friesenhan, a fighter, attack, and reconnaissance qualified pilot and a combat aircrew training officer, began a nonstop flight, piloting one of the two C-141 Starlifters attached to the air force reserve's 459th Military Airlift Wing. The Starlifters accompanied a group of fighters from the 1st Tactical Fighter Wing at Langley Air Force Base, Virginia, to their new posts at Dharan, Saudi Arabia. On August 8, Saddam Hussein defiantly announced the annexation of Kuwait. For the next six months, the United States and the UN sought

"Olsen Led Air Forces in Desert Storm," *Texas Aggie* (Dec., 1991), p. 34.

peaceful, diplomatic means to end the Iraqi occupation of Kuwait, while the United States moved naval, air force, and army units into the Persian Gulf area. Friesenhan, Maj. Gen. Thomas R. Olsen, and Col. William C. Bender ('65) were among the first troops to arrive in Saudi Arabia.[2] Deployment was fast, efficient, and, compared to previous engagements, remarkable in that many of the lead elements included special troops that were assigned to perform tasks that virtually did not exist even a decade earlier. It became very clear that, if this was to be war, war had assumed a different dimension.

Col. Bill Bender, task force director of the U.S. Air Force Electronic Security Command, arrived in Saudi Arabia on August 10 with about 150 men. Their job was to set up a security office for the Central Task Force Command and for the crews of the RC-135 reconnaissance aircraft. In a very short time "we deployed thousands of troops, hundreds of airplanes, and tons of supplies thousands of miles and arrived ready to wage war. It was (and is) an incredible effort," Bender wrote to Jerry Cooper ('63), editor of *Texas Aggie*. "And hot! Was it ever hot! It was, quite literally, like living in an oven. I drank so much water that I swore I'd never drink it again." But the Saudis, he said, were friendly and very supportive of the U.S. presence there. "It is a starkly beautiful country," and Bender prayed that peace could be established in that troubled area of the world without bloodshed.[3]

The United States hoped to make peace, not war, but was almost instantly ready for the latter. Among those who helped get ready was navy Lt. Cmdr. Andrew S. Griffith ('78), a civil engineer whose major job after he arrived in Saudi Arabia was to oversee the construction of a 92,000-square-foot building. That edifice would house the U.S. Transportation Command (TransCom), a joint army, navy, and air force staff whose business it was to get the troops and equipment in place for a 200,000-person combat force, should it be needed. Within a short time, TransCom had moved 185,000 people and more than 5 billion pounds of materials to Saudi Arabia—"everything from turkeys to tanks to portable hospitals." The task was likened to moving Missouri's capital, Jefferson City, with all of its people, cars, trucks, foodstuffs, water supplies, and household goods overseas.[4]

Capt. Tanya Mentzer ('83) also arrived in Saudi Arabia in August as the squadron section commander of the 27th Civil Engineer Squadron. Mentzer was deployed from Cannon Air Force Base in Clovis, New Mexico, with a large contingency of support personnel, including security police, doctors, nurses, civil engineers, and transportation, communications, and administrative personnel. Her duties were to oversee the erection of "tent cities" and to develop recreational facilities, "including a complete golf course in the sand" for deployed military personnel. That having been done, Captain Mentzer was designated "tent city commander" of two "cities" containing more than sixteen hundred personnel. Among the city's early visitors were Vice President Dan Quayle

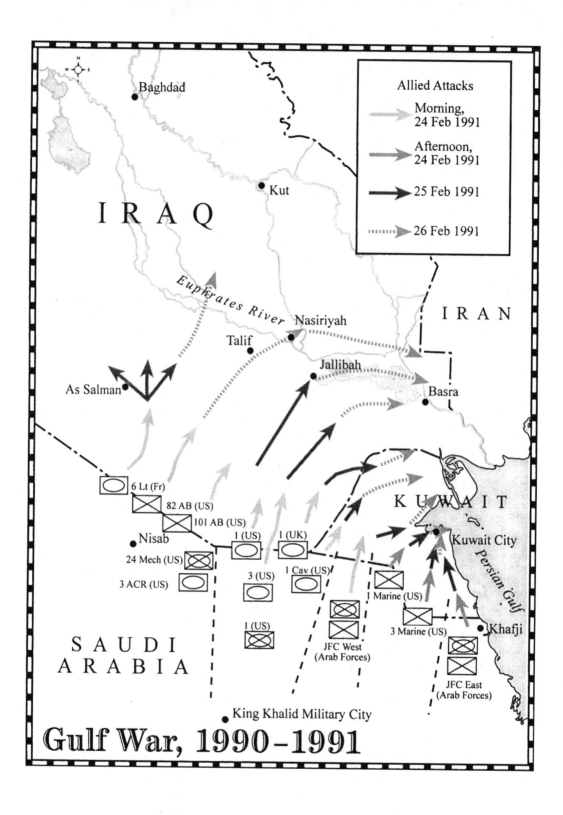

Allied Attacks

→	Morning, 24 Feb 1991
→	Afternoon, 24 Feb 1991
→	25 Feb 1991
⋯→	26 Feb 1991

Baghdad

Kut

I R A Q

Euphrates River

Nasiriyah

Talif

Jallibah

I R A N

As Salman

Basra

K U W A I T

6 Lt (Fr)

82 AB (US)

101 AB (US)

Nisab

1 (US)

1 (UK)

Kuwait City

24 Mech (US)

3 ACR (US)

3 (US)

1 Cav (US)

1 (US)

1 Marine (US)

Persian Gulf

JFC West
(Arab Forces)

3 Marine (US)

Khafji

S A U D I
A R A B I A

JFC East
(Arab Forces)

King Khalid Military City

Gulf War, 1990–1991

and Lt. Gen. Calvin Waller, second in command of Desert Storm operations. Mentzer's husband, Capt. Dwight Mentzer ('82), was back "home" at Cannon AFB, where he and fellow Aggie 1st Lt. Enoch Kent Wong ('86) were assigned to an F-111D Squadron, waiting for transfer to the Middle East if needed.[5]

Capt. Robert James ('85), with the 1703 Air Refueling Wing and maintenance supervisor for the KC-135 aircraft at his post, moved into one of the tent cities when he arrived on the scene but later shifted to a "dormitory style building," he said, which made the corps' dorms in College Station "look like suites at the Hyatt Hotel." Aggies working with him included Capt. Dale A. Cope ('82), whose job was to replace the UHF radios on the air tankers with VHF radios and then to help repair damaged aircraft. Others in the Desert Shield operations included Capt. James A. Rambo ('82) and Capt. I. Lee Patton ('82).[6]

Marine Capt. Harry L. Warren, MD ('79), also arrived in Saudi Arabia in August. After completing his undergraduate studies, Warren had enrolled in the Texas A&M University Medical School. Following graduation, Warren interned at Walter Reed Hospital before assignment to the 101st Airborne as a medical company commander (1984–1985). He then took special orthopedic surgery training at Fort Sam Houston in San Antonio from 1985 to 1989 before becoming chief of orthopedic surgery at Blaushfield Army Hospital, Fort Campbell, Kentucky, about the time Saddam Hussein's forces invaded Kuwait. Warren was immediately sent as a forward surgery team leader with the 326th Medical Battalion, 101st Airborne. His job, in the event of combat, was, in the MASH tradition, to provide battlefield medicine: "We move by helicopter in most cases with our tents and equipment slung beneath the aircraft in cargo nets. If an infantry brigade were to make a helicopter air assault, we would follow them in behind enemy lines to treat our wounded. Our equipment is first rate and by being closer to where the casualties occur we can perhaps save some lives that couldn't be saved without prompt intervention."[7]

Among other early arrivals in the Persian Gulf were Lt. Col. James L. Sachtleben ('69) and Lt. Edwin A. Klein ('88), both natives of Nacogdoches, Texas, and both marines. Sachtleben was commander of the 5th Battalion, 11th Marines, First Marine Division, and Klein was the guns platoon commander and assistant executive officer for Battery R, a 155-mm howitzer battery of the 5th Battalion. Four months after their arrival, they were still hoping for a diplomatic solution to the Iraq impasse but were prepared to do "whatever President Bush considers necessary to handle the situation." When they arrived, they secured equipment from ships of the marines' Maritime Preposition Force, a floating stockpile and supply system that helped make rapid deployments to remote overseas posts possible.[8] Thus, they were immediately combat ready.

Helping to prepare the military forces for combat were people such as air force Maj. Robert Reneau ('77) from Weatherford, whose job it would be to fly C-130 airlift missions and "airdrop or airland supplies and personnel to the army up front." He arrived in Abu Dhabi, Arab Emirates, on August 16 and found that nothing had been set up for the incoming military forces. "We ate a lot of MREs [meals ready to eat]," he said. And "[i]t was so hot in the summer that there were no bugs, no birds. . . . You drank so much water that you couldn't sleep through the night." The most depressing thing, he said, was the rotation plan. "It never happened."[9]

Maj. Richard M. ("Rick") Price ('74) was among the first casualties of Operation Desert Shield. He died on August 28 when his C-5A transport crashed at Ramstein Air Base, West Germany. A native of San Antonio, Price completed pilot training at Williams Air Force Base in Arizona, flew F-111s and T-39 Sabre jets, and became an instructor pilot. He joined the 68th Reserve Squadron in January, 1989, and, when the Desert Storm deployment began, he "repeatedly volunteered for every mission available." A friend, marine Maj. Robert S. ("Stew") Rayfield ('75), said that Price "was the epitome of soldiering, there wasn't anything he wouldn't do in the name of God, Country, and Corps."[10]

On August 22, President Bush mobilized additional military reserve units. By the end of August, the United States had four navy battle groups, three marine expeditionary brigades, four army divisions, and three air force tactical fighter wings in the Persian Gulf region, including assorted communications, logistics, and medical groups. During the initial deployment, Desert Shield commander Gen. Norman Schwarzkopf remained in Florida to organize the disposition of his forces. Brig. Gen. (later Lt. Gen.) Patrick P. Caruana ('72) was the 42nd Air Division commander with the Strategic Air Command (SAC) forces. Brig. Gen. Hal M. Hornburg ('68), a forward air controller in Vietnam, commanded the 4th Fighter Wing during Operation Desert Shield and Desert Storm. (Hornburg earned his fourth star in August, 2000, and became air component commander in 2002, in time for yet another armed conflict in Iraq.[11]) Lt. Gen. Charles A. Horner, who headed the U.S. Central Command Air Forces, was given responsibility for all military operations in the Middle East, while his deputy commander in Saudi Arabia, air force Maj. Gen. Thomas R. Olsen, oversaw all incoming air force units.

Olsen, who learned to fly when he was in high school, commanded the 615th Tactical Fighter Squadron in Vietnam and the 51st Tactical Fighter Wing in South Korea and had served as deputy commander of the Fourth Allied Tactical Air Force in West Germany. He arrived in Riyadh, Saudi Arabia, on the morning of August 8, and the first F-15 squadron landed at Dhahran about noon. F-16 fighters equipped with airborne warning-and-control systems (AWACS), electronic surveillance aircraft, and KC-135 and KC-10 tankers arrived thereafter around the clock. Olsen spent much of his time "getting organized" with coalition forces from the United Kingdom, France, Italy, Canada, Saudi Arabia, Kuwait, Bahrain, Qatar, the United Arab Emirates, and Oman.[12]

New communications and search technologies, Olsen noted, were crucial to the success of surveillance and the early operations of Desert Shield. Fighters equipped with infrared search-and-tracking systems provided unique night-strike capabilities, while electronic combat forces, notably the "Wild Weasels," provided detailed information and surveillance data. The "Weasels" included squadron leader Lt. Col. George W. Walton ('71), who led one of the first bombing missions of the Gulf War. Moreover, Olsen said, U.S. forces had almost instantaneous communications throughout the world using satellite systems. "We were electronically tied to all of the support bases and to the headquarters back in the U.S. . . . The deployment was overwhelming . . . not only to our allies, but also to the enemy."[13]

Important major elements of that deployment were four major navy battle groups clustered around carrier lead ships, including the USS *Saratoga*, USS *John F. Kennedy*, USS *Midway*, and USS *Ranger*. Aggies with the *Saratoga* included Lt. Cmdr. Larry D. Hall ('72), with VAQ-130, flying an EA6-B "Prowler" equipped for electronic warfare, and Ens. Steven H. Drexler ('88), one of the ship's officers. Marines and members of what Maj. Stew Rayfield from New Braunfels called the "Persian Gulf Yacht and Big-Bore Hunting Club" on board the assault ship USS *Raleigh* included Rayfield, 2nd Lt. Chris Rollins ('88) from Pass Christian, Mississippi; and 2nd Lt. John Mark Weideman ('83) from Midland.[14] Thus, the clouds of war and the resources for waging it gathered in the Persian Gulf. The days of Desert Shield lengthened into months—and soon into war and a Desert Storm.

On November 29, the UN Security Council authorized the use of force if Iraq failed to withdraw by January 15, 1991. Saddam again declined to withdraw. Thus, on January 17, the United States and its allies began strategic air strikes against Iraq and Iraqi military positions inside Kuwait. From the unique advantage of the control panel of a navy E-2C Hawkeye aircraft circling the skies over Iraq, Cmdr. Byron P. Compton ('75), executive officer of the "Sun Kings" Early Warning (Vertical Aircraft Warning) Squadron (VAW-16) aboard the *Ranger*, watched the beginning of what would become Operation Desert Storm. The AWACS aircraft were utilized to lead fighters to their targets and provide assistance and some combat direction. Flying their first real combat missions over Iraq, these aircraft could provide early warning of enemy targets over an area more than ten times the size of Texas and "simultaneously track more than 250 targets, control up to 30 airborne interceptions and detect approaching enemy aircraft at ranges of more than 3,000 miles."[15]

Capt. Craig W. ("Mole") Underhill ('81) from Houston, with the 58th Tactical Fighter Squadron (TFS), flew six combat missions over Iraq in his F-15 Eagle during the first two days of the operation. On his sixth mission, the AWACS escorts that were monitoring enemy air operations reported multiple groups of "bandits" in the distance and soon confirmed that they were hostile. Underhill locked onto a MiG-29. It "was there and then it was just a brown cloud. It didn't explode, it just disintegrated." MiGs were formidable aircraft, and, as in Vietnam and Korea, kills were difficult. Underhill was one of only five pilots who could claim he had dispatched a MiG during the opening days of the Iraqi air war. Capt. David Rose ('84) also flew F-15s with the 58th TFS and reported that they were "pressing the air war hard to ensure the ground troops a quick and decisive victory."[16]

At sea, naval forces targeted Iraqi sites far inland with missiles and pounded targets within the twenty-mile range of the 16-inch guns aboard ships such as the USS *Wisconsin* with deadly bombardments. Aboard the *Wisconsin*, turret one officer Ens. M. G. Fink ('89) helped direct the deadly fire, which was intended to pave the way for an amphibious assault "if needed." It was the job the *Wisconsin* was created for nearly fifty years ago, Fink explained, and "we're giving them hell!"[17]

Capt. Mark Rayfield ('79) was poised with his marine detachment in Kuwait, waiting for the naval bombardment and air war to end and the ground combat to begin. "We've finally begun doing what we came here for," he wrote to Thomas E. Wisdom ('60) in Houston. "Although none of us wanted it, it's what we're trained and prepared for and thus far, typical American ingenuity and courage are prevailing. . . . We receive harassing artillery rocket fire almost daily, but we have plenty of bunkers for protection." His sentiments were similar to those of Capt. Michael T. Minyard ('82) from Houston, who was awaiting action with a marine tank battalion. Marking time was the hardest part. With Minyard was Cpl. James M. Young ('90), who enrolled at Texas A&M before joining the marines and who arrived in Kuwait in August. Young was eager to "get it on" when his unit's Scud missile alarm sounded and he and his fellow troopers had to hunker down in their bunkers.[18]

A few days later, Lt. Brison Phillips ('87) wrote a brief note, without revealing his location, to the effect that the air war was not a week old, the flying was intense, and the missions were long. He reported that some of the aircraft and pilots had been lost in the action but, thus far, none with his own unit. One of the first Aggie casualties, Lt. Thomas C. Bland Jr. ('86), was shot down in his AC-130 on January 31. Phillips doubted that Saddam could take much more of the pounding. To help ensure that he could not, the USS *Theodore Roosevelt* with its fighter groups and AWACS aircraft arrived in the Persian Gulf on February 8 to join the action. Lt. (jg) Dennis L. Hassman ('88) was aboard the *Roosevelt* as the naval flight officer for VAW-120, an AWAC-Hawkeye squadron. Also at sea, the USS *Princeton* was struck by a mine shortly after Lt. Erich R. Roeder ('87) left his watch on the bridge. The crew responded magnificently, he reported, and the *Princeton* got a "purple heart" but was out of combat for the duration of the action. Also aboard the *Princeton* was Richard K. ("Rick") Holcomb ('89). When not flying or dodging Scuds, 1st Lt. David Smithhart ('86), navigator with an E-3 Sentry AWAC squadron flying "15 hr. sorties almost every day" from U.S. and overseas bases, tried to sleep.[19]

The USS *Princeton* CG-59, entering the Straits of Hormuz, January 13, 1991, en route to the Persian Gulf. Aboard are Lt (jg) Erich R. Roeder ('87) and Ens. Richard K. Holcomb ('89). The ship is flying a Texas Aggie flag and a Texas state flag donated by Rep. Richard A. Smith ('59).

The war assumed an almost surrealistic quality for many who were so near and yet so far removed from the combat. Maj. Gen. H. Hale Burr Jr. ('65), a forward air controller in the Vietnam War, "worked" this war from Washington, D.C., where he was deputy director of the National Military Command Center's joint staff. On January 1, a week before the air war began, Lt. Cmdr. Joseph A. Alexander ('89) arrived in Riyadh for duty with Central Command (CENTCOM). The scuttlebutt, he reported, "is that the Arabs want us to help free them from the maniac Saddam Hussein, but do not want us to remain permanently in their country. This is the dilemma that faces this command and the United States as we try to establish peace in the most violent portion of the world today."[20] The Persian Gulf War tested the post–Cold War cooperation that had developed between the United States and the former Soviet Union as well as the effectiveness and vitality of the United Nations and its commitment to the preservation of world peace. It also examined the relationships among the Arab nations and those between the Arab world, the United States, and the West.

The war, in terms of traditional land combat, began with a three-pronged ground attack on February 24 by coalition forces from neighboring Saudi Arabia that moved into Kuwait. U.S. forces struck across the border into southern Iraq toward Kuwait City; British and U.S. forces moved due north from central positions in Saudi Arabia into Iraq to engage the core elements of the estimated 650,000-man Iraqi army. At the same time, U.S. and French forces struck through central Iraq toward the Euphrates in an effort to cut off Iraqi supply lines. The "outer perimeter" attack was led by the 24th Infantry Division, under the command of Brig. Gen. James Terry Scott ('64), who pushed the division deep into Iraq to a junction with the Euphrates, thereby blocking the Iraqi soldiers' escape route, which the VII Corps was hammering.[21]

Led by the 2nd Armored Cavalry Regiment and followed by the 1st Armored, 3rd Armored, and 1st Infantry Divisions in company with the British 1st Armored Division, the U.S. VII Corps' mission was to attack into central Iraq and destroy the elite Republican Guard. Within twenty-four hours, a "modern day wagon train of men and heavy armor" had penetrated eighty miles north and east into Iraq, crushing virtually all resistance in its path. The 3rd Armored Division alone dealt destruction to three opposing Iraqi divisions.[22] During the brief combat, Iraqi special forces set fire to the vast oil fields of Kuwait and also to many of its own.

On February 27, Kuwait's capital was liberated. The next day—the fifth day of land combat—the commander in chief directed the disengagement of the coalition forces. On April 6, a formal withdrawal and cease-fire agreement with Saddam Hussein was negotiated and accepted by Iraq, and on April 11, the UN Security Council declared the war over. The war had been what some called a "one-hundred-hour war" and closely approached Gen. James R. Taylor's previously mentioned textbook example of a three-day war (that is, the day the war begins, the day it is fought, and the day it ends). Taylor's point was that the state of readiness tends to determine the outcome of future wars. This description, he predicted in 1982, will characterize wars of the future.[23]

Indeed, Maj. Stew Rayfield recalled that just three days after the ground campaign started, the war seemed to be winding down. He was hoping to soon see the "mother of all surrenders." Brig. Gen. James T. Scott commented, "No one could have anticipated that the ground war could have ended in 100 hours. My own estimate was two to four weeks. The air campaign stunned the Iraqis and we were able to move much faster than we thought." It was also a classic example of the military's new air-land battle (ALB) doctrine, a policy written and defined in part by Col. L. D. Holder, a 1966 history graduate from Texas A&M who commanded the 2nd Armored Cavalry Regiment during the attack on Iraq. The doctrine prescribed speed, teamwork, initiative, and flexibility at every level of command.[24] The combat ended, and U.S. and coalition forces began a withdrawal from Iraq, Kuwait, and Saudi Arabia, but real peace was elusive.

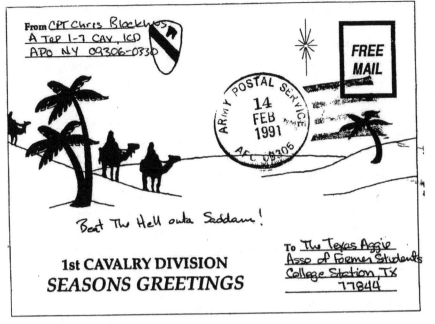

A 1st Cavalry cover dated February 14, 1991.

The 3rd Armored "Spearhead" Division was among the units that remained behind to help secure the demilitarized zone between Iraq and Kuwait, pending the arrival of UN observers and overseers. In addition to its military duties, the 3rd, like other occupation forces, provided aid and relief to the displaced civilian populations. Maj. Joseph C. Butler ('78), with the 3rd, reported that as of mid-April his division had provided humanitarian assistance to more than 12,000 residents of the Safwan, Iraq, area and given other relief to at least 7,000 additional displaced Iraqi civilians. On April 21, some of the 3rd Division's Texas Aggies gathered to celebrate Muster, including Capt. August G. Harder ('84), 2nd Lt. John T. Hubert ('88), Maj. Robert L. Reeves ('77), Major Butler, and Capt. Rick D. Hunter ('84).[25] With the combat at an end, disarmament and the preservation of peace became the focus of global concerns.

As part of the UN's effort to maintain peace in the Middle East and further deter Iraq from offensive warfare against its neighbors, no-fly and surveillance zones were designated over southern and northern Iraq (Operations Southern Watch and Northern Watch). For fully a decade thereafter, U.S. aircraft patrolled the zones and were not infrequently targeted by Iraqi surface-to-air missiles. Capt. Kevin C. Thompson ('95) piloted a C-130 reconnaissance plane in support of Operation Southern Watch, while Lt. Cmdr. Scott Wilmot ('88) and Lt. Cmdr. Mark Deardurff ('83) flew Seahawk helicopters from the USS *Kitty Hawk* in patrols along Iraq's coastal regions. Aggies involved in surveillance along the northern perimeters included Lt. John Bond ('88) from Athens, Texas, who flew an F-15 from Incirlik Air Force Base in Adana, Turkey, on Northern Watch duty. "Thirty minutes into his first mission protecting the Northern Fly Zone in Iraq, the Iraqis fired a surface-to-air missile at his plane"—and missed.[26] Although the situation in Iraq and the Middle East continued to deteriorate, relations between the United States and Russia warmed considerably.

The collapse of the Soviet Union and the broadening rapprochement between the United States and Russia resulted in the initiation of strategic-arms-reduction discussions between Pres. George H. W. Bush and Pres. Mikhail S. Gorbachev. The goal was to impose sharp reductions of and limits on nuclear warheads and strategic-delivery vehicles (including bombers and missiles). An initial strategic-arms-reduction treaty (START) was scheduled for completion in 1991. In other actions, the major world powers agreed to eliminate the use of chemical weapons, while the United States and the Soviet Union, in cooperation with the European Union and other nations, agreed to reduce their military presence in Europe and limit the number of troops stationed there to 195,000, with specific limits on battle tanks, armored carriers, artillery, combat aircraft, and helicopters. Concurrently, the United States began scaling back its conventional military forces, anticipating a troop-strength reduction of as much as 25 percent from Desert Storm levels, with projected budget savings of more than $100 billion.[27] Nonetheless, global peace and security remained elusive.

Hardly had the situation in Kuwait and Iraq begun to stabilize than trouble erupted in the historically troubled Balkans. Bosnia and Herzegovina declared their independence from Yugoslavia and then immediately became embroiled in a civil war that threatened to ignite violence, if not war, in the Middle East as well as Europe. Although the United States and the European community recognized Bosnia's independence, violence among the Muslim, Croatian, and Serbian peoples and "ethnic cleansing" spread through the region. The UN Security Council imposed a trade and oil embargo on Yugoslavia and authorized the use of force to protect humanitarian relief shipments. On November 20, 1992, the United States and European nations imposed a naval blockade on Yugoslavia in an effort to enforce the embargo and deter the spread of violence. "Operation Joint Guard" involved a number of Texas Aggies. Gen. Hal Hornburg ('68) directed air operations over Bosnia, while Maj. Bradley P. Presnal ('84), MD, who, after graduation from Texas A&M and medical school, spent a good part of his military service at Brooke Army Center in orthopedic surgery as chief of the Total Joint Service.[28]

Concurrently, Pres. Bill Clinton, again imposing the "social worker" mode on the military, ordered U.S. forces to begin providing humanitarian relief to civilian populations in the region, as had been done in the Congo, Somalia, Kosovo, and elsewhere. Col. Randy P. Durham ('71), who served from 1972 until his retirement in 1996 as chief of strategy and development for the U.S. Air Force Special Operations Command, spent most of his career in the diverse small

Gen. Thomas R. Olsen ('56)

First Sgt. Margarito Sendejas Jr. ('58)

Brig. Gen. James Terry Scott ('64)

Col. William C. Bender ('65)

Maj. Gen. H. Hale Burr Jr. ('65)

Maj. Richard H. McCall Jr. ('65)

Maj. Robert Reneau ('65)

Col. Leonard D. Holder Jr. ('66)

Col. John A. Van Alstyne ('66)

Col. Randolph W. House ('67)

Larry L. Landtroop ('67)

Col. Gene N. Patton ('67)

Col. John B. Sylvester ('67)

Lt. Col. William V. Cantú ('68)

Gen. Hal M. Hornburg ('68)

Lt. Col. John Randy Taylor ('68)

Lt. Col. James L. Sachtleben ('69)

Lt. Col. Jack Thompson ('69)

Lt. Col. Jimmy D. Dunham ('70)

Lt. Col. John R. Gingrich ('70)

Maj. Durell A. Hiller III ('70)

Sfc. Alexander L. Wisnoski Jr. ('70)

Lt. Col. James E. Albritton ('71)

Lt. Col. Robert H. Bishop ('71)

Lt. Col. Randy P. Durham ('71)

Lt. Col. Michael Moseley ('71)

Lt. Col. James E. Pritchett ('71)

Lt. Col. George W. Walton ('71)

Lt. Cdr. Larry D. Hall ('72)

Lt. Col. David H. Stone ('72)

Maj. Kenneth J. Allison ('73)

Maj. Glenn G. Burnside II ('73)

Maj. James W. DeLony ('73)

Lt. Col. James W. Green ('73)

Maj. Norman B. Taylor ('73)

Lt. Col. William A. White ('73)

Maj. Gary L. Buis ('74)

Maj. Chuck R. Friesenhahn ('74)

Maj. Douglas L. Horn Jr. ('74)★

Maj. John P. Imhoff ('74)

Cdr. Byron P. Compton ('75)

Maj. James F. Lane ('75)

Maj. Michael C. O'Neal ('75)

Maj. Richard M. Price ('74)★

Maj. R. S. Rayfield ('75)

Maj. David J. Speich ('75)

Maj. Lloyd ("Chip") Utterback ('75)

Maj. José A. Vazquez Jr. ('75)

Maj. Thomas S. Walker ('75)

Maj. Lewis W. Weber ('75)

Maj. N. M. DeBruin III ('76)

Maj. H. G. McCleskey ('76)

Maj. Robert D. Nossov ('76)

Maj. Thomas A. Owen ('76)

Maj. Steven T. Perrenot ('76)

Maj. W. A. Reed ('76)

Maj. John L. Ballantyne IV ('77)

Maj. Gayla J. Briles ('77)

Capt. H. Gregg Buescher ('77)

Brig. Gen. Floyd Carpenter ('77)

Maj. Larry W. Kruse ('77)

Maj. Vincent Pontani Jr. ('77)

Maj. Robert L. Reeves ('77)

Capt. Walter J. Rielley III ('77)

Capt. Thomas J. Felts ('78)

Maj. Joseph C. Butler ('78)

Maj. John H. Giesen ('78)

Lt. Cdr. Andrew S. Griffith ('78)

Maj. Jack W. Hampton Jr. ('78)

Maj. O. Robert Hilmo ('78)

Capt. Ronald L. Pearce ('78)

Capt. David D. Schneider ('78)

Maj. David B. Tagert ('78)

Maj. James E. Brooks ('79)

Capt. Mark Hryhorchuk ('79)

Capt. R. M. Rayfield ('79)

Capt. Kevin G. Troller ('79)

Maj. Harry L. Warren ('79)

Capt. Bobby L. Driesner ('80)

Capt. Kent M. Lasneske ('80)

Capt. Robert M. Namendorf ('80)

Capt. Mark H. Stroman ('80)

Capt. Edward G. Conger ('81)

Capt. Patrick W. Denton ('81)

Lt. Danny V. Hull ('81)★

Capt. Billy J. Jordan ('81)

(continued)

TABLE 17 *(continued)*

Capt. Charles A. Jumper ('81)

Lt. Lewis C. Nygard ('81)

Capt. Craig W. Underhill ('81)

Capt. Richard L. Barton ('82)

Capt. Allan M. Collier ('82)

Capt. Dale A. Cope ('82)

Capt. Kenneth G. Griffin ('82)

Capt. Clay M. Hamilton ('82)

Capt. Jeffrey R. Kregel ('82)

Capt. James W. McKellar ('82)

Capt. Dwight Mentzer ('82)

Capt. Michael T. Minyard ('82)

Capt. I. Lee Patton ('82)

Capt. Jennifer L. Pickett ('82)

Capt. James A. Ramb ('82)

Sgt. Sharon Randolph ('82)

Capt. David S. Reddin ('82)

Capt. Mark A. Traylor ('82)

G. Donald Baetge Jr. ('83)

Capt. Joseph E. Cleboski ('83)

Capt. Michael M. M. Davis ('83)

Lt. Cdr. Mark Deardurff ('83)

Capt. Robert W. Eoff ('83)

Capt. John D. Grigsby ('83)

Capt. David L. Jarratt ('83)

Capt. Christopher M. Jergens ('83)

Capt. Shelia A. Jones ('83)

Lt. Durwood L. Lewis ('83)

Capt. David R. Manning ('83)

Capt. Thomas D. Mayfield ('83)

Capt. James D. McCullough ('83)

Capt. Tanya D. Mentzer ('83)

Capt. John R. Motley ('83)

Capt. Michael S. O'Grady ('83)

Capt. William B. Pilcher ('83)

Pfc. Kurt E. Priest ('83)

1st Lt. Barry C. Stevens ('83)

Capt. Ronald K. Taylor Jr. ('83)

Capt. Cary D. Venden ('83)

1st Lt. John M. Weideman ('83)

Capt. Jeff C. Whitaker ('83)

Capt. Stuart B. Woods ('83)

Capt. Paul S. Anglin ('84)

Capt. Kenneth R. Barton ('84)

Lt. Christopher L. Breaux ('84)

1st Lt. Ronald G. Claiborne ('84)

Capt. Matthew A. Clay ('84)

Capt. August G. Harder ('84)

Capt. William V. Hill ('84)

Capt. Thomas M. Hood ('84)

Capt. Rick D. Hunter ('84)

Capt. Scott H. McVay ('84)

Capt. John K. Mikkelsen ('84)

1st Lt. James A Pollock ('84)

Capt. David G. Rose ('84)

Capt. Daniel L. Sharp ('84)

Capt. Christopher L. Blockhus ('85)

Capt. Gregory A. Byrd ('85)

Capt. Max A. Caramanian ('85)

Lt. Jeff C. Corder ('85)

1st Lt. Kenneth J. Crawford ('85)

Capt. Frank DeLeon Jr. ('85)

Capt. John C. Dvoracek ('85)

Capt. William B. Grimes ('85)

Lt. Patrick J. Heye ('85)

Capt. David C. Hill ('85)

Capt. Patrick R. Hollrah ('85)

1st Lt. Paul C. Hurley ('85)

Capt. Robert W. James ('85)

Capt. David L. Johnson ('85)

Greg J. Lackey ('85)

Lt. Thomas W. McAndrew ('85)

Capt. Russell O. McGee ('85)

Capt. Mark D. McGraw ('85)

S.Sgt. Richard A. McLeon IV ('85)

Capt. Scott E. Mitchell ('85)

Lt. (jg) William C. Nicholas ('85)

1st Lt. D. Grant Olbrich ('85)

Lt. Arcadio Alaniz Jr. ('86)

Capt. Thomas Clifford Bland ('86)★★

1st Lt. Jeff L. Brady ('86)

1st Lt. Michael W. Callaway ('86)

1st Lt. Gregory K. Cohen ('86)

Capt. Bruce R. Cox ('86)

1st Lt. Larry D. Cozine ('86)

1st Lt. Richard N. David ('86)

1st Lt. Cody D. Dowell ('86)

Lt. Joseph J. Candara ('86)

1st Lt. D. F. Hawkins ('86)

2nd Lt. Jeffrey M. Hines ('86)

Lt. Geof T. Hutton ('86)

1st Lt. James A. Laffey ('86)

1st Lt. Victor D. Lopez ('86)

1st Lt. David A. Smithhart ('86)

1st Lt. Curt A. Van de Walle ('86)

1st Lt. John F. Wegenhoft IV ('86)

1st Lt. Henry A. Werchan ('86)

1st Lt. Kent Wong ('86)

2nd Lt. Timothy L. Cahill ('87)

1st Lt. Jeffrey P. Davis ('87)

1st Lt. Gary F. Demers ('87)

Lt. John B. Dickson ('87)

1st Lt. Thomas A. Elkins Jr. ('87)

1st Lt. Hermann G. Hasken III ('87)

Lt. Bryan M. Holubec ('87)

Lt. Keith D. McBride ('87)

Lt. Brian D. Neumannn ('87)

Ens. James A. Perkins ('87)

1st Lt. Brison B. Phillips ('87)

Lt. Ken K. Regan ('87)

Ens. Erich R. Roeder ('87)

2nd Lt. Gregory C. Schmid ('87)

1st Lt. Anthony V. Scott ('87)

1st Lt. James C. Slaughter ('87)

1st Lt. Mike J. Youngson ('87)

Lt. Damon G. Baine ('88)

Lt. John Bond ('88)

2nd Lt. Brent M. Boyd ('88)

Lt. Tom Brown ('88)

Ens. Les T. Cardenas ('88)

2nd Lt. S. M. Cuningham ('88)

1st Lt. Stephen P. Cuningham ('88)

2nd Lt. Marc E. Cwiklik ('88)

Lt. Dale S. Daniel ('88)

Lt. Richard J. Diaz-Gonzales ('88)

Ens. Steven H. Drexler ('88)

1st Lt. Philip J. Faieta ('88)

1st Lt. William A. Ferro ('88)

Lt. Scott G. Fosdal ('88)

2nd Lt. Mark D. Freemyer ('88)

Lt. (jg) Richard C. Gallaher ('88)

Lt. Gordon P. Greaney ('88)

1st Lt. Bradley R. Hall ('88)

Lt. (jg) Dennis L. Hassman ('88)

Lt. James W. Hodge Jr. ('88)

1st Lt. Brian C. Hormberg ('88)

2nd Lt. John T. Hubert ('88)

2nd Lt. Jon C. Hunter ('88)

Spc. Scott Hunter ('88)

Lt. Joel S. Johnston ('88)

Pfc. John Kenneth Kelley ('88)

Lt. Edwin A. Klein ('88)

Ens. Miguel A. Lake ('88)

Lt. Gordon P. Greaney ('88)

Lt. (jg) Dennis L. Hassman ('88)

Lt. James W. Hodge Jr. ('88)

1st Lt. Brian C. Hormberg ('88)

2nd Lt. John T. Hubert ('88)

2nd Lt. Jon C. Hunter ('88)

Spc. Scott Hunter ('88)

Lt. Joel S. Johnston ('88)

Pfc. John Kenneth Kelley ('88)

Lt. Eddie A. Klein ('88)

Ens. Miguel A. Lake ('88)

1st Lt. Paul C. Landry ('88)

1st Lt. Rod Long ('88)

Lt. Patrick D. Marshall ('88)

2nd Lt. Craig A. McCrindle ('88)

1st Lt. Lance A. McDaniel ('88)

2nd Lt. John Q. Miller ('88)

1st Lt. Chris W. Rollins ('88)

1st Lt. Richard S. Schoeneberg ('88)

2nd Lt. Allen D. Soukup ('88)

1st Lt. John H. Steer ('88)

2nd Lt. David Symm ('88)

Lt. Cdr. Scott Wilmot ('88)

Lt. Homan M. Wilson ('88)

Lt. Howard W. Zuch ('88)

2nd Lt. Michael Bottiglieri ('89)

Lt. Cdr. Joseph A. Alexander ('89)

2nd Lt. Thomas Brown ('89)

2nd Lt. John A. Cavasos ('89)

2nd Lt. J. Darin Cowart ('89)

2nd Lt. Fitzhugh L. Duggan ('89)

Ens. Murray G. Fink ('89)

Ens. David W. Hodges ('89)

(continued)

TABLE 17 (*continued*)

Ens. Richard K. Holcomb ('89)	Sfc. Robert J. Bradley ('91)
2nd Lt. Kelly Jackson ('89)	Sgt. Dean W. Carey ('91)
2nd Lt. Michael A. Kelley ('89)	Pfc. Thaddeus A Bartholomew ('92)
Maj. Robert Redding ('89)	LCpl. Eric W. Edward ('92)
2nd Lt. Richard Lee Sechrist II ('89)	LCpl. Chris N. Morgan ('92)
Ens. David Earl Ward ('89)	Spc. Dwight Easton ('93)
2nd Lt. Chris Wilfong ('89)	Spc. Kirdk Allen Harrison ('93)
Ens. Gary E. Wohn ('89)	S.Sgt. James L. Stidfole ('93)
2nd Lt. Daniel P. Woulfe ('89)	LCpl. D. P. Banks ('94)
Pfc. Evan Ray Kirk ('90)	Pfc. Jean Christopher ('94)
Cpl. James Matt Young ('90)	Spc. Eric C. Gustavson ('94)
Sgt. Brian T. Beardsley ('91)	

*   Died in Operation Desert Shield
**   Killed in Action, Operation Desert Storm
These names were published in *Texas Aggie* (June, 1991), and the list is undoubtedly incomplete.

wars and humanitarian missions of the post–Vietnam War era. Lt. Cmdr. Harlan W. Ray ('73) from Troup, Texas, who commanded the 37th Airlift Squadron stationed at the Rhein-Main Air Base in Germany, made the first relief flight into war-torn Bosnia on July 3, 1992. By March, 1993, UN-sponsored Operation Provide Promise had delivered more than 9,800 tons of food and equipment into Sarajevo and an additional 930 tons of food and medicine by airdrop into more remote war-ravaged areas in eastern Bosnia-Herzegovina. Most of those supplies were delivered by Commander Ray's C-190 squadron. Independently, Texas Aggie Fred Cuny ('66), who had been styled a "renegade humanitarian" by the PBS news magazine, helped ferry emergency supplies of potable water into Sarajevo and then supervised the restoration of a water reservoir above the city. In March, 1995, Cuny disappeared in company with two Russian doctors who were attempting to provide emergency health care to devastated Chechnya in southern Russia. Col. John M. Braun ('71) commanded the 49th Aviation Brigade for seven months in Bosnia as part of NATO's peace-keeping force. However, peace and stability remained elusive. U.S. and UN forces later conducted air strikes against Bosnian Serb positions, and a resolution of the civil unrest throughout the region was long delayed. Violence and civil war subsided somewhat in 1994, when Serb, Croat, and Muslim groups agreed to a federated union, but that, too, soon failed despite continuing international pressure. Former Pres. Jimmy Carter finally succeeded in negotiating a seven-day cease-fire among the warring parties in December, 1994. That suspension of hostilities was later extended—but often violated. Navy Lt. Brian Anthony Riley ('95) from

Conroe piloted an F-14 during Bosnian operations when NATO aircraft briefly resumed strikes on Bosnian Serb ammunition dumps in 1995. This was followed by another cease-fire, and a more lasting peace settlement was finally put in place by the close of the year. Lt. Col. Gerald R. ("Jake") Betty ('73) was among those mobilized to serve with peace keeping forces in Bosnia, and a few years later he was ordered to Washington, D.C., in support of Operation Iraqi Freedom.[29]

Even as the United States and UN nations worked for peace in Bosnia, civil war, drought, and famine in Africa triggered a new crisis and a UN response that was code-named Operation Continue Hope. In response to famine conditions generated largely by tribal and ethnic warfare, the United States began delivering humanitarian aid to Somalia in November, 1992. In order to effect distribution to the multitudes who required assistance, the United States effectively secured control over Mogadishu and large sections of Somalia. Troops were pulled out in May, 1993, leaving behind a small military presence, including Capt. Steven A. Cook ('88), whose major responsibility was to maintain security and continue to dispense food and medicine. But local warring chiefs, and especially Muhammed Fara Aidid, seized the opportunity to attack the peace-keeping mission. When a special Army Ranger Task Force, including Maj. Joseph Dwayne Dinkins ('88) from Ft. Worth, arrived to provide assistance, the warlord launched a full-fledged assault. U.S. troops lost eighteen men killed in action and a considerable number of wounded. As a result, President Clinton decided to withdraw the American presence from Somalia by the close of the year. Major Dinkins commented later that he was very proud of the soldiers with whom he had served in Somalia: "All of them did their best to accomplish the mission, care for each other, and show compassion towards the Somali people."[30]

Civil war and local conflicts in Africa, the Middle East, the Balkans, Philippines, Southeast Asia, and Central America continually threatened regional and global peace and security. Americans and U.S. interests around the world were increasingly targeted for terrorist attack. In 1994, following the violent overthrow of Haiti's government under Pres. Jean Bertrand Aristide, U.S. and Canadian Special Forces attempting to land in Port au Prince to restore order were met with mob violence and withdrew until sufficient forces were in place to restore Aristide's government to power. In 1996, Lt. Col. John D. Bond's ('88) Northern Watch F-15 patrol squadron was moved from Turkey to Dhahran, Saudi Arabia, when a terrorist attack by car bombers destroyed Khobar Tower, killing nineteen American military personnel, including thirteen men in Bond's squadron. "I was lucky. I was outside the gate when it went off," he said. "I heard it. . . . I was out on a highway. I'd just been downtown. . . . I was one of the few in the squadron who was uninjured." That same year, in September, Lt. Col. Floyd L. Carpenter (' 77) commanded an air strike ordered by President Clinton against Iraqi forces threatening the Kurdish safe haven in northern Iraq.[31]

In the midst of these global troubles, air force Brig. Gen. Don Peterson ('66) assumed new duties as vice director of North American Aerospace Defense Command (NORAD). His job was to provide early detection of a missile, air, or space attack on North America and alert combat units. Working with Peterson was his executive officer, Maj. Steve Chichocki ('81). The duties of Brig. Gen. Wilbert D. ("Doug") Pearson Jr. ('69) were closely related to NORAD security. As vice commander of the Electronic Systems Center, Air Force Matériel Command, Pearson shared responsibility for, among other things, command and control, communications, and intelligence systems. During the Vietnam War he flew 364 combat hours, and later, in a test operation flying an F-15, Pearson became the first pilot to intercept and destroy a satellite in Earth orbit.[32] National security and readiness had become increasingly complex.

Col. Robert D. ("Danny") Barr ('68) was at once very near and yet very far from global flashpoints during his long service as presidential pilot aboard Air Force One, which began in 1980, during the administration of Pres. Ronald Reagan. During the Gulf War, Barr flew Pres. George H. W. Bush to Kuwait to visit the troops and later to Mogadishu, Somalia. Lt. Col. Everett De Wolfe III ('76) joined the Air Force One team as a flight navigator in 1993, logging more than 2,500 flight hours, while Colonel Barr logged more than 5,000 hours of flight time aboard Air Force One. After serving President Clinton, Barr retired as presidential aircraft commander in May, 1997. Texas Aggies continued the Air Force One pilot tradition during George W. Bush's administration. Maj. Michael G. McPherson ('91) and his brother, Maj. Sean C. McPherson ('91), both helicopter pilots for the Presidential Squadron, flew the president on his appointed rounds.[33]

After terrorist bombings of two U.S. embassies in Africa in 1998, the United States retaliated with cruise missile strikes from the Mediterranean against targets in the Sudan and Afghanistan, on the one hand demolishing a Sudanese "pharmaceutical plant" and on the other, "turning Osama bin Laden into a worldwide celebrity." Osama bin Laden's al-Qaeda terrorist network was committed to unremitting attacks against the United States and Israel. However, following the terrorist attacks in Dhahran and North Africa, America's increasing hesitancy to commit combat troops in troubled regions and the nonexistent, or seemingly ineffectual, responses "may have emboldened" the group to attempt yet more deadly attacks abroad as well as in the United States.[34] That tentativeness may also have encouraged further aggression by Yugoslavia's Slobodan Milosovik.

Yugoslav troops seized control of Kosovo in March, 1999. UN forces and the United States responded on March 23 with a bombing campaign accompanied by the directive "not to lose aircraft." The high-altitude bombing had relatively little impact on entrenched Yugoslav positions, but the increasing effectiveness of the resistance forces inside of Kosovo, coupled with the UN threat of a ground attack, finally caused Yugoslav troops to withdraw. U.S. soldiers then accompanied a multinational peace-keeping force into Kosovo, but they had little success. "Kosovo A&M Club" peacekeepers included Capt. Kurt Felpel ('92), Maj. Michael Mantey ('83), 2nd Lt. Jason Roberts ('99), Maj. Robert Broussard ('78), Maj. Darren Richardson ('88), Maj. David Spencer ('80), 2nd Lt. Matthew Broderick ('98), Capt. Shawn McManamy ('93), and Capt. William Riley ('95).

At home, training and preparation for war also took a toll. In March, 2000, air force Maj. Brison B. ("Tatoo") Phillips ('87) died when his F-16 Fighting Falcon crashed at Kingsville (Texas) Naval Air Station. Weeks later, Lt. Clayton J. Kennedy ('98) was killed in the crash of an MV-22 Osprey during training exercises near Tucson, Arizona.[35] Meanwhile, violence and terrorism soon spread from the Balkans, the Middle East, and Africa to America's own shores.

On the morning of September 11, 2001, Americans confronted the face of terror. Televised newscasts showed the north tower of New York's World Trade Center in flames after a commercial aircraft crashed into it. Even as the world watched, a second airliner and its civilian passengers, hijacked in the air by al-Qaeda suicide teams, collided with the south tower of the World Trade Center. Lee A. Adler ('84), who earned his PhD in nuclear chemistry at Texas A&M, and Jimmy Nevill Storey ('65), a business major at A&M, were among the three thousand people who died in that attack. Within the hour, another airliner loaded with al-Qaeda suicide bombers and innocent passengers was flown into the Pentagon. Lt. Col. Jerry Don Dickerson ('92), assistant executive officer for the U.S. Army Deputy Chief of Staff for Programs and who had served in Cold War Germany and fought in Korea, was one of the victims. Dickerson had earned his master's degree in industrial engineering at Texas A&M and spent most of his military career as a research analyst with the army staff. Jerry Henson ('59), a Vietnam veteran with seventy-two combat missions and who headed the interagency support office of the U.S. Navy Command Center, was trapped in his chair at his desk but was rescued by other naval officers as the building collapsed around them.[36]

Lt. Brian Anthony Riley ('95) from Conroe, Texas, like most Americans, stood motionless and speechless in front of the television. Unlike the condition in which most Americans found themselves, Riley was watching the news in the ready room of a navy F-14 Tomcat squadron. Within thirty minutes of the Pentagon attack, he and his squadron were in the air in F-14s loaded with ordnance and searching for possible intruders. Riley described it as a surreal experience. Wherever they flew up and down the east coast, there was only one emergency controller on the air. The customary chatter was gone. Civilian and most military air traffic had been grounded. There was general silence. No one had anything to say.[37]

Television reporter Melinda Murphy ('86), a journalism graduate with a New York City flagship station, felt the same way. She immediately took to the air with a photographer and helicopter pilot and spent the next seven hours providing news commentary and film of the twin towers' disaster. "We were all horrified. . . . I don't believe any of us uttered a word. We were awe struck."[38] That day marked the end of America's innocence, the beginning of a war on terrorism, and the inception of what would become Operation Enduring Freedom and Operation Iraqi Freedom.

Many Texas Aggies quickly became involved in combat and support roles in the new wars. In many ways they were but an extension of the old terrorist confrontations, including the devastations at the marine barracks in Beirut, Lebanon; the attack on the USS *Cole* in Yemen, the car bombing of the Khobar Tower in Kandahar, and the bombings of embassies in the Sudan, Afghanistan, and elsewhere. There was now a new resolve, determination, a target, and readiness. Within hours of the terrorist attack, Texas Aggies were with the 147th Fighter Wing, which participated in twenty-four-hour combat air patrol missions over New York City. They included Lt. Col. Stephan Higgs ('73), Maj. Gordon Niebergall ('91), Maj. Michael Smith ('89), and Senior Airman Frank Urbanic ('02). When the terrorists hit the twin towers, 1st Lt. Michael Eric La Coste ('98) from San Antonio was at Fort Polk, Louisiana, completing a mission-readiness exercise before deploying to Kosovo with the 7th Field Artillery Regiment. On September 11, Lt. Col. David Sahm ('82) was called to active duty from the reserves and soon was aboard the USS *Boxer* with the 1st Marine Expeditionary Force bound for the Persian Gulf. In response to the attack that day, Lt. Tobin C. Flinn ('96) left civilian employment and joined the marines and received his commission in April, 2002, before heading for the Middle East.[39]

Within ten days of the attack on the twin towers, Pres. George W. Bush, the son of the president who had ejected Iraqi armies from Kuwait a decade earlier, addressed a joint session of Congress. He outlined plans for the use of military force to destroy terrorist training camps in Afghanistan, eliminate the supportive and terrorist Taliban rulers of that country, and implement a global effort to detect and capture al-Qaeda and other terrorist operatives wherever they might be. The plan also called for the discovery and elimination of their financial resources and safe havens. On October 7, in an address to the nation, President Bush announced the beginning of combat—Operation Enduring Freedom—in Afghanistan.

Gen. Tommy Franks from Midland, Texas, commissioned a second lieutenant in 1967 as a distinguished graduate of the Artillery Officer Candidate School, commanded Operation Enduring Freedom from a central command post in the Middle East. A Vietnam veteran, Franks had been assistant division commander of the 1st Cavalry Division during Operation Desert Shield and Operation Desert Storm and had commanded the 2nd Infantry ("Warrior") Division in Korea. In the States, he assumed command of the Third Army, and, in June, 2000, he became commander in chief of the U.S. Central Command. With

Franks during the Afghanistan and Iraqi campaigns was Lt. Gen. Michael ("Buzz") Moseley ('71), who served under Franks as air component commander with oversight of air operations in a vast region sweeping from east Africa across the Arabian Peninsula into Southwest Asia and Pakistan. With a bachelor's and a master's degree in political science from Texas A&M and formerly an F-15 weapons and tactics officer and instructor pilot, Moseley had extensive training and experience in operations and political-military affairs.[40]

Because of the seemingly remote and very different character of the Taliban and hostile forces in Afghanistan and Iraq, there was considerable debate in the American press about how best to deal with the situation even as U.S. forces responded. When asked during a news conference about his reaction to "TV generals who were criticizing the war plan," Gen. "Buzz" Moseley, known as a plain-talking Texas cowboy, responded: "I grew up in Texas . . . [and] . . . I'm amused by the way they critique it. But in the end, it's a whole lot like listening to a cow pee on a flat rock. It just doesn't matter."[41]

Operation Enduring Freedom was again a different kind of warfare, part of a global war on terrorism sponsored by the United States and some sixty-eight supporting nations. For the moment it focused on Afghanistan as the leading incubator of global terrorism. The immediate goal was to search out and destroy terrorist training camps, eliminate al-Qaeda and Taliban leaders, and work with Afghani opposition groups in establishing a new government while providing humanitarian aid to the Afghani people.

As in Desert Storm, the United States sent carrier battle groups, including the USS *Kitty Hawk* and USS *Theodore Roosevelt*, into the Persian Gulf, accompanied by Tomahawk-firing surface ships and submarines, with navy, marine, and air force fighter and helicopter strike squadrons escorted by AWAC-type surveillance and control aircraft. Lt. Cmdr. Dane Denman ('84) from Tyler, Lt. (jg) James Cherry ('99) from Tolar, and Lt. (jg) Lori Steen ('98) from Davenport, Iowa, were among the "Texas A&M crew" aboard the *Roosevelt*. Among the specialists sent to the war front was Lt. Chad Allen Hesters ('96), a navy intelligence officer with previous experience in the Balkans, Iraq, North Africa, and South America. Capt. Steve Basso ('92) commanded the 7th Chemical Company of the 83rd Chemical Battalion, a very special unit that provided surveillance and support for defense against chemical warfare. With the medical teams sent to Afghanistan was Maj. Robert Nogueras ('92), operations officer for the Forty-fourth Medical Command. Nogueras's unit provided on-site "medical insight where it is really needed." Lt. Albert Kinkead ('00) with the 82nd Airborne Division and his father, Col. Bert Kinkead ('71), both provided "special services" during Operation Enduring Freedom. For a while they were the only father-son team in the region.[42] Helicopter pilots Capt. Marc Bertamini and Capt. Kristian Pfeiffer, both of the class of ('94), went ashore with the fast-moving Fifteenth Marine Expeditionary Force (MEF), while Capt. John Warren ('96), also with the

15th MEF, was an infantry officer. Air force Capt. Mike Flatten ('92) served as a combat air controller with U.S. Air Force Special Forces. Within two weeks of the initiation of combat, U.S. and coalition forces had destroyed Taliban air defenses, demolished known al-Qaeda training camps, and joined with anti-Taliban Afghans in rooting out al-Qaeda and Taliban positions. In November and December, the provincial capital of Mazar-e Sharif, along with the cities of Herat, Kabul, Jalalabad, and Qandahar, had fallen to the coalition. On December 22, a new Afghani interim government, headed by Hamid Karzai, was formally inaugurated. Lt. Justin Gray ('98), an air force KC-10 pilot with Operation Enduring Freedom, flew President Karzai to a number of his destinations.[43]

Although the major objectives of Operation Enduring Freedom had been achieved by the close of the year 2001, the mission did not end and now became closely associated with a new crisis—in neighboring Iraq. In the meantime, numerous Texas Aggies continued to serve in Operation Enduring Freedom. Army Maj. Robert Redding ('89), for example, was deployed to Afghanistan as part of the Coalition Joint Special Operations Task Force. That unit's assignment was to help train the new Afghani National Army and to continue search operations for remaining al-Qaeda and Taliban leaders and troops. Second Lt. Mike Zendejas ('99) with the 82nd Airborne Division operated on search-and-security missions out of Kandahar Airfield. Kevin Thompson ('95), a C-130 Hercules pilot, flew in and out of Kandahar and regional airfields in support of the operations in Afghanistan and the Middle East. Serving as air weapons officers for AWAC aircraft stationed in Oman, 1st Lt. Toni Tanner ('99) and 1st Lt. Amy Scott ('99) teamed up with Maj. Lisa Shoemaker ('92) and Anthony Fazzoli ('92). Together they worked "the skies of Afghanistan, searching out and destroying all of the Taliban and al-Qaeda cowards we can find."[44]

In November, 2002, Gen. Hal M. Hornburg ('68) was named commander of the U.S. Air Force Air Combat Command in Washington, D.C. That same month, Lt. Col. Joseph ("Rod") Matte ('76) moved from the Air Warfare Center in Nevada to Incirlik Air Base in Turkey as the executive officer for Operation Northern Watch. Brig. Gen. Loyd S. ("Chip") Utterback ('75) commanded the 366th Air Expeditionary Wing (as well as the 35th Fighter Wing stationed at Misawa Air Base, Japan), which flew twenty-four-hour-a-day surveillance and antiterror intelligence-gathering sorties over the Middle East. Other Texas Aggies who rotated in for Northern Watch duty included Lt. Martin Salinas II ('98). At his "unnamed" advanced deployment, Northern Watch Airfield, Salinas served as the deployed chief of standards and evaluation and mentioned that "All commanders in this deployed USAF unit happen to be Aggies and will be pinning on my Captain bars on January 13th." Those air force commanding officers included Lt. Col. Brad Vogt ('81), group deputy commander; Col. George Gagnon ('80), group commander; and Brig. Gen. Floyd Carpenter ('77), wing commander.[45] Very soon the Northern Watch, Southern Watch, and

Enduring Freedom Operations melded and coalesced with the more formidable Operation Iraqi Freedom.

On March 19, 2003, Pres. George W. Bush announced the commencement of Operation Iraqi Freedom, "a military operation to disarm Iraq, to free its people and to defend the world from grave danger." Thanks in part to the "immediate ready task force" concept, the armed forces were prepared. Capt. Patrick R. Seiber ('93), for example, had served as the armor liaison officer and planner from TF 1-63 Armor (1st Infantry Division) for the Southern European Task Force Airborne since December, 2002. His job was to help TF 1-63 Armor gear up for immediate ready task force responsibilities when and where needed. By March 28, Seiber was in Iraq, assisting in the deployment of armored forces into combat. For his outstanding work, he received the Bronze Star. Seiber returned to the United States in May, 2003, to resume duties with the army ROTC staff at Texas A&M.[46]

Indeed, by day one of the war, the United States had stationed in Kuwait, Saudi Arabia, and Afghanistan and at sea nearly 250,000 military personnel, complemented by an additional 45,000 British troops, 2,000 Australians, and other supporting units from Spain and Denmark, while Iraq's armies were estimated to number almost 650,000 troops. What the United States did not have was the support of the United Nations or of many of the coalition nations who had joined in the declaration of war on terrorism following the twin towers' attack. France, Germany, and especially Russia opposed U.S. unilateral military action in Iraq. Nevertheless, the United States and Great Britain, with other coalition support, commenced intensive and carefully selected air strikes against the military, Republican Guard, Baathist Party, the family palaces of Saddam Hussein, and facilities suspected of developing chemical weapons and weapons of mass destruction.

Marine Capt. Mike Riley ('94), who had recently served on a special mission in Aden, Yemen, and with Operation Enduring Freedom in Qatar, Uzbekistan, and Afghanistan, was on duty in the Pentagon when the terrorist attack occurred on September 11. He survived that attack and went on to provide direct support to the Joint Chiefs of Staff for Operation Iraqi Freedom.[47]

In the first major air strike of the campaign, technologically sophisticated F-18 Superhornets, accompanied by other aircraft and defended by a half-dozen escort F-18s from Carrier Wing 14, left the USS *Abraham Lincoln* on Friday night, March 21, bound for Baghdad. Lt. Eric Doyle ('95), piloting a Superhornet, flew for seven and a half hours over southern Iraq, providing protection and cover for aircraft headed to their targets. "It was pretty busy," he said. "A lot of communications going on. There were a whole lot of moving parts to that strike and it looked like it went pretty well." The attacks did go well, thanks in part to the work of Capt. Michael Downs ('92), stationed in Saudi Arabia, who was responsible for targeting in the air war over Iraq. Key targets destroyed during the intensive round-the-clock air strikes included those in Baghdad and other cities, at military positions, and at suspected chemical weapons sites. Damage to civilian and nonmilitary facilities during this operation was minimal.[48]

As in past wars, Texas Aggies played a prominent role in the air combat over Iraq. Capt. Brady V. Merrill ('91) served with the 71st ("Ironman") Squadron. Capt. Will Oliver ('95) flew the Chinook CH-46 helicopter from the USS *Boxer* in support of the 1st Marine Expeditionary Force. His brother Chris ('93) flew a CH-53E from the USS *Kearsage*. Capt. Dan T. Smith ('95) flew the AH-1W Cobra helicopter with the 24th Marine Expeditionary Force. Lt. Joe Bingham ('93) piloted an attack jet from the USS *Harry Truman*. Lt. Gordon N. Harwell ('99) flew a UH-1 in support of the 2nd Marine Expeditionary Battalion. Army Capt. Jason Arriaga ('97) flew a Blackhawk in support of ground actions, while Marine Corps Capt. Scott J. Luckie ('94) piloted the appropriately named Harrier jet.[49] And many others participated in direct attacks as well as in air- and ground-support roles.

Lt. Nathan Howard ('97), pilot of a KC-135 tanker, and his crew were awarded the Distinguished Flying Cross for their work in a search-and-rescue mission near Tikrit, Saddam Hussein's hometown. Lt. Craig Ilschner ('99), a C-130 pilot, served in Afghanistan during Operation Enduring Freedom and returned to serve in Operation Iraqi Freedom. A member of the staff of the CENTAF Combined Air Operations Center at al-Udeid Air Base in Qatar, 2nd Lt. Ernesto Garcia ('01) helped in the air war over Iraq. Ens. Charity Crismon ('02), maintenance officer for VRC-30, Detachment 2, which was deployed aboard the USS *Constellation*, helped provide logistical support, moving "people, parts, and pony (mail) to and from the carrier."[50] The round-the-clock attacks against strategic targets and enemy troop positions during the first week of combat greatly diminished the enemy's strength, effectiveness, and resolve.

On day one of the war, coalition forces were on the scene and fully prepared for combat. By the fifth day, targeted sites had been eliminated in Baghdad, Tikrit, Mosul (north of Baghdad), and An Nasiriyah to the south. The city of Basra in the south had been isolated, and Umm Qasr was under British and coalition control. In a forty-hour period, the 3rd Infantry Division had swept northward from Kuwait into Iraq and on to Najaf, about one hundred miles south of Baghdad. Kurdish and coalition forces had taken control of the northeastern sector of Iraq. At that point, some twenty-five Americans had died in combat, seven had been taken prisoner, and others were missing in action. Two days later, the marines moved through An Nasiriyah, crossed the Euphrates, and were advancing along an eastern route toward Baghdad. Meanwhile, the 3rd Infantry Division was moving through An Najaf and closing on Baghdad's suburbs. Umm Qasr's port was now open for the arrival of humanitarian aid and commerce. By April 3, despite a howling sandstorm that grounded air attacks and slowed armored columns, the Baghdad Airport and the perimeters of the

TURKEY

Tigris River

Al Mawsil (Mosel)

• Irbil

⊠ 173 AB Bde (US)

SYRIA

• Kirkuk

IRAN

"Sunni Triangle" • Tikrit

Euphrates River

• Samarra

Ar Ramadi

Al Fallujah • **Baghdad**

IRAQ

• Al Hillah

• Al Kut

Al Kufah •

• Ad Diwaniyah

• As Samawah

• An Nasiriyah

Al Basrah

⊠ 1 Marine (US)

SAUDI ARABIA

⊠ 3 (US)

KUWAIT

⊠ 101 AB (US)

★ Kuwait

⊠ 82 AB (US)

City

◯ 7th Bde (UK)
⊠ RMC Bde (UK)
⊠ 16 Air Assault Bde (UK)

Iraq War

city were being probed. Marine 2nd Lt. David C. Lewis ('00) fought with his Regimental Combat Team 1, the "tip of the spear," through al-Nasiriyah and al-Kut and into Baghdad. The first marines to cross the Tigris River, they then set up quarters in a state-owned cigarette factory in eastern Baghdad, where they were told they would remain "indefinitely." Central Baghdad was in U.S. hands by April 11. Iraqi combat losses had been substantial, and much of the regular army had melted away, but strong pockets of resistance remained. Iraqi anti-Hussein forces, the United States, and the coalition began to talk about the future government of Iraq.[51] But the war was not over, and peace was not yet secure.

The war was for the most part televised live to the American public and the global community by "embedded" journalists associated with combat units. One of the most dramatic moments involved the rescue of Pfc. Jessica Lynch, a member of the 507th Maintenance Company, which had been ambushed in the early days of the war just outside An Nasariyah. Lynch survived the ambush and was placed under guard in an Iraqi hospital. Almost two weeks later, Americans learned of her whereabouts and decided to attempt a rescue. A combined force of army, navy, and marine rangers and pilots, some of them engaged in a diversionary strike to draw the enemy away from the intended objective, flew the mission from the USS *Boxer*. The transport CH-46 Sea Knight helicopter carrying the assault-and-rescue team was flown by Capt. William Oliver ('95). Oliver's copter was first struck by enemy fire and then hit a tower cable, but it survived both and landed safely. The rangers and rescue crew members found Lynch. They also located the site where the bodies of eight soldiers with Lynch's company and a member of the 3rd Infantry Division's 3rd Forward Support Group were buried. Despite severe wounds, Lynch survived and returned home after a stay in a military hospital in Ramstein, Germany. In a somewhat similar engagement, marine 2nd Lt. Brett Eubank ('01), leading a platoon with the 3rd Light Armored Vehicle Division, found and freed seven prisoners of war in Samarra.[52]

Americans who were wounded in Operation Iraqi Freedom and many of the enemy soldiers and civilians were often able to receive on-site medical care and were moved to very advanced medical facilities within hours. Maj. Stephanie D. Redding ('85), MD, was among those who provided expert frontline care, as did Capt. Robert D. Payne ('98) with the 126th Forward Surgical Team and Col. Harry Warren ('79), MD, with the 86th Combat Support group in Kuwait. Many of the injured were speedily evacuated to Kuwait or the Landstuhl Medical Center in Ramstein, Germany, where Col. David Rubenstein ('77) commanded the medical center and Brig. Gen. James Mobley ('69), who commanded the 807th Medical Command, had located a large number of his doctors and care personnel. Among those who attended to the needs of Pfc. Jessica Lynch upon her removal to Ramstein was Mary C. ("Christi") Gantt (Majewski) ('86), a physical therapist.[53]

Major combat in Iraq effectively ended with the capture of the northern city of Mosul on April 11, followed by the seizure of Tikrit. U.S. Army units had filtered through the five-million-plus population of Baghdad and, by April 20, were nominally in control of the city and all of Iraq. Nevertheless, resistance, terrorist attacks, suicide bombings, threats, and other dangers persisted as American and coalition interests attempted to restore law, order, and stability to the country while also providing humanitarian aid. Additional U.S. forces, including the 2nd Armored Cavalry Regiment and 1st Lt. William J. Tolbert ('99), grandson of Maj. Gen. William A. Becker ('41), were deployed to Iraq. In May, Tolbert's howitzer battery occupied an abandoned cigarette factory in Sadr City, "a densely populated urban area . . . of 2.6 million Shiite Muslims who had been severely oppressed under Saddam's regime. . . . We received a warm welcome from the people." Tolbert was assigned the job of establishing a "civil military operations center" to facilitate meetings with local leaders and to meet the needs of the many Iraqis who came to the camp's gates. The greatest problems during the first five months involved looting, preserving order, and protecting property.[54]

In October, 2003, Tolbert was promoted to captain and assumed "information operations" duties, which largely had to do with disseminating information to the local populations and engaging local leaders, tribal chiefs, and religious leaders in supportive relationships. Because of the language and cultural barriers, it was a difficult assignment. Moreover, while Tolbert and most Americans were convinced that democracy would work in Iraq and that the Iraqis wanted to "live free and elect leaders they feel will best represent them," for the most part, Tolbert added, the Iraqis had "no idea or concept of what democracy is or how it works. Every meeting with local government representatives and leaders [we] affectionately called 'Democracy 101.'"[55]

The restoration and rehabilitation of Iraq, however, would take more time and patience and possibly exact more lives and money than did the military campaign to oust Saddam Hussein's government. On July 19, 1st Lt. Jonathan D. Rozier ('01) from Katy, Texas, one of only fifteen recipients of the Bronze Star awarded during Operation Iraqi Freedom, joined the number of American soldiers who died in Iraq after the close of combat. A tank commander assigned to B Company, 2-70th Armor Battalion, 1st Armored Division, Rozier was killed in Baghdad when his unit was fired upon by rocket-propelled grenades and small-arms fire while providing security at a municipal building. As one of the thousands stationed in Iraq, Rozier "gave his life to free an oppressed people, depose a brutal dictator, and provide peace and security for our nation."[56]

Despite the "end of hostilities" on May 1, throughout 2003, Operation Iraqi Freedom remained a work in progress. Lt. Eric Tapp ('01) with the 4th Infantry Division near Tikrit faced an increasing number of ambushes and bushwhacking incidents. "It is a fight every day," noted Col. James Hickey, commander of the 1st Brigade. For Tapp and the soldiers, pilots, and marines sent to Iraq, it was an exhausting and demanding business and one they were trained to do.[57] The elimination of Saddam Hussein's government offered an opportunity to build a different Iraq and a different Middle East and greatly improved the climate for substantially reducing the threat of global terrorism. But in early 2004, the fragile peace of Iraq was challenged as urban guerrilla warfare associated with radical Sunni elements erupted in Fallujah. That outbreak was accompanied by rising levels of terrorist attacks and violence at other locations in Iraq and by new terrorist strikes in Saudi Arabia, Pakistan, Afghanistan, Spain, and elsewhere. It heightened alerts from the Homeland Security Office in the United States. The greatest immediate threat to military forces in Iraq

09/07/2003

Capt. Daniel Hall ('98) prepares to inspect an abandoned
building in an unidentified town in Iraq.

CWO2 Scott McCrosky ('98) pilots the AH-64D Apache Longbow over the multipurpose range complex during target practice in Iraq.

were suicide bombers and improvised explosive devices (IEDs) planted along the public roadways. On December 28, 2003, an IED took the life of Capt. Ernesto Blanco-Caldes ('98), a soldier, Texas Aggie, and skilled guitarist who loved classical music. Casualties among the civilian populations in Iraq rose while those among U.S., British, and coalition forces also increased markedly, leading, among other things, to Spain's decision to evacuate its troops from Iraq.

Conditions were worsened in March, 2004, when radical Shiite cleric Muqtada al-Sadr raised his own rebellion against U.S. and coalition forces, with violence and resistance centered in Najaf and Karbala in south-central Iraq. Fighting flared throughout the country. Among the five people who were killed on March 31 by an IED in Habbaniyah near the Sunni-dominated Fallujah were 1st Lt. Doyle Hufstedler Jr. ('01) from Abilene and a medic from San Antonio. In the last conversation Hufstedler had with his parents, he asked for "prayers for himself and school supplies for Iraqi children."[58]

U.S. forces began offensive combat operations to protect and provide security for the creation of a new, transitional Iraqi government that assumed sovereignty on June 28, a date and a process stoutly defended by the administration of Pres. George W. Bush. The United States pledged to respond forcefully to

Secretary of Defense Robert M. Gates with members of Texas A&M University's Corps of Cadets at the Pentagon, March 14, 2007. The cadets presented Gates with a pair of signature "senior boots," to commemorate his service as president of the university from 2002–2006. Defense Dept. photo by Cherie A. Thurlby

challenges from insurgents and to protect roadways, power plants, utility lines, and the economic infrastructure. America also promised to continue to provide security for the interim government at least until the election of a legitimate Iraqi government, which would follow six months after the handover of sovereignty to the Iraqi Council—and beyond if required. Thus, by the close of 2004, as at the close of 2003, Iraqi Operation Freedom remained a work in progress.

During the ensuing years that work became increasingly complex as Shiite, Sunni, Kurd, and other tribal groups and extremists within those communities fought variously against the Taliban, al-Quaida, each other, the government of Iraq, and, on occasion, against U.S. and coalition forces. Neighboring nations were inevitably drawn into the arena of war. In 2005 and 2006 conditions worsened and U.S., coalition, and civilian casualties rose.

On December 18, 2006, Pres. George W. Bush appointed the then president of Texas A&M University, Dr. Robert M. Gates, as secretary of defense. A former deputy director and director of the Central Intelligence Agency, Gates had previously served under six presidents in the national intelligence community. Following his service as assistant to the president and deputy national security advisor, he had come to Texas as interim dean of Texas A&M's George Bush School of Government and Public Service before accepting the position as president of the university on August 1, 2002.

In January 2007, a month after Gates's appointment as secretary of defense and in the face of rising anti-war sentiment in the United States, President Bush announced that the situation in Iraq required the commitment of 21,500 additional troops—a "surge" that promised to resolve the decaying military situation. By March 2007 U.S. troop reinforcements began to arrive.

As he "Faced the Nation," Defense Secretary Gates advised Americans that the situation was improving and that a political reconciliation and a more stable civil government were developing in Iraq. U.S., coalition, Iraqi military, and civilian deaths began to decline markedly by mid-2007. However, the pursuit of peace and stability continued to be a long, difficult, and sometimes seemingly elusive process, and throughout that process many hundreds of Texas Aggies served in the Armed Forces of the United States in Iraq, Afghanistan, and in other critical areas throughout the world in the historic and unrelenting effort to halt terrorism and achieve world peace.

TABLE 18. A Sampling of Texas Aggies Serving in Operation Enduring Freedom and Operation Iraqi Freedom, and Associated Actions, 2001–2008

Bowden, Gary M. ('66), Command Master Chief, AF

Hornburg, Gen. Hal M. ('68), AF

Mobley, Brig. Gen. James A. ('69), MD/A

Walker, Col. Louis E. ('69), MC/A

Gass, Lt. Col. Jerry ('71), AF

Kinkead, Col. Bert ('71), A

Moseley, Lt. Gen. Michael ('71), AF

Lance, Capt. Lee Roy ('72), N

Weber, Lt. Gen. Joseph Weber ('72), MC

Betty, Lt. Col. Gerald R. (Jake) ('73), A

Gouge, Col. Steve ('74), MD/A

Utterback, Lt. Gen. Loyd S. "Chip" ('75), AF

Weber, Brig. Gen. Louis W. ('75), A

Fraser, Maj. John M., Jr. ('76), MC

*Howard, Sgt. 1st C Merideth. ('76), A

Matte, Lt. Col. Joseph "Rod" ('76), AF

Simmons, Col. Jimmie ('76), A

Carpenter, Brig. Gen. Floyd ('77), AF

Rubenstein, Brig. Gen. David ('77), MD/A

Franklin, Lt. Col. Gary W. ('78), A

Magee, Col. Jonathan ('78), A

Wilson, Col. Mike ('78), AF

Burnham, Lt. Col. Paul M. ('79)

Cates, Brig. Gen. Michael B. ('79), VMC

Cerda, Maj. Mark ('79), A

SantaAna, Lt. Col. Stephen ('79), MC

Thornton, Lt. Cdr. Scott A. ('79), MC/N

Warren, Col. Harry ('79), MD/A

Williams, Capt. John M., Sr. ('79), MC/A

Arroyo, Lt. Cdr. Erick ('80), N

Gagnon, Col. George ('80), AF

Garza, Col. Jorge ('80), AF

LaCrosse, Col. John ('80), A

Martin, Maj. Bonnie Jo ('80), VMC

Parker, Lt. Col. Robert A. ('80), A

Pena, Lt. Cdr. Ronald N. ('80), N

Hawes, Col. Sam ('81), A

Meyer, Lt. Col. Calvin ('81)

Traxler, Chief Steven ('81), N

Vogt, Lt. Col. Brad ('81), AF

TABLE 18 (continued)

Wilson, Maj. Marty ('81), A

Young, Lt. Col. Ed ('81), MC

Davis, Col. Jim ('82), A

Davis, Lt. Col. John M. ('82), A

Kregal, Maj. Jeff ('82), AF

Laughbaum, Lt. Col. Kent ('82), AF

Merkel, Capt. Chuck ('82), N

Minyard, Lt. Col. Mike ('82), A

Napper, Brig. Gen. Jennifer ('82), A

Nielson, Peter E. ('82), MC/A

Sahm, Col. David ('82), MC

Smith, Lt. Col. Jerry ('82), MC

Bone, Lt. Col. T. ('83), A

Dearduff, Capt. Mark ('83), N

Eoff, Lt. Col. Robert W. ('83), A

Ferris, Lt. Col. Mike ('83), A

Fuentes, Lt. Col. Rick ('83), AF

Huron, Lt. Col. Mark ('83), A

Kaminar, Lt. Col. John I. ('83), A

Mantey, Lt. Col. Michael D. ('83), A

Motley, Maj. John ('83), A

Ramirez, Lt. Col. Raul E., Jr. ('83), A

Andersibm, Lt. Col. West ('84), AF

Barr, Lt. Cdr. James ('84), N

Braunschweig, Cdr. John J. ('84), N

Burke, Lt. Col. Adrian ('84), MC

Denman, Lt. Cdr. Dane ('84), N

Hardy, Lt. Col. Jim ('84), A

Park, Maj. Glenn C. ('84), A

Polk, Maj. Patrick Brian ('84), MD/A

Restivo, Lt. Col. Philip G. ('84), MC

Vite, Lt. Col. Nick ('84), AF

Allen, Lt. Col. Jonathan ('85), MC

Becker, Lt. Col. Jim ('85), A

Bowling, Maj. John ('85)

Brunner, Maj. Carl ('85), AF

Cardenas, Lt. Col. Richard R. ('85), A

Crawford, Lt. Col. Kenny ('85), A

Davis, Maj. Donald ('85), AF

Irvin, Lt. Cdr. John ('85), N

Kelling, Maj. G. A. ('85), A

Nettles, Lt. Col. Bentley ('85), A

Olbrick, Lt. Col. Grant ('85), MC

Ransome, Maj. Charles W. ('85), A

*Salter, CWO Richard ('85), A

Schick, Cdr. Sam ('85), N

Stasney, Lt. Col. John A. ('85), A

Bearden, Lt. Col. Bryan ('86), AF

DeHaes, Lt. Col. Drew ('86), AF

Escalante, Lt. Col. Yori ('86), MC

Fink, Cdr. Paul A. ('86)

Frierson, CW3 Thomas ('86)

Gantt, Capt. Mary C. "Christi" ('86), A

Maples, Maj. W. C. "Curt" ('86), MC

Mittag, Maj. Michael ('86), A

Redding, Maj. Stephanie D. ('86), MD/A

Tate, Maj. Gordon ('86), A

Thomson, Lt. Col. Andy ('86), AF

Gehler, Maj. Gregory ('87), A

Kniskern, Maj. Kenny ('87), AF

Magruder, Capt. Jay W. ('87), A

Marble, Maj. Tom ('87), MC

McGuire, A1C John Samuel ('87)

Shaffer, Maj. Derek ('87), MC

Thames, Maj. Todd ('87), MD/AF

Wilson, Maj. Marty ('87), A

Acevedo, Capt. Rafael ('88), A

Brady, Capt. Patrick ('88), MC/A

Craig, SSgt. John H., III ('88), A

Henry, Lt. Col. Demitri ('88), A

Kurzy, Maj. Michael A. ('88), A

McDaniel, Maj. Lance ('88), MC

Mercurio, Maj. Joseph D. ('88), AF

Richardson, Lt. Col. Darren L. ('88), MC

Skrocki, Lt. Col. Thomas J. ('88), AF

Soukup, Lt. Col., Alan ('88), AF

Tate, Maj. Gordon ('88), A

Varner, Lt. Cdr. Andy ('88), N

Wilmot, Lt. Cdr. Scott ('88), N

Youngblood, Maj. Charlie ('88), AF

des Bordes, Capt. Chuck ('89), MC

Fink, Cdr. Murray ('89), N

Fink, Cdr. Paul ('89), N

Heye, Maj. John ('89), MC

Howell, Maj. Brent ('89), MC

Kelley, 2nd Lt. Michael A. ('89), A

Killian, Lt. Col. Dennis ('89), A

Korenek, Maj. Martin G. ('89)

Montgomery, Maj. William D. ('89), A

Redding, Maj. Robert ('89), A

Williams, Maj. Mike ('89), A

Coe, Maj. Adam ('90), AF

Cotton, Maj. John ('90), AF

DeLa Rosa, Lt. Renee ('90), MC/A

Emerson, Maj. Chris ('90), MC

Franks, Maj. Jim ('90), MC

Magee, Maj. Robert ('90), AF

Miller, Maj. Doug Miller ('90), A

Rowe, Lt. Col. Rusty ('90), A

Tamex, Capt. Carlos ('90), A

Weaver, Maj. Stephen L. ('90), A

Witte, Maj. Joel ('90), AF

Bellue, Lt. Col., Kyle G. ('91), AF

Bounds, Maj. James Yancy, II ('91), MC

Brumfeld, Maj. Timothy ('91), A

Cantrell, Maj. Chris ('91)

Delgado, Maj. Gil ('91), AF

Devora, Capt. Leo ('91), A

Hayes, Maj. Steve ('91), AF

McGuire, Sgt. 1C Sean ('91), A

McPherson, Maj. Michael G. ('91), MC

McPherson, Lt. Col. Sean C. ('91), MC

Merrill, Maj. Brady ('91), AF

Sanders, Maj. Brent ('91), A

Smitherman, Lt. Col. Jeffery ('91), MC

Williams, Capt. Mike ('91), MD/A

Allen, Capt. Jim ('92), A

Barr, Maj. Robert C. ('92), A

Basso, Capt. Steve ('92), A

Cantrell, Lt. Col. Christopher E. ('92), AF

Clark, Dr. Charlie ('92), MC/A

Costello, SSgt. Edward Costello, IV ('92), A

Dickerson, Capt. Richard L. ('92), MC/A

Downs, Capt. Michael ('92), AF

Espino, Lt. Cdr. Joseph C. ('92), N

Fazzoli, Maj. Anthony ('92), AF

Felpel, Maj. Kurt ('92), A

Floyd, Maj. Hunter ('92), A

Foltyn, Jason ('92)

Flatten, Capt. Mike ('92), AF

Gonzales, Maj. Adam G. ('92)

Heath, Maj. Ron ('92), MC

Hill, Maj. William D. ('92)

Imle, Lt. Chris ('92)

Janousek, Capt. Tom ('92), AMC

Johnson, Capt. Whit ('92), AF

Lister, Capt. Scott ('92), N

Lockett, Capt. Carl ('92), NG

Mitchell, Capt. Todd G. ('92), A

Nogueras, Maj. Robert ('92), A

Rawley, Lt. Cdr. Chris ('92), N

Ridgeway, Capt. Jason ('92), A

Rose, Maj. Mike ('92), AF

Ruth, Maj. Stephen G. ('92), A

Sanchez, Maj. Omar ('92), MC

Shoemaker, Maj. Lisa ('92), A

Bingham, Lt. Joseph ('93), N

Blake, Maj. Stephen ('93), A

Brown, Maj. Jason ('93)

Bryant, Capt. Craig ('93), A

Bushong, Maj. James T. ('93), A

Eiben, Capt. Stacy ('93), MC

Glasscock, Capt. Larry E. ('93), A

Healy, Capt. Michael J. Jr. ('93), A

Houghtby, Capt. Arthur C. ('93), MC

McCool, Sgt. M.J. ('93), A

Oliver, Capt. Chris ('93), MC

Parker, Capt. David E. ('93), A

Ripley, Maj. Michael ('93), A

Rogers, Capt. Ryan ('93), A

Seiber, Capt. Pat ('93), A

Shoemaker, Lt. Col. ('93), AF

Tucker, Maj. Patrick ('93), A

West, Capt. Tim ('93), A

Young, S/Sgt. Christopher ('93), AF

Anderson, Sgt. Jamie ('94), A

Bertamini, Capt. Mark ('94), MC

Bryant, Capt. Tom ('94), AF

Carey, Capt. David ('94), A

Clark, Maj. Todd ('94), A

Cohn, Capt. Warren ('94), AF

Denman, Lt. Cdr. ('94), N

Elchanan, Lt. Josef ('94), N

Elliott, Capt. Patrick ('94), AF

Estes, Capt. Greg ('94), AF

Healy, Capt. Mike ('94), A

King, Sgt. Steven ('94), A

Luckie, Capt. Scott J. ('94), MC

Maker, Maj. John ('94)

Marsh, Capt. Glenn E. ('94), A

TABLE 18 (continued)

Miller, Capt. Jeff ('94), A

Pfeiffer, Capt. Kristian ('94), MC

Reiley, Capt. Michael ('94), MC

Sanchez, Capt. Andy ('94), A

Scantlin, 1st Lt. Straus ('94), A

Sherrill, Capt. Matthew A. ('94), AF

*Sims, Capt. Sean Patrick ('94), A

Solleder, Capt. Drew ('94) AF

Spaid, Maj. John W. ('94), MC

*Worrell, Maj. Matthew W. ('94), A

Ybarra, Capt. Mark ('94), A

Zimmerman, Capt. David ('94), A

Baker, Lt. Cdr. Tim ('95), N

Brandon, Maj. J. Lewis ('95), AF

Brummett, Lt. Cdr. B. Mark ('95), N

Burwick, Lt. Cdr. Chuck ('95), N

Campbell, Capt. Russ ('95), A

Collins, Capt. Todd ('95), VMC

Doyle, Lt. Eric ('95), AF

Eberling, Capt. Brian ('95), AF

Fischl, Lt. Kurt E. ('95), N

Gilmore, Maj. Mark. A. ('95), A

Harper, Capt. Reggie ('95), A

Jeffery, Capt. Mark ('95), AF

Laauwe, Capt. Brad ('95), A

Murata, 1st Lt. Ryan ('95), MC

Oliver, Capt. William ('95), MC

Parker, Capt. Kevin ('95), A

Payne, Capt. Jayson ('95)

Ramirez, Capt. Gabe ('95), A

Riley, Lt. Brian Anthony ('95), AF

Rudd, Capt. Anthony ('95), A

Sammon, Capt. Nathan ('95), A

Smith, Capt. Daniel T. ('95), MC

Tillman, Capt. Jermon D. ('95), A

Thompson, Capt. Kevin ('95), AF

Tway, Capt. Marshall ('95), A

Valadez, Nah, Tim ('95), A

Vega, Maj. Sergi, Jr. ('95), AF

Washington, Capt. Robert S. ('95), MC

Watjus, Lt. S. Douglas ('95)

Worthington, Capt. Robert S. ('95), A

Zynda, Capt. Steve ('95), A

Alexander, Lt. Col. Jennifer C. ('96), AF

Bertakovich, Capt. Jeff ('96), A

Betik, 1st Lt. Bart "Pickle" ('96), A

Blackwell, Capt. Shelton ('96), A

Bucher, Capt. Kirk ('96), AF

Erickson, Capt. Bryan ('96), A

Flinn, Lt. Tobin C. ('96), MC

Gonzales, Ens. Marc C. ('96), N

Havard, Capt. Mike ('96), AF

Irwin, Capt. Lee ('96), AF

Laughlin, Lt. Christina ('96), A

Major, Capt. Trace ('96), A

Moreno, Capt. Jim ('96), AF

Thompson, Lt. Nicole E. ('96), AF

Traweek, Capt. Steven ('96), A

Voekel, Capt. Tyson ('96)

Warren, Capt. John ('96), MC

Arriaga, Capt. Jason ('97), A

Barrows, Capt. Jim ('97), A

Bell, Capt. Tyson ('97), A

Boyd, Capt. Stephanie L. ('97), VMC

Cimato, Michael ('97), A

Combs, Capt. Clayton L., ('97), A

Cones, Capt. Shawn ('97), A

Corcia, Capt. Trent J. ('97), A

Dellinger, Capt. Scott ('97), A

Dickson, Capt. Nicholas ('97), A

Erickson, Capt. Mike ('97), MC

Floyd, 1st Lt. Shane ('97), MC

Foster, Capt. Stephen R. ('97), A

*Gordon, Capt. Lyle L. ('97), MC

Hansford, Lt. James ('97), AF

Harrison, Capt. Jim ('97), A

Howard, Lt. Nathan ('97), AF

Martinez, Capt. Mike ('97), AF

McCullough, Capt. Adam ('97), A

McElwain, Lt. Mark ('97), A

Islam, Maj. Nadim ('97), A

Payne, Capt. Robert D. ('97), MC/A

Pope, Lt. Dallas ('97), AF

Sproat, Lt. Robert J. ('97), N

Thomas, Capt. Jesse ('97), MC

Tilson, Maj. Dennis A. ('97), A

Tran, 1st Lt. Alexander ('97), A

Williams, Capt. J. D. ('97), A

*Blanco-Caldas, Capt. Ernesto ('98), MC
Broaddus, 1st Lt. Jeff ('98), MC
Broderick, 1st Lt. Matthew ('98), A
Brown, Capt. Patrick ('98)
Chase, Capt. Chris ('98), A
Clark, Capt. Russell ('98), A
Davita, Capt. Mark ('98), MC
Dietz, Capt. Matt ('98), AF
Evans, Capt. Kenneth ('98), A
Fisher, 1st Lt. Richard J. ('98), MC
Floyd, 1st Lt. Shane ('98), MC
Fontaine, Capt. Donald E. ('98)
Gray, Lt. Justin ('98), AF
Gunn, 1st Lt. Richard ('98), A
Hall, Capt. Dan ('98), AF
Hesters, Lt. Chad Allen ('98), N
Hudson, 1st Lt. Jason M. ('98), M
Jaeger, 1st Lt. Jason Scot ('98), AF
Keith, Capt. Mitch L. ('98), A
King, Capt. Jeff ('98), A
Langley, Capt. Kevin S. ('98), MC
Lockard, Lt. Jim ('98), N
*Lyerly, Capt. Sean Edward ('98), A
McCrosky, CWO Scott ('98), A
Parker, Capt. Bryan ('98), A
Patterson, Maj. Craig R. ('98), A
Pinkerton, Sgt. Joshua ('98), A
Pontiff, Capt. Mike ('98), AF
Ramirez, Capt. Gabe ('98), A
Reeves, Capt. Matt ('98), A
*Russell, Capt. Blake H. ('98), A
Salinas, Lt. Martin II ('98), AF
Siefkin, Capt. Kathy ('98), A
Sproat, Lt. Bob ('98), MC
Stanley, 1st Lt. Dale ('98),
Steen, Lt. (jg) Lori ('98), N
Townsend, Capt. Ian ('98), A
Vest, Capt. Dickie J. ('98), VMC
Wilson, Capt. J. J. ('98), MC
Wilson, 1st Lt. Rawn M. ('98), A
Ballard, Capt. Jonathan ('99), A
Brand, 1st Lt. Mason ('99), MC
Brandenburg, Lt. Col. Bill ('99), MC
Bravo, 1st Lt. Ricardo ('99), A
Bluntzer, Capt. Sam ('99), A
Burrescia, Capt. John ('99), A

Cherry, Lt. (jg) James ('99), N
Clinkscales, Capt. Andrew ('99), A
Cody, Capt. Clint ('99), A
Cole, Capt. Seth ('99), A
Daniel, Lt. Andy ('99), AF
Fisher, 1st Lt. J. Troy ('99), A
Garcia, 1st Lt. Phillip ('99), A
Gerardot, Lt. Michael ('99), A
Gutierrez, Capt. Eric ('99), AF
Hart, Lt. Brian ('99), N
Harwell, Lt. Gordon N. ('99), MC
Ickles, 1st Lt. David H. ('99), MC
Ilschner, Lt. Craig ('99), A
Jones, 1st Lt. Kenneth M. ('99), MC
Kammeyer, Lt. (jg) Bryce ('99), N
Kinne, Capt. Megan ('99), A
Kulle, 1st Lt. Scott ('99), AF
Lattu, Capt. Alison ('99), A
McCaughrin, 1st Lt. David ('99), A
Moyer, Sgt. Heath ('99), A
Ostermann, Sgt. Nathan A. ('99), A
Phillips, CW2 Robert ('99), A
Roberts, Lt. Dustin ('99), MC
Rockwell, Lt. Kenneth ('99), A
Rustling, Lt. Aaron ('99), A
Saari, WO2 T.J. ('99), A
Scott, 1st Lt. Amy ('99), AF
Scott, Ens. Rebecca ('99), N
Shaw, Capt. Frederick ('99), AF
Sickinger, Lt. Damian K. ('99), A
Snelgrove, 2nd Lt. Jason ('99), A
Stancover, Lt. Brian W. ('99), A
Strye, Capt. Monica M. ('99), A
Sublette, Sgt. James ('99), MD/A
Tanner, 1st Lt. Toni J. ('99), AF
Templer, 1st Lt. John W. ('99), A
Tolbert, 1st Lt. Jason ('99), A
Tolbert, Capt. William J. ('99)
Tomberlain, Capt. Jonathan Lee ('99), A
Walther, 1st Lt. Robin ('99), MC
Webb, 1st Lt. John ('99), MC
Winnek, 1st Lt. Chris ('99), A
Zendejas, 1st Lt. Mike ('99), A
Amyx, Lt. Jim ('00), VMC
Bohne, Lt. Brett ('00), MC
*Christmas, Capt. Todd Tyler ('00), A

TABLE 18 (continued)

Dunn, Ens. Durwood ('00), N
Durham, 1st Lt. Jonathan ('00), A
Escobar, 1st Lt. Greg ('00), A
Ewing, Capt. James Cameron ('00), A
Franz, Capt. David ('00), A
French, Maj. Jeffrey ('00), A
Hayes, Sgt. Brian ('00), A
Hayes, 2nd Lt. John ('00), AF
Herbst, 1st Lt. Karl ('00), A
Huff, Capt. Jeremy ('00),
Humphreys, Lt. David ('00), A
Jones, Spc. Brandon ('00)
Kinkead, Lt. Albert ('00), A
Layton, 1st Lt. Robert Colby ('00), A
Lewis, 2nd Lt. David C. ('00), MC
Lewis, Lt. Shaun ('00), A
McDonald, Lt. Kenneth L. ('00), N
McDowell, 1st Lt. Afinju ('00), MC
Mikesa, SSgt. Joe E., III ('00), A
Miller, Capt. Jessica ('00), AF
Morgan, Capt. Rich ('00), A
Naylor, 1st Lt. Jeremiah ('00), A
Norris, 1st Lt. Andrew ('00), MC
Penrod, Capt.), Sean M. ('00), MC
Richmond, Sgt. Christopher L. ('00), A
Saullo, Lt. (jg) James Ryan ('00),N
Soule, 1st Lt. Patrick ('00), A
Strickland, Capt. Brian ('00), A
Tapp, 1st. Lt. Eric ('00), A
Thornton, Lt. Mike ('00), A
Tutt, 1st Lt. Casey ('00), A
Valadez, 1st Lt. Steve ('00), A
Weekley, 2nd Lt. C. Tyson ('00), A
Wolf, Capt. Mark ('00), AF
Abruzzo, 2nd Lt. Ben ('01), A
Diaz, 2nd Lt. Ben ('01), MC
Dressen, WO3 Dustin ('01), N
Eubank, 2nd Lt. Brett ('01), MC
Franks, Lt. Daniel ('01), MC
Garcia, 2nd Lt. Ernesto ('01), AF
Geyer, 1st Lt. Andrew J. ('01), A
Gorney, Lt. Luke ('01), A
Gue, Capt. Melissa ('01), A
Henley, 2nd Lt. Stephen ('01), A

Herndon, Capt. Troy ('01)
Homiller, 2nd Lt. Don ('01), A
*Hufstedler, 1st. Lt. Doyle M., III ('01), A
Hynniner, Lt. Onni ('01), A
Ingenloff, Maj. Christopher M. ('01), AF
Jackson, Ens. Christopher ('01), N
Jacob, Spc. Siefert ('01), A
Lyons, 2nd Lt. Joshua ('01), MC
Lutton, SSG Nicholas ('01), A
Maness, 2nd Lt. Austin ('01), A
McAlister, 1st Lt. John ('01), A
Nelson, 2nd Lt. Nathan K. ('01), A
Nickell, Melissa, Red Cross
Palermo, Sgt. Jeffrey ('01), A
Pesek, 2nd Lt. Jeff ('01), A
Reynolds, Cpl. John W. ('01), A
*Rozier, 1st Lt. Jonathan D. ('01), A
*Sanders, 1st Lt. Ryan T. ('01), A
Schindler, Ens. Christopher ('01), N
Scott, Lt. Dave ('01), A
Siefert, Spc. Jacob ('01), A
Simon, Ens. Wesley ('01), N
Sims, Ens. David ('01), N
Skinner, Lt. John A. ('01), A
Sorenson, Capt. Danny ('01), AF
Strictland, 2nd, Lt. Justin ('01), A
Tomberlain, Capt. Thomas David ('01), MC
Traweek, Maj. Kasandra ('01)
Tyner, Lt. Nathan S. ('01), A
Underwood, Ens. Pete ('01), N
Weatherall, Ens. E. Rollin ('01), N
Weaver, Capt. Kyle ('01), A
Whitaker, Lt. Nick ('01), A
Williams, 2nd Lt. Melvin ('01), A
Allison, Lt. Travis ('02), N
Aranda, Lt. Daniel III ('02), N
Armstrong, Capt. Patrick ('02), A
Bayars, Lt. jg. Matt Bayars ('02), N
Beto, 2nd Lt. Andrew ('02), MC
Betty, Capt. Joshua M. ('02), A
Billedo, 2nd Lt. Pamela ('02), A
Birch, 2nd Lt. Steven ('02), MC
Breidenback, Lt. Charity ('02), A
Channels, 1st Lt. Ben ('02), A

Crismon, Ens. Charity ('02), N

Chrismon, Ens. Charity ('02), N

Drake, 2nd Lt. David ('02), A

Eaves, Capt. Cassidy ('02), A

Enger, Capt. Jordon ('02), A

Franks, Lt Teresa ('02), A

Green, Capt. Dustin ('02)

Griese, Capt. Brandon ('02), A

Hans, Lt. Jordan ('02), AF

Imle, Lt. jg. Chris ('02), N

Jeffress, Capt. Clayton ('02), A

Kennedy, Capt. Clifton G. ('02), MC

Johnson, Capt. Colin ('02), A

Kresta, Capt. Kurt D. ('02), A

Murphy, Capt. Jonathon ('02), A

Richardson, 2nd Lt. Justin ('02), A

Rodriguez, Lt. Hector ('02), A

Rowan, 1st Lt. Josh ('02), A

Scogin, Lt. Alex W. ('02), N

Snider, Capt. Dale ('02), AF

Stoddard, Lt. Dusty ('02), N

Stone, 2nd Lt. Christian ('02), A

Tiller, Lt. J.C. ('02), A

Turner, Capt. Regan C. ('02), MC

Voelkel, Capt. Trevor S. ('02), A

Waggoner, Capt. Nat ('02), A

Walker, Capt. Burt ('02), A

Wetterauer, 1st Lt. Peter ('02), A

Abelson, 2nd Lt. Pete ('03), A

Alexander, Sgt. John C. ('03), A

Andreas, 1st Lt. Joshua ('03), A

Autry, Cody M. ('03), A

Autry, Jennifer ('03), A

*Burks, 2nd Lt. Peter Haskell ('03), A

Diggins, Brad ('03), AF

Figueroa, Capt. T. Christopher ('03), A

Gorney, 1st Lt. Michael John ('03), A

Grossman, Spc. Josh ('03), A

Harrison, Capt. John ('03), A

Henley, 1st Lt. Matthew D. ('03), AF

Hinton, Pfc. Seantoya ('03), AF

McMaughan, Spc. Sean Patrick ('03), A

Malone, Ens. Matthew ('03), N

*Meeuswen, Sgt. William ('03), A

Moran, Lt. Dan ('03), MC

Nethery, 1st Lt. Nick ('03), A

Payne, Lt. Adam ('03), A

Post, Capt. Ben ('03), A

Rich, Lt. jg. Joshua ('03), N

Schaumburg, Capt. Mark ('03), A

Senz, lt. George ('03), A

Smith, Lt. jg. Jarrod ('03), N

Sparks, Spc. Michael B. ('03), A

Soileau, Capt. Matt ('03), A

Use, 1st Lt. Charles ('03), A

Vernon, Capt. Mark ('03), A

Wathen, Sgt. Donny ('03), A

Wilson, Spc. Michael ('03), A

Alaniz, 1st Lt. J. Keith ('04), A

Barrett, 1st Lt. John M. ('04), AF

Brandes, Lt. Darrell ('04)

Brown, 1st Lt. Travis ('04), A

Burch, 1st Lt. Matt ('04), A

Dornhorst, 2nd. Lt. Christian ('04), A

Hensley, Spc. Philip Hensley ('04), A

Hernandez, 1st Lt. Mike ('04), A

Hince, 1st. Lt. Peter ('04), AF

Junick, Lt. Patrick W. ('04), MC

Kopecki, Lt. James ('04), A

Longmire, Capt. Melissa ('04), A

Lopez, Sgt. Juan ('04), A

McPudden, Lt. Ray ('04), A

Markos, Lt. ('04), A

Marshall, 1st Lt. Robert W. ('04), A

Mireur, 1st Lt. Patrick ('04), A

Muniz, Lt. Noe R. ('04), A

Nail, Kevin, Coast Guard

Natalino, 1st Lt. Mike ('04), A

Norton, S/Sgt. Thomas A. ('04), A

Oliveria, Lt. Chuck ('04), A

Osufsen, Lt. Jesse M. ('04), MC

Pinto, 1st Lt. Charles ('04), A

Platt, Capt. Jonathan S. ('04), A

*Ray, 1st Lt. Jeremy E. ('04), A

Sandoval, 1st Lt. Chris ('04), A

Shanks, 2nd Lt. David ('04), A

Sherman, Spc. Patrick ('04), A

*West, Cpl. Christopher J. ('04), A

Zinnecker, 1st Lt. Chad ('04), A

Baker, SSgt. Lewis W. ('05), AF

Bingham, Spec. Josh ('05), A

Clark, 1st Lt. Stephen ('05), A

TABLE 18 (*continued*)

Cruzen, Sgt. Tyler ('05), A

Dellinger, Lt. Russell ('05), A

Foran, Cpt. Charles D., III ('05), A

Haynes, 2nd Lt. Bryce ('05), A

Holtkamp, Lt. Christopher ('05), A

Horn, Lt. Michael ('05), A

Jaramillo, 1st Lt. Jeffrey ('05), A

Jones, 1st Lt. Kyle ('05), MC

Myers, Sgt. Kevin ('05), A

Renner, Cpl. Stephen ('05), A

Sherman, Spc. Patrick ('05), A

Teague, Maj. Leslie, III ('05), A

Vidotto, 1st Lt. Mark ('05), A

Bareilles, Sgt. Ryan ('06), A

Baumgardner, Capt. David E. ('06), A

Bliss, Capt. William ('06), A

Carter, 2nd Lt. Jared ('06), A

Comley, Lt. Eric ('06), A

*Edwards, Pvt. 1st C William L. ('06), A

Gonzales, Lt. Joe ('06), A

Kahler, Capt. Jeffrey ('06), A

Marselis, 2nd Lt. Zach ('06), A

Marshall, 1st Lt. Jonathan H. ('06), A

Postrigan, 2nd Lt. Andrey ('06), A

Prewitt, Maj. Daphany Lynn ('06), A

Souza, Sgt. Weston Anthony ('06), A

Terry, Spc.4, Steven ('06), A

Brambila, Sgt. Benjamin ('07), A

Damaske, Spc. Greg ('07), A

Flowers, Sgt. Geoffrey ('07), MC

Habhab, Capt. Travis ('07), A

Hinton, Pfc. Seantoya ('07), A

Wilcox, Spc. Charles ('07), A

Currie, Spc. Jason ('08), A

Davilla, Spc. Angel ('08), A

Darby, Spc. Colin ('08), A

Ehritch, Lt. Seth ('08), AF

Fleming, Sgt. Scott ('08), MC

Frazier, SrA, Adam B. ('08), AF

*Gomez, Spc. Daniel E. ('08), A

Huang, Sgt. Annie ('08), A

Kalina, SSgt. . Joshua S. ('08), AF

Klander, Spc. Sherry ('08), A

Kozel, Paul ('08), MC

Linnell, Sgt. K. Shane, Jr. ('08), A

Meyer, Cpl. Michael W. ('08), MC

Rogers, Sgt. Joshua ('08), A

Stephenson, Sgt. Sean ('08), MC

Woodward, SSgt. Ryan ('08), A

*Yepsen, Lance Cpl. Luke C. ('08), MC

Ball, Capt. David James ('09), A

Gorrell, Sgt. Gary W. ('09), A

Kahler, Sgt. Lawrence M. ('09), A

Smith, Sr.A, Mark J. ('09), AF

Steel, Cpl. Sean M. ('09), MC

Taylor, SSgt. Sean Robert ('09), MC

Y'Barbo, Sgt. Daniel ('09), MC

Robertson, OS2 Sara ('10), N

Note: This is an incomplete listing based on information available as of 1/30/08 from Aggienetwork.com and *Texas Aggie*, Corps of Cadets, and personal sources. Rank or rate and branch of service are listed when available. A = Army, AF = Air Force, N = Navy, MC = Marine Corps, MC/A = Medical Corps/Army, MC/AF = Medical Corps Air Force, MC/N = Medical Corps/Navy, VMC = Veterinary Medical Corps

Blanco-Caldas, Capt. Ernesto ('98), MC: Assigned to the 82nd Airborne, he was killed by an improvised explosive device destroyed his vehicle in Aaryat Ash Shababi, Iraq on December 28, 2003.

Burks, 2nd Lt. Peter Haskell ('03), A: 4th Squadron, 2nd Stryker Cavalry Regiment killed when his vehicle struck a roadside bomb utilizing an armor-penetrating projectile in Baghdad, Iraq on November 14, 2007.

Christmas, Capt. Todd Tyler ('00), A: Died in the crash of a UH-60 Black Hawk during exercises at Fort Hood, on November 29, 2004, shortly after returning from combat operations in Iraq.

Edwards, Pvt. 1st C William L. ('06), A: Killed on August 11, 2007 in an attack on his combat team during operations with the 1st Bn., 30th Infantry Regiment, 3rd Infantry Division in Arab Jabour, Iraq.

Gomez, Spc. Daniel E. ('08), A: Killed by mortar fire in operations in Tikrit, Iraq on March 16, 2006 during operations with the 1st Batt., 26th Infantry, 2nd Combat Team, 1st Infantry.

Gordon, Capt. Lyle L. ('97), MC: Died in the crash of a CH-53E helicopter near Ar Rutbah, Iraq during operations with Marine Heavy Helicopter Squadron 361 on January 26, 2005.

Howard, Sgt. 1st C Merideth ('76), A: Believed to be the oldest woman killed in combat, manned a machine gun on a Humvee struck by a suicide bomber who drove into their vehicle during operations in Kabul, Afghanistan on September 8, 2006.

Hufstedler, 1st. Lt. Doyle M., III ('01), A: Assigned to the 1st Engineer Batt., 1st Infantry Brigade, 1st Infantry Division, he was killed when a roadside bomb struck his armored personnel carrier near Habbaniya, Iraq, on March 31, 2004.

Lyerly, Capt. Sean Edward ('98), TxArmy Nat. Guard: One of twelve soldiers killed when their UH-60 Black Hawk helicopter crashed during operations near Baghdad on January 20, 2007.

Meeuswen, Sgt. William ('03), A: Assigned to the 101st Airborne Division, he was killed in action near Baghdad, Iraq on November 23, 2005.

Ray, 1st Lt. Jeremy E. ('04), A: Died of wounds suffered from a homemade bomb in an attack on the 1st Squadron, 3rd Army Cavalry Regiment operating in Kanaan, Iraq on December 20, 2007.

Rozier, 1st. Lt. Jonathan David ('01): Died in combat in Baghdad on July 19, 2003 with Bravo Company, 2–70 Armor Battalion, 1st Armor Division.

Russell, Capt. Blake H. ('98), A: Died of injuries sustained by enemy fire during combat operations with the 101st Airborne in Baghdad, Iraq on July 22, 2006.

Salter, CWO Richard ('85), A: Assigned to the Aviation Brigade, 4th Infantry Division, he died in a mid-air crash in an AH-64 Apache helicopter during operations in Baghdad, Iraq, on December 26, 2005.

Sanders, 1st Lt. Ryan T. ('01), A: Killed during combat operations with the 1st Batt., 66th Armor Regiment, 1st Brigade Combat Team, 4th Infantry Div. by a roadside bomb detonated near his M1A2 tank in Baghdad, Iraq on June 6, 2006.

Sims, Capt. Sean Patrick ('94), A: Killed by enemy fire during operations with 2nd Batt., 2nd Infantry Regiment, 1st Infantry Division in Fallujah, Iraq on November 13, 2004.

West, Cpl. Christopher J. ('04), A: A combat medic with the 1st Squadron, 73rd Cavalry Regiment, 2nd Brigade Combat Team, 82nd Airborne Division, died of injuries from an IED in Magdadiyah, Iraq, on Sunday, February 4, 2008.

Worrell, Maj. Matthew W. ('94), A: Assigned to the 160th Special Operations Aviation Regiment, he died when his AH-6M "Little Bird" helicopter was shot down by enemy fire during combat operations in Yusifiya, Iraq on May 14, 2006.

Yepsen, Lance Cpl. Luke C. ('08), MC: Assigned to the 1st Tank Battalion, 1st Marine Division, Marine Expeditionary Force, he died of injuries suffered from enemy action in Anbar Province, Iraq on December 14, 2006.

Suggested Reading

Blair, Arthur H. *At War in the Gulf: A Chronology* (College Station: Texas A&M University Press, 1992).

We in the military constitute the most antiwar group of
all. Our first job is to try to prevent war. The big difference
between us and other antiwar groups is the method of
prevention. We believe that only by maintaining strong
military forces can America prevent potential aggressor
nations from making war on us and our allies. The
responsibility of the U.S. military is not to wage war
but to deter it. . . . Its goal is peace.
—Gen. John D. Ryan, USAF Chief of Staff, 1971
Commissioning of 238 New Texas Aggie Officers

19

A TRADITION OF SERVICE THE CIVILIAN SOLDIER

Since the days of the American Revolution, the American military experience
has been conditioned by the distrust of a standing, professional army and by
dependence on the citizen soldier and a well-trained militia. Since 1898, distrust of a strong military presence has diminished as the United States has been
thrust into both great and small wars around the world. Americans are now
more than ever in accord with the sentiments of Pres. George Washington, who
envisioned a strong peacetime military establishment as a deterrent to war.
The only insurance against "insult, hostility and the calamities of war," he said,
as though foreseeing the needs and challenges of democratic societies in the
twenty-first century, "is to put the national militia in such a condition as that
they may appear truly respectable in the eyes of our friends and formidable to
those who would otherwise become our enemies."[1] From 1898 to 2005, in different worlds, different wars, and different times, American armies of citizen
soldiers have fought great wars and small ones, and prominent among them in
every instance, on every front, and on every continent have been Texas Aggies.

The American military has always relied on the citizen soldier and a well-
trained militia to supplement a standing army, a position explicitly incorporated in Article I of the U.S. Constitution. The citizen soldier and the militia
tradition of service in times of need have become an American historical experience and an integral part of the Texas A&M University tradition since the
school's founding in 1876. Most A&M graduates who have served on active military duty have served as commissioned officers. Until World War I, there was
no formalized mechanism for commissioning military college graduates.
Those who earned commissions did so largely through state militia training
programs. Then, between World War I and World War II, the Reserve Officer

Training Corps (ROTC) program produced thousands of Aggie officers for the Reserve Officer Corps—citizen soldiers in reserve for times of need. That need came soon. Following the attack on Pearl Harbor, America mobilized to fight World War II, and our military forces expanded about fortyfold. More than twenty thousand Texas Aggies served in that war.

Since then, a large U.S. military force has been maintained through the Cold War and the post–World War II conflicts. During this period, many Aggie officers have been integrated into the regular military services; others have been called to extended active duty, to return to reserve status on completion, and to be available for recall, if needed. War, combat, and military training, as an intrinsic part of Texas A&M's historic experience, helped mold the psyche and character of Texas Aggies who became soldiers.[2]

More than fifty thousand Texas Aggies have served in the military since 1898, most of them as officers and volunteers. The intensity and courage with which they fought and served are reflected by their numerous decorations and awards, the large number of flag rank officers, and the number who died while in the service of their country. During the dedication of a statue on the A&M campus honoring Lt. Gen. James F. Hollingsworth ('40), Maj. Gen. Marvin Ted Hopgood ('65), USMC, said, "the Corps of Cadets produces many special people and more than just a few truly heroic soldiers." General Hollingsworth's combat service in World War II, Korea, and Vietnam were of "legendary proportions," and he also contributed significantly to the military's effort to build and strengthen ROTC programs throughout the United States.[3]

When he addressed the graduating class of 1968, during a time of war and turbulence in Vietnam, U.S. Army Chief of Staff Gen. Harold K. Johnson recalled a conversation with an unnamed lieutenant who had just returned from Vietnam, where he had served as an infantry platoon leader and company commander. "He did not seem to be overly impressed with the dangers and the hardships he had faced, nor even with the enormous burdens of combat leadership." Instead, that soldier had come to understand "that always in our midst are the ready and the reluctant." And "indelibly etched on his mind was the staggering importance of personal responsibility." General Johnson stressed that Americans have a vision of a world "without conflict and bloodshed." But in attempting to create that world we must guard everything of value that is ours and help our neighbors protect what is theirs. "As a nation of paradoxes and anomalies, we have sometimes sought and sometimes dodged such involvement. Now, however, we can no longer avoid that responsibility if we intend to influence the course of international events in ways that are consistent with the visions we hold as a people."[4] It is a vision that was no less understood by the veterans of the Spanish-American War as well as those who served in Afghanistan and Iraq more than a hundred years later.

Texas A&M, its culture and traditions, and the Corps of Cadets have nurtured the school's students as they assumed their roles as citizens and soldiers and as leaders in peace and in war. Following his release in 2001 from "detainment" in China, Lt. (jg) Richard ("Rick") Payne ('97) from Pampa, Texas, spoke at the Aggie muster in Seattle, Washington. He said, "[I] can only say thank-you for your patriotism, support, thoughts, and prayers. It's great to be home." Payne entered naval flight training in 1998 and, after earning his wings, was deployed to the Pacific fleet for reconnaissance duties aboard an EP-3E Aires II. During one of Payne's routine flights over the China Sea, two Chinese fighters intercepted and began to closely observe the American aircraft, as was their routine, but this time the observation was too close. A midair collision forced the Aires into an 8,000-foot emergency descent and a forced, but safe, landing on China's Hainan Island. The crew were detained and interrogated but treated well, while negotiations proceeded for their release. Payne concluded his account of the trying experience by simply observing that "A&M helped me through this ordeal."[5]

The vision of world peace and the sense of an obligation to serve, shared by Texas Aggies over the centuries, has been a real-world view fraught with anxieties and the reality of the costs of service. As senior corps Cmdr. Spence Pennington ('03) noted in the spring of 2003, upon the approach of his being commissioned and readied for active duty in the Middle East, "I am more than willing to risk my life to protect the American way of life for my family and friends." Pennington was "anxious for the chance to repay America for the blessing of a good life that America has given me." But he and his fellow graduates were also aware of the harsh realities of war. "Everyone is afraid of dying. I don't think anyone in their right mind can say that going to war doesn't scare him," reflected their classmate Kyle Lippold.[6] That reality and that historic experience with war had also become a part of the A&M Corps of Cadets and the ROTC experience.

Over the years, Texas A&M has constantly reminded itself of that obligation to duty, commitment to service, and the costs of those obligations by planting oak trees to commemorate its World War I dead, building a memorial student center to honor its World War II students who died in the service of their country, and creating a memorial meditation garden and a corps plaza memorial to honor those who have died while defending America since World War II. Congressman Olin E. Teague ('32), a veteran of World War II, recognized the Memorial Meditation Garden dedicated in 1970 as "a quiet and inspiring place, a tribute to our dead and a living memorial to the spirit of Texas A&M which has made such a distinguished and continuing contribution to the safety and preservation of our nation and to the maintenance of the liberty of its citizens."[7]

In 1993, Texas A&M's Corps of Cadets established a hall of honor to recognize those former students who over the years contributed most significantly to the honor and reputation of the university and its military programs and traditions. The profiles of those selected to the Hall of Honor usually include distinctive service in the armed forces, service to the community, state, and nation, and attributes and values such as soldier, citizen, family, integrity, determination, leadership, and the indefinable "Aggie Spirit."[8]

The Corps of Cadets at Texas A&M University "is many things to many people," remarked commandant of cadets and head of the School of Military Sciences Lt. Gen. John A. Van Alstyne ('66). After being commissioned as an army second lieutenant, Van Alstyne served as an advisor to Vietnamese combat forces, chief of staff of the 24th Infantry Division in the Persian Gulf War, and deputy assistant secretary of defense for military personnel policy. After thirty-six years of service, he retired from active duty and returned "home" to Texas A&M to assume the duties of commandant. Texas A&M and the Corps of Cadets, Van Alstyne said, have provided unique and proven leadership opportunities to students for more than a century. The resulting citizen soldiers, who are volunteers in the militia tradition, are trained in leadership and in the technical skills and knowledge required by modern warfare and national defense. The most important aspect of the Corps of Cadets, he explained, has been its role in developing the capacity to lead and instilling the discipline and the traits of character required for leadership in peace and in war.[9] Texas A&M has contributed extensively to the pool of active and reserve officers and personnel the nation needs to provide insurance against the hostilities and calamities of war and to maintain the respect of our friends—and the apprehension of those who might be enemies.

Texas A&M's reputation as a provider of well-trained military officers has continued in contemporary times and especially since the Vietnam War. "Texas A&M has been a major producer of the nation's military officers," observed James C. Smith (master's degree '70 and PhD '76, both in civil engineering), who spent two tours of service in Vietnam plus ten years as a professional staffer for the U.S. Senate Armed Services Committee (1975–1985) and completed his active duty at the rank of lieutenant colonel. Smith explains that one of that committee's major tasks is to ensure the presence and readiness of a trained army of citizen soldiers. While the national service academies provide the nucleus of officers, that allotment consistently falls far below the armed services' total needs. The United States must rely on ROTC institutions and the Officer Candidate School (OCS) programs to meet the considerable and varying demands for additional officers.[10]

Texas A&M is at the top of the "top tier" of ROTC providers. The university's uniqueness is derived in part from the fact that Texas A&M students and officers are the products of a real-world experience, while the national service academies and some of the other key military officer incubators often offer a more controlled, less interactive, open, and public educational environment for their soldiers in training. Moreover, while Texas A&M officer candidates have a strong tradition in military leadership and discipline, as students they have a greater breadth and depth of academic exposure in many diverse fields. Thus, in addition to the Corps of Cadets, ROTC, and military training opportunities, Texas A&M offers a broad and diverse real-world educational experience that uniquely meets the demands of modern military service.[11]

The Texas A&M citizen soldier is versatile and adaptive in fulfilling the changing needs of the military in the dynamic technological and global environment. Through it all, the one thing that has "remained constant," reflected Bill J. Youngkin, former president of the Association of Former Students (1991), at the dedication of the Corps Plaza Memorial is that "when our country needs citizens to go forth and defend our freedom, our country and our democratic way of life, you've always found Aggies in the forefront. We've been marching off to war, offering up our service and our lives, helping to carry our country's colors since our inception, and so it continues today."[12]

NOTABLE AGGIES

The following individuals are prominent among the thousands of Texas Aggies who have served their country in peace and in war since 1898. They are representative of those who, as Bill J. Youngkin ('69) has observed, have been "marching off to war, offering up our service and our lives, and helping to carry our country's colors since our inception, and so it continues today."

Lt. Charles C. Todd ('97), Spanish-American War

Todd was the first captain of the Corps of Cadets and gave the valedictory address at his graduation. He was the first Aggie to receive a direct commission in the Regular Army and was among the first troops to land in the Philippines. He fought with the Filipino insurrectionists against Spanish forces and was wounded in action near Manila. Todd became the first former Aggie student to become commandant of the Corps of Cadets.

Lt. George P. F. Jouine ('07), World War I

Jouine sailed to France at his own expense in 1914, joined the French Army as a private, received a battlefield commission, and, despite six combat wounds, served thirty-four months on the front lines. With more than a dozen combat decorations from three nations, he was the most decorated former A&M student of World War I. A mechanical engineer, Jouine understood the mechanics of tanks and knew how best to use the innovative and deadly new weapon on the battlefield.

Lt. Jesse Easterwood ('17), World War I

Easterwood enlisted in the navy on April 7, 1917, the day after the declaration of war. Among the first class of navy officers to qualify as an aviator, he was loaned to the United Kingdom to fly its new Handley Page heavy bombers and flew sixteen combat missions behind German lines. Easterwood served variously with the British, Italian, and French air forces before completing his service as a highly decorated airman with the U.S. Army Air Corps.

Pvt. Norman G. Crocker ('17), World War I

Crocker, from Center, Texas, was the first from A&M to lose his life in World War I. He died, with more than a hundred soldiers and sailors, when German submarines sunk the British convoy troopship *Tuscania* on February 5, 1918.

Maj. Edward B. Cushing ('80), World War I

Cushing, a railroad engineer and master of logistics, received a direct commission as a major in the U.S. Army's 17th Engineer Regiment. By August, 1917, he was in France, where he served as director of debarkation at the ports of Antwerp and Brussels. Later on he became chief of the American Expeditionary Force transportation corps, for which he managed all of the Mediterranean supply ports and depots.

Maj. Gen. George F. Moore ('08), World War II

The first Texas Aggie to reach flag rank, General Moore received orders while serving as commandant at Texas A&M to report as commander of the garrison and defenses of Corregidor Island in the Philippines. Concurrently with the attack on Pearl Harbor, Japan attacked the Philippines and by December 24 had Corregidor under siege. Following heroic resistance, the Corregidor defenders, including Moore and twenty-five Texas Aggies, capitulated on May 6. Moore received the Distinguished Service Cross for extraordinary heroism.

Maj. John A. ("Jack") Hilger ('32), World War II

Hilger was second in command to Lt. Col. James Doolittle in the daring Tokyo bombing raid in April, 1942, which greatly bolstered American morale following the devastating attacks by Japan in the Pacific in the winter of 1941 and spring of 1942. Other Aggies on the mission were Lt. Robert M. Gray ('41), Lt. William M. Fitzhugh ('36), Lt. Glen C. Roloson ('40), and Lt. James M. Parker ('41).

Ens. George H. Gay Jr. ('40), World War II

Ensign Gay, the sole survivor of Torpedo Squadron 8 in the Battle of Midway (considered one of the most important naval battles of World War II), after having been wounded, made a final torpedo attack on the carrier Kaga and was shot down by Japanese fighters. His radioman was killed, but Gay survived the ditching and watched the rest of the battle while soaking his wounds in salt water for thirty hours before being rescued.

Lt. Lloyd H. Hughes ('43), World War II

On August 1, 1943, as the Allied invasion of Italy began, Lieutenant Hughes, piloting a B-24 Liberator bomber with the 564th Bomber Squadron, began a dangerous two-thousand-mile mission to strike the refineries of Ploesti at treetop level. During the attack, his aircraft received direct hits and was engulfed in flame, but Hughes continued the mission, dropping his bomb load precisely on target before being killed in an attempted forced landing. He was the first Texas Aggie to receive the Congressional Medal of Honor "for conspicuous gallantry in action and intrepidity at the risk of his life above and beyond the call of duty."

Lt. Col. James Earl Rudder ('32), World War II

Lieutenant Colonel Rudder led the initial Ranger Assault on Point du Hoc during the D-Day Allied invasion of Normandy, which helped define the successful course of the invasion. He received the Distinguished Service Cross for extraordinary heroism for this action and continued to fight in France and Germany. Rudder retired as a major general in the U.S. Army National Guard.

Lt. Turney W. Leonard ('42), World War II

On November 4, 1944, Lieutenant Leonard's 100-man tank-destroyer company and 1,100 infantrymen became trapped between two German divisions near Kommerscheidt, Germany. During the final German attack, with most of the infantry officers dead, Leonard took command. Using only a submachine gun and grenades, he knocked out German snipers, a half-track, and a .50-cal. machine gun while directing fire that destroyed six enemy tanks. After a shell blew off the lower part of his arm, Leonard managed to tie a tourniquet around the stump. He then headed for a first-aid station but was never seen again. He was posthumously awarded the Congressional Medal of Honor.

Lt. Eli Whiteley ('41), World War II

During the Battle of the Bulge, on the day after Christmas, 1945, Lieutenant Whiteley's I Company was ordered to attack heavily fortified German positions in Sigolsheim, France. In the first attack the company commander was severely wounded, and 40 of the unit's 96 men were killed. Whiteley assumed command. While wounded, he led his men in a house-to-house attack, during which he killed 9 of the enemy, captured 23, and cracked the core of enemy resistance. Pres. Harry S. Truman awarded Whiteley the Medal of Honor.

Lt. Thomas W. Fowler ('43), World War II

In the drive toward Rome while reconnoitering for mines, Fowler found a disorganized infantry platoon lost in a German minefield. He took charge of the men, clearing a path through the minefield by proceeding ahead to personally remove antipersonnel mines. While in an advanced position, his troops came under a German tank attack. When an American tank was set afire in the midst of battle, Fowler attempted to save the wounded tank crew and administered aid to the wounded infantry. His actions earned him the Medal of Honor and "exemplify the high traditions of the military service for which he later gave his life."

Staff Sgt. George D. Keathley ('37), World War II

When all of the officers of the 2nd and 3rd platoons of Company B, 338th Infantry Regiment, 85th Division, were killed in an assault on Mt. Altruzzo, Staff Sergeant Keathley reorganized the survivors and assumed command. When attacked by two German infantry companies, Keathley passed out ammunition and encouragement, and although mortally wounded, Keathley continued to fight until the enemy withdrew. He was posthumously awarded the Congressional Medal of Honor.

Gen. Bernard Schriever ('31), World War II, Cold War

During World War II, General Schriever, a former U.S. Air Corps test pilot, flew sixty-three combat missions in B-17 and B-24 bombers, earning the Legion of Merit, Air Medal, and a Purple Heart. In 1944 and 1945, he commanded air-combat-support operations in the South Pacific. In 1957, he headed the Air Force Ballistic Missile Division in developing the Atlas, Titan, and Minuteman booster and missile systems and helped to pioneer America's entry into space flight.

Maj. Horace S. Carswell Jr. ('38), World War II

During the air and sea battles of Leyte Gulf, Major Carswell, piloting a B-24 bomber on a solo reconnaissance mission over the South China Sea, discovered an enemy task force of twelve ships escorted by two or more destroyers. Carswell attacked, severely damaging one of the warships, and attacked again, releasing his bombs but taking heavy flak. "Carswell gave his life in a supreme effort to save all members of his crew." He was posthumously awarded the Medal of Honor.

Maj. Gen. Raymond L. Murray ('35), World War II, Korea

Colonel Murray received a Silver Star for action at Guadalcanal, another for combat on Tarawa, and the U.S. Navy Cross for heroism in the battle of Saipan. In one of the most successful amphibious landings in the history of warfare, he led the 5th Marine Regiment's 1st Battalion at Inchon in Korea, resulting in the retreat of the North Korean forces toward China. Then, after confronting six Chinese communist divisions at Chosin Reservoir, Murray and his marines conducted one of the bloodiest fighting withdrawals of the war, for which he received the Distinguished Service Cross.

Sgt. William G. Harrell ('43), World War II

On March 3, 1945, Sergeant Harrell led his marine assault group against Japanese troops located in rugged terrain on Iwo Jima. The enemy's forces infiltrated his division's positions and attacked. Harrell killed two enemy at close range, lost his left hand, and was wounded in the thigh. In continuing close combat he killed an enemy officer who was about to strike him with a saber, shot two enemy soldiers who placed a grenade near his head, and pushed the grenade toward another charging soldier, who was killed. At dawn, medics extracted Harrell from a mound of twelve enemy dead. He was still alive but had by then lost his remaining hand as well. He received the Medal of Honor "for exceptional valor and indomitable fighting spirit against almost insurmountable odds."

Gen. Otto P. ("Opie") Weyland ('25), World War II, Cold War, Korea

In the drive across Europe following the Normandy landings, while commander of the Nineteenth Tactical Air Command, Brigadier General Weyland developed standards of air-land cooperation between the army and the air force. During the Korean War he was the architect of new tactics and strategies that defined air-to-air and air-to-land combat. In 1954, he was promoted to four-star general in command of all U.S. tactical air forces worldwide.

Lt. Gen. Ormond R. Simpson ('36), World War II, Cold War, Korea, Vietnam

General Simpson served on Gen. Douglas MacArthur's staff during World War II and was a regimental commander in Korea, commander of the Thailand expedition in May, 1962, and marine division commander at Da Nang, Vietnam, in 1969. Upon his retirement from the U.S. Marine Corps in 1974, General Simpson joined the administration at Texas A&M University as assistant vice president for student services and supervisor of military programs. A long-term advocate of and advisor to the Corps of Cadets, Simpson held that the corps is "absolutely essential to the existence of Texas A&M, not because of what it has been in the past, but what it can be to the future."

Capt. Robert L. ("Bob") Acklen Jr. ('63), Vietnam

Among the most decorated Aggies in the Vietnam War, Captain Acklen served almost three full years in combat as a helicopter pilot and infantry company commander. Awarded more than 60 decorations—17 for valor in combat, including the Silver Star, 6 Bronze Stars, and 3 Vietnamese crosses—Acklen suffered a broken back in a helicopter crash but recovered. He subsequently became a U.S. Army Ranger and resumed his military duties in Korea.

Adm. Jerome L. ("Jerry") Johnson ('56), Cold War, Vietnam, Iraq

Admiral Johnson became the third Texas A&M graduate to achieve four-star rank. He commanded Carrier Group Four, NATO's carrier striking force, and, in 1988, assumed command of the U.S. Second Fleet, Joint Task Force 120, which provided security for 38 million square miles of ocean in the Atlantic theater.

Lt. Gen. James F. Hollingsworth ('40), World War II, Korea, Vietnam

General Hollingsworth is one of the most decorated general officers in American military history. He earned three Distinguished Service Crosses, four Distinguished Service Medals, four Silver Stars, three Legion of Merit awards, three Distinguished Flying Crosses, four Bronze Stars, and six Purple Hearts. General Hollingsworth commanded the Third Regional Assistance Command in Vietnam and directed the critical and successful defense in the battle of An Loc.

Maj. Gen. T. Michael Moseley ('71), Vietnam, Afghanistan, Iraq

A former pilot instructor and F-15 weapons and tactics officer, General Moseley served as combined forces air component commander for Operations Southern Watch, Enduring Freedom, and Iraqi Freedom. He was combat director of operations for Joint Task Force–Southwest Asia and air component commander in charge of air operations during the Afghanistan and Iraq campaigns. His assignments have included the National War College, Joint Chiefs of Staff, and Office of the Secretary of the Air Force. He has served as commander, Fifty-seventh Wing; commander, Ninth Air Force and U.S. Central Command Air Forces; and chief of staff.

APPENDIX A RANKS AND GRADES (U.S. ARMED SERVICES)

Grade	Army	Air Force	Marine Corps	Navy/Coast Guard
O–11	General of the army	General of the air force	(no equivalent)	(no equivalent)
O–10	General	General	General	Admiral
O–9	Lieutenant general	Lieutenant general	Lieutenant general	Vice admiral
O–8	Major general	Major general	Major general	Rear admiral (upper half)
O–7	Brigadier general	Brigadier general	Brigadier general	Rear admiral (lower half)
O–6	Colonel	Colonel	Colonel	Captain
O–5	Lieutenant colonel	Lieutenant colonel	Lieutenant colonel	Commander
O–4	Major	Major	Major	Lieutenant commander
O–3	Captain	Captain	Captain	Lieutenant
O–2	1st Lieutenant	1st Lieutenant	1st lieutenant	Lieutenant (junior grade)
O–1	2nd Lieutenant	2nd Lieutenant	2nd lieutenant	Ensign
W–4	Chief warrant officer	Chief warrant officer	Chief warrant officer	Chief warrant officer
W–3				
W–2				
E9	Sergeant major of the army	(no equivalent)	(no equivalent)	(no equivalent)
E8	Master sergeant specialist 9	Chief master sergeant	Master gunnery sergeant	Master chief petty officer
E7	Sergeant 1st class platoon sergeant	Master sergeant	Gunnery sergeant	Chief petty officer
E6	Staff sergeant	Technical sergeant	Staff sergeant	Petty officer 1st class
E5	Sergeant	Staff sergeant	Sergeant	Petty officer 2nd
E4	Corporal	Airman 1st class	Corporal	Petty officer 3rd
E3	Private 1st class	Airman 2nd class	Lance corporal	Seaman
E2	Private	Airman 3rd class	Private 1st class	Seaman apprentice
E1	Recruit	Recruit	Private	Seaman recruit

APPENDIX B ARMY AND MARINE ORGANIZATION: LEVELS OF COMMAND

Unit	Number of Personnel	Rank of C/O	Basic Composition
Theater operations[1]	Varied	General	Headquarters (HQ), two or more corps
Corps	Varied	Lieutenant general	HQ and two or more divisions
Division	Airborne 13,250	Major general	HQ and three or more brigades:
	Air assault 15,700		aviation, infantry, engineer, artillery,
	Armored 17,300		and up to fifteen combat battalions
	Mech. infantry 17,900		
	Light infantry 11,500		
Brigade[2]	3,000–4,000	Colonel	HQ and two or more battalions
			and support units
Battalion[3]	300–1,000	Lieutenant colonel	HQ and two or more companies
			or detachments
Company and battery	60–190	Captain	HQ and two or more platoons
Platoon	16–44	Lieutenant	Three or four squads
Squad	10	Staff sergeant	Smallest unit

1. In Korea, the field army was subordinate to the theater HQ and superior to the corps. In World War II, the army group was over field armies.

2. In Korea and World War II, the regiment was next subordinate to the division; now it is the brigade.

3. Today, battalion unit designations still identify with their historic regiments (e.g., the 1st Battalion, 3rd Infantry Regiment is abbreviated 1/3 Infantry).

APPENDIX C AIR FORCE ORGANIZATION: LEVELS OF COMMAND

Unit	Number of Personnel	Rank of C/O	Basic Composition
Theater of operations	Varied	General	HQ, two or more air forces
Air force (numbered)	Varied	Lieutenant or major general	Two or more wings
Wing	3,000–5,000	Brigadier general or colonel	Basic combat unit with three or more squadrons of 10–24 aircraft, with combat support groups
Air base wing	3,000–5,000		
Group[1]	1,000–1,500	Colonel or lieutenant colonel	Two or more squadrons of 10–24 aircraft
Squadron	200–400	Lieutenant colonel or major	Two or more flights
Flight	Varied (about 100, including support personnel)	Captain or major	Smallest tactical unit (usually 4 or more aircraft)

1. The air group was the basic World War II combat unit assigned to an air base. Historically it contained three or four flying squadrons plus support personnel numbering several thousand. In 1947, the air force adopted the wing-based plan, and flying squadrons thereafter have reported to the wing, while the air group is primarily staff.

APPENDIX D NAVY ORGANIZATION: LEVELS OF COMMAND

Unit	Number of Personnel	Rank of C/O	Basic Composition
Theater of operations	Varied	Admiral	U.S. Atlantic Fleet U.S. Pacific Fleet
Fleet	55,000–87,000, depending on number of assigned vessels and aircraft	Vice admiral	About 100 ships distributed among four battle groups
Battle group	9,000–10,000	Rear admiral	1 carrier 2 cruisers 5 destroyers 1 attack submarine
Amphibious group	Varied	Major general (marine)	Element within a battle group
Squadron	Varied	Commodore (or lower half rear admiral since World War II)	2 or more divisions of vessels or aircraft
Ship	50–500	Lieutenant to captain (depending on size and class of ship)	5–6 departments
Air wing	50–500		2–5 air squadrons
Department	50–75	Lieutenant to commander	3–5 divisions
Squadron	50–75		
Division	10–50	Ensign to lieutenant commander	Deck, engineering administration, gunnery, air, etc.

APPENDIX E AIRCRAFT IDENTIFICATION AND DESCRIPTION

This appendix presents those aircraft that are most prominently referenced in the text. For additional information, see David Donald, ed, *The Complete Encyclopedia of World Aircraft* (New York: Barnes and Noble Books, 1997; repr. 1998).

A-3D (Douglas) Skywarrior. A navy carrier-based, swept-wing, twin-engine jet attack bomber that entered service in 1956 and, with modifications, continued in use as a tanker through the twentieth century.

A-7 (Vought) Corsair. A very successful subsonic attack aircraft introduced into the navy in 1967 and adopted by the air force as a tactical fighter (A-7D). The navy Corsairs flew more than ninety thousand missions during the Vietnam War and were last used in operations during Desert Storm.

A-20/DB-7 (Douglas) Boston/Havoc Series. One of the most widely used twin-engine (Pratt and Whitney; 1,100 hp) light bombers of World War II.

AH-1 (Bell) Cobra. Introduced by the army as the "Huey" Cobra in 1967, the aircraft was the primary antiarmor weapon of the war in Vietnam and has been modernized and modified since then.

AH-64 (McDonnell-Douglas) Apache. Originally designed by Hughes Helicopters as an attack helicopter, the Apache was first delivered to the army in 1985. The Apache has superceded the Cobra and was used extensively in Operations Just Cause in Panama and Desert Storm in Iraq.

B-1 (Rockwell) Lancer bomber. Under development between 1969 and 1983, the first production model, B-1B, with a speed of Mach 1.25, came out in 1985 and replaced the B-52 in long-range strike missions.

B-2 (Northrop) Stealth bomber. A flying-V-wing, radar-absorbent aircraft with two pilots that flew first in 1989. It was originally intended as a replacement for the B-52 that would be capable of carrying missiles or strategic nuclear bombs, but costs deterred large-scale acquisition.

B-17 (Boeing) Flying Fortress. Designed as a high-altitude, long-range, four-engine bomber with a speed of 200–250 mph., the Flying Fortress (produced in numerous models and variations) was first used operationally over Germany in July, 1941.

B-24 (Consolidated) Liberator. Produced in a number of configurations, this four-engine, long-range bomber carried an 8,000-lb. bomb load and defensive armaments in the nose and tail and on the upper and lower fuselage. It entered service in 1941 and was the key bomber used in the 1942–1943 raids over Italy, Romania, and southern Europe. Some nineteen thousand aircraft were produced during World War II.

B-25 (North American) Mitchell. A twin-engine, five-seat medium attack bomber introduced in 1940 and modified during World War II in a number of variations, the bomber was used by James H. Doolittle's squadron in the 1942 raids over Japan.

B-29 (Boeing) Superfortress. Production began in 1943 on this very heavy, four-engine bomber that was used during the closing years of World War II and in the Korean War. Over time there were a number of modifications in armaments, fire-control systems, and capability for tanker utilization.

B-47 Stratojet. Built by Boeing, Douglas, and Lockheed, the B-47, the world's first swept-wing, six-engine turbojet bomber entered service in 1951. An improved (B-47E) model entered service in 1953. The aircraft was withdrawn in 1966.

B-52 (Boeing) Stratofortress. The first prototype flew in April, 1952. Equipped with eight Pratt and Whitney J57 turbojet (and later TF33) engines in regularly improved models, the aircraft remained in production until 1962. B-52s were deployed in the Vietnam War and were later modified as air-launch cruise and short-range missile carriers.

B-58 (Convair) Hustler. The first delta-wing, supersonic bomber (c. 1,385 mph) began tests in 1952, entered service in 1959, and was withdrawn from service in 1970.

C-47 (Douglas) Skytrain. A military derivative of the twin-engine DC-3, the C-47 transported troops and supplies and towed gliders in actions in Sicily, Burma, and Normandy during World War II. It was also used extensively in the Berlin airlift and the Korean and Vietnam Wars.

C-54 (Douglas) DC-4/C-54 Skymaster. First produced for the military in 1942 for cargo and troop transport, this four-engine aircraft remained in use through many models and variations.

C-130 (Lockheed) Hercules. A major military air-transport turboprop aircraft introduced into service in 1956 and subsequently adapted to numerous tasks (including use as a gunship), the Hercules remained in use and production into the 1990s.

C-141 (Lockheed). The first air force military jet cargo transport. It was introduced in 1964 and used extensively in all theaters of operation through the remainder of the twentieth century.

CH-47 (Boeing Vertol) Chinook helicopter. Used for heavy transport and troop assault operations, the twin-engine, tandem-rotor Chinook was introduced in 1959 and continually improved and modified thereafter. It was used very effectively in Southeast Asia for troop and supply transport and for airlift and evacuation operations.

CH-54 (Sikorsky) Tarhe Skycrane helicopter. A powerful, heavy-lift, twin-rotor vehicle that was used very successfully in Vietnam and elsewhere and adapted from the S-60 and S-64 "flying crane" models first flown in 1961.

F-4 (McDonnell) Phantom. Adopted by the air force, navy, and marines after test flights in 1958, the twin-jet Phantom II all-weather attack fighter set speed (1,606 mph) and altitude (98,556 ft.) records between 1959 and 1961. It is recognized as one of the world's finest all-around military combat aircraft.

F-4D (Douglas) Skyray. A navy carrier-based, delta-wing interceptor, single-engine jet that first began service in 1956. A prototype set the world speed record in 1953 at 752.9 mph.

F-16 (General Dynamics) Fighting Falcon. A multirole single-engine fighter for the United States and NATO Allies that entered service in 1978. Later variations offered a Mach 2.0 capability.

F-86 (North American) Sabre. Designed as a single-engine fighter, escort fighter, or dive bomber with a maximum speed of 707 mph, the F-86 entered service in 1949 and saw considerable service during the Korean War.

F-105 (Republic) Thunderchief. A single-engine, all-weather fighter-bomber introduced in 1958. It was used extensively during the Vietnam War.

F-111 (General Dynamics). Designed as an air force and navy tactical fighter, the twin-engine F-111 (A and B) entered service in 1967 and was widely used in operations over Vietnam.

H-37 (Sikorsky) Mojave helicopter. An adaptation of the Sikorsky S-56 assault helicopter capable of carrying twenty-six troops, the Mojave entered service in 1958 and continued in use throughout the Vietnam War.

MiG-15 (Mikoyan-Gurevich). Introduced into combat in Korea, the MiG-15 had a better rate of climb, tighter turning circle, and higher ceiling than the opposing U.S. F-86 Sabre.

MiG-17. This improved successor to the MiG-15 entered service in 1952, and later adaptations made it the first missile-armed fighter interceptor to be used by the Soviet Union.

OH-13 (Bell) Sioux helicopter. A 1960s' modification of the low-cost, simplified, and widely used H-13/model 47 series utility and trainer helicopters first introduced in 1948. Later versions included three-seat modifications.

OH-58 (Bell/Commonwealth Aircraft Corp.) Kiowa helicopter. An upgraded special-tasks patrol, target observation, and support helicopter introduced in 1969. It was used widely in Vietnam and subsequently produced with varying modifications.

P-38 (Lockheed) Lightning. A highly effective twin-engine fighter that entered service in late 1939 and was used in every theater of war during World War II. The pilot's nacelle was centered between two booms that supported the engines, wings, tail fins, and twin rudders.

P-40 Curtiss Warhawk (and improved versions such as the Tomahawk and Kittyhawk). These single-engine primary fighter aircraft of World War II were produced from 1939 through 1944. This was the aircraft used by the "Flying Tigers" in China.

P-47 (Republic) Thunderbolt. The P-47 entered service in 1943. More than fifteen thousand were produced during World War II. The single-engine aircraft is credited with the destruction of 4.6 enemy aircraft for each one lost during a total of 546,000 combat sorties.

P-51 (North American) Mustang. A highly effective, low-altitude, long-range, single-engine fighter aircraft used by the USAAF and RAF during World War II and refitted with various engines and equipment, including 20-mm cannon and cameras.

P-80 (Lockheed) Shooting Star. This single-engine jet entered USAAF service in early 1945 and saw limited service during World War II but was a major fighter of the Korean War. Lockheed later produced 5,691 T-33s, an adaptation of the P-80, as a primary jet trainer.

PBY (Consolidated) Catalina. A twin-engine, patrol-flying boat with long-range and high load-carrying capabilities, the PBY entered service in 1935 and was used by the United States, Canada, and the UK during World War II.

RAF (Supermarine) Spitfire. A single-seat fighter with retractable landing gear and eight machine guns, the Spitfire was used in the Atlantic and Pacific theaters during World War II and remained operational until 1967.

SR-71 (Lockheed) Blackbird. A two-seat, high-altitude, high-speed (Mach 3.2) "secret eye in the sky" reconnaissance aircraft equipped with radar and electromagnetic sensors introduced about 1964. It remained operational into the 1990s.

T-33 (jet trainer). See P-80 Lockheed Shooting Star.

U-2 (Lockheed). A high-speed, single-engine, high-altitude reconnaissance aircraft designed by Lockheed's secretive "Skunk Works." It first flew in 1955 and complemented and effectively superceded the SR-71 Blackbird.

UH-1 (Bell) Huey helicopter (or Bell model 204). The helicopter was introduced as the "Iroquois" in 1955 and nicknamed the "Huey" (through several adaptations as HU-1A, HU-1B, HU-1C, UH-1E, UH-1F, UH-1L, and UH-1M (night sensors). It has been widely used by all services (and prominently in Vietnam) as a utility helicopter and gunship.

UH-60A (Sikorsky) Black Hawk helicopter. This tactical transport vehicle entered service in 1979 with the 101st Airborne Division. Variations are used for assault, medevac, electronic warfare, and special operations.

V-22 (Bell-Boeing) Osprey. A prototype tilt-rotor Osprey combining the vertical landing and takeoff capability of the helicopter and the relatively high speed of a turboprop and designed as a quick-response combat-troop carrier (twenty-four troops with full combat equipment) first flew in 1989, although deliveries to the Marine Corps did not begin until after 2000.

APPENDIX F AWARDS AND DECORATIONS

Medal of Honor (often called the Congressional Medal of Honor). The nation's highest award established by Congress in 1862 is awarded by the president in the name of Congress to members of the armed services who distinguish themselves by gallantry and intrepidity at the risk of life and beyond the call of duty while engaged in military operations against an enemy force. As of 2004, the award has been presented to 3,459 recipients.

Distinguished Service Cross (DSC). Awarded to those serving in the armed forces who distinguish themselves by extraordinary heroism in action against an enemy of the United States, an act so notable or extraordinary as to set the individuals apart from their comrades but one not justifying the award of a Medal of Honor.

Distinguished Service Medal. Awarded for service not related to war and given to those who have distinguished themselves by exceptionally meritorious service.

Silver Star. Established by Congress in 1918, the Silver Star is awarded to a person in military services cited for gallantry in action against an enemy of the United States while engaging in military operations.

Legion of Merit. Awarded for exceptionally meritorious conduct in the performance of outstanding services.

Distinguished Flying Cross (DFC). Established by Congress in 1926, the DFC is awarded to those who have distinguished themselves by heroism or extraordinary achievement while participating in aerial flight in action involving enemies of the United States.

Soldiers Medal. Established by Congress in 1926 for heroism in situations not involving combat but which involved personal hazard and the voluntary risk of life.

Bronze Star. Established by executive order in 1944, the Bronze Star is awarded to military personnel who distinguish themselves by heroic or meritorious achievement (not involving aerial flight) in connection with military operations against an armed enemy.

Purple Heart. Established by Gen. George Washington during the Revolutionary War, the Purple Heart is awarded to a member of the armed services who, while serving under military authority, is killed or wounded. An oak-leaf cluster is given for subsequent awards.

Meritorious Service Medal. Established by executive order in 1969 as an award for distinguished or meritorious service while serving in a noncombat area.

Air Medal. Established by executive order in 1942, the Air Medal is awarded for acts of heroism in connection with military operations involving conflict with opposing armed forces and that are of a lesser degree than those required for the Distinguished Flying Cross.

APPENDIX G TEXAS AGGIES WHO DIED IN THE MILITARY SERVICE OF THEIR COUNTRY DURING WORLD WAR II

Class of 1906
John H. Pirie

Class of 1908
Douglas B. Netherwood

Class of 1910
James G. Ellis Jr.

Class of 1911
John William Butts
Clinton Warden Russell
Benjamin Fiske Wright

Class of 1914
J. H. Burford
Hugh Andrew Wear

Class of 1915
Crawford H. Booth Jr.
James Herbert Hinds

Class of 1916
Claudius Miller Easley
Walter Gustave Schultz
George Watson Splawn

Class of 1917
Myron J. Conway
John August Otto Jr.
Stanley Ezra Perrin
George A. Woody

Class of 1918
J. M. Woodson
Horace Conrad Yates

Class of 1919
C. Barfield
Manson Franklin Curtis

Class of 1921
Roswell G. Higginbotham
John Allen Pierce
Maynard Goldman Snell

Class of 1923
Welborn B. Griffith Jr.

Class of 1926
Elbert Beard Anding
Adolph Hartung Giesecke
Rufus Hayden Rogers

Class of 1927
Clarence Reid Davis
Earl Emerson Jackson
Ralph T. Smith

Class of 1928
Lacy Noel Bourland
Paul Armstrong Brown
George Edward Miller
James McKinzie Thompson

Class of 1929
John August E. Bergstrom
William Edwin Davis
John Hopkins Dodge
John Robertson Jefferson
Jack William Kelly
John Looney Lester

Class of 1930
William L. Hughes Jr.
Joe Burke Michael
Oscar Stanley Tom

Class of 1931
Gideon Henry Bigham
Graham McFee Hatch Jr.

William Cruse McMurrey
Wesley John Neumann
J. Wesley Ray
John Finis Rettiger
James Donald Richter

Class of 1932

James Otis Beasley
Joseph Hunt Bourland
James Thomas Connally
William Mark Curtis
Jeth Wesley Dodson
Courtney W. Fichtner
Felix Berkeley Lester
Edward Albert Obergfell
James Howard Perkins
William Clinton Vincent

Class of 1933

Joseph J. Backloupe
Madison D. Beaty
Harold Furman Blodgett
George Cooke Brundrett
George Perry Cook Jr.
Hamey Estes Jr.
Oliver Edwin Ford
Claude Lewis Madeley
Chester Alan Peyton
William P. Ragsdale Jr.
Jackson McLane Tarver

Class of 1934

Cary McClure Abney Jr.
Harold B. Chamberlain
William J. Collier Jr.
Lewis Griffin Compton Jr.
Earl Oxford Hall
Ted Adair Hilger
William Lester Jameson
Stephen Anson Jones
Travis Edward Perrenot
Rosson Nat Reid
Thomas Knox Smithwick
Warren D. Srubblefield Jr.
Bill Jeff Williams
Harold Edward Wright

Class of 1935

John Franklin Bamett Jr.
Henry Vincent Baushausen
Aubrey Roy Biggs
Robert Wayne Blodgett
John William Crow
Charles Martin Dempwolf
Gustave Herman Froebel
Sydney Robert Greer
Aubrey Peter Meador Jr.
James Randolph Oppenheim
Perkins Gardner Post
Joe Aluis Rosprim
Robert Wilson Russi
Roy McMahan Vick Jr.

Class of 1936

James Carlton Barham
John Letcher Chapin
Raymond Scott Evans
Bose Gorman
Marvin Earl Hiner
James Russell Holmes
Marshall Arlon Langley
Paul Ostis Mayberry
John Brown McCluskey Jr.
Louis Oliver Moss
Hollis Ulrich Mustain
Paul Edison Payne

Class of 1937

Olen Williford Abbott
Newton Bryan Birkes
James Madison Blanks
Wilbert Adair Calvert
Bailey Gordon Carnahan
Maxey Cleburne Chenault
Ray Esther Dickson Jr.
Clifford Hardwick
Otto Heye
George Dennis Keathley
Norman Jarvis McKendry
John Henry Morehead
James Edwin Rountree
Joseph Eugene Routt
Willis Arthur Scrivener

Lee Marion Sommers

Chester Isaac Tims

John Thomas Whitfield

S. Theodore Willis Jr.

Class of 1938

Woodrow Radford Allen

Edwin Park Arneson Jr.

Edgar Beaumont Burgess

Horace Scaver Carswell Jr.

Weldon Davis Cauthan

Dale P. Cleveland

Frank Monroe Colburn

John Charles Conly

George Stevens Gay Jr.

Henry Troy Gillespie

Rudyard Kipling Grimes

Joe Benjamin Guerra

James Albert Harris

Addie Joss Hogan

Noah Horn

James Frank House

Truman DeWitt Peale

Orville Kennard Puryear

Hiram Aldine Putnam

August Max Schmidt

Lee Joseph Shudde

Robert Neal Smith

William J. Stringer Jr.

William Marion Taylor Jr.

Carol Hightower Thomas

Joe Gordon Turner

Warner Rox Underwood

Jack McGee Vinson

James Barclay Whitley

Lillard Graham Wilmeth

Class of 1939

Augustus Jared Allen

Johnson Butler Allen

Robert Balch

Robert Clinton Beck

Freeman Harold Bokenkamp

Gaines Maness Boyle

Joe Wayne Bradford

John Pierre Bradley

Floyd Edwin Breedlove

Jesse Lee Brown

John Frank Burns

William Arthur Burton Jr.

Daniel Lynell Cajka

Charles W. Carpenter

Jack Whalon Clark

Jack Grady Wilson Cooper

David Elworth DeLong

Hugh Alan Derrick

Gerald Parker Elder

Allen Tatum Fowler

Harry Franklin Goodloe

Robert Edward Greenwell

Raymond Louie Gregg

James Richard Griffin

Howard Preston Hardegree

Frank Petty Haynes

Charles Daniel Heller

Philip S. Isis

James Herman Kaden

Lloyd Wyatt Kelly

Boyd Calfee Knetsar

Kenneth Edwin Krug Jr.

Leonard Gage Larsen

Henry Archer Lowrance Jr.

David B. McCorquodale

Birdwell J. McKnight

Ernest Benge Miller

Ross lyon Miller

Herbert Moss Mills

Maurice Allen Morgan

John B. Naughton

James William Parker

Herbert Hoover Perritte

Francis Morgan Potts

Warren Purman Rece

William Robert Ross

Henry John Schutte Jr.

Harold Thomas Scott

William Harvey Shuler

David Louis Silverman

Clarence E. Simpson Jr.

Marvin Judson Smith

Claud Paul Strother
Willis Albert Teller
Milton David Wallace
John Chapin Watkins
Marl Avant Westerman
Robert Joseph Williams
Paul Oscar Wofford

Class of 1940

Charles Benton Adams
William Andrew Adams
T. P. Aycock
Robert Miller Baird
Alfo Leroy Baker
Samuel Johnson Baldwin
Percy Berten Bennett
William Mayo Bills
Howard Louis Bowman
Rolland John Bowman
James Hugh Brantley
Foster Cochran Burch
Wilson B. Buster Jr.
Walter Mark Cabaniss Jr.
John Erwin Carpenter Jr.
Foster Lawson Cash
Walter Junior Clemans
Walter Pershing Crump
Jessie Cleveland Draper
John Henry Duncan
Ioland Edmund Dutton
John Evans Edge
Allen William Erck
Orman Lester Fitzhugh
Thomas Rex Francis
Stanley Friedline
Clifford Patrick Garney
Arthur Edward Gary
Paul Raymond Gregory
Charles Hugh Hamner
John L. Hanby
Duke W. Harrison Jr.
William Lee Hastings Jr.
Douglas Henderson
John Jefferson Keeter Jr.
Marshall H. Kennady Jr.

Paul Allard Kirk
John Clifford Knight
John Poiterent Lackey Jr.
Ollie Jack Laird
Sam Winston Lane Jr.
Louis Jules Lippman
Samuel Webb Lipscomb
Tommie Grantham Martin
Ashbell Green McClung
Charles Robert McIntire
Melvin Royce Millard
Joe Clifton Moseley
Chester Ellis Moudy
Wayne Livingston Mueller
John Willis Muse
Conrad John Netting III
Roy Adolphus Nichols
Hansford George Olney
Ferdinand B. Paris Jr.
Brady Oscar Parker
Ralph Isaiah Parlette
Hugh Buster Parris
Marvin Mather Pearson Jr.
Philip Edgar Pearson
Boyce Penrod Jr.
Carl Harold Pipkin
William Harrison Reeder
William Conner Richards
Charles L. Ricks Jr.
William Riley Roberts
Fred Sullivan Rodway
Glen C. Roloson
John Jacob Sanders
Radcliffe S. Simpson
Herbert Everett Smith
Gordon S. Stephens
John Darrell Stukenburg
Rollins C. Syfan Jr.
George Elias Turner
Henry William Waters
George Walton Wells Jr.
Richard Djalma Williams
Dennis H. Woodruff
Albert Boyce Yearwood Jr.

Class of 1941

Thomas Hubert Arkarman
James Marvin Atkins Jr.
Jack Bruner Bailer
Dwight Watkins Barry
Clyde Webb Beatty Jr.
Alexander Henry Beville
August John Bischoff
Rex Harvey Blankenship
Howard Leo Blessington
Edmund Francis Boyle
Claude Francis Brewster
Billy Dean Brundidge
Ben Davis Cannan Jr.
Gus Calhoun Cardwell Jr.
Daniel R. Chamberlain
Austin Wilkins Clark
Roger Bently Clements
Albert Dale Cotton
Alvin Cowling Jr.
Herbert Winfield Cumming
Jerral Walter Derryberry
Vincent DeSalvo
James Thomas Drake
James Musick Drummond
Ballard Powell Durham
John Lindsey Eddins
John Green Ellzey
Meinrad Joseph Endres
Walter Lafayette Evans
Ed A. Felder
Barry Church Francks Jr.
William Faris Gammon
Charles Earl Gaskell
Warren George Jr.
Tommy Glass
Robert Manning Gray
Lawrence Smith Gready Jr.
Robert Bruce Gregory Jr.
Burt Olney Griffin
Paul Grabow Haines Jr.
Miller Hammons Jr.
Curtis Olen Hancock
John Robert Harshey
Ralph Beaver Hartgraves

Henry William Heitmann III
Richard Gordon Hill
Travis Vestal Hodges
Edward D. Hughey
Kenneth McFarland Irby
Andy Marmaduke James Jr.
Abraham Simon Kahn
Sidney Caldwell Kimball
Edward Carr King
Robert Trimble Kissinger
Clarence Leroy Korth
Jim Lewis Kuykendall
George Lawrence Leger
Arthur Cornelius LePage
Henry Arthur Lewis
Joseph Paul Lindsey Jr.
Hugh Bland Lockhart
Joe Wallace McCrary
John Easton McCrary
John Preston McKinney
Herbert Welton McMinn
Lynn Howard Mead Jr.
Kenneth Taylor Merritt
Wendell Deering Neely
Patrick Cluney Noel
Samuel Jackson Parks
William Henry Paschal
Harvey Claude Pollay
Edward Herman Prove
John Daniel Ragland
Robert Smith Roddy
James McDonald Rowland
John Doyle Scoggin Jr.
Leo Theodore Sharum Jr.
Charles Thomas Sherman
Keith Willard Short
Charles Savage Simmons
Frank Pierce Smart
Paul Jones Stach
Joel Bryan Stratton
Herbert Carl Stucke
Robert Jackson Sudbury
Charles Vernon Thornton
Aubry Lawless Tobias Jr.
Leo Tomaso

Richard Herley Torrence
Vester Lamar Turner
Richard Lee Vickrey
Charles Oldham Watts
Percy Alton Weaver
M. J. White
Clarence Emil Phillip Wisrodt Jr.

Class of 1942

John Harold Allen
Barney R. Anderson Jr.
Michael Joseph Arisco
William Henry Baker
Jack Michael Balagia
William Spencer Barstow
Frank Parrish Blassingame
H. O. Borgfeld Jr.
Byron Leo Bostick
David Lee Braunig
Howard Horace Brians
Aaron Lewis Brinkoeter
William Lee Bryce
Raymond Salter Carter
William Brame Cartwright
Newton Vincent Craig
Paul Howard Damrel
Frank Percy Daugherty Jr.
Brice Coulter Diedrick
Clayton Norwood Duvall
Robert Cromwell Elliott
Robert Smith English
Worthington A. Franks
Virgil Dewey Fugler
Porter Frederick Fuqua
Charles William Gerhardt
Thomas Henry Gilliland
John Pershing Gilreath
Bobby Mack Godwin
Jack Emitt Golden
William Richard Grady
Earl Vetten Green
James Haywood Gulley
Henry Buford Hales Jr.
Gambrell W. Haltom
Rex Woodrow Hamilton

John Emmett Harris
Walter Manning Hart
Weldon Henderson Holland
J. D. Holzheauser
Joe Berl Huddleston
George Arthur Huser
Charles Largent Hynds
James Edward Inglehart
Henry Douglas Jackson
Gaines H. Jenkins Jr.
William Charles Jenn
Robert Guy Johnson
Ransom Dudley Kenny Jr.
Thomas Sylvester King Jr.
Ivy D. Kuykendall
Foster Lee Lemly
Turney White Leonard
Edwin Robert Lewis
Otis Forest Lowry
George Leslie Mauldin Jr.
James Walter McCaslin
Willis Douglas Michie
Roger Morwood
Robert Derace Moser
Kirby Clarence Musick
William Lynn Oler
John Paul Olsen
Robert Brownwell Parker
Edwin Forrest Patterson
Robert Lawrence Plagens
George W. Proctor
William Marion Rascoe
Robert Lee Ravey
Charles Glynn Ray Jr.
Arthur Mills Rider
Addison C. Rumbaugh Jr.
James Roan Sanders
Otto Eugene Schroeter
Raymond Carl Schuette
Edward Miles Schuyler
Felix Ernest Scott
Sam Fred Semo Jr.
Henry R. Smith
Reuben Alonzo Smith Jr.
Herman Henry Spoede Jr.

Theodore R. Stellmacher
George Lawson Stidham
William Conwell Swain
Anthony Tirk Jr.
Victor Pat Tumlinson
Lisle Reed Van Burgh Jr.
John Charles Walden
Raymond Frank Watson
Frank Gordon Weisiger
Goode Shockley Wier Jr.
James Maurice Williams
Theophulus A. Williams
Eugene Dickens Wilmeth
Tom Fred Wilson
Jack Preston Wolfe
John Shelton Zimmer

Class of 1943

Charles L. Babcock Jr.
Newell Moore Ballard
Clarence Vance Berdine
James Edgar Bragg
Charles Earl Butler
William B. Caraway Jr.
Paul D. Chaney
Joe Robert Clark Jr.
Thomas Ray Coffey
Wiley Harold Craft
Joe Brooks Dalton
Robert Earnest Daw
Garland Edwin Dennis
Louden Charles Doney III
Kyle Nichols Drake
Carl Bill Ehman
Alfred Anthony Esposite
Joseph Edward Fisher Jr.
Thomas Weldon Fowler
William Gerard Fraser Jr.
Edward Fry
Ben Prentice Gafford
William Byron Gibbs
Sam Tom Gillespie
Louis Vinc Girard
William Gammon Goodman
Henry G. Goodwin Jr.

William Soul Gordon
Dulane P. Gunn
Ferris Sam Harris
Ralph Edwin Hill
Richard Lloyd Hoefle
William Murray Holland
Lloyd Herbert Hughes
Clifford Clark Hutchison
James Hull Japhet
Stephen Charles Kaffer
Charles Edwin Kingery
Jimmie Stewart Knight
James Wafer Mabry Jr.
William P. Malone Jr.
Joe Townley Mann
Horace Lowell Markland
Randolph Magruder Martin
Harold M. Massey
Albert Lee Matteson
J. C. McCrary
Donald W. McIntyre
George Perry McMillan Jr.
William Walter Miller Jr.
Marvin Claude Mitchell
William Brooks Morehouse
Durward Duvon Morrison
Robert Frederick Mumm
James Tom Myers
Jack Cameron Nagel
Otto Austin Nance Jr.
John Negri Jr.
Joseph Terry Newman
William Pinner Noa Jr.
Sam Oliver
Philip Hackley Parker
William Waldo Partlow
James Perry Passons
Thomas Albert Patton
Herbert Gamble Perkins
Zug Chesley Phelps
Thomas Sharp Porter Jr.
Patrick Benjamin Quinn
Amos Clyde Railey
William D. Richardson
George Eugene Roberts

Walter Eugene Rogers
Julian Warner Saunders
Harry Oscar Schellhase
George Thomas Schleier
James Henry Scholl
James Adam Scott Jr.
Carlton A. Sheram Jr.
Blwyn Marvin Shinn
Charles Willard Smith Jr.
Lucian E. Taliaferro
Quincy W. Thompson Jr.
Raymond Leon Tucker
George William Turrill
William Stone Tyler
Archibald S. Ware Jr.
Harold Douglas Weedon
Warren Henry Welch Jr.
William B. Wetzel
Howell Roy Young

Class of 1944

Bob John Aderhold
Earnest R. Alexander
Richard Eugene Alston
Lee Ernest Barton
Charles M. Brazelton Jr.
Thomas Cleo Brown
Joseph Henry Bunch
Jack Coogan Cameron
Robert H. Canterbury
Roy James Cantlon Jr.
James Durham Cantrell
Elbert Sheridan Clark
Harold Tyrus Cobb
James Wilson Coke
Harrell Leonard Cole
John Daniel Connell
Granville William Cowan
Paul Clifford Crouch
Harry Pearston Curl
John Grandison Delamater
Weldon Warren Dyess
Herbert Dave Erp Jr.
Cloy Donald Farley Jr.
Harold Fink

Ralph Leroy Fisher
William Gonzalez
Leslie Talbert Gordy
Edward Allen Gripp Jr.
Croswell Hall Jr.
Charles E. Harrington Jr.
Melvin G. Hass
Richard L. Haxthausen
Roy David Hughes
Luther Gordon Kent
Joe Don Kunkel
Willard Leo Kunze
Robert Morris Livingston
Joseph Courand Maroney
Bobby Lee Massey
Joe John Maucini Jr.
John Lomax May Jr.
Forrest Warren McCargo
Edward Albert MeKelvey
Charles Carroll McKivett
Raymond Lee Merritt
Frank Allen Milliken
Ben Frank Mills
William Mason Moran
John Marshall Mullins
Irving Murland
James Elias Naham Jr.
James Earl Newberry
Roy Herbert Nunn Jr.
Harland Brady Parks
Garrett Columbus Pamell
Robert Alton Pegues
Frank Edward Phenicie
Aubry Durward Poindexter
Robert King Porter Jr.
Anson Farrand Rideout
Claude Archer Riggs
Howell Clay Robinson
Howell Raymond Rollings
Isaac Samarel
Wilbur Reginald Sanders
John Henry Seay
Forrest David Sharpe
Gerald E. Spofford
Louis Thomas Statton

James Harold Steward
Frederick D. Storey Jr.
Richard Andrew Stromberg
Fred William Sutherland
Lonnie Collins Tucker Jr.
Oscar Glenn Turner
Carl R. Van Hook
Kenneth Glenn Varvel
Burton Leon Wade
George Amos Williams
Otto Thomas Willrich

Class of 1945

Frank G. Albritton
Billy Lavern Allman
Theodore E. Armstrong
Addison A. Bachman
William P. Ballard Jr.
Max Hoyt Barrett
David Irving Binder
James Carlock Black
Jeff George Blair
William B. Blocker Jr.
Carl Andrew Brannen Jr.
Edwin Earnest Brashear
Robert Reese Braswell
Doyle Lee Brown
Jarvis Orr Butler
Henry Joseph Canavespe
Victor Clesi Jr.
James Rufus Collins Jr.
James Edward Connolly
Donald Hugh Cooper
George Lafayette Davis
Harry Lewis Davis
John Joseph Dee Jr.
Roy Young Deveny Jr.
Charles Leroy Dickens
Marshall Clyde Dunn
Weldon Eugene Duty
Alfred Robert Ehlers Jr.
Raymond Arthur Emery Jr.
Leslie Andrew Evans Jr.
Wilbur Randal Flenner Jr.
Marion Flynt Jr.

Henry Lee Forrest
Paul Froberg
Warren Kay Garrett
Bryce Charles Gibson Jr.
Jack Harold Glenn
Norbert Joseph Gorski
Taswell Fielden Hackler
George Allen Halsell Jr.
Charles E. Harrell Jr.
Mark Willard Hertz
Cecil Martin Holekamp
Robert Martin Hyde
Ben Barton Isbell Jr.
William Perkins Johnson
Rufus Jefferson Lackland III
Daniel Richard Lamberson
Joseph Dan Longley
William F. Lovett Jr.
Paul Manning Jr.
Edmundo Martinez
Joe Thornton Mason Jr.
Cyrus Marion McCaskill
Jim Ragsdale McCutcheon
Maxey Ward McGuire
Lee Earl Meyer
James Philip Miller
Melvin Wesley Miller
James Richard Mitchell
Roger Taylor Newton
James Bertrand Noland
Robert Francis Olsen
David Harrison Payne
John A. Pennington
Harold Stacy Pettit
Fred Philip Pipkin Jr.
Ira Elbert Pritchett
Walter Sidney Radley Jr.
Winifred Thomas Rapp
William Walter Redus
Henry King Roark
Pat Neff Roberts Jr.
Harry Connor Robison
Edward William Roeder
Henry Andrew Rougagnac
Theophilus M. Schnell

William Bradbury Sieber
Billy E. Smith
Herbert Gibson Smith Jr.
Leonard Roy Steidel Jr.
Lewis Albert Stein
Homer Jordan Stengel
Charles Henry Taylor
Leonard Tracy Tew
Odis Bert Torbett
Hal Wayne Townsend
Bill Trodlier
Arthur Milton Tubb Jr.
J. T. Turbeville Jr.
Alfred W. Walker Jr.
Benton Joseph Walker Jr.
George Wilbur Wallace Jr.
John Earl Watkins Jr.
Frank Felix Weaver Jr.
Herbert John Weeren Jr.
Grady A. Whitehead Jr.
Burl Tankersley Wiley Jr.
Robert Willis Willeford
Rual H. Williams
James Murphy Willis III
James Hamilton Wilson
Tommy Hereford Winn
Lawrence Miller Wolf
Guy Booth Wyrick
John Marvin Young

Class of 1946

Mercer Greene Abernathy
Johnnie Mack Allman
Calvin Floyd Ballard
Max B. Ernst Bergfeld Jr.
Lynwood Weldon Beyer
Maurice Block Jr.
William Gary Boatright
Dwight Kendall Booth
Earl Taylor Brown Jr.
Ormiston Dalton Brown
William Emmett Bruton
Fred Gordon Buckner
Albert Basil Capt
Arthur Aymar Cater

Donald Marion Cortimilia
Philip Albert Davidson
Ben Luker Dean
John Allsrin DeBell
Eduardo Diego DeLachica
Albert C. Deutsch Jr.
Kenneth Horace Doke
Roger Eugene Edwards
Ernest William Genthner
Ward Crockett Gillespie
Connie Claude Hagemeier
Samuel David Hanks
Elwood Henry Herrmann
Jack Copeland Herron
Gano Ladon Hobgood
Gus Thomas Hodge Jr.
Donald Edgar Hudson
David Reynolds Hughes
Robert Winston Hull
George Norwood Jackson
Jay Neal Jones
William David Jones
Monte William Kaufman
George Henry King
David Vance Lamun
Sam David Lasser
John Galen Lawrence
Thomas Ross Leary
Monteith T. Lincecum
Miles Joseph Luster
Billy Maurice Magee
Warner Harrison Marsh Jr.
William Gould McCarter
Theodore R. McCrocklin
Lawrence Howell McGinnes
William G. Medaris Jr.
John Frankiin Mingos
Cyril Dwight Moreland
Thomas Jackson Paul
Thomas Ray Perkins
James Francis Perry
James Byron Price Jr.
Charles Appelt Ragsdale
Hubert T. Roussel Jr.
John Clovis Sanford

Charles Douglas Saur
Robert Henry Shimer
Ray Parks Shipley
Stanley Dean Smith
Hugh Albert Stanberry Jr.
Leander C. Stedman Jr.
William James Summy
Luther Marney Tillery
John Wiley Waldrop
Fred Shelfer Wilcox Jr.
Robert Vardy Wynne
Horace Edwin Yeary Jr.
Bobby Joe Younger

Class of 1947
Bland Massie Barnes Jr.
John Vernon Cox Jr.

David Allen Harris
Herbert Allan Heinemeier
James Harold Henry
Herbert Otto Koehler Jr.
Jack Storey Lipscomb
Sam William Noto Jr.
William Levert Pietzsch
Thomas Lee Sirman
Douglas B. Stillwagon
Arthur G. Stricklin
Harrell Gene Tilley

Class of 1948
Rodman Laferne Boggs
John Batiste Roemer

NOTES

Chapter 1

1. *Bryan–College Station Eagle* (Mar. 24, 1898); Texas A&M Biennial Report, Dec., 1898, p. 31.
2. *Bryan–College Station Eagle* (Apr. 6, 1917); Texas A&M Biennial Report, 1917–1918, pp. 23–124; Minutes of the Board of Directors, vol. 3 (Mar. 23, 1917), pp. 212–13.
3. "A&M Men Present at Famous Aggie Muster on Apr. 21, 1942, on Island of Corregidor," Corregidor Muster file, Association of Former Students Office (hereinafter cited as AFS), Texas A&M University.
4. Agricultural and Mechanical College of Texas (hereinafter cited as Texas A&M), *Alumni Quarterly* 3 (Feb., 1918): 8; *College Station (Tex.) Battalion* (Dec. 9, 1941; Apr. 23, 1942); *Houston Post* (Nov. 11, 1942); "A&M Men Present at Famous Aggie Muster." In a 1946 address at Texas A&M, Pres. Dwight D. Eisenhower mentioned 700 as the number of soldiers killed in the war, but the number identified has increased to almost 1,000.
5. Col. Thomas Parsons ('49), interview by John A. Adams Jr., Feb. 5, 1999.
6. Texas A&M University Archives (hereinafter cited as TAMU Archives), Vietnam War files; *College Station (Tex.) Battalion* (Nov. 11, 1986); *Bryan–College Station Eagle* (Mar. 14, 1987); *The Texas Military Experience: From the Texas Revolution through World War II*, ed. Joseph G. Dawson (College Station: Texas A&M University Press, 1995), p. 167.
7. Michael A. Kelly, Gulf War file, TAMU Archives and Manuscripts Collection.
8. Gen. Omar Bradley, address to the graduating class of 1950, at Texas A&M's seventy-fifth anniversary, Oct. 4, 1950.
9. James Peeler Anderson, ed., "Address by A. J. Peeler," in *Laws Relating to the Agricultural and Mechanical College of Texas and the Proceedings of the Board of Directors of Said College from June 1, 1875, to January 23, 1878* (Austin, Tex., 1878).
10. "Who Ought to Supply and Control the Education Needed by the People?" in Charles Judson Crane Papers, TAMU Archives.
11. Charles W. Crawford, "One Hundred Years of Engineering at Texas A&M, 1876–1976" (n.p., 1976), pp. 3–97.
12. Henry C. Dethloff, ed., *Thomas Jefferson and American Democracy* (Lexington, Mass.: D. C. Heath, 1971); see William E. Simons, ed., *Professional Military Education in the United States: A Historical Dictionary* (Westport, Conn.: Greenwood Press, 2000), 7, 203–205, 307–309, 327–31.
13. Dethloff, ed., *Thomas Jefferson*, pp. vii–xii, 1–19; Simons, ed., *Professional Military Education*, pp. 8, 203–205, 242–44.
14. Simons, ed., *Professional Military Education*, pp. 203–205, 230–33, 242–44.
15. Rod Andrew Jr., *Long Gray Lines: The Southern Military School Tradition, 1839–1915* (Chapel Hill: University of North Carolina Press, 2001), pp. 2–45.
16. Walter Prescott Webb, *The Texas Rangers: A Century of Frontier Defense* (1935; repr., Austin: University of Texas Press, 1993), pp. 92–93.

17. Marcus J. Wright and Harold B. Simpson, *Texas in the War, 1861–1865* (Hillsboro, Tex.: Hill Junior College Press), pp. 3–70.

18. Ibid., pp. 726–30.

19. Henry C. Dethloff, *Centennial History of Texas A&M University, 1876–1976*, vol. 1 (College Station: Texas A&M University Press, 1975), pp. 38–49.

20. Ibid., pp. 32, 41–43; John A. Adams Jr., *Keepers of the Spirit: The Corps of Cadets at Texas A&M University, 1876–2001* (College Station: Texas A&M University Press, 2001), pp. 14–20.

21. See details of Army Officers Act, 1866; Adams, *Keepers of the Spirit*, pp. 20–23; Dethloff, *Centennial History*, vol. 1, pp. 45–49.

22. See U.S. Congress, House of Representatives, *Depredations on the Frontiers of Texas*, 42nd Cong., 3d sess., exec. doc. 39, Dec. 16, 1872.

23. Bessie Ross Clarke, "S. P. Ross and Sul Ross," pp. 1–35, unpublished manuscript (copy) by the daughter of Lawrence Sullivan Ross in Ross Biographical Papers, Texas A&M University, original in the L. S. Ross Papers, Texas Collection, Baylor University; see J. W. Wilbarger, *Indian Depredations in Texas* (1889; repr., Austin, Tex.: Steck-Vaughn, 1935), pp. 333–39; Ron Tyler, ed., *New Handbook of Texas*, vol. 5 (Austin: Texas State Historical Association, 1996), pp. 688–89; Judith Ann Benner, *Sul Ross: Soldier, Statesman, Educator* (College Station: Texas A&M University Press, 1983).

24. Bessie Ross Clarke, "S. P. Ross and Sul Ross," pp. 1–35, unpublished manuscript (copy) by the daughter of Lawrence Sullivan Ross in Ross Biographical Papers, Texas A&M University, original in the L. S. Ross Papers, Texas Collection, Baylor University; see J. W. Wilbarger, *Indian Depredations in Texas* (1889; repr., Austin, Tex.: Steck-Vaughn, 1935), pp. 333–39; Tyler, ed., *New Handbook of Texas*, vol. 5, pp. 688–89; Judith Ann Benner, *Sul Ross: Soldier, Statesman, Educator* (College Station: Texas A&M University Press, 1983).

Chapter 2

1. *Report of the Agricultural and Mechanical College of Texas, September, 1896–December, 1898* (College Station: A&M College of Texas, 1898), p. 93; G. W. Hardy Letters, AFS war memorial files.

2. H. G. Rickover, *How the Battleship Maine Was Destroyed* (Annapolis, Md.: Naval Institute Press, 1995), p. 3; Graham A. Cosmas, *An Army for Empire: The United States Army in the Spanish American War* (1971; repr., Shippending, Penn.: White Mane, 1994), pp. 34–35.

3. *Olio* (1895), p. 32.

4. Cosmas, *Army for Empire*, pp. 2–6, 34–46.

5. Ibid., pp. 88, 101; see Theodore Roosevelt, *America and the World War* (New York: Charles Scribner's Sons, 1915), pp. 179–83.

6. See Henry C. Dethloff and Allen E. Begnaud, *The American People: Their History to 1900* (Austin, Tex.: Steck-Vaughn, 1972), p. 139.

7. *Bryan–College Station Eagle* (Jan. 20, 1898).

8. Rickover, *Battleship Maine*, pp. 3–45.

9. John C. Hemment, *Cannon and Camera: Sea and Land Battles of the Spanish-American War in Cuba, Camp Life, and the Return of the Soldiers* (New York: D. Appleton, 1898), p. 4.

10. *Bryan–College Station Eagle* (Mar. 3, 1898).

11. The defense appropriation bill is referred to as the Fifty Million Bill. See Walter Millis, *The Martial Spirit* (Chicago: Elephant Paperbacks, 1989), pp. 109–39.

12. Ibid., pp. 85–122; G. W. Hardy Letters, AFS files and letters.

13. This was called the "Volunteer Bill." See Cosmas, *Army for Empire*, pp. 88–100.

14. Gen. Marcus J. Wright, *Leslie's Official History of the Spanish-American War* (Washington, D.C.: War Records Office, 1899), p. 159; "Report of the Agricultural and Mechanical College of Texas, September 1896–December 1898," p. 93; Will E. Hutson to "Dear Mamma," Oct. 21, 1898, and Henry L. Hutson to "Dear Mamma," June 3, 1898, Hutson Papers, TAMU Archives and Manuscripts.

15. G. W. Hardy to E. E. McQuillen, Aug. 19, 1946, G. W. Hardy Letters, AFS files and letters.

16. Nichols to Hardy, Sept. 13, 1946; Gebhart to Hardy, Sept. 13, 1946, G. W. Hardy Letters, AFS files and letters.

17. Gen. Marcus J. Wright, *Leslie's Official History of the Spanish-American War* (Washington, D.C.: War Records Office, 1899), p. 159; "Report of the Agricultural and Mechanical College of Texas, September 1896–December 1898," p. 93.

18. Cosmas, *Army for Empire*, pp. 101–19.

19. Ibid.

20. *Bryan–College Station Eagle* (May 19 and May 26, 1898).

21. Ibid. (June 7, 1898). Camp Mabry was named for Col. Woodford Hayword Mabry, who resigned his post as adjutant general of Texas to assume command of the 1st Texas Volunteers.

22. Bonney Youngblood to G. W. Hardy, Sept. 18, 1946, G. W. Hardy Letters, AFS war memorial files; Henry C. Dethloff, *Centennial History of Texas A&M University, 1876–1976*, vol. 1 (College Station: Texas A&M University Press, 1975), p. 225. Youngblood received an M.S. degree at Texas A&M in 1907 and headed the Texas Agricultural Experiment Station from 1914 to 1927. He served as the principal agricultural economist for the U.S. experiment stations in Washington, D.C., from 1927 until his retirement in 1950.

23. Millis, *Martial Spirit*, pp. 310–15; Cosmas, *Army for Empire*, pp. 276–78.

24. Cosmas, *Army for Empire*, pp. 229–41. Richmond Pearson Hobson, who commanded the attempt, became the first real hero of the war despite the failure of the mission.

25. Ibid., p. 255.

26. *The Spanish-American War: The Cuban Land Campaign, Order of Battle*, booklet no. 4 (Miami: South and Central American Military Historians Society), pp. 76–95; Theodore Roosevelt, *The Rough Riders* (1902; repr., New York: De Capo Press, 1990), pp. 1–54; Millis, *Martial Spirit*, p. 241. The army comprised two infantry brigades under Maj. Gen. Joseph Wheeler, plus cavalry. The Rough Riders, or 1st Volunteer Cavalry Regiment, were partnered with the 10th Cavalry Brigade, while the 9th Cavalry Regiment was assigned to the 1st Brigade, as were the 3rd and 6th Cavalry Regiments. The 9th and 10th Cavalry Regiments were black "Buffalo Soldier" units that had achieved distinction on the western outposts, as they would again in Cuba.

27. Millis, *Martial Spirit*, pp. 281–315; Roosevelt, *Rough Riders*, pp. 156–214.

28. Millis, *Martial Spirit*, pp. 281–315; Roosevelt, *Rough Riders*, pp. 156–214.

29. Milby Porter Scrapbook, TAMU Archives, Cushing Library; *A&M College Battalion* (Jan.–Feb., 1900); H. E. Rawlins ('98) obituary, G. W. Hardy Letters, AFS war memorial files.

30. Milby Porter Scrapbook, TAMU Archives, Cushing Library; *A&M College Battalion* (Jan.–Feb., 1900); H. E. Rawlins ('98) obituary, G. W. Hardy Letters, AFS war memorial files.

31. John A. Adams Jr., *Keepers of the Spirit: The Corps of Cadets at Texas A&M University, 1876–2001* (College Station: Texas A&M University Press, 2001), pp. 52–53.

32. Ibid., pp. 52–53, 118, 125. When the commandant of cadets, Lt. George Bartlett, was promoted and called to active duty, newly commissioned Lt. Charles C. Todd was named interim commandant. He served in that capacity for two months before he himself was called to the Pacific front.

33. Collins C. Brown (Company M) and Eugene Appleby (Company D), *A&M College Battalion* (Mar., 1900).

34. Ibid.

35. Ibid., p. 54.

36. Report of the Agricultural and Mechanical College of Texas (Sept., 1896–Dec., 1898).

Chapter 3

1. See Walter Prescott Webb, *The Great Plains* (Boston: Ginn, 1931); Joseph Bernardo and Eugene H. Bacon, *American Military Policy: Its Development since 1775* (Harrisburg, Penn.: Military Services Publishing, 1955), pp. 278–89.

2. Webb, *The Great Plains*; Bernardo and Bacon, *American Military Policy*, pp. 278–89.

3. Bernardo and Bacon, *American Military Policy*, pp. 290–91.

4. Ibid., pp. 313–16. Largely at the instigation of Elihu Root and with the support of Pres. T. R. Roosevelt, Congress passed the Dick Act on Jan. 21, 1903, which effectively created the National Guard.

5. Walter H. Bradford, "Aggie Fashion: A Survey of the Texas A&M Cadet Uniform through the Years" (n.p., Feb. 23, 1975).

6. Bernardo and Bacon, *American Military Policy*, pp. 314–15. The Texas A&M commandants between 1907 and 1916 included Capt. Andrew M. Moses (1907–1911), Lt. Chauncey L. Fenton (1911–1912), Lt. Levi G. Brown (1912–1914), and Lt. James R. Hill (1914–1916).

7. Ibid.

8. Gen. Peyton C. March, *The Nation at War* (Garden City, N.Y.: Doubleday, Doran, 1932), p. 1.

9. John M. Hart, *Empire and Revolution: The Americans in Mexico since the Civil War* (Berkeley: University of California Press, 2002), pp. 280–304; Thomas R. Fehrenbach, *Lone Star: A History of Texas and the Texans* (New York: Collier Books, 1985), pp. 381, 585–86, 690–92.

10. Hart, *Empire and Revolution*, pp. 305–307. The five Texans in Wilson's cabinet included Thomas W. Gregory (attorney general); former governor Charles A. Culberson (chair, Senate Committee on the Judiciary, 1913–1919); Albert S. Burleson (postmaster, who also served as a member of Congress from 1899 to 1913 and was closely associated with Col. Edwin M. House); Sidney E. Mezes (special advisor); and former Texas A&M president David F. Houston (July, 1902–Sept., 1905; Secretary of Agriculture).

11. John S. D. Eisenhower, *Intervention! The United States and the Mexican Revolution, 1913–1917* (New York: Norton, 1993), pp. 79–138.

12. "Pershing Takes Command of U.S. Troops 'Somewhere along Border,'" *St. Louis Star* (Mar. 14, 1916); Ron Tyler, ed., *New Handbook of Texas*, vol. 5 (Austin: Texas State Historical Association, 1996), p. 164.

13. National Defense Act of 1916, *U.S. Statutes at Large* (1917), pp. 116–217; Edwin P. Parker,

"The Development of the Field Artillery Reserve Officers' Training Corps," *Field Artillery Journal* (July, 1935): 334–42; Timothy J. Dunn, *The Militarization of the U.S.-Mexico Border, 1978–1992: Low-intensity Conflict Doctrine Comes Home* (Austin: CMAS Books, University of Texas at Austin, 1996), pp. 9–10; John Eisenhower with Joanne Thompson Eisenhower, *Yanks: The Epic Story of the American Army in World War I* (New York: Free Press, 2001), p. 23.

14. "Brig. Gen. Claudius M. Easley, 1916," World War II, KIA files, AFS; *Waco News-Tribune* (June, 1945).

15. National Defense Act of 1916; Pearson Menoher, "The Reserve Officers Training Corps," *Cavalry Journal* (Apr., 1920): 70–80; Bowers Davis, "On the Reserve Officers' Training Corps," *Infantry Journal* (Sept., 1930): 290–94; Henry C. Dethloff, *Centennial History of Texas A&M University, 1876–1976*, vol. 1 (College Station: Texas A&M University Press, 1975), pp. 267–69; John A. Adams Jr., *Keepers of the Spirit: The Corps of Cadets at Texas A&M University, 1876–2001* (College Station: Texas A&M University Press, 2001), pp. 90–92; "Officers Reserve Corps," *Alumni Quarterly* (Jan., 1917): 6–8.

16. Victor A. Barraco, interview by Terry H. Anderson, June 4, 1981, TAMU Archives.

17. Barbara W. Tuchman, *The Zimmermann Telegram* (New York: Ballantine, 1985), p. 146. British Naval Intelligence intercepted the secret proposal and decoded it, but, fearing the Germans would detect that their secret code had been broken, withheld its contents for three weeks, even though the British government hoped the contents of this telegram might bring America into the war. Meanwhile, some officials in the Mexican foreign secretary's office actually expressed an interest in the Germans' offer. Great Britain finally chose to inform President Wilson of the contents of the Zimmerman telegram. Even then, Wilson withheld a public release of the note pending Mexico's drafting and acceptance of its new constitution. He delayed its release again until it appeared that Carranza would become the next president of Mexico. On the day before the election of President Carranza, March 1, 1917, Pres. Woodrow Wilson disclosed the contents of the Zimmerman telegram to the American public.

18. Minutes of the Board of Directors, vol. 3 (Mar. 23, 1917), pp. 212–13; *Bryan–College Station Eagle* (Mar. 26, 1917). One of the earliest use of the term "Aggies" appears in the *Alumni Quarterly* (Nov., 1917).

19. Camp Funston was redesignated Camp Stanley in 1918 as a part of the Leon Spring Military Reservation, better known today as Camp Bullis. General Funston's name was given to a camp in his home state of Kansas.

20. *Bryan (Tex.) Daily Eagle and Pilot* (May 18 and June 2, 1917); *San Antonio Express* (June 4, 1917).

21. *San Antonio Express* (June 17, 1917); Texas A&M, "Biennial Report, 1917–1918," p. 125.

22. "At New Post in Puerto Rico," *Texas Aggie* (Sept., 1942). A number of the Aggies who fought in World War I also served again in World War II, as did Ashton and Perrine. Ashton became an Aggie legend by composing the Aggie Muster poem during the Battle of Corregidor. Perrine received a commission in the U.S. Army and remained on active duty. He assumed command of the 141st Infantry in 1941, and in Aug., 1942, he was promoted to brigadier general.

23. Letter, E. E. McQuillen to Ernest Langford, Mar. 11, 1958, G. P. F. Jouine Collections, TAMU Archives; "Jouine Receives His Sixth Wound," *Alumni Quarterly* (Nov., 1918): 19.

Decorations included the Croix de la Légion d'Honneur, Croix de Guerre, three silver stars, the Croix de Combattant, Médaille Interalliée, Médaille de la Grand Guerre, Médaille de Verdun, and Médaille des Blesses (i.e., the French Purple Heart). The U.S. Army awarded him the Purple Heart and four oak-leaf clusters.

24. Letter, E. E. McQuillen to Ernest Langford, Mar. 11, 1958; "Jouine Receives His Sixth Wound," p. 19.

25. "Gold Book: A Tribute to Her Loyal Sons Who Paid the Supreme Sacrifice in the World War," *Alumni Quarterly* (Aug., 1919): 9.

26. William B. Bizzell, "The Service of the College to the Nation," *Alumni Quarterly* (Nov., 1917): 4.

Chapter 4

1. Leonard P. Ayres, *The War with Germany: A Statistical Summary* (Washington, D.C.: GPO, 1919), pp. 17–18; John J. Pershing, *My Experiences in the War*, vol. 1 (New York: Frederick A. Stokes, 1931), pp. 8–13.

2. Ayres, *The War with Germany*, pp. 17–18; Pershing, *My Experiences in the War*, vol. 1, pp. 8–13.

3. William B. Bizzell, "The Service of the College to the Nation," *Alumni Quarterly* (Nov., 1917): 3–6; "General Pershing Praises the American Farmer," *Alumni Quarterly* (Feb., 1917): 23. As of the outbreak of war, funds for military training scheduled under the National Defense Act of 1916 had not been received by the college.

4. John A. Adams Jr., *Keepers of the Spirit: The Corps of Cadets at Texas A&M University, 1876–2001* (College Station: Texas A&M University Press, 2001), pp. 89–92; "Officer Reserve Corps," *Alumni Quarterly* (Jan., 1917): 6–8; Henry C. Dethloff, *Centennial History of Texas A&M University, 1876–1976*, vol. 1 (College Station: Texas A&M University Press, 1975), p. 274.

5. W. L. Driver, "Texas 'Aggies' 1917 Southwest Champions," *Alumni Quarterly* (Feb., 1918): 3–4; "The A. and M. Pep," *Alumni Quarterly* (May, 1918): 14; "Captains of the Four Major Sports for 1918–1919 Session Are in the Service," *Alumni Quarterly* (Nov., 1918): 19; Wilbur Evans and H. B. McElroy, *The Twelfth Man: The Story of Texas A&M Football* (Huntsville, Ala.: Strode, 1974), pp. 77–84.

6. Minutes of the Board of Directors (June 13, 1916); Adams, *Keepers of the Spirit*, pp. 92–94.

7. Dethloff, *Centennial History*, vol. 1, pp. 276–77; *Texas A&M Longhorn* (1919), p. 113; war training enrollments included 1,731 military personnel who completed the course in auto mechanics, 1,305 in signal corps and radio, 338 in meteorology, 82 in machining, 30 in horseshoeing, 56 in blacksmithing, 82 in carpentry, 6 in general mechanics, 12 in surveying, and 6 in topographical drafting.

8. Charles Puryear, "The War and College," *Alumni Quarterly* (Nov., 1918): 3–4; "War Work at the College," *Alumni Quarterly* (Aug., 1918): 4–5, and "Faculty Recommends War Certificates," *Alumni Quarterly* (Aug., 1918): 7; Frank C. Bolton, "With the School of Radio Mechanics," and R. A. Andree, "With the School of Auto and Motor Mechanics," *Alumni Quarterly* (May, 1818): 4–5, 10; *Bryan (Tex.) Daily Eagle and Pilot* (May 25, 1918; Aug. 31, 1918; Sept. 10, 1018). An "Honor War Certificate" was conferred on cadets who "were called to service prior to completing their degree requirements" if they otherwise had "every purpose of receiving a degree."

9. Joe Utay ('08), interview by John A. Adams Jr., May 21, 1976, Dallas; "A. and M. Men to Organize a Cavalry Regiment," *Alumni Quarterly* (Feb., 1918): 12; *Alumni Quarterly* (Aug., 1918): 15.

10. "A. and M. Regiment Is Ready for Federalization," *Alumni Quarterly* (Nov., 1918): 10; "New Draft Expressions," *Waco Daily Times-Herald* (Aug. 25, 1918).

11. "A. and M. Regiment Is Ready for Federalization"; "New Draft Expressions"; Frank E. Vandiver, *Blackjack: The Life and Times of John J. Pershing*, vols. 1–2 (College Station: Texas A&M University Press, 1977), pp. 89–95, 195–213, 360–87, 390, 719–22, 724, 727.

12. Laurence Stallings, *The Doughboys: The Story of the AEF, 1917–1918* (Harper and Row: New York, 1963), pp. 25–27; and see Colonel Frank Tompkins, *Chasing Villa: The Last Campaign of the U.S. Cavalry* (Silver City, New Mexico: High-Lonesome Books, 1996), pp. 231–45.

13. Vandiver, *Blackjack*, p. 738. Training and coordination are now combined.

14. Ibid.; *War Memoirs of David Lloyd George*, vol. 5 (Boston: Little, Brown, 1936), p. 397. The view that the French military plight "teetered toward ruin," notes Vandiver, was a "fetish charmed by the British commanders." In the summer of 1917, the British and French had a combined force of 2,545,500 troops, as compared with 2,149,000 Germans.

15. Joseph Bernardo and Eugene H. Bacon, *American Military Policy: Its Development since 1775* (Harrisburg, Penn.: Military Services Publishing, 1955), pp. 356–57.

16. Ayres, *The War with Germany*, pp. 37–42, 52–54.

17. Ibid., pp. 54–56; Pershing, *My Experiences in the War*, vol. 1, pp. 80–83.

18. *Alumni Quarterly* (Feb., 1918): 20; (Aug., 1919): 8.

19. Frank E. Vandiver, *Blackjack: The Life and Times of John J. Pershing*, vols. 1 and 2 (College Station: Texas A&M University Press, 1977), pp. 89–95, 195–213, 360–87, 390, 719–22, 724, 727.

20. Edward B. Cushing Papers, TAMU Archives, College Station.

21. "The 'OoLaLa' Times," *Alumni Quarterly* (May, 1918): 14; "The OoLaLa Times Feature," *Alumni Quarterly* (Feb., 1919): 22–23.

22. "The Tyree Bell Scholarship," *Texas Aggie* (Oct., 1971); Bell was named a Distinguished Alumni of Texas A&M in 1964.

23. World War I letters, AFS files and records, TAMU Archives.

24. Vandiver, *Blackjack*, pp. 840–41, 864–66, 871, 883; Stallings, *Doughboys*, pp. 43–47, 77; B. D. Liddell Hart, "The Strategy of 1918," in *Strategy* (New York: Frederick A. Praeger, 1968), pp. 202–19.

25. Pershing, *My Experiences in the War*, vol. 1, pp. 9–11; Larry I. Bland, *The Papers of George Catlett Marshall*, vol. 1 (Baltimore: John Hopkins University Press, 1981), pp. 136–42; Stallings, *Doughboys*, pp. 56–74.

26. Pershing, *My Experiences in the War*, vol. 1, pp. 9–11; Bland, *The Papers of George Catlett Marshall*, vol. 1, pp. 136–42; Stallings, *Doughboys*, pp. 56–74.

27. Stallings, *Doughboys*, pp. 80–83.

28. "Captain Trickey Has a Narrow Escape," *Alumni Quarterly* (Nov., 1918): 11.

29. Ayres, *War with Germany*, pp. 85–100.

30. "Captain George F. Wellage Cited for Bravery," *Alumni Quarterly* (Aug., 1918): 13.

31. Ayres, *War with Germany*, pp. 85–100; World War I KIA, AFS files and records, TAMU Archives.

32. Pershing, *My Experiences in the War*, vol. 2, p. 211; Stallings, *Doughboys*, pp. 141–57; E. L. Stephens to "Ernest" (n.d.) [Dec., 1918], E. L. Stephens Papers, Southwestern Archives and Manuscripts Collections, University of Southwestern Louisiana, Lafayette, La.

33. George C. Marshall, *Memoirs of My Services in the World War* (Boston: Houghton Mifflin, 1976), p. 117.

34. World War I KIA, AFS files and records, TAMU Archives.

35. Letter from Maj. Chester A. Davis, commander, 3rd Machine Gun Bn., to Mrs. S. L. Moore, *Alumni Quarterly* (Nov., 1918): 6.

36. *New York Times* (July 14, 1918).

37. Ayres, *War with Germany*, p. 46; Pershing, *My Experiences in the War*, vol. 2, pp. 171–75.

38. *The Americans in the Great War*, vol. 3 (Clermont-Ferrand, France: Michelin, 1920), pp. 22–29; Stallings, *Doughboys*, pp. 207–14; Marshall, *Memoirs*, pp. 141–47. The U.S. divisions in the action included the 1st, 2nd, 5th, 19th, 26th, 42nd, 82nd, and 90th.

39. "Major Morris Writes an Interesting Letter from France," *Alumni Quarterly* (Nov., 1918): 8–9.

40. "Major Ashburn Cited for Bravery and Awarded the DSC," *Alumni Quarterly* (Feb., 1919): 21: Adams, *Keepers of the Spirit*, pp. 107–109.

41. "Gold Book," *Alumni Quarterly* (Aug., 1919): 4–24.

42. Ibid.

43. *Alumni Quarterly* 3 (Feb., 1918): 8; Dethloff, *Centennial History*, vol. 1, pp. 281–82; John A. Adams Jr., *Softly Call the Muster* (College Station: Texas A&M University Press, 1994), pp. 10–11.

Chapter 5

1. *Alumni Quarterly* (Feb., 1919): 11, 16; (May, 1919): 21.

2. Walter H. Bradford, "Aggie Fashion: A Survey of the Texas A&M Cadet Uniform through the Years" (n.p.: Feb. 23, 1875), p. 6.

3. W. O. Thompson, "Military Training at Educational Institutions," *Infantry Journal* (May, 1929): 500.

4. Ibid., pp. 104–105.

5. The advisory board of the War Department, *Committee on Education and Special Training: A Review of Its Work during 1918* (Washington, D.C.: War Department, June 19, 1919), pp. 33–37, 143–44; "War Department Closes Up Its Affairs at College," *Alumni Quarterly* (Nov., 1919): 19; Col. Waldo C. Potter, "Field Artillery Units of the Reserve Officers' Training Corps," *Field Artillery Journal* 9 (1919): 20–21. See also Maj. Person Menoher, "The Reserve Officers Training Corps," *Cavalry Journal* (Apr., 1920): 70–80.

6. Frank C. Bolton, "Reserve Officer Training Corps on a New Basis," *Alumni Quarterly* (Feb., 1919): 7–8.

7. Ibid., pp. 7, 24; *Alumni Quarterly* (May, 1919): 26; "Artillery Unit Organized at A. & M. College," *A&M College Battalion* (May 1, 1919), p. 1; Raymond Walters, "Field Artillery in American Colleges," *Field Artillery Journal* (Nov.–Dec., 1919): 543–55; Edwin Parker, "The Development of the Field Artillery Reserve Officers' Training Corps," *Field Artillery Journal* (July, 1935): 334–40; *Texas A&M Longhorn* (1919), pp. 119–24.

8. "College Once Again Designated a Distinguished Institution," *Reveille* (June 15, 1919), p. 1; John A. Adams Jr., *Keepers of the Spirit: The Corps of Cadets at Texas A&M University,*

1876–2001 (College Station: Texas A&M University Press, 2001), pp. 105–10; Bess Stephenson, "Texas A&M Has Provided More U.S. Army Officers Than Any Other Institution," *College Station* (Tex.) *Battalion* (Mar. 6, 1942), p. 1.

9. Peyton C. March, *The Nation at War* (New York: Doubleday, 1932), pp. 340–43; Joseph Bernardo and Eugene H. Bacon, *American Military Policy: Its Development since 1775* (Harrisburg, Penn.: Military Services Publishing, 1955), pp. 385, 387. In his memoir, General March notes (with some irony) that the defeated postwar German army, "in order to make her impotent," was limited to one hundred thousand soldiers.

10. Henry Dethloff and Donald H. Dyal, *Special Kind of Doctor: A History of Veterinary Medicine in Texas* (College Station: Texas A&M University Press, 1991), pp. 58–73. Colleges and universities often provided housing, medical facilities, and other amenities that would otherwise have been constructed by the military.

11. Monroe MacCloskey, *Reserve Officers Training Corps: Campus Pathways to Service Commissions* (New York: Richards Rosen Press, 1965), pp. 36–37; David L. Chapman, *Wings over Aggieland* (College Station: Texas A&M Friends of the Library, 1944), pp. 18–20.

12. MacCloskey, *Reserve Officers Training Corps*, pp. 36–37; Chapman, *Wings over Aggieland*, pp. 18–20.

13. "A Cavalry Unit Has Been Authorized Established at College," *Alumni Quarterly* (Nov., 1919): 9; "R.O.T.C. Units Highly Commended," *Alumni Quarterly* (Feb., 1920): 21–23; Adams, *Keepers of the Spirit*, pp. 107–10.

14. George B. Tindall, *America* (New York: W. W. Norton, 1988), p. 1155.

15. Bernardo and Bacon, *American Military Policy*, p. 389.

16. Herbert Hoover, *The Ordeal of Woodrow Wilson: 1874–1964* (New York: McGraw-Hill, 1958), pp. 279–93; Bernard M. Baruch, *Baruch: The Public Years* (New York: Holt, Rinehart, and Winston, 1960), pp. 140–45; P. L. Miles, "Orientation of R.O.T.C. Freshmen," *Infantry Journal* (Sept., 1931): 439–42.

17. Newton A. McCully, *The McCully Report: The Russo-Japanese War, 1904–1905* (Annapolis, Md.: Naval Institute, 1977), pp. vii–ix, 243–56.

18. Ronald H. Spector, *At War at Sea: Sailors and Naval Combat in the Twentieth Century* (New York: Viking, 2001), pp. 144, 152–53.

19. Baruch, *Baruch*, pp. 265–66. According to Baruch, the American public strongly endorsed the idea that the nation should "lighten the costly burden of arms and diminish the danger of loaded guns."

20. Adams, *Keepers of the Spirit*, pp. 117–21.

21. Ibid.; "A. & M. Cadet Corps Largest in Country," *College Station* (Tex.) *Battalion* (Feb. 19, 1924), p. 5; "Texas A. and M.," *Texas A&M Longhorn* (1925), pp. 20–21; John A. Adams Jr., *We Are the Aggies: The Texas A&M University Association of Former Students* (College Station: Texas A&M University Press, 1979), pp. 131–33; statement of Gen. Douglas MacArthur, chief of staff, *Annual Report of the Secretary of War* (Washington, D.C.: GPO, 1931), pp. 44–45; Gen. C. P. Summerall, "The Officers' Reserve Corps," *Infantry Journal* (Nov., 1930): 461–65.

22. Minutes of the Board of Directors, vol. 4 (Oct. 15, 1926), p. 86, and vol. 4 (May 30, 1930), p. 53; see Henry C. Dethloff, *Centennial History of Texas A&M University, 1876–1976*, vol. 2 (College Station: Texas A&M University Press, 1975), pp. 409, 414; Bowers Davis, "On the Reserve Officers Training Corps," *Infantry Journal* (Sept., 1930): 290.

23. Barrington Boardman, *Isaac Asimov Presents from Harding to Hiroshima: an Anecdotal History of the United States from 1923 to 1945 Based on Little-known Facts and the Lives of the People Who Made History—and Some Who Didn't* (New York: Dembner Books, 1988), p. 128.

24. "War!" *College Station* (Tex.) *Battalion* (Feb. 3, 1932), p. 2.

25. "Aggies Oppose Disarmament and Prohibition but Uphold ROTC," *College Station* (Tex.) *Battalion* (Apr. 6, 1932), p. 2; "War Lords or Thinkers?" *College Station* (Tex.) *Battalion* (Mar. 30, 1932), p. 2; Haynes W. Dugan, "The History of the Great Class of 1934" (College Station, Tex.), pp. 33–40, 86–89; "ROTC Is Upheld by Supreme Court of United States," *College Station* (Tex.) *Battalion* (Dec. 6, 1933), p. 1

26. *College Station* (Tex.) *Battalion* (Nov. 8, 1933), p. 1.

27. Dethloff, *Centennial History*, vol. 2, pp. 432–33; Bernardo and Bacon, *American Military Policy*, p. 401.

28. Ion M. Bethel, "Aggie Generals," AFS files and records, TAMU Archives.

29. See "Aggie Generals," AFS files and records, TAMU Archives. Davis's title was "General de Brigada, Ejericito Nacional de Guatemala."

30. Dugan, "Class of 1934," pp. 36–37.

31. Gen. Bernard Schriever, interview by John A. Adams Jr., Aug. 9, 1999; U.S. Air Force, *Of Flight and Bold Men* (Washington, D.C.: GPO, 1968); "Aviation Hall of Fame Honors Schriever," *Texas Aggie* (Sept., 1980), p. 21.

32. Spector, *At War at Sea*, pp. 141–43.

33. J. E. Volonte, "Our Future Navy: Toward a Two-ocean Supremacy," *Army-Navy*, 1941 (Nov. 29, 1941), p. 180; George H. Beverley biographical, AFS files and records, TAMU Archives.

34. John Mack Faragher, Mari Jo Buhle, Daniel Czitrom, and Susan H. Armitage, *Out of Many: A History of the American People*, vol. 2 (Upper Saddle River, N.J.: Prentice-Hall, 1997), pp. 794–95.

35. Text of President Roosevelt's May 11, 1937, address in president's personal file, p. 1053, Franklin D. Roosevelt Papers, Hyde Park, N.Y.; "FDR Tells A&M Students of Opportunities to Serve," *Houston Post* (May 12, 1937), p. 1; Joe Utay ('08), interview by John A. Adams Jr., May 21, 1976, Dallas. See also Edna M. Smith, ed., *Aggies, Moms, and Apple Pie* (College Station: Texas A&M University Press, 1987), p. xvi.

36. Dethloff, *Centennial History*, vol. 2, pp. 438, 445–46; Adams, *Keepers of the Spirit*, pp. 135–37. The military science building opened in 1924 as the Extension Service Building.

37. "A&M Cadets to Be Offered One-Year Regular Training," *College Station* (Tex.) *Battalion* (Mar. 31, 1937), p. 1; Maj. Gen. Ray Murray ('35), interview by John A. Adams Jr., Oct. 16, 1999, College Station, Tex. In July, 1937, the Thompson Act allowed one thousand reserve officers to come on active duty for a one-year tenure.

38. Dugan, "Class of 1934," p. 180.

39. Minutes of the Board of Directors, vol. 6 (Aug. 6, 1940), p. 39; *College Station* (Tex.) *Battalion* (Mar. 7, 1942); Charles Monroe Johnson, *Action with the Seaforths* (New York: Vantage Press, 1954), flyleaf.

40. *College Station* (Tex.) *Battalion* (Dec. 9, 1941); KIA files, AFS files and records, TAMU Archives; "He Was Just Doing His Duty," *Texas Aggie* (June, 1999), p. 30.

41. Franklin Delano Roosevelt, address to Congress, December 8, 1941.

Chapter 6

1. Keyes Carson to Richard O. ("Buck") Weirus, Dec. 5, 1960, AFS World War II KIA files and records, TAMU Archives; Martin Gilbert, *The Second World War: A Complete History* (New York: Henry Holt, 1989), pp. 272–95.

2. "Buck Jordan," clippings and notes, Aggies in War papers, TAMU Archives.

3. "He Was Just Doing His Duty," *Texas Aggie* (June, 1999), p. 30.

4. Gilbert, *The Second World War*, pp. 272–95; Capt. Sydney R. Greer ('35), AFS World War II files, TAMU Archives.

5. Louis Morton, *Strategy and Command: The First Two Years*, vol. 10, *The U.S. Army in World War II: The War in the Pacific* series (Washington, D.C.: GPO, 1962), pp. 16–18; Newton A. McCully, *The McCully Report: The Russo-Japanese War, 1904–1905* (Annapolis, Md.: Naval Institute Press, 1977), pp. vii–ix, 243–56.

6. Edward S. Miller, *War Plan Orange: The U.S. Strategy to defeat Japan, 1897–1945* (Annapolis, Md.: Naval Institute Press, 1991), pp. 19–30.

7. Morton, *Strategy and Command*, pp. 24–25.

8. Ibid., pp. 28–29.

9. Ibid., p. 35.

10. *Texas A&M Longhorn* (1908), p. 166; John A. Adams Jr., *Keepers of the Spirit: The Corps of Cadets at Texas A&M University, 1876–2001* (College Station: Texas A&M University Press, 2001), pp. 136–45.

11. Joe Utay, interview by John A. Adams Jr., May 21, 1976, Dallas; *Texas Aggie* Apr. 15, 1937; May 12, 1938; Mar. 1, 1939; "A. & M. Loses," College Station (Tex.) *Battalion*, July 4, 1940.

12. Miller, *War Plan Orange*, pp. 56–60, 153–55, 362; Tom Hanson, "The Guns of Corregidor: A Close-up Look at an Island Fortress," *Pacific Stars and Stripes* (Dec. 29, 1991); F. M. Flanagan, *Corregidor: The Rock Force Assault* (Novato, Calif.: Presidio Press, 1988), pp. 21–33.

13. *Reports of General MacArthur: The Campaigns of MacArthur in the Pacific*, vol. 1 (Washington, D.C.: GPO, 1966), pp. 14–16; Jonathan M. Wainwright, *General Wainwright's Story* (New York: Doubleday, 1946), pp. 9–10; Morton, *Strategy and Command*, pp. 136–39.

14. *Reports of General MacArthur*, pp. 14–16; Wainwright, *General Wainwright's Story*, pp. 9–10; Morton, *Strategy and Command*, pp. 136–39.

15. John Toland, *But Not in Shame: The Six Months after Pearl Harbor* (New York: Random House, 1961), p. 270; Tom Dooley ('35), interview by John A. Adams Jr., Oct. 21, 1991; Morton, *Strategy and Command*, pp. 541–47. See also John J. Beck, *MacArthur and Wainwright: Sacrifice of the Philippines* (Albuquerque: University of New Mexico Press, 1974), p. 144.

16. Harry A. Gailey, *War in the Pacific: From Pearl Harbor to Tokyo Bay* (Novato, Calif.: Presidio Press, 1997), pp. 117–23.

17. Wainwright, *General Wainwright's Story*, pp. 104–16; *Texas A&M Longhorn* (1943), p. 69.

18. Morton, *Strategy and Command*, pp. 181–97, 265; Flanagan, *Corregidor*, p. 54.

19. John C. Adams, *The Voices of a Proud Tradition: A Collection of Aggie Muster Speeches* (Bryan: Brazos Valley Printing, 1985), pp. 154–55.

20. Col. Tom Dooley, interview by John A. Adams Jr., Oct. 21, 1991. See also *Texas Aggie* (Apr. 22 and May 2, 1942).

21. Felix McKnight, "Aggies Sure Corregidor in Capable Hands," *Dallas Morning News*

(Apr. 22, 1942); *Time* (Jan. 12, 1942; May 4, 1942); "Historic Meeting Held by Texas Aggies on Corregidor," *Eagle* (Nov. 11, 1942); *Congressional Record*, Apr. 20, 1942, p. A1453. See also 1942 Muster file, TAMU Archives.

22. Coleman, *Bataan and Beyond*, p. 72; Flanagan, *Corregidor*, pp. 67–77; Gerard M. Devlin, *Back to Corregidor* (New York: St. Martin's Press, 1992), pp. 20–23; Beck, *MacArthur and Wainwright*, pp. 216–21.

23. *Atlanta Journal Constitution* (Apr. 20, 1942).

24. Col. Tom Dooley ('35), interview by John A. Adams Jr., Oct. 21, 1991; *Texas Aggie* (Apr. 22 and May 5, 1942).

25. Wainwright, *General Wainwright's Story*, pp. 110–13.

26. Flanagan, *Corregidor*, pp. 67–77; Gerard M. Devlin, *Back to Corregidor* (New York: St. Martin's Press, 1992), pp. 20–23; Beck, *MacArthur and Wainwright*, pp. 216–21.

27. Jim Black, interview by John A. Adams Jr., Apr. 20–21, 1992, and site visit to Malinta tunnels on Corregidor.

28. John S. Coleman Jr., *Bataan and Beyond: Memories of an American POW* (College Station: Texas A&M University Press, 1978), pp. 76–77.

29. Elizabeth H. Lewis to Tina Evans Wright, editorial assistant, *Texas Aggie*, May 30, 1994, with affidavit from William E. Lewis, Lubbock County, Tex. (n.d.), AFS WW II veteran files, TAMU Archives.

30. Ibid.

31. Ibid.

32. AFS KIA files, TAMU Archives.

33. Speech delivered by Lt. Col. Y. Nagatomo to Allied prisoners of war at Thanbuyuzhat, Burma, on Oct. 28, 1942, AFS World War II files, TAMU Archives.

34. "Aggie Heroes Freed from Japs," *College Station* (Tex.) *Battalion* (Sept. 6, 1945); press release, Armed Forces Public Information Service, July 28, 1949, George Moore biographical file, TAMU Archives.

35. Adams, *Softly Call the Muster*, pp. 25–28.

36. Henry C. Dethloff, *Centennial History of Texas A&M University, 1876–1976*, vol. 2 (College Station: Texas A&M University Press, 1975), pp. 461–62.

Chapter 7

1. Bill Adams, interview by Terry H. Anderson, Aug. 20, 2002, College Station, Tex., TAMU Archives; draft memorandum from Pres. Earl Rudder to the Honorable Steven Ailes, AFS World War II files and records, TAMU Archives.

2. Keyes Carson to Richard O. ("Buck") Weirus, Dec. 5, 1960, AFS World War II KIA files and records, TAMU Archives; Eric Morris, *The American Alamo of World War II: Corregidor* (1981; repr., New York: Cooper Square Press, 2000).

3. Bill Adams, interview by Terry H. Anderson, Aug. 20, 2002, College Station, Tex., TAMU Archives.

4. Dedication of Bruce Memorial Hall, Nov. 10, 1972; biography, Lt. Gen. Andrew Davis Bruce; "A Salute to Dad," by A. D. Bruce, in AFC WW II files and records, TAMU Archives.

5. Brig. Gen. Kay Halsell II, interview by Terry H. Anderson, Sept. 17, 1981, TAMU Archives.

6. Ibid.

7. Bill Adams, interview by Terry H. Anderson, Aug. 20, 2002, College Station, Tex., TAMU Archives.

8. Maj. Gen. Frederick H. Weston, military questionnaire, TAMU Archives.

9. Brig. Gen. Aubry L. Moore, military questionnaire, TAMU Archives.

10. Ibid.

11. Brig. Gen. William L. Lee, military questionnaire, TAMU Archives.

12. Robert Francis Worden, USAF, biographical, TAMU Archives.

13. Brig. Gen. Kyle L. Riddle, USAF biography, TAMU Archives.

14. Maj. Gen. Guy H. Goddard, U.S. Air Force biography, TAMU Archives; Brig. Gen., Durant S. Buchanan, USMC, military questionnaire, TAMU Archives; Henry C. Dethloff, *Centennial History of Texas A&M University, 1876–1976*, vol. 2 (College Station: Texas A&M University Press, 1975), pp. 474–75.

15. Albert MacQueen Bledsoe, biography and military questionnaire, TAMU Archives.

16. Maj. Gen. John H. Buckner, military questionnaire, TAMU Archives; Brig. Gen. George H. Beverley; Brig. Gen. Durant S. Buchanan, AFS military questionnaire, TAMU Archives.

17. Brig. Gen. Guy M. Townsend, USAF biography, TAMU Archives.

18. Hiram Broiles obituary (Redding, Calif.), TAMU Archives; *Texas Aggie* (Nov., 1992), p. 9.

19. *Texas Aggie* (June, 1966), p. 7 (Nov., 1966), pp. 9–10; Dethloff, *Centennial History of Texas A&M University*, vol. 2, pp. 471–72.

20. Ibid.; *Texas Aggie* (Sept., 1980), p. 21.

21. *Texas Aggie* (June, 1966); Dethloff, *Centennial History*, vol. 2, pp. 578–79.

22. Brig. Gen. Manning Eugene Tillery, military questionnaire, TAMU Archives; Maj. Gen. Robert B. Williams, military questionnaire, TAMU Archives.

23. Dethloff, *Centennial History*, vol. 2, pp. 470–74; Maj. Gen. Guy H. Goddard, military questionnaire, TAMU Archives; Brig. Gen. George H. Beverley, AFS military questionnaire, TAMU Archives.

24. *Texas Aggie* (May, 1976), p. 13; AFS generals' biographical file, TAMU Archives.

25. *Texas Aggie* (Mar., 1975), p. 11; Robert R. ("Bob") Herring, AFS World War II biographies, TAMU Archives.

26. *Texas Aggie* (July, 1967), p. 27.

27. AFS KIA lists, TAMU Archives.

28. Brig. Gen. George H. Beverley, interview by Terry H. Anderson, July 16, 1981, TAMU Archives.

29. Newsletter, 385th *Bomb Group (Heavy) Memorial Association* (BGMA) (Aug., 1992), p. 18; letter, Lawrence Oliver to "Dear Ed," written in 1989, under cover of Ed Morton to Henry C. Dethloff, July 26, 2002, in Aggies in War papers and correspondence, TAMU Archives.

30. Maj. Gen. Homer S. Hill, military questionnaire, TAMU Archives.

31. AFS KIA lists, TAMU Archives.

32. AFS World War II biographies, TAMU Archives.

33. *Sacramento Union* (July 7, 1971); AFS William C. Tinus biography, TAMU Archives; Travis M. Hetherington, interview by Terry H. Anderson, Aug. 12, 1980, TAMU Archives.

34. *Texas Aggie* (Jan., 1973), p. 14; very successful in the electronics industry after the war, McMullin established a Presidential Endowed Scholarship at Texas A&M in 1972.

35. Army Strategic Communications Command, press release, Apr. 6, 1970, AFS biography, TAMU Archives.

36. AFS Henry C. Wendler biography, TAMU Archives.

37. Joe G. Hanover, biographical sketch, TAMU Archives.

38. Maj. Gen. George P. Munson Jr., military questionnaire; AFS Frank H. Newnam Jr. biography, TAMU Archives.

39. Andy Rollins to Richard ("Buck") Weirus, July 1, 1971; Maj. Gen. Andrew P. Rollins, military questionnaire; Distinguished Service Medal Award to Brig. Gen. Andrew P. Rollins Jr., TAMU Archives.

40. AFS Lt. Col. Crawford H. Booth, TAMU Archives.

41. Note to Henry Dethloff from Gen. William A. Becker, Dec. 12, 2002, in Aggies in War papers, TAMU Archives.

42. *The Biography of Robert H. Haight, D.V.M.* (n.p, n.d.), pp. 7–22, TAMU Archives.

43. Ibid.

44. News from the U.S. Army Medical Department (Apr. 28, 1972), TAMU Archives.

45. Ogbourne D. Butler, interview by Terry H. Anderson, Apr. 29, 1983, TAMU Archives.

46. Fred W. Dollar, interview by Terry H. Anderson, Sept. 7, 2002, College Station, Tex., TAMU Archives.

Chapter 8

1. Ed Rector, "The Original Flying Tigers," http://www.flyingtigersavg.com.

2. Ibid.

3. Maj. Gen. Charles R. Bond Jr., USAF (ret.), résumé, AFS files and records, TAMU Archives; and see Charles R. Bond Jr. and Terry H. Anderson, *A Flying Tiger's Diary* (College Station: Texas A&M University Press, 1984).

4. Sir Knight Joseph E. Bennett, "Brother Tex Hill: Flying Tiger Ace," *Knight Templar* (Oct., 2000), pp. 25–29.

5. James Doolittle, in "The Reminiscences of James Harold Doolittle in the Aviation Project collection of the Columbia University Oral History Research Office," interview by Kenneth W. Leish, 1960 (see http://www.fathom.com/feature/122209, hereinafter cited as "The Reminiscences of James H. Doolittle"); Harry A. Gailey, *War in the Pacific: From Pearl Harbor to Tokyo Bay* (Novato, Calif.: Presidio Press, 1997), pp. 146–47.

6. Craig Nelson, *The First Heroes: The Extraordinary Story of the Doolittle Raid—America's First World War II Victory* (New York: Viking, 2002), p. 58.

7. Ibid., pp. 12–15; Ted W. Lawson, *Thirty Seconds over Tokyo* (New York: Penguin, 1944), pp. 3–27.

8. Nelson, *The First Heroes*, p. 51.

9. James H. ("Jimmy") Doolittle with Carroll V. Glines, *I Could Never Be So Lucky Again* (New York: Bantam Books, 1991), p. 2.

10. Nelson, *The First Heroes*, p. 61.

11. Mitsuo Fuchida and Masatake Okumiya, *Midway: The Battle That Doomed Japan* (Annapolis, Md.: Naval Institute Press, 1955), pp. 66–71. This is the Japanese version (translated into English) of the war in the Pacific during the first half of 1942.

12. Louis Morton, *Strategy and Command: The First Two Years*, vol. 10, *The U.S. Army in World War II: The War in the Pacific* series (Washington, D.C.: GPO, 1962), pp. 270–73.

13. Fuchida and Okumiya, *Midway*, pp. 70–71.

14. William Boyd, interview by John A. Adams Jr., Feb. 17, 1992; Morton, *Strategy and Command*, p. 274.

15. Carroll V. Glines, *Doolittle's Tokyo Raiders* (New York: Ayers, 1992), pp. 270–73; "Doolittle's Raid: Here's One for Allied 'Captives' in Philippines," *Officer* (Apr., 1992), pp. 50–56; Morton, *Strategy and Command*, pp. 273–74.

16. Ibid.; Vonda L. Parker to Jerry Cooper, Feb. 21, 1992, and clipping, Cindy Hicks, "James M. Parker, Local WW II Hero" (n.d.), TAMU Archives. Also see Glines, *Doolittle's Tokyo Raiders*.

17. Capt. Robert M. Gray ('41), Killeen, Tex., and Lt. Bobby M. Godwin ('42), Fort Worth, Tex., AFS World War II KIA files, TAMU Archives.

18. "The Reminiscences of James H. Doolittle"; and see Gailey, *War in the Pacific*, pp. 133–40.

19. Lt. Ted Adair Hilger, Houston, Tex., AFS World War II KIA files, TAMU Archives.

20. Ibid.; *Texas Aggie* (Nov., 1996), p. 21; Lost Battalion Association, files and records, TAMU Archives.

21. Address by Gavin Daws at the dedication of the monument honoring the Lost Battalion and Houston survivors, National Memorial Cemetery of the Pacific, Honolulu, Hawaii, May 4, 1994, AFS World War II files and records, TAMU Archives.

22. Gailey, *War in the Pacific*, pp. 147–53.

23. Ibid., pp. 152–71.

24. "And Then There Were None," *Texas Aggie* (Jan., 1995); *Houston Chronicle* (June 3, 2002), p. 6A; Henry C. Dethloff, *Centennial History of Texas A&M University, 1876–1976*, vol. 2 (College Station: Texas A&M University Press, 1975), p. 455.

25. "And Then There Were None"; *Houston Chronicle* (June 3, 2002), p. 6A; Dethloff, *Centennial History of Texas A&M University, 1876–1976*, vol. 2, p. 455.; George H. Gay Jr., *Sole Survivor: The Battle of Midway and Its Effect on His Life* (Naples, Fla: Naples Ad/Graphics Services, 1979); Gay died of a heart attack in Marietta, Ga., on Oct. 21, 1994.

26. Maj. Earl O. Hall, AFS World War II KIA files, TAMU Archives; Thomas Hubert Akarman, AFS World War II KIA files, TAMU Archives.

27. Gailey, *War in the Pacific*, pp. 170–71; Mavis P. Kelsey Sr., *Twentieth Century Doctor: House Calls to Space Medicine* (College Station: Texas A&M University Press, 1999), pp. 140–47.

28. Kelsey, *Twentieth Century Doctor*, pp. 140–47.

29. Ibid.

30. Ibid.

31. Ibid., pp. 147–51.

32. First Lt. Roy Kasson Bliler, interview by John R. Hatch, Nov. 18, 1985, TAMU Archives. Alaskan outposts often contributed to alcoholism and serious psychological problems. Hypothermia was a constant danger, and accidents occurred not infrequently.

33. Ibid.

34. Ibid.

35. Stan Cohen, *A Pictorial History of World War II in Alaska and Northwestern Canada* (Missoula, Mont.: Pictorial Histories, 1981), pp. 188–93.

36. Martin Gilbert, *The Second World War: A Complete History* (New York: Henry Holt, 1989), p. 350; Patrick K. O'Donnell, *Into the Rising Sun* (New York: Free Press, 2002), pp. 17–23.

37. O'Donnell, *Into the Rising Sun*, pp. 40–42.

38. Lt. (jg) Warren K. Garrett, Lt. Wiley H. Craft, Samuel T. Gillespie, AFS World War II KIA files, TAMU Archives.

39. *Fort Bend County Herald–Coaster* (July 27, 2003); C. C. Taylor, memorandum re: Lindsey I. Lipscomb (n.d.); Aggies in War files, TAMU Archives; see respective names at http://lib-oldweb.tamu.edu/aggiesinwar/.

40. O'Donnell, *Into the Rising Sun*, pp. 53–68; Lt. Felix B. Lester, AFS World War II KIA files, TAMU Archives.

41. First Lt. John William Crow ('35), AFS World War II KIA files, TAMU Archives.

42. Flying officer William Byron ("Billy") Gibbs ('43); Lt. James Albert Harris ('38), AFS World War II KIA files, TAMU Archives.

43. Brig. Gen. Victor A. Barraco, interview by Terry H. Anderson, June 4, 1981, TAMU Archives.

44. Ibid.

45. Brig. Gen. James P. Newberry, interview by Terry H. Anderson, June 10, 1982, TAMU Archives.

46. Capt. Elbert B. ("Tex") Anding ('26), AFS World War II KIA files, TAMU Archives.

47. William P. Ballard Jr. ('45), S1/c, AFS World War II KIA files, TAMU Archives.

48. Lt. William Henry Baker, AFS KIA files, TAMU Archives; Gilbert, *The Second World War*, pp. 353–54.

49. Walter J. Boyne, *Clash of Wings: World War II in the Air* (New York: Simon and Schuster/Touchstone Books, 1994), pp. 282–320.

50. Maj. Gen. John Buckner, interview by Terry H. Anderson, July 30, 1981, Jacksonville, Tex., TAMU Archives.

51. Ibid. Later, as assistant group operations officer, Buckner participated in and directed the escort of the paratroopers and gliders during the Normandy invasion and soon commanded the 365th Fighter Squadron, fighting throughout Europe to the close of the war.

52. Lt. T. P. Aycock ('40), AFS World War II KIA files; Lt. John Harold Allen, AFS World War II KIA files; Tech. Sgt. Thomas H. Gilliland ('42), AFS World War II KIA files, TAMU Archives.

53. Lt. Warren George Jr., AFS KIA files; S.Sgt. Robert C. Elliott ('42); TAMU Archives.

54. Glenn H. Reynolds to Henry Dethloff, May 8, 2004, Aggies in War Papers, TAMU Archives.

Chapter 9

1. Rick Atkinson, *An Army at Dawn: The War in North Africa, 1942–1943* (New York: Henry Holt, 2002), pp. 4, 160; Lt. Gen. James F. Hollingsworth, interview by Terry H. Anderson, Aug. 18, 1982, TAMU Archives.

2. John Keegan, ed., *World War II: A Visual Encyclopedia* (London: PRC, 1999), pp. 482–83, 485.

3. Brig. Gen. George H. Beverley, interview by Terry H. Anderson, July 16, 1981, TAMU Archives.

4. Atkinson, *An Army at Dawn*, pp. 44–45.

5. Ibid., pp. 62, 66; Keegan, *World War II*, pp. 17–19.

6. Atkinson, *An Army at Dawn*; Keegan, *World War II*, pp. 26, 36, 44–45, 70–77, 91, 112, 129–44.

7. Atkinson, *An Army at Dawn*; Keegan, *World War II*, pp. 70–77, 129–30; Lt. (jg) Charles W. Gerhardt, AFS KIA files, TAMU Archives.

8. Atkinson, *An Army at Dawn*, pp. 129–30; 1st Lt. Gambrell W. Haltom, AFS KIA files, TAMU Archives.

9. Atkinson, *An Army at Dawn*, pp. 117–39.

10. Col. Jack Nahas, "Lebanese-American Aggie Vet," in ASF World War II files, TAMU Archives.

11. Brig. Gen. George H. Beverley, interview by Terry H. Anderson, July 16, 1981, TAMU Archives.

12. See 1st Lt. Frank Petty Haynes, AFS KIA files, TAMU Archives; Atkinson, *An Army at Dawn*, p. 210.

13. Atkinson, *An Army at Dawn*, p. 217; Martin Gilbert, *The Second World War: A Complete History* (New York: Henry Holt, 1989), p. 383. There is a discrepancy in these accounts in the actual numbers of ships scuttled.

14. Lt. Gen. James F. Hollingsworth, interview by Terry H. Anderson, Aug. 18, 1982, TAMU Archives.

15. Jack Milton Ilfrey, interview by John A. Adams Jr., Sept. 25, 2002. After a training stint back in the United States, Ilfrey returned to Europe to command a fighter squadron in the battle of Germany.

16. Memorandum, Maj. Gen. William A. Becker to C. C. Taylor, Dec. 29, 2003; Atkinson, *An Army at Dawn*, pp. 259, 271–438. Specifically, American positions at Sidibou Zid, Gafsa, and Skeitler were overrun.

17. Atkinson, *An Army at Dawn*, pp. 259, 271–438; 1st Lt. John Pershing Gilreath, Capt. Jack E. Golden, AFS KIA files, TAMU Archives.

18. Cindy Hicks, "James M. Parker, Local World War II Hero," unpublished manuscript, TAMU Archives; Carroll V. Glines, *Doolittle's Tokyo Raiders* (New York: Van Nostrand Rheinhold, 1971); and see Capt. Robert Edward Greenwell, Capt. Kenneth McFarland Irby, S.Sgt. Lindsey C. Hoskins Jr., AFS KIA files, TAMU Archives. At the end of the war, Lieutenant Commander Parker returned to Texas to work with the Soil Conservation Service and the U.S. Bureau of Reclamation as a hydrology engineer.

19. Capt. Jack E. Golden, Lt. Howard H. Brians, 1st Lt. Harold B. Chamberlain, Lt. Walter Mark Cabaniss Jr., AFS KIA files, TAMU Archives.

20. *Brady (Tex.) Standard-Herald* (Jan. 25, 2002).

21. Gilbert, *Second World War*, pp. 446–47, 451, 459–60.

22. Lloyd H. Hughes, Medal of Honor citation and biographical papers, TAMU Archives; Lt. Gen. Ira C. Eaker, "Strategic Air Power over Europe," in *Bombs Away! Your Air Force in Action*, vol. 7 of *Pictorial History of the Second World War*, ed. Clary Thompson (New York: W. H. Wise, 1947), p. 206; *Bryan–College Station Eagle* (Apr. 20, 1946).

23. Ray O. Hargis, telephone interview by Henry C. Dethloff, Dec. 8, 2003; Lt. Brice C. Diedrick, AFS KIA files, TAMU Archives.

24. Brig. Gen. Theodore H. Andrews, AFS biographical files, TAMU Archives.

25. Capt. John L. Chapin, AFS KIA files; "School Name Honors WW II Hero," *Association of the United States Army News* (Feb., 2001); *Texas Aggie* (Dec., 1999), p. 24; Brig. Gen. Richard J. Werner, AFS biographical files; Brig. Gen. Theodore H. Andrews, AFS biographical files; Percy W. Clarkson, noted in Werner AFS biography; Lt. James O. Beasley, AFS KIA files, TAMU Archives.

26. Capt. Charles H. Hamner, AFS KIA files, TAMU Archives.

27. "Ft. Bliss School Named for World War II Aggie Hero," *Texas Aggie* (Dec., 1999), p. 24; Texas Military Forces Museum, "443rd Antiaircraft Artillery Automatic Weapons Battalion (SP), Rapido River Operation," at http://kwanan.com/txmilmus/36thdivision/archives/443/44566.htm.

28. Capt. Gerald P. Elder, Lt. Elbert Sheridan Clark, AFS KIA files; Brig. Gen. Theodore H. Andrews, AFS biographical, TAMU Archives; Gilbert, *The Second World War*, pp. 491–98.

29. O. Wayne Crisman, AFS biographical; Thomas W. Fowler, Medal of Honor citation, AFS files and records, TAMU Archives.

30. Thomas W. Fowler, Medal of Honor citation, AFS files and records, TAMU Archives.

31. John Keegan, ed., *World War II: A Visual Encyclopedia*, p. 429.

32. George D. Keathley, Medal of Honor citation, AFS files and records, TAMU Archives.

33. Pfc. John Daniel Connell; Lt. John F. Barnett Jr., AFS KIA files, TAMU Archives.

34. Pfc. Marvin Earl Hiner; Capt. John Poitevent Lackey Jr., Capt. Daniel L. Cajka, AFS KIA files, TAMU Archives.

35. Lt. Robert G. Johnson Jr., Lt. Joseph Pane Lindsly Jr., Lt. Norbert J. Gorski, Lt. Jack C. Herron, Lt. Clarence Leroy Korth, AFS KIA files, TAMU Archives.

36. Sgt. John Lindsey Eddins, Lt. Lloyd W. Kelly, Lt. Jim Kuykendall, Lt. Brice C. Diedrick, AFS KIA files, TAMU Archives.

37. Sgt. Samuel David Lasser, Lt. Bland Massie Barnes Jr., Lt. Robert Martin Hyde, AFS KIA files, TAMU Archives.

38. Lt. Maurice Block Jr.; letter from Brig. Gen. Leon W. Johnson to M. I. Block, Aug. 20, 1945, AFS KIA files, TAMU Archives.

Chapter 10

1. Brig. Gen. O. D. Butler, interview by Terry H. Anderson, Apr. 29, 1983, TAMU Archives.

2. Memorandum, Lindsey I. Lipscomb biographical, TAMU Archives.

3. Gordon A. Harrison, *Cross-channel Attack* (Washington, D.C.: GPO, 1951), pp. 1–126, 158–267, 274. Rick Atkinson, *An Army at Dawn: The War in North Africa, 1942–1943* (New York: Henry Holt, 2002), pp. 293–95, 540; Kent R. Greenfield, *American Strategy in World War II* (Malabar, Fla: Krieger, 1963), pp. 33–41, 71–78; Military Intelligence Service, "Notes and Lessons on Operations in the Middle East," campaign study no. 5 (Washington, D.C.: War Department, Jan. 30, 1943), pp. 1–24. The major powers also held conferences in Quebec in Aug., 1943, and Tehran in Nov., 1943, sealing the pact to land in France in mid-1944.

4. Frank C. Litterst Jr. ('43), interview by John A. Adams Jr., Dec. 18, 2002; Brig. Gen. O. D. Butler ('36), interview by Terry H. Anderson, Apr. 29, 1983, TAMU Archives.

5. Jack Ilfrey, *Happy Jack's Go Buggy: A Fighter Pilot's Story* (Atglen, Penn.: Schiffer Military and Aviation History, 1998), pp. 8–117.

6. Chief of Air Staff, Intelligence, "Year of Feverish Preparation for Normandy," *Impact*

(May, 1945): 11–17; "First A&M Four-Star General Dies," *Texas Aggie* (Nov., 1979), p. 14, and (Feb. 1, 1944); Office of the Air Staff, Intelligence, "German Fighter Tactics against Flying Fortresses," no. 43-17 (Washington, D.C.: War Department, Dec. 31, 1943), pp. 1–27; "The Invasion and the Days That Followed," *Impact* (May, 1945): 24–25.

7. Ed Morton to Henry C. Dethloff, July 26, 2002, with attached 385th BGMA newsletter (Aug., 1992), TAMU Archives.

8. Ed Ivey to C. C. Taylor, May 31, 2003, TAMU Archives. A brother, Robert W. Ivey ('44), and two brothers-in-law, Joe B. Randol ('39) and Robert T. Randol ('50), also served in WW II.

9. Maj. Gen. Jim Dan Hill, interview by Terry H. Anderson, Aug. 20, 1982, TAMU Archives; Harrison, *Cross-channel Attack*, pp. 158–97; AFS biographical memorandum, Bennie L. Zinn (n.d.), TAMU Archives.

10. B. H. Liddell Hart, *The German Generals Talk* (New York: William Morrow, 1948), p. 238; Cornelius Ryan, *The Longest Day: June 6, 1944* (New York: Simon and Schuster, 1959), p. 8; Harrison, *Cross-channel Attack*, pp. 8, 12, 271–78.

11. See http://www.lebanondailyrecord.com/articles/2004/07/16/specia11/www2staffel.txt; copy in Aggies in War papers, chapter 10, TAMU Archives.

12. Louis Hudson, telephone interview by Henry C. Dethloff, June 6, 2004.

13. Joseph Balkoski, *Beyond the Beachhead: The 29th Infantry Division in Normandy* (Harrisburg, Penn.: Stackpole Books, 1989), p. 157.

14. Harrison, *Cross-channel Attack*, pp. 318–24; Robert Edlin, 2nd Ranger Battalion lieutenant and D-day veteran, interview by John A. Adams Jr., Nov. 9, 2002, College Station, Tex.; Marcia Moen and Margo Heinen, *The Fool Lieutenant: A Personal Account of D-day and World War II* (Elk River, Minn.: Meadowlark, 2000), p. 84.

15. Omar Bradley, *A Soldier's Story* (New York: Henry Holt, 1951), pp. 269–70.

16. Ryan, *The Longest Day*, pp. 237–39.

17. Harrison, *Cross-channel Attack*, p. 322; Ronald L. Lane, *Rudder's Rangers* (Manassas, Va.: Ranger Associates, 1979), pp. 1–198; "Gen. Earl Rudder's Military Decorations Given to Texas A&M," *Texas Aggie* (June, 1985), p. 46. See also Christopher J. Anderson, "Screaming Eagles at Point-du-Hoc," *World War II* [magazine] (July, 2001), pp. 34–40; Rebecca Zimmermann and Donn Friedman, "Only Echoes of War Remain on Pastoral French Coast," *Texas Aggie* (Apr., 1987), pp. 4–6; Jim Hiney, "Magnitude of Sacrifice," *Texas Shores* (Spring, 2001), pp. 2–16.

18. Papers of Jack E. Golden ('42), Jan., 1943–May, 1945, TAMU Archives; Ralph G. Martin, "From D-day to St. Lo," in *Highlights from Yank, the Army Weekly* (New York: Royal Books, 1953), pp. 121–34.

19. Joe Simnacher, "John Forrest Smith: Decorated WW II Hero," *Dallas Morning News* (Dec. 18, 2001).

20. Johnny Mitchell, *The Secret War of Johnny Mitchell* (Houston: Pacesetter Press, 1976), pp. 20–26; Gen. James F. Hollingsworth ('40), interview by Terry H. Anderson, Aug. 18, 1982, TAMU Archives.

21. AFS KIA files, TAMU Archives; *Houston Chronicle* (July 26, 2003), p. 32A; letter to "Dear A&M" from the Morris family, May 6, 2004, TAMU Archives.

22. Letter from Charlotte Jackson to "Dear Sir," June 26, 1944, World War II casualties file, AFS, TAMU Archives.

23. Balkoski, *Beyond the Beachhead*, pp. 236–78.

24. Letter, Calvin C. Boykin Jr. to David Dewhurst, May 11, 1999, TAMU Archives. Boykin is president of the WW II Tank Destroyer Society.

25. Harrison, *Cross-channel Attack*, pp. 422–49.

26. "Comanche Man," news clipping, Mar. 5, 1945, World War II casualties files, AFS.

27. Alexander McKee, *The Race for the Rhine Bridges* (New York: Stein and Day, 1971), pp. 182–302; papers of Capt. Jack Golden ('42), authors' collection; World War II casualties file, AFS.

28. U.S. Senate, "Medal of Honor Recipients, 1863–1973," 93rd Cong., 1st sess., no. 15, Oct. 22, 1973, p. 609; *Dallas Morning News* (Apr. 18, 1946); *Texas Aggie* (Dec. 1, 1945).

29. "Report from the 95th [Division]," *Texas Aggie* (Feb. 1, 1945), p. 1.

30. Peter Elstob, *Hitler's Last Offensive: The Full Story of the Battle of the Ardennes* (New York: Macmillan, 1971), pp. 24–33; Kent R. Greenfield, ed., *The War against Germany: Europe and Adjacent Areas* (Washington, D.C.: GPO, 1951), pp. 211–15. See also H. M. Cole, *The Lorraine Campaign* (Washington, D.C.: GPO, 1950); World War II casualties files, AFS.

31. Letter, Capt. Jack Golden to "Mother" [Mrs. Emitt P. Golden], Dec. 12, 1944, Jack E. Golden Papers. When Golden was promoted to captain, his pay was $241.00 per month.

32. Karl von Clausewitz, *On War* (1832; repr., Middlesex, UK: Penguin Classics, 1987), p. 258.

33. Hanson W. Baldwin, *Battles Lost and Won: Great Campaigns of World War II* (New York: Harper and Row, 1966), pp. 319–20.

34. Elstob, *Hitler's Last Offensive*, pp. 24–77; memorandum, Rick Crow to Henry Dethloff, March 24, 2008.

35. *Texas Aggie* (May, 2003), p. 15; James L. Huffines Jr., AFS Files and Records, TAMU Archives. A. P. Wiley Jr., "War at Ground Level: The Experiences of a Combat Infantryman in Europe during World War II" (personal account), 62 pp., TAMU Archives.

36. Letter, Col. Branner P. Purdue, 120th Infantry, to all officers and men of Infantry Regiment 120, Jan. 16, 1945, in Wiley, "War at Ground Level," TAMU Archives.

37. William M. Peña, *As Far as Schleiden: A Memoir of World War II* (Houston: William M. Peña, 1991).

38. Memorandum, Charles A. Girand to Henry C. Dethloff, May 23, 2002, with letter, "Dear Wife & Boy, Jan. 8, Somewhere in Belgium," and attachments, both in AFS WW II Papers, TAMU Archives.

39. Myra Fisher and Stewart Fisher, compilers, "Some Uncommon Men" (Spring, 2001), unpublished ms., TAMU Archives.

40. Ibid.; letter, Jett J. Johnson to *Texas Aggie* [Jan., 2001], Aggies in War files and records, TAMU Archives.

41. Fisher and Fisher, "Some Uncommon Men"; John Toland, *Battle: The Story of the Bulge* (New York: Random House, 1959), pp. 205–88; Stephen Ambrose, *Citizen Soldiers* (New York: Touchstone, 1998), pp. 226–48; "Aggies in Germany," *Texas Aggie* (Feb. 1, 1945), p. 1. Sorelle's awards included the Air Medal and seventeen oak-leaf clusters.

42. Toland, *Battle*, pp. 205–88; Ambrose, *Citizen Soldiers*, pp. 226–48; "Aggies in Germany," *Texas Aggie* (Feb. 1, 1945), p. 1.

43. U.S. Senate, "Medal of Honor Recipients 1863–1973," 93rd Cong., 1st sess., no. 15, Oct. 22, 1973, p. 717; *New York Times* (Aug. 19, 1945).

44. Heywood C. Clemons, telephone interview by Henry C. Dethloff, Oct. 18, 2003.

45. John A. Adams Jr., *Keepers of the Spirit: The Corps of Cadets at Texas A&M University, 1876–2001* (College Station: Texas A&M University Press, 2001), p. 162; letter, Eleanor M. Allen to Ernest Langford, Sept. 18, 1970, Roderick R. Allen Papers, TAMU Archives; *Texas Aggie* (July 18, 1952; May 7, 1945; June 19, 1951); Trevor N. Dupuy, *Hitler's Last Gamble: The Battle of the Bulge* (New York: Harper Collins, 1994), p. 104; Hugh M. Cole, *The Ardennes: Battle of the Bulge* (Washington, D.C.: GPO, 1965), pp. 214–17.

46. Gen. James F. Hollingsworth ('40), interview by Terry H. Anderson, Aug. 18, 1982, TAMU Archives; Cornelius Ryan, *The Last Battle* (New York: Simon and Schuster, 1966), pp. 305–10: Donald E. Houston, *Hell on Wheels: The 2nd Armored Division* (Novato, Calif.: Presidio Press, 1977), pp. 367, 417.

47. "Joe Routt Will Become Aggie Legend," *Houston Post* (Dec. 12, 1944); World War II casualties file, AFS; "Former Ag Gridsters of Past 5 Years Serving in Army," *Texas Aggie* (May 5, 1942), p. 1; Wilbur Evan and H. B. McElroy, *The Twelfth Man* (Huntsville, Ala.: Strode, 1974), pp. 291, 295.

48. Ken Hechler, *The Bridge at Remagen* (New York: Ballantine, 1957), pp. 183–90: "Patton Dashes across Rhine," *Stars and Stripes* (Mar. 24, 1944), p. 1; *Military History* (Oct., 1997), p. 52.

49. World War II casualties files, AFS, TAMU Archives.

50. Roy McCaldin to Henry C. Dethloff, Aug. 22, 2003, with Eighth Air Force Historical Society newsletter dated Feb., 2002, TAMU Archives.

51. Mark Scott and Semyon Krasilshchik, eds., *Yanks Meet Reds: Recollections of U.S. and Soviet Vets from the Linkup in World War II* (Santa Barbara: Copra Press, 1988), pp. 1–224; "Russian and Aggie Who Met at Elbe Meet Again 43 Years Later," *Texas Aggie* (Nov., 1988), p. 7; John A. Adams Jr., *Softly Call the Muster* (College Station: Texas A&M University Press, 1994), pp. 39–41. See also *Texas Aggie* (Aug. 1, 1945; May 31, 1945).

52. Jack Golden to "Geneva," Apr. 3, 1945, Jack E. Golden Papers, TAMU Archives.

53. Supreme Headquarters of the Allied Expeditionary Forces (SHAEF), confidential, "Unconditional Surrender," May 7, 1945, in Gen. Roderick R. Allen Papers, TAMU Archives; Hart, *The German Generals Talk*, pp. 292–93.

Chapter 11

1. Harry A. Gailey, *War in the Pacific: From Pearl Harbor to Tokyo Bay* (Novato, Calif.: Presidio Press, 1995), pp. 458–70; *Texas Aggie* (July, 1967), p. 28; William S. Bacon, membership director, Military Order of the Purple Heart, to *Texas Aggie*, Feb. 17, 2002, AFS files and records, TAMU Archives.

2. Lt. Albert Dale Cotton, Lt. Bobbie Livingston, Lt. Carl Bill Ehman, Lt. Thomas Ray Coffey, memoranda, AFS KIA files, TAMU Archives.

3. Gailey, *War in the Pacific*, pp. 234–35; Capt. Lewis G. Compton Jr., AFS KIA files, TAMU Archives.

4. Henry Bismark Ferguson, booklet and clipping file, TAMU Archives.

5. Letter, Mrs. Max Bergfeld to C. E. McQuillen, executive secretary of the AFS (n.d.), AFS KIA files and records, TAMU Archives.

6. Gailey, *War in the Pacific*, pp. 256–62.

7. *Houston Chronicle* (Apr. 2, 2001), pp. 15, 17A.

8. Lt. Gen. George I. Forsythe, U.S. Army, chief of information, biography; Gailey, *War in the Pacific*, pp. 312–16; *Texas Aggie* (Aug. 15, 1950).

9. Gailey, *War in the Pacific*, pp. 305–25.

10. Ibid.; Lt. Clayton N. Duvall, AFS KIA files, TAMU Archives.

11. Calvin C. Boykin Jr., *General A. D. Bruce: Father of Fort Hood* (College Station, Tex.: C&R Publications, 2002), pp. 45–52.

12. Maj. Gen. Victor A. Barraco, USMC, AFS military questionnaire, TAMU Archives.

13. San Antonio A&M Club, *Alamo Aggie* (Apr., 2002).

14. Memorandum, Gen. William A. Becker to Henry Dethloff, Mar. 28, 2003, TAMU Archives.

15. Ibid.

16. Ibid.

17. Charles McQueen Taylor, AFS WW II files and records, TAMU Archives; Gailey, *War in the Pacific*, pp. 337–73; H. Stephen Jones ('74) to ASF, Dec. 14, 2000, TAMU Archives.

18. Memorandum, Gen. William A. Becker to Henry Dethloff, Mar. 28, 2003, TAMU Archives.

19. Gailey, *War in the Pacific*, pp. 337–73; Horace S. Carswell Jr., Medal of Honor citation, AFS KIA files, TAMU Archives; Lt. Sidney Caldwell Kimball, Maj. Raymond Scott Evans, Lt. (jg) H. B. Hales, Lt. James Edward Inglehart, Lt. Melvin G. Hass, AFS KIA files, TAMU Archives.

20. Memorandum, Gen. William A. Becker to Henry Dethloff, Mar. 28, 2003, TAMU Archives; William A. Becker, interview by Terry H. Anderson, July 1, 1981, TAMU Archives.

21. Memorandum, Gen. William A. Becker to Henry Dethloff, Mar. 28, 2003, TAMU Archives.

22. Ibid.

23. *Texas Aggie* (Nov. 1, 1945); see Hampton Sides, *Ghost Soldiers* (New York: Doubleday, 2001).

24. *Texas Aggie* (Nov. 1, 1945); Sides, *Ghost Soldiers*; Maj. Paul Armstrong Brown, Lt. Andy M. James Jr., Capt. Gary M. Abney Jr., Capt. Sydney R. Greer, and Lt. Andy M. James Jr., AFS KIA files and records, TAMU Archives.

25. Email from Noel Garland, Dallas, Tex., to Jerry Cooper, AFS, College Station, Tex., June 18, 2002, AFS KIA files and records, TAMU Archives.

26. Gailey, *War in the Pacific*, pp. 376–406; Lt. James H. Collins Jr.; Lt. Albert B. Capt, AFS KIA files, TAMU Archives.

27. Memorandum, Gen. William A. Becker to Henry Dethloff, Mar. 28, 2003, TAMU Archives.

28. Ibid.; World War II memorial newsletter (Fall, 2002), TAMU Archives.

29. Memorandum, Gen. William A. Becker to Henry Dethloff, Mar. 28, 2003, TAMU Archives; World War II memorial newsletter (Fall, 2002), TAMU Archives; Maj. Gen. William A. Becker, interview by Terry H. Anderson, July 2, 1981, TAMU Archives; memorandum, Sam E. Harris to Bill Becker, Mar. 5, 2003, TAMU Archives. The famous dash to Manila is still celebrated on Feb. 3 each year by veterans of the operation, rescued internees, and reportedly some Philippinos.

30. Maj. Charles Benton Adams, Maj. Robert Balch, AFS KIA files, TAMU Archives; Gailey, *War in the Pacific*, pp. 376–406.

31. Capt. Newton Vincent Craig, AFS KIA files, TAMU Archives; see Patrick O'Donnell,

Into the Rising Sun (New York: Free Press, 2002), pp. 12–13, 89–117; *Texas Aggie* (May 5, 1943; May 30, 1951).

32. Alvin Roubal Luedecke, *Who's Who in America* (1966–1967) p. 1305 (After retiring from military service in 1968, Luedecke returned to Texas A&M as an associate dean and served as acting president of that institution following the death of James Earl Rudder); *Texas Aggie* (Oct. 15, 1942; May 7, 1945); *New York Times* (May 27, 1956); *Texas Aggie* (Aug. 20, 1942); Robert Sherrod, "Toughest Guy in the Air Force," *Saturday Evening Post* (Mar. 26, 1955), pp. 144, 147.

33. See *Houston Post* (Nov. 11, 1942); Bryce O. Templeton, Mountain Lake, N.J., to F. C. Bolton, College Station, Tex., Mar. 14, 1948, honorary degree file, TAMU Archives; Maj. Gen. Robert Boyd Williams, honorary degree file, TAMU Archives; *Texas Aggie* (July 15, 1943).

34. Gailey, *War in the Pacific*, pp. 407–20; letter, Benton H. Elliott to Bill Becker, June 27, 2003, TAMU Archives; J. C. Grady, interview by Henry C. Dethloff, June 13, 2004, College Station, Tex.

35. Sgt. William G. Harrell, Congressional Medal of Honor citation, AFS WW II files and records, TAMU Archives; Samuel David Hanks, Monteith Talmadge Lincecum Jr., Cpl. Philip Albert Davidson, AFS KIA files and records, TAMU Archives.

36. Jack S. Lipscomb, Charles E. Harrington Jr., AFS KIA files and records, TAMU Archives.

37. Charles Montgomery Nettles, obituary in Aggies in War files and records, TAMU Archives.

38. J. R. Spiller Jr., memorandum, "Memories from WW II Navy Days," Aggies in War files and records, TAMU Archives.

39. Boykin, *A. D. Bruce*, pp. 59–60; memorandum, Gen. William A. Becker to Henry Dethloff, Mar. 28, 2003, TAMU Archives.

40. Radioman Third Class Calvin Floyd Ballard, Lt. Charles Glynn Ray Jr., Sgt. Cecil Martin Holekamp, AFS KIA files and records, TAMU Archives.

41. Boykin, *A. D. Bruce*, pp. 62–63; Gailey, *War in the Pacific*, pp. 433–35.

42. Capt. Joe Benjamin Guerra, Pvt. James Harold Henry, Lt. William Bryant Caraway Jr., Lt. Jesse Lee Brown, Pvt. Miles Joseph Luster, Pvt. John Galen Lawrence, AFS KIA files and records, TAMU Archives; see George Feifer, *The Battle of Okinawa: The Blood and the Bomb* (Lyons, Conn.: Guilford Press, 2001).

43. Brig. Gen. Claudius M. Easley, AFS KIA files and records, TAMU Archives; *Waco News Tribune* (June 22, 1945).

44. Lt. Roger Eugene Edwards, Lt. Ransom D. Kenny Jr., S 1/c John Batiste Roemer, Pvt. Phillip Francis Schaefer, AFS KIA files and records, TAMU Archives; memorandum, Emil Joe Chromcak, "My U.S. Navy Experience in World War II," TAMU Archives.

45. Gailey, *War in the Pacific*, pp. 425–46.

46. Ibid., pp. 449–75.

47. *Texas Aggie* (Nov. 1, 1945).

48. Lt. Leonard Gage Larsen, Sgt. Rex W. Hamilton, F/O Frank G. Albritton, Maj. John Charles Conly, Capt. Walter Junior Clemans, AFS KIA files and records, TAMU Archives.

49. Lt. Henry W. Heitmann, 1st Lt. John P. Bradley, Lt. Lawrence Smith Gready Jr., AFS KIA files and records, TAMU Archives.

50. *Alumni Salute* (Nov., 1995).

51. Robert Karl Manoff, "American Victims of Hiroshima," *New York Times Magazine* (Dec. 2, 1984).

52. Email memorandum, Rip Collins to Henry C. Dethloff, Jan. 16, 2004, TAMU Archives.

53. Gailey, *War in the Pacific*, pp. 490–97; Edmond H. Leavey to Richard O. ("Buck") Weirus, Jan. 3, 1975, AFS WW II files and records, TAMU Archives; Henry C. Dethloff, *A Pictorial History of Texas A&M University, 1876–1976* (College Station: Texas A&M University Press, 1975), pp. 156–57; Maj. Gen. William A. Becker, interview by Terry H. Anderson, July 2, 1981, TAMU Archives.

54. Memorandum, Gen. William A. Becker to Henry Dethloff, Mar. 28, 2003, TAMU Archives.

Chapter 12

1. Brig. Gen. Kay Halsell II, interview by Terry H. Anderson, Sept. 17, 1981, TAMU Archives.

2. Mark Scott and Semyon Krasilshchik, eds., *Yanks Meet Reds: Recollections of U.S. and Soviet Vets from the Linkup in World War II* (Santa Barbara, Calif.: Capra Press, 1988), pp. 23–28; "Aggie Pursues Memorial to Lasting Peace," *Texas Aggie* (Oct., 1992), pp. 12–13.

3. Scott and Krasilshchik, eds., *Yanks Meet Reds*, p. 28.

4. Maj. Gen. William A. Becker, interview by Terry H. Anderson, July 2, 1981, TAMU Archives.

5. Brig. Gen. Kay Halsell II, interview by Terry H. Anderson, Sept. 17, 1981, TAMU Archives. The Meiji Stadium in Tokyo became the home base of the Japanese team.

6. Memorandum, Charles A. Girand to Henry C. Dethloff, May 22, 2002; James E. Wiley ('46), biographical; John Allen Ater (directory information); Maj. Gen. William A. Becker, biographical, AFS WW II files, TAMU Archives.

7. AFS KIA files, TAMU Archives.

8. Lt. Charles L. Babcock Jr., Flying Cadet Duke W. Harrison Jr., AFS KIA files, TAMU Archives.

9. Jim Carroll, "Texas A&M in World War II," *Houston Press* (Apr. 18, 1946).

10. Henry C. Dethloff, *Centennial History of Texas A&M University*, vol. 2, pp. 476–91.

11. Jim Carroll, "Texas A&M in World War II," *Houston Press* (Apr. 18, 1946).

12. Ibid.

13. Ibid.

14. Ibid.

15. Ibid.

16. Ibid.

17. Ibid.

18. Ibid.

19. Dethloff, *Centennial History*, vol. 2, pp. 476–91; Harrington later became president and chancellor of Texas A&M.

20. Memo, W. A. Becker to Henry Dethloff, May 15, 2003, TAMU Archives.

21. Ibid.

22. *Texas Aggie* (May, 1946).

23. Capt. Ralph R. Thomas to E. E. McQuillen, c. Apr. 21, 1946, AFS WW II files and records, TAMU Archives.

24. Letter, Max McCullar to E. E. McQuillen, Calcutta, India, Apr. 21, 1946, AFS WW II files and records, TAMU Archives.

25. Letter, Neil S. Madeley to E. E. McQuillen, Okinawa, Apr. 30, 1946, AFS WW II files and records, TAMU Archives.

26. Ibid. The identifying branches are as used by Madeley. Presumably "AC" is Air Corps, "CE" is Civil Engineering, "VC" is Veterinary Corps, and "QMC" is Quartermaster Corps; for several soldiers, however, the branches are unidentified.

27. Letter, 1st Lt. Jack J. Keith to E. E. McQuillen, Paris, Apr. 22, 1946; Lt. Hap Russell to E. E. McQuillen, Munich, Apr. 27, 1946, AFS WW II Papers, TAMU Archives.

28. Dethloff, *Centennial History*, vol. 2, pp. 476–500.

29. Ibid., p. 450.

30. Brig. Gen. Kay Halsell II, interview by Terry H. Anderson, Sept. 17, 1981, Bryan, Tex., TAMU Archives.

31. Brig. Gen. Kyle L. Riddle, interview by Terry H. Anderson, June 28, 1982.

32. Ibid.

33. Ibid.

34. Maj. Gen. Frederick H. Weston, interview by Terry H. Anderson, July 20, 1981, TAMU Archives.

35. Brig. Gen. Clarence Wilson, interview by Terry H. Anderson, June 11, 1982, TAMU Archives.

36. Ibid.

37. Brig. Gen. Joe G. Hanover, interview by Terry H. Anderson, July 29, 1980, TAMU Archives.

38. Ibid.

Chapter 13

1. Robert M. Shuffler, Berlin Muster report, Apr. 21, 1946, AFS files, TAMU Archives.

2. Edwin Glazener, registry, http://lib-oldweb.tamu.edu/aggiesinwar/; Brig. Gen. John M. Kenderdine, AFS general officer files, TAMU Archives; OMGUS is the acronym for Office of the Military Governor, United States.

3. Red Scott, TAMU Class of 1953 Military History, text and notes, TAMU Archives; *Texas Aggie* (Oct., 1968), p. 34.

4. Eivand H. Johansen biographical, AFS general office files, TAMU Archives.

5. Hugh O. Walker Jr. to E. E. McQuillen, May 5, 1946; William A. ("Kizer") Wright to E. E. McQuillen, Apr. 26, 1946, AFS WW II files, TAMU Archives.

6. Red Scott, TAMU Class of 1953 Military History, text and notes, TAMU Archives; *Texas Aggie* (Oct., 1968), p. 34.

7. Red Scott, TAMU Class of 1953 Military History, text and notes, TAMU Archives; *Texas Aggie* (Oct., 1968), p. 34, and (Mar., 1993), pp. 14–15.

8. Red Scott, TAMU Class of 1953 Military History, text and notes, TAMU Archives; *Texas Aggie* (Oct., 1968), p. 34, and (Mar., 1993), pp. 14–15.

9. Red Scott, TAMU Class of 1953 Military History, text and notes, TAMU Archives; *Texas Aggie* (Oct., 1968), p. 34, and (Mar., 1993), pp. 14–15.

10. Texas A&M University Library register of Aggies in service at http://lib-oldweb.tamu.edu/aggiesinwar/; *Texas Aggie* (Aug., 1994), p. 39.

11. Texas A&M University Library register of Aggies in service at http://lib-oldweb.tamu .edu/aggiesinwar/; *Texas Aggie* (Aug., 1994), p. 39.

12. Texas A&M University Library register of Aggies in service at http://lib-oldweb.tamu .edu/aggiesinwar/; *Texas Aggie* (Aug., 1994), p. 39.

13. *Texas Aggie* (Nov., 1994).

14. Red Scott, TAMC Class of 1953 Military History, text and notes, TAMU Archives; *Texas Aggie* (Oct., 1968), p. 34.

15. *Texas Aggie* (May, 1981).

16. "Young Man on the Go: Bill Libby," *Texas Aggie* (Sept., 1967), p. 34; Alaska Department of Military Affairs, news release, June 14, 1971; *Texas Aggie* (Jan., 1969), p. 30; (May, 1972), p. 21; (Nov., 1980), p. 16.

17. *Texas Aggie* (May, 1980), p. 33; (Oct., 1984), p. 33.

18. "Young Man on the Go: Bill Libby," *Texas Aggie* (Sept., 1967), p. 34.

19. Brig. Gen. Kyle Ridde, interview by Terry H. Anderson, Aug. 17, 1980, TAMU Archives.

20. *Houston Chronicle* (Apr. 15, 2002).

21. *Texas Aggie* (Dec., 1969).

22. *Texas Aggie* (June, 1966); Henry C. Dethloff, *Centennial History of Texas A&M University, 1876–1976*, vol. 2 (College Station: Texas A&M University Press, 1975), pp. 473–74.

23. *Texas Aggie* (Nov., 1966).

24. Ibid.; Walter J. Boyne, *Beyond the Wild Blue: A History of the United States Air Force* (New York: St. Martin's Griffin Press, 1998); and see Henry C. Dethloff, *Suddenly . . . Tomorrow Came: A History of Johnson Space Center* (Washington, D.C.: NASA, SP4307), 1993; Walter A. McDougall, *The Heavens and the Earth: A Political History of the Space Age* (New York: Basic Books, 1985), pp. 107, 128, 155, 173, 190–99, 312–19, 336–39.

25. Gen. Bernard A. Schriever, "The Role of Management in Technological Conflict," *Air University Quarterly Review* (Winter-Spring, 1962–1963): 19–29.

26. *Texas Aggie* (Feb., 1970), p. 28; (Nov., 1967), pp. 34–35; (Nov., 1984), p. 18; Maj. Gen. Michael C. Kostelnik, USAF biography, TAMU Archives.

27. *Texas Aggie* (Nov.–Dec., 1971; July, 1977; Dec., 1987).

28. Dethloff, *Suddenly . . . Tomorrow Came*, pp. 310–12, 316–18, 336–39.

29. Ibid., p. 336.

30. Ibid., pp. 181, 184, 197–99, 307–19; Gerald D. ("Gerry") Griffin biographical, TAMU Archives; *Texas Aggie* (Nov., 1969).

31. Dethloff, *Suddenly . . . Tomorrow Came*; Gerald D. ("Gerry") Griffin biographical, TAMU Archives; *Texas Aggie* (Nov., 1969).

32. Rotary National Award for Space Achievement, news release, Jan. 10, 1994, TAMU Archives.

33. Dethloff, *Suddenly . . . Tomorrow Came*, pp. 18, 41, 320.

34. "Texas A&M, 1876–1951, 75th Anniversary" commemorative booklet [p. 11].

35. D. M. Giangreco, *War in Korea, 1950–1953* (Novato, Calif.: Presidio Press, 1990).

Chapter 14

1. Memorandum, "The Korean War as Experienced by Robert L. (Bob) Middleton, Texas A&M, Class of 1951," TAMU Archives.

2. Ibid.; "Aggies Who Died in Korea to Be on Memorial," *Texas Aggie* (June, 1996), p. 24;

James Proffitt, "Notes on Aggies Known by Me in Korea, Mid 1951–Mid 1952" (Apr. 8, 2003), TAMU Archives; Fred Dollar, interview by Terry H. Anderson, Sept. 7, 2003, College Station, Tex., TAMU Archives.

3. Record group 330, office of the secretary of defense, Korean Conflict casualties file, National Archives, College Park, Md., copy in AFS files, TAMU Archives; memorandum, "Special to the *Texas Aggie* Magazine," undated [1996], copy in AFS files, TAMU Archives.

4. Paul Y. Hammond, *Cold War and Détente: The American Foreign Policy Process since 1945* (New York: Harcourt Brace Jovanovich, 1975), pp. 58–64; John Toland, *In Mortal Combat: Korea, 1950–1953* (New York: William Morrow, 1991), pp. 18–37; Ernest May, "America's Berlin: Heart of the Cold War," *Foreign Affairs* (July, 1998): 148–55.

5. U.S. State Department, *Korea, 1945 to 1948: A Report on Political Developments and Economic Resources with Selected Documents* (1948; repr., New York: Greenwood Press, 1969), pp. 3–5; Toland, *In Mortal Combat*, p. 16.

6. David G. McCullough, *Truman* (New York: Simon and Schuster, 1992), p. 777. See also Glenn Paige, *1950: Truman's Decision* (New York: Chelsea House, 1970), pp. 1–172, for an excellent collection of documents and dispatches covering the period from January to July, 1950.

7. Paige, *Truman's Decision*, p. 42.

8. McCullough, *Truman*, pp. 46, 55, 59–60, 63–68; Walter J. Boyne, *Beyond the Wild Blue: A History of the U.S. Air Force, 1947–1997* (New York: St. Martin's Griffin Press, 1997), p. 51.

9. Col. John A. Adams, interview by John A. Adams Jr., Jan. 4, 2003, Norcross, Ga.

10. William Appleman Williams, *The Tragedy of American Diplomacy* (New York: Norton, 1988), pp. 254, 268–69, 273; McCullough, *Truman*, p. 772; Robert L. O'Connell, *Of Arms and Men* (New York: Oxford University Press, 1989), p. 296. See also George F. Kennan, *Memoirs: 1925–1950* (New York: Little, Brown, 1967), pp. 361–67, and paper no. 68 of the National Security Council, Washington, D.C., Mar., 1950.

11. McCullough, *Truman*, pp. 771–73; John R. Bruning, *Crimson Sky: The Air Battle for Korea* (Dulles, Va.: Brassey's, 1999), pp. xii–xiv; Boyne, *Beyond the Wild Blue*, p. 53.

12. Boyne, *Beyond the Wild Blue*, pp. 61–62.

13. Ibid., p. 56.

14. "PMS&T Responsible for Control and Discipline of Cadet Corps," *College Station (Tex.) Battalion* (Jan. 24, 1947), p. 1; John A. Adams Jr., *Keepers of the Spirit: The Corps of Cadets at Texas A&M University, 1876–2001* (College Station: Texas A&M University Press, 2001), pp. 168–75.

15. Memorandum, Jim McGuire to Henry Dethloff, Apr. 15, 2003, TAMU Archives; "Meloy Awarded DSC for Heroism," *College Station (Tex.) Battalion* (Sept. 26, 1950); Adams, *Keepers of the Spirit*, p. 175; Toland, *In Mortal Combat*, pp. 91–97; Guy S. Meloy Jr., "The Eighth Army Story," *Army Digest* (June, 1963), pp. 2–13.

16. Memorandum, Jim McGuire to Henry Dethloff, Apr. 15, 2003, TAMU Archives; "Meloy Awarded DSC for Heroism," *College Station (Tex.) Battalion* (Sept. 26, 1950); Adams, *Keepers of the Spirit*, p. 175; Toland, *In Mortal Combat*, pp. 91–97; Guy S. Meloy Jr., "The Eighth Army Story," *Army Digest* (June, 1963), pp. 2–13; Korean War casualties file, AFS, TAMU Archives.

17. Memorandum, Jim McGuire to Henry Dethloff, Apr. 15, 2003, TAMU Archives; "Meloy

Awarded DSC for Heroism," *College Station* (Tex.) *Battalion* (Sept. 26, 1950); Adams, *Keepers of the Spirit*, p. 175; Toland, *In Mortal Combat*, pp. 91–97; Guy S. Meloy Jr., "The Eighth Army Story," *Army Digest* (June, 1963), pp. 2–13; Korean War casualties file, AFS, TAMU Archives.

18. Roy E. Appleman, *South to the Naktong, North to the Yalu, June–November 1940* (Washington, D.C.: GPO, Office of the Chief of Military History, Dept. of the Army, 1961), pp. 488–504; Eugene F. Clark, *The Secrets of Inchon: The Untold Story* (New York: Putnam's Sons, 2002), pp. 17–231.

19. Matthew B. Ridgway, *The Korean War: How We Met the Challenge: How All-out Asian War Was Averted: Why MacArthur Was Dismissed: Why Today's War Objectives Must Be Limited* (Garden City, N.Y.: Doubleday, 1967), p. 40; Brig. Gen. Edwin H. Simmons, *Over the Seawall: U.S. Marines at Inchon*, Korean War Commemorative Series (Washington, D.C.: Marine Corps Historical Center, 2000), pp. 1–68.

20. "Col. Ray Murray ('35) Relates Recent Korean Experiences," *Texas Aggie* (Apr. 30, 1951); "Aggie-Ex Wins Promotion to Marine High Position," *College Station* (Tex.) *Battalion* (July 26, 1962); Clay Blair, *The Forgotten War: America in Korea, 1950–1953* (New York: Times Books, 1987), p. 194.

21. Blair, *Forgotten War*, pp. 233–60; Adams, *Keepers of the Spirit*, p. 133; Appleman, *South to the Naktong*, pp. 510–15; Brian Catchpole, *The Korean War* (New York: Carroll and Graf, 2001), p. 45.

22. Lt. Gen. John H. Miller (ret.), interview by John A. Adams Jr. and Henry C. Dethloff, June 21, 2003, College Station, Tex.

23. Memorandum, "My Mission during the Korean War," by Richard R. ("Dick") Tumlinson; memorandum, "Bert Beecroft in the United States Air Force," TAMU Archives.

24. Blair, *Forgotten War*, pp. 270–321; Tom Parsons, interview by John A. Adams Jr., Feb. 4, 1999; Jon E. Lewis, ed., *Book of Battles: The Art and Science of Modern Warfare* (New York: Carroll and Graf, 1995), pp. 403–10. There were only three dates on which the tides would have been high enough to allow the landing craft (LSTs [landing ship tank]), which drew twenty-nine feet, to avoid the mudflats and land: Sept. 15, Oct. 11, and Nov. 3; even then, only a three-hour window was available.

25. Toland, *In Mortal Combat*, pp. 238–54.

26. Quote in Martin Russ, *Breakout: The Chosin Reservoir Campaign—Korea 1950* (New York: Penguin, 2000), p. 77.

27. Allen S. Whiting, *China Crosses the Yalu: The Decision to Enter the Korean War* (New York: Macmillan, 1960), pp. 5–96; Carter Malkasian, *The Korean War 1950–1953* (Oxford, UK: Osprey, 2001), pp. 28–29; Appleman, *South to the Naktong*, pp. 667–774.

28. Roy E. Appleman, *East of Chosin: Entrapment and Breakout in Korea, 1950* (College Station: Texas A&M University Press, 1987), pp. 3–194; Russ, *Breakout*, pp. 14–105.

29. Email memorandum, Jim McGuire to Henry Dethloff, Apr. 15, 2003, TAMU Archives; see Brig. Gen. W. W. Harris (commander of the 65th), *Puerto Rico's Fighting 65th U.S. Infantry: From San Juan to Chorwan* (San Rafael, Calif.: Presidio Press, 1980).

30. Harris, *Puerto Rico's Fighting 65th*, pp. 139, 163. See also Toland, *In Mortal Combat*, pp. 346–47, and Blair, *Forgotten War*, pp. 458–59.

31. Robert Leckie, *The March to Glory* (New York: World, 1959), p. 169.

32. Toland, *In Mortal Combat*, p. 346.

33. Russ, *Breakout*, pp. 186, 204, 235, 285–92, 312–14, 328; Blair, *Forgotten War*, pp. 534–47; Roy Appleman, *Escaping the Trap: The U.S. Army X Corps in Northeast Korea, 1950* (College Station: Texas A&M University Press, 1990), pp. 247–66.

34. "Col. Ray Murray '35, Relates Recent Korean Experiences," *Texas Aggie* (Apr. 30, 1951), p. 18.

35. Appleman, *Escaping the Trap*, pp. 366–73; Ridgway, *Korean War*, pp. 47–124; Blair, *Forgotten War*, p. 464; Lt. Gen. John H. Miller, interview by John A. Adams and Henry C. Dethloff, June 21, 2003, College Station, Tex.

36. Gen. Waymond C. Nutt ('51), interview by John A. Adams Jr., Feb. 18, 2003; "Silver Taps," *Texas Aggie* (Jan., 2003; Mar., 2003).

37. Gen. Waymond C. Nutt ('51), interview by John A. Adams Jr., Feb. 18, 2003, TAMU Archives; "Silver Taps," *Texas Aggie* (Jan., 2003; Mar., 2003).

38. Ridgway, *Korean War*, pp. 79–121; Conrad C. Crane, *American Airpower Strategy in Korea, 1950–1953* (Lawrence: University Press of Kansas, 2000), pp. 80–84; Bill Vaughn to C. C. Taylor, Mar. 18, 2004, with report dated Apr. 3, 1951, TAMU Archives.

39. Ridgway, *Korean War*, pp. 79–121; Conrad C. Crane, *American Airpower Strategy in Korea, 1950–1953* (Lawrence: University Press of Kansas, 2000), pp. 80–84; Bill Vaughn to C. C. Taylor, Mar. 18, 2004, with report dated Apr. 3, 1951, TAMU Archives.

40. Letter, Ken Schaake ('51), class agent, to John A. Adams Jr., Mar. 3, 2003; Texas A&M College, commissioning exercises, Guion Hall, June 1, 1951, College Station, Tex.

41. "Former Commandant of A&M Sends Letter from Korea Post," *College Station* (Tex.) *Battalion* (Oct. 9, 1951).

42. Memorandum, "Highlights of Military Career of Wilman D. Barnes, Class of 1951," TAMU Archives; memorandum, Thomas Harvey Royder III, "Recalling and Sharing My Experiences of War," TAMU Archives; G. M. Giangreco, *War in Korea, 1950–1953* (Novato, Calif.: Presidio Press, 2001), pp. 203–49.

43. Royder, "Recalling and Sharing My Experiences."

44. Memorandum, "Highlights of Military Career of Wilman D. Barnes, Class of 1951," TAMU Archives.

45. Crane, *American Airpower Strategy*, pp. 11–53.

46. John R. Bruning, *Crimson Sky: The Air Battle for Korea* (Dulles, Va.: Brassey's, 2000), p. 206; Xiaoming Zhang, *Red Wings over the Yalu: China, the Soviet Union, and the Air War in Korea* (College Station: Texas A&M University Press, 2002), pp. 42–98.

Chapter 15

1. D. M. Giangreco, *War in Korea, 1950–1953* (Novato, Calif.: Presidio Press, 2001), pp. 204–49.

2. Robert F. Futrell, *The United States Air Force in Korea, 1950–1953* (Washington, D.C.: Office of Air Force History, United States Air Force, 1983), p. 52.

3. Ibid., p. 44; Conrad C. Crane, *American Airpower Strategy in Korea, 1950–1953* (Lawrence: University Press of Kansas, 2000), pp. 31–34.

4. Futrell, *USAF in Korea*, pp. 118–19, 534–44; Crane, *American Airpower Strategy*, pp. 117–28.

5. Futrell, *USAF in Korea*, pp. 118–19, 534–44; Crane, *American Airpower Strategy*, pp. 117–128.

6. Memorandum, "Bert Beecroft in the United States Air Force," by Bert E. Beecroft, Apr. 19, 2003, TAMU Archives.

7. Ibid.

8. Ibid.

9. James V. Proffitt ('47), interview by John A. Adams Jr., Apr. 6, 2003, Laredo, Tex.; Gen. Waymond C. Nutt, interview by John A. Adams Jr., Apr. 11, 2003, San Antonio, Tex.; *Texas Aggie Magazine* (Nov., 1952–July, 1953).

10. Gen. Waymond C. Nutt, interview by John A. Adams Jr., Apr. 11, 2003, San Antonio, Tex.; "Moody Pilot Bags Red MiG in Korea," *Waco Times* (Jan. 15, 1953). See also Zhang, *Red Wings over the Yalu*, pp. 55–67.

11. Richard R. Tumlinson, interview by John A. Adams Jr., Apr. 25, 2003; James P. McCarthy and Drue L. DeBerry, *The Air Force* (Washington, D.C: Air Force Historical Foundation, 2002), pp. 136–37, 142.

12. Letter, J. L. McFarling Jr. to C. C. Taylor, Apr. 16, 2004, and citation, TAMU Archives.

13. Memorandum, "B29 Bombing Strikes into North Korea," by 1st Lt. Dare K. Keelan (n.d.), TAMU Archives.

14. Letter and memorandum, Frederick P. Henry to C. C. Taylor, Mar. 19, 2004; citation, 2nd Lt. Winston A. McKenzie; *Houston Post* (July 5, 1953), in Aggies in War files and records, TAMU Archives.

15. Robert Leach Pierson, accident report, July 10, 1953, TAMU Archives.

16. Edwin P. Hoyt, *The Bloody Road to Panmunjom* (New York: Stein and Day, 1985), pp. 213–83; Appleman, *Ridgway Duels for Korea*, p. 651; *Army Times* (Pacific) (Dec. 10, 1953), p. 18.

17. Memorandum, "The Korean War as Experienced by Robert L. (Bob) Middleton," TAMU Archives.

18. Ibid.

19. Headquarters, 40th Infantry Division, APO 6, general orders no. 66, Feb. 21, 1953, Award of the Silver Star, TAMU Archives; see Arned Hinshaw, *Heartbreak Ridge* (New York: Praeger, 1989), pp. 7–123.

20. Memoranda and citation, L. D. Ross to C. C. Taylor, Mar. 5, 2004, TAMU Archives.

21. Memorandum, "Quad 50s in Infantry Combat during the Third Korean Winter Campaign," by Dudley J. Hughes, TAMU Archives.

22. Headquarters, 40th Infantry Division, general order no. 115, Mar. 24, 1953, Award of the Silver Star, TAMU Archives.

23. Mrs. J. R. Holland, Belton, Tex., to Mr. Hervey, Nov. 21, 1952, AFS files.

24. "Bill Knapp Dies Hero in Korean Battle Oct. 18," *Texas A&M System News* (Dec., 1952); "DSC Given Late Hero, Lt. Knapp," Houston Post News Service (n.d, n.p.), AFS casualty files.

25. Walter G. Hermes, *Truce Tent and the Fighting Front* (Washington, D.C.: GPO, 1966), pp. 283–512; "Aggies Who Died in Korea to Be on Memorial," *Texas Aggie* (June, 1996). The number of deaths during the war in Korea has been revised upward to 63 from the 58 former students reported in the *Texas Aggie* (Nov., 1953) and as noted in John A. Adams Jr., *Keepers of the Spirit: The Corps of Cadets at Texas A&M University, 1876–2001* (College Station: Texas A&M University Press, 2001), p. 182; Robert E. Thompson, email to Henry Dethloff, Apr. 11, 2004; email, McIver to C. C. Taylor, Mar. 14, 2003; and see Levine, in Aggies in War file, TAMU Archives.

26. Col. Joseph B. Murphy, biographical, in Aggies in War Files and Letters, TAMU Archives; and see Joseph B. Murphy, http://lib-oldweb.tamu.edu/aggiesinwar.

27. "Soft Measure Out, Says Gen. Boatner," *Dallas Morning News* (May 16, 1952); "New 'Stern' Policy Is Instituted," *Houston Chronicle* (May 19, 1952).

28. Arned L. Hinshaw, *Heartbreak Ridge* (New York: Praeger, 1989), pp. 63–64; Historical Division, *Merrill's Marauders (February–May, 1944)* (Washington, D.C.: GPO, Military Intelligence Division, U.S. War Dept., June, 1945), pp. 1–115; Brian Catchpole, *The Korean War* (New York: Carroll and Graf, 2001), pp. 207–26; Hermes, *Truce Tent*, pp. 248–62. A highly decorated member of Merrill's Marauders, Capt. Logan E. Weston returned to the A&M campus to serve as chaplain at All Faiths' Chapel.

29. Edward E. Thomas and Jack D. Gressett, interview by Henry C. Dethloff, June 21, 2004, College Station, Tex.

30. See Leo J. Daugherty and Gregory Louis Mattson, *NAM: A Photographic History* (New York: Metro Books, 2001); James R. Arnold, *The First Domino: Eisenhower, the Military, and America's Intervention in Vietnam* (New York: William Morrow, 1991), pp. 55–58, 83–84.

31. See Marvin E. Gettleman, *Vietnam: History, Documents, and Opinions* (New York: Fawcett, 1965), pp. 62–181; Harry G. Summers Jr., *On Strategy: A Critical Analysis of the Vietnam War* (New York: Dell, 1984), pp. 94–95; Adm. U. S. Grant Sharp (USN, commander in chief, Pacific), *Report on the War in Vietnam as of 30 June 1968*, sec. 1 (Washington, D.C.: GPO, 1968), pp. 4–5; Gen. William C. Westmoreland (commander, U.S. Military Assistance Command, Vietnam), *Report on Operations in South Vietnam, January 1964–June 1968*, sec. 2 (Washington, D.C.: GPO, 1968), p. 79; Jules Roy, *The Battle of Dienbienphu* (New York: Carroll and Graf, 1984), pp. 288–310.

32. "Thailand Album" and "Light on the Twilight War," *Army Digest* (Jan., 1963), pp. 8–9, 36–41.

Chapter 16

1. Bruce Palmer Jr., *The 25-Year War: America's Military Role in Vietnam* (Lexington: University of Kentucky Press, 1984), pp. 5, 28–31; John A. Adams Jr., *Keepers of the Spirit: The Corps of Cadets at Texas A&M University, 1876–2001* (College Station: Texas A&M University Press, 2001), p. 225.

2. Palmer, *The 25-Year War*, pp. 5, 28–31; Bernard Newman, *Background to Vietnam* (New York: Signet, 1965), pp. 144–49; Harry G. Summers Jr., *On Strategy: A Critical Analysis of the Vietnam War* (New York: Dell, 1984), pp. 87–95. See also Military Assistance Command, Vietnam (MACV) HQ, *Strategy since 1954* (Saigon: Office of Joint General Staff J-2, June 29, 1967), pp. 1–45.

3. Palmer, *The 25-Year War*, p. 39; Adams, *Keepers of the Spirit*, p. 225.

4. Adams, *Keepers of the Spirit*, pp. 200–11; "Texas A&M Diplomas Go to 900," *Austin American Statesman* (May 29, 1960).

5. Thomas R. Hargrove, *A Dragon Lives Forever: War and Rice in Vietnam's Mekong Delta, 1969–1991 and Beyond* (New York: Ivy Books, 1994), pp. 186–88.

6. Department of the Army, *Jungle Operations* (Washington, D.C.: GPO, FM 31-30, Oct., 1960); Tom Mangold and John Penycate, *The Tunnels of Cu Chi* (New York: Berkley Books, 1986), pp. 1–282.

7. Biographical, TAMU Archives; *A&M Spirit and Sharing* (35) (Summer, 2003).

8. Len Layne ('59), unpublished manuscript (Feb. 20, 2002), Aggies in War files and records, TAMU Archives; Peter Arnett, "Four Stood Ground, Died in Ambush," *Birmingham News* (Aug. 23, 1964), p. 1.

9. Layne ('59), unpublished manuscript (Feb. 20, 2002), Aggies in War files and records, TAMU Archives; Arnett, "Four Stood Ground," p. 1; Harold Moore and Joseph L. Galloway, *We Were Soldiers Once . . . and Young* (New York: Random House, 1992), p. 337; Lyndon B. Johnson, *The Vantage Point* (New York: Popular Library, 1971), pp. 116–19; Robert S. McNamara, *In Retrospect: The Tragedy and Lessons of Vietnam* (New York: Random House, 1995), pp. 127–43. Passing the Senate by a vote of 88 to 2 and the House by a unanimous voice vote, the Gulf of Tonkin Resolution became Public Law 88-408; "South Vietnam: A New Kind of War," *Time* (Oct. 22, 1965), pp. 32–45.

10. Peter B. Mersky and Norman Polmar, *The Naval Air War in Vietnam* (Annapolis, Md.: Nautical and Aviation Publishing, 1981), pp. 121–23.

11. Maj. Gen. Thomas Darling ('54), interview by John A. Adams Jr., June 8, 2003.

12. Memo, William A. Becker to Henry C. Dethloff, Oct. 2, 2003, TAMU Archives.

13. Moore and Galloway, *We Were Soldiers Once*, p. 258.

14. Memo, William A. Becker to Henry C. Dethloff, Oct. 2, 2003, TAMU Archives.

15. General order no. 4264, Award of the Silver Star to Boyce A. Cates, Sept. 9, 1967; general order no. 3132, Award of the Distinguished Flying Cross, July 5, 1967, TAMU Archives.

16. Letter, Frank M. Muller to C. C. Taylor, Mar. 21, 2004, TAMU Archives.

17. Frederick H. Mitchell, Award of the Silver Star, TAMU Archives.

18. William A. Becker to Henry C. Dethloff, memo and inserts to chap. 16, Oct. 2, 2003, in Aggies in War Papers, TAMU Archives.

19. Paul McKay, "Ormond Simpson Fights Winning Battles," *Bryan–College Station Eagle* (May 1, 1983); "Maj. Gen. W. B. Kyle Commands 3d Div.," *Sea Tiger* (Mar. 25, 1966); "A South Texas Marine," *Dallas News* (Jan. 23, 1967); Hans Eric von Dorp, "Someone Has to Be Division Commander," *Texas Aggie* (Apr., 1968), pp. 4–7.

20. Silver Star citation to 2nd Lt. Richard L. Daerr Jr., USMCR, TAMU Archives.

21. Ann Robinette to Bill Lonquist (n.d.), with Silver Star citation and letter of commendation, TAMU Archives.

22. Zalon Grant, *Facing the Phoenix* (New York: Norton, 1991), pp. 21–30, 293–97.

23. William Hearn to John A. Adams Jr., June 20, 2003, and June 23, 2003; Department of the Army, Headquarters, 1st Infantry Division, general order no. 2012, Award of the Silver Star to William C. Hearne, TAMU Archives.

24. *Texas Aggie* (Feb.–Mar., 1967), pp. 3–4.

25. Ibid.; Paul Joseph, *Crack in the Empire: State Politics in the Vietnam War* (New York: Columbia University Press, 1987), pp. 209–44.

26. "Marine Corps Reunion Brings Memories of 'Why There Is a Fourth of July Celebration,'" article by USMC Maj. M. N. Chafey, written twenty-six years after the incident. *Clifton (Tex.) Record* (n.d.), TAMU Archives.

27. Charles E. Burge to C. C. Taylor, June 6, 2003, TAMU Archives.

28. Award of the Silver Star, general orders no. 4511, Aug. 9, 1967, in Aggies in War files and records, TAMU Archives; "Spy on Uncle Ho's Trail," *Texas Aggie* (Feb., 1967), pp. 33–34.

29. Address of Pres. Lyndon B. Johnson, White House, Mar. 31, 1968, in "Air Force Policy Letter for Commanders" (Washington, D.C.: May, 1968); Summers, *On Strategy,* pp. 43, 182–86; Doris Kearns, *Lyndon Johnson and the American Dream* (New York: Harper and Row, 1976), p. 356; "Twenty Years Later, Tet Recalled as 'Beginning of the End,'" *New*

York Times news service, in Gwinnett (Ga.) Daily News (Jan. 31, 1988); letter of appreciation, attn: Maj. Clarence H. Woliver, May 10, 1968; Houston Chronicle, staff report by Lynwood Abram on Clancy Woliver, Apr. 25, 2002, TAMU Archives.

30. Biographical sketch files and interviews, TAMU Archives.

31. General order no. 202, Award of the Silver Star to James R. Woodall, Apr. 11, 1969, TAMU Archives.

32. "Hi. Well, Today Is Another Day in Vietnam," Texas Aggie (Feb., 1967), pp. 3–4; Edward Y. Hall ('60), Valley of the Shadow (Spartanburg, S.C.: Honoribus Press, 1986), pp. 4–265.

33. Email and attachments from Arthur W. Noll to C. C. Taylor, Apr. 1, 2002, TAMU Archives.

34. Palmer, The 25-Year War, p. 26. Before 1968, the Huey troops in Vietnam were moved by the H-21, nicknamed the "Flying Banana." "U.S. 'Copter: Experimental Ace Now in Viet Nam," College Station (Tex.) Battalion (Oct. 3, 1962); Adams, Keepers of the Spirit, pp. 224–25.

35. Capt. Robert Acklen ('67), Corps Hall of Honor, Sam Houston Sanders Corps Center, College Station, Tex.; "One of A&M's Most Decorated Graduates, He Never Talked about It," Texas Aggie (June, 1999), p. 7.

36. General order no. 3639, Award of Distinguished Flying Cross to Billy M. Vaughn, Feb. 25, 1971, TAMU Archives.

37. Email from Jeff Murray of Fort Worth to John A. Adams Jr., Apr. 24, 2003.

38. Hargrove, A Dragon Lives Forever, pp. 287–99; "A&M Grad Likes Job in Vietnam," Bryan (Tex.) Daily Eagle (Jan. 25, 1967), p. 5; email from Edward Y. Hall to John A. Adams Jr., June 11, 2003.

39. Jerry Houston, interview by John A. Adams Jr., June 6, 2003.

40. "Aggies on the Go: Farmers Fight at Sea," Texas Aggie (Sept., 1972), pp. 20–21. For a detailed account of Houston and Teague, see Sally Rawlings, ed., Phantoms over Vietnam: U.S. Navy F4 Phantoms, 1965–1973 (Oxford, UK: Osprey, 2002), pp. 111–13, 116.

41. Citation to accompany the Award of the Distinguished Flying Cross to Frederick F. Nye III, TAMU Archives.

42. Not all combat missions were equal. There was an elaborate system for counting missions. Those to North Vietnam were the most significant. One hundred sorties to North Vietnam was a very prized achievement and generally resulted in rotation back to the States regardless of the length of tour.

43. http://lib-oldweb.tamu.edu/aggiesinwar/; Jack Swift, "The Mini-plane World of Major Ellis," Texas Aggie (May, 1969), pp. 5–8.

44. Maj. Gen. Thomas Darling, interview by John A. Adams Jr., Apr. 25, 1991, TAMU Archives; G. B. Simler, "Airpower in Southeast Asia," U.S. Air Force policy letter for commanders, Washington, D.C., June, 1968, pp. 10–15; Jack Broughton, Going Downtown: The War against Hanoi and Washington (New York: Orion, 1988), pp. 171–288.

45. http://lib-oldweb.tamu.edu/aggiesinwar/. The fire cost 134 lives, and sixty-four aircraft were either destroyed or badly damaged.

46. Letter, Col. Homer D. Smith to Richard Weirus, May 15, 1970, AFS Papers; Adams, Softly Call the Muster, p. 54; John M. Economidy, "The Aggie Muster Mission: 25 Years Later," Texas Aggie (Apr., 1995), pp. 2–3; "Aggie Veteran [Kirk] Receives Top Honor," Texas Aggie (Feb., 1972), p. 23; John A. Adams Jr., We Are the Aggies: The Texas A&M

University Association of Former Students (College Station: Texas A&M University Press, 1979), p. 196.

47. Letter, Col. Homer D. Smith to Richard Weirus, May 15, 1970, AFS Papers; Adams, *Softly Call the Muster*, p. 54; John M. Economidy, "The Aggie Muster Mission: 25 Years Later," *Texas Aggie* (Apr., 1995), pp. 2–3; "Aggie Veteran [Kirk] Receives Top Honor," *Texas Aggie* (Feb., 1972), p. 23; Adams, *We Are the Aggies*, p. 196; *Texas Aggie* (Nov., 1996), p. 6.

48. John L. Frisbee, "Long Night at Mo Doc," *Air Force Magazine* (Mar., 1987); Christopher Robbins, *The Ravens: The Men Who Flew in America's Secret War in Laos* (New York: Crown Pocket Books, 1987), pp. 175–79; John A. Adams, *The Noise Never Dies: Ton San Nhut, 1970–1971* (College Station, Tex.: Intaglio Press, 2003), pp. 12–68; Susan Levine, "Three Houstonians Still on Vietnam War MIA List," *Houston Chronicle* (Sept. 1, 1978), p. 18.

49. *Los Angeles Times* (Mar. 8, 1970), p. 2.

50. Memorandum, Col. John B. Ferrata, USAF (ret.), TAMU Archives.

51. Robbins, *The Ravens*, pp. 175–79; Adams, *The Noise Never Dies*, pp. 12–68; Levine, "Three Houstonians," p. 18; "Air Force Honors Tijerina," *Texas Aggie* (Nov., 1985), p. 4.

52. H. Bruce Franklin, "Missing in Action in the 21st Century," *Long Term View* 5 (Summer, 2000): 39–52; Rod Colvin, *First Heroes: The POWs Left Behind in Vietnam* (New York: Irvington, 1987), pp. 285–341; press release, "Summary of ARC Action on Behalf of U.S. Prisoners of War in Vietnam," American Red Cross News Service, Washington, D.C., Jan. 4, 1971, AFS Vietnam MIA/POW file; "American Prisoners of War and Missing in Action in Southeast Asia, 1973," 93rd Cong., 1st sess., hearings before the Subcommittee on National Security Policy and Scientific Developments, part 4, May 23, 1973. In contrast, the International Committee of the Red Cross estimated that some thirty-eight thousand communist troops were held as POWs in South Vietnam. Alton Meyer ('60), interview by John A. Adams Jr., May 30, 2003, College Station, Tex.; "Reds Kept POWs at Strategic Point," *Ft. Worth Press* (Apr. 22, 1973). See also Returned POWs file, AFS Papers; "The Plight of the Prisoners: Acting to Aid the Forgotten Men," *Time* (Dec. 7, 1970), pp. 15–22; Louis R. Stockstill, "The Forgotten Americans in the Vietnam War," *Air Force and Space Digest* (Oct., 1969); "But When Are They Coming Home?" *Texas Aggie* (Oct., 1970), pp. 8–10; "Scarred Legacy: Aggies in Vietnam," *College Station* (Tex.) *Battalion* (Nov. 11, 1986), supplement, pp. 1–8; "In the Enemy Hands" (n.p., n.d.); Aggies in the Military file, TAMU Archives. See also Jeremiah A. Denton Jr., *When Hell Was in Session* (Clover, S.C.: Riverhills Press, 1976), pp. 1–237, and Larry Chesley, *Seven Years in Hanoi: A POW Tells His Story* (Salt Lake City: Bookcraft, 1973), pp. 1–158; U.S. Congress, "American Prisoners of War and Missing in Action in Southeast Asia, 1973," 93rd Cong., 1st sess., hearings before the Subcommittee of National Security Policy and Scientific Developments, part 4, May 23, 30, 31, 1973.

53. Joe D. Boyd ('57), "Faith, Hope, and (Perot's) Charity," *Texas Aggie* (July, 1970), pp. 11–17; Maurice L. Lien, "The Plight of the Prisoners We Have Not Forgotten," *Air Force and Space Digest* (June, 1970), pp. 32–40.

54. *Texas Aggie* (Jan.–Mar., 1971).

55. Ibid. (Mar., 1971); "On to Paris" file, AFS Papers; Kent Caperton, interview by John A. Adams Jr., June 3, 2003.

56. Jeffery Clarke, *Advice and Support: The Final Years, 1965–1973* (Washington, D.C.: GPO,

Center of Military History, 1988), pp. 449–60; Palmer, *The 25-Year War*, pp. 83, 93; William Shawcross, *Sideshow: Kissinger, Nixon, and the Destruction of Cambodia* (New York: Cooper Square Press, 2002), pp. 112–87.

57. Clarke, *Advice and Support*, pp. 474–75; Adams, *The Noise Never Dies*, pp. 45–60; Ray L. Bowers, *Tactical Airlift* (Washington, D.C.: GPO, Office of Air Force History, 1983), p. 517; Stanley Karnow, *Vietnam: A History* (New York: Viking Press, 1983), pp. 628–31.

58. James Willbanks, interview by John A. Adams Jr., June 8, 2003. See also James H. Willbanks ('69), *Thiet Giap! The Battle of An Loc, April 1972* (Fort Leavenworth, Kans.: U.S. Army Command and General Staff College, 1993), pp. 1–11.

59. Col. Chuck Holt, interview by John A. Adams Jr., June 9, 2003.

60. Memorandum by Col. Robert V. Reid regarding the mission in "Aircraft 043" on June 18, 1972, TAMU Archives.

61. Willbanks, *Thiet Giap!* pp. 10–40, 70; Frank Muller, interview by John A. Adams Jr., June 16, 2003; Earl H. Tilford Jr., *Crosswinds: The Air Force's Setup in Vietnam* (College Station: Texas A&M University Press, 1993), p. 146; Drew Middleton, *Air War Vietnam* (New York: Bobbs-Merrill, 1978), p. 201; Bowers, *Tactical Airlift*, pp. 539–79. See also A. J. C. Lavalle, ed., *Airpower and the 1972 Spring Invasion* (Washington, D.C.: GPO, 1976); Henry Kissinger, *The White House Years* (Boston: Little, Brown, 1979), p. 1196.

62. Marilyn B. Young, *The Vietnam Wars, 1945–1990* (New York: Harper, 1991), pp. 202–203; Lawrence M. Baskir and William A. Strauss, *Chance and Circumstance: The Draft, the War, and the Vietnam Generation* (New York: Vantage Books, 1978), p. 53.

63. Letter from Brig. Gen. Melvin A. Goers, director of the U.S. Army ROTC, to "Parents," May 1, 1969, in authors' papers; Adams, *Keepers of the Spirit*, chart titled "Vietnam Era Officer Production at Texas A&M, 1962–1973," p. 223.

64. Keith Shelton, "Sanger General Goes Where Action Is," *Denton Record-Chronicle* (June 19, 1966); and see McNamara, *In Retrospect*, pp. 320–35; Paul Joseph, *Cracks in the Empire: State Politics in the Vietnam War* (New York: Columbia University Press, 1987), pp. 287–305; Harrison E. Salisbury, ed., *Vietnam Reconsidered: Lessons from a War* (New York: Harper and Row, 1984), pp. 284–320; James Burk, "How Vietnam Shaped the All-volunteer Force," *Long Term View* 5 (Summer, 2000): 53–66; Loren Baritz, *Backfire* (New York: William Morrow, 1985), pp. 21–350; Donald Mruzek, *Air Power and the Ground War in Vietnam* (Montgomery, Ala.: Air University Press, Maxwell AFB, Jan., 1988), pp. 1–187; Kissinger, *White House Years*, pp. 1446–68; Robert A. Pape, *Bombing to Win: Airpower and Coercion in War* (Ithaca, N.Y.: Cornell University Press, 1996), pp. 174–210; Marshall L. Michel, *The Eleven Days of Christmas: America's Last Vietnam Battle* (San Francisco: Encounter Books, 2000), pp. 41–242.

65. "A&M Congressmen Look at Vietnam," *Texas Aggie* (Jan., 1968), p. 28. Congressman Olin ("Tiger") Teague ('32) made three inspection trips to Vietnam between 1965 and 1967.

66. Gen. Ormond R. Simpson, USMC (ret.), interview by Terry H. Anderson and Benis M. Frank, TAMU Archives, 1985.

Chapter 17

1. Robert Keeney, http://lib-oldweb.tamu.edu/aggiesinwar/.

2. Memorandum, Donald E. Ellis to C. C. Taylor, Apr. 2, 2004, TAMU Archives. Not all of the POWs were returned, and the search continues to the present.

3. Brig. Gen. James R. Taylor, interview by Mariane Vardaman, Nov. 8, 1982, TAMU Archives.

4. "R. James Woolsey, a Long War," *New York Times* (Apr. 15, 2003).

5. Ibid.

6. *Texas Aggie* (June, 1986; Mar., 1988).

7. "In Memorium, Brigadier General Donald L. Moore, 1935 to 1987," AFC4A, in Aggies in War files and records, TAMU Archives; *Texas Aggie* (June, 1985; Mar., 1986; June, 1988; June, 1989).

8. *Texas Aggie* (Oct., 1982).

9. Ibid. (May, 1977; July, 1981).

10. Ibid. (Aug., 1994).

11. Ibid. (June, 1988).

12. Ibid. (Mar., 1989)

13. Ibid. (Mar., 1982).

14. Ibid. (Dec., 1988; Aug., 1988; Aug., 1990).

15. Ibid. (Dec., 1988; Aug., 1988).

16. Bossier City, La., *Bossier Press-Tribune* (June 21, 1999).

17. *Texas Aggie* (Feb., 1982).

18. Memorandum, Corps Hall of Honor inductees, TAMU Archives.

19. *Texas Aggie* (June, 1986; Aug., 1989).

20. Ibid. (Mar., 1989).

21. Ibid. (Dec., 1989).

22. Vita synopsis, Charles Dewey McMullan, TAMU Archives.

23. *Texas Aggie* (Jan., 2002), p. 38.

24. Ibid. (June, 1987; Nov., 1990); Gen. Waymond C. Nutt, interview by John A. Adams Jr., Apr. 11, 2003.

25. Maj. Gen. Thomas R. Olsen, U.S. Air Force biography; Maj. Gen. Thomas R. Olsen, interview by Jerry Cooper, Sept. 28, 1994, TAMU Archives.

26. *Texas Aggie* (Sept., 1983; Nov., 1983; Oct., 1989).

27. Ibid. (Mar., 1986).

28. Ibid. (Aug., 1988).

29. Ibid. (Mar., 1995).

30. Ibid. (Aug., 1989).

31. Ibid. (Oct., 1989). *The Complete Encyclopedia of World Aircraft* (New York: Barnes and Noble, 1997), p. 707, incorrectly identifies Richard S. Couch as Richard S. Cough.

32. *Texas Aggie* (Nov., 1983).

33. Bryan P. Austin, fax to Jerry Cooper, May 12, 2002; Austin, email to Jerry Cooper, May 13, 2002, TAMU Archives.

34. Bryan P. Austin, fax to Jerry Cooper, May 12, 2002; Austin, email to Jerry Cooper, May 13, 2002, TAMU Archives; *Texas Aggie* (May, 2001; July, 2002); see the respective NASA biographical data, TAMU Archives.

35. Bryan P. Austin, fax to Jerry Cooper, May 12, 2002; Austin, email to Jerry Cooper, May 13, 2002, TAMU Archives; *Texas Aggie* (May, 2001; July, 2002); see the respective NASA biographical data, TAMU Archives.

36. *Texas Aggie* (May, 2001).

37. Emailed news account from Robert Gosney, June 7, 2001, to Marie Martch (and

others), copying a news article by Chris Menczer, *Herald* staff writer, "Liberia's Past Tied with Local Career Soldier," in Aggies in War papers, TAMU Archives.

38. Ibid.

39. Allen Bettisworth, http://lib-oldweb.tamu.edu/aggiesinwar/.

40. John Mack Faragher, Mari Jo Buhle, Daniel Czitrom, Susan H. Armitage, *Out of Many: A History of the American People*, 2d ed., vol. 2 (Saddle River, N.J.: Prentice Hall, 1997), p. 1027.

Chapter 18

1. U.S. Air Force, news release, PAI91-08-12-01, TAMU Archives.

2. Ibid.; Bill Bender to Jerry Cooper, Nov. 22, 1990, TAMU Archives.

3. Bender to Cooper, Nov. 22, 1990, TAMU Archives.

4. Release no. 1488-00, Navy Public Affairs Center, Norfolk, Va., TAMU Archives.

5. Letter, 1st Lt. Enoch Kent Wong to Jerry Cooper, Feb. 25, 1991, TAMU Archives.

6. Letter, Dale A. Cope (n.d.) to Jerry Cooper; Capt. Robert James to *Texas Aggie* (received Jan. 24, 1991), TAMU Archives.

7. Harry L. Warren, MD, to Jerry Cooper, Feb. 24, 1991, TAMU Archives.

8. Memo and clipping, Roy A. Julian Jr. ('69), to *Texas Aggie*, Feb. 27, 1991, TAMU Archives.

9. Sue Alland, "Navigator Served in Desert Storm," *Weatherford* (Tex.) *Democrat Reporter* (Apr. 11, 1991).

10. *Texas Aggie* (Nov., 1990); Stew Rayfield to *Texas Aggie*, Sept. 6, 1990, TAMU Archives.

11. Maj. Gen. H. Hale Burr Jr., USAF biography; Gen. Hal M. Hornburg biography, headquarters, Air Combat Command, TAMU Archives.

12. Jerry C. Cooper, "Olsen Led Air Forces in Desert Storm," *Texas Aggie* (Dec., 1991).

13. Ibid.

14. Stew Rayfield to *Texas Aggie*, Sept. 1, 1990, TAMU Archives.

15. Marilyn M. Wesley, "Texas A&M University Alumnus Sees Persian Gulf War from Unique Perspective," Navy Public Affairs Center, Norfolk, Va., press release no. 1221-91, TAMU Archives. The area of surveillance is identified as three million cubic miles.

16. Jim I. ("Jake") Swinson Jr., "Eglin Nomad Blasts MiG from the Sky" (n.d.), untitled clipping, TAMU Archives.

17. M. G. Fink to Thomas E. Wisdom, Feb. 7, 1991, TAMU Archives.

18. R. M. Rayfield to Thomas E. Wisdom, Jan. 21, 1991; Mike Minyard to Wisdom, Jan. 26, 1991; letter to "Dear Aggies" from James M. Young, Jan. 19, 1991, TAMU Archives.

19. David Smithhart to *Texas Aggie*, Feb. 10, 1991, TAMU Archives; *Washington Times* (Mar. 28, 1992).

20. Lt. Cdr. Joe A. Alexander to "Dear Friends," Jan. 28, 1991, TAMU Archives.

21. *Houston Chronicle* (Feb. 26, 1991); unidentified news clipping, Feb. 24, 1991, TAMU Archives.

22. *Houston Chronicle* (Feb. 26, 1991); unidentified news clipping, Feb. 24, 1991, TAMU Archives; Department of the Army, asst. chief of staff, G3, to AFS, Apr. 24, 1991, TAMU Archives.

23. Brig. Gen. James R. Taylor, interview by Mariane Vardaman, Nov. 8, 1982, TAMU Archives; see R. James Woolsey, "A Long War," *New York Times* (Apr. 15, 2003.)

24. "War in the Gulf," *Stars and Stripes* (Feb. 12, 1991); unidentified news clipping, Feb. 24, 1991, TAMU Archives; *Texas Aggie* (June, 1991).

25. Department of the Army, ass't. chief of staff, G3, to AFS, Apr. 24, 1991, TAMU Archives.

26. Article from *Athens* (Tex.) *Review*, cited in email text from BJames8249@aol.com to F15BONDO@aol.com, Mar. 18, 2002, TAMU Archives; Jodi Wilmot ('91) to http://www .aggienetwork.com/troopsupport, Mar. 18, 2003, p. 22 of 30, TAMU Archives.

27. See David A. Deese, "Persian Gulf War of 1991," World Book Online, Americas' Edition, at www.worldbookonline.com, and related entries under "Desert Shield," "Desert Storm," and "Persian Gulf War."

28. Bradley Presnal, http://lib-oldweb.tamu.edu/aggiesinwar/.

29. *Texas Aggie* (June, 1993); Brian Anthony Riley, http://lib-oldweb.tamu.edu/aggiesinwar/; memorandum, John A. Adams Jr. to Henry Dethloff, May 4, 2003, in Aggie in War Papers, TAMU Archives.

30. Memorandum, Joseph Dinkins to Henry Dethloff (n.d.); email, Aug. 5, 2003, Dinkins to Dethloff, TAMU Archives.

31. Max Boot, *The Savage Wars of Peace: Small Wars and the Rise of American Power* (New York: Basic Books, 2002), pp. 326–29; article from *Athens* (Tex.) *Review* cited in email text from BJames8249@aol.com to F15BONDO@aol.com, Mar. 18, 2002, TAMU Archives; *Bryan–College Station Eagle* (Sept. 5, 1996).

32. *Texas Aggie* (Aug., 1997), p. 27.

33. "Danny Barr ('68) Piloted Air Force One for Four Presidents," *Texas Aggie* (Jan., 1998), pp. 14–15; *Texas Aggie* (Mar., 2002), p. 34; memorandum, Rick McPherson to John A. Adams Jr., June 17, 2004, TAMU Archives.

34. Boot, *The Savage Wars of Peace*, p. 326.

35. Kosovo Club Muster Report, AFS Papers, TAMU Archives; *Texas Aggie* (June, 2000), p. 15.

36. Memorandum from Jerry Cooper, *Texas Aggie* files, Lt. Col. Jerry Don Dickerson, Lee A. Adler, TAMU Archives; *Texas Aggie* (Sept., 2002).

37. Brian Anthony Riley, http://lib-oldweb.tamu.edu/aggiesinwar/.

38. *Texas Aggie* (Sept., 2002).

39. Michael La Coste, Lt. Tobin C. Flinn, and Lt. Col. David Sahm, all at http://aggienetwork. com/troopsupport/.

40. Gen. Tommy Franks, biographical, Wikipedia Encyclopedia, TAMU Archives; Lt. Gen. T. Michael Moseley, U.S. Air Force biography.

41. *Dallas Morning News* (Aug. 23, 2003).

42. Chad Allen Hesters, http://lib-oldweb.tamu.edu/aggiesinwar/; and see Steve Basso, Robert Nogueras, Albert Kinkead, all at http://aggienetwork.com/troopsupport/, copy, TAMU Archives.

43. Justin Gray, http://aggienetwork.com/troopsupport/, copy, TAMU Archives.

44. Lt. Toni Tanner, Maj. Robert Redding, 2nd Lt. Mike Zendejas, http://aggienetwork .com/troopsupport/; Kevin Thompson, http://lib-oldweb.tamu.edu/aggiesinwar/, copy, TAMU Archives.

45. Lt. Col. Joseph R. Matte, Lt. Martin Salinas II, http://aggienetwork.com/troopsupport/, copy, TAMU Archives; *Texas Aggie* (Mar., 2002), p. 35.

46. Memorandum, Capt. Patrick R. Seiber, Iraq experiences with 173rd ABN in BDE, TAMU Archives.

47. Capt. Mike Riley, http://aggienetwork.com/troopsupport/, copy, TAMU Archives.

48. Report by Kent Willis ('97) with article attached by Chris Barron, *Bremerton* (Wash.) *Sun* staff; and Leah Downs to "Dear Sir or Madam" at http://aggienetwork.com/troopsupport/, copy, TAMU Archives.

49. See named person as reported at http://aggienetwork.com/troopsupport/, copy, TAMU Archives.

50. See named people as reported at http://aggienetwork.com/troopsupport/, copy, TAMU Archives.

51. David C. Lewis, at http://aggienetwork.com/troopsupport/, copy, TAMU Archives; and for a useful synopsis and chronology of Operation Iraqi Freedom, see Houston Chronicle.com/Iraq.

52. *Houston Chronicle* (Apr. 6, 2003); Brett Eubank at http://aggienetwork.com/troopsupport/, copy, TAMU Archives.

53. See named people as reported at http://aggienetwork.com/troopsupport/, copy, TAMU Archives.

54. Memorandum to William A. Becker from Jason Tolbert, "A Summary of My Duties in OIF," May 6, 2004, TAMU Archives.

55. Ibid.

56. Rosanna Ruíz, "Katy Man, 25, Killed in Iraq," *Houston Chronicle* (July 21, 2003).

57. *Houston Chronicle* (Oct. 20, 2003).

58. Ibid. (Apr. 3, 2004).

Chapter 19

1. John C. Fitzpatrick, ed., *Writings of George Washington from the Original Manuscript Sources, 1745–1799*, v. 26 (Washington, D.C.: GPO, 1934), p. 388.

2. Gen. Omar Bradley, address to the graduating class of 1950, at Texas A&M's 75th Anniversary.

3. Memorandum, dedication of Hollingsworth statue on Texas A&M campus (n.d.), TAMU Archives.

4. "There Are People Who Live in America and There Are Americans," *Texas Aggie* (July, 1968), pp. 6–7.

5. *Texas Aggie* (July, 2001), pp. 12–15.

6. *College Station* (Tex.) *Battalion* (Jan. 14, 2003).

7. "Student Efforts on Garden Put into *Congressional Record*," *Texas Aggie* (Feb., 1970), p. 12.

8. Ibid.

9. Lt. Gen. John A. Van Alstyne, interview by Henry C. Dethloff, July 29, 2003, College Station, Tex.

10. James C. Smith, interview by Henry C. Dethloff, Sept. 1, 2003, College Station, Tex. Smith holds two graduate degrees from Texas A&M and at the time of the interview headed the Department of Construction Science there.

11. Ibid.

12. Memorandum, Corps Plaza Memorial dedication, July 2, 1992, TAMU Archives.

GLOSSARY

American Expeditionary Force (AEF). Composed of the U.S. Army of regular and National Guard units sent to France under the command of Gen. John J. ("Blackjack") Pershing in the summer of 1917.

ARVN. Army of the Republic of Vietnam.

Atlantic Charter. An agreement initiated by Pres. Franklin D. Roosevelt and Prime Minister Winston Churchill in August, 1941. Established common principles and objectives of war, including the right of all peoples to live in freedom from fear, want, and tyranny; the principles of free trade among all nations; an end to territorial seizures; and the advocacy of disarmament.

Camp Funston. Originally a subpost of the San Antonio Arsenal and an ammunition storage depot located at Leon Springs, Texas, this Spanish-American War mobilization post was renamed Camp Stanley in 1917 and has continued in use as a military installation.

Camp Logan. A World War I emergency training center on the then western city limits of Houston, including the present Memorial Park.

Camp Mabry. A training encampment located northwest of Austin in the early 1890s for the Texas Volunteer Guard and used as a mobilization area for the Spanish-American War. It is the present headquarters of the Texas Air National Guard, the Texas State Guard, and other military, state, and federal offices.

Camp Travis. Originally called Camp Wilson and located five miles northeast of downtown San Antonio, Camp Travis was renamed in honor of William B. Travis in 1917 and became the base for the organization of the thirty-one-thousand-man 90th Infantry Division sent to Europe in World War I.

CCF. Chinese Communist Forces.

Dick Militia Act of 1903. This act reorganized the militia along military lines and provided federal funding and limited federal control over the state militia.

DMZ. Demilitarized zone.

KATUSA. Korean Augmentation to the U.S. Army (untrained troops).

KIA. Killed in action.

Marshall Plan. A post–World War II plan for European recovery initiated by Secretary of State George C. Marshall in June, 1947. Seeking to reduce hunger, poverty, desperation, and chaos, the plan led to massive U.S. financial aid to the Allies and Western European nations not under Soviet control.

MIA. Missing in action.

National Defense Act of 1916. Instituted the Reserve Officer Training Corps and established the national guard as the nation's first military reserve.

National Defense Act of 1920. Expanded the size of the peacetime Regular Army to 280,000 enlisted personnel and 17,700 officers; authorized the continuation and expansion of the National Guard, U.S. Army Reserve, and Reserve Officer Training Corps.

National Security Act of 1947. Established the Department of Defense and the National Security Council to administer and coordinate defense policies and advise the president. Also created the Central Intelligence Agency to obtain political, military, and economic information for national security and defense.

NATO. North Atlantic Treaty Organization. A defense pact by ten European nations, Canada, and the United States entered into in April, 1949, following the Berlin blockade and airlift. The alliance is based on the understanding that an armed attack against one or more of its members is considered an attack against them all. The coalition established a joint mechanism for military enforcement.

NKPA. North Korean People's Army.

NVA. Regular forces of the Army of North Vietnam.

POW. Prisoner of war.

ROK. Armies of the Republic of Korea.

RVN. Armies of the Republic of South Vietnam.

Serviceman's Readjustment Act (GI Bill of Rights). Approved by Congress in 1944, the legislation provided veterans educational grants and loans, low-interest mortgages, low-interest business loans, and the right to return to their previous employment.

Texas National Guard. Volunteer citizen soldiers were organized as the "uniformed militia" until 1879, the "Texas Volunteer Guard" until 1903, and the "Texas National Guard" thereafter. The group was responsible for repelling invasions, suppressing insurrections, and executing state laws and, after 1903, those of the union.

Thompson Act. Approved by Congress in July, 1937, the Thompson Act allowed one thousand reserve officers to return to active duty for a one-year tour, thus enhancing the cadre of trained officers available for military service.

Truman Doctrine. Enunciated in March, 1947, the Truman Doctrine asserted both the necessity for the United States to contain communism and the right to intervene in order to save other nations from communist subversion.

VC/NVA. Viet Cong. Forces (usually infiltrators) of the armies of North Korea.

Vichy. Refers to the French forces in Vichy, France, who operated under the authority of the government of Marshall Henri Petain, who collaborated with the occupying German forces.

Viet Minh. Communist insurgents in North and South Vietnam during the early phases of the Vietnam War.

INDEX